AMERICAN GOVERNMENT

AMERICAN GOVERNMENT
Readings and Cases

SEVENTH EDITION

PETER WOLL
Brandeis University

Little, Brown and Company
BOSTON · TORONTO

Library of Congress Catalog Card No. 80-83037

ISBN 0-316-951439

9   8   7   6   5   4   3   2

MV

Published simultaneously in Canada
by Little, Brown & Company (Canada) Limited

Printed in the United States of America

This book is dedicated to
JOHN W. WOLL
and
RUTH C. WOLL

Preface

This book provides key readings and cases to introduce students to the underpinnings and contemporary practices of American government. As a sourcebook, it complements regular texts by illustrating and amplifying important issues and concepts. At the same time, the organization and design of the book make it suitable for use as a core text. Extensive notes are included that introduce, connect, and comment upon the selections within the broader context of American government.

This new edition contains up-to-date and relevant material designed to stimulate student interest and discussion and at the same time to show how our government functions. As in previous editions, a balance is maintained among classical readings, important historical and current constitutional law cases, and contemporary readings that pinpoint and analyze evolving political trends.

The basic areas covered in this edition include the nature and origins of constitutional theory and practice; federalism and intergovernmental relations; the civil liberties and civil rights of citizens; the organization and functions of political parties; elections and electoral behavior; political campaigning; the nature and functions of interest groups; the powers, responsibilities, and limitations of the presidency; the presidential establishment; presidential character and style; presidential transition; the scope of executive privilege; the nature and functions of the bureaucracy and its key role as part of the Washington establishment; the organization and activities of Congress, including the relationship between members of Congress and their constituencies, and the quest for personal power on Capitol Hill that has spawned an increased role for committee and personal staffs; the Supreme Court, the nature of judicial decision making, and the effects of Supreme Court rulings.

The selections for this edition were chosen with a view not only to presenting students with important readings and cases that give new perspectives on American constitutional development and political institutions, but also to heightening their interest and appreciation of the richness and excitement of politics.

In Chapter 1 on constitutional government, a new selection by Gary Wills helps students to understand the relationship between the Declaration of Independence and the Constitution. Wills's selection is taken from his book, *Inventing America,* and it nicely complements the preceding views on the Constitution by John P. Roche and Charles A. Beard. A selection from John Locke's Second Treatise rounds out Chapter 1 by giving a general theoretical perspective on the nature of political society and government.

Chapter 2, which covers federalism, has been strengthened through the addition of a selection by Samuel H. Beer dealing with the future of the states in the federal system.

The conflict between the First Amendment freedom of the press, and the Sixth Amendment's right to a fair trial, are the focus of *Nebraska Press Association* v. *Stuart,* an important new case in Chapter 3, which covers civil liberties and civil rights. Also new in Chapter 3 is *Regents of the University of California* v. *Bakke,* in which the Court ruled on the issue of reverse discrimination.

The discussion of political parties and the electorate in Chapter 4 has been enlivened by the addition of two selections that students should find particularly interesting and readable. *Washington Post* reporter Haynes Johnson describes contemporary voter attitudes and their meaning for parties and candidates. Timothy Crouse depicts the frenzied, harrowing, but at the same time exhalted experience of a presidential campaign and the highly charged emotional environment of its last days.

A new case study in pressure group politics in Chapter 5 portrays the often-criticized but highly effective oil lobbyists who roam the corridors, offices, and lobbies of Capitol Hill and who frequently touch base with the President and the bureaucracy as well.

For Chapter 6 on the presidency, Thomas E. Cronin has updated his analysis of the presidential establishment, and Henry Kissinger examines the promises and realities of a presidential transition from the vantage point of a top member of the White House staff.

A new selection in Chapter 7 on the bureaucracy and Congress by Robert Sherrill concludes that "the iron triangle," which is supposed to link administrative agencies and the congressional committees with pressure groups, is not as solid as the term implies. Administrative agencies must battle for political support, and if they alienate their Capitol Hill allies their powers may be reduced and their very life threatened. Agencies must delicately balance private interests, which in turn are reflected on Capitol Hill, if they are to serve the public interest.

Chapter 8 on Congress has been strengthened and made more interesting for students through the addition of lively and provocative writings concerning the activities of members of Congress and their staffs. David Mayhew describes the activities of Congressmen who constantly must strive for reelection, while Richard Fenno, Jr., suggests that the linkage between Washington careers and the activities of Congressmen in constituencies may be remote. Eric Redman gives a firsthand account of his experiences as a junior staffer in the Senate who attempted to secure the passage of legislation to establish a National Health Service Corps. Members of congressional staffs are described as the "surrogates of power" in a new selection by Rochelle Jones and Peter Woll. Elizabeth Drew completes the chapter on Congress with a lively discussion of a day in the life of a United States Senator.

In his epilogue to *Gideon's Trumpet,* a new selection on the judiciary in Chapter 9, Anthony Lewis examines the aftermath of the Supreme Court decision in *Gideon* v. *Wainwright* that extended the right to counsel to all criminal defendants.

As in previous editions, an extensive Instructors Manual accompanies the text. The Manual provides a comprehensive guide to the selections in the text. Background material is provided to help place the selections in an appropriate historical and contemporary context.

Over the years numerous individuals have generously given their time, energy, and ideas to help the author make this work a major sourcebook in American government. Sam Beer has continued to review the federalism chapter and has made an important personal contribution to it in this edition. Ted Lowi has always made provocative and useful suggestions for the entire book. Henry J. Abraham's expertise in the judiciary continues to buttress that section of the book, as have his suggestions for other parts. Tom Cronin reviewed the chapter on the presidency, which contains his own updated selection on the presidential establishment. Frederick Zuercher has taken an interest in the book from the very beginning, and has helped to shape its contents over the years. Neil Sullivan has acted as a valuable research assistant for the book in the past and continues critically and effectively to review and recommend selections. Rochelle Jones, from her vantage point at the center of the Washington political maelstrom, has given me an insider's knowledge that would be impossible to obtain without her. Her contributions to the book and her encouragement are deeply appreciated.

Finally, I would like to thank William T. Ethridge, who read the entire manuscript with the eye of a skillful editor and a person with a broad knowledge of politics. His astute recommendations contributed importantly to the book. Thanks are also due to Cynthia Chapin, who handled the production of the book, and to Barbara Nagy, who adeptly typed the manuscript.

P. W.

Contents

conflict between the two documents, and that they reflect, respectively, humanitarian democratic ideals and a desire to protect minorities against the unbridled rule of the majority.

LIMITATION OF GOVERNMENTAL POWER AND OF MAJORITY RULE

CONSTITUTIONAL DEMOCRACY: THE RULE OF LAW

CONSTITUTIONAL BACKGROUND: NATIONAL v. STATE POWER

allowing the national government to act directly upon the people on national matters.

Alexis de Tocqueville came to America in the early 19th century and was astonished by what he found. He was sanguine about the future of democracy, yet was also concerned about a possible tyranny of the majority. He particularly admired the federal system, which gave the national government the necessary power to act for the nation while preserving the interests of the states.

THE SUPREMACY OF NATIONAL LAW

Congress may exercise powers that can be implied from its enumerated powers in Article 1 of the Constitution. The Constitution and laws based upon it are supreme over conflicting state laws.

A PERSPECTIVE ON FEDERALISM: PRESENT AND FUTURE

The nature of intergovernmental relations reflects underlying political conditions and realities. The original constitutional scheme represented a delicate balance between national and state interests, which is continually changing as the national government and the states struggle for political power.

CONSTITUTIONAL BACKGROUND: THE DEBATE OVER THE INCLUSION OF A BILL OF RIGHTS IN THE CONSTITUTION

The inclusion of a separate Bill of Rights in the Constitution would be redundant, because the people retain all of the rights that are proposed to be added through a Bill of Rights. There is no power given to the central government to curb any of the rights in question. The listing of rights in the main body of the Constitution is similar to many state constitutions and affords whatever protections are necessary to the people.

THE NATIONALIZATION OF THE BILL OF RIGHTS

The right to counsel is fundamental to a fair trial and must be guaranteed by the states under the Due Process Clause of the Fourteenth Amendment.

FREEDOM OF SPEECH AND PRESS

Freedom of speech and press is essential to constitutional democracy, because all people are fallible and no one person has the right to enforce views arbitrarily upon others.

Congress can abridge freedoms of speech and press where there is a clear and probable danger that the exercise of these freedoms will undermine the government.

FREE PRESS AND FAIR TRIAL

A judge's attempt to restrict what the press may report from a preliminary hearing constitutes prior censorship that is unconstitutional under the First Amendment guaranty of freedom of the press.

FREEDOM OF RELIGION

A state law providing for the recitation of a daily prayer in the public schools violates the Establishment Clause of the First Amendment, which requires the separation of church and state.

EQUAL PROTECTION OF THE LAWS: SCHOOL DESEGREGATION

State laws that establish separate public educational facilities based on race violate the Equal Protection of the Laws Clause of the Fourteenth Amendment. Separate facilities are inherently unequal even though they may be equal physically.

Because of varied local school problems relating to desegregation, the federal district courts are delegated the authority to implement the 1954 *Brown* decision. These courts are to proceed "with all deliberate speed," while balancing the community and personal interests involved.

EQUAL PROTECTION OF THE LAWS: REVERSE DISCRIMINATION

The use of quotas by a university to give preference to racial groups in an admissions program is a violation of the Equal Protection Clause of the Fourteenth Amendment. However, an applicant's race can be considered as one factor in the admissions process.

EQUAL PROTECTION OF THE LAWS: ELECTORAL REAPPORTIONMENT

The apportionment of state legislative electoral districts is a proper matter for judicial determination under the Equal Protection of the Laws Clause of the Fourteenth Amendment.

CONSTITUTIONAL BACKGROUND

Factions are groups that unite to serve selfish goals, not the national interest. It is necessary to control factions through constitutional means, one of which is the creation of a large republic that helps to disperse factions and reduces their influence on the national legislature.

Interest groups are controlled by a variety of constitutional provisions, including the separation of powers and checks and balances. Moreover, groups are checked because of their inability to claim the total loyalty of their members.

FUNCTIONS AND TYPES OF ELECTIONS

Critical elections are those in which voting patterns suggest that there has been a permanent realignment of the electorate between parties.

VOTING BEHAVIOR: RATIONAL OR IRRATIONAL?

Although democratic theory assumes that all voters are rational and interested in participating in elections, in fact many citizens are irrational in making political choices and often apathetic.

The attitudes of contemporary voters reflect not political apathy but strong skepticism about ever being able to know the facts. Voters tend to believe that no matter who is President the real problems of the nation are unlikely to be solved. The electorate craves a fresh political voice, a political outsider who will magically make the government a responsible and accountable body that acts in accordance with the wishes of the people.

THE ROLE OF PARTIES IN THE POLITICAL PROCESS

The decline of voter identification with political parties is producing a trend toward politics without parties. This threatens the democratic process, because parties are the major link between the general public and government.

POLITICAL CAMPAIGNING

Political campaigning is primarily a public relations job. Voters are to be treated as largely irrational and, in order to gain votes, appeals must be made more to emotion than to reason.

PRESIDENTIAL CAMPAIGNS AND THE PRESS

large, and foreign governments — that presidential policies are in their interests.

THE PRESIDENTIAL ESTABLISHMENT

The Executive Office of the President has become a dominant force in the White House, often overshadowing the person who occupies the Oval Office. Presidents often promise to reduce the size of the presidential bureaucracy, but the political realities that buttress a large presidential establishment have remained unchanged.

PRESIDENTIAL CHARACTER AND STYLE

It is the total character of the person who occupies the White House that is the determinant of presidential performance.

Discussions between President Nixon and his staff about Watergate and related matters reveal the impact of personal and institutional factors in the Watergate affair.

PRESIDENTIAL TRANSITION: FORMING A NEW ADMINISTRATION

The change from one presidential administration to another is never easy and is usually characterized by muddling through on the part of the President-Elect, his staff, new cabinet officials, and the transition team. Henry Kissinger describes the poignant moments and the spells of elation and frenzy that characterized the presidential transition of which he was a part. The selection is from his memoirs, *White House Years.*

PRESIDENTIAL POWER AND EXECUTIVE PRIVILEGE

The President cannot claim executive privilege and refuse to obey a court subpoena to produce evidence relative to a criminal case on the general grounds that the material sought is confidential,

and that it would be inconsistent with the public interest to release it.

JUDGING THE PRESIDENCY

sists of powerful members of Congress and their aides, top career civil servants, the Cabinet and other political appointees.

The functions of the House and Senate are fundamentally different. The House, popularly elected for a two year term, stands close to the people and represents popular interests in matters of local concern. Senators, indirectly elected for staggered six year terms, are more detached, deliberative, and conservative. A primary responsibility of the Senate is to act as a conservative check on the House.

The Power of Jamie Whitten, Chairman of the House Appropriations Subcommittee on Agriculture, illustrates how committee chairmen can single-handedly control the policies of administrative departments and agencies.

People apply different standards in judging Congressmen and the institution of Congress. The member is judged for personality, style, and representativeness, while the institution is judged by its ability to recognize and solve the nation's problems.

The primary incentive of members of Congress is to achieve reelection. The organization and the procedures of Congress have been designed to give members the necessary flexibility to accomplish their reelection goals.

The constituency careers of members of Congress primarily involve the pursuit of the goal of reelection. The Washington careers of Congressmen are often separate from their constituency
careers, and are characterized by the pursuit of influence within
Congress and the making of good public policy.

CONGRESSIONAL STAFF:
THE SURROGATES OF POWER

A junior aide to a powerful senior Senator describes some of the
lessons he learned as a beginner on Capitol Hill. A loyal staffer
protects the turf of his Senator, making certain that the Senator
receives credit for new programs initiated at the staff level. The
power of the staffer redounds to the member.

While staff tends to be more an attribute of power in the Senate
than in the House, politically astute Congressmen know that they
too can build their Capitol Hill careers through a talented and
adroit staff. Deft and aggressive staff work has placed congressmen in the public eye at the same that it has boosted their status
on Capitol Hill.

A DAY IN THE UNITED STATES SENATE

A hectic day in the life of a United States Senator illustrates that
a spirit of collegiality still prevails in the Senate. Norms of hard
work, expertise, courtesy, and respect for the institution continue
to characterize those Senators who seek power and status in the
body.

CONSTITUTIONAL BACKGROUND:
JUDICIAL INDEPENDENCE AND
JUDICIAL REVIEW

An independent judiciary is essential in a limited constitution to
check arbitrary and unconstitutional acts by the legislature. It is

the duty of the courts "to declare all acts contrary to the manifest tenor of the Constitution void."

AMERICAN GOVERNMENT

PART ONE

The Setting of the American System

CHAPTER 1

Constitutional Government

A remarkable fact about the United States government is that it has operated for over 180 years on the basis of a written Constitution. Does this
suggest unusual sagacity on the part of the Founding Fathers, or exceptional luck? What was involved in framing the Constitution?

Framing the Constitution:
Elitist or Democratic Process?

In the following selection John P. Roche suggests that the framing of the
Constitution was essentially a democratic process involving the reconciliation of a variety of state, political, and economic interests. Roche writes
that "The Philadelphia Convention was not a College of Cardinals or a
council of Platonic guardians working in a manipulative, predemocratic
framework; it was a *nationalist* reform caucus that had to operate with great
delicacy and skill in a political cosmos full of enemies to achieve one
definitive goal — popular approbation." Roche recognizes that the framers,
collectively, were an elite, but he is careful to point out that they were a
political elite dedicated for the most part to establishing an effective and
at the same time controlled national government that would be able to
overcome the weaknesses of the Articles of Confederation. The framers
were not, says Roche, a cohesive elite dedicated to a particular set of
political or economic assumptions beyond the simple need to create a
national government that would be capable of reconciling disparate state
interests. The Constitution was "a vivid demonstration of effective democratic political action, and of the forging of a national elite which literally
persuaded its countrymen to hoist themselves by their own bootstraps."

1
John P. Roche

THE FOUNDING FATHERS:
A REFORM CAUCUS IN ACTION

Over the last century and a half, the work of the Constitutional Convention and the motives of the Founding Fathers have been analyzed under a number of different ideological auspices. To one generation of historians, the hand of God was moving in the assembly; under a later dispensation, the dialectic (at various levels of philosophical sophistication) replaced the Deity: "relationships of production" moved into the niche previously reserved for Love of Country. Thus in counterpart to the zeitgeist, the framers have undergone miraculous metamorphoses: at one time acclaimed as liberals and bold social engineers, today they appear in the guise of sound Burkean conservatives, men who in our time would subscribe to *Fortune,* look to Walter Lippmann for political theory, and chuckle patronizingly at the antics of Barry Goldwater. The implicit assumption is that if James Madison were among us, he would be President of the Ford Foundation, while Alexander Hamilton would chair the Committee for Economic Development.

The "Fathers" have thus been admitted to our best circles; the revolutionary ferocity which confiscated all Tory property in reach and populated New Brunswick with outlaws has been converted by the "Miltown School" of American historians into a benign dedication to "consensus" and "prescriptive rights." The Daughters of the American Revolution have, through the ministrations of Professors Boorstin, Hartz, and Rossiter, at last found ancestors worthy of their descendants. It is not my purpose here to argue that the "Fathers" were, in fact, radical revolutionaries; that proposition has been brilliantly demonstrated by Robert R. Palmer in his *Age of the Democratic Revolution.* My concern is with the future position that not only were they revolutionaries, but also they were democrats. Indeed, in my view, there is one fundamental truth about the Founding Fathers that *every* generation of zeitgeisters has done its best to obscure: they were first and foremost superb democratic politicians. I suspect that in a contemporary setting, James Madison would be Speaker of the House of Representatives and Hamilton would be the *eminence grise* dominating (*pace* Theodore Sorensen or Sherman Adams) the Executive Office of the President. They were, with their colleagues, *political men* — not metaphysicians, disembodied

From John P. Roche, "The Founding Fathers: A Reform Caucus in Action," *American Political Science Review* (December 1961). Reprinted by permission.

conservatives or Agents of History — and as recent research into the nature of American politics in the 1780s confirms, they were committed (perhaps willy-nilly) to working within the democratic framework, within a universe of public approval. Charles Beard *and* the filiopietists to the contrary notwithstanding, the Philadelphia Convention was not a College of Cardinals or a council of Platonic guardians working within a manipulative, predemocratic framework; it was a *nationalist* reform caucus which had to operate with great delicacy and skill in a political cosmos full of enemies to achieve the one definitive goal — popular approbation.

Perhaps the time has come, to borrow Walton Hamilton's fine phrase, to raise the framers from immortality to mortality, to give them credit for their magnificent demonstration of the art of democratic politics. The point must be reemphasized; they *made* history and did it within the limits of consensus. There was nothing inevitable about the future in 1787; the *zeitgeist,* that fine Hegelian technique of begging causal questions, could only be discerned in retrospect. What they did was to hammer out a pragmatic compromise which would both bolster the "National interest" and be acceptable to the people. What inspiration they got came from their collective experience as professional politicians in a democratic society. As John Dickinson put it to his fellow delegates on August 13, "Experience must be our guide. Reason may mislead us."

In this context, let us examine the problems they confronted and the solutions they evolved. The Convention has been described picturesquely as a counter-revolutionary junta and the Constitution as a coup d'état, but this has been accomplished by withdrawing the whole history of the movement for constitutional reform from its true context. No doubt the goals of the constitutional elite were "subversive" to the existing political order, but it is overlooked that their subversion could only have succeeded if the people of the United States endorsed it by regularized procedures. Indubitably they were "plotting" to establish a much stronger central government than existed under the Articles, but only in the sense in which one could argue equally well that John F. Kennedy was, from 1956 to 1960, "plotting" to become President. In short, on the fundamental *procedural* level, the Constitutionalists had to work according to the prevailing rules of the game. Whether they liked it or not is a topic for spiritualists — and is irrelevant: one may be quite certain that had Washington agreed to play the de Gaulle (as the Cincinnati once urged), Hamilton would willingly have held his horse, but such fertile speculation in no way alters the actual context in which events took place.

I

When the Constitutionalists went forth to subvert the Confederation, they utilized the mechanisms of political legitimacy. And the roadblocks which confronted them were formidable. At the same time, they were endowed with certain potent political assets. The history of the United States from 1786 to 1790 was largely one of a masterful employment of political expertise by the Constitutionalists as against bumbling, erratic behavior by the opponents of reform. Effectively, the Constitutionalists had to induce the states, by democratic techniques of coercion, to emasculate themselves. To be specific, if New York had refused to join the new Union, the project was doomed; yet before New York was safely in, the reluctant state legislature had *suasponte* to take the following steps: (1) agree to send delegates to the Philadelphia Convention; (2) provide maintenance for these delegates (these were distinct stages: New Hampshire was early in naming delegates, but did not provide for their maintenance until July); (3) set up the special ad hoc convention to decide on ratification; and (4) concede to the decision of the ad hoc convention that New York should participate. New York admittedly was a tricky state, with a strong interest in a status quo which permitted her to exploit New Jersey and Connecticut, but the same legal hurdles existed in every state. And at the risk of becoming boring, it must be reiterated that the *only* weapon in the Constitutionalist arsenal was an effective mobilization of public opinion.

The group which undertook this struggle was an interesting amalgam of a few dedicated nationalists with the self-interested spokesmen of various parochial bailiwicks. The Georgians, for example, wanted a strong central authority to provide military protection for their huge, underpopulated state against the Creek Confederacy; Jerseymen and Connecticuters wanted to escape from economic bondage to New York; the Virginians hoped to establish a system which would give that great state its rightful place in the councils of the republic. The dominant figures in the politics of these states therefore cooperated in the call for the Convention. In other states, the thrust towards national reform was taken up by opposition groups who added the "national interest" to their weapons system; in Pennsylvania, for instance, the group fighting to revise the Constitution of 1776 came out four-square behind the Constitutionalists, and in New York, Hamilton and the Schuyler *ambiance* took the same tack against George Clinton. There was, of course, a large element of personality in the affair: there is reason to suspect that Patrick Henry's opposition to the Convention and the Constitution was founded on his conviction that Jefferson was behind both, and a close study of local politics elsewhere would surely reveal that others supported the Constitution for the simple (and politically quite sufficient) reason that the "wrong" people were against it.

To say this is not to suggest that the Constitution rested on a foundation of impure or base motives. It is rather to argue that in politics there are no immaculate conceptions, and that in the drive for a stronger general government, motives of all sorts played a part. Few men in the history of mankind have espoused a view of the "common good" or "public interest" that militated against their private status; even Plato with all his reverence for disembodied reason managed to put philosophers on top of the pile. Thus it is not surprising that a number of diversified private interests joined to push the nationalist public interest; what would have been surprising was the absence of such a pragmatic united front. And the fact remains that, however motivated, these men did demonstrate a willingness to compromise their parochial interests in behalf of an ideal which took shape before their eyes and under their ministrations.

As Stanley Elkins and Eric McKitrick have suggested in a perceptive essay [76 *Political Science Quarterly* 181 (1961)], what distinguished the leaders of the Constitutionalist caucus from their enemies was a "Continental" approach to political, economic and military issues. To the extent that they shared an institutional base of operations, it was the Continental Congress (thirty-nine of the delegates to the Federal Convention had served in Congress), and this was hardly a locale which inspired respect for the state governments. Robert de Jouvenal observed French politics half a century ago and noted that a revolutionary Deputy had more in common with a nonrevolutionary Deputy than he had with a revolutionary non-Deputy; similarly one can surmise that membership in the Congress under the Articles of Confederation worked to establish a continental frame of reference, that a Congressman from Pennsylvania and one from South Carolina would share a universe of discourse which provided them with a conceptual common denominator vis-à-vis their respective state legislatures. This was particularly true with respect to external affairs: the average state legislator was probably about as concerned with foreign policy then as he is today, but Congressmen were constantly forced to take the broad view of American prestige, were compelled to listen to the reports of Secretary John Jay and to the dispatches and pleas from their frustrated envoys in Britain, France and Spain. From considerations such as these, a "Continental" ideology developed which seems to have demanded a revision of our domestic institutions primarily on the ground that only by invigorating our general government could we assume our rightful place in the international arena. Indeed, an argument with great force — particularly since Washington was its incarnation — urged that our very survival in the Hobbesian jungle of world politics depended upon a reordering and strengthening of our national sovereignty.

The great achievement of the Constitutionalists was their ultimate success in convincing the elected representatives of a majority of the white male population that change was imperative. A small group of political leaders with a Continental vision and essentially a consciousness of the United States' *international* impotence, provided the matrix of the movement. To their standard other leaders rallied with their own parallel ambitions. Their great assets were (1) the presence in their caucus of the one authentic American "father figure," George Washington, whose prestige was enormous; (2) the energy and talent of their leadership (in which one must include the towering intellectuals of the time, John Adams and Thomas Jefferson, despite their absence abroad), and their communications "network," which was far superior to anything on the opposition side; (3) the preemptive skill which made "their" issue The Issue and kept the locally oriented opposition permanently on the defensive; and (4) the subjective consideration that these men were spokesmen of a new and compelling credo: *American* nationalism, that ill-defined but nonetheless potent sense of collective purpose that emerged from the American Revolution.

Despite great institutional handicaps, the Constitutionalists managed in the mid-1780s to mount an offensive which gained momentum as years went by. Their greatest problem was lethargy, and paradoxically, the number of barriers in their path may have proved an advantage in the long run. Beginning with the initial battle to get the Constitutional Convention called and delegates appointed, they could never relax, never let up the pressure. In practical terms, this meant that the local "organizations" created by the Constitutionalists were perpetually in movement building up their cadres for the next fight. (The word *organization* has to be used with great caution: a political organization in the United States — as in contemporary England — generally consisted of a magnate and his following, or a coalition of magnates. This did not necessarily mean that it was "undemocratic" or "aristocratic," in the Aristotelian sense of the word: while a few magnates such as the Livingstons could draft their followings, most exercised their leadership without coercion on the basis of popular endorsement. The absence of organized opposition did not imply the impossibility of competition any more than low public participation in elections necessarily indicated an undemocratic suffrage.)

The Constitutionalists got the jump on the "opposition" (a collective noun: oppositions would be more correct) at the outset with the demand for a Convention. Their opponents were caught in an old political trap: they were not being asked to approve any specific program of reform, but only to endorse a meeting to discuss and recommend needed reforms. If they took a hard line at the first stage, they were put in the position of glorifying the status quo and of denying the need for *any* changes. Moreover, the Constitutionalists could go to the people with a persuasive argument for "fair play" — "How can you condemn reform before you know precisely what is involved?" Since the state legislatures obviously would have the final say on any proposals that might emerge from the Convention, the Constitutionalists were merely reasonable men asking for a chance. Besides, since they did not make any concrete proposals at that stage, they were in a position to capitalize on every sort of generalized discontent with the Confederation.

Perhaps because of their poor intelligence system, perhaps because of overconfidence generated by the failure of all previous efforts to alter the

Articles, the opposition awoke too late to the dangers that confronted them in 1787. Not only did the Constitutionalists manage to get every state but Rhode Island (where politics was enlivened by a party system reminiscent of the "Blues" and the "Greens" in the Byzantine Empire) to appoint delegates to Philadelphia, but when the results were in, it appeared that they dominated the delegations. Given the apathy of the opposition, this was a natural phenomenon: in an ideologically nonpolarized political atmosphere those who get appointed to a special committee are likely to be the men who supported the movement for its creation. Even George Clinton, who seems to have been the first opposition leader to awake to the possibility of trouble, could not prevent the New York legislature from appointing Alexander Hamilton — though he did have the foresight to send two of his henchmen to dominate the delegation. Incidentally, much has been made of the fact that the delegates to Philadelphia were not elected by the people; some have adduced this fact as evidence of the "undemocratic" character of the gathering. But put in the context of the time, this argument is wholly specious: the central government under the Articles was considered a creature of the component states and in all the states but Rhode Island, Connecticut, and New Hampshire, members of the national Congress were chosen by the state legislatures. This was not a consequence of elitism or fear of the mob; it was a logical extension of states' rights doctrine to guarantee that the national institution did not end-run the state legislatures and make direct contact with the people.

II

With delegations safely named, the focus shifted to Philadelphia. While waiting for a quorum to assemble, James Madison got busy and drafted the so-called Randolph or Virginia Plan with the aid of the Virginia delegation. This was a political master-stroke. Its consequence was that once business got underway, the framework of discussion was established on Madison's terms. There was no interminable argument over agenda; instead the delegates took the Virginia Resolutions — "just for purposes of discussion" — as their point of departure. And along with Madison's proposals, many of which were buried in the course of the summer, went his major premise: a new start on a Constitution rather than piecemeal amendment. This was not necessarily revolutionary — a little exegesis could demonstrate that a new Constitution might be formulated as "amendments" to the Articles of Confederation — but Madison's proposal that this "lump sum" amendment go into effect after approval by nine states (the Articles required unanimous state approval for any amendment) was thoroughly subversive.

Standard treatments of the Convention divide the delegates into "nationalists" and "states' righters" with various improvised shadings ("moderate nationalists," etc.), but these are *a posteriori* categories which obfuscate more than they clarify. What is striking to one who analyzes the Convention as a case study in democratic politics is the lack of clear-cut ideological divisions in the Convention. Indeed, I submit that the evidence — Madison's *Notes,* the correspondence of the delegates, and debates on ratification — indicates that this was a remarkably homogeneous body on the ideological level. Yates and Lansing, Clinton's two chaperones for Hamilton, left in disgust on July 10. (Is there anything more tedious than sitting through endless disputes on matters one deems fundamentally misconceived? It takes an iron will to spend a hot summer as an ideological *agent provocateur.*) Luther Martin, Maryland's bibulous narcissist, left on September 4 in a huff when he discovered that others did not share his self-esteem; others went home for personal reasons. But the hard core of delegates accepted a grinding regimen throughout the attrition of a Philadelphia summer precisely because they shared the Constitutionalist goal.

Basic differences of opinion emerged, of course, but these were not ideological; they were *structural.* If the so-called "states' rights" group had not accepted the fundamental purposes of the Convention, they could simply have pulled out and by doing so have aborted the whole enterprise. Instead of bolting, they returned day after day to argue and to compromise. An interesting symbol of this basic homogeneity was the initial agreement on secrecy: these professional politicians did not want to become prisoners of publicity; they wanted to retain that freedom of maneuver which is only possible when men are not forced to take public stands in the preliminary stages of negotiation. There was no legal means of binding the tongues of the delegates: at any stage in the game a delegate with basic principled objections to the emerging project could have taken the stump (as Luther Martin did after his exit) and denounced the convention to the skies. Yet Madison did not even inform Thomas Jefferson in Paris of the course of the deliberations and available correspondence indicates that the delegates generally observed the injunction. Secrecy is certainly uncharacteristic of any assembly marked by strong ideological polarization. This was noted at the time: the *New York Daily Advertiser,* August 14, 1787, commented that the "profound secrecy hitherto observed by the Convention [we consider] a happy omen, as it demonstrates that the spirit of party on any great and essential point cannot have arisen to any height."

Commentators on the Constitution who have read *The Federalist* in lieu of reading the actual debates have credited the Fathers with the invention of a sublime concept called "Federalism." Unfortunately *The Federalist* is probative evidence for only one proposition: that Hamilton and Madison were inspired propagandists with a genius for retrospective symmetry. Federalism, as the theory is generally defined, was an improvisation which was later promoted into a political theory. Experts on "federalism" should take to heart the advice of David Hume, who warned in his *Of the Rise and Progress of the Arts and Sciences* that "there is no subject in which we must proceed with more caution than in [history], lest we assign causes which never existed and reduce what is merely contingent to stable and universal principles." In any event, the final balance in the Constitution between the states and the nation must have come as a great disappointment to Madison, while Hamilton's unitary views are too well known to need elucidation.

It is indeed astonishing how those who have glibly designated James Madison the "father" of Federalism have overlooked the solid body of fact which indicates that he shared Hamilton's quest for a unitary central government. To be specific, they have avoided examining the clear import of the Madison-Virginia Plan, and have disregarded Madison's dogged inch-by-inch retreat from the bastions of centralization. The Virginia Plan envisioned a unitary national government effectively freed from and dominant over the states. The lower house of the national legislature was to be elected directly by the people of the states with membership proportional to population. The upper house was to be selected by the lower and the two chambers would elect the executive and choose the judges. The national government would be thus cut completely loose from the states.

The structure of the general government was freed from state control in a truly radical fashion, but the scope of the authority of the national sovereign as Madison initially formulated it was breathtaking — it was a formulation worthy of the Sage of Malmesbury himself. The national legislature was to be empowered to disallow the acts of state legislatures, and the central government was vested, in addition to the powers of the nation under the Articles of Confederation, with plenary authority wherever "the separate States are incompetent or in which the harmony of the United States may be interrupted by the exercise of individual legislation." Finally, just to lock the door against state intrusion, the national Congress was to be given the power to use military force on recalcitrant states. This was Madison's "model" of an ideal national government, though it later received little publicity in *The Federalist*.

The interesting thing was the reaction of the Convention to this militant program for a strong autonomous central government. Some delegates were startled, some obviously leery of so comprehensive a project of reform, but nobody set off any fireworks and nobody walked out. Moreover, in the two weeks that followed, the Virginia Plan received substantial endorsement *en principe;* the initial temper of the gathering can be deduced from the approval "without debate or dissent," on May 31, of the Sixth Resolution which granted Congress the authority to disallow state legislation "contravening *in its opinion* the Articles of Union." Indeed, an amendment was included to bar states from contravening national treaties.

The Virginia Plan may therefore be considered, in ideological terms, as the delegates' Utopia, but as the discussions continued and became more specific, many of those present began to have second thoughts. After all, they were not residents of Utopia or guardians in Plato's Republic who could simply impose a philosophical ideal on subordinate strata of the population. They were practical politicians in a democratic society, and no matter what their private dreams might be, they had to take home an acceptable package and defend it — and their own political futures — against predictable attack. On June 14 the breaking point between dream and reality took place. Apparently realizing that under the Virginia Plan, Massachusetts, Virginia, and Pennsylvania could virtually dominate the national government — and probably appreciating that to sell this program to "the folks back home" would be impossible — the delegates from the small states dug in their heels and demanded time for a consideration of alternatives. One gets a graphic sense of the inner politics from John Dickinson's reproach to Madison: "You see the consequences of pushing things too far. Some of the members from the small States wish for two branches in the General Legislature and are friends to a good National Government; but we would sooner submit to a foreign power than . . . be deprived of an equality of suffrage in both branches of the Legislature, and thereby be thrown under the domination of the large States."

The bare outline of the *Journal* entry for Tuesday, June 14, is suggestive to anyone with extensive experience in deliberative bodies. "It was moved by Mr. Patterson [*sic,* Paterson's name was one of those consistently misspelled by Madison and everybody else] seconded by Mr. Randolph that the further consideration of the report from the Committee of the whole House [endorsing the Virginia Plan] be postponed til tomorrow and before the question for postponement was taken. It was moved by Mr. Randolph seconded by Mr. Patterson that the House adjourn." The House adjourned by obvious prearrangement of the two principals: since the preceding Saturday when Brearley and Paterson of New Jersey had announced their fundamental discontent with the representational features of the Virginia Plan, the informal pressure had certainly been building up to slow down the steamroller. Doubtless there were extended arguments at the Indian Queen between Madison and Paterson, the latter insisting that events were moving rapidly towards a probably disastrous conclusion, towards a political suicide pact. Now the process of accommodation was put into action smoothly — and wisely, given the character and strength of the doubters. Madison had the votes, but this was one of those situations where the enforcement of mechanical majoritarianism could easily have destroyed the objectives of the majority: the Constitutionalists were in quest of a qualitative as well as a quantitative consensus. This was hardly from deference to local Quaker custom; it was a political imperative if they were to attain ratification.

III

According to the standard script, at this point the "states' rights" group intervened in force behind the New Jersey Plan, which has been characteristically portrayed as a reversion to the status quo under the Articles of

Confederation with but minor modifications. A careful examination of the evidence indicates that only in a marginal sense is this an accurate description. It is true that the New Jersey Plan put the states back into the institutional picture, but one could argue that to do so was a recognition of political reality rather than an affirmation of states' rights. A serious case can be made that the advocates of the New Jersey Plan, far from being ideological addicts of states' rights, intended to substitute for the Virginia Plan a system which would both retain strong national power and have a chance of adoption in the states. The leading spokesman for the project asserted quite clearly that his views were based more on counsels of expediency than on principle; said Paterson on June 16: "I came here not to speak my own sentiments, but the sentiments of those who sent me. Our object is not such a Governmt. as may be best in itself, but such a one as our Constituents have authorized us to prepare, and as they will approve." This is Madison's version; in Yates's transcription, there is a crucial sentence following the remarks above: "I believe that a little practical virtue is to be preferred to the finest theoretical principles, which cannot be carried into effect." In his preliminary speech on June 9, Paterson had stated "to the public mind we must accommodate ourselves," and in his notes for this and his later effort as well, the emphasis is the same. The *structure* of government under the Articles should be retained:

> 2. Because it accords with the Sentiments of the People
> [Proof:] 1. Coms. [Commissions from state legislatures defining the jurisdiction of the delegates]
> 2. News-papers — Political Barometer. Jersey never would have sent Delegates under the first [Virginia] Plan —
> Not here to sport Opinions of my own. Wt. [What] can be done. A little practicable Virtue preferrable to Theory.

This was a defense of political acumen, not of states' rights. In fact, Paterson's notes of his speech can easily be construed as an argument for attaining the substantive objectives of the Virginia Plan by a sound political route, i.e., pouring the new wine in the old bottles. With a shrewd eye, Paterson queried:

> Will the Operation, and Force of the [central] Govt. depend upon the mode of Representn. — No — it will depend upon the Quantum of Power lodged in the leg. ex. and judy. Departments — Give [the existing] Congress the same Powers that you intend to give the two Branches, [under the Virginia Plan] and I apprehend they will act with as much Propriety and more Energy. . . .

In other words, the advocates of the New Jersey Plan concentrated their fire on what they held to be the *political liabilities* of the Virginia Plan — which were matters of institutional structure — rather than on the proposed scope of national authority. Indeed, the Supremacy Clause of the Constitution first saw the light of day in Paterson's Sixth Resolution; the New Jersey Plan contemplated the use of military force to secure compliance with national law; and finally Paterson made clear his view that under either the Virginia or the New Jersey systems, the general government would ". . . act on individuals and not on states." From the states' rights viewpoint, this was heresy: the fundament of that doctrine was the proposition that any central government had as its constituents the states, not the people, and could only reach the people through the agency of the state government.

Paterson then reopened the agenda of the Convention, but he did so within a distinctly nationalist framework. Paterson's position was one of favoring a strong central government in principle, but opposing one which in fact *put the big states in the saddle.* (The Virginia Plan, for all its abstract merits, did very well by Virginia.) As evidence for this speculation, there is a curious and intriguing proposal among Paterson's preliminary drafts of the New Jersey Plan:

> Whereas it is necessary in Order to form the People of the U.S. of America in to a Nation, that the States should be consolidated, by which means all the Citizens thereof will become equally intitled to and will equally participate in the same Privileges and Rights . . . it is therefore resolved, that all the Lands contained within the Limits of each state individually, and of the U.S. generally be considered as constituting one Body or Mass, and be divided into thirteen or more integral parts.
>
> Resolved, That such Divisions or integral Parts shall be styled Districts.

This makes it sound as though Paterson was prepared to accept a strong unified central government along the lines of the Virginia Plan if the existing states were eliminated. He may have gotten the idea from his New Jersey colleague Judge David Brearley, who on June 9 had commented that the only remedy to the dilemma over representation was "that a map of the U.S. be spread out, that all the existing boundaries be erased, and that a new partition of the whole be made into 13 equal parts." According to Yates, Brearley added at this point, "then a government on the present [Virginia Plan] system will be just."

This proposition was never pushed — it was patently unrealistic — but one can appreciate its purpose: it would have separated the men from the boys in the large-state delegations. How attached would the Virginians have been to their reform principles if Virginia were to disappear as a component geographical unit (the largest) for representational purposes? Up to this point, the Virginians had been in the happy position of supporting high ideals with that inner confidence born of knowledge that the "public interest" they endorsed would nourish their private interest. Worse, they had shown little willingness to compromise. Now the delegates from the small states announced that they were unprepared to be offered up as sacrificial victims to a "national interest" which reflected Virginia's parochial ambition. Caustic Charles Pinckney was not far off when he remarked sardonically that "the whole [conflict] comes to this": "Give N. Jersey an equal vote, and she will dismiss her scruples, and concur in the Natl. system." What he rather unfairly did not add was that the Jersey delegates were not free agents who could adhere to their private convictions; they had to take back, sponsor and risk their reputations on the reforms approved by the Convention — and in New Jersey, not in Virginia.

Paterson spoke on Saturday, and one can surmise that over the weekend there was a good deal of consultation, argument, and caucusing among the delegates. One member at least prepared a full length address: on Monday Alexander Hamilton, previously mute, rose and delivered a six-hour oration. It was a remarkably apolitical speech; the gist of his position was that *both* the Virginia and New Jersey Plans were inadequately centralist, and he detailed a reform program which was reminiscent of the Protectorate under the Cromwellian *Instrument of Government* of 1653. It has been suggested that Hamilton did this in the best political tradition to emphasize the moderate character of the Viriginia Plan, to give the cautious delegates something *really* to worry about; but this interpretation seems somehow too clever. Particularly since the sentiments Hamilton expressed happened to be completely consistent with those he privately — and sometimes publicly — expressed throughout his life. He wanted, to take a striking phrase from a letter to George Washington, a "strong well mounted government"; in essence, the Hamilton Plan contemplated an elected life monarch, virtually free of public control, on the Hobbesian ground that only in this fashion could strength and stability be achieved. The other alternatives, he argued, would put policy-making at the mercy of the passions of the mob; only if the sovereign was beyond the reach of selfish influence would it be possible to have government in the interests of the whole community.

From all accounts, this was a masterful and compelling speech, but (aside from furnishing John Lansing and Luther Martin with ammunition for later use against the Constitution) it made little impact. Hamilton was simply transmitting on a different wavelength from the rest of the delegates; the latter adjourned after his great effort, admired his rhetoric, and then returned to business. It was rather as if they had taken a day off to attend the opera. Hamilton, never a particularly patient man or much of a negotiator, stayed for another ten days and then left, in considerable disgust, for New York. Although he came back to Philadelphia sporadically and attended the last two weeks of the Convention, Hamilton played no part in the laborious task of hammering out the Constitution. His day came later when he led the New York Constitutionalists into the savage imbroglio over ratification — an arena in which his unmatched talent for dirty political infighting may well have won the day. For instance, in the New York Ratifying Convention, Lansing threw back into Hamilton's teeth the sentiments the latter had expressed in his June 18 oration in the Convention. However, having since retreated to the fine defensive positions immortalized in *The Federalist,* the Colonel flatly denied that he had ever been an enemy of the states, or had believed that conflict between states and nation was inexorable! As Madison's authoritative *Notes* did not appear until 1840, and there had been no press coverage, there was no way to verify his assertions, so in the words of the reporter, "a warm personal altercation between [Lansing and Hamilton] engrossed the remainder of the day [June 28, 1788]."

IV

On Tuesday morning, June 19, the vacation was over. James Madison led off with a long, carefully reasoned speech analyzing the New Jersey Plan which, while intellectually vigorous in its criticisms, was quite conciliatory in mood. "The great difficulty," he observed, "lies in the affair of Representation; and if this could be adjusted, all others would be surmountable." (As events were to demonstrate, this diagnosis was correct.) When he finished, a vote was taken on whether to continue with the Virginia Plan as the nucleus for a new constitution: seven states voted "Yes"; New York, New Jersey, and Delaware voted "No"; and Maryland, whose position often depended on which delegates happened to be on the floor, divided. Paterson, it seems, lost decisively; yet in a fundamental sense he and his allies had achieved their purpose: from that day onward, it could never be forgotten that the state governments loomed ominously in the background and that no verbal incantations could exorcise their power. Moreover, nobody bolted the Convention: Paterson and his colleagues took their defeat in stride and set to work to modify the Virginia Plan, particularly with respect to its provisions on representation in the national legislature. Indeed, they won an immediate rhetorical bonus; when Oliver Ellsworth of Connecticut rose to move that the word "national" be expunged from the Third Virginia Resolution ("Resolved that a *national* Government ought to be established consisting of a *supreme* Legislative, Executive and Judiciary"), Randolph agreed and the motion passed unanimously. The process of compromise had begun.

For the next two weeks, the delegates circled around the problem of legislative representation. The Connecticut delegation appears to have evolved a possible compromise quite early in the debates, but the Virginians and particularly Madison (unaware that he would later be acclaimed as the prophet of "federalism") fought obdurately against providing for equal representation of states in the second chamber. There was a good deal of acrimony and at one point Benjamin Franklin — of all people — proposed the institution of a daily prayer; practical politicians in the gathering, however, were meditating more on the merits of a good committee than on the utility of Divine intervention. On July 2, the ice began to break when through a number of fortuitous events — and one that seems deliberate — the majority against equality of representation was converted into a dead tie. The Convention had reached the stage where it was "ripe" for a solution (presumably all the therapeutic speeches had been made), and the South Carolinians proposed a committee. Madison and James Wilson wanted none of it, but with only Pennsylvania dissenting, the body voted to establish a working party on the problem of representation.

The members of this committee, one from each state, were elected by the delegates — and a very interesting committee it was. Despite the fact that the Virginia Plan had held majority support up to that date, neither Madison nor Randolph was selected (Mason was the Virginian) and Baldwin of Georgia, whose shift in position had resulted in the tie, was chosen. From the composition, it was clear that this was not to be a "fighting" committee: the emphasis in membership was on what might be described as "second-level political entrepreneurs." On the basis of the discussions up to that time, only Luther Martin of Maryland could be described as a "bitter-ender." Admittedly, some divination enters into this sort of analysis, but one does get a sense of the mood of the delegates from these choices — including the interesting selection of Benjamin Franklin, despite his age and intellectual wobbliness, over the brilliant and incisive Wilson or the sharp, polemical Gouverneur Morris, to represent Pennsylvania. His passion for conciliation was more valuable at this juncture than Wilson's logical genius, or Morris's acerbic wit.

There is a common rumor that the framers divided their time between philosophical discussions of government and reading the classics in political theory. Perhaps this is as good a time as any to note that their concerns were highly practical, that they spent little time canvassing abstractions. A number of them had some acquaintance with the history of political theory (probably gained from reading John Adams's monumental compilation *A Defense of the Constitutions of Government,* the first volume of which appeared in 1786), and it was a poor rhetorician indeed who could not cite Locke, Montesquieu, or Harrington *in support* of a desired goal. Yet up to this point in the deliberations, no one had expounded a defense of states' rights or the "separation of powers" on anything resembling a theoretical basis. It should be reiterated that the Madison model had no room either for the states or for the "separation of powers": effectively *all* governmental power was vested in the national legislature. The merits of Montesquieu did not turn up until *The Federalist;* and although a perverse argument could be made that Madison's ideal was truly in the tradition of John Locke's *Second Treatise of Government,* the Locke whom the American rebels treated as an honorary president was a pluralistic defender of vested rights, not of parliamentary supremacy.

It would be tedious to continue a blow-by-blow analysis of the work of the delegates; the critical fight was over representation of the states and once the Connecticut Compromise was adopted on July 17, the Convention was over the hump. Madison, James Wilson, and Gouverneur Morris of New York (who was there representing Pennsylvania!) fought the compromise all the way in a last-ditch effort to get a unitary state with parliamentary supremacy. But their allies deserted them and they demonstrated after their defeat the essential opportunist character of their objections — using "opportunist" here in a nonpejorative sense, to indicate a willingness to swallow their objections and get on with the business. Moreover, once the compromise had carried (by five states to four, with one state divided), its advocates threw themselves vigorously into the job of strengthening the general government's substantive powers — as might have been predicted, indeed, from Paterson's early statements. It nourishes an increased respect for Madison's devotion to the art of politics, to realize that this dogged fighter could sit down six months later and prepare essays for *The Federalist* in contradiction to his basic convictions about the true course the Convention should have taken.

V

Two tricky issues will serve to illustrate the later process of accommodation. The first was the institutional position of the Executive. Madison argued for an executive chosen by the national legislature and on May 29 this had been adopted with a provision that after his seven-year term was concluded, the chief magistrate should not be eligible for reelection. In late July this was reopened and for a week the matter was argued from several different points of view. A good deal of desultory speech-making ensued, but the gist of the problem was the opposition from two sources to election by the legislature. One group felt that the states should have a hand in the process; another small but influential circle urged direct election by the people. There were a number of proposals: election by the people, election by state governors, by electors chosen by state legislatures, by the national legislature (James Wilson, perhaps ironically, proposed at one point that an Electoral College be chosen by lot from the national legislature!), and there was some resemblance to three-dimensional chess in the dispute because of the presence of two other variables, length of tenure and reeligibility. Finally, after opening, reopening, and re-reopening the debate, the thorny problem was consigned to a committee for absolution.

The Brearley Committee on Postponed Matters was a superb aggregation of talent and its compromise on the Executive was a masterpiece of political improvisation. (The Electoral College, its creation, however, had little in its favor as an *institution* — as the delegates well appreciated.) The point of departure for all discussion about the presidency in the Convention was that in immediate terms, the problem was nonexistent; in other words, everybody present knew that under any system devised, George Washington would be President. Thus they were dealing in the future tense and to a body of working politicians the merits of the Brearley proposal were obvious: everybody got a piece of cake. (Or to put it more academically, each viewpoint could leave the Convention and argue to its constituents that it had *really* won the day.) First, the state legislatures had the right to determine the mode of selection of the electors; second, the small states received a bonus in the Electoral College in the form of a guaranteed minimum of three votes while the big states got acceptance of the principle of proportional power; third, if the state legislatures agreed (as six did in the first presidential election), the people could be involved directly in the choice of electors; and finally, if no candidate received a majority in the College, the right of decision passed to the national legislature with each state exercising equal strength. (In the Brearley recommendation, the election went to the Senate, but a motion from the floor substituted the House; this was accepted on the ground that the Senate already had enough authority over the executive in its treaty and appointment powers.)

This compromise was almost too good to be true, and the framers snapped it up with little debate or controversy. No one seemed to think well of the College as an *institution;* indeed, what evidence there is suggests that there was an assumption that once Washington had finished his tenure as President, the electors would cease to produce majorities and the Chief Executive would usually be chosen in the House. George Mason observed casually that the selection would be made in the House nineteen times in twenty and no one seriously disputed this point. The vital aspect of the Electoral College was that it got the Convention over the hurdle and protected everybody's interests. The future was left to cope with the problem of what to do with this Rube Goldberg mechanism.

In short, the framers did not in their wisdom endow the United States with a college of Cardinals — the Electoral College was neither an exercise in applied Platonism nor an experiment in indirect government based on elitist distrust of the masses. It was merely a jerry-rigged improvisation which has subsequently been endowed with a high theoretical content. When an elector from Oklahoma in 1960 refused to cast his vote for Nixon (naming Byrd and Goldwater instead) on the ground that the Founding Fathers intended him to exercise his great independent wisdom, he was indulging in historical fantasy. If one were to indulge in counter-fantasy, he would be tempted to suggest that the Fathers would be startled to find the College still in operation — and perhaps even dismayed at their descendants' lack of judgment or inventiveness.

The second issue on which some substantial practical bargaining took place was slavery. The morality of slavery was, by design, not at issue; but in its other concrete aspects, slavery colored the arguments over taxation, commerce, and representation. The "Three-Fifths Compromise," that three-fifths of the slaves would be counted both for representation and for purposes of direct taxation (which was drawn from the past — it was a formula of Madison's utilized by Congress in 1783 to establish the basis of state contributions to the Confederation treasury) had allayed some Northern fears about Southern overrepresentation (no one then foresaw the trivial role that direct taxation would play in later federal financial policy), but doubts still remained. The Southerners, on the other hand, were afraid that Congressional control over commerce would lead to the exclusion of slaves or to their excessive taxation as imports. Moreover, the Southerners were disturbed over "navigation acts," i.e., tariffs, or special legislation providing, for example, that exports be carried only in American ships; as a section depending upon exports, they wanted protection from the potential voracity of their commercial brethren of the Eastern states. To achieve this end, Mason and others urged that the Constitution include a proviso that navigation and commercial laws should require a two-thirds vote in Congress.

These problems came to a head in late August and, as usual, were handed to a committee in the hope that, in Gouverneur Morris's words, "these things may form a bargain among the Northern and Southern States." The Committee reported its measures of reconciliation on August 25, and on August 29 the package was wrapped up and delivered. What occurred can best be described in George Mason's dour version (he anticipated Calhoun in his conviction that permitting navigation acts to pass by majority vote would put the South in economic bondage to the North — it was mainly on this ground that he refused to sign the Constitution):

> The Constitution as agreed to till a fortnight before the Convention rose was such a one as he would have set his hand and heart to. . . . [Until that time] The 3 New England States were constantly with us in all questions . . . so that it was these three States with the 5 Southern ones against Pennsylvania, Jersey and Delaware. With respect to the importation of slaves, [decision-making] was left to Congress. This disturbed the two Southern-most States who knew that Congress would immediately suppress the importation of slaves. Those two States therefore struck up a bargain with the three New England States. If they would join to admit slaves for some years, the two Southern-most States would join in changing the clause which required the ⅔ of the Legislature in any vote [on navigation acts]. It was done.

On the floor of the Convention there was a virtual love-feast on this happy occasion. Charles Pinckney of South Carolina attempted to overturn the committee's decision, when the compromise was reported to the Convention, by insisting that the South needed protection from the imperialism of the Northern states. But his Southern colleagues were not prepared to rock the boat and General C. C. Pinckney arose to spread oil on the suddenly ruffled waters; he admitted that:

> It was in the true interest of the S[outhern] States to have no regulation of
> commerce; but considering the loss brought on the commerce of the East-
> ern States by the Revolution, their liberal conduct towards the views of
> South Carolina [on the regulation of the slave trade] and the interests the
> weak Southn. States had in being united with the strong Eastern states, he
> thought it proper that no fetters should be imposed on the power of mak-
> ing commercial regulations; *and that his constituents, though prejudiced
> against the Eastern States, would be reconciled to this liberality.* He had
> himself prejudices agst the Eastern States before he came here, but would
> acknowledge that he had found them as liberal and candid as any men
> whatever. (Italics added.)

Pierce Butler took the same tack, essentially arguing that he was not too
happy about the possible consequences, but that a deal was a deal. Many
Southern leaders were later — in the wake of the "Tariff of Abominations"
— to rue this day of reconciliation; Calhoun's *Disquisition on Government*
was little more than an extension of the argument in the Convention against
permitting a Congressional majority to enact navigation acts.

VI

Drawing on their vast collective political experience, utilizing every weapon
in the politician's arsenal, looking constantly over their shoulders at their
constituents, the delegates put together a Constitution. It was a makeshift
affair; some sticky issues (for example, the qualification of voters) they
ducked entirely; others they mastered with that ancient instrument of political sagacity, studied ambiguity (for example, citizenship), and some they
just overlooked. In this last category, I suspect, fell the matter of the power
of the federal courts to determine the constitutionality of acts of Congress.
When the judicial article was formulated (Article III of the Constitution),
deliberations were still in the stage where the legislature was endowed with
broad power under the Randolph formulation, authority which by its own
terms was scarcely amenable to judicial review. In essence, courts could
hardly determine when "the separate States are incompetent or . . . the harmony of the United States may be interrupted"; the national legislature, as
critics pointed out, was free to define its own jurisdiction. Later the definition of legislative authority was changed into the form we know, a series of
stipulated powers, *but the delegates never seriously reexamined the jurisdiction of the judiciary under this new limited formulation.* All arguments
on the intention of the framers in this matter are thus deductive and *a posteriori,* though some obviously make more sense than others.

The framers were busy and distinguished men, anxious to get back to
their families, their positions, and their constituents, not members of the
French Academy devoting a lifetime to a dictionary. They were trying to do
an important job, and do it in such a fashion that their handiwork would

be acceptable to very diverse constituencies. No one was rhapsodic about the final document, but it was a beginning, a move in the right direction, and one they had reason to believe the people would endorse. In addition, since they had modified the impossible amendment provisions of the Articles (the requirement of unanimity which could always be frustrated by Rogues Island") to one demanding approval by only three-quarters of the states, they seemed confident that gaps in the fabric which experience would reveal could be rewoven without undue difficulty.

So with a neat phrase introduced by Benjamin Franklin (but devised by Gouverneur Morris) which made their decision sound unanimous, and an inspired benediction by the Old Doctor urging doubters to doubt their own infallibility, the Constitution was accepted and signed. Curiously, Edmund Randolph, who had played so vital a role throughout, refused to sign, as did his fellow Virginian George Mason and Elbridge Gerry of Massachusetts. Randolph's behavior was eccentric, to say the least — his excuses for refusing his signature have a factitious ring even at this late date; the best explanation seems to be that he was afraid that the Constitution would prove to be a liability in Virginia politics, where Patrick Henry was burning up the countryside with impassioned denunciations. Presumably, Randolph wanted to check the temper of the populace before he risked his reputation, and perhaps his job, in a fight with both Henry and Richard Henry Lee. Events lend some justification to this speculation: after much temporizing and use of the conditional subjunctive tense, Randolph endorsed ratification in Virginia and ended up getting the best of both worlds.

Madison, despite his reservations about the Constitution, was the campaign manager in ratification. His first task was to get the Congress in New York to light its own funeral pyre by approving the "amendments" to the Articles and sending them on to the state legislatures. Above all, momentum had to be maintained. The anti-Constitutionalists, now thoroughly alarmed and no novices in politics, realized that their best tactic was attrition rather than direct opposition. Thus they settled on a position expressing qualified approval but calling for a second Convention to remedy various defects (the one with the most demagogic appeal was the lack of a Bill of Rights). Madison knew that to accede to this demand would be equivalent to losing the battle, nor would he agree to conditional approval (despite wavering even by Hamilton). This was an all-or-nothing proposition: national salvation or national impotence with no intermediate positions possible. Unable to get Congressional approval, he settled for second best: a unanimous resolution of Congress transmitting the Constitution to the states for whatever action they saw fit to take. The opponents then moved from New York and the Congress, where they had attempted to attach amendments and conditions, to the states for the final battle.

At first the campaign for ratification went beautifully: within eight months after the delegates set their names to the document, eight states had ratified. Only in Massachusetts had the result been close (187–168). Theoretically, a ratification by one more state convention would set the new government in motion, but in fact until Virginia and New York acceded to the new Union, the latter was a fiction. New Hampshire was the next to ratify; Rhode Island was involved in its characteristic political convulsions (the legislature there sent the Constitution out to the towns for decision by popular vote and it got lost among a series of local issues); North Carolina's convention did not meet until July and then postponed a final decision. This is hardly the place for an extensive analysis of the conventions of New York and Virginia. Suffice it to say that the Constitutionalists clearly outmaneuvered their opponents, forced them into impossible political positions, and won both states narrowly. The Virginia Convention could serve as a classic study in effective floor management: Patrick Henry had to be contained, and a reading of the debates discloses a standard two-stage technique. Henry would give a four- or five-hour speech denouncing some section of the Constitution on every conceivable ground (the federal district, he averred at one point, would become a haven for convicts escaping from state authority!); when Henry subsided, "Mr. Lee of Westmoreland" would rise and literally poleax him with sardonic invective (when Henry complained about the militia power, "Lighthorse Harry" really punched below the belt: observing that while the former Governor had been sitting in Richmond during the Revolution, *he* had been out in the trenches with the troops and thus felt better qualified to discuss military affairs). Then the gentlemanly Constitutionalists (Madison, Pendleton, and Marshall) would pick up the matters at issue and examine them in the light of reason.

Indeed, modern Americans who tend to think of James Madison as a rather desiccated character should spend some time with this transcript. Probably Madison put on his most spectacular demonstration of nimble rhetoric in what might be called "The Battle of the Absent Authorities." Patrick Henry in the course of one of his harangues alleged that Jefferson was known to be opposed to Virginia's approving the Constitution. This was clever: Henry hated Jefferson, but was prepared to use any weapon that came to hand. Madison's riposte was superb: First, he said that with all due respect to the great reputation of Jefferson, he was not in the country and therefore could not formulate an adequate judgment; second, no one should utilize the reputation of an outsider — the Virginia Convention was there to think for itself; third, if there were to be recourse to outsiders, the opinions of George Washington should certainly be taken into consideration; and finally, he knew from privileged personal communications from Jefferson that in fact the latter *strongly favored* the Constitution. To devise an assault route into this rhetorical fortress was literally impossible.

VII

The fight was over; all that remained now was to establish the new frame of government in the spirit of its framers. And who were better qualified for this task than the framers themselves? Thus victory for the Constitution meant simultaneous victory for the Constitutionalists; the anti-Constitutionalists either capitulated or vanished into limbo — soon Patrick Henry would be offered a seat on the Supreme Court and Luther Martin would be known as the Federalist "bull-dog." And irony of ironies, Alexander Hamilton and James Madison would shortly accumulate a reputation as the formulators of what is often alleged to be our political theory, the concept of "federalism." Also, on the other side of the ledger, the arguments would soon appear over what the framers "really meant"; while these disputes have assumed the proportions of a big scholarly business in the last century, they began almost before the ink on the Constitution was dry. One of the best early ones featured Hamilton versus Madison on the scope of presidential power, and other framers characteristically assumed positions in this and other disputes on the basis of their political convictions.

Probably our greatest difficulty is that we know so much more about what the framers *should have meant* than they themselves did. We are intimately acquainted with the problems that their Constitution should have been designed to master; in short, we have read the mystery story backwards. If we are to get the right "feel" for their time and their circumstances, we must in Maitland's phrase, "think ourselves back into a twilight." Obviously, no one can pretend completely to escape from the solipsistic web of his own environment, but if the effort is made, it is possible to appreciate the past roughly on its own terms. The first step in this process is to abandon the academic premise that because we can ask a question, there must be an answer.

Thus we can ask what the framers meant when they gave Congress the power to regulate interstate and foreign commerce, and we emerge, reluctantly perhaps, with the reply that they may not have known what they meant, that there may not have been any semantic consensus. The Convention was not a seminar in analytic philosophy or linguistic analysis. Commerce was *commerce* — and if different interpretations of the word arose, later generations could worry about the problem of definition. The delegates were in a hurry to get a new government established; when definitional arguments arose, they characteristically took refuge in ambiguity. If different men voted for the same proposition for varying reasons, that was politics (and still is); if later generations were unsettled by this lack of precision, that would be their problem.

There was a good deal of definitional pluralism with respect to the problems the delegates did discuss, but when we move to the question of extrapolated intentions, we enter the realm of spiritualism. When men in our time, for instance, launch into elaborate talmudic exegesis to demonstrate that federal aid to parochial schools is (or is not) in accord with the intentions of the men who established the Republic and endorsed the Bill of Rights, they are engaging in historical Extra-Sensory Perception. (If one were to join this E.S.P. contingent for a minute, he might suggest that the hard-boiled politicians who wrote the Constitution and Bill of Rights would chuckle scornfully at such an invocation of authority: obviously a politician would chart his course on the intentions of the living, not of the dead, and count the number of Catholics in his constituency.)

The Constitution, then, was not an apotheosis of "constitutionalism," a triumph of architectonic genius; it was a patch-work sewn together under the pressure of both time and events by a group of extremely talented democratic politicians. They refused to attempt the establishment of a strong, centralized sovereignty on the principle of legislative supremacy for the excellent reason that the people would not accept it. They risked their political fortunes by opposing the established doctrines of state sovereignty because they were convinced that the existing system was leading to national impotence and probably foreign domination. For two years, they worked to get a convention established. For over three months, in what must have seemed to the faithful participants an endless process of give-and-take, they reasoned, cajoled, threatened, and bargained amongst themselves. The result was a Constitution which the people, in fact, by democratic processes, did accept, and a new and far better national government was established.

Beginning with the inspired propaganda of Hamilton, Madison, and Jay, the ideological build-up got under way. *The Federalist* had little impact on the ratification of the Constitution, except perhaps in New York, but this volume had enormous influence on the image of the Constitution in the minds of future generations, particularly on historians and political scientists who have an innate fondness for theoretical symmetry. Yet, while the shades of Locke and Montesquieu *may* have been hovering in the background, and the delegates *may* have been unconscious instruments of a transcendent *telos,* the careful observer of the day-to-day work of the Convention finds no overarching principles. The "separation of powers" to him seems to be a by-product of suspicion, and "federalism" he views as a *pis aller,* as the farthest point the delegates felt they could go in the destruction of state power without themselves inviting repudiation.

To conclude, the Constitution was neither a victory for abstract theory nor a great practical success. Well over half a million men had to die on the battlefields of the Civil War before certain constitutional principles could be defined — a baleful consideration which is somehow overlooked in our customary tributes to the farsighted genius of the framers and to the supposed American talent for "constitutionalism." The Constitution was, however, a vivid demonstration of effective democratic political action, and of the forging of a national elite which literally persuaded its countrymen to hoist themselves by their own boot straps. American pro-consuls would be wise not to translate the Constitution into Japanese, or Swahili, or treat it as a work of semi-Divine origin; but when students of comparative politics examine the process of nation-building in countries newly freed from colonial rule, they may find the American experience instructive as a classic example of the potentialities of a democratic elite.

John Roche's article on the framing of the Constitution was written as an attack upon a variety of views that suggested the Constitution was not so much a practical political document, as an expression of elitist views based upon political philosophy and economic interests. One such elitist view was that of Charles A. Beard, who published his famous *An Economic Interpretation of the Constitution* in 1913. He suggested that the Constitution was nothing more than the work of an economic elite that was seeking to preserve its property. This elite, according to Beard, consisted of landholders, creditors, merchants, public bondholders, and wealthy lawyers. Beard demonstrated that many of the delegates to the convention fell into one of these categories.

According to Beard's thesis, as the delegates met, the primary concern of most of them was to limit the power of popular majorities and thus protect their own property interests. To Beard, the antimajoritarian attributes that he felt existed in the Constitution were a reflection of the less numerous creditor class attempting to protect itself against incursions by the majority. Specific provisions as well were put into the Constitution with a view towards protecting property, such as the clause prohibiting states from impairing contracts, coining money, or emitting bills of credit. Control over money was placed in the hands of the national government, and in Article VI of the Constitution it was provided that the new government was to guarantee all debts that had been incurred by the national government under the Articles of Confederation.

Ironically, Beard, like Roche, was attempting to dispel the prevailing notions of his time that the Constitution had been formulated by philosopher kings whose wisdom could not be challenged. But while Roche postulates a loosely knit practical political elite, Beard suggests the existence of a cohesive and even conspiratorial economic elite. The limitation on majority rule was an essential component of this economic conspiracy.

The Constitution does contain many provisions that limit majority rule. Beard claimed that the Constitution from initial adoption to final ratification was never supported by the majority of the people. Holding a constitutional convention in the first place was never submitted to a popular vote, nor was the Constitution that was finally agreed upon ratified by a popular referendum. The selection of delegates to state ratifying conventions was not executed through universal suffrage, but on the basis of the suffrage qualifications that applied in the states and that were within the discretion of state legislatures. The limited suffrage in the states severely restricted popular participation in ratification of the Constitution.

Beard's thesis was startling at the time it was published in 1913. As it came under close examination, it was revealed that the evidence simply did not support Beard's hypothesis. Key leaders of the convention, including Madison, were not substantial property owners. Several important opponents to ratification of the Constitution were the very members of the economic elite that Beard said conspired to thrust the Constitution upon an unknowing public.

Before Beard presented his narrow thesis in 1913, he had published in 1912 *The Supreme Court and the Constitution.* The major theme of the book was that the Supreme Court was intended to have the authority to review acts of Congress under the terms of the original Constitution. At the same time, the book presents Beard's elitist view of the framing of the Constitution in a somewhat broader context than it was presented in *An Economic Interpretation of the Constitution* published a year later. But the earlier work clearly contains the economic theme, as in the passage where Beard states that the framers of the Constitution were "anxious above everything else to safeguard the rights of private property against any levelling tendencies on the part of the propertyless masses." The following selection contains Beard's overview of the framing and adoption of the Constitution, and highlights his economic theme and his belief in the antimajoritarian attributes of the Constitution.

2
Charles A. Beard

FRAMING THE CONSTITUTION

As Blackstone[1] shows by happy illustration the reason and spirit of a law are to be understood only by an inquiry into the circumstances of its enactment. The underlying purposes of the Constitution [of the United States], therefore, are to be revealed only by a study of the conditions and events which led to its formation and adoption.

At the outset it must be remembered that there were two great parties at the time of the adoption of the Constitution — one laying emphasis on strength and efficiency in government and the other on its popular aspects. Quite naturally the men who led in stirring up the revolt against Great Britain and in keeping the fighting temper of the Revolutionists at the proper heat were the boldest and most radical thinkers — men like Samuel Adams, Thomas Paine, Patrick Henry, and Thomas Jefferson. They were

---

From Chapter X from *The Economic Basis of Politics and Related Writings by Charles A. Beard,* compiled and annotated by William Beard, © 1957 by William Beard and Miriam B. Vagts. Reprinted here by permission of the copyright holders. The original text is The Supreme Court and the Constitution. Footnotes are renumbered.

[1] *Compiler's Note:* Blackstone, Sir William (1723–1780). Distinguished commentator on the laws of England, judge, and teacher.

not, generally speaking, men of large property interests or of much practical business experience. In a time of disorder, they could consistently lay more stress upon personal liberty than upon social control; and they pushed to the extreme limits those doctrines of individual rights which had been evolved in England during the struggles of the small landed proprietors and commercial classes against royal prerogative, and which corresponded to the economic conditions prevailing in America at the close of the eighteenth century. They associated strong government with monarchy, and came to believe that the best political system was one which governed least. A majority of the radicals viewed all government, especially if highly centralized, as a species of evil, tolerable only because necessary and always to be kept down to an irreducible minimum by a jealous vigilance.

Jefferson put the doctrine in concrete form when he declared that he preferred newspapers without government to government without newspapers. The Declaration of Independence, the first state Constitutions, and the Articles of Confederation bore the impress of this philosophy. In their anxiety to defend the individual against all federal interference and to preserve to the states a large sphere of local autonomy, these Revolutionists had set up a system too weak to accomplish the accepted objects of government; namely, national defense, the protection of property, and the advancement of commerce. They were not unaware of the character of their handiwork, but they believed with Jefferson that "man was a rational animal endowed by nature with rights and with an innate sense of justice and that he could be restrained from wrong and protected in right by moderate powers confided to persons of his own choice." Occasional riots and disorders, they held, were preferable to too much government.

The new American political system based on these doctrines had scarcely gone into effect before it began to incur opposition from many sources. The close of the Revolutionary struggle removed the prime cause for radical agitation and brought a new group of thinkers into prominence. When independence had been gained, the practical work to be done was the maintenance of social order, the payment of the public debt, the provision of a sound financial system, and the establishment of conditions favorable to the development of the economic resources of the new country. The men who were principally concerned in this work of peaceful enterprise were not the philosophers, but men of business and property and the holders of public securities. For the most part they had had no quarrel with the system of class rule and the strong centralization of government which existed in England. It was on the question of policy, not of governmental structure, that they had broken with the British authorities. By no means all of them, in fact, had even resisted the policy of the mother country, for within the ranks of the conservatives were large numbers of Loyalists who had remained in America, and, as was to have been expected, cherished a bitter feeling against the Revolutionists, especially the radical section which had been boldest in denouncing the English system root and branch. In other words, after the heat and excitement of the War of Independence were over and the new government, state and national, was tested by the ordinary experiences of traders, financiers, and manufacturers, it was found inadequate, and these groups accordingly grew more and more determined to reconstruct the political system in such a fashion as to make it subserve their permanent interests.

Under the state constitutions and the Articles of Confederation established during the Revolution, every powerful economic class in the nation suffered either immediate losses or from impediments placed in the way of the development of their enterprises. The holders of the securities of the Confederate government did not receive the interest on their loans. Those who owned Western lands or looked with longing eyes upon the rich opportunities for speculation there chaffed at the weakness of the government and its delays in establishing order on the frontiers. Traders and commercial men found their plans for commerce on a national scale impeded by local interference with interstate commerce. The currency of the states and the nation was hopelessly muddled. Creditors everywhere were angry about the depreciated paper money which the agrarians had made and were attempting to force upon those from whom they had borrowed specie. In short, it was a war between business and populism. Under the Articles of Confederation populism had a free hand, for majorities in the state legislatures were omnipotent. Anyone who reads the economic history of the time will see why the solid conservative interests of the country were weary of talk about the "rights of the people" and bent upon establishing firm guarantees for the rights of property.

The Congress of the Confederation was not long in discovering the true character of the futile authority which the Articles had conferred upon it. The necessity for new sources of revenue became apparent even while the struggle for independence was yet undecided, and, in 1781, Congress carried a resolution to the effect that it should be authorized to lay a duty of five percent on certain goods. This moderate proposition was defeated because Rhode Island rejected it on the grounds that "she regarded it the most precious jewel of sovereignty that no state shall be called upon to open its purse but by the authority of the state and by her own officers." Two years later Congress prepared another amendment to the Articles providing for certain import duties, the receipts from which, collected by state officers, were to be applied to the payment of the public debt; but three years after the introduction of the measure, four states, including New York, still held out against its ratification, and the project was allowed to drop. At last, in 1786, Congress in a resolution declared that the requisitions for the last eight years had been so irregular in their operation, so uncertain in their collection, and so evidently unproductive, that a reliance on them in the future would be no less dishonorable to the understandings of those who entertained it than it would be dangerous to the welfare and peace of the Union. Congress, thereupon, solemnly added that it had become its duty "to declare most explicitly that the crisis had arrived when the people of the United States, by whose will and for whose benefit the federal government was instituted, must decide whether they will support their rank as a nation by maintaining the public faith at home and abroad, or whether for the want of a timely exertion in establishing a general revenue and thereby giving strength to the Confederacy, they will hazard not only the existence of the Union but those great and invaluable privileges for which they have so arduously and so honorably contended."

In fact, the Articles of Confederation had hardly gone into effect before the leading citizens also began to feel that the powers of Congress were wholly inadequate. In 1780, even before their adoption, Alexander Hamilton proposed a general convention to frame a new constitution, and from that time forward he labored with remarkable zeal and wisdom to extend and popularize the idea of a strong national government. Two years later, the Assembly of the State of New York recommended a convention to revise the Articles and increase the power of Congress. In 1783, Washington, in a circular letter to the governors, urged that it was indispensable to the happiness of the individual states that there should be lodged somewhere a supreme power to regulate and govern the general concerns of the confederation. Shortly afterward (1785), Governor Bowdoin, of Massachusetts, suggested to his state legislature the advisability of calling a national assembly to settle upon and define the powers of Congress; and the legislature resolved that the government under the Articles of Confederation was inadequate and should be reformed; but the resolution was never laid before Congress.

In January, 1786, Virginia invited all the other states to send delegates to a convention at Annapolis to consider the question of duties on imports and commerce in general. When this convention assembled in 1786, delegates from only five states were present, and they were disheartened at the limitations on their powers and the lack of interest the other states had shown in the project. With characteristic foresight, however, Alexander Hamilton seized the occasion to secure the adoption of a recommendation advising the states to choose representatives for another convention to meet in Philadelphia the following year "to consider the Articles of Confederation and to propose such changes therein as might render them adequate to the exigencies of the union." This recommendation was cautiously worded, for Hamilton did not want to raise any unnecessary alarm. He doubtless believed that a complete revolution in the old system was desirable, but he knew that, in the existing state of popular temper, it was not expedient to announce his complete program. Accordingly no general reconstruction of the political system was suggested; the Articles of Confederation were merely to be "revised"; and the amendments were to be approved by the state legislatures as provided by that instrument.

The proposal of the Annapolis convention was transmitted to the state legislatures and laid before Congress. Congress thereupon resolved in February, 1787, that a convention should be held for the sole and express purpose of revising the Articles of Confederation and reporting to itself and the legislatures of the several states such alterations and provisions as would when agreed to by Congress and confirmed by the states render the federal constitution adequate to the exigencies of government and the preservation of the union.

In pursuance of this call, delegates to the new convention were chosen by the legislatures of the states or by the governors in conformity to authority conferred by the legislative assemblies.[2] The delegates were given instructions of a general nature by their respective states, none of which, apparently, contemplated any very far-reaching changes. In fact, almost all of them expressly limited their representatives to a mere revision of the Articles of Confederation. For example, Connecticut authorized her delegates to represent and confer for the purpose mentioned in the resolution of Congress and to discuss such measures "agreeably to the general principles of Republican government" as they should think proper to render the Union adequate. Delaware, however, went so far as to provide that none of the proposed alterations should extend to the fifth part of the Articles of Confederation guaranteeing that each state should be entitled to one vote.

It was a truly remarkable assembly of men that gathered in Philadelphia on May 14, 1787, to undertake the work of reconstructing the American system of government. It is not merely patriotic pride that compels one to assert that never in the history of assemblies has there been a convention of men richer in political experience and in practical knowledge, or endowed with a profounder insight into the springs of human action and the intimate essence of government. It is indeed an astounding fact that at one time so many men skilled in statecraft could be found on the very frontiers of civilization among a population numbering about four million whites. It is no less a cause for admiration that their instrument of government should have survived the trials and crises of a century that saw the wreck of more than a score of paper constitutions.

All the members had had a practical training in politics. Washington, as commander-in-chief of the Revolutionary forces, had learned well the lessons and problems of war, and mastered successfully the no less difficult problems of administration. The two Morrises had distinguished themselves in grappling with financial questions as trying and perplexing as any which statesmen had ever been compelled to face. Seven of the delegates had gained political wisdom as governors of their native states; and no less than

---

[2] Rhode Island alone was unrepresented. In all, sixty-two delegates were appointed by the states; fifty-five of these attended sometime during the sessions; but only thirty-nine signed the finished document.

twenty-eight had served in Congress either during the Revolution or under the Articles of Confederation. These were men trained in the law, versed in finance, skilled in administration, and learned in the political philosophy of their own and all earlier times. Moreover, they were men destined to continue public service under the government which they had met to construct — Presidents, Vice-Presidents, heads of departments, Justices of the Supreme Court were in that imposing body. . . .

As Woodrow Wilson has concisely put it, the framers of the Constitution represented "a strong and intelligent class possessed of unity and informed by a conscious solidarity of interests." [3] . . .

The makers of the federal Constitution represented the solid, conservative, commercial and financial interests of the country — not the interests which denounced and proscribed judges in Rhode Island, New Jersey, and North Carolina, and stoned their houses in New York. The conservative interests, made desperate by the imbecilities of the Confederation and harried by state legislatures, roused themselves from their lethargy, drew together in a mighty effort to establish a government that would be strong enough to pay the national debt, regulate interstate and foreign commerce, provide for national defense, prevent fluctuations in the currency created by paper emissions, and control the propensities of legislative majorities to attack private rights. . . . The radicals, however, like Patrick Henry, Jefferson, and Samuel Adams, were conspicuous by their absence from the convention.[4] . . .

[The makers of the Constitution were convened] to frame a government which would meet the practical issues that had arisen under the Articles of Confederation. The objections they entertained to direct popular government, and they were undoubtedly many, were based upon their experience with popular assemblies during the immediately preceding years. With many of the plain lessons of history before them, they naturally feared that the rights and privileges of the minority would be insecure if the principle of majority rule was definitely adopted and provisions made for its exercise. Furthermore, it will be remembered that up to that time the right of all men, as men, to share in the government had never been recognized in practice. Everywhere in Europe the government was in the hands of a ruling monarch or at best a ruling class; everywhere the mass of the people had been regarded principally as an arms-bearing and tax-paying multitude, uneducated, and with little hope or capacity for advancement. Two years were to elapse after the meeting of the grave assembly at Philadelphia be-

---

[3] Woodrow Wilson, *Division and Reunion* (New York: Longmans, Green, & Co., 1893), p. 12.

[4] *Compiler's Note:* The contents of this paragraph have been taken from positions on pp. 75–76 and 88 of the original text of The Supreme Court and the Constitution and placed here to emphasize the economic theme.

fore the transformation of the Estates General into the National Convention in France opened the floodgates of revolutionary ideas on human rights before whose rising tide old landmarks of government are still being submerged. It is small wonder, therefore, that, under the circumstances, many of the members of that august body held popular government in slight esteem and took the people into consideration only as far as it was imperative "to inspire them with the necessary confidence," as Mr. Gerry frankly put it.[5]

Indeed, every page of the laconic record of the proceedings of the convention preserved to posterity by Mr. Madison shows conclusively that the members of that assembly were not seeking to realize any fine notions about democracy and equality, but were striving with all the resources of political wisdom at their command to set up a system of government that would be stable and efficient, safeguarded on one hand against the possibilities of despotism and on the other against the onslaught of majorities. In the mind of Mr. Gerry, the evils they had experienced flowed "from the excess of democracy," and he confessed that while he was still republican, he "had been taught by experience the danger of the levelling spirit." [6] Mr. Randolph in offering to the consideration of the convention his plan of government, observed "that the general object was to provide a cure for the evils under which the United States labored; that, in tracing these evils to their origin, every man had found it in the turbulence and follies of democracy; that some check therefore was to be sought for against this tendency of our governments; and that a good Senate seemed most likely to answer the purpose." [7] Mr. Hamilton, in advocating a life term for Senators, urged that "all communities divide themselves into the few and the many. The first are rich and well born and the other the mass of the people who seldom judge or determine right."

Gouverneur Morris wanted to check the "precipitancy, changeableness, and excess" of the representatives of the people by the ability and virtue of men "of great and established property — aristocracy; men who from pride will support consistency and permanency. . . . Such an aristocratic body will keep down the turbulence of democracy." While these extreme doctrines were somewhat counterbalanced by the democratic principles of Mr. Wilson who urged that "the government ought to possess, not only first, the force, but second the mind or sense of the people at large," Madison doubtless summed up in a brief sentence the general opinion of the convention when he said that to secure private rights against major-

---

[5] Jonathan Elliot, *The Debates in the Several State Conventions on the Adoption of the Federal Constitution* (Washington, D.C.: The Editor, 1827–1830), vol. v, p. 160.

[6] *Ibid.*, vol. v, p. 136.

[7] *Ibid.*, vol. v, p. 138.

ity factions, and at the same time to preserve the spirit and form of popular government, was the great object to which their inquiries had been directed.[8]

They were anxious above everything else to safeguard the rights of private property against any leveling tendencies on the part of the propertyless masses. Gouverneur Morris, in speaking on the problem of apportioning representatives, correctly stated the sound historical fact when he declared: "Life and liberty were generally said to be of more value than property. An accurate view of the matter would, nevertheless, prove that property was the main object of society. . . . If property, then, was the main object of government, certainly it ought to be one measure of the influence due to those who were to be affected by the government." [9] Mr. King also agreed that "property was the primary object of society";[10] and Mr. Madison warned the convention that in framing a system which they wished to last for ages they must not lose sight of the changes which the ages would produce in the forms and distribution of property. In advocating a long term in order to give independence and firmness to the Senate, he described these impending changes: "An increase of population will of necessity increase the proportion of those who will labor under all the hardships of life and secretly sigh for a more equal distribution of its blessings. These may in time outnumber those who are placed above the feelings of indigence. According to the equal laws of suffrage, the power will slide into the hands of the former. No agrarian attempts have yet been made in this country, but symptoms of a levelling spirit, as we have understood have sufficiently appeared, in a certain quarter, to give notice of the future danger." [11] And again, in support of the argument for a property qualification on voters, Madison urged: "In future times, a great majority of the people will not only be without landed, but any other sort of property. These will either combine, under the influence of their common situation, — in which case the rights of property and the public liberty will not be secure in their hands, — or, what is more probable, they will become the tools of opulence and ambition; in which case there will be equal danger on another side." [12] Various projects for setting up class rule by the establishment of property qualifications for voters and officers were advanced in the convention, but they were defeated. . . .

The absence of such property qualifications is certainly not due to any belief in Jefferson's free-and-equal doctrine. It is due rather to the fact that the

---

[8] *The Federalist,* No. 10.

[9] Elliot's *Debates,* op. cit., vol. v, p. 279.

[10] *Ibid.,* vol. v, p. 280.

[11] *Ibid.,* vol. v, p. 243.

[12] Elliot's *Debates,* op. cit., vol. v, p. 387.

members of the convention could not agree on the nature and amount of the qualifications. Naturally a landed qualification was suggested, but for obvious reasons it was rejected. Although it was satisfactory to the landed gentry of the South, it did not suit the financial, commercial, and manufacturing gentry of the North. If it was high, the latter would be excluded; if it was low it would let in the populistic farmers who had already made so much trouble in the state legislatures with paper-money schemes and other devices for "relieving agriculture." One of the chief reasons for calling the convention and framing the Constitution was to promote commerce and industry and to protect personal property against the "depredations" of Jefferson's noble freeholders. On the other hand a personal-property qualification, high enough to please merchant princes like Robert Morris and Nathaniel Gorham would shut out the Southern planters. Again, an alternative of land or personal property, high enough to afford safeguards to large interests, would doubtless bring about the rejection of the whole Constitution by the trouble-making farmers who had to pass upon the question of ratification.[13] . . .

Nevertheless, by the system of checks and balances placed in the government, the convention safeguarded the interests of property against attacks by majorities. The House of Representatives, Mr. Hamilton pointed out, "was so formed as to render it particularly the guardian of the poorer orders of citizens," [14] while the Senate was to preserve the rights of property and the interests of the minority against the demands of the majority.[15] In the tenth number of *The Federalist,* Mr. Madison argued in a philosophic vein in support of the proposition that it was necessary to base the political system on the actual conditions of "natural inequality." Uniformity of interests throughout the state, he contended, was impossible on account of the diversity in the faculties of men, from which the rights of property originated; the protection of these faculties was the first object of government; from the protection of different and unequal faculties of acquiring property the possession of different degrees and kinds of property immediately resulted; from the influence of these on the sentiments and views of the respective proprietors ensued a division of society into different interests and parties; the unequal distribution of wealth inevitably led to a clash of interests in which the majority was liable to carry out its policies at the expense of the minority; hence, he added, in concluding this splendid piece of logic, "the majority, having such coexistent passion or interest, must be rendered by

---

[13] *Compiler's Note:* This single paragraph from "Whom Does Congress Represent?" *Harper's Magazine,* Jan., 1930, pp. 144–152, has been inserted here because of its value in amplifying the passages from *The Supreme Court and the Constitution.* Reprinting from this article by Beard has been done with the permission of *Harper's Magazine.*

[14] Elliot's *Debates,* op. cit., vol. v, p. 244.

[15] *Ibid.,* vol. v, p. 203.

their number and local situation unable to concert and carry into effect schemes of oppression"; and in his opinion it was the great merit of the newly framed Constitution that it secured the rights of the minority against "the superior force of an interested and overbearing majority."

This very system of checks and balances, which is undeniably the essential element of the Constitution, is built upon the doctrine that the popular branch of the government cannot be allowed full sway, and least of all in the enactment of laws touching the rights of property. The exclusion of the direct popular vote in the election of the President; the creation, again by indirect election, of a Senate which the framers hoped would represent the wealth and conservative interests of the country;[16] and the establishment of an independent judiciary appointed by the President with the concurrence of the Senate — all these devices bear witness to the fact that the underlying purpose of the Constitution was not the establishment of popular government by means of parliamentary majorities.

Page after page of *The Federalist* is directed to that portion of the electorate which was disgusted with the "mutability of the public councils." Writing on the presidential veto Hamilton says: "The propensity of the legislative department to intrude upon the rights, and absorb the powers, of the other departments has already been suggested and repeated. . . . It may perhaps be said that the power of preventing bad laws included the power of preventing good ones; and may be used to the one purpose as well as the other. But this objection will have little weight with those who can properly estimate the mischiefs of that inconstancy and mutability in the laws which form the greatest blemish in the character and genius of our governments. They will consider every institution calculated to restrain the excess of law-making and to keep things in the same state in which they happen to be at any given period, as more likely to do good than harm; because it is favorable to greater stability in the system of legislation. The injury which may be possibly done by defeating a few good laws will be amply compensated by the advantage of preventing a number of bad ones."

When the framers of the Constitution had completed the remarkable instrument which was to establish a national government capable of discharging effectively certain great functions and checking the propensities of popular legislatures to attack the rights of private property, a formidable task remained before them — the task of securing the adoption of the new frame of government by states torn with popular dissensions. They knew very well that the state legislatures which had been so negligent in paying their quotas [of money] under the Articles [of Confederation] and which had been so jealous of their rights, would probably stick at ratifying such

---

[16] *Compiler's Note:* Popular election of Senators was achieved in 1913 through the XVIIth Amendment to the Constitution.

a national instrument of government. Accordingly they cast aside that clause in the Articles requiring amendments to be ratified by the legislatures of all the states; and advised that the new Constitution should be ratified by conventions in the several states composed of delegates chosen by the voters.[17] They furthermore declared — and this is a fundamental matter — that when the conventions of nine states had ratified the Constitution the new government should go into effect so far as those states were concerned. The chief reason for resorting to ratifications by conventions is laid down by Hamilton in the twenty-second number of *The Federalist*: "It has not a little contributed to the infirmities of the existing federal system that it never had a ratification by the people. Resting on no better foundation than the consent of the several legislatures, it has been exposed to frequent and intricate questions concerning the validity of its powers; and has in some instances given birth to the enormous doctrine of a right of legislative repeal. Owing its ratification to the law of a state, it has been contended that the same authority might repeal the law by which it was ratified. However gross a heresy it may be to maintain that a party to a compact has a right to revoke that compact, the doctrine itself has respectable advocates. The possibility of a question of this nature proves the necessity of laying the foundations of our national government deeper than in the mere sanction of delegated authority. The fabric of American empire ought to rest on the solid basis of the consent of the people. The streams of national power ought to flow immediately from that pure original fountain of all legitimate authority."

Of course, the convention did not resort to the revolutionary policy of transmitting the Constitution directly to the conventions of the several states. It merely laid the finished instrument before the Confederate Congress with the suggestion that it should be submitted to "a convention of delegates chosen in each state by the people thereof, under the recommendation of its legislature, for their assent and ratification; and each convention assenting thereto and ratifying the same should give notice thereof to the United States in Congress assembled." The convention went on to suggest that when nine states had ratified the Constitution, the Confederate Congress should extinguish itself by making provision for the elections necessary to put the new government into effect. . . .

After the new Constitution was published and transmitted to the states, there began a long and bitter fight over ratification. A veritable flood of pamphlet literature descended upon the country, and a collection of these pamphlets by Hamilton, Madison, and Jay, brought together under the title

---

[17] *Compiler's Note:* The original text, p. 75, comments: "It was largely because the framers of the Constitution knew the temper and class bias of the state legislatures that they arranged that the new Constitution should be ratified by conventions."

of *The Federalist* — though clearly a piece of campaign literature — has remained a permanent part of the contemporary sources on the Constitution and has been regarded by many lawyers as a commentary second in value only to the decisions of the Supreme Court. Within a year the champions of the new government found themselves victorious, for on June 21, 1788, the ninth state, New Hampshire, ratified the Constitution, and accordingly the new government might go into effect as between the agreeing states. Within a few weeks, the nationalist party in Virginia and New York succeeded in winning these two states, and in spite of the fact that North Carolina and Rhode Island had not yet ratified the Constitution, Congress determined to put the instrument into effect in accordance with the recommendations of the convention. Elections for the new government were held; the date March 4, 1789, was fixed for the formal establishment of the new system; Congress secured a quorum on April 6; and on April 30 Washington was inaugurated at the Federal Hall in Wall Street, New York.

Charles A. Beard suggests that there is a dichotomy between the values of the Constitution and those of the Declaration of Independence, between Jefferson and his followers on the one hand, and Madison and Hamilton on the other. He suggests that Jefferson and the Revolutionists supported political equality and individual freedom and opposed a strong central government. The spirit of the Revolution, argues Beard, spawned the Articles of Confederation, which purposely created a weak and ineffective government. The Revolutionists, in general, were not men of property and thus did not believe that a strong central government was necessary to protect their interests. By contrast, the framers of the Constitution reflected the spirit of Alexander Hamilton, who ironically was not a man of substantial property himself, but who advocated an energetic and dominant national government. Hamilton, like many of the framers, was a strong proponent of governmental protection of property interests.

In the following selection, Gary Wills discusses the philosophy of the leaders of eighteenth-century America, a century that produced both the Declaration of Independence and the Constitution. He suggests that there is no conflict between the two documents and that they reflect, respectively, humanitarian democratic ideals and a desire to protect minorities against the unbridled rule of the majority.

3

Gary Wills

THE CONSTITUTION AND THE DECLARATION OF INDEPENDENCE: CONFLICT OR CONGRUENCE?

"...NO PART OF OUR CONSTITUTION..."

It is not easy to understand today why since Civil War days intelligent Americans should so strangely have confused the Declaration of Independence and the Constitution, and have come to accept them as complementary statements of the democratic purpose of America. Their unlikeness is unmistakable: the one a classical statement of French humanitarian democracy, the other an organic law designed to safeguard the minority under republican rule.

— Vernon L. Parrington

Scholars long ago demolished Parrington's thesis that American history has been "largely a struggle between the spirit of the Declaration of Independence and the spirit of the Constitution, the one primarily concerned with the rights of man, the other more practically concerned with the rights of property." Yet the notion of antagonism between the documents lingers in the popular mind. I have just read a new book and a new article, both by well-known authors, trotting out this tired idea as the secret of American politics.

I mentioned in my Prologue the odd charm many Americans find in the notion that the Declaration proclaimed a revolution which the Constitution betrayed. To use Parrington's own phrase, "it is not easy to understand today" how such a notion could have grown up and attracted otherwise bright people, considering the facts that:

— the principal formulator of the Constitution's doctrine was James Madison, friend and disciple of Jefferson;

— Madison under Witherspoon, like Jefferson under Small, had shaped his politics to Scottish Enlightenment ways;

— there is not a single reference, by *participants* of either transaction, to any disparity in spirit between the passage of the Declaration and that of the Constitution;

From Chapter 27, *Inventing America* by Gary Wills. Copyright © 1978 by Gary Wills. Reprinted by permission of Doubleday & Company, Inc.

— in fact, seven of the Declaration's Signers were at the constitutional convention;

— and, more to the point, thirty of the forty-three living Signers supported the Constitution;

— while the Signers opposed were, as we shall see, defenders of local (state) establishments;

— those at the constitutional convention were younger, poorer, and less powerful in their states than the men who met in Philadelphia from 1774 through 1776 (including the Signers);

— the ratifying procedures for the Constitution, which Parrington (following Beard) called undemocratic, were *more* democratic than those used to adopt the Articles or the state constitutions that preceded them;

— so were the amending procedures and the lack of religious test for office more democratic even than the "radical" constitution of Pennsylvania (which had not been passed by popular vote);

— George Washington, the principal symbol and vindicator of the Revolution from the outset, stood warrant for the Constitution;

— Jefferson, though he criticized some aspects of the Constitution (no more than he had the defects of the Virginia state constitution), still thought it "unquestionably the wisest ever yet presented to men;"

— had Jefferson been a delegate to the convention, he would undoubtedly have voted with Madison, as did many who felt some objection to one or other parts of the document; since he wrote that — while not being of the Federalist faction — "I am much farther from that of the Antifederalists."

It is not surprising that criticism of the Constitution grew up after the Gilded Age, during the populist movement at the end of the nineteenth century, when America's plutocracy had learned so well how to hide behind constitutional provisos. Time had revealed some defects, though amendment was always possible. Yet why was it assumed that those defects were imposed on a *prior* and purer republic? If the framers of the Constitution were a selfish lot, prompted mainly by economic interests, what had happened to the nobler race of their predecessors that signed the Declaration of Independence? Had the revolutionary experience itself taught men to adopt what they had opposed in arms?

Parrington thought Beard had solved this problem by contrasting the older "Declaration men," who were landholders, with a new kind of entrepreneur formed by the war's debts — the holders of "personalities" (mainly public securities). But Robert E. Brown proved that the treasury records Beard relied on, covering the period *after* the convention, showed little about the holdings of men as they came into the convention, and practically nothing about those who had sat at the Continental Congresses a decade before that. Besides, the actual delegates did not behave the way Beard thought their interests dictated. Forrest McDonald carried further this analysis and found anomalies like this: The seven men who walked out of the Convention or refused to sign the Constitution were among the heaviest owners of public securities, while the three states that ratified the Constitution unanimously — Delaware, New Jersey, and Georgia — were controlled by agrarian interests. Sectional and state issues, even in an economic sense, did not fall into the symmetrical scheme Beard constructed.

Other attempts to create a continental division along consistent economic lines — e.g., Carl Becker's merchants versus "mechanics" — have failed for lack of evidence or because of unconscious anachronism. These were efforts to impose a theory of proletarian revolt on the essentially bourgeois scheme of eighteenth-century revolution. That kind of revolution fought the religious and monarchic establishment, along with mercantilism, in the name of free speech and free trade. To the embarrassment of some Beckerites, the "radicals" they looked for were often religious enthusiasts, like those who put the religious qualification in the Pennsylvania constitution. Moderate whig deists were philosophically more "open" in their attitudes.

The Antifederalists, as people have realized since Cecilia Kenyon made her study of them, were not the champions of democracy against privilege. They were often men of established power within their states, who did not want to yield that power to a federal apparatus. They talked of defending the individual by interposing the state's power against any rival. Patrick Henry began his speech against the Constitution by arguing for the status quo — the new Constitution would upset the web of treaties established with other countries in the name of the Confederation. He went on: "Give me leave to demand what right had they to say, We the people? My political curiosity, exclusive of my anxious solicitude for the public welfare, leads me to ask who authorized them to speak the language of We the people instead of We the States? States are the characteristics and soul of a confederation."

The idealization of agrarian virtue by progressive historians overlooked the way plantation owners were bound by tradition as well as by slaveholding, by rural isolation and the desire to retain local autocracies of various sorts. Stanley Elkins and Eric McKitrick have argued that it was the younger generation — formed almost entirely in the revolutionary experience, and with little stake in the old ways — that made up the federalist vanguard, willing to risk and innovate at Philadelphia. A number of them had fought with Washington and knew how much his efforts had been hampered by local pride and obstructionism. They had served in the Confederation congresses, while many of the Antifederalists stayed home, exercising the familiar powers of their provincial legislatures. Even Merrill Jensen, in fighting his rearguard action for Beardism, came up with lists of Federalists and Antifederalists that showed the leaders separated by an average of eleven years. Four of the nine Federalist leaders were still in their twenties. Of the Antifederalists, only three were under forty (and one of those was the anomalous sixteen-year-old son of George Bryan).

The Constitution has, at various times, been attacked as "conservative" on grounds not only anachronistic in themselves but mutually contradictory. It is attacked by Jensen for dangerously concentrating power, yet attacked by James McGregor Burns for inefficiently dividing and checking power.

Did the Constitution concentrate power? It created new powers, not so much over individuals as over these old loci of power, the states. Indeed, the main task was to get those old centers to surrender certain prerogatives; and the effort at reassuring them led to lingering ambiguities in our use of the very term "federalism." In itself, this has to do with treaties (*foedera*) or alliances — the neutral use at, e.g., Jefferson, *Papers,* 1:311. But there was an emphasis, in the 1780s, on the ties that connect those under treaty — on *union* and united force, as in the term "federal [i.e., covenant] theology." Federalists were, therefore, thought to stand for federal power over against the states. But in explaining their position, Madison and Hamilton labored in the *Federalist Papers* to show the states they had nothing to fear from this central (federal) power. Thus federalism has come, in modern parlance, to mean the division or *dispersal* of central power.

Gordon Wood has shown that the framers tried to muster popular support by calling for freshly elected conventions, not the sitting legislatures, to ratify the Constitution. This was more "democratic" than the procedure used in ratifying the state constitutions themselves. Even the issue of a bill of rights was not the simple battle between democracy and privilege often presented to us. Having a bill of rights was, of course, a whig tradition, harking back to Magna Carta through the 1689 Bill of Rights. In that sense it was "conservative" and represented concessions wrung from an executive by a legislature. Most states put bills of rights in their constitutions as a matter of course. Those who opposed a bill of rights at the Constitutional Convention — including, at first, Madison himself, who drafted and steered through the final bill — were assuming that the individual was already protected by the states' bills; that the central government could not reach the individual except through the states, which had put impenetrable barriers around individual rights. Would it not be an act of usurpation to imply that the federal power could go around those barriers? The growth of the Bill of Rights was nudged along by antithetical developments. On the one hand, the states used the Bill of Rights as a further statement of limit on the central power; while, on the other, the effort to solicit popular support against state establishments made the framers themselves see their instrument as reaching individuals in new ways, who must therefore assured of the customary exemptions.

As the progressive era gave way to the New Deal, liberal support for an active executive made some people look at the constitution in an entirely different way. "Concentration" of power was no longer, in itself, the issue. Concentration was benign so long as it was democratic. After all, the radical Pennsylvania constitution had what John Adams called a dangerous concentration of power in its unicameral legislature.

The Constitution was an ingeniously constructed Enlightenment machine of "counterpoises"; and it was recognized as such in Europe. The Declaration, which more recent celebrants have thought a pure voice of the Enlightenment, had no impact at all on the European continent. But the state and federal constitutions were studied with enthusiasm and much debate; it was to explain their novelties that John Adams launched his three-volume *Defense* toward a foreign audience. Constitution-making was a favorite Enlightenment exercise, as Rousseau showed with his plans for Geneva and Poland. Jefferson was himself engaged in this pastime, while the convention sat in Philadelphia, discussing amendment procedures with Lafayette and Condorcet in Paris. Intricate mechanics were "progressive," not inhibiting, to these men. Frenchmen thought they saw how to tie the *"parlements"* to a central government as they watched Americans combine local government with a central power neither monarchic nor merely symbolic. Washington was almost as much a hero in France as in America, and his presence at the helm meant the Revolution was steering forward true to its origins.

The Constitution had the virtue, for its contemporaries, of specificity. They liked their machinery well-made. The propaganda effort of Madison and Hamilton stressed the Constitution's complexity and predictability of function. But that first strength became a later liability. When things did not work well, or did not work as expected, the Constitution could be blamed for causing things it merely countenanced. The problem of slavery, for instance, had to be deferred to accomplish any kind of constitution. But then it was used as a bulwark for state authority to enslave. Its powerlessness looked like complicity.

The Declaration did not labor under those particular disadvantages. It did not (any more than the Constitution would) express a desire or form a plan to end slavery in America. That was even less thinkable to the delegates in 1776 than in 1789 (and it would have run up against just that *agrarian* power Beard tried to call the source of democracy). But the Declaration did say "all men are created equal," and that could be used as a pledge of future actions. . . .

The Declaration, as it was passed and as it is generally read, looks just as vague as the Constitution looks concrete. Even its defenders and admirers think there is some virtue to its vagueness, its idealism, its general statement of nice goals, unencumbered by too precise and transient instructions over the means to be taken to such ends. Liberal apologists for an active presidency saw in "the pursuit of happiness" a general mandate for strong government measures that could promise happiness to those affected. "Self-evident truths" — ill-defined as their grounds might be — conveniently became any speaker's favorite truths of the moment.

In time it became psychically important for men to keep the Declaration vague. When the Constitution or some part of the actual government had to be criticized, this reality could be contrasted with the ideal. One could oppose the American government without becoming un-American. After all, what is more American than the Declaration of Independence? So radicals of the 1960s read the Declaration at gatherings meant to end in acts of civil disobedience. One could repudiate the mere *letter* of the law, the Constitution, in the name of a higher law, containing the *spirit* of America.

And what was true of Jefferson's document was also true of his person. There was a vested interest in keeping him vague. The Jefferson cult offers endless cases of vagueness in the service of anachronism. At times he seems to sidle through our history in odd dance steps that keep pairing him with another man to belittle that man's achievements — Jefferson versus Hamilton, or Adams, or Washington, or even Madison. When earth was to be rebuked by heaven, men brought the Declaration to sit in judgment on the Constitution. In the same way would Claude Bowers bring Jefferson to the condemnation of Hamilton.

The conflict between Jefferson and Hamilton was real, almost as much a matter of personality as of principle. Jefferson, a gentleman farmer, disliked the professional politician, the man without independent land to stand on, one who must live by serving a constituency. Neither position is, in itself, "democratic." It is said that Hamilton loved power, and he certainly admired efficiency — a spirit that was necessary to the Revolution, and one that always needs watching. Jefferson's own dreams would have come to nought if Washington had been forced to depend on soldiering no more efficient than his fellow Virginian's. Hamilton fought the revolution that Jefferson, as war governor, could barely bring himself to attend. In the first administration, Hamilton's kind of efficiency, expertly used by Washington, helped stave off that chaos from which dictatorships are bred. The highest aims can lead to disaster if one is unwilling to adopt the necessary means for their attainment. Jefferson could not even run his own plantation profitably — which meant, among other things, that he could not free his slaves, nor escape the necessity of selling some of them at times, which broke up families. Washington could free his own slaves because he made Mount Vernon pay.

This is not said to disparage Jefferson, but to show how unfair it is to use his quite different gifts to denigrate a man like Hamilton. Jefferson was in some ways as nationalist as Hamilton. He wanted an American ethos protected from European ways. It was he, not Hamilton (as Woodrow Wilson and others have said), who warned against "entangling alliances." Many of his finer schemes would have called for extensive state powers he was unwilling to envisage — e.g., the effort to secure control of the whole continent for America, from Cuba to Canada; his plan for allotting free acreage to citizens; his slave-deportation scheme. Hamilton is vulnerable to "idealistic" criticism because he realistically saw what was necessary when vague schemes and ideals were discussed. But even where Jefferson was not vague in fact, his defenders try to keep him mercifully unspecific.

Since Adams died on the same day as Jefferson, it has been customary to pair them. Their very reconciliation brought their final letters together in a way that made for convenient contrast between the Federalist President and the Republican one. James MacGregor Burns presents them as the type of the fearful aristocrat and the democrat who trusts the people. Adams makes an odd-looking aristocrat; and he collaborated in one of the most radical actions of the struggle for independence, the Philadelphia coup of May 1776. With his cousin Samuel, he had deeper experience of the democracy of town meetings and the presence of mobs than did Jefferson in his deferential Virginia society. One of the things that caused Jefferson to dislike New England so much during his second term was precisely the tradition of direct action on matters like his embargo, a tradition that had helped bring on the Revolution in the first place.

Some of the differences between the two men ran deep. Jefferson *was* always more optimistic, almost eerily so; he felt the Revolution's outcome was foreordained when there was no very solid evidence for thinking so. Adams, though he ended fully as rationalist in his theology as Jefferson, retained a Calvinist vision of fallen man's limitations. Adams can be condescended to. Jefferson could be hated, but never dismissed. Perhaps that explains why so many tend to think the failings of Adams's presidency an *expression* of the man's character, while President Jefferson's faults are considered an *exception* to his general virtue — though the Alien and Sedition Acts were less personal efforts for Adams than were the embargo and the pursuit of Burr on Jefferson's part. Once again, comparison does not generally enlighten us — it just reduces Adams, while fuzzing the Jefferson image in aureole.

Jefferson has even been played off against Madison, his friend and student. Madison's political thought was more earthbound, as we saw from his reaction to Jefferson's scheme of letting contracts run no longer than twenty years. Madison was perhaps the best political thinker this country has produced; but he is forced to play second fiddle to his mentor, even in this one matter of his supremacy. As the author of the basic draft for the Constitution, he is felt to have betrayed his master's Declaration in some unspecified way, and he is made the more partisan leader in forming the first party system. It was hard to be Jefferson's friend. Madison shows it could be, in the long run, hurtful.

The two greatest Virginians of their day were clearly Washington and Jefferson. But no contemporaries thought they had even roughly similar stature. Dazzling as was the galaxy of founders and framers, there was no doubt in their midst who was pre-eminent among them. It was impossible to think there could be another man than Washington at the helm of the Constitutional Convention or of the first administration. Washington was Cincinnatus, the world hero as famous for his surrender of power as for his achievement of it. He took the lead at each crucial moment, in the war, in the framing and passage of the Constitution, in the governing of the country through its precarious first experiments — without Napoleonic excess, yet without weakness or pettiness.

One of the most astonishing reversals in public attitudes toward American history is the one that makes it possible for people, now, to think Jefferson was a greater man than Washington himself. The process of this change was a complex one; a full account of it would involve most major changes that took place in our politics over the last century and more. But the result of that process gives us still another use for Jefferson's putative vagueness. Washington was "merely" practical, "just" a general and good manager. Not a thinker. He worked out some details for the ideals Jefferson formulated. He was a man of the day-to-day; of compromise; of the Constitution. Chance removed him from the scene of the Declaration (where he would certainly have been a signer if he had not been on the battlefield), just as chance removed Jefferson from America when the Constitution was being drafted. A fortuitous symmetry was thus established — Jefferson as the man of the Declaration, the idea, the dream; Washington the man of the Constitution, of the real, of power.

Jefferson did not share the ideals some of his defenders use to enhance his stature. They say Washington, for all his restraint in power, was still in love with glory and honor. True. But so was Jefferson. The ideal of earned public honor was posed to all men of the Enlightenment. Jefferson held honor sacred, and arranged for the glorification of American heroes, including himself. He made sure that Houdon and Trumbull would make his features imperishable, along with Franklin's and Washington's. Nor would Jefferson have scorned the "merely practical" work of making a constitution, and making it work — as we see from his labors on the Virginia constitution and the revision of Virginia's laws. Those laws — including the harsh ones against freed slaves — are not a high point in Jefferson's work, nor are some of his measures as President. But the cult of Jefferson looks only briefly, if at all, toward his "practical" problems as governor or politician. It prefers to linger in his study, pronouncing self-evident truths.

Douglass Adair reminded us that the Enlightenment's highest ideal was the law-giver, who had been the supreme hero since Bacon's time. Though Jefferson called the three greatest men Bacon and Newton and Locke, he would not have denied Bacon's praise for the "founders of states and commonwealths, such as were Romulus, Cyrus, Ottoman, and

Julius Caesar." A much later concept of democracy than Jefferson's had to develop before men would question Washington's greatness as recent decades have.

Jefferson has been made a vague idealist despite himself, despite his empiricism and love of precision. This has made him hard to understand but easy to use. It has made him and his Declaration a touchstone by which other men and ideas are found wanting. . . . Jefferson and Lincoln are the twinned saints of our politics. The Gettysburg Address, another piece of war propaganda with no legal force, has entered the empyrean with the Declaration, bathed in a light that makes them easy to see but hard to read.

Limitation of Governmental Power and of Majority Rule

The most accurate and helpful way to characterize our political system is to call it a constitutional democracy. The term implies a system in which the government is regulated by laws that control and limit the exercise of political power. In a constitutional democracy people participate in government on a limited basis. A distinction should be made between an unlimited democratic government and a constitutional democracy. In the former, the people govern through the operation of a principle such as majority rule without legal restraint; in the latter, majority rule is curtailed and checked through various legal devices. A constitutional system is one in which the formal authority of government is restrained. The checks upon government in a constitutional society customarily include a division or fragmentation of authority that prevents government from controlling all sectors of human life.

Hamilton noted in *Federalist 1,* "It seems to have been reserved to the people of this country, to decide by their conduct and example, the important question, whether societies of men are really capable or not, o⁢ establishing good government from reflection and choice, or whether they are forever destined to depend, for their political constitutions, on accident and force." The framers of our Constitution attempted to structure the government in such a way that it would meet the needs and aspirations of the people and at the same time check the arbitrary exercise of political power. The doctrine of the separation of powers was designed to prevent any one group from gaining control of the national governmental apparatus. The selections reprinted here from *The Federalist,* which was written between October, 1787, and August, 1788, outline the theory and mechanism of the separation of powers.

4
Alexander Hamilton

FEDERALIST 1

I propose, in a series of papers to discuss the following interesting particulars . . . The utility of the UNION to your political prosperity . . . The insufficiency of the present confederation to preserve that Union . . . The necessity of a government, at least equally energetic with the one proposed, to the attainment of this object . . . The conformity of the proposed constitution to the true principles of republican government . . . Its analogy to your own state constitution . . . and lastly, The additional security, which its adoption will afford to the preservation of that species of government, to liberty, and to property.

5
James Madison

FEDERALIST 47

I proceed to examine the particular structure of this government, and the distribution of this mass of power among its constituent parts.

One of the principal objections inculcated by the more respectable adversaries to the constitution, is its supposed violation of the political maxim, that the legislative, executive, and judiciary departments, ought to be separate and distinct. In the structure of the federal government, no regard, it is said, seems to have been paid to this essential precaution in favor of liberty. The several departments of power are distributed and blended in such a manner, as at once to destroy all symmetry and beauty of form; and to expose some of the essential parts of the edifice to the danger of being crushed by the disproportionate weight of other parts.

No political truth is certainly of greater intrinsic value, or is stamped with the authority of more enlightened patrons of liberty, than that on which the objection is founded. The accumulation of all powers, legislative, executive, and judiciary, in the same hands, whether of one, a few, or many, and whether hereditary, self-appointed, or elective, may justly be pro-

nounced the very definition of tyranny. Were the federal constitution, therefore, really chargeable with this accumulation of power, or with a mixture
of powers, having a dangerous tendency to such an accumulation, no further
arguments would be necessary to inspire a universal reprobation of the
system. I persuade myself, however, that it will be made apparent to every
one, that the charge cannot be supported, and that the maxim on which it
relies has been totally misconceived and misapplied.

The oracle who is always consulted and cited on this subject, is the
celebrated Montesquieu. If he be not the author of this invaluable precept in
the science of politics, he has the merit of at least displaying and recom-
mending it most effectually to the attention of mankind. . . .

From . . . facts, by which Montesquieu was guided, it may clearly be
inferred, that in saying, "there can be no liberty, where the legislative and
executive powers are united in the same person, or body of magistrates"; or
"if the power of judging, be not separated from the legislative and executive
powers," he did not mean that these departments ought to have no *partial
agency* in, or no *control* over, the acts of each other. His meaning . . . can
amount to no more than this, that where the *whole* power of one department
is exercised by the same hands which possess the *whole* power of another
department, the fundamental principles of a free constitution are sub-
verted. . . .

If we look into the constitutions of the several states, we find, that notwithstanding the emphatical, and, in some instances, the unqualified terms
in which this axiom has been laid down, there is not a single instance in
which the several departments of power have been kept absolutely separate
and distinct. . . .

The constitution of Massachusetts has observed a sufficient, though
less pointed caution, in expressing this fundamental article of liberty. It
declares, "that the legislative department shall never exercise the executive
and judicial powers, or either of them: the executive shall never exercise the
legislative and judicial powers, or either of them: the judicial shall never
exercise the legislative and executive powers, or either of them." This declaration corresponds precisely with the doctrine of Montesquieu. . . . It goes
no farther than to prohibit any one of the entire departments from exercising the powers of another department. In the very constitution to which it
is prefixed, a partial mixture of powers has been admitted. . . .

FEDERALIST 48

. . . I shall undertake in the next place to show, that unless these departments be so far connected and blended, as to give to each a constitutional
control over the others, the degree of separation which the maxim requires,

as essential to a free government, can never in practice be duly maintained.

It is agreed on all sides, that the powers properly belonging to one of the departments ought not to be directly and completely administered by either of the other departments. It is equally evident, that neither of them ought to possess, directly or indirectly, an overruling influence over the others in the administration of their respective powers. It will not be denied, that power is of an encroaching nature, and that it ought to be effectually restrained from passing the limits assigned to it. After discriminating, therefore, in theory, the several classes of power, as they may in their nature be legislative, executive, or judiciary; the next, and most difficult task, is to provide some practical security for each, against the invasion of the others. What this security ought to be, is the great problem to be solved.

Will it be sufficient to mark, with precision, the boundaries of these departments, in the constitution of the government, and to trust to these parchment barriers against the encroaching spirit of power? This is the security which appears to have been principally relied on by the compilers of most American constitutions. But experience assures us, that the efficacy of the provision has been greatly overrated; and that some more adequate defense is indispensably necessary for the more feeble, against the more powerful members of the government. The legislative department is everywhere extending the sphere of its activity, and drawing all power into its impetuous vortex. . . .

In a government where numerous and extensive prerogatives are placed in the hands of an hereditary monarch, the executive department is very justly regarded as the source of danger, and watched with all the jealousy which a zeal for liberty ought to inspire. In a democracy, where a multitude of people exercise in person the legislative functions, and are continually exposed, by their incapacity for regular deliberation and concerted measures, to the ambitious intrigues of their executive magistrates, tyranny may well be apprehended on some favorable emergency, to start up in the same quarter. But in a representative republic, where the executive magistracy is carefully limited, both in the extent and the duration of its power; and where the legislative is exercised by an assembly, which is inspired by a supposed influence over the people, with an intrepid confidence in its own strength; which is sufficiently numerous to feel all the passions which actuate a multitude; yet not so numerous as to be incapable of pursuing the objects of its passions, by means which reason prescribes; it is against the enterprising ambition of this department, that the people ought to indulge all their jealousy and exhaust all their precautions.

The legislative department derives a superiority in our governments from other circumstances. Its constitutional powers being at once more extensive, and less susceptible of precise limits, it can, with the greater facility, mask, under complicated and indirect measures, the encroachment which it makes on the coordinate departments. It is not infrequently a question of real nicety in legislative bodies, whether the operation of a particular measure will, or will not extend beyond the legislative sphere. On the other side, the executive power being restrained within a narrower compass, and being more simple in its nature; and the judiciary being described by land-marks, still less uncertain, projects of usurpation by either of these depart-ments would immediately betray and defeat themselves. Nor is this all: as the legislative department alone has access to the pockets of the people, and has in some constitutions full discretion, and in all a prevailing influence over the pecuniary rewards of those who fill the other departments; a de-pendence is thus created in the latter, which gives still greater facility to en-croachments of the former. . . .

FEDERALIST 51

To what expedient then shall we finally resort, for maintaining in practice the necessary partition of power among the several departments, as laid down in the constitution? The only answer that can be given is, that as all these exterior provisions are found to be inadequate, the defect must be supplied, by so contriving the interior structure of the government, as that its several constituent parts may, by their mutual relations, be the means of keeping each other in their proper places. . . .

In order to lay a due foundation for that separate and distinct exercise of the different powers of government, which, to a certain extent, is ad-mitted on all hands to be essential to the preservation of liberty, it is evident that each department should have a will of its own; and consequently should be so constituted, that the members of each should have as little agency as possible in the appointment of the members of the others. . . .

It is equally evident, that the members of each department should be as little dependent as possible on those of the others, for the emoluments annexed to their offices. Were the executive magistrate, or the judges, not independent of the legislature in this particular, their independence in every other, would be merely nominal.

But the great security against a gradual concentration of the several powers in the same department, consists in giving to those who administer each department, the necessary constitutional means, and personal motives, to resist encroachments of the others. The provision for defense must in this, as in all other cases, be made commensurate to the danger of attack. Ambi-tion must be made to counteract ambition. The interest of the man must be connected with the constitutional rights of the place. It may be a reflection on human nature, that such devices should be necessary to control the abuses of government. But what is government itself, but the greatest of all reflections on human nature? If men were angels, no government would be necessary. If angels were to govern men, neither external nor internal controls on government would be necessary. In framing a government, which is to be administered by men over men, the great difficulty lies in this: You must first enable the government to control the governed; and in the next place, oblige it to control itself. A dependence on the people is, no doubt, the primary control on the government; but experience has taught mankind the necessity of auxiliary precautions.

This policy of supplying by opposite and rival interests, the defect of better motives, might be traced through the whole system of human affairs, private as well as public. We see it particularly displayed in all the subordinate distributions of power; where the constant aim is, to divide and arrange the several offices in such a manner, as that each may be a check on the other; that the private interest of every individual, may be a sentinel over the public rights. These inventions of prudence cannot be less requisite to the distribution of the supreme powers of the state.

But it is not possible to give to each department an equal power of self-defense. In republican government, the legislative authority necessarily predominates. The remedy for this inconvenience is, to divide the legislature into different branches; and to render them by different modes of election, and different principles of action, as little connected with each other, as the nature of their common functions, and their common dependence on the society will admit. It may even be necessary to guard against dangerous encroachments, by still further precautions. As the weight of the legislative authority requires that it should be thus divided, the weakness of the executive may require, on the other hand, that it should be fortified. An absolute negative on the legislature, appears, at first view, to be the natural defense with which the executive magistrate should be armed. But perhaps it would be neither altogether safe, nor alone sufficient. On ordinary occasions, it might not be exerted with the requisite firmness; and on extraordinary occasions, it might be perfidiously abused. May not this defect of an absolute negative be supplied by some qualified connection between this weaker department, and the weaker branch of the stronger department, by which the latter may be led to support the constitutional rights of the former, without being too much detached from the rights of its own department?

Constitutional Democracy: The Rule of Law

The Western political heritage has emphasized the importance of democracy and the rule of law. As early as Aristotle's *Politics,* the viability of democracy, provided there are sufficient checks upon unlimited popular rule, has been stressed.

The American constitutional tradition reflects the beliefs of many political philosophers. One of the most dominating figures is John Locke. It is not suggested that Locke was read by most of the colonists, but only that his ideas invariably found their way into many writings of eighteenth-century America, most importantly the Declaration of Independence. In a letter to Henry Lee in 1825, Thomas Jefferson wrote:

"When forced . . . to resort to arms for redress, an appeal to the tribunal of the world was deemed proper for our justification. This was the object of the Declaration of Independence. Not to find out new principles, or new arguments, never before thought of, not merely to say things which had never been said before; but to place before mankind the common sense of the subject, in terms so plain and firm as to command their assent, and to justify ourselves in the independent stand we are compelled to take. Neither aiming at originality of principle or sentiment, nor yet copied from any particular and previous writing, it was intended to be an expression of the American mind, and to give to that expression the proper tone and spirit called for by the occasion. All its authority rests then on the harmonizing sentiments of the day, whether expressed in conversation, in letters, printed essays, or in the elementary books of public right [such] as Aristotle, Cicero, Locke, Sidney, etc. . . . "

In May of 1790, Jefferson wrote: "Locke's little book on government is perfect as far as it goes." Although Jefferson's admiration of Locke was perhaps greater than that of many other colonists, his views did reflect a mood of eighteenth-century America. Locke's *Second Treatise, Of Civil Government* attempted to trace the reasons why men enter into political societies in the first place. The eighteenth century, no less than the twentieth, was an era characterized by attempts to be "scientific" in political formulations. Locke's *Second Treatise,* first published in 1690, reflected the scientific emphasis that was to prevail so widely beginning in the eighteenth century. To Locke, natural law was objectively valid, and therefore once ascertained, governments based upon it would have a superior claim to legitimacy. Locke is notable for his discussions of natural law, from which he derived the "best" form of government. In reading Locke, one should observe how much importance he placed upon property rights and the right of the people to dissolve government once it no longer meets their legitimate expectations.

6

John Locke

SECOND TREATISE,
OF CIVIL GOVERNMENT

OF THE STATE OF NATURE

To understand political power aright, and derive it from its original, we must consider what estate all men are naturally in, and that is, a state of perfect freedom to order their actions, and dispose of their possessions and persons as they think fit, within the bounds of the laws of Nature, without asking leave or depending upon the will of any other man.

A state also of equality, wherein all the power and jurisdiction is reciprocal, no one having more than another, there being nothing more evident than that creatures of the same species and rank, promiscuously born to all the same advantages of Nature, and the use of the same faculties, should also be equal one amongst another, without subordination or subjection, unless the lord and master of them all should, by any manifest declaration of his will, set one above another, and confer on him, by an evident and clear appointment, an undoubted right to dominion and sovereignty. . . .

But though this be a state of liberty, yet it is not a state of license; though man in that state have an uncontrollable liberty to dispose of his person or possessions, yet he has not liberty to destroy himself, or so much as any creature in his possession, but where some nobler use than its bare preservation calls for it. The state of Nature has a law of Nature to govern it, which obliges every one, and reason, which is that law, teaches all mankind who will but consult it, that being all equal and independent, no one ought to harm another in his life, health, liberty or possessions. . . . And, being furnished with like faculties, sharing all in one community of Nature, there cannot be supposed any such subordination among us that may authorize us to destroy one another, as if we were made for one another's uses, as the inferior ranks of creatures are for ours. Every one as he is bound to preserve himself, and not to quit his station wilfully, so by the like reason, when his own preservation comes not in competition, ought he as much as he can to preserve the rest of mankind, and not unless it be to do justice on an offender, take away or impair the life, or what tends to the preservation of the life, the liberty, health, limb, or goods of another.

And that all men may be restrained from invading others' rights, and from doing hurt to one another, and the law of Nature be observed, which willeth the peace and preservation of all mankind, the execution of the law of Nature is in that state put into every man's hands, whereby every one has a right to punish the transgressors of that law to such a degree as may hinder its violation. For the law of Nature would, as all other laws that concern men in this world, be in vain if there were nobody that in the state of Nature had a power to execute that law, and thereby preserve the innocent and restrain offenders; and if any one in the state of Nature may punish another for any evil he has done, every one may do so. For in that state of perfect equality, where naturally there is no superiority or jurisdiction of one over another, what any may do in prosecution of that law, every one must needs have a right to do.

And thus, in the state of Nature, one man comes by a power over another, but yet no absolute or arbitrary power to use a criminal, when he has got him in his hands, according to the passionate heats or boundless extravagancy of his own will, but only to retribute to him so far as calm reason and conscience dictate, what is proportionate to his transgression, which is so much as may serve for reparation and restraint. . . .

Every offence that can be committed in the state of Nature may, in the state of Nature, be also punished equally, and as far forth, as it may, in a commonwealth. For-though it would be beside my present purpose to enter here into the particulars of the law of Nature, or its measures of punishment, yet it is certain there is such a law, and that too as intelligible and plain to a rational creature and a studier of that law as the positive laws of commonwealths, nay, possibly plainer; as much as reason is easier to be understood than the fancies and intricate contrivances of men, following contrary and hidden interests put into words. . . .

OF THE ENDS OF POLITICAL SOCIETY AND GOVERNMENT

If man in the state of Nature be so free as has been said, if he be absolute lord of his own person and possessions, equal to the greatest and subject to nobody, why will he part with his freedom, this empire, and subject himself to the dominion and control of any other power? To which it is obvious to answer, that though in the state of Nature he hath such a right, yet the enjoyment of it is very uncertain and constantly exposed to the invasion of others; for all being kings as much as he, every man his equal, and the greater part no strict observers of equity and justice, the enjoyment of the property he has in this state is very unsafe, very insecure. This makes him willing to quit this condition which, however free, is full of fears and continual dangers; and it is not without reason that he seeks out and is willing to join in society with others who are already united, or have a mind to unite for the mutual preservation of their lives, liberties, and estates, which I call by the general name—property.

The great and chief end, therefore, of men uniting into commonwealths, and putting themselves under government, is the preservation of their property; to which in the state of Nature there are many things wanting.

Firstly, there wants an established, settled, known law, received and allowed by common consent to be the standard of right and wrong, and the common measure to decide all controversies between them. For though the law of Nature be plain and intelligible to all rational creatures, yet men, being biased by their interest, as well as ignorant for want of study of it, are not apt to allow of it as a law binding to them in the application of it to their particular cases.

Secondly, in the state of Nature there wants a known and indifferent judge, with authority to determine all differences according to the established law. For every one in that state being both judge and executioner of the law of Nature, men being partial to themselves, passion and revenge is very apt to carry them too far, and with too much heat in their own cases, as well as negligence and unconcernedness, make them too remiss in other men's.

Thirdly, in the state of Nature there often wants power to back and support the sentence when right, and to give it due execution. They who by any injustice offended will seldom fail where they are able by force to make good their injustice. Such resistance many times makes the punishment dangerous, and frequently destructive to those who attempt it.

Thus mankind, notwithstanding all the privileges of the state of Nature, being but in an ill condition while they remain in it are quickly driven into society. Hence it comes to pass, that we seldom find any number of men live any time together in this state. The inconveniences that they are therein exposed to by the irregular and uncertain exercise of the power every man has of punishing the transgressions of others, make them take sanctuary under the established laws of government, and therein seek the preservation of their property. It is this makes them so willingly give up every one his single power of punishing to be exercised by such alone as shall be appointed to it amongst them, and by such rules as the community, or those authorised by them to that purpose, shall agree on. And in this we have the original right and rise of both the legislative and executive power as well as of the governments and societies themselves.

For in the state of Nature to omit the liberty he has of innocent delights, a man has two powers. The first is to do whatsoever he thinks fit for the preservation of himself and others within the permission of the law of Nature; by which law, common to them all, he and all the rest of mankind are one community, make up one society distinct from all other creatures, and were it not for the corruption and viciousness of degenerate men, there would be no need of any other, no necessity that men should separate from this great and natural community, and associate into lesser combinations. The other power a man has in the state of Nature is the power to punish the crimes committed against that law. Both these he gives up when he joins in a private, if I may so call it, or particular political society, and incorporates into any commonwealth separate from the rest of mankind.

The first power—viz., of doing whatsoever he thought fit for the preservation of himself and the rest of mankind, he gives up to be regulated by laws made by the society, so far forth as the preservation of himself and the rest of that society shall require; which laws of the society in many things confine the liberty he had by the law of Nature.

Secondly, the power of punishing he wholly gives up, and engages his natural force, which he might before employ in the execution of the law of Nature, by his own single authority, as he thought fit, to assist the executive power of the society as the law thereof shall require. For being now in a new state, wherein he is to enjoy many conveniences from the labor, assistance, and society of others in the same community, as well as protection from its whole strength, he is to part also with as much of his natural liberty, in providing for himself, as the good, prosperity, and safety of the society shall require, which is not only necessary but just, since the other members of the society do the like.

But though men when they enter into society give up the equality, liberty, and executive power they had in the state of Nature into the hands of the society, to be so far disposed of by the legislative as the good of the society shall require, yet it being only with an intention in every one the better to preserve himself, his liberty and property (for no rational creature can be supposed to change his condition with an intention to be worse), the power of the society or legislative constituted by them can never be supposed to extend farther than the common against those three defects above mentioned that made the state of Nature so unsafe and uneasy. And so, whoever has the legislative or supreme power of any commonwealth, is bound to govern by established standing laws, promulgated and known to the people, and not by extemporary decrees, by indifferent and upright judges, who are to decide controversies by those laws; and to employ the force of the community at home only in the execution of such laws, or abroad to prevent or redress foreign injuries and secure the community from inroads and invasion. And all this to be directed to no other end but the peace, safety, and public good of the people. . . .

OF THE EXTENT OF THE LEGISLATIVE POWER

The great end of men's entering into society being the enjoyment of their properties in peace and safety, and the great instrument and means of that being the laws established in that society, the first and fundamental positive law of all commonwealths is the establishing of the legislative power, as the first and fundamental natural law, which is to govern even the legislative itself, is the preservation of the society and (as far as will consist with the public good) of every person in it. This legislative is not only the supreme power of the commonwealth, but sacred and unalterable in the hands where the community have once placed it. Nor can any edict of anybody else, in what form soever conceived, or by what power soever backed, have the force and obligation of a law which has not its sanction from that legislative which the public has chosen and appointed; for without this the law could not have that which is absolutely necessary to its being a law, the consent of the society, over whom nobody can have a power to make laws but by their own consent and by authority received from them. . . .

These are the bounds which the trust that is put in them by the society and the law of God and Nature have set to the legislative power of every commonwealth, in all forms of government. First: They are to govern by promulgated established laws, not to be varied in particular cases, but to have one rule for rich and poor, for the favorite at Court and the countryman at plough. Secondly: These laws also ought to be designed for no other end ultimately but the good of the people. Thirdly: They must not raise taxes on the property of the people without the consent of the people given by themselves or their deputies. And this properly concerns only such governments where the legislative is always in being, or at least where the people have not reserved any part of the legislative to deputies, to be from time to time chosen by themselves. Fourthly: Legislative neither must nor can transfer the power of making laws to anybody else, or place it anywhere but where the people have. . . .

OF THE DISSOLUTION OF GOVERNMENT

The constitution of the legislative [authority] is the first and fundamental act of society, whereby provision is made for the continuation of their union under the direction of persons and bonds of laws, made by persons authorised thereunto, by the consent and appointment of the people, without which no one man, or number of men, amongst them can have authority of making laws that shall be binding to the rest. When any one, or more, shall take upon them to make laws whom the people have not appointed so to do, they make laws without authority, which the people are not therefore bound to obey; by which means they come again to be out of subjection, and may constitute to themselves a new legislative, as they think best, being in full liberty to resist the force of those who, without authority, would impose anything upon them. . . .

Whosoever uses force without right—as every one does in society who does it without law—puts himself into a state of war with those against whom he so uses it, and in that state all former ties are cancelled, all other rights cease, and every one has a right to defend himself, and to resist the aggressor. . . .

Here it is like the common question will be made: Who shall be judge whether the prince or legislative act contrary to their trust? This, perhaps, ill-affected and factious men may spread amongst the people, when the prince only makes use of his due prerogative. To this I reply, The people shall be judge; for who shall be judge whether his trustee or deputy acts well and according to the trust reposed in him, but he who deputes him and must, by having deputed him, have still a power to discard him when he fails in his trust? If this be reasonable in particular cases of private men, why should it be otherwise in that of the greatest moment, where the welfare of millions is concerned and also where the evil, if not prevented, is greater, and the redress very difficult, dear, and dangerous? . . .

To conclude. The power that every individual gave the society when he entered into it can never revert to the individuals again, as long as the society lasts, but will always remain in the community; because without this there can be no community—no commonwealth, which is contrary to the original agreement; so also when the society hath placed the legislative in any assembly of men, to continue in them and their successors, with direction and authority for providing such successors, the legislative can never revert to the people whilst that government lasts; because, having provided a legislative with power to continue for ever, they have given up their political power to the legislative, and cannot resume it. But if they have set limits to the duration of their legislative, and made this supreme power in any person or assembly only temporary; or else when, by the miscarriages of those in authority, it is forfeited; upon the forfeiture of their rulers, or at the determination of the time set, it reverts to the society, and the people have a right to act as supreme, and continue the legislative in themselves or place it in a new form, or new hands, as they think good.

The influence of John Locke goes far beyond his impact on the thinking of the founding fathers of the United States, such as Thomas Jefferson. Some scholars (among them, Louis Hartz, *The Liberal Tradition in America*) have interpreted the American political tradition in terms of the pervasive attachment to the ideas and values set forth in the writings of Locke. There is little question that American political life has been uniquely characterized by widespread adherence to the fundamental principles about the relations among men, society, and government expressed in Locke's writings.

It is not just that we have representative government, with institutions similar in structure and function to those of the constitutional democracy described in Locke's *Second Treatise,* but that through the years we have probably maintained, more than any other society, a widespread agreement about the fundamental human values cherished by Locke. His emphasis upon the sanctity of private property has been paramount in the American political tradition from the very beginning. Moreover, Locke's views on the nature of man are shared by most Americans. All our governmental institutions, processes, and traditions rest upon principles such as the primacy of the individual, man's inborn ability to exercise reason in order to discern truth and higher principles of order and justice, and a political and social equality among men in which no man shall count for more than another in determining the actions of government and their application. We may not have always practiced these ideals, but we have been *theoretically* committed to them.

CHAPTER 2

Federalism

The United States government utilizes a "federal" form to secure certain political and economic objectives. This chapter identifies both the traditional and modern goals of American federalism from the writings of important theorists who have examined general and specific problems in national-state relationships. The validity of federalism is also analyzed.

Constitutional Background: National v. State Power

No subject attracted greater attention or was more carefully analyzed at the time of the framing of the Constitution than federalism. *The Federalist* devoted a great deal of space to proving the advantages of a federal form of government relative to a confederacy, since the Constitution was going to take some of the power traditionally within the jurisdiction of state governments and give it to a newly constituted national government.

The victory of the nationalists at the Constitutional Convention of 1787, which resulted in sovereign states giving up a significant portion of their authority to a new national government, is remarkable by any standard of measurement. Today, when the creation of the Union is largely taken for granted, it is difficult to appreciate the environment of the Revolutionary period, a time when the states wanted at all costs to protect their newly won freedom from an oppressive British government. The Constitution of 1787 was accepted as a matter of necessity as much as desire.

It was against the background of the Articles of Confederation that Hamilton wrote in *The Federalist* about the advantages of the new "federal" system that would be created by the Constitution. The Articles of Confederation had been submitted to the states in 1777 and was finally ratified by all of the states in 1781, Maryland being the only holdout after 1779. The "League of Friendship" that had been created among the states by the Articles had proved inadequate to meeting even the minimum needs of union. The government of the Articles of Confederation had many weaknesses, for it was essentially a league of sovereign states, joined together more in accordance with principles of international agreement than in accordance with the rules of nation states. Most of the provisions of the Articles of Confederation concerned the foreign relations of the new government, and matters of national defense and security. For this purpose a minimum number of powers were granted to the national government, which, however, had no executive or judicial authority and was therefore incapable of independent enforcement. National actions were dependent upon the states for enforcement, and under Article Two "each state retains its sovereignty, freedom and independence, and every power, jurisdiction and right, which is not by this confederation expressly delegated to the United States, in Congress assembled." The paucity of authority delegated to the central government under the Articles left the sovereignty of the states intact. And, the national government was totally dependent upon the states as agents of enforcement of what little authority it could exercise. The government of the Articles of Confederation then, without an executive or judicial branch, and without such crucial authority as the power to tax and regulate commerce, required a drastic overhaul if it was to become a national government in fact as well as in name.

In the following selections from *The Federalist* Alexander Hamilton argues the advantages of the new federal Constitution, and at the same time attempts to alleviate the fears of his opponents that the new government would intrude upon and possibly eventually destroy the sovereignty of the states. The national government, he wrote, must be able to act directly upon the citizens of the states to regulate the common concerns of the nation. He found the system of the Articles of Confederation too weak, allowing state evasion of national power. Augmenting the authority of the national government would not destroy state sovereignty, because of the inherent strength of the individual states (which at the time Hamilton wrote were singly and collectively far more powerful than any proposed national government). Moreover, there would be no incentives for ambitious politicians to look to the states to realize their goals, for the scope of national power was sufficient to occupy temptations for political aggrandizement.

7

Alexander Hamilton

FEDERALIST 16

The . . . death of the confederacy . . . is what we now seem to be on the point of experiencing, if the federal system be not speedily renovated in a more substantial form. It is not probable, considering the genius of this country, that the complying states would often be inclined to support the authority of the union, by engaging in a war against the noncomplying states. They would always be more ready to pursue the milder course of putting themselves upon an equal footing with the delinquent members, by an imitation of their example. And the guilt of all would thus become the security of all. Our past experience has exhibited the operation of this spirit in its full light. There would, in fact, be an insuperable difficulty in ascertaining when force would with propriety be employed. In the article of pecuniary contribution, which would be the most usual source of delinquency, it would often be impossible to decide whether it had proceeded from disinclination, or inability. The pretense of the latter would always be at hand. And the case must be very flagrant in which its fallacy could be detected with sufficient certainty to justify the harsh expedient of compulsion. It is easy to see that this problem alone, as often as it should occur, would open a wide field to the majority that happened to prevail in the national council, for the exercise of factious views, of partiality, and of oppression.

It seems to require no pains to prove that the states ought not to prefer a national constitution, which could only be kept in motion by the instrumentality of a large army, continually on foot to execute the ordinary requisitions or decrees of the government. And yet this is the plain alternative involved by those who wish to deny it the power of extending its operations to individuals. Such a scheme, if practicable at all, would instantly degenerate into a military despotism; but it will be found in every light impracticable. The resources of the union would not be equal to the maintenance of any army considerable enough to confine the larger states within the limits of their duty; nor would the means ever be furnished of forming such an army in the first instance. Whoever considers the populousness and strength of several of these states singly at the present juncture, and looks forward to what they will become, even at the distance of half a century, will at once dismiss as idle and visionary any scheme which aims at regulating their movements by laws, to operate upon them in their collective capacities, and to be executed by a coercion applicable to them in the same capacities. A project of this kind is little less romantic than the monster-taming spirit attributed to the fabulous heroes and demigods of antiquity. . . .

The result of these observations to an intelligent mind must clearly be this, that if it be possible at any rate to construct a federal government capable of regulating the common concerns, and preserving the general tranquillity, it must be founded, as to the objects committed to its case, upon the reverse of the principle contended for by the opponents of the proposed constitution [i.e., a confederacy]. It must carry its agency to the persons of the citizens. It must stand in need of no intermediate legislations; but must itself be empowered to employ the arm of the ordinary magistrate to execute its own resolutions. The majesty of the national authority must be manifested through the medium of the courts of justice. The government of the union, like that of each state, must be able to address itself immediately to the hopes and fears of individuals; and to attract to its support, those passions which have the strongest influence upon the human heart. It must, in short, possess all the means, and have a right to resort to all the methods, of executing the powers with which it is entrusted, that are possessed and exercised by the governments of the particular states.

To this reasoning it may perhaps be objected, that if any state should be disaffected to the authority of the union, it could at any time obstruct the execution of its laws, and bring the matter to the same issue of force, with the necessity of which the opposite scheme is reproached.

The plausibility of this objection will vanish the moment we advert to the essential difference between a mere NONCOMPLIANCE and a DIRECT and ACTIVE RESISTANCE. If the interposition of the state legislatures be necessary to give effect to a measure of the union [as in a confederacy], they have only NOT TO ACT, OR TO ACT EVASIVELY, and the measure is defeated. This neglect of duty may be disguised under affected but unsubstantial provisions so as not to appear, and of course not to excite any alarm in the people for the safety of the constitution. The state leaders may even make a merit of their surreptitious invasions of it, on the ground of some temporary convenience, exemption, or advantage.

But if the execution of the laws of the national government should not require the intervention of the state legislatures; if they were to pass into immediate operation upon the citizens themselves, the particular governments could not interrupt their progress without an open and violent exertion of an unconstitutional power. No omission, nor evasions, would answer the end. They would be obliged to act, and in such a manner, as would leave no doubt that they had encroached on the national rights. An experiment of this nature would always be hazardous in the face of a constitution in any degree competent to its own defense, and of a people enlightened enough to distinguish between a legal exercise and an illegal usurpation of authority. The success of it would require not merely a factious majority in the legislature, but the concurrence of the courts of justice, and of the body of the people. . . .

FEDERALIST 17

An objection, of a nature different from that which has been stated and answered in my last address, may, perhaps, be urged against the principle of legislation for the individual citizens of America. It may be said, that it would tend to render the government of the union too powerful, and to enable it to absorb those residuary authorities, which it might be judged proper to leave with the states for local purposes. Allowing the utmost latitude to the love of power, which any reasonable man can require, I confess I am at a loss to discover what temptation the persons entrusted with the administration of the general government could ever feel to divest the states of the authorities of that description. The regulation of the mere domestic police of a state, appears to me to hold out slender allurements to ambition. Commerce, finance, negotiation, and war, seem to comprehend all the objects which have charms for minds governed by that passion; and all the powers necessary to those objects, ought, in the first instance, to be lodged in the national depository. The administration of private justice between the citizens of the same state; the supervision of agriculture, and of other concerns of a similar nature; all those things, in short, which are proper to be provided for by local legislation, can never be desirable cares of a general jurisdiction. It is therefore improbable, that there should exist a disposition in the federal councils, to usurp the powers with which they are connected; because the attempt to exercise them would be as troublesome as it would be nugatory; and the possession of them, for that reason, would contribute nothing to the dignity, to the importance, or to the splendor, of the national government.

But let it be admitted, for argument's sake, that mere wantonness, and lust of domination, would be sufficient to beget that disposition; still, it may be safely affirmed, that the sense of the constituent body of the national representatives, or in other words, of the people of the several states, would control the indulgence of so extravagant an appetite. It will always be far more easy for the state governments to encroach upon the national authorities, than for the national government to encroach upon the state authorities. The proof of this proposition turns upon the greater degree of influence which the state governments, if they administer their affairs with uprightness and prudence, will generally possess over the people; a circumstance which at the same time teaches us, that there is an inherent and intrinsic weakness in all federal constitutions; and that too much pains cannot be taken in their organization, to give them all the force which is compatible with the principles of liberty.

The superiority of influence in favor of the particular governments, would result partly from the diffusive construction of the national government; but chiefly from the nature of the objects to which the attention of the state administrations would be directed.

It is a known fact in human nature, that its affections are commonly weak in proportion to the distance of diffusiveness of the object. Upon the same principle that a man is more attached to his family than to his neighborhood, to his neighborhood than to the community at large, the people of each state would be apt to feel a stronger bias towards their local governments, than towards the government of the union, unless the force of that principle should be destroyed by a much better administration of the latter.

This strong propensity of the human heart, would find powerful auxiliaries in the objects of state regulation.

The variety of more minute interests, which will necessarily fall under the superintendence of the local administrations, and which will form so many rivulets of influence, running through every part of the society, cannot be particularized, without involving a detail too tedious and uninteresting to compensate for the instruction it might afford.

There is one transcendent advantage belonging to the province of the state governments, which alone suffices to place the matter in a clear and satisfactory light — I mean the ordinary administration of criminal and civil justice. This, of all others, is the most powerful, most universal and most attractive source of popular obedience and attachment. It is this, which, being the immediate and visible guardian of life and property; having its benefits and its terrors in constant activity before the public eye; regulating all those personal interests, and familiar concerns, to which the sensibility of individuals is more immediately awake; contributes, more than any other circumstance, to impress upon the minds of the people affection, esteem, and reverence towards the government. This great cement of society, which will diffuse itself almost wholly through the channels of the particular governments, independent of all other causes of influence, would insure them so decided an empire over their respective citizens, as to render them at all times a complete counterpoise, and not infrequently dangerous rivals to the power of the union.

In *Federalist 39,* James Madison stated that the new Constitution was both federal and national. He attempted to answer arguments that the Constitution destroyed the confederacy of sovereign states and replaced it with a national government. In answering this argument Madison used the term "federal" as it was used by the objectors to the constitution he was attempting to answer. They essentially used "federal" and "confederacy" interchangeably, each term referring to a system requiring agreement among the states before certain actions could be taken. Because agreement was required among the states for ratification, for example, Madison referred to the establishment of the Constitution as a *federal* and not a national act. Madison suggested that the character of the House of Representatives, which derives its powers from the people, was national rather than federal. Conversely, the Senate, representing the states equally, was federal, not national. With regard to the powers of the national government, Madison claimed that in operation they are national because they allow the national government to act directly upon the people, but in extent they are federal because they are limited, the states having agreed to delegate only a certain number of powers to the national government. A truly national government would not be limited in the scope of its powers.

8

James Madison

FEDERALIST 39

The last paper having concluded the observations which were meant to introduce a candid survey of the plan of government reported by the convention, we now proceed to the execution of that part of our undertaking.

The first question that offers itself is whether the general form and aspect of the government be strictly republican. It is evident that no other form would be reconcilable with the genius of the people of America; with the fundamental principles of the Revolution; or with that honorable determination which animates every votary of freedom to rest all our political experiments on the capacity of mankind for self-government. If the plan of the convention, therefore, be found to depart from the republican character, its advocates must abandon it as no longer defensible.

What, then, are the distinctive characters of the republican form? Were an answer to this question to be sought, not by recurring to principles but in the application of the term by political writers to the constitutions of different States, no satisfactory one would ever be found. Holland, in which no particle of the supreme authority is derived from the people, has passed almost universally under the denomination of a republic. The same title has been bestowed on Venice, where absolute power over the great body of the people is exercised in the most absolute manner by a small body of hereditary nobles. Poland, which is a mixture of aristocracy and of monarchy in their worst forms, has been dignified with the same appellation. The government of England, which has one republican branch only, combined with an hereditary aristocracy and monarchy, has with equal impropriety been frequently placed on the list of republics. These examples, which are nearly as dissimilar to each other as to a genuine republic, show the extreme inaccuracy with which the term has been used in political disquisitions.

If we resort for a criterion to the different principles on which different forms of government are established, we may define a republic to be, or at least may bestow that name on, a government which derives all its powers directly or indirectly from the great body of the people, and is administered by persons holding their offices during pleasure for a limited period, or during good behavior. It is *essential* to such a government that it be derived from the great body of the society, not from an inconsiderable proportion or a favored class of it; otherwise a handful of tyrannical nobles, exercising their oppressions by a delegation of their powers, might aspire to the rank of republicans and claim for their government the honorable title of republic. It is *sufficient* for such a government that the persons administering it be appointed, either directly or indirectly, by the people; and that they hold their appointments by either of the tenures just specified; otherwise every government in the United States, as well as every other popular government that has been or can be well organized or well executed, would be degraded from the republican character. According to the constitution of every State in the Union, some or other of the officers of government are appointed indirectly only by the people. According to most of them, the chief magistrate himself is so appointed. And according to one, this mode of appointment is extended to one of the co-ordinate branches of the legislature. According to all the constitutions, also, the tenure of the highest offices is extended to a definite period, and in many instances, both within the legislative and executive departments, to a period of years. According to the provisions of most of the constitutions, again, as well as according to the most respectable and received opinions on the subject, the members of the judiciary department are to retain their offices by the firm tenure of good behavior.

On comparing the Constitution planned by the convention with the standard here fixed, we perceived at once that it is, in the most rigid sense, conformable to it. The House of Representatives, like that of one branch at least of all the State legislatures, is elected immediately by the great body of the people. The Senate, like the present Congress and the Senate of Maryland, derives its appointment indirectly from the people. The President is indirectly derived from the choice of the people, according to the example in most of the States. Even the judges, with all other officers of the Union, will, as in the several States, be the choice, though a remote choice, of the people themselves. The duration of the appointments is equally conformable to the republican standard and to the model of State constitutions. The House of Representatives is periodically elective, as in all the States; and for the period of two years, as in the State of South Carolina. The

Senate is elective for the period of six years, which is but one year more than the period of the Senate of Maryland, and but two more than that of the Senates of New York and Virginia. The President is to continue in office for the period of four years; as in New York and Delaware the chief magistrate is elected for three years, and in South Carolina for two years. In the other States the election is annual. In several of the States, however, no explicit provision is made for the impeachment of the chief magistrate. And in Delaware and Virginia he is not impeachable till out of office. The President of the United States is impeachable at any time during his continuance in office. The tenure by which the judges are to hold their places is, as it unquestionably ought to be, that of good behavior. The tenure of the ministerial offices generally will be a subject of legal regulation, conformably to the reason of the case and the example of the State constitutions.

Could any further proof be required of the republican complexion of this system, the most decisive one might be found in its absolute prohibition of titles of nobility, both under the federal and the State governments; and in its express guaranty of the republican form to each of the latter.

"But it was not sufficient," say the adversaries of the proposed Constitution, "for the convention to adhere to the republican form. They ought with equal care to have preserved the *federal* form, which regards the Union as a *Confederacy* of sovereign states; instead of which they have framed a *national* government, which regards the Union as a *consolidation* of the States." And it is asked by what authority this bold and radical innovation was undertaken. The handle which has been made of this objection requires that it should be examined with some precision.

Without inquiring into the accuracy of the distinction on which the objection is founded, it will be necessary to a just estimate of its force, first, to ascertain the real character of the government in question; secondly, to inquire how far the convention were authorized to propose such a government; and thirdly, how far the duty they owed to their country could supply any defect of regular authority.

First. — In order to ascertain the real character of the government, it may be considered in relation to the foundation on which it is to be established; to the sources from which its ordinary powers are to be drawn; to the operation of those powers; to the extent of them; and to the authority by which future changes in the government are to be introduced.

On examining the first relation, it appears, on one hand, that the Constitution is to be founded on the assent and ratification of the people of America, given by deputies elected for the special purpose; but, on the other, that this assent and ratification is to be given by the people, not as individuals composing one entire nation, but as composing the distinct and independent States to which they respectively belong. It is to be the assent and ratification of the several States, derived from the supreme authority in each State — the authority of the people themselves. The act, therefore, establishing the Constitution will not be a *national* but a *federal* act.

That it will be a federal and not a national act, as these terms are understood by the objectors — the act of the people, as forming so many independent States, not as forming one aggregate nation — is obvious from this single consideration: that it is to result neither from the decision of a *majority* of the people of the Union, nor from that of a *majority* of the States. It must result from the *unanimous* assent of the several States that are parties to it, differing no otherwise from their ordinary assent than in its being expressed, not by the legislative authority, but by that of the people themselves. Were the people regarded in this transaction as forming one nation, the will of the majority of the whole people of the United States would bind the minority, in the same manner as the majority in each State must bind the minority; and the will of the majority must be determined either by a comparison of the individual votes, or by considering the will of the majority of the States as evidence of the will of a majority of the people of the United States. Neither of these rules has been adopted. Each State, in ratifying the Constitution, is considered as a sovereign body independent of all others, and only to be bound by its own voluntary act. In this relation, then, the new Constitution will, if established, be a *federal* and not a *national* constitution.

The next relation is to the sources from which the ordinary powers of government are to be derived. The House of Representatives will derive its powers from the people of America; and the people will be represented in the same proportion and on the same principle as they are in the legislature of a particular State. So far the government is *national, not federal.* The Senate, on the other hand, will derive its powers from the States as political and coequal societies; and these will be represented on the principle of equality in the Senate, as they now are in the existing Congress. So far the government is *federal, not national.* The executive power will be derived from a very compound source. The immediate election of the President is to be made by the States in their political characters. The votes allotted to them are in a compound ratio, which considers them partly as distinct and coequal societies, partly as unequal members of the same society. The eventual election, again, is to be made by that branch of the legislature which consists of the national representatives; but in this particular act they are to be thrown into the form of individual delegations from so many distinct and coequal bodies politic. From this aspect of the government it appears to be of a mixed character, presenting at least as many *federal* as *national* features.

The difference between a federal and national government, as it relates to the *operation of the government,* is by the adversaries of the plan of the convention supposed to consist in this, that in the former the powers operate on the political bodies composing the Confederacy in their political capacities; in the latter, on the individual citizens composing the nation in their individual capacities. On trying the Constitution by this criterion, it falls under the *national* not the *federal* character; though perhaps not so completely as has been understood. In several cases, and particularly in the trial of controversies to which States may be parties, they must be viewed and. proceeded against in their collective and political capacities only. But the operation of the government on the people in their individual capacities, in its ordinary and most essential proceedings, will, in the sense of its opponents, on the whole, designate it, in this relation, a *national* government.

But if the government be national with regard to the *operation* of its powers, it changes its aspect again when we contemplate it in relation to the extent of its powers. The idea of a national government involves in it not only an authority over the individual citizens, but an indefinite supremacy over all persons and things, so far as they are objects of lawful government. Among a people consolidated into one nation, this supremacy is completely vested in the national legislature. Among communities united for particular purposes, it is vested partly in the general and partly in the municipal legislatures. In the former case, all local authorities are subordinate to the supreme; and may be controlled, directed, or abolished by it at pleasure. In the latter, the local or municipal authorities form distinct and independent portions of the supremacy, no more subject, within their respective spheres, to the general authority than the general authority is subject to them, within its own sphere. In this relation, then, the proposed government cannot be deemed a *national* one; since its jurisdiction extends to certain enumerated objects only, and leaves to the several States a residuary and inviolable sovereignty over all other objects. It is true that in controversies relating to the boundary between the two jurisdictions, the tribunal which is ultimately to decide is to be established under the general government. But this does not change the principle of the case. The decision is to be impartially made, according to the rules of the Constitution; and all the usual and most effectual precautions are taken to secure this impartiality. Some such tribunal is clearly essential to prevent an appeal to the sword and a dissolution of the compact; and that it ought to be established under the general rather than under the local governments, or, to speak more properly, that it could be safely established under the first alone, is a position not likely to be combated.

If we try the Constitution by its last relation to the authority by which amendments are to be made, we find it neither wholly *national* nor wholly *federal*. Were it wholly national, the supreme and ultimate authority would reside in the *majority* of the people of the Union; and this authority would be competent at all times, like that of a majority of every national society to alter or abolish its established government. Were it wholly federal, on the other hand, the concurrence of each State in the Union would be essential to every alteration that would be binding on all. The mode provided by the plan of the convention is not founded on either of these principles. In requiring more than a majority, and particularly in computing the proportion by *States,* not by *citizens,* it departs from the national and advances towards the *federal* character; in rendering the concurrence of less than the whole number of States sufficient, it loses again the *federal* and partakes of the *national* character.

The proposed Constitution, therefore, even when tested by the rules laid down by its antagonists, is, in strictness, neither a national nor a federal Constitution, but a composition of both. In its foundation it is federal, not national; in the sources from which the ordinary powers of the government are drawn, it is partly federal and partly national; in the operation of these powers, it is national, not federal; in the extent of them, again, it is federal, not national; and, finally in the authoritative mode of introducing amendments, it is neither wholly federal nor wholly national.

PUBLIUS

In *The Federalist,* Alexander Hamilton and James Madison were careful to point out the advantages of the federal form of government that would be established by the Constitution, both over the government that had existed under the Articles of Confederation and in general terms. Because many state political leaders were highly suspicious of the national government that would be created by the new Constitution, much of the efforts of Hamilton and Madison were directed toward allaying their fears. Above all, they both stated, the energy of the national government would never be sufficient to coerce the states into giving up any portion of their sovereignty. Moreover, Hamilton stated in *Federalist 17* that there would be no incentive for national politicians to take away the reserved powers of the states. The sphere of national power, although limited, was considered entirely adequate to absorb even the most ambitious politicians. And James Madison, in *Federalist 39,* was careful to point out that the jurisdiction of the national government extended only to certain enumerated objects, implying that the residual sovereignty of the states was in fact greater than the sovereignty of the national government.

Alexis de Tocqueville, an aristocratic French observer of the American political and social scene in the early 1830s, acknowledged his debt to the writers of *The Federalist* in helping him to understand American government. Many of the sanguine views of Hamilton and Madison about the prospects for the new Constitution were echoed in Tocqueville's analysis of American institutions forty years later.

Tocqueville had set out for the United States in 1831, with his friend Gustave de Beaumont, ostensibly to examine the American prison system with a view toward prison reform in France. Tocqueville was a French judicial officer, who after the July Revolution of 1830 became disenchanted with the new government of Louis Philippe, and, in a broader context, with the continual turmoil that he saw in French political institutions. While the investigation of prisons served as a ready excuse for a leave of absence from governmental duties, Tocqueville and Beaumont's real interest was in studying American society and government. It was their feeling that democracy was probably the wave of the future and whatever lessons that could be learned from the American experiment would undoubtedly be a useful guide to the future of European society.

Tocqueville was in the United States for only nine months, from May 1831 until February 1832, but during this time he traveled over most of the country east of the Mississippi, staying long enough in various places to gain wide knowledge of local customs and institutions. Most of Tocqueville's observations about the United States were objectively optimistic about the future of democracy, yet his most hopeful expectations were not always realized. In particular, after leaving the United States, he became concerned with the possibility of what he called "tyranny of the majority" which he wrote would be an inevitable consequence of egalitarian tendencies in democratic societies such as the United States. The framers of the Constitution too were worried about unbridled majority rule in government, and felt that governmental tyranny by the majority would be curtailed by such institutional devices as the separation of powers, checks and balances, and federalism, the latter being a division of authority between the national government and the states. While the framers of the Constitution felt that the possibility of the tyranny of the majority was primarily a governmental problem, Tocqueville saw it as a societal dilemma, produced by the egalitarian ethic. Therefore, to Tocqueville, constitutional devices by themselves would not be sufficient to control the inevitable tendency toward majority despotism in an egalitarian society.

The following selection is taken from Tocqueville's discussion of the characteristics of federalism as he saw it in operation in 1831. In his discussion Tocqueville uses the terms "confederation" and "federalism" interchangeably. To him, the American federal system was one type of confederation. This is important to note because Hamilton, in his discussion of federalism in The Federalist, spoke of federalism in the new Constitution as replacing the "confederacy," by which he meant the government that existed under the Articles of Confederation. Most American writers on politics distinguish federalism and confederacy in the same way that Hamilton did, essentially by identifying federalism with the system of the Constitution, and a confederacy with the system of the Articles of Confederation. Under this more common definition of federalism, a federal system is one in which the national government has authority that is separate and distinct from that of the constituent states, an authority that operates directly upon the citizens of the states rather than upon the states as entities. Dual sovereignty is a characteristic of American federalism, whereas under the Articles of Confederation the national government had no authority distinct from the states, and it could not operate without their consent.

The breadth of Tocqueville's analytical method is revealed in his discussion of American federalism. He examines the broad social and political forces operating in society, refers to historical and comparative experience, and analyzes constitutional forms and institutional characteristics. His approach is both empirical and analytical. Tocqueville recognizes that while the theory of federalism may be clear, it is very difficult to apply it without some further clarification. This has certainly been true of the American federal system. As Tocqueville noted: "The sovereignty of the union is so involved in that of the states that it is impossible to distinguish its boundaries at the first glance. The whole structure of the government is artificial and conventional, and it would be ill adapted to a people which has not been long accustomed to conduct its own affairs, or to one in which the science of politics has not descended to the humblest classes of society. I have never been more struck by the good sense and the practical judgment of the Americans than in the manner in which they elude the numberless difficulties resulting from their federal constitution." Tocqueville implied that after all is said and done, federalism as well as other constitutional forms worked because of the good sense and pragmatism of the American people, which overcame constitutional ambiguity. This is why federalism worked in the United States, but, according to Tocqueville, failed in other countries that attempted to imitate the United States Constitution.

In reading the following selection, students should look for Tocqueville's views on: (1) the outstanding characteristics of American federalism; (2) the major advantages of federalism; (3) significant disadvantages of the federal form of government. What evidence does Tocqueville use to buttress his arguments for the advantages and disadvantages of federalism? What changes have occurred since 1831 that might lead to a different perspective on federalism today?

9

Alexis de Tocqueville

DEMOCRACY IN AMERICA: THE FEDERAL CONSTITUTION

CHARACTERISTICS OF THE FEDERAL CONSTITUTION OF THE UNITED STATES OF AMERICA AS COMPARED WITH ALL OTHER FEDERAL CONSTITUTIONS

The United States of America does not afford the first or the only instance of a confederation, several of which have existed in modern Europe, without referring to those of antiquity. Switzerland, the Germanic Empire, and the Republic of the Low Countries either have been or still are confederations. In studying the constitutions of these different countries one is surprised to see that the powers with which they invested the federal government are nearly the same as those awarded by the American Constitution to the government of the United States. They confer upon the central power the same rights of making peace and war, of raising money and troops, and of providing for the general exigencies and the common interests of the nation. Nevertheless, the federal government of these different states has always been as remarkable for its weakness and inefficiency as that of the American Union is for its vigor and capacity. Again, the first American Confederation perished through the excessive weakness of its government; and yet this weak government has as large rights and privileges as those of the Federal government of the present day, and in some respects even larger. But the present Constitution of the United States contains certain novel principles which exercise a most important influence, although they do not at once strike the observer.

This Constitution, which may at first sight be confused with the federal constitutions that have preceded it, rests in truth upon a wholly novel theory, which may be considered as a great discovery in modern political science. In all the confederations that preceded the American Constitution of 1789, the states allied for a common object agreed to obey the injunctions of a federal government; but they reserved to themselves the right of ordaining and enforcing the execution of the laws of the union. The American states which combined in 1789 agreed that the Federal government should not only dictate the laws, but execute its own enactments. In both cases the right is the same, but the exercise of the right is different; and this difference produced the most momentous consequences.

In all the confederations that preceded the American Union the federal government, in order to provide for its wants, had to apply to the separate governments; and if what it prescribed was disagreeable to any one of them, means were found to evade its claims. If it was powerful, it then had recourse to arms; if it was weak, it connived at the resistance which the law of the union, its sovereign, met with, and did nothing, under the plea of inability. Under these circumstances one of two results invariably followed: either the strongest of the allied states assumed the privileges of the federal authority and ruled all the others in its name;[1] or the federal government

---

[1] This was the case in Greece when Philip undertook to execute the decrees of the Amphictyons; in the Low Countries, where the province of Holland always gave the law; and in our own time in the Germanic Confederation, in which Austria and Prussia make themselves the agents of the Diet and rule the whole confederation in its name.

was abandoned by its natural supporters, anarchy arose between the confederates, and the union lost all power of action.[2]

In America the subjects of the Union are not states, but private citizens: the national government levies a tax, not upon the state of Massachusetts, but upon each inhabitant of Massachusetts. The old confederate governments presided over communities, but that of the Union presides over individuals. Its force is not borrowed, but self-derived; and it is served by its own civil and military officers, its own army, and its own courts of justice. It cannot be doubted that the national spirit, the passions of the multitude, and the provincial prejudices of each state still tend singularly to diminish the extent of the Federal authority thus constituted and to facilitate resistance to its mandates; but the comparative weakness of a restricted sovereignty is an evil inherent in the federal system. In America each state has fewer opportunities and temptations to resist; nor can such a design be put in execution (if indeed it be entertained) without an open violation of the laws of the Union, a direct interruption of the ordinary course of justice, and a bold declaration of revolt; in a word, without taking the decisive step that men always hesitate to adopt.

In all former confederations the privileges of the union furnished more elements of discord than of power, since they multiplied the claims of the nation without augmenting the means of enforcing them; and hence the real weakness of federal governments has almost always been in the exact ratio of their nominal power. Such is not the case in the American Union, in which, as in ordinary governments, the Federal power has the means of enforcing all it is empowered to demand. . . .

ADVANTAGES OF THE FEDERAL SYSTEM IN GENERAL, AND ITS SPECIAL UTILITY IN AMERICA

. . . In small states, the watchfulness of society penetrates everywhere, and a desire for improvement pervades the smallest details; the ambition of the people being necessarily checked by its weakness, all the efforts and resources of the citizens are turned to the internal well-being of the community and are not likely to be wasted upon an empty pursuit of glory. The powers of every individual being generally limited, his desires are proportionally small. Mediocrity of fortune makes the various conditions of life nearly equal, and the manners of the inhabitants are orderly and simple. Thus, all things considered, and allowance being made for the various de-

---

[2] Such has always been the situation of the Swiss Confederation, which would have perished ages ago but for the mutual jealousies of its neighbors.

grees of morality and enlightenment, we shall generally find more persons in easy circumstances, more contentment and tranquillity, in small nations than in large ones.

When tyranny is established in the bosom of a small state, it is more galling than elsewhere, because, acting in a narrower circle, everything in that circle is affected by it. It supplies the place of those great designs which it cannot entertain, by a violent or exasperating interference in a multitude of minute details; and it leaves the political world, to which it properly belongs, to meddle with the arrangements of private life. Tastes as well as actions are to be regulated; and the families of the citizens, as well as the state, are to be governed. This invasion of rights occurs but seldom, however, freedom being in truth the natural state of small communities. The temptations that the government offers to ambition are too weak and the resources of private individuals are too slender for the sovereign power easily to fall into the grasp of a single man; and should such an event occur, the subjects of the state can easily unite and overthrow the tyrant and the tyranny at once by a common effort.

Small nations have therefore always been the cradle of political liberty; and the fact that many of them have lost their liberty by becoming larger shows that their freedom was more a consequence of their small size than of the character of the people.

The history of the world affords no instance of a great nation retaining the form of republican government for a long series of years;[3] and this has led to the conclusion that such a thing is impracticable. For my own part, I think it imprudent for men who are every day deceived in relation to the actual and the present, and often taken by surprise in the circumstances with which they are most familiar, to attempt to limit what is possible and to judge the future. But it may be said with confidence, that a great republic will always be exposed to more perils than a small one.

All the passions that are most fatal to republican institutions increase with an increasing territory, while the virtues that favor them do not augment in the same proportion. The ambition of private citizens increases with the power of the state; the strength of parties with the importance of the ends they have in view; but the love of country, which ought to check these destructive agencies, is not stronger in a large than in a small republic. It might, indeed, be easily proved that it is less powerful and less developed. Great wealth and extreme poverty, capital cities of large size, a lax morality, selfishness, and antagonism of interests are the dangers which almost invariably arise from the magnitude of states. Several of these evils scarcely

---

[3] I do not speak of a confederation of small republics, but of a great consolidated republic.

injure a monarchy, and some of them even contribute to its strength and duration. In monarchical states the government has its peculiar strength; it may use, but it does not depend on, the community; and the more numerous the people, the stronger is the prince. But the only security that a republican government possesses against these evils lies in the support of the majority. This support is not, however, proportionably greater in a large republic than in a small one; and thus, while the means of attack perpetually increase, in both number and influence, the power of resistance remains the same; or it may rather be said to diminish, since the inclinations and interests of the people are more diversified by the increase of the population, and the difficulty of forming a compact majority is constantly augmented. It has been observed, moreover, that the intensity of human passions is heightened not only by the importance of the end which they propose to attain, but by the multitude of individuals who are animated by them at the same time. Everyone has had occasion to remark that his emotions in the midst of a sympathizing crowd are far greater than those which he would have felt in solitude. In great republics, political passions become irresistible, not only because they aim at gigantic objects, but because they are felt and shared by millions of men at the same time.

It may therefore be asserted as a general proposition that nothing is more opposed to the well-being and the freedom of men than vast empires. Nevertheless, it is important to acknowledge the peculiar advantages of great states. For the very reason that the desire for power is more intense in these communities than among ordinary men, the love of glory is also more developed in the hearts of certain citizens, who regard the applause of a great people as a reward worthy of their exertions and an elevating encouragement to man. If we would learn why great nations contribute more powerfully to the increase of knowledge and the advance of civilization than small states, we shall discover an adequate cause in the more rapid and energetic circulation of ideas and in those great cities which are the intellectual centers where all the rays of human genius are reflected and combined. To this it may be added that most important discoveries demand a use of national power which the government of a small state is unable to make: in great nations the government has more enlarged ideas, and is more completely disengaged from the routine of precedent and the selfishness of local feeling; its designs are conceived with more talent and executed with more boldness.

In time of peace the well-being of small nations is undoubtedly more general and complete; but they are apt to suffer more acutely from the calamities of war than those great empires whose distant frontiers may long avert the presence of the danger from the mass of the people, who are therefore more frequently afflicted than ruined by the contest.

But in this matter, as in many others, the decisive argument is the necessity of the case. If none but small nations existed, I do not doubt that mankind would be more happy and more free; but the existence of great nations is unavoidable.

Political strength thus becomes a condition of national prosperity. It profits a state but little to be affluent and free if it is perpetually exposed to be pillaged or subjugated; its manufactures and commerce are of small advantage if another nation has the empire of the seas and gives the law in all the markets of the globe. Small nations are often miserable, not because they are small, but because they are weak; and great empires prosper less because they are great than because they are strong. Physical strength is therefore one of the first conditions of the happiness and even of the existence of nations. Hence it occurs that, unless very peculiar circumstances intervene, small nations are always united to large empires in the end, either by force or by their own consent. I do not know a more deplorable condition than that of a people unable to defend itself or to provide for its own wants.

The federal system was created with the intention of combining the different advantages which result from the magnitude and the littleness of nations; and a glance at the United States of America discovers the advantages which they have derived from its adoption.

In great centralized nations the legislator is obliged to give a character of uniformity to the laws, which does not always suit the diversity of customs and of districts; as he takes no cognizance of special cases, he can only proceed upon general principles; and the population are obliged to conform to the requirements of the laws, since legislation cannot adapt itself to the exigencies and the customs of the population, which is a great cause of trouble and misery. This disadvantage does not exist in confederations; Congress regulates the principal measures of the national government, and all the details of the administration are reserved to the provincial legislatures. One can hardly imagine how much this division of sovereignty contributes to the well-being of each of the states that compose the Union. In these small communities, which are never agitated by the desire of aggrandizement or the care of self-defense, all public authority and private energy are turned towards internal improvements. The central government of each state, which is in immediate relationship with the citizens, is daily apprised of the wants that arise in society; and new projects are proposed every year, which are discussed at town meetings or by the legislature, and which are transmitted by the press to stimulate the zeal and to excite the interest of the citizens. This spirit of improvement is constantly alive in the American republics, without compromising their tranquillity; the ambition of power yields to the less refined and less dangerous desire for well-being. It is generally believed in America that the existence and the permanence of the republican form of government in the New World depend upon the existence and the duration of the federal system; and it is not unusual to attribute a large share of the misfortunes that have befallen the new states of South America to the injudicious erection of great republics instead of a divided and confederate sovereignty.

It is incontestably true that the tastes and the habits of republican government in the United States were first created in the townships and the provincial assemblies. In a small state, like that of Connecticut, for instance, where cutting a canal or laying down a road is a great political question, where the state has no army to pay and no wars to carry on, and where much wealth or much honor cannot be given to the rulers, no form of government can be more natural or more appropriate than a republic. But it is this same republican spirit, it is these manners and customs of a free people, which have been created and nurtured in the different states, that must be afterwards applied to the country at large. The public spirit of the Union is, so to speak, nothing more than an aggregate or summary of the patriotic zeal of the separate provinces. Every citizen of the United States transfers, so to speak, his attachment to his little republic into the common store of American patriotism. In defending the Union he defends the increasing prosperity of his own state or county, the right of conducting its affairs, and the hope of causing measures of improvement to be adopted in it which may be favorable to his own interests; and these are motives that are wont to stir men more than the general interests of the country and the glory of the nation.

On the other hand, if the temper and the manners of the inhabitants especially fitted them to promote the welfare of a great republic, the federal system renders their task less difficult. The confederation of all the American states presents none of the ordinary inconveniences resulting from large associations of men. The Union is a great republic in extent, but the paucity of objects for which its government acts assimilates it to a small state. Its acts are important, but they are rare. As the sovereignty of the Union is limited and incomplete, its exercise is not dangerous to liberty; for it does not excite those insatiable desires for fame and power which have proved so fatal to great republics. As there is no common center to the country, great capital cities, colossal wealth, abject poverty, and sudden revolutions are alike unknown; and political passion, instead of spreading over the land like a fire on the prairies, spends its strength against the interests and the individual passions of every state.

Nevertheless, tangible objects and ideas circulate throughout the Union as freely as in a country inhabited by one people. Nothing checks the spirit of enterprise. The government invites the aid of all who have talents or knowledge to serve it. Inside of the frontiers of the Union profound peace prevails, as within the heart of some great empire; abroad it ranks with the most powerful nations of the earth: two thousand miles of coast are open to the commerce of the world; and as it holds the keys of a new world, its flag is respected in the most remote seas. The Union is happy and free as a small people, and glorious and strong as a great nation.

WHY THE FEDERAL SYSTEM IS NOT PRACTICABLE
FOR ALL NATIONS, AND HOW THE ANGLO-AMERICANS
WERE ENABLED TO ADOPT IT

. . . I have shown the advantages that the Americans derive from their federal system; it remains for me to point out the circumstances that enabled them to adopt it, as its benefits cannot be enjoyed by all nations. The accidental defects of the federal system which originate in the laws may be corrected by the skill of the legislator, but there are evils inherent in the system which cannot be remedied by any effort. The people must therefore find in themselves the strength necessary to bear the natural imperfections of their government.

The most prominent evil of all federal systems is the complicated nature of the means they employ. Two sovereignties are necessarily in presence of each other. The legislator may simplify and equalize as far as possible the action of these two sovereignties, by limiting each of them to a sphere of authority accurately defined; but he cannot combine them into one or prevent them from coming into collision at certain points. The federal system, therefore, rests upon a theory which is complicated at the best, and which demands the daily exercise of a considerable share of discretion on the part of those it governs. . . .

In examining the Constitution of the United States, which is the most perfect federal constitution that ever existed, one is startled at the variety of information and the amount of discernment that it presupposes in the people whom it is meant to govern. The government of the Union depends almost entirely upon legal fictions; the Union is an ideal nation, which exists, so to speak, only in the mind, and whose limits and extent can only be discerned by the understanding.

After the general theory is comprehended, many difficulties remain to be solved in its application; for the sovereignty of the Union is so involved in that of the states that it is impossible to distinguish its boundaries at the first glance. The whole structure of the government is artificial and conventional, and it would be ill adapted to a people which has not been long accustomed to conduct its own affairs, or to one in which the science of politics has not descended to the humblest classes of society. I have never been more struck by the good sense and the practical judgment of the Americans than in the manner in which they elude the numberless difficulties resulting from their Federal Constitution. I scarcely ever met with a plain American citizen who could not distinguish with surprising facility the obligations created by the laws of Congress from those created by the laws of his own state, and who, after having discriminated between the matters which come under the cognizance of the Union and those which the local legislature is competent to regulate, could not point out the exact limit of the separate jurisdictions of the Federal courts and the tribunals of the state.

The Constitution of the United States resembles those fine creations of human industry which ensure wealth and renown to their inventors, but which are profitless in other hands. . . .

The second and most fatal of all defects, and that which I believe to be inherent in the federal system, is the relative weakness of the government of the Union. The principle upon which all confederations rest is that of a divided sovereignty. Legislators may render this partition less perceptible, they may even conceal it for a time from the public eye, but they cannot prevent it from existing; and a divided sovereignty must always be weaker than an entire one. The remarks made on the Constitution of the United States have shown with what skill the Americans, while restraining the power of the Union within the narrow limits of a federal government, have given it the semblance, and to a certain extent the force, of a national government. By this means the legislators of the Union have diminished the natural danger of confederations, but have not entirely obviated it.

The American government, it is said, does not address itself to the states, but transmits its injunctions directly to the citizens and compels them individually to comply with its demands. But if the Federal law were to clash with the interests and the prejudices of a state, it might be feared that all the citizens of that state would conceive themselves to be interested in the cause of a single individual who refused to obey. If all the citizens of the state were aggrieved at the same time and in the same manner by the authority of the Union, the Federal government would vainly attempt to subdue them individually; they would instinctively unite in a common defense and would find an organization already prepared for them in the sovereignty that their state is allowed to enjoy. Fiction would give way to reality, and an organized portion of the nation might then contest the central authority.

The same observation holds good with regard to the Federal jurisdiction. If the courts of the Union violated an important law of a state in a private case, the real though not the apparent contest would be between the aggrieved state represented by a citizen and the Union represented by its courts of justice.

He would have but a partial knowledge of the world who should imagine that it is possible by the aid of legal fictions to prevent men from finding out and employing those means of gratifying their passions which have been left open to them. The American legislators, though they have rendered a collision between the two sovereignties less probable, have not destroyed the causes of such a misfortune. It may even be affirmed that, in case of such a collision, they have not been able to ensure the victory of the Federal element. The Union is possessed of money and troops, but the states have kept the affections and the prejudices of the people. The sovereignty of the Union is an abstract being, which is connected with but few external objects; the sovereignty of the states is perceptible by the senses, easily understood, and constantly active. The former is of recent creation, the latter is coeval with the people itself. The sovereignty of the Union is factitious, that of the states is natural and self-existent, without effort, like the authority of a parent. The sovereignty of the nation affects a few of the chief interests of society; it represents an immense but remote country, a vague and ill-defined sentiment. The authority of the states controls every individual citizen at every hour and in all circumstances; it protects his property, his freedom, and his life; it affects at every moment his well-being or his misery. When we recollect the traditions, the customs, the prejudices of local and familiar attachment with which it is connected, we cannot doubt the superiority of a power that rests on the instinct of patriotism, so natural to the human heart.

Since legislators cannot prevent such dangerous collisions as occur between the two sovereignties which coexist in the Federal system, their first object must be, not only to dissuade the confederate states from warfare, but to encourage such dispositions as lead to peace. Hence it is that the Federal compact cannot be lasting unless there exists in the communities which are leagued together a certain number of inducements to union which render their common dependence agreeable and the task of the government light. The Federal system cannot succeed without the presence of favorable circumstances added to the influence of good laws. All the nations that have ever formed a confederation have been held together by some common interests, which served as the intellectual ties of association. . . .

The circumstance which makes it easy to maintain a Federal government in America is not only that the states have similar interests, a common origin, and a common language, but that they have also arrived at the same stage of civilization, which almost always renders a union feasible. I do not know of any European nation, however small, that does not present less uniformity in its different provinces than the American people, which occupy a territory as extensive as one half of Europe. The distance from Maine to Georgia is about one thousand miles; but the difference between the civilization of Maine and that of Georgia is slighter than the difference between the habits of Normandy and those of Brittany. Maine and Georgia, which are placed at the opposite extremities of a great empire, have therefore more real inducements to form a confederation than Normandy and Brittany, which are separated only by a brook.

The geographical position of the country increased the facilities that the American legislators derived from the usages and customs of the inhabitants; and it is to this circumstance that the adoption and the maintenance of the Federal system are mainly attributable.

The most important occurrence in the life of a nation is the breaking out of a war. . . . A long war almost always reduces nations to the wretched alternative of being abandoned to ruin by defeat or to despotism by success. War therefore renders the weakness of a government most apparent and most alarming; and I have shown that the inherent defect of federal governments is that of being weak.

The federal system not only has no centralized administration, and nothing that resembles one, but the central government itself is imperfectly organized, which is always a great cause of weakness when the nation is opposed to other countries which are themselves governed by a single authority. In the Federal Constitution of the United States, where the central government has more real force than in any other confederation, this evil is extremely evident. . . .

How does it happen, then, that the American Union, with all the relative perfection of its laws, is not dissolved by the occurrence of a great war? It is because it has no great wars to fear. Placed in the center of an immense continent, which offers a boundless field for human industry, the Union is almost as much insulated from the world as if all its frontiers were girt by the ocean. . . .

The great advantage of the United States does not, then, consist in a Federal Constitution which allows it to carry on great wars, but in a geographical position which renders such wars extremely improbable.

No one can be more inclined than I am to appreciate the advantages of the federal system, which I hold to be one of the combinations most favorable to the prosperity and freedom of man. I envy the lot of those nations which have been able to adopt it; but I cannot believe that any confederate people could maintain a long or an equal contest with a nation of similar strength in which the government is centralized. A people which, in the presence of the great military monarchies of Europe, should divide its sovereignty into fractional parts would, in my opinion, by that very act abdicate its power, and perhaps its existence and its name. But such is the admirable position of the New World that man has no other enemy than himself, and that, in order to be happy and to be free, he has only to determine that he will be so.

The Supremacy of National Law

Tracing the historical development of national-state relationships, one finds that there has been constant strife over the determination of the boundaries of national power in relation to the reserved powers of the states. The Civil War did not settle once and for all the difficult question of national versus state power. The Supreme Court has played an important role in the development of the federal system, and some of its most historic opinions have upheld national power at the expense of the states. In the early period of the Court, Chief Justice John Marshall in *McCulloch v. Maryland,* 4 Wheaton 316 (1819), stated two doctrines that have had a profound effect upon the federal system: (1) the doctrine of implied powers; (2) the doctrine of the supremacy of national law. The former enables Congress to expand its power into numerous areas affecting states directly. By utilizing the commerce clause, for example, Congress may now regulate what is essentially *intrastate* commerce, for the Court has held that this is implied in the original clause giving Congress the power to regulate commerce among the several states. The immediate issues in *McCulloch* v. *Maryland* were, first, whether or not Congress had the power to incorporate, or charter, a national bank; second, if Congress did have such a power, although nowhere stated in the Constitution, did the existence of such a bank prevent state action that would interfere in its operation?

10
McCULLOCH v. MARYLAND
4 Wheaton 316 (1819)

Mr. Chief Justice Marshall delivered the opinion of the Court, saying in part:

In the case now to be determined, the defendant, a sovereign state, denies the obligation of a law enacted by the legislature of the Union; and the plaintiff, on his part, contests the validity of an act which has been passed by the legislature of that state. The Constitution of our country, in its most interesting and vital parts, is to be considered; the conflicting powers of the government of the Union and of its members, as marked in that Constitution, are to be discussed; and an opinion given, which may essentially influence the great operations of the government. . . .

If any one proposition could command the universal assent of mankind, we might expect it would be this: that the government of the Union, though limited in its powers, is supreme within its sphere of action. This would seem to result necessarily from its nature. It is the government of all; its powers are delegated by all; it represents all, and acts for all. Though any one state may be willing to control its operations, no state is willing to allow others to control them. The nation, on those subjects on which it can act, must necessarily bind its component parts. But this question is not left to mere reason: the people have, in express terms, decided it, by saying, "this Constitution, and the laws of the United States, which shall be made in pursuance thereof," "shall be the supreme law of the land," and by requiring that the members of the state legislatures, and the officers of the executive and judicial departments of the states, shall take the oath of fidelity to it. . . .

A constitution, to contain an accurate detail of all the subdivisions of which its great powers will admit, and of all the means by which they may be carried into execution, would partake of the prolixity of a legal code, and could scarcely be embraced by the human mind. It would probably never be understood by the public. Its nature, therefore, requires that only its great outlines should be marked, its important objects designated, and the minor ingredients which compose those objects be deduced from the nature of the objects themselves. That this idea was entertained by the framers of the American Constitution, is not only to be inferred from the nature of the instrument, but from the language. . . .

Although, among the enumerated powers of government, we do not find the word "bank," or "incorporation," we find the great powers to lay and collect taxes; to borrow money; to regulate commerce; to declare and conduct a war; and to raise and support armies and navies. The sword and the purse, all the external relations, and no inconsiderable portion of the industry of the nation, are entrusted to its government. It can never be pretended that these vast powers draw after them others of inferior importance, merely because they are inferior. Such an idea can never be advanced. But it may, with great reason, be contended, that a government, entrusted with such ample powers, on the due execution of which the happiness and prosperity of the nation so vitally depends, must also be entrusted with ample means for their execution. The power being given, it is the interest of the nation to facilitate its execution. It can never be their interest, and cannot be presumed to have been their intention, to clog and embarrass its execution by withholding the most appropriate means. Throughout this vast republic, from the St. Croix to the Gulf of Mexico, from the Atlantic to the Pacific, revenue is to be collected and expended, armies are to be marched and supported. The exigencies of the nation may require, that the treasure raised in the North should be transported to the South, that raised in the East conveyed to the West, or that this order should be reversed. Is that construction of the Constitution to be preferred which would render these operations difficult, hazardous, and expensive? Can we adopt that construction (unless the words imperiously require it) which would impute to the framers of that instrument, when granting these powers for the public good, the intention of impeding their exercise by withholding a choice of means? If, indeed, such be the mandate of the Constitution, we have only to obey; but that instrument does not profess to enumerate the means by which the powers it confers may be executed; nor does it prohibit the creation of a corporation, if the existence of such a being be essential to the beneficial exercise of those powers. It is, then, the subject of fair inquiry, how far such means may be employed. . . .

We admit, as all must admit, that the powers of the government are limited, and that its limits are not to be transcended. But we think the sound construction of the Constitution must allow to the national legislature that discretion, with respect to the means by which the powers it confers are to be carried into execution, which will enable that body to perform the high duties assigned to it, in the manner most beneficial to the people. Let the end be legitimate, let it be within the scope of the Constitution, and all means which are appropriate, which are plainly adapted to that end, which are not prohibited, but consist with the letter and spirit of the Constitution, are constitutional. . . .

It being the opinion of the court that the act incorporating the bank is constitutional; and that the power of establishing a branch in the state of Maryland might be properly exercised by the bank itself, we proceed to inquire:

Whether the state of Maryland may, without violating the Constitution, tax that branch? . . .

That the power of taxation is one of vital importance; that it is retained by the states; that it is not abridged by the grant of a similar power to the government of the Union; that it is to be concurrently exercised by the two governments: are truths which have never been denied. But, such is the paramount character of the Constitution, that its capacity to withdraw any subject from the action of even this power, is admitted. The states are expressly forbidden to lay any duties on imports or exports, except what may be absolutely necessary for executing their inspection laws. If the obligation of this prohibition must be conceded — if it may restrain a state from the exercise of its taxing power on imports and exports; the same paramount character would seem to restrain, as it certainly may restrain, a state from such other exercise of this power, as is in its nature incompatible with, and repugnant to, the constitutional laws of the Union. A law, absolutely repugnant to another, as entirely repeals that other as if express terms of repeal were used.

On this ground the counsel for the bank place its claim to be exempted from the power of a state to tax its operations. There is no express provision for the case, but the claim has been sustained on a principle which so entirely pervades the Constitution, is so intermixed with the materials which compose it, so interwoven with its web, so blended with its texture, as to be incapable of being separated from it, without rending it into shreds.

This great principle is, that the Constitution and the laws made in pursuance thereof are supreme; that they control the Constitution and laws of the respective states, and cannot be controlled by them. From this, which may be almost termed an axiom, other propositions are deduced as corollaries, on the truth or error of which, and on their application to this case, the cause has been supposed to depend. These are, 1. That a power to create implies a power to preserve. 2. That a power to destroy, if wielded by a different hand, is hostile to, and incompatible with, these powers to create and preserve. 3. That where this repugnancy exists, that authority which is supreme must control, not yield to that over which it is supreme. . . .

If we apply the principle for which the state of Maryland contends, to the Constitution generally, we shall find it capable of changing totally the character of that instrument. We shall find it capable of arresting all the measures of the government, and of prostrating it at the foot of the states. The American people have declared their Constitution, and the laws made in pursuance thereof, to be supreme; but this principle would transfer the supremacy, in fact, to the states. . . .

The court has bestowed on this subject its most deliberate consideration. The result is a conviction that the states have no power, by taxation or otherwise, to retard, impede, burden, or in any manner control, the operations of the constitutional laws enacted by Congress to carry into execution the powers vested in the general government. That is, we think, the unavoidable consequence of that supremacy which the Constitution has declared. . . .

Constitutional doctrine regarding the power of the national government to regulate commerce among the states to promote general prosperity has been clarified in a series of Supreme Court cases. At issue is the interpretation of the power to "regulate commerce with foreign nations, and among the several States," granted to Congress in Article 1. Some of these cases have emphasized the role of the national government as umpire, enforcing certain rules of the game within which the free enterprise system functions; others have emphasized the positive role of the government in regulating the economy.

A key case supporting the supremacy of the national government in commercial regulation was *Gibbons* v. *Ogden,* 9 Wheaton 1 (1824). The New York legislature, in 1798, granted Robert R. Livingston the exclusive privilege to navigate by steam the rivers and other waters of the state, provided he could build a boat that would travel at four miles an hour against the current of the Hudson River. A two-year time limitation was imposed, and the conditions were not met; however, New York renewed its grant for two years in 1803 and again in 1807. In 1807 Robert Fulton, who now held the exclusive license with Livingston, completed and put into operation a steamboat which met the legislative conditions. The New York legislature now provided that a five-year extension of their monopoly would be given to Livingston and Fulton for each new steamboat they placed into operation on New York waters. The monopoly could not exceed thirty years, but during that period anyone wishing to navigate New York waters by steam had first to obtain a license from Livingston and Fulton, who were given the power to confiscate unlicensed boats. New Jersey and Connecticut passed retaliatory laws, the former authorizing confiscation of any New York ship for each ship confiscated by Livingston and Fulton, the latter prohibiting boats licensed in New York from entering Connecticut waters. Ohio also passed retaliatory legislation. Open commercial warfare seemed a possibility among the states of the union.

In 1793 Congress passed an act providing for the licensing of vessels engaged in the coasting trade, and Gibbons obtained under this statute a license to operate boats between New York and New Jersey. Ogden was engaged in a similar operation under an exclusive license issued by Livingston and Fulton, and thus sought to enjoin Gibbons from further operation. The New York court upheld the exclusive grants given to Livingston and Fulton, and Gibbons appealed to the Supreme Court. Chief Justice Marshall made it quite clear that (1) states cannot interfere with a power granted to Congress by passing conflicting state legislation, and (2) the commerce power includes anything affecting "commerce among the states" and thus may include *intrastate* as well as interstate commerce. In this way the foundation was laid for broad national control over commercial activity.

Congress has used its constitutional power to regulate "commerce among the several States" to justify broad regulatory programs. In *Champion* v. *Ames,* 188 U.S. 321 (1903), the Court stated that Congress could bar transportation of objectionable articles in interstate commerce. This was in reference to an 1895 lottery law prohibiting lottery tickets from being sent through the channels of interstate commerce. After this decision Congress prohibited transportation of numerous other "objectionable" articles in interstate commerce; e.g., impure food and drugs, uninspected meat and fabrics, stolen automobiles, kidnapped persons, and women for immoral purposes. In this way a national police power was developed similar to that of the states in intent — i.e., the power to protect the health, welfare, and morals of the community — initially within the "reserved" powers of the states.

In 1916 Congress attempted to regulate child labor conditions within states by preventing the transportation in interstate commerce of goods produced by children under conditions that violated the standards of the Child Labor Act of 1916. Although the initial attempt was declared unconstitutional in *Hammer* v. *Dagenhart,* 247 U.S. 251 (1918), the device of regulation through controlling the transportation of goods in interstate commerce is now an accepted constitutional practice. Furthermore, the regulatory power of Congress extends to all economic areas — production, distribution, etc. — that in any way affect interstate commerce. Thus labor disputes that burden or obstruct interstate commerce are controlled under the Wagner Labor Relations Act of 1935 and the Taft-Hartley Act of 1947. The radio and television industry, because it uses the channels of interstate commerce, is regulated by the Federal Communications Act of 1934. The same is true of banks, securities dealers and exchanges, railroads, telephone companies, petroleum firms and natural gas companies, and trucking firms. The list of industries subject to national regulation through the commerce clause could be extended indefinitely. Marshall's decision in *Gibbons* v. *Ogden* set the stage for extensive national regulation through its broad and flexible interpretation of the commerce clause.

Both *McCulloch* v. *Maryland* and *Gibbons* v. *Ogden* clearly held that the states cannot take action that will impinge upon the legitimate authority of Congress. These opinions reflected judicial acceptance of the fact that when the federal government acts, it generally preempts the field. But this does not mean that the states can never legislate concurrently with the national government. It depends upon the circumstances. For example, in *Pennsylvania* v. *Nelson,* 350 U.S. 497 (1956), the Supreme Court found that the Smith Act superseded a Pennsylvania sedition statute under which Nelson had been convicted. The Pennsylvania law, like the Smith Act, made it a crime to advocate the violent overthrow of the government of the United States or the government of Pennsylvania. The Supreme Court found that the Smith Act, in combination with a number of other federal subversive control statutes such as the Internal Security Act of 1950 and the Communist Control Act of 1954, proscribed advocacy to overthrow any government, whether federal, state, or local. On the basis of the aggregate of federal statutes in the sedition field, the Court concluded: "Congress had intended to occupy the field of sedition. Taken as a whole, they [the statutes] evince a Congressional plan which makes it reasonable to determine that no room has been left for the state to supplement it. Therefore, a state's sedition statute is superseded regardless of whether it purports to supplement the federal law. . . ." Although the *Nelson* case apparently nullified more than forty state sedition statutes, the issue has not been finally resolved. Several cases since the *Nelson* decision reflect a judicial hesitancy to prevent state and local authorities from enforcing statutes controlling subversive activities. (See *Beilan* v. *Board of Education,* 357 U.S. 399 [1958], and *Lerner* v. *Casey,* 357 U.S. 468 [1958].) The real problems that arise concerning the doctrine of national supremacy do not develop where there is clear state defiance of a federal law or a federal court order, for in these situations the enforcement of the principle of the supremacy of the Constitution and of national law can easily and clearly be carried out. Thus in *Cooper* v. *Aaron,* 358 U.S. 1 (1958), a federal district court order to proceed with integration at Central High School in Little Rock was upheld by the Supreme Court in face of the defiance of the Governor of Arkansas. The supremacy of the national government was clear, and the opinion of the Court was not ambiguous.

Another example of the problem of concurrent jurisdiction arose in the case of *Colorado Anti-Discrimination Commission* v. *Continental Air Lines,* 372 U.S. 714 (1963). This case involved the constitutionality of the Colorado Anti-Discrimination Act, which made it an unfair employment practice to refuse to hire qualified individuals because of race, creed, color, national origin, or ancestry. Under the Act a commission was established to investigate complaints. Marlon D. Green, a black, applied for a job as a pilot with Continental Air Lines, a small interstate carrier whose route passes through Colorado. He was refused a position, and he filed a complaint with the Anti-Discrimination Commission, claiming that the only reason he was not hired was because he was a black. The Commission held extensive hearings to determine the validity of his charge, and finally upheld it. Continental Air Lines was ordered to cease and desist from this particular discrimination and from any other discriminatory practices. The Commission directed the air line to enroll the applicant for its first opening in its pilot training school.

The validity of the Commission's cease and desist order was immediately attacked by Continental, which secured a judgment vacating the order from a lower State District Court. On appeal, the Supreme Court of Colorado affirmed the judgment. Both state courts held that the Colorado statute placed an undue burden upon interstate commerce, which was within the exclusive jurisdiction of the national government. However, the Supreme Court found that the Colorado statute merely extended, rather than conflicted with, the federal laws dealing with the same subject.

A Perspective on Federalism: Present and Future

In the following selection, the role of the states in the political system is discussed from the perspective that the nature of intergovernmental relations reflects underlying political conditions and realities. As James Madison pointed out in *Federalist 39,* the original constitutional scheme of federalism represented a delicate balance between national and state ("federal") interests. But, under the original constitutional design, the national government was not to intervene directly in the affairs of state governments; and the problems of subsidiary local governments within states were not considered to be separate from the problems of the states themselves, and therefore, they were a proper matter for resolution by the individual state governments.

Morton Grodzins, in his article "The Federal System," pointed out that strict separation of national and state functions has never really existed, and that even before the Constitution of 1787 a national statute passed by the Continental Congress gave grants-in-aid of land to the states for public schools.[1] Tocqueville also comments on the difficulties of formally separating, in theory, the responsibilities of national, state, and local governments. The history of the federal system has seen the ebb and flow of national dominance over the states; centralization and decentralization have been the cyclical themes of federalism and intergovernmental relations. The thrust of the New Deal was toward centralization through the use of federal grant-in-aid programs, a philosophy that dominated the government until the emergence of the "New Federalism" of the Nixon administration, which supported decentralization of power from the national to the state governments. The move toward decentralization was broadly supported by the Republican party. Revenue-sharing was inaugurated by President Nixon to transfer national funds to the states, without stipulation of how the money was to be spent. The revenue-sharing procedure was in direct contrast to the grant-in-aid programs, which

---

[1] Morton Grodzins, ed., *Goals for Americans* (Englewood Cliffs, N.J.: Prentice-Hall, 1960).

allowed for state receipt of federal money upon the condition of state adherence to national standards. The continuing conflict between the themes and realities of centralization and decentralization are examined in the following selection.

11

Samuel H. Beer

THE FUTURE OF THE STATES IN THE FEDERAL SYSTEM

Since the founding of the republic, the role of the states has been determined by the stage of our national development. The power accorded the states, and their use of it, has been the outcome of federal response to national needs.

In the early days of the founding of the Republic the states could have been thought of as "commonwealths" — John Adams's term for Massachusetts — laying down the infrastructure of a developing country. In the Jacksonian period they were vigorous centers of mercantilistic democracy contributing to the booming national economy and the languishing national polity. In the great Republican era of nation building that extended from the Civil War to the New Deal they acted as experimental laboratories for testing the precedents that led to gradual centralization of the federal system. In the years of New Deal liberalism, from the 1930s to the 1960s, they were agents for redistribution of wealth and power in the American version of the welfare state.

This quick review of the role of the states shows two principles at work. First, the American federal system has never been static. It has changed radically over the years, as tides of centralization and decentralization have altered the balance of power and the allocation of functions among the different levels of government. We cannot, therefore, solve the problem of the future role of the states by trying to return to some ideal blueprint that prevailed in the past. Second, if the present and future role of the states is questioned, it is because there is much uncertainty about the direction of our national life. The proper function of the states is hard to

Presented at a seminar conducted jointly by the Woodrow Wilson International Center for Scholars and the National Governors Association, December 12, 1979 and included in this volume by permission.

define because the public philosophy of our time is obscure and confused.

If and when the role of the states is clarified, it will not be simply by a return to the past. Nor will this clarification consist of a new consensus on the allocation of functions among levels of government. It will be the outcome of factors that shape our public life: a new public philosophy broadly shared by a coherent political coalition — and, no doubt, hotly contested by another coalition — that requires a specific allocation of functions to pursue its goals of national development.

THE NEW FEDERAL SYSTEM OF THE 1960s

In the 1960s the development of the American welfare state took a radical turn. Although like the New Deal the Great Society was strongly centralist, in other crucial respects it differed. The key contrast was the new role of professionalism in the public service, reflecting the rapid advance in the postwar years of the scientific revolution in both natural and social sciences.

The faith that science can transform society goes back to the beginning of the modern era. It found a particularly warm welcome in America, and from the days of Benjamin Franklin the ideals of popular government were joined with great expectations of what science would do in the service of humanity. This promise of power came into its own during and after World War II. Physicists invented nuclear weapons, transforming defense and foreign policy, and in the late 1950s they launched the space program that culminated in the moonshot of 1969. Advances in medicine encouraged the development of the National Institutes of Health and the great expansion of federal medical programs, even under the cautious administration of Eisenhower. In perhaps the greatest step forward of all, the social sciences, psychology, economics, sociology, and even political science, seemed to have achieved the capacity for creating a behavioral revolution. Their ability to formulate principles of social control made them the foundations for government action. Social engineering based on the policy sciences gained new prestige and influence. In the fields of health, housing, urban renewal, transportation, welfare, education, the environment, energy, and poverty, the new programs of the 1960s and 1970s drew heavily upon specialized and technical knowledge for conception advocacy, and implementation. Stripped of its apocalyptic overtones, the term technocracy suggests the orientation of the new public philosophy and the consequent shift of influence toward bureaucratic professionals.

Needless to say, the programs and policies of these years have displayed great variety in their goals and methods. Some, such as the civil rights acts, sought to protect certain legal rights; others aimed at redistributing income or power in the spirit of the New Deal reforms. But the new technocratic programs had a distinctive and ambitious rationale. They were concerned not merely with the output of government action, but rather with the outcome; that is, with the actual effects on social behavior of the services or other actions. In this spirit, it was hoped that the new knowledge derived from advances in the social and natural sciences would be applied to combat heart disease, lessen mental illness, raise reading scores, increase work skills, cut down juvenile delinquency, and even cure poverty. While the "people" programs were especially concerned with altering social behavior, the "physical" programs, such as housing and urban renewal, sought success that could be measured not by mere bricks and mortar but by social outcome. The new outlook on public policy marked a shift from the redistributive welfare state to the reformative welfare state.

This technocratic trend has had a transforming effect on federalism in two ways: first by its services strategy, and second by its intergovernmental strategy. The service strategy consisted of new programs that depended on government spending to provide specific services, delivered by professionally trained persons, to certain categories of consumers, for a designated behavioral outcome. The intergovernmental strategy developed because the fields these programs entered usually were already occupied by state and local governments. It was natural that the federal government should use the administrative agencies of state and local governments when it moved into their fields on so massive a scale.

Given this derivation and rationale, the new programs found their chosen vehicle for implementation in categorical grants in aid designed by federal professionals and carried out by their counterparts at the state and local levels. As a consequence a new component was added to the federal system: the professional bureaucratic complex. The term is singular, but the examples have multiplied with the prodigious growth of the categorical system in the 1960s and 1970s, including the health syndicate, the highway lobby, and the educational establishment, among others (see Table 1). The main element in any such complex is a core of bureaucratic professionals linked by a common program across levels of government. This technocratic core also works closely with other elements: interested legislators, especially the chairmen of the specialized committees in Congress, and the local beneficiaries, or their spokespersons. With different shades of meaning, these complexes have also been called whirlpools, iron triangles, or perhaps most accurately, issue networks. As they have multiplied they have transformed the actual operation of American federalism, not only by adding a new system of implementation, but also by eliciting an array of powerful new electoral forces. The new centralism has done much to create its own sustaining political base at the level of delivery.

The effect of all this on the role of the states in the federal system has been radical. Any exact estimate is made impossible by the interactive flow of influence between levels of government. But by the end of the 1960s the fundamental change was already obvious: a sharp shift in the balance of power toward the center.

Table 1 Growth of the Categorical System: Federal Aid to State and Local Governments, 1938–1978 (amounts in billions)

| Year | Categorical Grants | | Other Aid | Total Federal Aid |
	Number of Programs	Amount of Aid		
1938	30	.8	—	.8
1962	160	7.9	—	7.9
1967	379	15.2	—	15.2
1975	442	37.4	12.3	49.7
1978	492	59.1	22.6	81.7

SOURCES: Advisory Commission on Intergovernmental Relations, *Categorical Grants: Their Role and Design.* A-52. Washington, D.C.: U.S. Government Printing Office, 1977, pp. 19, 25, 26, 28, 32, 35. *A Catalog of Federal Grant-In-Aid Programs to State and Local Governments: Grants Funded FY 1978.* A-72. Washington, D.C.: U.S. Government Printing Office, 1979, p. 1.

Whether one likes it or not, it is important to understand the grounds of the new centralism. Many features of the American political system were, of course, necessary conditions for this development, but they had been in existence well before it took place. Congressmen have been interested in getting material benefits for their constituencies from the earliest days of the Republic. The progressive income tax dates back to a generation before the New Deal. Economic causes for categorical grants existed during and after the 1930s, but they produced a modest number of programs in comparison with those that came later. The vast growth of the categorical system dating from the 1960s derives, to a large extent, from one of the profound, formative influences on all contemporary societies — the new phase of the scientific revolution that set in after World War II (see Table 1). Its radical effects upon the role of the states will not be easily reversed.

THE REACTION TOWARD AUTONOMY

There were two reactions against the new centralism of the 1960s: the first, a reaction seeking greater autonomy for state and local governments; the second, a reaction seeking more effective representation for these governments in federal policy-making and implementation.

The reaction toward autonomy aimed at a reallocation, or sorting out, of functions between the various levels of government, so that state and local governments would gain a greater control over certain aspects of government activity. It was a break from the "marble cake" model, in which all functions were shared by all levels; and it was an attempt to recover, with due allowance for late twentieth-century realities, a division of power in the spirit of the older dual federalism. The central thrust was suggested by Dan Elazar when he wrote:

> The true role of the states in the federal system is to function as polities, not as middle managers. . . . The United States consists of a national polity with the whole country for its arena and served by the general government plus the several state polities each with its state for an arena and served by its own government.

For those interested in strengthening the power of the states today, it is important to see that this earlier attempt was prolonged, well-thought out, and politically powerful. Support for an effort of this kind had been gathering, especially in the Republican party, from the late 1950s. Although it acquired its name from the New Federalism launched by President Nixon in 1969, one could reasonably think of Eisenhower as the first of the New Federalists, to be followed by other advocates, such as Laird, Rockefeller, Romney, Goodell, and John Anderson, as well as presidents Nixon and Ford.

The rhetoric of New Federalism, which called for " a revitalization of state and local governments," was meaningful and operational. Grounded in the American conservative's high regard for liberty, it sought to heighten self-determination by subnational communities. Richard Nathan, who served under Nixon in the Office of Management and Budget (OMB) and the Department of Health, Education, and Welfare (HEW), gave programmatic form to this aspiration. His proposals for a reallocation of functions can be presented schematically according to four major budget categories.

Primarily for the federal government with regard to policy-making, administration, and finance:

1. Income security, for example, social insurance and welfare. In these matters, uniformity is desired as a national value, and the federal government has access to the resources of the whole country. Income transfers, moreover, can be more readily centralized than services.
2. Natural resources, for example, air and water pollution and energy. Interstate spillovers in these fields require action by a central authority.

Primarily for state and local governments with regard to policy-making and administration, but with federal financial assistance:

3. Human services programs, for example, education, health, manpower. These programs provide services that require close contact with recipients in the communities where the services are delivered.
4. Community service programs, for example, urban development, police and fire protection, zoning, sanitation. To be decentralized for much the same reasons as the programs in the previous category.

During the Nixon administration these proposals were embodied in more specific measures. They included bills to federalize welfare, especially the Family Assistance Plan, as well as general revenue sharing, the six major grant consolidations known as special revenue sharing, and certain administrative reforms. While the New Federalism recognized the virtues of local government, its preference for the states was marked. The earlier Republican plans for general revenue sharing, such as the measure proposed by Laird in 1958 and by the Republican platform in 1964, would have made payments exclusively to state governments. Nixon's first proposal of August 1969 provided for grants to the states with a pass-through to local governments of no more than 30 percent, and accordingly his message to Congress stressed only "the restoration of a rightful balance between the state capitals and the national capital."

The New Federalism was not concerned merely with narrow technical reform of intergovernmental relations. On the contrary, its advocates saw it as a challenge to the rationale of the reformative Welfare State inaugurated by the New Frontier and the Great Society. In presenting his bill for general revenue sharing in 1966, Senator Goodell explicitly set forth its claims as an alternative public philosophy:

> This proposal seeks to provide for the great public needs of the 1960s and 1970s by equipping state and local governments to meet these needs. It is an alternative to the philosophy of the Great Society which would meet these needs by massive expansion of Federal programs and by further proliferation of narrow categorical grant-in-aid programs that end up in administrative confusion, waste and centralized control.

This major emphasis continued under Republican presidents. As Nathan reports, "this term [the New Federalism] . . . eventually came to . . . characterize Nixon's domestic program."

Although distinctly conservative in outlook, the New Federalists departed sharply from certain crucial positions taken by earlier conservative critics of federal centralization. The New Federalists sought to decentralize not by transferring legal or fiscal powers to subnational governments, but by transferring funds. They acknowledged the massive taxing and borrowing powers of the federal government and proposed to use these superior "extractive" powers to carry out their program of federal renewal. Above all, in contrast with the fiscal conservatism of the older decentralizers, they recognized the need for substantial government spending and sought not so much to reduce spending as to decentralize the decisions that directed it. Indeed, they were prepared to reward a taste for public goods on the part of state and local governments, as Nixon emphasized when he pointed out that the formula of his 1969 revenue sharing bill would "provide the States with some incentive to maintain (and even expand) their efforts to use their own tax resources to meet their needs."

The accomplishments of the New Federalism were substantial. General revenue sharing was instituted in 1972 and renewed in 1976. It was more difficult to enact special revenue sharing legislation, but the manpower and urban development proposals, after considerable modification, were approved by Congress in the form of two block grant programs: the Community Development Act of 1973 and the Comprehensive Employment and Training Act of 1974. While nearly all Federal aid before 1972 had been in the form of categorical programs, by 1975 other less conditional aid amounted to $12 billion, one-quarter of the growing total (see Table 1). As for the actual political outcome of this financial output, advocates of decentralization could hope that recipient governments would use the new money to produce public goods reflecting the distinctive preferences of the respective state and local communities. From his careful monitoring studies of general revenue sharing, which sought, among other things, to measure how far the shared revenue was used for innovation rather than substitution, Richard Nathan concluded affirmatively that, "persons with a pro-spending orientation may be encouraged by the significant amounts of new spending uses."

During the 1970s, even in those years when Republican presidents were in office, developments radically contrary to the spirit of the New Federalism took place. The increase in categorical programs slacked off from its dizzy pace at the height of the Great Society legislation when, between 1962 and 1967, the number had risen from 160 to 379. But the total continued to mount steadily, reaching 442 in 1975 and 492 in 1978. Moreover, existing aid programs increasingly were made the basis for new measures of regulation, so that when a state or local government received a federal grant, it also became responsible not only for fulfilling the directly enacted purpose of the grant, but also for assuring that the funds were administered according to certain specified national policy requirements. A few of these requirements dated back to the 1930s, but most of them had been added in the 1960s and 1970s and concerned such questions as nondiscrimination on the grounds of race, sex, and handicaps; environmental protection; labor and procurement standards; citizen participation; and freedom of information and privacy. By 1977 there were thirty-one such requirements.

Even more significant for the future of federalism than this continuing tendency toward categorical control was the growth in direct relations between the federal and local governments, as grant programs increasingly bypassed state governments. Traditionally, federal aid has been given exclusively to state governments, except on such occasions as the emergency grants to cities and local governments during the Great Depression. Even as late as 1965, grants directly to local governments included only 10 percent of total federal aid. By 1978 the figure had risen to 30 percent. This percentage included the two-thirds of the general revenue-sharing

Table 2 Relative Extractive Power: Government Expenditure on Domestic Programs from Own Source Revenues, as Percent of GNP

Year	Federal Government (domestic only)	State Governments	Local Governments
1929	1.5	2.0	5.3
1939	8.1	4.1	5.3
1949	7.5	3.4	3.5
1959	7.7	3.8	4.4
1964	8.5	4.3	4.8
1969	9.9	5.3	5.1
1975	15.8	6.3	5.3
1979 est.	15.0	6.2	4.8

SOURCE: Advisory Commission on Intergovernmental Relations, *Significant Features of Fiscal Federalism*. 1978–1979 edition. M-115. Washington, D.C.: U.S. Government Printing Office, 1979, Table 1.

money that went directly to local governments, all the block grants for community development, and most of the block grants for the Comprehensive Employment and Training Act (CETA).

The growing dependence on federal money on the part of big cities is particularly striking. A study of the 15 largest cities showed that the average percent of revenue supplied by federal aid rose from 1 percent in 1957 to 5 percent in 1967, and then shot up to 46 percent by 1978. And this is only an average, masking a much higher degree of dependence for some communities, such as Cleveland, for which the figure was 70 percent. Overall, the dependence of both state and local governments on Washington steadily increased, with the percent of state and local revenues derived from federal aid doubling from about 12 percent in 1960 to 26 percent in 1978.

Looking back on the New Federalist reaction against the centralism of the 1960s, one must admit that at the beginning of the 1980s federal dominance, if measured by the relative autonomy of state and local governments, is more pronounced than ever. No single index can measure the complex and interactive balance of power in the federal system, but Table 2 is suggestive of it. The table shows the trend in spending on domestic programs from own source revenues over the past fifty years; that is, what each level has been able to do with its own "extractive" power. The most striking contrast is between the federal government and all local governments. With some ups and downs, the latter have continued to spend from their own resources about the same percent of the national product, while the federal ratio has increased by a factor of ten. (The steadiness of local spending must seem curious in view of the growing outcry against local property taxation.) State governments have by no means lagged as taxers and spenders. They have inched up to equality with local governments and

Table 3 Government Expenditures After Intergovernmental Transfers, as Percent of GNP

| Year | Federal Government | | | State Governments | Local Governments |
	Total	Defense	Domestic		
1929	2.4	1.1	1.4	1.6	5.9
1939	8.7	1.7	7.0	3.3	7.3
1949	15.2	8.5	6.7	3.0	4.8
1959	17.3	11.0	6.3	3.6	6.0
1964	17.0	10.0	6.9	4.0	6.8
1969	18.0	10.2	7.8	4.7	7.8
1975	19.8	7.5	12.3	5.9	9.2
1979 est.	18.3	6.7	11.6	5.9	8.4

SOURCE: Advisory Commission on Intergovernmental Relations, *Significant Features of Fiscal Federalism.* 1978–1979 edition. M-115. Washington, D.C.: U.S. Government Printing Office, 1979, Table 2.

then forged ahead, the rise from 1959 to 1969 being even sharper than the federal increase. Federal self-financed spending, however, towers over the other totals and would, of course, be even more disproportionate if defense spendings were included. Intergovernmental transfers change the spending ratios, but given the pervasive controls on federal aid, do not greatly modify the impression of federal dominance (see Table 3).

THE POLITICS OF THE NEW FEDERALISM

If the New Federalist thrust toward autonomy was only a limited success, the reasons are primarily political. These reasons must be understood if any future effort to strengthen the states or to reform the federal structure is to succeed.

In the first place, the minority status of the Republican party meant that the New Federalism, primarily a Republican initiative, would have to find Democratic allies if it was to build a successful coalition. And within the GOP the strength of the old fiscal conservatism made this dependence upon Democratic support even greater. To be sure, pressure from state and local governments could bring over some Democrats, as the big-city mayors did in helping ensure the enactment of general revenue sharing. But the bulk of the Democrats, especially those who, coming from outside the South, were ready to support social spending, remained attached to the centralizing approach of the Great Society. This was not simply a matter of outlook or ideology. As chairmen and majority members of the committees that authorized and supervised the categorical programs, Democrats were in a good position to attract electoral support from the beneficiaries of these programs and their spokespersons. Indeed, one should not put great emphasis on the partisan aspect of the problem. With the decline of both parties that set in strongly during the 1960s, the new sources of electoral support arising from the categorical system tended to take the place of the older ties of partisanship between congressmen and voters. In spite of the New Federalist presidency in the years of Nixon and Ford, therefore, the technocratic thrust continued to exert great influence on the development of federal domestic policy. With such dubious political backing the New Federalism could only marginally modify, not radically redirect, the new centralism.

Despite the increase in influence of the professional bureaucratic complex relative to the political parties, the technocrats were unable to perform what is, perhaps, the primary task of a political party and its leaders. They could not present a coherent view of government action that reflected an overall view of national needs. The fragmentation of the professionals among their many functional fields renders them unfit for this task. However cooperative they may be with their fellows in the same discipline and program, their dispersion among the many vertical hierarchies of contemporary functional federalism gives them little opportunity or occasion for concerted action toward common national programs. The pluralism of the professional bureaucratic complex is one main ground for the present disorientation of public policy.

THE REACTION TOWARD REPRESENTATION

The new centralism also bred another reaction — a reaction that may prove to be more significant for the actual distribution of power in the federal system than the attempt to revive dual federalism. From the latter part of the 1960s, state and local governments, increasingly the vehicles of federal programs, made their presence felt in Washington as an influence on the design and execution of these programs. In addition to trying to fight the system, they also sought to join it. In response to the rise of the professional bureaucratic complex, there has arisen the intergovernmental lobby. This consists of the officials, usually elected, who are charged with the general responsibilities in state and local governments — the governors, mayors, county supervisors, city managers, and state legislators. These officials act through their various organizations: the National Governors Association, the Council of State Governments, the United States Conference of Mayors, the National League of Cities, the National Association of Counties, the International City Management Association, and the National Legislative Conference. A no less important front involves the continual, almost day-to-day activity of individual officeholders and their agents, offering advice and pressing requests before the legislative and executive branches of the federal government.

So important is this new class of political actors in this country — and in other Western democracies — that I would like to offer a common term to identify them: "topocrat" (from the Greek, *topos,* meaning "place" or "locality," and *kratos,* meaning "authority"). The rise of the topocratic influence in relation to federal policy-making and administration is something more than mere lobbying. It adds a whole new dimension of representation to our political system, and the interplay between topocratic and technocratic influences is one of the more important, growing forums of decision making today — which deserves much more study than it has received so far.

The states have played a leading part in raising topocratic organizations to their new level of influence in Washington. It was a governor — Pat Brown of California — who, in 1964, first urged that the state chief executives be given "a more direct voice in policy-making at the federal level." Remarking that governors have more knowledge of the diverse conditions in their states than either bureaucrats or congressmen can have, he regretted that they were not brought into the process that produced the programs they later had the responsibility for carrying out. His proposal was that a small council of governors, elected by the then National Governors' Conference, would act as consultants to the federal government with regard to federal-state programs. Ten years later, greater influence on federal action became the prime objective of the reorganized National Governors' Association. The governors resolved no longer merely to react to federal initiatives, but to take the initiative themselves by assembling the necessary staff, research facilities, and organizational apparatus. In recent years the governors have brought their organized influence to bear on specific legislation, such as revenue sharing, welfare reform, Medicaid, and economic development programs. Perhaps the most interesting of all for federalism was the effort launched in 1978 to exchange, so to speak, money for power, by offering to lobby Congress in support of President Carter's restricted budget for federal aid on the understanding that his Administration would sharply reduce the strings attached to that aid. At the present writing, as the budget for 1981 makes its way through Congress, this effort is still very much alive. The outcome could make a difference to the future balance of power in the federal system.

As the story of the New Federalism demonstrates, the governors confront a very tough political problem if they are to make their influence felt more effectively in Washington. The centralizing tendencies are deeply rooted in the formative forces of modern society and are sustained by powerful sources of electoral support. These barriers confront the whole array of topocratic aspirants to greater influence and autonomy — states, cities, and counties alike. The governors also face the further problem of maintaining their influence within the intergovernmental lobby itself. They have been resourceful and successful in helping to mobilize the "New Coalition" of topocrats to bring pressure to bear on the federal executive and legislature. But that coalition is and always has been a tenuous and limited alliance, threatened by conflicts of interest, among which the growth of direct federalism — the bypassing of the states in favor of the cities — has produced the most acute differences. In short, if the governors are to strengthen themselves and the states in the new relationships of representative federalism, they must develop their political base. As former Governor Dukakis recently remarked, "the next phase in rebuilding the NGA is to develop its capacity as a lobbying force in its own right so it can bring strong influence to bear upon the Administration and on Congress." This complex and difficult problem has three dimensions.

The first is the party political role of the governor. If the governor, as the spokesman for his state, is to be listened to by Congress or the Administration, it will help if he is believed to have political resources with which he can reward friends and punish enemies. As former Governor Askew observed, "You see Congressmen being attentive to Governors when the Governors have a political base that bears attention." At one time, the position of leader of his party in his state gave a governor access to such resources. The decline of party affiliations among voters, activists, and politicians, however, has greatly diminished this source of gubernatorial influence. We need more case studies if we are to be more precise as to the actual influence of governors, and how it might be strengthened. The political relations of governors, mayors, and other topocrats with members of the federal legislature and executive are among the great unexplored mysteries that beckon the aspiring political scientist.

The role of governors in presidential politics, however, is a rough index of their standing. From 1876, when both parties nominated governors, presidential candidates typically were drawn from the ranks of the state chief executives. Governors remained great powers in both parties into the 1950s. Consider, for instance, the role of Republican governors in securing the nomination for Eisenhower against Taft in 1952, or the influence of Democratic governors at the conventions of 1952 and 1956. The decline of the convention, to which the spread of the presidential primary has greatly contributed, has deprived the governor of his traditional role in the "smoke-filled room." Governors were few at the Democratic convention of 1972, and their numbers were insignificant in 1976. Recent changes in the democratic rules have sought to increase their numbers and possibly enhance their power. Further steps may be in order. But the general decline of party, it cannot be doubted, has reduced the ability of state chief executives to mobilize party political power to put pressure on Congress or the Administration on behalf of their states.

Pressure, however, is too narrow a word to characterize all the main channels of influence. Information, the second dimension in gubernatorial influence, is also a major source of power in policy-making. The present is the age of the professional in government service precisely because the problems of public policy are so complex that participants can rarely perceive what is in their interest or in the public interest without the aid of research. The National Governors' Association recognized this new necessity when it created the Center for Policy Research. One of its recent studies illustrates the potential of the Center in influencing political decisions. A critique of federal aid for cities that bypasses state government, this study claims to show, on the basis of careful, quantitative policy analysis, that federal money is more likely to reach the needy and distressed communities if it goes through state governments than if it goes directly from a federal agency to the cities. This assessment of the facts is totally at variance with the opinion that is commonly held among mayors and their experts and that supports their preference for direct federalism. Imagine the impact on the politics of the New Coalition if this new assessment by the NGA research arm comes to be accepted by the mayors of such cities as Detroit, Cleveland, or Baltimore.

But there is another kind of information that potentially has great influence also. Its character was suggested by Governor Pat Brown when he spoke of the understanding of the diverse and special conditions in their states that governors can bring to bear on policy-making by the federal government. It embraces a sense of local values, a knowledge of local people, and a feeling for the unique characteristics of a specific community in a certain place and time. Information of this kind does not lend itself to scientific inquiry. It is, rather, the know-how of the practitioner who has learned from doing — and getting elected. It is, of course, not limited to chief executives but also forms the contribution of the responsive legislator. Such is its value that it makes the topocrat, whether executive or legislative, an indispensable channel of information for effective government at any level, as congressmen and federal officials increasingly recognize.

The political problem of strengthening the states has a crucial third dimension. This is their performance as agencies of not only responsive but also coherent government. The task of imposing a coordinated outlook and a scale of priorities upon the far-flung activities of a typical state government today is primarily the responsibility of its chief executive. The question is: Can he get his act together? Whether or not governors will be listened to in Washington as spokesmen for their states depends in no small part on the answer to that question.

Measured by their willingness to tax and spend, the responsiveness of the states to the presumed demands of their citizens cannot be questioned. As Table 2 shows, the rise in self-financed spending by the states goes back to the New Deal era and parallels the federal effort. Indeed, as we have seen, for some periods the state increase has been at a higher rate than the federal. The huge growth of the public sector dating from the 1930s has been a cooperative project of all levels of government. If growing use of extractive power is a sign of health, then the states are hale and hearty. Small may be beautiful; it certainly can be expensive.

At $145 billion, state self-financed expenditure is a significant slice even of a two-trillion-dollar economy. During its recent decades of growth, we have normally thought of this complex of activity and money as an aspect of the demand side of the economy. Major government functions regarding the supply side, specifically economic stabilization and economic growth, seemed to belong to the federal level. The states functioned mainly as agents for delivering — directly through state agencies or indirectly through their local governments — goods and services for public consumption. Their concern with the demand side of economic life meant that the states were largely occupied with social rather than economic policy.

As Norton Long has pointed out, recent experience has shaken the theoretical foundations of centralized management of the supply side of the economy and suggested the need for a regional, "bottoms up" approach. At the same time, the prospect of basic scarcities, of which energy is only the most acute, confronts the nation with the need to husband its productive capacities as well as share its product. The great increase in the defense effort, on which the federal government has recently embarked, heightens these pressures, promising a new "battle of production" reminiscent of wartime efforts. It appears, in short, that the country may be entering a new phase of mercantilism in public policy in which the main stress will be on developing the supply side of the economy. If so, the states may find themselves called upon to fill a new role, emphasizing their economic rather than social policy. In their legal powers and their taxing-spending leverage, the potential is there.

If the states are to realize this potential as "political economies" in a new mercantilism, they must, as Norton Long has emphasized, show a capacity for economic management. "The states," he writes, "as territorial polities could serve both to coordinate their own unifunctional agencies and those of the federal government in the service of their own people." Specifically, he asks that the states provide "horizontal coordination" by "action to positively and favorably affect the performance of the state's economy."

When the talk turns to coordination and management and comprehensive planning, the practical man may well think that, once again, the academic mind is losing contact with reality. Hard experience echoes from Arthur Bauer's sober conclusion that "as a practical matter, it is difficult for legislatures to develop grand designs." His specific concern is with urban strategies and urban initiatives and the severe limits set on such aspirations by the realities of state politics. But the general sense of his comment must also qualify the hope for coherent policy management or resource management in broad fields of state activity, such as economic development, in a new phase of mercantilism. A great deal of research has been devoted to the problem of management in state government. The amounts spent on "financial administration" and "general control" have steadily risen year by year. Constitutional reform and government modernization have made much progress. But when one examines the outcomes of the major efforts to improve management performance, the record is disappointing. Shining exceptions can be named. On balance, however, little has been accomplished to cope with the organization of governments in metropolitan areas, to establish comprehensive controls over land use, to give teeth to plans for urban development, or to create effective systems of program budgeting.

The management problem is recognized by both federal and state governments, although their spokespersons look at it rather differently. During the period of the New Federalism, an OMB report, after observing that "some states and localities have made significant progress in upgrading their management capacity," set forth its view of the source of the difficulties as follows:

> Most, however, have an extremely limited ability to plan and direct on a long-term basis for the total needs of their particular jurisdiction. The usual management style is the functional approach — presiding over a fractionalized set of programs with little attention to the whole. The jurisdictional approach — which requires integration of needs analysis, goal setting, long-term planning and evaluation with daily operation — is usually beyond their existing management capacity.

A subsequent study authorized by the governors replied:

> Increasingly . . . the nation's Governors recognize the need for a comprehensive approach to carrying out the public's business. In State after State, the chief executive is attempting to build mechanisms to initiate comprehensive policy development. . . .
>
> Unfortunately, almost as quickly as the attempt is begun, the governor and his staff run headlong into the problems which underlie the rhetoric of the "new federalism." Chief among these is the tendency of the grant-in-aid network to compound issue fragmentation and to impede, if not actually prevent, a comprehensive approach to policy formulation. The federal grant-in-aid system promotes pulverization or fragmentation of scope in many ways.

These familiar themes of the intergovernmental dialogue arise from problems that specific reforms of federal legislation and administration can help resolve. President Carter has been unable to get congressional cooperation with his major proposal, which would have led to substantial consolidations of categorical grants. He has set up an interagency committee in the White House to coordinate urban and rural programs and to direct the OMB in an effort to simplify regulations and management procedures in the federal aid system.

The thrust of this paper is that the basic conditions which underlie incoherence and lack of direction in public policy at all levels of government will not yield merely to administrative or procedural reforms. They can neither be blamed on nor cured by the isolated action of one level of government alone. They are deeply political in nature. They arise as much from the confusion of our public philosophy as from the pluralism of our Welfare State. A new mercantilism, accepted at all levels of government, could give direction to our national life again and a future to the states as political economies. Needless to say, such a new role for the states would be the expression of a certain public philosophy. Conceivably, however, another outlook expressing different value preferences may come to dominate the climate of opinion and give the states a radically different role. It is these deep political tides that have shaped the federal system in the past and that will continue to do so in the future.

CHAPTER 3

Civil Liberties and Civil Rights

Civil liberties and civil rights cover a very broad area. Among the most fundamental civil liberties are those governing the extent to which individuals can speak, write, and read what they choose. The democratic process requires the free exchange of ideas. Constitutional government requires the protection of minority rights and, above all, the right to dissent.

Constitutional Background: The Debate over the Inclusion of a Bill of Rights in the Constitution

The Bill of Rights, which every American takes for granted, was not part of the original Constitution of 1787.[1] The Anglo-American legal tradition up to the time of the writing of the Constitution had emphasized the importance of independent rights and liberties of citizens that were to be protected by government. This was recognized in the Magna Carta in 1215, in the English Bill of Rights of 1689, and in numerous common law precedents. The colonists brought their rights as Englishmen to America, and through struggles with colonial governors they emphasized new rights of local self-government. The struggle with England as well brought out the need for such rights as protection against unreasonable search and seizure (British troops constantly were searching private premises for

---

[1] Moreover, the original Bill of Rights that was ratified by ten states in 1791, thus accomplishing the necessary three-fourths majority required for adoption, was not applied to the states until *Gitlow* v. *New York* in 1925, and then only the First Amendment was considered fundamental enough to make it applicable to state action under the due process clause of the Fourteenth Amendment. At the time of original adoption, Connecticut, Massachusetts, and Georgia failed to consider the Bill of Rights sufficiently important to ratify it. They "corrected" this mistake by belatedly "ratifying" the Bill of Rights upon the 150th anniversary celebration of its adoption in 1941,

smuggled goods), and the right to bear arms, which was seen as a protection against standing armies. The third amendment, prohibiting the quartering in any house of soldiers without the consent of the owner, was also the outgrowth of the struggle of the colonists with Great Britain.

The strong Anglo-American tradition of civil liberties and civil rights was not reflected in all of the state constitutions that were written during the revolutionary period. Only seven of the new state constitutions contained separate bills of rights, the remainder incorporating various rights in the main bodies of their constitutions.[2] The Virginia Bill of Rights was the most comprehensive of all of the state constitutions, containing in addition to the fundamental rights growing out of the English tradition, the new right of revolution which Jefferson was to proclaim in the Declaration of Independence.

Given the long tradition of civil liberties and civil rights in Anglo-American history, it is somewhat surprising that a separate bill of rights was not part of the original Constitution. The main body of the Constitution did contain provisions that protected civil rights and liberties, such as the prohibition upon suspension of the writ of habeas corpus, and upon the passage of ex post facto laws and bills of attainder. But whether or not the Constitution should go beyond stating these rights was not a matter of debate during the proceedings, and moreover, a motion that was made shortly before the close of the convention to draft a bill of rights did not receive a single state vote. This would suggest that the state delegations to the convention were not overly concerned about the need for a bill of rights, being preoccupied with the difficult task of forging a national constitution that would receive support in the states.

While the Constitutional Convention did not feel a separate bill of rights was appropriate, it soon became evident that there was opposition in the states to the ratification of a constitution without a separate bill of rights. Thomas Jefferson, who was in Paris at that time, reflected the view that a bill of rights was important in a letter to James Madison on December 20, 1787. After noting that he liked most of the provisions of the Constitution, he pointed out to Madison that:

> I will now tell you what I do not like. First, the omission of a bill of rights, providing clearly, and without the aid of sophism, for freedom of religion, freedom of the press, protection against standing armies, restriction of monopoly, the eternal and unremitting force of the habeas corpus laws, and trials by jury in all matters of fact triable by the laws of the land, and not by the laws of nations. To say, as Mr. Wilson [a delegate from Philadelphia to the Pennsylvania ratifying convention] does, that a bill of rights was not necessary, because all is reserved [to the states] in the case of the general government which is not given, while in the particular ones [the states] all is given which is not reserved, might do for the audience for which it was addressed; but it is surely a *gratis dictum*, the reverse of which might just as well be said; and it

---

[2] Connecticut and Rhode Island retained their colonial charters as their form of government into the nineteenth century.

is opposed by strong inferences from the body of the instrument [the national constitution], as well as from the omission of the cause of our present confederation, which had made the reservation in expressed terms. It was hard to conclude, because there has been a want of uniformity among the states as to the cases triable by jury, because some have been so incautious as to dispense with this mode of trial in certain cases, therefore, the more prudent states shall be reduced to the same level of calamity. It would have been much more just and wise to have concluded the other way, that as most of the states had preserved with jealousy this sacred palladium of liberty, those who had wandered, should be brought back to it; and to have established general right rather than general wrong. For I consider all the ill as established, which may be established. I have the right to nothing, which another has a right to take away; and Congress will have a right to take away trials by jury in all civil cases. Let me add, that a bill of rights is what the people are entitled to against every government on earth, general or particular; and what no just government should refuse, or rest on inference.

James Wilson, the Philadelphia delegate to the Pennsylvania ratifying convention, to whom Jefferson refers in the above quote, argued before his state ratifying convention that a bill of rights was not only unnecessary but dangerous, an argument that was to be repeated by Alexander Hamilton in *Federalist 84.* In debating before the Pennsylvania convention, Wilson noted that:

A bill of rights annexed to a constitution is an enumeration of the powers reserved. If we attempt an enumeration, everything that is not enumerated is presumed to be given. The consequence is, that an imperfect enumeration would throw all implied power into the scale [power] of the government, and the rights of the people would be rendered incomplete. On the other hand, an imperfect enumeration of the powers of government reserves all implied power to the people; and by that means the constitution becomes incomplete. But of the two, it is much safer to run the risk on the side of the constitution; for an omission in the enumeration of the powers of government is neither so dangerous or important as an omission in the enumeration of the rights of the people.

In the following selection from *The Federalist,* Alexander Hamilton is addressing the people of New York, and contrasting the New York constitution with the proposed national constitution of 1787. He argues that the inclusion of a separate bill of rights would be redundant, because the people retain all of the rights that are proposed to be added through a bill of rights. Hamilton even suggests that the addition of a bill of rights would be dangerous, because it would imply that the national government has authority to curb the very rights that are enumerated. In fact, however, Hamilton states that there is no power given to the central government to curb any of the rights in question. Continuing his argument against a separate bill of rights, Hamilton points out that the national constitution and many of the state constitutions are the same in their treatment of rights, listing them in the main body of the document, rather than in a separate bill of rights. The Constitution is in itself, in its entirety, a general bill of rights, says Hamilton. In contrasting the federal constitution with that of New York, he concludes that the former contains more safeguards than the latter. Therefore, the people of New York should not complain about the lack of protection of rights in the national constitution. When the state constitutions and the federal constitution are viewed together, Hamilton concludes that they collectively contain all of the protections of rights that can reasonably be desired.

12

Alexander Hamilton

FEDERALIST 84

In the course of the foregoing review of the Constitution, I have taken notice of, and endeavored to answer most of the objections which have appeared against it. There however remain a few which either did not fall naturally under any particular head or were forgotten in their proper places. These shall now be discussed; but as the subject has been drawn into great length, I shall so far consult brevity as to comprise all my observations on these miscellaneous points in a single paper.

The most considerable of these remaining objections is that the plan of the convention contains no bill of rights. Among other answers given to this, it has been upon different occasions remarked that the constitutions of several of the States are in a similar predicament. I add that New York is of this number. And yet the opposers of the new system, in this State [N.Y.], who profess an unlimited admiration for its constitution, are among the most intemperate partisans of a bill of rights. To justify their zeal in this matter they allege two things: one is that, though the constitution of New York has no bill of rights prefixed to it, yet it contains, in the body of it, various provisions in favor of particular privileges and rights which, in substance, amount to the same thing; the other is that the Constitution [of N.Y.] adopts, in their full extent, the common and statute law of Great Britain, by which many other rights not expressed in it are equally secured.

To the first I answer that the Constitution proposed by the convention contains, as well as the constitution of this State, a number of such provisions.

Independent of those which relate to the structure of the government, we find the following: Article 1, section 3, clause 7 — "Judgment in cases of impeachment shall not extend further than to removal from office and disqualification to hold and enjoy any office of honor, trust, or profit under the United States; but the party convicted shall, nevertheless, be liable and subject to indictment, trial, judgment, and punishment according to law."

Section 9, of the same article, clause 2 — "The privilege of the writ of *habeas corpus* shall not be suspended, unless when in cases of rebellion or invasion the public safety may require it." Clause 3 — "No bill of attainder or *ex post facto* law shall be passed." Clause 7 — "No title of nobility shall be granted by the United States; and no person holding any office of profit or trust under them shall, without the consent of the Congress, accept of any present, emolument, office, or title of any kind whatever, from any king, prince, or foreign state." Article 3, section 2, clause 3 — "The trial of all crimes, except in cases of impeachment, shall be by jury; and such trial shall be held in the State where the said crimes shall have been committed; but when not committed within any State, the trial shall be at such place or places as the Congress may by law have directed." Section 3, of the same article — "Treason against the United States shall consist only in levying war against them, or in adhering to their enemies, giving them aid and comfort. No person shall be convicted of treason, unless on the testimony of two witnesses to the same overt act, or on confession in open court." And clause 3, of the same section — "The Congress shall have power to declare the punishment of treason; but no attainder of treason shall work corruption of blood, or forfeiture, except during the life of the person attainted."

It may well be a question whether these are not, upon the whole, of equal importance with any which are to be found in the constitution of this State. The establishment of the writ of *habeas corpus,* the prohibition of *ex post facto* laws, and of TITLES OF NOBILITY, *to which we have no corresponding provision in our* [N.Y.] *Constitution,* are perhaps greater securities to liberty and republicanism than any it contains. The creation of crimes after the commission of the fact, or, in other words, the subjecting of men to punishment for things which, when they were done, were breaches of no law, and the practice of arbitrary imprisonments, have been, in all ages, the favorite and most formidable instruments of tyranny. The observations of the judicious Blackstone,[1] in reference to the latter, are well worthy of recital: "To bereave a man of life [says he] or by violence to confiscate his estate, without accusation or trial, would be so gross and notorious an act of despotism as must at once convey the alarm of tyranny throughout the whole nation; but confinement of the person, by secretly hurrying him to jail, where his sufferings are unknown or forgotten, is a less public, a less striking, and therefore a *more dangerous engine* of arbitrary government." And as a remedy for this fatal evil he is everywhere peculiarly emphatical in his encomiums on the *habeas corpus* act, which in one place he calls "the BULWARK of the British Constitution." [2]

---

[1] *Vide* Blackstone's *Commentaries,* Vol. 1, Page 136.
[2] Idem, Vol. 4, Page 438.

Nothing need be said to illustrate the importance of the prohibition of titles of nobility. This may truly be denominated the cornerstone of republican government; for so long as they are excluded there can never be serious danger that the government will be any other than that of the people.

To the second, that is, to the pretended establishment of the common and statute law by the Constitution [of N.Y.], I answer that they are expressly made subject "to such alterations and provisions as the legislature shall from time to time make concerning the same." They are therefore at any moment liable to repeal by the ordinary legislative power, and of course have no constitutional sanction. The only use of the declaration was to recognize the ancient law and to remove doubts which might have been occasioned by the Revolution. This consequently can be considered as no part of a declaration of rights, which under our constitutions must be intended as limitations of the power of the government itself.

It has been several times truly remarked that bills of rights are, in their origin, stipulations between kings and their subjects, abridgments of prerogative in favor of privilege, reservations of rights not surrendered to the prince. Such was MAGNA CHARTA, obtained by the barons, sword in hand, from King John. Such were the subsequent confirmations of that charter by subsequent princes. Such was the *Petition of Right* assented to by Charles the First in the beginning of his reign. Such, also, was the Declaration of Right presented by the Lords and Commons to the Prince of Orange in 1688, and afterwards thrown into the form of an act of Parliament called the Bill of Rights. It is evident, therefore, that, according to their primitive signification, they have no application to constitutions, professedly founded upon the power of the people and executed by their immediate representatives and servants. Here, in strictness, the people surrender nothing; and as they retain everything they have no need of particular reservations, "WE, THE PEOPLE of the United States, to secure the blessings of liberty to ourselves and our posterity, do *ordain* and *establish* this Constitution for the United States of America." Here is a better recognition of popular rights than volumes of those aphorisms which make the principal figure in several of our State bills of rights and which would sound much better in a treatise of ethics than in a constitution of government.

But a minute detail of particular rights is certainly far less applicable to a Constitution like that under consideration, which is merely intended to regulate the general political interests of the nation, than to a constitution which has the regulation of every species of personal and private concerns. If, therefore, the loud clamors against the plan of the convention, on this score, are well founded, no epithets of reprobation will be too strong for the constitution of this State. But the truth is that both of them contain all which, in relation to their objects, is reasonably to be desired.

I go further and affirm that bills of rights, in the sense and to the extent in which they are contended for, are not only unnecessary in the proposed Constitution but would even be dangerous. They would contain various exceptions to powers which are not granted; and, on this very account, would afford a colorable pretext to claim more than were granted. For why declare that things shall not be done which there is no power to do? Why, for instance, should it be said that the liberty of the press shall not be restrained, when no power is given by which restrictions may be imposed? I will not contend that such a provision would confer a regulating power; but it is evident that it would furnish, to men disposed to usurp, a plausible pretense for claiming that power. They might urge with a semblance of reason that the Constitution ought not to be charged with the absurdity of providing against the abuse of an authority which was not given, and that the provision against restraining the liberty of the press afforded a clear implication that a power to prescribe proper regulations concerning it was intended to be vested in the national government. This may serve as a specimen of the numerous handles which would be given to the doctrine of constructive powers, by the indulgence of an injudicious zeal for bills of rights.

On the subject of the liberty of the press, as much as has been said, I cannot forbear adding a remark or two: in the first place, I observe, that there is not a syllable concerning it in the constitution of this State; in the next, I contend that whatever has been said about it in that of any other State amounts to nothing. What signifies a declaration that "the liberty of the press shall be inviolably preserved"? What is the liberty of the press? Who can give it any definition which would not leave the utmost latitude for evasion? I hold it to be impracticable; and from this I infer that its security, whatever fine declarations may be inserted in any constitution respecting it, must altogether depend on public opinion, and on the general spirit of the people and of the government.[3] And here, after all, as is intimated upon another occasion, must we seek for the only solid basis of all our rights.

---

[3] To show that there is a power in the Constitution by which the liberty of the press may be affected, recourse has been had to the power of taxation. It is said that duties may be laid upon the publications so high as to amount to a prohibition. I know not by what logic it could be maintained that the declarations in the State constitutions, in favor of the freedom of the press, would be a constitutional impediment to the imposition of duties upon publications by the State legislatures. It cannot certainly be pretended that any degree of duties, however low, would be an abridgment of the liberty of the press. We know that newspapers are taxed in Great Britain, and yet it is notorious that the press nowhere enjoys greater liberty than in that country. And if duties of any kind may be laid without a violation of that liberty, it is evident that the extent must depend on legislative discretion, regulated by public opinion; so that, after all, general declarations respecting the liberty of the press will give it no greater security than it will have without them. The same invasions of it may be effected under the State constitutions which contain those declarations through the means of taxation, as under the proposed Constitution, which has nothing of the kind. It would be quite as significant to declare that government ought to be free, that taxes ought not to be excessive, etc., as that the liberty of the press ought not to be restrained.

There remains but one other view of this matter to conclude the point. The truth is, after all the declamations we have heard, that the Constitution is itself, in every rational sense, and to every useful purpose, A BILL OF RIGHTS. The several bills of rights in Great Britain form its Constitution, and conversely the constitution of each State is its bill of rights. And the proposed Constitution, if adopted, will be the bill of rights of the Union. Is it one object of a bill of rights to declare and specify the political privileges of the citizens in the structure and administration of the government? This is done in the most ample and precise manner in the plan of the convention; comprehending various precautions for the public security which are not to be found in any of the State constitutions. Is another object of a bill of rights to define certain immunities and modes of proceeding, which are relative to personal and private concerns? This we have seen has also been attended to in a variety of cases in the same plan. Adverting therefore to the substantial meaning of a bill of rights, it is absurd to allege that it is not to be found in the work of the convention. It may be said that it does not go far enough though it will not be easy to make this appear; but it can with no propriety be contended that there is no such thing. It certainly must be immaterial what mode is observed as to the order of declaring the rights of the citizens if they are to be found in any part of the instrument which establishes the government. And hence it must be apparent that much of what has been said on this subject rests merely on verbal and nominal distinctions, entirely foreign from the substance of the thing. . . .

The Nationalization of the Bill of Rights

It is clear from the debate over the inclusion of the Bill of Rights in the Constitution of 1787 that its provisions were certainly never intended to be prohibitions upon state action. The Bill of Rights was added to the Constitution to satisfy state governments that the same rights which they generally accorded to their own citizens under state constitutions would apply with respect to the national government, and act as a check upon abridgments by the national government of civil liberties and civil rights. Proponents of a separate bill of rights wanted specific provisions to limit the powers of the national government which, *in its own sphere,* could act directly upon citizens of the state.

Article Ten, which is not so much a part of the Bill of Rights as an expression of the balance of authority that exists between the national government and the states in the Constitution, provides that "the powers not delegated to the United States by the Constitution, nor prohibited by it to the states are reserved to the states respectively, or to the people." Under the federal system each member of the community is both (1) a citizen of the United States and (2) a citizen of the particular state in which he resides. The rights and obligations of each citizenship class are determined by the legal divisions of authority set up in the Constitution. Apart from specific limits upon state power to abridge civil liberties and civil rights, as for example the prohibitions of section ten against state passage of any bills of attainder or ex post facto laws, there is nothing in the main body of the Constitution or the Bill of Rights that controls state action. Originally it was up to the states to determine the protections they would give to their own citizens against state actions. The applicability of the Bill of Rights to national action only was affirmed in *Barron* v. *Baltimore,* 7 Peters 243 (1833).

The adoption of the Fourteenth Amendment in 1868 potentially limited the discretion that the states had possessed to determine the civil liberties and rights of citizens within their sphere of authority. The Fourteenth Amendment provided that:

> 1.   All persons born or naturalized in the United States, and subject to the jurisdiction thereof, are citizens of the United States and of the state wherein they reside. No state shall make or enforce any law which shall abridge the privileges or immunities of citizens of the United States; nor shall any state deprive any person of life, liberty, or property, without due process of law; nor deny to any person within its jurisdiction the equal protection of the laws. . . .
>
> 5.   The Congress shall have power to enforce, by appropriate legislation, the provisions of this article.

Although the Fourteenth Amendment appeared to be a tough restriction upon state action, its provisions were equivocal and required clarification by the Supreme Court before they could take effect. The history of the Fourteenth Amendment suggested that it was designed to protect the legal and political rights of Blacks against state encroachment, and was not to have a broader application. In the *Slaughterhouse Cases,* 16 Wallace 36 (1873), the Supreme Court held that the privileges and immunities clause of the Fourteenth Amendment did nothing to alter the authority of the states to determine the rights and obligations of citizens subject to state action. Under this doctrine the Bill of Rights could not be made applicable to the states.

It was not until *Gitlow* v. *New York,* 268 U.S. 652 (1925), that the Court finally announced that the substantive areas of freedom of speech and of press of the First Amendment are part of the "liberty" protected by the Fourteenth Amendment due process clause; however, in Gitlow's case the Court found that the procedures that had been used in New York to restrict his freedom of speech did not violate due process. In *Near* v. *Minnesota,* 283 U.S. 697 (1931), the Court for the first time overturned a state statute as a violation of the Fourteenth Amendment due process clause because it permitted prior censorship of the press. *Gitlow* and *Near* were limited because they incorporated only the freedom of speech and press provisions of the First Amendment under the due process clause of the Fourteenth Amendment. The cases marked the beginning of a slow and tedious process of "incorporation" of most of the provisions of the Bill of Rights as part of the due process clause of the Fourteenth Amendment.

The process of incorporation did not begin in earnest until the Warren Court, and then not until the 1960s. By the late 1970s all of the Bill of Rights were incorporated as protections against state action with the exceptions of the rights to grand jury indictment, trial by jury in *civil* cases, the right to bear arms, protection against excessive bail and fines, and against involuntary quartering of troops in private homes.[1]

The following case presents an example of incorporation of the right to counsel under the due process clause of the Fourteenth Amendment. In cases prior to *Gideon* v. *Wainwright,* decided in 1963, the Court had upheld an ad hoc right to counsel in individual cases. That is, it had held that the facts of a particular case warranted granting the right to counsel as part of due process under the Fourteenth Amendment for that particular case only. By such ad hoc determinations, the Court was able to exercise self-restraint in relation to federal-state relations, by not requiring a general right to counsel in all state criminal cases. *Powell* v. *Alabama,* 287 U.S. 45 (1932), was an example of such an ad hoc inclusion of the right to counsel in a specific case, where, in a one-day trial, seven Blacks had been convicted of raping two white girls, and sentenced to death. The Court held that under the circumstances of the case the denial of counsel by the Alabama courts to the defendants violated the due process clause of the Fourteenth Amendment. In *Powell,* however, the Court did not incorporate the right to counsel in all criminal cases under this due process clause. It only provided that "in a capital case, where the defendant is unable to employ counsel, and is incapable adequately of making his own defense because of ignorance, feeblemindedness, illiteracy, or the like, it is the duty of the court, whether requested or not, to assign counsel for him as a necessary requisite of due process of law. . . ." The *Powell* case was widely interpreted as nationalizing (incorporating) the right to counsel in all *capital* cases. The Court reaffirmed its refusal to incorporate the right to counsel in all criminal cases in *Betts* v. *Brady,* 316 U.S. 455 (1942). There the Court held that the Sixth Amendment applies only to trials in federal courts and that the right to counsel is not a fundamental right, essential to a fair trial, and therefore is not required in all cases under the due process clause of the Fourteenth Amendment. The Court emphasized that whether or not the right to counsel would be required depended upon the circumstances of the case in which it was requested.

In *Gideon* v. *Wainwright* the Court finally nationalized the right to counsel in all criminal cases under the due process clause of the Fourteenth Amendment. The case represented, in 1963, an important step in the progression toward nationalization of most of the Bill of Rights. While Justice Roberts, writing for the majority of the Court in the *Betts* case in 1942, found that the right to counsel was not fundamental to a fair trial, Justice Black, who had dissented in the *Betts* case, writing for the majority

---

[1] For an excellent discussion of the incorporation of most of the Bill of Rights under the due process clause of the Fourteenth Amendment, see Henry J. Abraham, *Freedom and the Court* (3rd edition, New York: Oxford University Press, 1977), Chapter 3.

in *Gideon* v. *Wainwright* in 1962, held that the right to counsel was fundamental and essential to a fair trial and therefore was protected by the due
process clause of the Fourteenth Amendment. In *Gideon,* Justice Black
noted:

> We accept that the *Brady* assumption, based as it was on our prior cases,
> that a provision of the Bill of Rights which is "fundamental and essential to
> a fair trial" is made obligatory upon the states by the Fourteenth Amendment.
> We think the Court in *Betts* was wrong, however, in concluding that the Sixth
> Amendment's guarantee of counsel is not one of the fundamental rights.

The history of Supreme Court interpretation of the Fourteenth Amendment due process clause reveals the Court acting both politically and
ideologically. In the period from 1868 to 1925 the Court was careful to
exercise judicial self-restraint in interpreting the Fourteenth Amendment,
in part because of the conservative views of most of the justices that the
Court should not impose national standards of civil liberties and civil
rights upon the states. The Court did not believe in self-restraint in all
areas, as is demonstrated by its use of the due process clause of the
Fourteenth Amendment to impose its own views on the proper relationship
between the states and business. The Court read the Fourteenth Amendment due process clause in such a way as to protect the property interests
of business against state regulation. Many such laws were found to be
taking the liberty or property of business without due process. Beginning
with *Gitlow* v. *New York* in 1925, the Court for the first time added substance to the due process clause of the Fourteenth Amendment in the
area of civil liberties by including First Amendment freedoms of speech
and press as part of the "liberty" of the due process clause.

While the Supreme Court is sensitive to the political environment in
which it functions, the ways in which it has interpreted the due process
clause of the Fourteenth Amendment suggests that ideological convictions
are more important than pressure from political majorities. During the era
of economic substantive due process under the Fourteenth Amendment,
which ended in 1937, the Court was really taking an elitist position that did
not agree with the political majorities in many states that were behind the
regulatory laws that the Court struck down. Nor can it be said that when
the Court began to add substance in civil liberties and civil rights to the
due process clause and extend procedural protections that it was supported by political majorities. In fact, the Warren Court's extension of the
Fourteenth Amendment due process clause, particularly in the area of
criminal rights, caused a political outcry among the states and their citizens who felt that law enforcement efforts would be unduly impeded. When
the Court, in *Griswold* v. *Connecticut* in 1965, went beyond the explicit
provisions of the Bill of Rights to find a right of privacy to strike down
Connecticut's birth control statute that prevented the use of contracep-
tives in the state, even Justice Black, a strong supporter of incorporating
the Bill of Rights under the due process clause, took objection. He found
in the *Griswold* decision a return to substantive due process in a form that
was unacceptable, because it was adding substance to the clause that
was not explicitly provided for in the intent of the Fourteenth Amendment,

which he had held in *Adamson* v. *California* in 1946 to be total inclusion of the Bill of Rights. The *Griswold* decision was not unpopular politically, but when the Court in *Roe* v. *Wade* in 1973 used the right of privacy to strike down a Texas abortion statute, and in effect declare all state laws that absolutely prohibited abortion to be unconstitutional, a nationwide anti-abortion movement was organized to overturn the decision by mobilizing political support behind a constitutional amendment. The Supreme Court has certainly not, in the area of interpretation of the Fourteenth Amendment, acted solely out of political motives.[2]

The following case presents an example of the way in which the Supreme Court gradually incorporated the Bill of Rights under the Fourteenth Amendment. Behind the decision to nationalize the right to counsel in *Gideon* v. *Wainwright* a fascinating series of events had occurred.[3] By the time the *Gideon* case was called up the Court was purposely looking for an appropriate case from which it could incorporate the right to counsel under the due process clause of the Fourteenth Amendment. The Court felt that Gideon's case presented the kind of circumstances that would be publicly accepted as requiring the right to counsel to ensure fairness. In granting certiorari to Gideon's *in forma pauperis* ("in the manner of the pauper," a permission to sue without incurring liability for costs) the Court had in effect already made up its mind what decision would result. By the appointment of Attorney Abe Fortas, later to become a member of the Court (although eventually forced to resign because of conflict of interest charges), one of the most distinguished lawyers in the country, the Court guaranteed an eloquent and persuasive brief for the petitioner, Earl Gideon. The Court felt that the right to counsel was a right whose time had come by 1963.

---

[2] The forces affecting Supreme Court decision making are discussed in the selections by William J. Brennan, Jr., John P. Roche, and Earl Warren, in Chapter 9.

[3] The story of the case is brilliantly told by Anthony Lewis, in *Gideon's Trumpet* (New York: Random House, 1964).

13

GIDEON v. WAINWRIGHT
372 U.S. 335 (1963)

... Mr. Justice BLACK delivered the opinion of the Court, saying in part:

Petitioner was charged in a Florida state court with having broken and entered a poolroom with intent to commit a misdemeanor. This offense is a felony under Florida law. Appearing in court without funds and without a lawyer, petitioner asked the court to appoint counsel for him, whereupon the following colloquy took place:

> The COURT: Mr. Gideon, I am sorry, but I cannot appoint Counsel to represent you in this case. Under the laws of the State of Florida, the only time the Court can appoint Counsel to represent a Defendant is when that person is charged with a capital offense. I am sorry, but I will have to deny your request to appoint Counsel to defend you in this case.

> The DEFENDANT: The United States Supreme Court says I am entitled to be represented by Counsel.

Put to trial before a jury, Gideon conducted his defense about as well as could be expected from a layman. He made an opening statement to the jury, cross-examined the State's witnesses, presented witnesses in his own defense, declined to testify himself, and made a short argument "emphasizing his innocence to the charge contained in the Information filed in this case." The jury returned a verdict of guilty, and petitioner was sentenced to serve five years in the state prison. Later, petitioner filed in the Florida Supreme Court this habeas corpus petition attacking his conviction and sentence on the ground that the trial court's refusal to appoint counsel for him denied him rights "guaranteed by the Constitution and the Bill of Rights by the United States Government." [1] Treating the petition for habeas corpus as properly before it, the State Supreme Court, "upon consideration thereof" but without an opinion, denied all relief. Since 1942, when *Betts v. Brady,* 316 U.S. 455 ... was decided by a divided Court, the problem of a defendant's federal constitutional right to counsel in a state court has been a continuing source of controversy and litigation in both state and

---

In this selection some footnotes are omitted; all are renumbered.

[1] Later in the petition for habeas corpus, signed and apparently prepared by the petitioner himself, he stated, "I, Clarence Earl Gideon, claim that I was denied the rights of the 4th, 5th and 14th amendments of the Bill of Rights."

federal courts. To give this problem another review here, we granted certiorari. 370 U.S. 908. . . . Since Gideon was proceeding *in forma pauperis,* we appointed counsel to represent him and requested both sides to discuss in their briefs and oral arguments the following: "Should this Court's holding in *Betts* v. *Brady* . . . be reconsidered?"

I.

The facts upon which Betts claimed that he had been unconstitutionally denied the right to have counsel appointed to assist him are strikingly like the facts upon which Gideon here bases his federal constitutional claim. Betts was indicted for robbery in a Maryland state court. On arraignment, he told the trial judge of his lack of funds to hire a lawyer and asked the court to appoint one for him. Betts was advised that it was not the practice in that county to appoint counsel for indigent defendants except in murder and rape cases. He then pleaded not guilty, had witnesses summoned, cross-examined the State's witnesses, examined his own, and chose not to testify himself. He was found guilty by the judge, sitting without a jury, and sentenced to eight years in prison. Like Gideon, Betts sought release by habeas corpus, alleging that he had been denied the right to assistance of counsel in violation of the Fourteenth Amendment. Betts was denied any relief, and on review this Court affirmed. It was held that a refusal to appoint counsel for an indigent defendant charged with a felony did not necessarily violate the Due Process Clause of the Fourteenth Amendment, which for reasons given the Court deemed to be the only applicable federal constitutional provision. The Court said:

> Asserted denial [of due process] is to be tested by an appraisal of the totality of facts in a given case. That which may, in one setting, constitute a denial of fundamental fairness, shocking to the universal sense of justice, may, in other circumstances, and in the light of other considerations, fall short of such denial. 316 U.S., at 462. . . .

Treating due process as "a concept less rigid and more fluid than those envisaged in other specific and particular provisions of the Bill of Rights," the Court held that refusal to appoint counsel under the particular facts and circumstances in the Betts case was not so "offensive to the common and fundamental ideas of fairness" as to amount to a denial of due process. Since the facts and circumstances of the two cases are so nearly indistinguishable, we think the *Betts* v. *Brady* holding if left standing would require us to reject Gideon's claim that the Constitution guarantees him the assistance of counsel. Upon full reconsideration we conclude that *Betts* v. *Brady* should be overruled.

II.

The Sixth Amendment provides, "In all criminal prosecutions, the accused shall enjoy the right . . . to have the Assistance of Counsel for his defence."

We have construed this to mean that in federal courts counsel must be provided for defendants unable to employ counsel unless the right is competently and intelligently waived. Betts argued that this right is extended to indigent defendants in state courts by the Fourteenth Amendment. In response the Court stated that, while the Sixth Amendment laid down "no rule for the conduct of the states, the question recurs whether the constraint laid by the amendment upon the national courts expresses a rule so fundamental and essential to a fair trial, and so, to due process of law, that it is made obligatory upon the states by the Fourteenth Amendment." 316 U.S., at 465. . . . In order to decide whether the Sixth Amendment's guarantee of counsel is of this fundamental nature, the Court in Betts set out and considered "[r]elevant data on the subject . . . afforded by constitutional and statutory provisions subsisting in the colonies and the states prior to the inclusion of the Bill of Rights in the national Constitution, and in the constitutional, legislative, and judicial history of the states to the present date." 316 U.S., at 465. . . . On the basis of this historical data the Court concluded that "appointment of counsel is not a fundamental right, essential to a fair trial." 316 U.S. at 471. . . . It was for this reason the Betts Court refused to accept the contention that the Sixth Amendment's guarantee of counsel for indigent federal defendants was extended to or, in the words of that Court, "made obligatory upon the states by the Fourteenth Amendment." Plainly, had the Court concluded that appointment of counsel for an indigent criminal defendant was "a fundamental right, essential to a fair trial," it would have held that the Fourteenth Amendment requires appointment of counsel in a state court, just as the Sixth Amendment requires in a federal court.

We think the Court in Betts had ample precedent for acknowledging that those guarantees of the Bill of Rights which are fundamental safeguards of liberty immune from federal abridgment are equally protected against state invasion by the Due Process Clause of the Fourteenth Amendment. This same principle was recognized, explained, and applied in *Powell* v. *Alabama,* 287 U.S. 45 (1932), a case upholding the right of counsel, where the Court held that despite sweeping language to the contrary in *Hurtado* v. *California,* 110 U.S. 516 (1884), the Fourteenth Amendment "embraced" those " 'fundamental principles of liberty and justice which lie at the base of all our civil and political institutions,' " even though they had been "specifically dealt with in another part of the Federal Constitution." 287 U.S., at 67. . . . In many cases other than Powell and Betts, this Court has looked to the fundamental nature of original Bill of Rights guarantees to decide whether the Fourteenth Amendment makes them obligatory on the States. Explicitly recognized to be of this "fundamental nature" and therefore made immune from state invasion by the Fourteenth, or some part of it, are the First Amendment's freedoms of speech, press, religion, assembly, association, and petition for redress of grievances. For the same reason, though not always in precisely the same terminology, the Court has made obligatory on the States the Fifth Amendment's command that private property shall not be taken for public use without just compensation, the Fourth Amendment's prohibition of unreasonable searches and seizures, and the Eighth's ban on cruel and unusual punishment. On the other hand, this Court in *Palko* v. *Connecticut,* 302 U.S. 319 . . . (1937), refused to hold that the Fourteenth Amendment made the double jeopardy provision of the Fifth Amendment obligatory on the States. In so refusing, however, the Court, speaking through Mr. Justice Cardozo, was careful to emphasize that "immunities that are valid as against the federal government by force of the specific pledges of particular amendments have been found to be implicit in the concept of ordered liberty, and thus, through the Fourteenth Amendment, become valid as against the states" and that guarantees "in their origin . . . effective against the federal government alone" had by prior cases "been taken over from the earlier articles of the Federal Bill of Rights and brought within the Fourteenth Amendment by a process of absorption." 302 U.S., at 324–325, 326. . . .

We accept *Betts* v. *Brady*'s assumption, based as it was on our prior cases, that a provision of the Bill of Rights which is "fundamental and essential to a fair trial" is made obligatory upon the States by the Fourteenth Amendment. We think the Court in Betts was wrong, however, in concluding that the Sixth Amendment's guarantee of counsel is not one of these fundamental rights. Ten years before *Betts* v. *Brady*, this Court, after full consideration of all the historical data examined in Betts, had unequivocally declared that "the right to the aid of counsel is of this fundamental character." *Powell* v. *Alabama,* 287 U.S. 45 . . . (1932). While the Court at the close of its Powell opinion did by its language, as this Court frequently does, limit its holding to the particular facts and circumstances of that case, its conclusions about the fundamental nature of the right to counsel are unmistakable. Several years later, in 1936, the Court reemphasized what it had said about the fundamental nature of the right to counsel in this language:

> We concluded that certain fundamental rights, safeguarded by the first eight amendments against federal action, were also safeguarded against state action by the due process of law clause of the Fourteenth Amendment, and among them the fundamental right of the accused to the aid of counsel in a criminal prosecution." *Grosjean* v. *American Press Co.,* 297 U.S. 233 . . . (1936).

And again in 1938 this Court said:

> [The assistance of counsel] is one of the safeguards of the Sixth Amendment deemed necessary to insure fundamental human rights of life and liberty. . . . The Sixth Amendment stands as a constant admonition that if the constitutional safeguards it provides be lost, justice will not 'still be done.' " *Johnson* v. *Zerbst,* 304 U.S. 458 . . . (1938). To the same effect,

see *Avery* v. *Alabama,* 308 U.S. 444 . . . (1940), and *Smith* v. *O'Grady,* 312 U.S. 329 . . . (1941).

In light of these and many other prior decisions of this Court, it is not surprising that the Betts Court, when faced with the contention that "one charged with crime, who is unable to obtain counsel, must be furnished counsel by the state," conceded that "[e]xpressions in the opinions of this court lend color to the argument . . ." 316 U.S., at 462–463. . . . The fact is that in deciding as it did — that "appointment of counsel is not a fundamental right, essential to a fair trial" — the Court in *Betts* v. *Brady* made an abrupt break with its own well-considered precedents. In returning to these old precedents, sounder we believe than the new, we but restore constitutional principles established to achieve a fair system of justice. Not only these precedents but also reason and reflection require us to recognize that in our adversary system of criminal justice, any person haled into court, who is too poor to hire a lawyer, cannot be assured a fair trial unless counsel is provided for him. This seems to us to be an obvious truth. Governments, both state and federal, quite properly spend vast sums of money to establish machinery to try defendants accused of crime. Lawyers to prosecute are everywhere deemed essential to protect the public's interest in an orderly society. Similarly, there are few defendants charged with crime, few indeed, who fail to hire the best lawyers they can get to prepare and present their defenses. That government hires lawyers to prosecute and defendants who have the money hire lawyers to defend are the strongest indications of the widespread belief that lawyers in criminal courts are necessities, not luxuries. The right of one charged with crime to counsel may not be deemed fundamental and essential to fair trials in some countries, but it is in ours. From the very beginning, our state and national constitutions and laws have laid great emphasis on procedural and substantive safeguards designed to assure fair trials before impartial tribunals in which every defendant stands equal before the law. This noble ideal cannot be realized if the poor man charged with crime has to face his accusers without a lawyer to assist him. A defendant's need for a lawyer is nowhere better stated than in the moving words of Mr. Justice Sutherland in *Powell* v. *Alabama:*

> The right to be heard would be, in many cases, of little avail if it did not comprehend the right to be heard by counsel. Even the intelligent and educated layman has small and sometimes no skill in the science of law. If charged with crime, he is incapable, generally, of determining for himself whether the indictment is good or bad. He is unfamiliar with the rules of evidence. Left without the aid of counsel he may be put on trial without a proper charge, and convicted upon incompetent evidence, or evidence irrelevant to the issue or otherwise inadmissible. He lacks both the skill and knowledge adequately to prepare his defense, even though he have a perfect one. He requires the guiding hand of counsel at every step in the

proceedings against him. Without it, though he be not guilty, he faces the danger of conviction because he does not know how to establish his innocence. 287 U.S., at 68–69. . . .

The Court in *Betts* v. *Brady* departed from the sound wisdom upon which the Court's holding in *Powell* v. *Alabama* rested. Florida, supported by two other States, has asked that *Betts* v. *Brady* be left intact. Twenty-two States, as friends of the Court, argue that Betts was "an anachronism when handed down" and that it should now be overruled. We agree.

The judgment is reversed and the cause is remanded to the Supreme Court of Florida for further action not inconsistent with this opinion.

Reversed.

Chief Justice Warren, and Justices Brennan, Stewart, White, and Goldberg join in the opinion of the Court.

Mr. Justice DOUGLAS joins the opinion, giving a brief historical resume of the relation between the Bill of Rights and the Fourteenth Amendment. Mr. Justice Clark concurs in the result. Mr. Justice Harlan concurs in the result.

Freedom of Speech and Press

There are many reasons why we should support freedom of speech and press. One of these is the impossibility of proving the existence of an Absolute Truth. No person nor group can be infallible. The "best" decisions are those that are made on the basis of the most widespread information available pertaining to the subject at hand. Freedom of information is an integral part of the democratic process. In this selection from John Stuart Mill's famous essay *On Liberty,* published in 1859, the justifications for permitting liberty of speech and press are discussed.

14
John Stuart Mill

LIBERTY OF THOUGHT
AND DISCUSSION

The time, it is to be hoped, is gone by when any defence would be necessary of the "liberty of the press" as one of the securities against corrupt or tyrannical government. No argument, we may suppose, can now be needed, against permitting a legislature or an executive, not identified in interest with the people, to prescribe opinions to them, and determine what doctrines or what arguments they shall be allowed to hear. This aspect of the question, besides, has been so often and so triumphantly enforced by preceding writers, that it needs not be specially insisted on in this place. Though the law of England, on the subject of the press, is as servile to this day as it was in the time of the Tudors, there is little danger of its being actually put in force against political discussion, except during some temporary panic, when fear of insurrection drives ministers and judges from their propriety; and, speaking generally, it is not, in constitutional countries, to be apprehended, that the government, whether completely responsible to the people or not, will often attempt to control the expression of opinion, except when in doing so it makes itself the organ of the general intolerance of the public. Let us suppose, therefore, that the government is entirely at one with the people, and never thinks of exerting any power of coercion unless in agreement with what it conceives to be their voice. But I deny the right of the people to exercise such coercion, either by themselves or by their government. The power itself is illegitimate. The best government has no more title to it than the worst. It is as noxious, or more noxious, when exerted in accordance with public opinion, than when in opposition to it. If all mankind minus one, were of one opinion, and only one person were of the contrary opinion, mankind would be no more justified in silencing that one person, than he, if he had the power, would be justified in silencing mankind. Were an opinion a personal possession of no value except to the owner; if to be obstructed in the enjoyment of it were simply a private injury, it would make some difference whether the injury was inflicted only on a few persons or on many. But the peculiar evil of silencing the expression of an opinion is, that it is robbing the human race; posterity as well as the existing generation; those who dissent from the opinion, still more than those who hold it. If the opinion is right, they are deprived of the opportunity of exchanging error for truth: if wrong, they lose, what is almost as great a benefit, the clearer perception and livelier impression of truth, produced by its collision with error.

It is necessary to consider separately these two hypotheses, each of which has a distinct branch of the argument corresponding to it. We can never be sure that the opinion we are endeavoring to stifle is a false opinion; and if we were sure, stifling it would be an evil still.

First: the opinion which it is attempted to suppress by authority may possibly be true. Those who desire to suppress it, of course deny its truth; but they are not infallible. They have no authority to decide the question for all mankind, and exclude every other person from the means of judging. To refuse a hearing to an opinion, because they are sure that it is false, is to assume that *their* certainty is the same thing as *absolute* certainty. All silencing of discussion is an assumption of infallibility. Its condemnation may be allowed to rest on this common argument, not the worse for being common.

Unfortunately for the good sense of mankind, the fact of their fallibility is far from carrying the weight in their practical judgment, which is always allowed to it in theory; for while every one well knows himself to be fallible, few think it necessary to take any precautions against their own fallibility, or admit the supposition that any opinion, of which they feel very certain, may be one of the examples of the error to which they acknowledge themselves to be liable. Absolute princes, or others who are accustomed to unlimited deference, usually feel this complete confidence in their own opinions on nearly all subjects. People more happily situated, who sometimes hear their opinions disputed, and are not wholly unused to be set right when they are wrong, place the same unbounded reliance only on such of their opinions as are shared by all who surround them, or to whom they habitually defer: for in proportion to a man's want of confidence in his own solitary judgment, does he usually repose, with implicit trust, on the infallibility of "the world" in general. And the world, to each individual, means the part of it with which he comes in contact; his party, his sect, his church, his class of society: the man may be called, by comparison, almost liberal and large-minded to whom it means anything so comprehensive as his own country or his own age. Nor is his faith in this collective authority at all shaken by his being aware that other ages, countries, sects, churches, classes, and parties have thought, and even now think, the exact reverse. He devolves upon his own world the responsibility of being in the right against the dissentient worlds of other people; and it never troubles him that mere accident has decided which of these numerous worlds is the object of his reliance, and that the same causes which make him a Churchman in London, would have made him a Buddhist or a Confucian in Peking. Yet it is as evident in itself, as any amount of argument can make it, that ages are no more infallible than individuals; every age having held many opinions which subsequent ages have deemed not only false but absurd; and it is as certain that many opinions, now general, will be rejected by future ages, as it is that many, once general, are rejected by the present.

The objection likely to be made to this argument, would probably take some such form as the following. There is no greater assumption of infallibility in forbidding the propagation of error, than in any other thing which is done by public authority on its own judgment and responsibility. Judgment is given to men that they may use it. Because it may be used erroneously, are men to be told that they ought not to use it at all? To prohibit what they think pernicious, is not claiming exemption from error, but fulfilling the duty incumbent on them, although fallible, of acting on their conscientious conviction. If we were never to act on our opinions, because those opinions may be wrong, we should leave all our interests uncared for, and all our duties unperformed. An objection which applies to all conduct, can be no valid objection to any conduct in particular. It is the duty of governments, and of individuals, to form the truest opinions they can; to form them carefully, and never impose them upon others unless they are quite sure of being right. But when they are sure (such reasoners may say), it is not conscientiousness but cowardice to shrink from acting on their opinions, and allow doctrines which they honestly think dangerous to the welfare of mankind, either in this life or in another, to be scattered abroad without restraint, because other people, in less enlightened times, have persecuted opinions now believed to be true. Let us take care, it may be said, not to make the same mistake: but governments and nations have made mistakes in other things, which are not denied to be fit subjects for the exercise of authority: they have laid on bad taxes, made unjust wars. Ought we therefore to lay on no taxes, and, under whatever provocation, make no wars? Men, and governments, must act to the best of their ability. There is no such thing as absolute certainty, but there is assurance sufficient for the purposes of human life. We may, and must, assume our opinion to be true for the guidance of our own conduct: and it is assuming no more when we forbid bad men to pervert society by the propagation of opinions which we regard as false and pernicious.

I answer, that it is assuming very much more. There is the greatest difference between presuming an opinion to be true, because, with every opportunity for contesting it, it has not been refuted, and assuming its truth for the purpose of not permitting its refutation. Complete liberty of contradicting and disproving our opinion, is the very condition which justifies us in assuming its truth for purposes of action; and on no other terms can a being with human faculties have any rational assurance of being right.

When we consider either the history of opinion, or the ordinary conduct of human life, to what is it to be ascribed that the one and the other are no worse than they are? Not certainly to the inherent force of the human understanding; for, on any matter not self-evident, there are ninety-nine persons totally incapable of judging of it, for one who is capable; and the capacity of the hundredth person is only comparative; for the majority of the eminent men of every past generation held many opinions now known to be erroneous, and did or approved numerous things which no one will now justify. Why is it, then, that there is on the whole a preponderance among mankind of rational opinions and rational conduct? If there really is this preponderance — which there must be, unless human affairs are, and have always been, in an almost desperate state — it is owing to a quality of the human mind, the source of everything respectable in man either as an intellectual or as a moral being, namely, that his errors are corrigible. He is capable of rectifying his mistakes, by discussion and experience. Not by experience alone. There must be discussion, to show how experience is to be interpreted. Wrong opinions and practices gradually yield to fact and argument: but facts and arguments, to produce any effect on the mind, must be brought before it. Very few facts are able to tell their own story, without comments to bring out their meaning. The whole strength and value, then, of human judgment, depending on the one property, that it can be set when it is wrong, reliance can be placed on it only when the means of setting it right are kept constantly at hand. In the case of any person whose judgment is really deserving of confidence, how has it become so? Because he has kept his mind open to criticism of his opinions and conduct. Because it has been his practice to listen to all that could be said against him; to profit by as much of it as was just, and expound to himself, and upon occasion to others, the fallacy of what was fallacious. Because he has felt, that the only way in which a human being can make some approach to knowing the whole of a subject, is by hearing what can be said about it by persons of every variety of opinion, and studying all modes in which it can be looked at by every character of mind. No wise man ever acquired his wisdom in any mode but this; nor is it in the nature of human intellect to become wise in any other manner. The steady habit of correcting and completing his own opinion by collating it with those of others, so far from causing doubt and hesitation in carrying it into practice, is the only stable foundation for a just reliance on it: for, being cognizant of all that can, at least obviously, be said against him, and having taken up his position against all gainsayers — knowing that he has sought for objections and difficulties, instead of avoiding them, and has shut out no light which can be thrown upon the subject from any quarter — he has a right to think his judgment better than that of any person, or any multitude, who have not gone through a similar process.

It is not too much to require that what the wisest of mankind, those who are best entitled to trust their own judgment, find necessary to warrant their relying on it, should be submitted to by that miscellaneous collection of a few wise and many foolish individuals, called the public. The most intolerant of churches, the Roman Catholic Church, even at the canonization of a saint, admits, and listens patiently to, a "devil's advocate." The holiest of men, it appears, cannot be admitted to posthumous honors, until all that the devil could say against him is known and weighed. If even the

Newtonian philosophy were not permitted to be questioned, mankind could not feel as complete assurance of its truth as they now do. The beliefs which we have most warrant for, have no safeguard to rest on, but a standing invitation to the whole world to prove them unfounded. . . .

We have now recognized the necessity to the mental well-being of mankind (on which all their other well-being depends) of freedom of opinion, and freedom of the expression of opinion, on four distinct grounds; which we will now briefly recapitulate.

First, if any opinion is compelled to silence, that opinion may, for aught we can certainly know, be true. To deny this is to assume our own infallibility.

Secondly, though the silenced opinion be an error, it may, and very commonly does, contain a portion of truth; and since the general or prevailing opinion on any subject is rarely or never the whole truth, it is only by the collision of adverse opinions that the remainder of the truth has any chance of being supplied.

Thirdly, even if the received opinion be not only true, but the whole truth; unless it is suffered to be, and actually is, vigorously and earnestly contested, it will, by most of those who receive it, be held in the manner of a prejudice, with little comprehension of feeling of its rational grounds. And not only this, but, fourthly, the meaning of the doctrine itself will be in danger of being lost, or enfeebled, and deprived of its vital effect on the character and conduct: the dogma becoming a mere formal profession, inefficacious for good, but cumbering the ground, and preventing the growth of any real and heartfelt conviction from reason or personal experience.

Before quitting the subject of freedom of opinion, it is fit to take some notice of those who say, that the free expression of all opinions should be permitted, on condition that the manner be temperate, and do not pass the bounds of fair discussion. Much might be said on the impossibility of fixing where these supposed bounds are to be placed; for if the test be offence to those whose opinion is attacked, I think experience testifies that this offence is given whenever the attack is telling and powerful, and that every opponent who pushes them hard, and whom they find it difficult to answer, appears to them, if he shows any strong feeling on the subject, an intemperate opponent. But this, though an important consideration in a practical point of view, merges in a more fundamental objection. Undoubtedly the manner of asserting an opinion, even though it be a true one, may be very objectionable, and may justly incur severe censure. But the principal offences of the kind are such as it is mostly impossible, unless by accidental self-betrayal, to bring home to conviction. The gravest of them is, to argue sophistically, to suppress facts or arguments, to misstate the elements of the case, or misrepresent the opposite opinion. But all this, even to the most aggravated degree, is so continually done in perfect good faith, by persons who are not considered, and in many other respects may not deserve to be considered, ignorant or incompetent, that it is rarely possible on adequate grounds conscientiously to stamp the misrepresentation as morally culpable; and still less could law presume to interfere with this kind of controversial misconduct. With regard to what is commonly meant by intemperate discussion, namely, invective, sarcasm, personality, and the like, the denunciation of these weapons would deserve more sympathy if it were ever proposed to interdict them equally to both sides; but it is only desired to restrain the employment of them against the prevailing opinion: against the unprevailing they may not only be used without general disapproval, but will be likely to obtain for him who uses them the praise of honest zeal and righteous indignation. Yet whatever mischief arises from their use, is greatest when they are employed against the comparatively defenceless; and whatever unfair advantage can be derived by any opinion from this mode of asserting it, accrues almost exclusively to received opinions. The worst offence of this kind which can be committed by a polemic, is to stigmatize those who hold the contrary opinion as bad and immoral men. To calumny of this sort, those who hold any unpopular opinion are peculiarly exposed, because they are in general few and uninfluential, and nobody but themselves feels much interest in seeing justice done them; but this weapon is, from the nature of the case, denied to those who attack a prevailing opinion: they can neither use it with safety to themselves, nor, if they could, would it do anything but recoil on their own cause. In general, opinions contrary to those commonly received can only obtain a hearing by studied moderation of language, and the most cautious avoidance of unnecessary offence, from which they hardly ever deviate even in a slight degree without losing ground: while unmeasured vituperation employed on the side of the prevailing opinion, really does deter people from professing contrary opinions, and from listening to those who profess them. For the interest, therefore, of truth and justice, it is far more important to restrain this employment of vituperative language than the other; and, for example, if it were necessary to choose, there would be much more need to discourage offensive attacks on infidelity, than on religion. It is, however, obvious that law and authority have no business with restraining either, while opinion ought, in every instance, to determine its verdict by the circumstances of the individual case; condemning every one, on whichever side of the argument he places himself, in whose mode of advocacy either want of candor, or malignity, bigotry, or intolerance of feeling manifest themselves; but not inferring these vices from the side which a person takes, though it be the contrary side of the question to our own: and giving merited honor to every one, whatever opinion he may hold, who has calmness to see and honesty to state what his opponents and their opinions really are, exaggerating nothing to their discredit, keeping nothing back which tells, or can be supposed to tell, in their favor. This is the real morality of public discussion; and if often violated, I am happy to think that there are many controversialists who to a great extent observe it, and a still greater number who conscientiously strive towards it.

Mill does not justify absolute liberty of speech and press but implies that there are boundaries — although difficult to determine — to public debate. Democratic governments have always been faced with this dilemma: At what point can freedom of speech and press be curtailed? The Supreme Court has had difficulty in making decisions in areas involving censorship and loyalty and security. Freedom of speech and press cannot be used to destroy the very government that protects civil liberties.

Justice Holmes, in *Schenck* v. *United States,* 249 U.S. 47 (1919), stated his famous "clear and present danger" test, which subsequently was applied at both the national and state levels, for deciding whether or not Congress could abridge freedom of speech under the First Amendment:

"The most stringent protection of free speech would not protect a man in falsely shouting fire in a theatre and causing a panic. It does not protect a man from an injunction against uttering words that may have all the effects of force. . . . The question in every case is whether the words used are used in such circumstances and are of such a nature as to create a clear and present danger that they will bring about the substantive evils that Congress has a right to prevent. It is a question of proximity and degree. When a nation is at war many things that might be said in time of peace are such a hindrance to its efforts that their utterance will not be endured so long as men fight and that no Court could regard them as protected by any constitutional right."

In 1940 Congress passed the Smith Act, Section 2 of which made it unlawful for any person:

"(1) to knowingly or willfully advocate, abet, advise, or teach the duty, necessity, desirability, or propriety of overthrowing or destroying any government in the United States by force or violence . . . ; (2) with intent to cause the overthrow or destruction of any government in the United States, to print, publish, edit, issue, circulate, sell, distribute, or publicly display any written or printed matter advocating, advising, or teaching the duty, necessity, desirability, or propriety of overthrowing or destroying any government in the United States by force or violence; (3) to organize or help to organize any society, group, or assembly of persons who teach, advocate, or encourage the overthrow or destruction of any government in the United States by force or violence; or to be or become a member of, or affiliate with, any such society . . . , knowing the purposes thereof."

The constitutionality of this act was tested in *Dennis* v. *United States,* 341 U.S. 494 (1951), which contained five opinions. Vinson spoke for the Court, with Frankfurter and Jackson concurring; Black and Douglas dissented.

15

DENNIS v. UNITED STATES
341 U.S. 494 (1951)

Mr. Chief Justice Vinson announced the judgment of the Court, saying in part:

Petitioners were indicted in July, 1948, for violation of the conspiracy provisions of the Smith Act. . . . A verdict of guilty as to all the petitioners was returned by the jury on October 14, 1949. The Court of Appeals affirmed the convictions. . . . We granted certiorari. . . .

. . . Our limited grant of the writ of certiorari has removed from our consideration any question as to the sufficiency of the evidence to support the jury's determination that petitioners are guilty of the offense charged. Whether on this record petitioners did in fact advocate the overthrow of the government by force and violence is not before us, and we must base any discussion of this point upon the conclusions stated in the opinion of the Court of Appeals, which treated the issue in great detail. That court held that the record in this case amply supports the necessary finding of the jury that petitioners, the leaders of the Communist Party in this country, were unwilling to work within our framework of democracy, but intended to initiate a violent revolution whenever the propitious occasion appeared. . . .

I

It will be helpful in clarifying the issues to treat next the contention that the trial judge improperly interpreted the statute by charging that the statute required an unlawful intent before the jury could convict. More specifically, he charged that the jury could not find the petitioners guilty under the indictment unless they found that petitioners had the intent to "overthrow . . . the Government of the United States by force and violence as speedily as circumstances would permit."

. . . The structure and purpose of the statute demand the inclusion of intent as an element of the crime. Congress was concerned with those who advocate and organize for the overthrow of the government. Certainly those who recruit and combine for the purpose of advocating overthrow intend to bring about that overthrow. We hold that the statute requires as an essential element of the crime proof of the intent of those who are charged with its violation to overthrow the government by force and violence. . . .

II

The obvious purpose of the statute is to protect existing government, not from change by peaceable, lawful and constitutional means, but from change by violence, revolution, and terrorism. That it is within the *power* of the Congress to protect the government of the United States from armed rebellion is a proposition which requires little discussion. Whatever theoretical merit there may be to the argument that there is a "right" to rebellion against dictatorial governments is without force where the existing structure of the government provides for peaceful and orderly change. We reject any principle of governmental helplessness in the face of preparation for revolution, which principle, carried to its logical conclusion, must lead to anarchy. No one could conceive that it is not within the power of Congress to prohibit acts intended to overthrow the government by force and violence. The question with which we are concerned here is not whether Congress has such *power,* but whether the *means* that it has employed conflict with the First and Fifth Amendments to the Constitution.

One of the bases for the contention that the means which Congress has employed are invalid takes the form of an attack on the face of the statute on the grounds that by its terms it prohibits academic discussion of the merits of Marxism–Leninism, that it stifles ideas and is contrary to all concepts of a free speech and a free press. Although we do not agree that the language itself has that significance, we must bear in mind that it is the duty of the federal courts to interpret federal legislation in a manner not inconsistent with the demands of the Constitution. . . . This is a federal statute which we must interpret as well as judge. . . .

The very language of the Smith Act negates the interpretation which petitioners would have us impose on that Act. It is directed at advocacy, not discussion. Thus, the trial judge properly charged the jury that they could not convict if they found that petitioners did "no more than pursue peaceful studies and discussions or teaching and advocacy in the realm of ideas." He further charged that it was not unlawful "to conduct in an American college or university a course explaining the philosophical theories set forth in the books which have been placed in evidence." Such a charge is in strict accord with the statutory language, and illustrates the meaning to be placed on those words. Congress did not intend to eradicate the free discussion of political theories, to destroy the traditional rights of Americans to discuss and evaluate ideas without fear of governmental sanction. Rather Congress was concerned with the very kind of activity in which the evidence showed these petitioners engaged.

III

But although the statute is not directed at the hypothetical cases which petitioners have conjured, its application in this case has resulted in convictions for the teaching and advocacy of the overthrow of the government by force and violence, which, even though coupled with the intent to accomplish that overthrow, contains an element of speech. For this reason, we must pay special heed to the demands of the First Amendment marking out the boundaries of speech.

We pointed out in *Douds, supra,* that the basis of the First Amendment is the hypothesis that speech can rebut speech, propaganda will answer propaganda, free debate of ideas will result in the wisest governmental policies. It is for this reason that this Court has recognized the inherent value of free discourse. An analysis of the leading cases in this Court which have involved direct limitations on speech, however, will demonstrate that both the majority of the Court and the dissenters in particular cases have recognized that this is not an unlimited, unqualified right, but that the societal value of speech must, on occasion, be subordinated to other values and considerations. . . .

The rule we deduce from these cases [*Schenck* and others] is that where an offense is specified by a statute in nonspeech or nonpress terms, a conviction relying upon speech or press as evidence of violation may be sustained only when the speech or publication created a "clear and present danger" of attempting or accomplishing the prohibited crime, e.g. interference with enlistment. The dissents . . . in emphasizing the value of speech, were addressed to the argument of the sufficiency of the evidence. . . .

In this case we are squarely presented with the application of the "clear and present danger" test, and must decide what that phrase imports. We first note that many of the cases in which this Court has reversed convictions by use of this or similar tests have been based on the fact that the interest which the state was attempting to protect was itself too insubstantial to warrant restriction of speech. . . . Overthrow of the government by force and violence is certainly a substantial enough interest for the government to limit speech. Indeed, this is the ultimate value of any society, for if a society cannot protect its structure from armed internal attack, it must follow that no subordinate value can be protected. If, then, this interest may be protected, the literal problem which is presented is what has been meant by the use of the phrase "clear and present danger" of the utterances bringing about the evil within the power of Congress to punish.

Obviously, the words cannot mean that before the government may act, it must wait until the *putsch* is about to be executed, the plans have been laid and the signal is awaited. If government is aware that a group aiming at its overthrow is attempting to indoctrinate its members and to commit them to a course whereby they will strike when the leaders feel the circumstances permit, action by the government is required. The argument that there is no need for government to concern itself, for government is strong, it possesses ample powers to put down a rebellion, it may defeat the revolution with ease needs no answer. For that is not the question. Certainly an attempt to overthrow the government by force, even though doomed from the outset because of inadequate numbers or power of the revolutionists, is a sufficient evil for Congress to prevent. The damage which such attempts create both physically and politically to a nation makes it impossible to measure the validity in terms of the probability of success, or the immediacy of a successful attempt. In the instant case the trial judge charged the jury that they could not convict unless they found that petitioners intended to overthrow the government "as speedily as circumstances would permit." This does not mean, and could not properly mean, that they would not strike until there was certainty of success. What was meant was that the revolutionists would strike when they thought the time was ripe. We must therefore reject the contention that success or probability of success is the criterion.

The situation with which Justices Holmes and Brandeis were concerned in *Gitlow* was a comparatively isolated event [involving a conviction for criminal anarchy in New York of one Gitlow for circulating Communist literature], bearing little relation in their minds to any substantial threat to the safety of the community. . . . They were not confronted with any situation comparable to the instant one — the development of an apparatus designed and dedicated to the overthrow of the government, in the context of world crisis after crisis.

Chief Justice Learned Hand, writing for the majority below, interpreted the phrase as follows: "In each case [courts] must ask whether the gravity of the 'evil,' discounted by its improbability, justifies such invasion of free speech as is necessary to avoid the danger." 183 F.2d at 212. We adopt this statement of the rule. . . .

Likewise, we are in accord with the court below, which affirmed the trial court's finding that the requisite danger existed. The mere fact that from the period 1945 to 1948 petitioners' activities did not result in an attempt to overthrow the government by force and violence is of course no answer to the fact that there was a group that was ready to make the attempt. The formation by petitioners of such a highly organized conspiracy, with rigidly disciplined members subject to call when the leaders, these petitioners, felt that the time had come for action, coupled with the inflammable nature of world conditions, similar uprisings in other countries, and the touch-and-go nature of our relations with countries with whom petitioners were in the very least ideologically attuned, convince us that their convictions were justified on this score. And this analysis disposes of the contention that a conspiracy to advocate, as distinguished from the advocacy itself, cannot be constitutionally restrained, because it comprises only the preparation. It is the existence of the conspiracy which creates the danger. . . . If the ingredients of the reaction are present, we cannot bind the government to wait until the catalyst is added. . . .

We hold that §§ 2(a) (1), 2(a) (2) and (3) of the Smith Act, do not inherently, or as construed or applied in the instant case, violate the First Amendment and other provisions of the Bill of Rights, or the First and Fifth Amendments because of indefiniteness. Petitioners intended to overthrow the government of the United States as speedily as the circumstances would permit. Their conspiracy to organize the Communist Party and to teach and advocate the overthrow of the government of the United States by force and violence created a "clear and present danger" of an attempt to overthrow the government by force and violence. They were properly and constitutionally convicted for violation of the Smith Act. The judgments of conviction are affirmed. . . .

Mr. Justice Black, dissenting, said in part:

. . . At the outset I want to emphasize what the crime involved in this case is, and what it is not. These petitioners were not charged with an attempt to overthrow the government. They were not charged with overt acts of any kind designed to overthrow the government. They were not even charged with saying anything or writing anything designed to overthrow the government. The charge was that they agreed to assemble and to talk and publish certain ideas at a later date: The indictment is that they conspired to organize the Communist Party and to use speech or newspapers and other publications in the future to teach and advocate the forcible overthrow of the government. No matter how it is worded, this is a virulent form of prior censorship of speech and press, which I believe the First Amendment forbids. . . .

But let us assume, contrary to all constitutional ideas of fair criminal procedure, that petitioners although not indicted for the crime of actual advocacy, may be punished for it. Even on this radical assumption, the other opinions in this case show that the only way to affirm these convictions is to repudiate directly or indirectly the established "clear and present danger" rule. This the Court does in a way which greatly restricts the protections afforded by the First Amendment. The opinions for affirmance indicate that the chief reason for jettisoning the rule is the expressed fear that advocacy of Communist doctrine endangers the safety of the Republic. Undoubtedly, a governmental policy of unfettered communication of ideas does entail dangers. To the Founders of this nation, however, the benefits derived from free expression were worth the risk. They embodied this philosophy in the First Amendment's command that "Congress shall make no law . . . abridging the freedom of speech, or of the press. . . ." I have always believed that the First Amendment is the keystone of our government, that the freedoms it guarantees provide the best insurance against destruction of all freedom. At least as to speech in the realm of public matters, I believe that the "clear and present danger" test does not "mark the furthermost constitutional boundaries of protected expression" but does "no more than recognize a minimum compulsion of the Bill of Rights." . . .

So long as this Court exercises the power of judicial review of legislation, I cannot agree that the First Amendment permits us to sustain laws suppressing freedom of speech and press on the basis of Congress's or our own notions of mere "reasonableness." Such a doctrine waters down the First Amendment so that it amounts to little more than an admonition to Congress. The Amendment as so construed is not likely to protect any but those "safe" or orthodox views which rarely need its protection. I must also express my objection to the holding because, as Mr. Justice Douglas's dissent shows, it sanctions the determination of a crucial issue of fact by the judge rather than by the jury. Nor can I let this opportunity pass without expressing my objection to the severely limited grant of certiorari in this case which precluded consideration here of at least two other reasons for reversing these convictions: (1) the record shows a discriminatory selection of the jury panel which prevented trial before a representative cross-section of the community; (2) the record shows that one member of the trial jury was violently hostile to petitioners before and during the trial.

Public opinion being what it now is, few will protest the conviction of these Communist petitioners. There is hope, however, that in calmer times, when present pressure, passions and fears subside, this or some later Court will restore the First Amendment liberties to the high preferred place where they belong in a free society.

Mr. Justice Douglas, dissenting, said in part:

. . . [N]ever until today has anyone seriously thought that the ancient law of conspiracy could constitutionally be used to turn speech into seditious conduct. Yet that is precisely what is suggested. I repeat that we deal here with speech alone, not with speech *plus* acts of sabotage or unlawful conduct. Not a single seditious act is charged in the indictment. . . .

Free speech has occupied an exalted position because of the high service it has given our society. Its protection is essential to the very existence of a democracy. The airing of ideas releases pressures which otherwise might become destructive. When ideas compete in the market for acceptance, full and free discussion exposes the false and they gain few adherents. Full and free discussion even of ideas we hate encourages the testing of our own prejudices and preconceptions. Full and free discussion keeps a society from becoming stagnant and unprepared for the stresses and strains that work to tear all civilizations apart.

Full and free discussion has indeed been the first article of our faith. We have founded our political system on it. It has been the safeguard of every religious, political, philosophical, economic, and racial group amongst us. We have counted on it to keep us from embracing what is cheap and false; we have trusted the common sense of our people to choose the doctrine true to our genius and to reject the rest. This has been the one single outstanding tenet that has made our institutions the symbol of freedom and equality. We have deemed it more costly to liberty to suppress a despised minority than to let them vent their spleen. We have above all else feared the political censor. We have wanted a land where our people can be exposed to all the diverse creeds and cultures of the world.

There comes a time when even speech loses its constitutional immunity. Speech innocuous one year may at another time fan such destructive flames that it must be halted in the interest of the safety of the Republic.

That is the meaning of the clear and present danger test. When conditions are so critical that there will be no time to avoid the evil that the speech threatens, it is time to call a halt. Otherwise, free speech which is the strength of the nation will be the cause of its destruction.

Yet free speech is the rule, not the exception. The restraint to be constitutional must be based on more than fear, on more than passionate opposition against the speech, on more than a revolted dislike for its contents. There must be some immediate injury to society that is likely if speech is allowed. . . .

. . . This record . . . contains no evidence whatsoever showing that the acts charged, viz., the teaching of the Soviet theory of revolution with the hope that it will be realized, have created any clear and present danger to the nation. The Court, however, rules to the contrary. . . .

The political impotence of the Communists in this country does not, of course, dispose of the problem. Their numbers; their positions in industry and government; the extent to which they have in fact infiltrated the police, the armed services, transportation, stevedoring, power plants, munition works, and other critical places — these facts all bear on the likelihood that their advocacy of the Soviet theory of revolution will endanger the Republic. But the record is silent on these facts. If we are to proceed on the basis of judicial notice, it is impossible for me to say that the Communists in this country are so potent or so strategically deployed that they must be suppressed for their speech. I could not so hold unless I were willing to conclude that the activities in recent years of committees of Congress, of the Attorney General, of labor unions, of state legislatures, and of Loyalty Boards were so futile as to leave the country on the edge of grave peril. To believe that petitioners and their following are placed in such critical positions as to endanger the nation is to believe the incredible. It is safe to say that the followers of the creed of Soviet Communism are known to the FBI; that in case of war with Russia they will be picked up overnight as were all prospective saboteurs at the commencement of World War II; that the invisible army of petitioners is the best known, the most beset, and the least thriving of any fifth column in history. Only those held by fear and panic could think otherwise. . . .

. . . The political censor has no place in our public debates. Unless and until extreme and necessitous circumstances are shown, our aim should be to keep speech unfettered and to allow the processes of law to be invoked only when the provocateurs among us move from speech to action.

Vishinsky wrote in 1938 in the Law of the Soviet State, "In our state, naturally, there is and can be no place for freedom of speech, press, and so on for the foes of socialism."

Our concern should be that we accept no such standard for the United States. Our faith should be that our people will never give support to those advocates of revolution, so long as we remain loyal to the purposes for which our nation was founded.

Free Press and Fair Trial

The free speech and press standards of the First Amendment have always been ranked by the Supreme Court as among the most fundamental of our constitutional liberties. But even fundamental liberties can be restricted by government if there is a clear demonstration that the restraint of freedom is required by a compelling public interest. In *Dennis* v. *United States,* presented above, the Court upheld the restrictions on the First Amendment freedoms of expression in the Smith Act on the grounds that they were justified by a compelling governmental interest to prevent the probability of a *putsch.*

The First Amendment freedoms of expression may also be limited on grounds other than the showing of a clear and present danger of the overthrow of the government. An area of increasing controversy over the extent of First Amendment rights concerns the conflict that may occur between the requirements of a free press and those of a fair trial. Under certain circumstances press and electronic media coverage of a criminal trial may create an atmosphere of hostility toward the defendants that makes it difficult, if not impossible, to try them fairly and impartially. The state, which acts in the name of the people in criminal proceedings, has a clear and legitimate interest in assuring criminal defendants a fair trial. When there is glaring and prejudicial publicity surrounding persons accused of a crime, judges, defense attorneys, and the criminal defendants have argued that press and media coverage should be curtailed to guarantee a fair and impartial trial.

The Sixth Amendment provides: "In all criminal prosecutions, the accused shall enjoy the right to a speedy and public trial, by an impartial jury of the state and district wherein the crime shall have been committed." The rights of the Sixth Amendment, which have been nationalized under the due process clause of the Fourteenth Amendment to apply to the states, sometimes may conflict with the free press demands of the First Amendment. When confronted with a request to confine the press coverage of a criminal trial, the court must weigh the requirements of freedom of the press of the First Amendment against the requisites of the Sixth Amendment.

In *Sheppard* v. *Maxwell,* 384 U.S. 333 (1966), the Court reversed a murder conviction that was obtained in an atmosphere of extreme prejudice, caused largely by strident press accounts of the murder and direct accusations against the accused. The judge made no effort to control the accuracy of press and radio accounts of the trial, and he allowed reporters and radio commentators to have unlimited access to the rooms of the court and to prosecution witnesses. Radio broadcasts were made in a room next to one where the jury recessed and deliberated. Private courtroom proceedings were overheard and reported by the press. The noise and commotion surrounding the trial that was created by the newsmen often made it difficult for the counsel and witnesses to be heard. In the Sheppard case the Supreme Court concluded that the trial judge should have taken appropriate measures to reduce the carnival atmosphere of the trial, such as warning the newspapers to check the accuracy of their accounts, controlling prejudicial statements to the news media made by prosecution witnesses, and warning the press not to publish or broadcast prejudicial stories and material that had not been introduced in the proceedings. None of these measures would constitute a censorship of press accounts of the trial, nor did the Court imply that such censorship would be constitutionally permissible.

The Court confronted the question of the constitutionality of direct trial court censorship of the press in the following case, which involved a particularly heinous and brutal crime in which six members of a family were murdered in cold blood. The crime attracted widespread press coverage and pretrial publicity that was clearly prejudicial to the defendant. At the request of the county attorney and the counsel for the defendant, the trial court judge prohibited the public release of any testimony given or evidence produced at the *preliminary* hearing for the defendant. The Nebraska Press Association challenged the order in the state district court, which issued another restrictive order prohibiting the press from reporting certain facts surrounding the trial. The district court judge found: "Because of the nature of the crimes charged in the complaint, there is a clear and present danger that pretrial publicity could impinge upon the defendant's right to a fair trial." The order was to apply only until a jury was impaneled. On appeal, the Nebraska Supreme Court, after balancing the presumption against prior censorship against the defendant's right to a fair trial, found that a restrictive order upon the press was justified. Noting that under Nebraska law pretrial hearings could be closed entirely to the press and the public, the Nebraska Supreme Court remanded the case to the district judge to determine whether or not this should be done. The United States Supreme Court granted certiorari to the Nebraska Supreme Court to review its decision. The restrictive order that had been issued was a prior restraint on the press, against which there was a strong presumption of unconstitutionality based upon *Near* v. *Minnesota,* 283 U.S. 697 (1931), and *New York Times Company* v. *United States,* 403 U.S. 713 (1971).

16
NEBRASKA PRESS ASSOCIATION v. STUART
427 U.S. 539 (1976)

Mr. Chief Justice Burger delivered the opinion of the Court, saying in part:

III

The problems presented by this case are almost as old as the Republic. Neither in the Constitution nor in contemporaneous writings do we find that the conflict between these two important rights was anticipated, yet it is inconceivable that the authors of the Constitution were unaware of the potential conflicts between the right to an unbiased jury and the guarantee of freedom of the press. The unusually able lawyers who helped write the Constitution and later drafted the Bill of Rights were familiar with the historic episode in which John Adams defended British soldiers charged with homicide for firing into a crowd of Boston demonstrators; they were intimately familiar with the clash of the adversary system and the part that passions of the populace sometimes play in influencing potential jurors. They did not address themselves directly to the situation presented by this case; their chief concern was the need for freedom of expression in the political arena and the dialogue in ideas. But they recognized that there were risks to private rights from an unfettered press. . . .

The trial of Aaron Burr in 1807 presented Mr. Chief Justice Marshall, presiding as a trial judge, with acute problems in selecting an unbiased jury. Few people in the area of Virginia from which jurors were drawn had not formed some opinions concerning Mr. Burr or the case, from newspaper accounts and heightened discussion both private and public. The Chief Justice conducted a searching *voir dire* of the two panels eventually called, and rendered a substantial opinion on the purposes of *voir dire* and the standards to be applied. . . . Burr was acquitted, so there was no occasion for appellate review to examine the problem of prejudicial pretrial publicity. Mr. Chief Justice Marshall's careful *voir dire* inquiry into the matter of possible bias makes clear that the problem is not a new one.

The speed of communication and the pervasiveness of the modern news media have exacerbated these problems, however, as numerous appeals demonstrate. The trial of Bruno Hauptmann in a small New Jersey community for the abduction and murder of the Charles Lindberghs' infant child probably was the most widely covered trial up to that time, and the nature of the coverage produced widespread public reaction. Criticism was directed at the "carnival" atmosphere that pervaded the community and the courtroom itself. Responsible leaders of press and the legal profession

— including other judges — pointed out that much of this sorry performance could have been controlled by a vigilant trial judge and by other public officers subject to the control of the court. . . .

The excesses of press and radio and lack of responsibility of those in authority in the *Hauptmann* case and others of that era led to efforts to develop voluntary guidelines for courts, lawyers, press, and broadcasters. . . . The effort was renewed in 1965 when the American Bar Association embarked on a project to develop standards for all aspects of criminal justice, including guidelines to accommodate the right to a fair trial and the rights of a free press. . . . The resulting standards, approved by the Association in 1968, received support from most of the legal profession. . . . In the wake of these efforts, the cooperation between bar associations and members of the press led to the adoption of voluntary guidelines like Nebraska's. . . .

In practice, of course, even the most ideal guidelines are subjected to powerful strains when a case such as Simants' arises, with reporters from many parts of the country on the scene. Reporters from distant places are unlikely to consider themselves bound by local standards. They report to editors outside the area covered by the guidelines, and their editors are likely to be guided only by their own standards. To contemplate how a state court can control acts of a newspaper or broadcaster outside its jurisdiction, even though the newspapers and broadcasts reach the very community from which jurors are to be selected, suggests something of the practical difficulties of managing such guidelines. . . .

IV

The Sixth Amendment in terms guarantees "trial, by an impartial jury . . ." in federal criminal prosecutions. Because "trial by jury in criminal cases is fundamental to the American scheme of justice," the due process clause of the Fourteenth Amendment guarantees the same right in state criminal prosecutions. *Duncan* v. *Louisiana* [1968] . . .

In the overwhelming majority of criminal trials, pretrial publicity presents few unmanageable threats to this important right. But when the case is a "sensational" one tensions develop between the right of the accused to trial by an impartial jury and the rights guaranteed others by the First Amendment. The relevant decisions of this Court, even if not dispositive, are instructive by way of background. . . .

In *Sheppard* v. *Maxwell* (1966), the Court focused sharply on the impact of pretrial publicity and a trial court's duty to protect the defendant's constitutional right to a fair trial. With only Mr. Justice Black dissenting, and he without opinion, the Court ordered a new trial for the petitioner, even though the first trial had occurred 12 years before. Beyond doubt the press had shown no responsible concern for the constitutional guarantee of a fair trial; the community from which the jury was drawn had been inundated by publicity hostile to the defendant. But the trial judge "did not fulfill his duty to protect [the defendant] from the inherently prejudicial publicity which saturated the community and to control disruptive influences in the courtroom." The Court noted that "unfair and prejudicial news comment on pending trials has become increasingly prevalent," and issued a strong warning:

> Due process requires that the accused receive a trial by an impartial jury free from outside influences. Given the pervasiveness of modern communications and the difficulty of effacing prejudicial publicity from the minds of the jurors, *the trial courts must take strong measures to ensure that the balance is never weighed against the accused. . . .* Of course, there is nothing that proscribes the press from reporting events that transpire in the courtroom. But where there is a reasonable likelihood that prejudicial news prior to trial will prevent a fair trial, the judge should *continue the case* until the threat abates, *or transfer it* to another county not so permeated with publicity. In addition, *sequestration of the jury* was something the judge should have raised *sua sponte* with counsel. If publicity during the proceedings threatens the fairness of the trial, a new trial should be ordered. But we must remember that reversals are but palliatives; the cure lies in those remedial measures that will prevent the prejudice at its inception. The courts must take such steps by rule and regulation that will protect their processes from prejudicial outside interferences. *Neither prosecutors, counsel for defense, the accused, witnesses, court staff nor enforcement officers coming under the jurisdiction of the court should be permitted to frustrate its function.* Collaboration between counsel and the press as to information affecting the fairness of a criminal trial is not only subject to regulation, but is highly censurable and worthy of disciplinary measures." (Emphasis added.)

Because the trial court had failed to use even minimal efforts to insulate the trial and the jurors from the "deluge of publicity," the Court vacated the judgment of conviction and a new trial followed, in which the accused was acquitted. . . .

Cases such as these are relatively rare, and we have held in other cases that trials have been fair in spite of widespread publicity.

Taken together, these cases demonstrate that pretrial publicity — even pervasive, adverse publicity — does not inevitably lead to an unfair trial. The capacity of the jury eventually impaneled to decide the case fairly is influenced by the tone and extent of the publicity, which is in part, and often in large part, shaped by what attorneys, police, and other officials do to precipitate news coverage. The trial judge has a major responsibility. What the judge says about a case, in or out of the courtroom, is likely to appear in newspapers and broadcasts. More important, the measures a judge takes or fails to take to mitigate the effects of pretrial publicity — the measures described in *Sheppard* — may well determine whether the defendant receives a trial consistent with the requirements of due process. That this responsibility has not always been properly discharged is apparent from the decisions just reviewed.

The costs of failure to afford a fair trial are high. In the most extreme cases, like *Sheppard* and *Estes,* the risk of injustice was avoided when the convictions were reversed. But a reversal means that justice has been delayed for both the defendant and the State; in some cases, because of lapse of time retrial is impossible or further prosecution is gravely handicapped. Moreover, in borderline cases in which the conviction is not reversed, there is some possibility of an injustice unredressed. The "strong measures" outlined in *Sheppard* v. *Maxwell* are means by which a trial judge can try to avoid exacting these costs from society or from the accused.

The state trial judge in the case before us acted responsibly, out of a legitimate concern, in an effort to protect the defendant's right to a fair trial. What we must decide is not simply whether the Nebraska courts erred in seeing the possibility of real danger to the defendant's rights, but whether in the circumstances of this case the means employed were foreclosed by another provision of the Constitution.

V

The First Amendment provides that "Congress shall make no law . . . abridging the freedom . . . of the press," and it is "no longer open to doubt that the liberty of the press, and of speech, is within the liberty safeguarded by the due process clause of the Fourteenth Amendment from invasion by state action." *Near* v. *Minnesota* [1931]. . . . The Court has interpreted these guarantees to afford special protection against orders that prohibit the publication or broadcast of particular information or commentary — orders that impose a "previous" or "prior" restraint on speech. None of our decided cases on prior restraint involved restrictive orders entered to protect a defendant's right to a fair and impartial jury, but the opinions on prior restraint have a common thread relevant to this case. . . .

More recently in *New York Times Co.* v. *United States* [1971], the Government sought to enjoin the publication of excerpts from a massive, classified study of this Nation's involvement in the Vietnam conflict, going back to the end of the Second World War. The dispositive opinion of the Court simply concluded that the Government had not met its heavy burden of showing justification for the prior restraint. Each of the six concurring Justices and the three dissenting Justices expressed his views separately, but "every member of the Court, tacitly or explicitly, accepted the *Near* . . . condemnation of prior restraint as presumptively unconstitutional." . . . The Court's conclusion in *New York Times* suggests that the burden on the Government is not reduced by the temporary nature of a restraint; in that case the Government asked for a temporary restraint solely to permit it to study and assess the impact on national security of the lengthy documents at issue.

The thread running through all these cases is that prior restraints on speech and publication are the most serious and the least tolerable infringement on First Amendment rights. . . .

. . . The extraordinary protections afforded by the First Amendment carry with them something in the nature of a fiduciary duty to exercise the protected rights responsibly — a duty widely acknowledged but not always observed by editors and publishers. It is not asking too much to suggest that those who exercise First Amendment rights in newspapers or broadcasting enterprises direct some effort to protect the rights of an accused to a fair trial by unbiased jurors.

Of course, the order at issue — like the order requested in *New York Times* — does not prohibit but only postpones publication. Some news can be delayed and most commentary can even more readily be delayed without serious injury, and there often is a self-imposed delay when responsible editors call for verification of information. But such delays are normally slight and they are self-imposed. Delays imposed by governmental authority are a different matter.

> We have learned, and continue to learn, from what we view as the unhappy experiences of other nations where government has been allowed to meddle in the internal editorial affairs of newspapers. Regardless of how beneficent-sounding the purposes of controlling the press might be, we . . . remain intensely skeptical about those measures that would allow government to insinuate itself into the editorial rooms of this Nation's press. *Miami Herald Publishing Co.* v. *Tornillo* [1974]

As a practical matter, moreover, the element of time is not unimportant if press coverage is to fulfill its traditional function of bringing news to the public promptly.

The authors of the Bill of Rights did not undertake to assign priorities as between First Amendment and Sixth Amendment rights, ranking one as superior to the other. In this case, the petitioners would have us declare the right of an accused subordinate to their right to publish in all circumstances. But if the authors of these guarantees, fully aware of the potential conflicts between them, were unwilling or unable to resolve the issue by assigning to one priority over the other, it is not for us to rewrite the Constitution by undertaking what they declined to do. It is unnecessary, after nearly two centuries, to establish a priority applicable in all circumstances. Yet it is nonetheless clear that the barriers to prior restraint remain high unless we are to abandon what the Court has said for nearly a quarter of our national existence and implied throughout all of it. The history of even wartime suspension of categorical guarantees, such as habeas corpus or the right to trial by civilian courts, see *Ex parte Milligan* [1867] cautions against suspending explicit guarantees.

The Nebraska courts in this case enjoined the publication of certain kinds of information about the *Simants* case. There are, as we suggested earlier, marked differences in setting and purpose between the order entered here and the orders in *Near* . . . and *New York Times,* but as to the underlying issue — the right of the press to be free from *prior* restraints on publication — those cases form the backdrop against which we must decide this case.

VI

We turn now to the record in this case to determine whether, as Learned Hand put it, "the gravity of the 'evil,' discounted by its improbability, justifies such invasion of free speech as is necessary to avoid the danger." *United States* v. *Dennis* [1951]. . . . To do so, we must examine the evidence before the trial judge when the order was entered to determine (a) the nature and extent of pretrial news coverage; (b) whether other measures would be likely to mitigate the effects of unrestrained pretrial publicity; and (c) how effectively a restraining order would operate to prevent the threatened danger. The precise terms of the restraining order are also important. We must then consider whether the record supports the entry of a prior restraint on publication, one of the most extraordinary remedies known to our jurisprudence.

A

. . . Our review of the pretrial record persuades us that the trial judge was justified in concluding that there would be intense and pervasive pretrial publicity concerning this case. He could also reasonably conclude, based on common human experience, that publicity might impair the defendant's right to a fair trial. He did not purport to say more, for he found only "a clear and present danger that pre-trial publicity *could* impinge upon the defendant's right to a fair trial." (Emphasis added.) His conclusion as to the impact of such publicity on prospective jurors was of necessity speculative, dealing as he was with factors unknown and unknowable.

B

We find little in the record that goes to another aspect of our task, determining whether measures short of an order restraining all publication would have insured the defendant a fair trial. . . .

We have noted earlier that pretrial publicity, even if pervasive and concentrated, cannot be regarded as leading automatically and in every kind of criminal case to an unfair trial. . . . There is no finding that alternative measures would not have protected Simants' rights, and the Nebraska Supreme Court did no more than imply that such measures might not be adequate. Moreover, the record is lacking in evidence to support such a finding.

C

We must also assess the probable efficacy of prior restraint on publication as a workable method of protecting Simants' right to a fair trial, and we cannot ignore the reality of the problems of managing and enforcing pretrial restraining orders. . . .

Finally, we note that the events disclosed by the record took place in a community of 850 people. It is reasonable to assume that, without any news accounts being printed or broadcast, rumors would travel swiftly by word of mouth. One can only speculate on the accuracy of such reports, given the generative propensities of rumors; they could well be more damaging than reasonably accurate news accounts. But plainly a whole community cannot be restrained from discussing a subject intimately affecting life within it.

Given these practical problems, it is far from clear that prior restraint on publication would have protected Simants' rights.

D

Finally, another feature of this case leads us to conclude that the restrictive order entered here is not supportable. At the outset the County Court entered a very broad restrictive order, the terms of which are not before us; it then held a preliminary hearing open to the public and the press. There was testimony concerning at least two incriminating statements made by Simants to private persons; the statement — evidently a confession — that he gave to law enforcement officials was also introduced. . . .

To the extent that this order prohibited the reporting of evidence adduced at the open preliminary hearing, it plainly violated settled principles: "[T]here is nothing that proscribes the press from reporting events that transpire in the courtroom." *Sheppard* v. *Maxwell* [1966]. . . . The County Court could not know that closure of the preliminary hearing was an alternative open to it until the Nebraska Supreme Court so construed state law; but once a public hearing had been held, what transpired there could not be subject to prior restraint. . . .

E

The record demonstrates, as the Nebraska courts held, that there was indeed a risk that pretrial news accounts, true or false, would have some adverse impact on the attitudes of those who might be called as jurors. But on the record now before us it is not clear that further publicity, unchecked, would so distort the views of potential jurors that 12 could not be found who would, under proper instructions, fulfill their sworn duty to render a just verdict exclusively on the evidence presented in open court.

We cannot say on this record that alternatives to a prior restraint on petitioners would not have sufficiently mitigated the adverse effects of pretrial publicity so as to make prior restraint unnecessary. Nor can we conclude that the restraining order actually entered would serve its intended purpose. Reasonable minds can have few doubts about the gravity of the evil pretrial publicity can work, but the probability that it would do so here was not demonstrated with the degree of certainty our cases on prior restraint require. . . .

Our analysis ends as it began, with a confrontation between prior restraint imposed to protect one vital constitutional guarantee and the explicit command of another that the freedom to speak and publish shall not be abridged. We reaffirm that the guarantees of freedom of expression are not an absolute prohibition under all circumstances, but the barriers to prior restraint remain high and the presumption against its use continues intact. We hold that, with respect to the order entered in this case prohibiting reporting or commentary on judicial proceedings held in public, the barriers have not been overcome; to the extent that this order restrained publication of such material, it is clearly invalid. To the extent that it prohibited publication based on information gained from other sources, we conclude that the heavy burden imposed as a condition to securing a prior restraint was not met and the judgment of the Nebraska Supreme Court is therefore

Reversed.

Mr. Justice White, concurring.

Technically there is no need to go farther than the Court does to dispose of this case, and I join the Court's opinion. I should add, however, that for the reasons which the Court itself canvasses there is grave doubt in my mind whether orders with respect to the press such as were entered in this case would ever be justifiable. It may be the better part of discretion, however, not to announce such a rule in the first case in which the issue has been squarely presented here. Perhaps we should go no further than absolutely necessary until the federal courts, and ourselves, have been exposed to a broader spectrum of cases presenting similar issues. If the recurring result, however, in case after case is to be similar to our judgment today, we should at some point announce a more general rule and avoid the interminable litigation that our failure to do so would necessarily entail.

Mr. Justice Powell wrote a separate concurring opinion. . . .

Mr. Justice Brennan, with whom Mr. Justice Stewart and Mr. Justice Marshall join, concurring in the judgment.

. . . The right to a fair trial by a jury of one's peers is unquestionably one of the most precious and sacred safeguards enshrined in the Bill of

Rights. I would hold, however, that resort to prior restraints on the freedom of the press is a constitutionally impermissible method for enforcing that right; judges have at their disposal a broad spectrum of devices for ensuring that fundamental fairness is accorded the accused without necessitating so drastic an incursion on the equally fundamental and salutary constitutional mandate that discussion of public affairs in a free society cannot depend on the preliminary grace of judicial censors. . . .

I unreservedly agree with Mr. Justice Black that "free speech and fair trials are two of the most cherished policies of our civilization, and it would be a trying task to choose between them." *Bridges* v. *California* [1961]. . . . But I would reject the notion that a choice is necessary, that there is an inherent conflict that cannot be resolved without essentially abrogating one right or the other. To hold that courts cannot impose any prior restraints on the reporting of or commentary upon information revealed in open court proceedings, disclosed in public documents, or divulged by other sources with respect to the criminal justice system is not, I must emphasize, to countenance the sacrifice of precious Sixth Amendment rights on the altar of the First Amendment. For although there may in some instances be tension between uninhibited and robust reporting by the press and fair trials for criminal defendants, judges possess adequate tools short of injunctions against reporting for relieving that tension. To be sure, these alternatives may require greater sensitivity and effort on the part of judges conducting criminal trials than would the stifling of publicity through the simple expedient of issuing a restrictive order on the press; but that sensitivity and effort is required in order to ensure the full enjoyment and proper accommodation of both First and Sixth Amendment rights.

There is, beyond peradventure, a clear and substantial damage to freedom of the press whenever even a temporary restraint is imposed on reporting of material concerning the operations of the criminal justice system, an institution of such pervasive influence in our constitutional scheme. And the necessary impact of reporting even confessions can never be so direct, immediate, and irreparable that I would give credence to any notion that prior restraints may be imposed on that rationale. It may be that such incriminating material would be of such slight news value or so inflammatory in particular cases that responsible organs of the media, in an exercise of self-restraint, would choose not to publicize that material, and not make the judicial task of safeguarding precious rights of criminal defendants more difficult. Voluntary codes such as the Nebraska Bar-Press Guidelines are a commendable acknowledgment by the media that constitutional prerogatives bring enormous responsibilities, and I would encourage continuation of such voluntary cooperative efforts between the bar and the media. However, the press may be arrogant, tyrannical, abusive, and sensationalist, just as it may be incisive, probing, and informative. But at least in the context of prior restraints on publication, the decision of what, when, and how to publish is for editors, not judges. . . . Every restrictive order imposed on the press in this case was accordingly an unconstitutional prior restraint on the freedom of the press, and I would therefore reverse the judgment of the Nebraska Supreme Court and remand for further proceedings not inconsistent with this opinion.

Mr. Justice Stevens, concurring in the judgment.

For the reasons eloquently stated by Mr. Justice Brennan, I agree that the judiciary is capable of protecting the defendant's right to a fair trial without enjoining the press from publishing information in the public domain, and that it may not do so. Whether the same absolute protection would apply no matter how shabby or illegal the means by which the information is obtained, no matter how serious an intrusion on privacy might be involved, no matter how demonstrably false the information might be, no matter how prejudicial it might be to the interest of innocent persons, and no matter how perverse the motivation for publishing it, is a question I would not answer without further argument. . . . I do, however, subscribe to most of what Mr. Justice Brennan says and, if ever required to face the issue squarely, may well accept his ultimate conclusion.

In the *Nebraska Press Association* case the Supreme Court emphasized that since closure of the preliminary hearing had not been invoked, the pretrial hearing was open to the public and the press, making the restrictive order, in effect, one of prior censorship of what could be reported. The court emphasized that the press cannot be proscribed from reporting what transpires in the courtroom, for "once a public hearing had been held, what transpired there could not be subject to prior restraint." However, the Supreme Court held in *Gannett Co.* v. *DePasquale* (1979) that a trial court could close a *pretrial* hearing to prevent prejudicial and adverse publicity. Justice Powell pointed out in a concurring opinion, "Excluding all members of the press from the courtroom . . . differs substantially from the 'gag order' at issue in *Nebraska Press,* as the latter involved a classic prior restraint . . . and applied to information irrespective of its source. In the present case, on the other hand, we are confronted with a trial court's order that in effect denies access to only one, albeit important, source. It does not in any way tell the press what it may or may not publish." The majority of the Court found that since there was no prior censorship, the freedom of the press guaranteed by the First and Fourteenth Amendments was not violated. Moreover, stated the majority, the Sixth Amendment requirement for public trials in criminal prosecutions does not extend to pretrial proceedings, which may be closed to prevent adverse publicity, provided there is evidence that the trial judge has carefully weighed the rights of access of the press under the First and Sixth Amendments with the requirements of a fair trial.

Freedom of Religion

The Establishment Clause of the First Amendment states: "Congress shall make no law respecting an establishment of religion, or prohibiting the free exercise thereof." How does this affect the rights of the individual? First, every person is free to worship in his own way. In line with this meaning, the establishment of religion cannot be curtailed by government; that is, government cannot take action that would prevent religious groups from operating in accordance with their beliefs. There are, however, exceptions, and the meaning of the protection of religion in the First Amendment has varied from one case to another. In this area as in all others involving civil liberties and civil rights the Supreme Court has had to try to balance the needs of the state with the rights of the individual. Religious freedom is not absolute.

In 1962, the Court rendered one of its most controversial decisions, *Engel v. Vitale,* 370 U.S. 421 (1962), based upon the Establishment Clause. This opinion banned the recitation of prayers in public schools.

17
ENGEL v. VITALE
370 U.S. 421 (1962)

Mr. Justice Black delivered the opinion of the Court, saying in part:

The respondent Board of Education of Union Free School District No. 9, New Hyde Park, New York, acting in its official capacity under state law, directed the School District's principal to cause the following prayer to be said aloud by each class in the presence of a teacher at the beginning of each school day:

> Almighty God, we acknowledge our dependence upon Thee, and we beg Thy blessings upon us, our parents, our teachers and our country.

This daily procedure was adopted on the recommendation of the State Board of Regents, a governmental agency created by the state Constitution to which the New York Legislature has granted broad supervisory, executive, and legislative powers over the state's public school system. These state officials composed the prayer which they recommended and published as a part of their "Statement on Moral and Spiritual Training in the Schools," saying: "We believe that this Statement will be subscribed to by all men and women of good will, and we call upon all of them to aid in giving life to our program."

Shortly after the practice of reciting the Regents' prayer was adopted by the School District, the parents of ten pupils brought this action in a New York State Court insisting that use of this official prayer in the public schools was contrary to the beliefs, religions, or religious practices of both themselves and their children. Among other things, these parents challenged the constitutionality of both the state law authorizing the School District to direct the use of prayer in public schools and the School District's regulation ordering the recitation of this particular prayer on the ground that these actions of official governmental agencies violate that part of the First Amendment of the federal Constitution which commands that "Congress shall make no law respecting an establishment of religion" — a command which was "made applicable to the state of New York by the Fourteenth Amendment of the said Constitution." The New York Court of Appeals, over the dissents of Judges Dye and Fuld, sustained an order of the lower state courts which had upheld the power of New York to use the Regents' prayer as a part of the daily procedures of its public schools so long as the schools did not compel any pupil to join in the prayer over his or her parents' objection. We granted certiorari to review this important decision involving rights protected by the First and Fourteenth Amendments.

We think that by using its public school system to encourage recitation of the Regents' prayer, the state of New York has adopted a practice wholly inconsistent with the Establishment Clause. There can, of course, be no doubt that New York's program of daily classroom invocation of God's blessings as prescribed in the Regents' prayer is a religious activity. It is a solemn avowal of divine faith and supplication for the blessings of the Almighty. The nature of such a prayer has always been religious, none of the respondents has denied this and the trial court expressly so found. . . .

The petitioners contend among other things that the state laws requiring or permitting use of the Regents' prayer must be struck down as a violation of the Establishment Clause because that prayer was composed by governmental officials as a part of a governmental program to further religious beliefs. For this reason, petitioners argue, the state's use of the Regents' prayer in its public school system breaches the constitutional wall of separation between church and state. We agree with that contention since we think that the constitutional prohibition against laws respecting an establishment of religion must at least mean that in this country it is no part of the business of government to compose official prayers for any group of the American people to recite as a part of a religious program carried on by government.

It is a matter of history that this very practice of establishing governmentally composed prayers for religious services was one of the reasons which caused many of our early colonists to leave England and seek religious freedom in America. The Book of Common Prayer, which was created under governmental direction and which was approved by Acts of Parliament in 1548 and 1549, set out in minute detail the accepted form and content of prayer and other religious ceremonies to be used in the established, tax-supported Church of England. The controversies over the Book and what should be its content repeatedly threatened to disrupt the peace of that country as the accepted forms of prayer in the established church changed with the views of the particular ruler that happened to be in control at the time. Powerful groups representing some of the varying religious views of the people struggled among themselves to impress their particular views upon the government and obtain amendments of the Book more suitable to their respective notions of how religious services should be conducted in order that the official religious establishment would advance their particular religious beliefs. Other groups, lacking the necessary political power to influence the government on the matter, decided to leave England and its established church and seek freedom in America from England's governmentally ordained and supported religion.

It is an unfortunate fact of history that when some of the very groups which had most strenuously opposed the established Church of England found themselves sufficiently in control of colonial governments in this country to write their own prayers into law, they passed laws making their own religion the official religion of their respective colonies. Indeed, as late as the time of the Revolutionary War, there were established churches in at least eight of the thirteen former colonies and established religions in at least four of the other five. But the successful Revolution against English political domination was shortly followed by intense opposition to the practice of establishing religion by law. . . .

By the time of the adoption of the Constitution, our history shows that there was a widespread awareness among many Americans of the dangers of a union of church and state. . . . The First Amendment was added to the Constitution to stand as a guarantee that neither the power nor the prestige of the federal government would be used to control, support or influence the kinds of prayer the American people can say — that the people's religions must not be subjected to the pressures of government for change each time a new political administration is elected to office. Under that amendment's prohibition against governmental establishment of religion, as reinforced by the provisions of the Fourteenth Amendment, government in this country, be it state or federal, is without power to prescribe by law any particular form of prayer which is to be used as an official prayer in carrying on any program of governmentally sponsored religious activity.

There can be no doubt that New York's state prayer program officially establishes the religious beliefs embodied in the Regents' prayer. The respondents' argument to the contrary, which is largely based upon the contention that the Regents' prayer is "nondenominational" and the fact that the program, as modified and approved by state courts, does not require all pupils to recite the prayer but permits those who wish to do so to remain silent or be excused from the room, ignores the essential nature of the program's constitutional defects. Neither the fact that the prayer may be denominationally neutral, nor the fact that its observance on the part of the students is voluntary can serve to free it from the limitations of the Establishment Clause, as it might from the Free Exercise Clause, of the First Amendment, both of which are operative against the states by virtue of the Fourteenth Amendment. Although these two clauses may in certain instances overlap, they forbid two quite different kinds of governmental encroachment upon religious freedom. The Establishment Clause, unlike the Free Exercise Clause, does not depend upon any showing of direct governmental compulsion and is violated by the enactment of laws which establish an official religion whether those laws operate directly to coerce nonobserving individuals or not. This is not to say, of course, that laws officially prescribing a particular form of religious worship do not involve coercion of such individuals. When the power, prestige and financial support of government is placed behind a particular religious belief, the indirect coercive pressure upon religious minorities to conform to the prevailing officially approved religion is plain. But the purposes underlying the Establishment Clause go much further than that. Its first and most immediate purpose rested on the belief that a union of government and religion tends to destroy government and to degrade religion. The history of governmentally established religion, both in England and in this country, showed that whenever government had allied itself with one particular form of religion, the inevitable result has been that it had incurred the hatred, disrespect and even contempt of those who held contrary beliefs. That same history showed that many people had lost their respect for any religion that had relied upon the support of government to spread its faith. The Establishment Clause thus stands as an expression of principle on the part of the Founders of our Constitution that religion is too personal, too sacred, too holy, to permit its "unhallowed perversion" by a civil magistrate. Another purpose of the Establishment Clause rested upon an awareness of the historical fact that governmentally established religions and religious persecutions go hand in hand. The founders knew that only a few years after the Book of Common Prayer became the only accepted form of religious services in the established Church of England, an Act of Uniformity was passed to compel all Englishmen to attend those services and to make it a criminal offense to conduct or attend religious gatherings of any other kind — a law which was consistently flouted by dissenting religious groups in England and which contributed to widespread persecutions of people like John Bunyan who persisted in holding "unlawful [religious] meetings . . . to the great disturbance and distraction of the good subjects of this kingdom. . . ." And they knew that similar persecutions had received the sanction of law in several of the colonies in this country soon after the establishment of official religions in those colonies. It was in large part to get completely away from this sort of systematic religious persecution that the Founders brought into being our Nation, our Constitution, and our Bill of Rights with its prohibition against any governmental establishment of religion. The New York laws officially prescribing the Regents' prayer are inconsistent with both the purposes of the Establishment Clause and with the Establishment Clause itself.

It has been argued that to apply the Constitution in such a way as to prohibit state laws respecting an establishment of religious services in public schools is to indicate a hostility toward religion or toward prayer. Nothing, of course, could be more wrong. The history of man is inseparable from the history of religion. And perhaps it is not too much to say that since the beginning of that history many people have devoutly believed that "More things are wrought by prayer than this world dreams of." It was doubtless largely due to men who believed this that there grew up a sentiment that caused men to leave the cross-currents of officially established state religions and religious persecution in Europe and come to this country filled with the hope that they could find a place in which they could pray when they pleased to the God of their faith in the language they chose. And there were men of this same faith in the power of prayer who led the fight for adoption of our Constitution and also for our Bill of Rights with the very guarantees of religious freedom that forbid the sort of governmental activity which New York has attempted here. These men knew that the First Amendment, which tried to put an end to governmental control of religion and of prayer, was not written to destroy either. They knew rather that it was written to quite well-justified fears which nearly all of them felt arising out of an awareness that governments of the past had shackled men's tongues to make them speak only the religious thoughts that government wanted them to speak and to pray only to the God that government wanted them to pray to. It is neither sacrilegious nor antireligious to say that each separate government in this country should stay out of the business of writing or sanctioning official prayers and leave that purely religious function to the people themselves and to those the people choose to look to for religious guidance.

It is true that New York's establishment of its Regents' prayer as an officially approved religious doctrine of that state does not amount to a total establishment of one particular religious sect to the exclusion of all others — that, indeed, the governmental endorsement of that prayer seems relatively insignificant when compared to the governmental encroachments upon religion which were commonplace 200 years ago. To those who may subscribe to the view that because the Regents' official prayer is so brief and general there can be no danger to religious freedom in its governmental establishment, however, it may be appropriate to say in the words of James Madison, the author of the First Amendment:

> [I]t is proper to take alarm at the first experiment on our liberties. . . . Who does not see that the same authority which can establish Christianity, in

exclusion of all other Religions, may establish with the same ease any particular sect of Christians, in exclusion of all other Sects? That the same authority which can force a citizen to contribute three pence only of his property for the support of any one establishment, may force him to conform to any other establishment in all cases whatsoever?

The judgment of the Court of Appeals of New York is reversed and the cause remanded for further proceedings not inconsistent with this opinion.

Reversed and remanded.

Mr. Justice Frankfurter took no part in the decision of this case.

Mr. Justice White took no part in the consideration or decision of this case.

Mr. Justice Douglas concurred in a separate opinion.

Mr. Justice Stewart, dissenting.

A local school board in New York has provided that those pupils who wish to do so may join in a brief prayer at the beginning of each school day, acknowledging their dependence upon God and asking His blessing upon them and upon their parents, their teachers, and their country. The court today decides that in permitting this brief nondenominational prayer the school board has violated the Constitution of the United States. I think this decision is wrong.

The Court does not hold, nor could it, that New York has interfered with the free exercise of anybody's religion. For the state courts have made clear that those who object to reciting the prayer must be entirely free of any compulsion to do so, including any "embarrassments and pressure." Cf. *West Virginia State Board of Education* v. *Barnette,* 319 U.S. 624. But the Court says that in permitting school children to say this simple prayer, the New York authorities have established "an official religion."

With all respect, I think the Court has misapplied a great constitutional principle. I cannot see how an "official religion" is established by letting those who want to say a prayer say it. On the contrary, I think that to deny the wish of these school children to join in reciting this prayer is to deny them the opportunity of sharing in the spiritual heritage of our nation.

The Court's historical review of the quarrels over the Book of Common Prayer in England throws no light for me on the issue before us in this case. England had then and has now an established church. Equally unenlightening, I think, is the history of the early establishment and later rejection of an official church in our own states. For we deal here not with the establishment of a state church, which would, of course, be constitutionally impermissible, but with whether school children who want to begin their day by joining in prayer must be prohibited from doing so. Moreover, I think that the Court's task, in this as in all areas of constitutional adjudication, is not responsibly aided by the uncritical invocation of metaphors like the "wall of separation," a phrase nowhere to be found in the Constitution. What is relevant to the issue here is not the history of an established church in sixteenth-century England or in eighteenth-century America, but the history of the religious traditions of our people, reflected in countless practices of the institutions and officials of our government.

At the opening of each day's session of this Court we stand, while one of our officials invokes the protection of God. Since the days of John Marshall our Crier has said, "God save the United States and this Honorable Court." Both the Senate and the House of Representatives open their daily sessions with prayer. Each of our Presidents, from George Washington to John F. Kennedy, has upon assuming his office asked the protection and help of God.

The Court today says that the state and federal governments are without constitutional power to prescribe any particular form of words to be recited by any group of the American people on any subject touching religion. The third stanza of "The Star-Spangled Banner," made our national anthem by Act of Congress in 1931, contains these verses:

Blest with victory and peace, may the heav'n rescued land
Praise the Pow'r that hath made and preserved us a nation!
Then conquer we must, when our cause it is just,
And this be our motto, "In God is our Trust."

In 1954 Congress added a phrase to the Pledge of Allegiance to the Flag so that it now contains the words "one Nation *under God* indivisible, with liberty and justice for all." In 1952 Congress enacted legislation calling upon the President each year to proclaim a National Day of Prayer. Since 1865 the words "IN GOD WE TRUST" have been impressed on our coins.

Countless similar examples could be listed, but there is no need to belabor the obvious. It was all summed up by this Court just ten years ago in a single sentence: "We are a religious people whose institutions presuppose a Supreme Being." *Zoarch* v. *Clauson,* 343 U.S. 306, 313.

I do not believe that this Court, or the Congress, or the President has by the actions and practices I have mentioned established an "official religion" in violation of the Constitution. And I do not believe the state of New York has done so in this case. What each has done has been to recognize and to follow the deeply entrenched and highly cherished spiritual traditions of our nation — traditions which come down to us from those who almost two hundred years ago avowed their "firm reliance on the Protection of Divine Providence" when they proclaimed the freedom and independence of this brave new world.

I dissent.

A storm of controversy arose over the Supreme Court's decision in *Engel* v. *Vitale.* Misunderstanding the intention of the Supreme Court, which was clearly to *increase* religious freedom rather than restrict it, opponents of the school prayer decision succeeded in introducing a proposed constitutional amendment in Congress, that would have overruled the Supreme Court's decision. Known as the Becker Amendment, it had the support of extremist groups throughout the country as well as many well-intentioned citizens who felt that the Court's decision unduly restricted their religious freedom and indeed implied a bias against religion. The proposed amendment, on which the key House Judiciary Committee refused to act, had virtually no chance of passing the first Congressional hurdle. It clearly overruled decisions of the Supreme Court that had prevented the use of public school facilities for religious exercises, as well as its opinion in the school prayer case. A similar amendment failed by only twenty-eight votes to pass the House in 1971.

The Supreme Court has long held that there must be a wall of separation between church and state, which means that government cannot discriminate among religious creeds. There has always been a controversy over federal aid to parochial schools. It has been virtually impossible for Congress to reach an agreement upon the extent to which private schools with religious affiliations should receive federal aid. It is questionable how much aid can be given without jeopardizing the separation of church and state.

At the state and local level, separation between church and state has raised many questions. Should bus transportation be given to private school students as well as those attending the public schools? Should released time be given for religious exercises in the public schools? And, perhaps the most controversial of all, should public schools have officially sanctioned prayers?

In the case of *Everson* v. *Board of Education,* 330 U.S. 1 (1947), the Supreme Court had to face the issue of how far local government could go in aiding Roman Catholic parochial schools. New Jersey had authorized local boards of education to reimburse parents for money they spent on bus transportation without regard to the nature of the school attended. Both those going to public and private schools could receive reimbursement. When this statute was challenged as a violation of the wall of separation doctrine, the Supreme Court upheld it. In its opinion the Court pointed out that secular education serves a public purpose, and therefore tax money can be spent on private nonprofit schools as well as on public education. Although reimbursement for bus transportation to parochial schools constituted a degree of aid to religion, it was not in this case considered sufficient to justify a holding that it violated the First Amendment. The state was not acting as an agent of any religion, but remained neutral. It was providing a public service for all school children, in much the same way as it provides policemen and traffic control to assist children in reaching school safely.

Another issue that has developed concerning freedom of religion is whether the public schools may institute a "released time" program to permit religious instruction during the school day. In *McCollum* v. *Board of Education,* 333 U.S. 203 (1948), the Court held that a board of education could not use tax-supported property for religious instruction. An Illinois program had been providing for released time for students while they received religious instruction on school property. In *Zorach* v. *Clauson,* 343 U.S. 306 (1952), the Court retreated slightly from its decision in *McCollum* when it upheld a New York program that permitted students to go to religious centers beyond school property for religious instruction during the school day.

The status of the wall of separation doctrine today is ambiguous. The Supreme Court has held that a religious oath for office requiring an expressed belief in God is unconstitutional. (See *Torcaso* v. *Watkins,* 367 U.S. 488 [1961].) But Sunday closing laws are not unconstitutional, for even though they may once have had a religious motivation, today they achieve secular goals. (See *McGowan* v. *Maryland,* 366 U.S. 420 [1961].) In the educational area, the Court held in *Tilton* v. *Richardson,* 403 U.S. 672 (1971) that Congress could give some aid to secular higher education, although in companion cases it barred state aid to elementary and secondary education.

Equal Protection of the Laws: School Desegregation

By now most students are thoroughly familiar with the evolution of the "separate but equal" doctrine first enunciated by the Supreme Court in *Plessy* v. *Ferguson,* 163 U.S. 537 (1896). Students should note that what is involved in cases in this area is legal interpretation of the provision in the Fourteenth Amendment that no state may deny "to any person within its jurisdiction the equal protection of the laws." The *Plessy* case stated that separate but equal accommodations, required by state law to be established on railroads in Louisiana, did not violate the equal protection of the laws clause of the Fourteenth Amendment. The Court went on to say that the object of the Fourteenth Amendment:

> ... was undoubtedly to enforce the absolute equality of the two races before the law, but in the nature of things it could not have been intended to abolish distinction based upon color, or to enforce social, as distinguished from political, equality, or a commingling of the two races upon terms unsatisfactory to either. Laws permitting, and even requiring, their separation in places where they are liable to be brought into contact do not necessarily imply the inferiority of either race to the other, and have been generally, if not universally, recognized as within the competency of the state legislatures in the exercise of their police power. The most common instance of this is connected with the establishment of separate schools for white and colored children, which has been held to be a valid exercise of the legislative power even by courts of States where the political rights of the colored race have been longest and most earnestly enforced.

Both the police power and education are within the reserved powers of the states; they are reserved, however, only insofar as they do not conflict with provisions of the Constitution. The Supreme Court, in *Brown* v.

Board of Education, 347 U.S. 483 (1954), finally crystallized its interpretation of the equal protection of the laws clause in a way that resulted in a significant decrease in state power in an area traditionally reserved to states, viz., education. In addition, a general principle was established which extended far beyond the field of education.

18
BROWN v. BOARD OF EDUCATION OF TOPEKA
347 U.S. 483 (1954)

Mr. Chief Justice Warren delivered the opinion of the Court, saying in part:

These cases come to us from the states of Kansas, South Carolina, Virginia, and Delaware. They are premised on different facts and different local conditions, but a common legal question justifies their consideration together in this consolidated opinion.

In each of the cases, minors of the Negro race, through their legal representatives, seek the aid of the courts in obtaining admission to the public schools of their community on a nonsegregated basis. In each instance, they had been denied admission to schools attended by white children under laws requiring or permitting segregation according to race. This segregation was alleged to deprive the plaintiffs of the equal protection of the laws under the Fourteenth Amendment. In each of the cases other than the Delaware case, a three-judge federal district court denied relief to the plaintiffs on the so-called "separate but equal" doctrine announced by this Court in *Plessy* v. *Ferguson*. . . .

The plaintiffs contend that segregated public schools are not "equal" and cannot be made "equal," and that hence they are deprived of the equal protection of the laws. Because of the obvious importance of the question presented, the Court took jurisdiction. . . .

In the first cases in this Court construing the Fourteenth Amendment, decided shortly after its adoption, the Court interpreted it as proscribing all state-imposed discriminations against the Negro race. The doctrine of "separate but equal" did not make its appearance in this Court until 1896 in the case of *Plessy* v. *Ferguson, supra,* involving not education but transportation. American courts have since labored with the doctrine for over half a century. In this Court, there have been six cases involving the "separate but equal" doctrine in the field of public education. . . . In more recent cases, all on the graduate school level, inequality was found in that specific benefits enjoyed by white students were denied to Negro students of the same educational qualifications. . . . In none of these cases was it necessary to re-examine the doctrine to grant relief to the Negro plaintiff. And in *Sweatt* v. *Painter* [339 U.S. 629 (1950)], the Court expressly reserved decision on the question whether *Plessy* v. *Ferguson* should be held inapplicable to public education.

In the instant cases, that question is directly presented. Here, unlike *Sweatt* v. *Painter,* there are findings below that the Negro and white schools involved have been equalized, or are being equalized, with respect to buildings, curricula, qualifications and salaries of teachers, and other "tangible" factors. Our decision, therefore, cannot turn on merely a comparison of these tangible factors in the Negro and white schools involved in each of the cases. We must look instead to the effect of segregation itself on public education.

In approaching this problem, we cannot turn the clock back to 1868 when the Amendment was adopted, or even to 1896 when *Plessy* v. *Ferguson* was written. We must consider public education in the light of its full development and its present place in American life throughout the Nation. Only in this way can it be determined if segregation in public schools deprives these plaintiffs of the equal protection of the laws.

Today, education is perhaps the most important function of state and local governments. Compulsory school attendance laws and the great expenditures for education both demonstrate our recognition of the importance of education to our democratic society. It is required in the performance of our most basic public responsibilities, even service in the armed forces. It is the very foundation of good citizenship. Today it is a principal instrument in awakening the child to cultural values, in preparing him for later professional training, and in helping him to adjust normally to his environment. In these days, it is doubtful that any child may reasonably be expected to succeed in life if he is denied the opportunity of an education. Such an opportunity, where the state has undertaken to provide it, is a right which must be made available to all on equal terms.

We come then to the question presented: Does segregation of children in public schools solely on the basis of race, even though the physical facilities and other "tangible" factors may be equal, deprive the children of the minority group of equal educational opportunities? We believe that it does.

In *Sweatt* v. *Painter, supra,* in finding that a segregated law school for Negroes could not provide them equal educational opportunities, this Court relied in large part on "those qualities which are incapable of objective measurement but which make for greatness in a law school." In *McLaurin* v. *Oklahoma State Regents, supra* [339 U.S. 637 (1950)], the Court, in requiring that a Negro admitted to a white graduate school be treated like all other students, again resorted to intangible considerations: "his ability to study, to engage in discussions and exchange views with other students, and, in general, to learn his profession." Such considerations apply with added force to children in grade and high schools. To separate them from others of similar age and qualifications solely because of their race generates a feeling of inferiority as to their status in the community that may affect their hearts and minds in a way unlikely ever to be undone. The effect of this separation of their educational opportunities was well stated by a finding in the Kansas case by a court which nevertheless felt compelled to rule against the Negro plaintiffs:

> Segregation of white and colored children in public schools has a detrimental effect upon the colored children. The impact is greater when it has the sanction of the law; for the policy of separating the races is usually interpreted as denoting the inferiority of the Negro group. A sense of inferiority affects the motivation of a child to learn. Segregation with the sanction of law, therefore, has a tendency to retard the educational and mental development of Negro children and to deprive them of some of the benefits they would receive in a racially integrated school system.

Whatever may have been the extent of psychological knowledge at the time of *Plessy* v. *Ferguson,* this finding is amply supported by modern authority. Any language in *Plessy* v. *Ferguson* contrary to this finding is rejected.

We conclude that in the field of public education the doctrine of "separate but equal" has no place. Separate educational facilities are inherently unequal. Therefore, we hold that the plaintiffs and others similarly situated for whom the actions have been brought are by reason of the segregation complained of, deprived of the equal protection of the laws guaranteed by the Fourteenth Amendment. This disposition makes unnecessary any discussion whether such segregation also violates the Due Process Clause of the Fourteenth Amendment.

Because these are class actions, because of the wide applicability of this decision, and because of the great variety of local conditions, the formulation of decrees in these cases presents problems of considerable complexity. On re-argument, the consideration of appropriate relief was necessarily subordinate to the primary question — the constitutionality of segregation in public education. We have now announced that such segregation is a denial of the equal protection of the laws. In order that we may have the full assistance of the parties in formulating decrees, the cases will be restored to the docket, and the parties are requested to present further argument on Questions 4 and 5 previously propounded by the Court for the re-argument this Term [which deal with the implementation of desegregation]. The Attorney General of the United States is again invited to participate. The Attorneys General of the states requiring or permitting segregation in public education will also be permitted to appear as *amici curiae* upon request to do so by September 15, 1954, and submission of briefs by October 1, 1954. It is so ordered.

On the same day the decision was announced in the *Brown* case (1954), the Court held that segregation in the District of Columbia was unconstitutional on the basis of the due process clause of the Fifth Amendment. (See *Bolling* v. *Sharpe,* 347 U.S. 497 [1954].) This situation reversed the normal one in that a protection explicitly afforded citizens of states was not expressly applicable against the national government, and could be made so only through interpreting it into the concept of due process of law.

After hearing the views of all interested parties in the *Brown* case the Court, on May 31, 1955, announced its decision concerning the implementation of desegregation in public schools.

19

BROWN v. BOARD OF EDUCATION OF TOPEKA
349 U.S. 294 (1955)

Mr. Chief Justice Warren delivered the opinion of the Court, saying in part:

These cases were decided on May 17, 1954. The opinions of that date, declaring the fundamental principle that racial discrimination in public education is unconstitutional, are incorporated herein by reference. All provisions of federal, state, or local law requiring or permitting such discrimination must yield to this principle. There remains for consideration the manner in which relief is to be accorded.

Because these cases arose under different local conditions and their disposition will involve a variety of local problems, we requested further argument on the question of relief. . . . The parties, the United States, and the states of Florida, North Carolina, Arkansas, Oklahoma, Maryland, and Texas filed briefs and participated in the oral argument.

These presentations were informative and helpful to the Court in its consideration of the complexities arising from the transition to a system of public education freed of racial discrimination. The presentations also demonstrated that substantial steps to eliminate racial discrimination in public schools have already been taken, not only in some of the communities in which these cases arose, but in some of the states appearing as *amici curiae,* and in other states as well. Substantial progress has been made in the District of Columbia and in the communities in Kansas and Delaware involved in this litigation. The defendants in the cases coming to us from South Carolina and Virginia are awaiting the decision of this Court concerning relief.

Full implementation of these constitutional principles may require solution of varied local school problems. School authorities have the primary responsibility for elucidating, assessing, and solving these problems; courts will have to consider whether the action of school authorities constitutes good faith implementation of the governing constitutional principles. Because of their proximity to local conditions and the possible need for further hearings, the courts which originally heard these cases can best perform this judicial appraisal. Accordingly, we believe it appropriate to remand the cases to those courts.

In fashioning and effectuating the decrees, the courts will be guided by equitable principles. Traditionally, equity has been characterized by a practical flexibility in shaping its remedies and by a facility for adjusting and reconciling public and private needs. These cases call for the exercise of these traditional attributes of equity power. At stake is the personal interest of the plaintiffs in admission to public schools as soon as practicable on a nondiscriminatory basis. To effectuate this interest may call for elimination of a variety of obstacles in making the transition to school systems operated in accordance with the constitutional principles set forth in our May 17, 1954, decision. Courts of equity may properly take into account the public interest in the elimination of such obstacles in a systematic and effective manner. But it should go without saying that the vitality of these constitutional principles cannot be allowed to yield simply because of disagreement with them.

While giving weight to these public and private considerations, the courts will require that the defendants make a prompt and reasonable start toward full compliance with our May 17, 1954, ruling. Once such a start has been made, the courts may find that additional time is necessary to carry out the ruling in an effective manner. The burden rests upon the defendants to establish such time is necessary in the public interest and is consistent with good faith compliance at the earliest practicable date. To that end, the courts may consider problems related to administration, arising from the physical condition of the school plant, the school transportation system, personnel, revision of school districts and attendance areas into compact units to achieve a system of determining admission to the public schools on a nonracial basis, and revision of local laws and regulations which may be necessary in solving the foregoing problems. They will also consider the adequacy of any plans the defendants may propose to meet these problems and to effectuate a transition to a racially nondiscriminatory school system. During this period of transition, the courts will retain jurisdiction of these cases.

The judgments below, except that in the Delaware case, are accordingly reversed and the cases are remanded to the District Courts to take such proceedings and enter such orders and decrees consistent with this opinion as are necessary and proper to admit to public schools on a racially nondiscriminatory basis with all deliberate speed the parties to these cases. The judgment in the Delaware case — ordering the immediate admission of the plaintiffs to schools previously attended only by white children — is affirmed on the basis of the principles stated in our May 17, 1954, opinion, but the case is remanded to the Supreme Court of Delaware for such further proceedings as that Court may deem necessary in the light of this opinion.

It is so ordered.

After the second decision of the Supreme Court in *Brown* v. *Board of Education* in 1955, it soon became clear that many Southern states would proceed with deliberate speed not to implement the desegregation of public schools but to obstruct the intent of the Supreme Court. The Southern Manifesto, signed by 101 Congressmen from 11 Southern states in 1956, clearly indicated the line that would be taken by many Southern Congressmen to justify defiance of the Supreme Court. The gist of the Manifesto was simply that the Supreme Court did not have the constitutional authority to interfere in an area such as education, which falls within the reserved powers of the states.

After the two *Brown* decisions in 1954 and 1955, the implementation for desegregation in the South was very slow. Ten years later, less than 10 percent of the black pupils in the lower educational levels in the Southern states that had had legally segregated education before were enrolled in integrated schools. It was not until 1970 that substantial progress was made in the South. Between 1968 and 1970 the percentage of black students in all-black schools in eleven Southern states decreased from 68.0 percent to 18.4 percent. One device used to circumvent the Supreme Court's decisions was to establish de facto dual school systems, similar to those that exist in most Northern cities, whereby students are assigned to schools on the basis of the neighborhoods in which they live. Such systems are not de jure segregation because they are not based upon a law requiring segregation per se, but simply upon school board regulations assigning pupils on the basis of where they live. De facto school systems can be as segregated as were the de jure systems previously existing in the South, but the question is to what extent can courts interfere to break up de facto segregation patterns since they are not based upon legal stipulations?

In *Swann* v. *Charlotte-Mecklenburg County Board of Education,* 402 U.S. 1 (1971), the Supreme Court held that in Southern states with a history of legally segregated education the District Courts have broad power to assure "unitary" school systems by requiring: (1) reassignment of teachers, so that each school faculty will reflect a racial balance similar to that which exists in the community as a whole; (2) reassignment of pupils to reflect a racial ratio similar to that which exists within the total community; (3) the use of noncontiguous school zones and the grouping of schools for the purpose of attendance to bring about racial balance; and (4) the use of busing of elementary and secondary school students within the school system to achieve racial balance.

This case and companion cases were referred to at the time as school "busing" cases, and caused tremendous controversy within the South because communities felt they were not being treated on an equal basis with their Northern counterparts, where de facto segregation is for the most part not subject to judicial intervention. The Nixon Administration, which favored neighborhood schools, was firmly opposed to the transportation of students beyond normal geographic school zones to achieve racial balance. Democratic Senator Ribicoff of Connecticut attempted to attach an amendment to an administration-sponsored bill providing $1.5 billion to aid school districts in the South in the desegregation of facilities that would have required nationwide integration of pupils from intercity schools with children from the suburbs. The amendment was defeated on April 21, 1971, by a vote of 51 to 35, with most Republicans voting against it and 13 of 34 Northern Democrats opposed. Busing remains a highly controversial political issue.

Swann v. *Charlotte-Mecklenburg County Board* (1971) held that the courts could order busing of school children within the limits of the city school district if necessary to achieve desegrated educational facilities. In the case of Charlotte-Mecklenburg the limits of the city school district included the surrounding county. However, only eighteen of the country's 100 largest city school districts contain both the inner city and the surrounding county. In cities such as San Francisco, Denver, Pasadena, and Boston, court-ordered busing plans pertained only to the central city school district. In 1974 the Supreme Court reviewed a busing plan for Detroit ordered by a federal District Court and sustained by the Court of Appeals that would have required the busing of students among fifty-four separate school districts in the Detroit metropolitan area to achieve racially balanced schools. The decision of the lower federal court in the Detroit case set a new precedent that required busing among legally separate school districts. Proponents of the Detroit busing plan argued that the central city of Detroit was 70 percent Black, and that the only way integration could be achieved would be to link the school district of Detroit with the surrounding white suburban school districts. In *Milliken* v. *Bradley,* 418 U.S. 717 (1974), the Supreme Court held that the court-ordered Detroit busing plan could not be sustained under the Equal Protection Clause of the Fourteenth Amendment, which was the constitutional provision relied upon in the lower court's decision to require busing. The Supreme Court found that there was no evidence of disparate treatment of white and Black students among the fifty-three outlying school districts that surround Detroit. The only evidence of discrimination was within the city limits of Detroit itself. Therefore, since the outlying districts did not violate the Equal Protection Clause they could not be ordered to integrate their systems with that of Detroit. Since discrimination was limited to Detroit, the court order to remedy the situation must be limited to Detroit also. The effect of the decision is to leave standing court orders for busing within school districts, but to prevent the forced merger of inner city schools with legally separate suburban school districts.

Equal Protection of the Laws: Reverse Discrimination

When the law treats racial groups differently, it is almost invariably the case that the Court will declare the law to be a violation of the equal protection clause of the Fourteenth Amendment or, where federal action is involved, the standards of equal protection required under the due process clause of the Fifth Amendment.[1]

Before the era of the Warren court, which began in 1953 and led immediately to the *Brown* decision, the Supreme Court applied a "rational-relation" or "conceivable-basis" test to determine if legislative classifications that treated separate groups of people differently constituted a violation of equal protection standards. Generally, under these tests the Court upheld the legislative classifications if it found there was a rational relationship between the classifications and legislative goals. Such classifications were also upheld if the Court found a conceivable basis upon which to support the reasoning of the legislature in creating classifications. These equal protection standards are referred to as the "old equal protection."

The Warren court inaugurated the "new equal protection" standards to apply to legislative classifications based on race or other "suspect" group classifications. For example, gender-classifications have come to be regarded by the Burger court as at least semi-suspect.[2] The new equal protection standards required the demonstration of a "compelling" governmental interest to uphold the legislative classifications under review. The new equal protection standards also required the demonstration of a compelling governmental interest to sustain legislative classifications that burdened fundamental rights. For example, in *Shapiro* v. *Thompson,* 394 U.S. 618 (1969), the Warren court reviewed challenges to state and District of Columbia laws denying welfare assistance to persons who had not resided within their jurisdictions for at least one year immediately prior to applying for assistance. The Court found that the laws burdened the fundamental right to travel, and therefore could be sustained only upon the demonstration of a compelling governmental interest. The Court found no such compelling interest present and held the laws to be unconstitutional. The application of the new equal protection standard is called *strict judicial scrutiny.* When the Court employs this

---

[1] An important exception to the rigid application of equal protection standards to racial classification was the holding of the Supreme Court in *Korematsu* v. *United States,* 323 U.S. 214 (1944), which upheld a racial classification that treated Japanese-Americans differently than other citizens. The Court found that the federal government could exclude Japanese-Americans from military zones on the West Coast on the ground of national security, a holding that in effect supported the establishment of relocation centers for Japanese-American citizens during World War II.

[2] See, for example, *Frontiero* v. *Richardson,* 411 U.S. 677 (1973).

strict judicial scrutiny, the invariable effect is to declare unconstitutional the classification in the law under review.

In the *Bakke* case, presented below, the opinions of justices Powell and Brennan discuss the circumstances under which strict judicial scrutiny is required by the equal protection clause of the Fourteenth Amendment. This case arose out of a complex set of circumstances. Title VI of the Civil Rights Act of 1964 provided that no person was to be "subjected to discrimination under any program or activity receiving federal financial assistance." The Department of Health, Education and Welfare found this section to require affirmative action programs by private institutions receiving federal aid, to achieve a racial balance among employees and, in institutions of higher learning, within their student bodies as well. Under pressure from civil rights groups, women, and other minorities, many affirmative action plans were adopted throughout the country that contained racial classifications providing for the favored treatment of racial minorities in school admissions and private employment.

The *Bakke* case was initiated by Allan Bakke, a 36-year-old white engineer who decided that he wanted to become a doctor. In 1973 and 1974 he applied, unsuccessfully, for admission to the University of California Medical School at Davis. The school informed Bakke that there were too many qualified applicants and that it could admit only one out of 26 in 1973, and one out of 37 in 1974. However, 16 of the 100 openings in the Davis medical school were set aside for minority applicants. Bakke's objective qualifications, such as his Medical College Admission Test scores and his undergraduate grades, were better than those of some of the minority applicants that were accepted during the years when he was rejected. The minority applicants competed among themselves for the 16 places reserved for them, making it possible to admit minority students with different qualifications than were required of nonminority applicants. Bakke claimed that the admissions procedures violated the equal protection clause and Title VI of the Civil Rights Act of 1964.

The trial court in the *Bakke* case held that the admissions program established racial quotas in violation of the equal protection clause and Title VI. However, the court refused to order the admission of Bakke to the medical school because of his failure to prove that he would have been admitted in the absence of the special program for minorities. The California Supreme Court sustained the trial court's finding that the program violated the equal protection clause and the Civil Rights Act but overruled the trial court's denial of an order that Bakke be admitted. The United States Supreme Court granted certiorari to the California Supreme Court to review the case.

The California Supreme Court, by a five-four vote, ruled that Bakke should be admitted to the Davis Medical School. The majority on the issue of admittance agreed that the racial quota system at the school was not an acceptable means to decide who should be admitted. The majority justices favoring admission and a ban on quotas were Powell, Burger, Stevens, Rehnquist, and Stewart. Brennan, White, Marshall, and Blackmun dissented on these issues, arguing that "Davis's special admissions program cannot be said to violate the Constitution simply because it has set aside a predetermined number of places for qualified minority applicants. . . ."

Justice Louis F. Powell, who was in the majority favoring admission and a ban on quotas, joined with the four justices who dissented from the Court's decision and opinion on those issues to form another majority that held that an applicant's race can be considered in deciding who should be admitted to a university program.

20
REGENTS OF THE UNIVERSITY OF CALIFORNIA v. BAKKE
438 U.S. 265 (1978)

Mr. Justice Powell announced the judgment of the Court and wrote an opinion:

For the reasons stated in the following opinion, I believe that so much of the judgment of the California court as holds petitioner's special admissions program unlawful and directs that respondent be admitted to the Medical School must be affirmed. For the reasons expressed in a separate opinion, my Brothers The Chief Justice, Mr. Justice Stewart, Mr. Justice Rehnquist, and Mr. Justice Stevens concur in this judgment.

I also conclude for the reasons stated in the following opinion that the portion of the court's judgment enjoining petitioner from according any consideration to race in its admissions process must be reversed. For reasons expressed in separate opinions, My Brothers Mr. Justice Brennan, Mr. Justice White, Mr. Justice Marshall, and Mr. Justice Blackmun concur in this judgment.

Affirmed in part and reversed in part.

II

B

The language of § 601 [of the Civil Rights Act of 1964], like that of the Equal Protection Clause, is majestic in its sweep:

> No person in the United States shall, on the ground of race, color, or national origin, be excluded from participation in, be denied the benefits

of, or be subjected to discrimination under any program or activity receiving Federal financial assistance.

The concept of "discrimination," like the phrase "equal protection of the laws," is susceptible of varying interpretations, for as Mr. Justice Holmes declared, "[a] word is not a crystal, transparent and unchanged, it is the skin of a living thought and may vary greatly in color and content according to the circumstances and the time in which it is used." . . . We must, therefore, seek whatever aid is available in determining the precise meaning of the statute before us. . . . Examination of the voluminous legislative history of Title VI reveals a congressional intent to halt federal funding of entities that violate a prohibition of racial discrimination similar to that of the Constitution. Although isolated statements of various legislators, taken out of context, can be marshaled in support of the proposition that § 601 enacted a purely color-blind scheme, without regard to the reach of the Equal Protection Clause, these comments must be read against the background of both the problem that Congress was addressing and the broader view of the statute that emerges from a full examination of the legislative debates.

The problem confronting Congress was discrimination against Negro citizens at the hands of recipients of federal moneys. Indeed, the color blindness pronouncements [of Congress] generally occur in the midst of extended remarks dealing with the evils of segregation in federally funded programs. Over and over again, proponents of the bill detailed the plight of Negroes seeking equal treatment in such programs. There simply was no reason for Congress to consider the validity of hypothetical preferences that might be accorded minority citizens; the legislators were dealing with the real and pressing problem of how to guarantee those citizens equal treatment.

In addressing that problem, supporters of Title VI repeatedly declared that the bill enacted constitutional principles. . . .

In the Senate, Senator Humphrey declared that the purpose of Title VI was "to insure that Federal funds are spent in accordance with the Constitution and the moral sense of the Nation." . . .

Further evidence of the incorporation of a constitutional standard into Title VI appears in the repeated refusals of the legislation's supporters precisely to define the term "discrimination." Opponents sharply criticized this failure, but proponents of the bill merely replied that the meaning of "discrimination" would be made clear by reference to the Constitution or other existing law. . . .

In view of the clear legislative intent, Title VI must be held to proscribe only those racial classifications that would violate the Equal Protection Clause or the Fifth Amendment.

III

A

Petitioner does not deny that decisions based on race or ethnic origin by faculties and administrations of state universities are reviewable under the Fourteenth Amendment. . . . For his part, respondent does not argue that all racial or ethnic classifications are *per se* invalid. . . . The parties do disagree as to the level of judicial scrutiny to be applied to the special admissions program. Petitioner argues that the court below erred in applying strict scrutiny, as this inexact term has been applied in our cases. . . .

En route to this crucial battle over the scope of judicial review, the parties fight a sharp preliminary action over the proper characterization of the special admissions program. Petitioner prefers to view it as establishing a "goal" of minority representation in the Medical School. Respondent, echoing the courts below, labels it a racial quota.

This semantic distinction is beside the point: The special admissions program is undeniably a classification based on race and ethnic background. To the extent that there existed a pool of at least minimally qualified minority applicants to fill the 16 special admissions seats, white applicants could compete only for 84 seats in the entering class, rather than the 100 open to minority applicants. Whether this limitation is described as a quota or a goal, it is a line drawn on the basis of race and ethnic status.

The guarantees of the Fourteenth Amendment extend to all persons. Its language is explicit: "No State shall . . . deny to any person within its jurisdiction the equal protection of the laws." It is settled beyond question that the "rights created by the first section of the Fourteenth Amendment are, by its terms, guaranteed to the individual. The rights established are personal rights" . . . . The guarantee of equal protection cannot mean one thing when applied to one individual and something else when applied to a person of another color. If both are not accorded the same protection, then it is not equal.

Nevertheless, petitioner argues that the court below erred in applying strict scrutiny to the special admissions program because white males, such as respondent, are not a "discrete and insular minority" requiring extraordinary protection from the majoritarian political process. . . . This rationale, however, has never been invoked in our decisions as a prerequisite to subjecting racial or ethnic distinctions to strict scrutiny. Nor has this Court held that discreteness and insularity constitute necessary preconditions to a holding that a particular classification is invidious. . . . These characteristics may be relevant in deciding whether or not to add new types of classifications to the list of "suspect" categories or whether a particular classification survives close examination. . . . Racial and ethnic classifications, however, are subject to stringent examination without regard to these additional characteristics. We declared as much in the first cases explicitly to recognize racial distinctions as suspect:

> Distinctions between citizens solely because of their ancestry are by their very nature odious to a free people whose institutions are founded upon the doctrine of equality. *Hirabayashi* [v. *United States* (1943)].

> [A]ll legal restrictions which curtail the civil rights of a single racial group are immediately suspect. That is not to say that all such restrictions are unconstitutional. It is to say that courts must subject them to the most rigid scrutiny. *Korematsu* [v. *United States* (1944)].

The Court has never questioned the validity of those pronouncements. Racial and ethnic distinctions of any sort are inherently suspect and thus call for the most exacting judicial examination. . . .

Although many of the Framers of the Fourteenth Amendment conceived of its primary function as bridging the vast distance between members of the Negro race and the white "majority" . . . the amendment itself was framed in universal terms, without reference to color, ethnic origin, or condition of prior servitude. As this Court recently remarked in interpreting the 1866 Civil Rights Act to extend to claims of racial discrimination against white persons, "the 39th Congress was intent upon establishing in the federal law a broader principle than would have been necessary simply to meet the particular and immediate plight of the newly freed Negro slaves." . . .

Over the past 30 years, this Court has embarked upon the crucial mission of interpreting the Equal Protection Clause with the view of assuring to all persons "the protection of equal laws . . ." in a Nation confronting a legacy of slavery and racial discrimination. . . . Because the landmark decisions in this area arose in response to the continued exclusion of Negroes from the mainstream of American society, they could be characterized as involving discrimination by the "majority" white race against the Negro minority. But they need not be read as depending upon that characterization for their results. It suffices to say that "[o]ver the years, this Court has consistently repudiated '[d]istinctions between citizens solely because of their ancestry' as being 'odious to a free people whose institutions are founded upon the doctrine of equality.' " . . .

Petitioner urges us to adopt for the first time a more restrictive view of the Equal Protection Clause and hold that discrimination against members of the white "majority" cannot be suspect if its purpose can be characterized as "benign." The clock of our liberties, however, cannot be turned back to 1868. . . . It is far too late to argue that the guarantee of equal protection to *all* persons permits the recognition of special wards entitled to a degree of protection greater than that accorded others. "The Fourteenth Amendment is not directed solely against discrimination due to a 'two-class theory' — that is, based upon differences between 'white' and Negro." . . .

Once the artificial line of a "two-class theory" of the Fourteenth Amendment is put aside, the difficulties entailed in varying the level of judicial review according to a perceived "preferred" status of a particular racial or ethnic minority are intractable. The concepts of "majority" and "minority" necessarily reflect temporary arrangements and political judgments. As observed above, the white "majority" itself is composed of various minority groups, most of which can lay claim to a history of prior discrimination at the hands of the State and private individuals. Not all of these groups can receive preferential treatment and corresponding judicial tolerance of distinctions drawn in terms of race and nationality, for then the only "majority" left would be a new minority of white Anglo-Saxon Protestants. There is no principled basis for deciding which groups would merit "heightened judicial solicitude" and which would not. Courts would be asked to evaluate the extent of the prejudice and consequent harm suffered by various minority groups. Those whose societal injury is thought to exceed some arbitrary level of tolerability then would be entitled to preferential classifications at the expense of individuals belonging to other groups. Those classifications would be free from exacting judicial scrutiny. As these preferences began to have their desired effect, and the consequences of past discrimination were undone, new judicial rankings would be necessary. The kind of variable sociological and political analysis necessary to produce such rankings simply does not lie within the judicial competence — even if they otherwise were politically feasible and socially desirable.

Moreover, there are serious problems of justice connected with the idea of preference itself. First, it may not always be clear that a so-called preference is in fact benign. . . . Second, preferential programs may only reinforce common stereotypes holding that certain groups are unable to achieve success without special protection based on a factor having no relationship to individual worth. . . . Third, there is a measure of inequity in forcing innocent persons in respondent's position to bear the burdens of redressing grievances not of their making.

By hitching the meaning of the Equal Protection Clause to these transitory considerations, we would be holding, as a constitutional principle, that judicial scrutiny of classifications touching on racial and ethnic background may vary with the ebb and flow of political forces. Disparate constitutional tolerance of such classifications well may serve to exacerbate racial and ethnic antagonisms rather than alleviate them. . . . Also, the mutability of a constitutional principle, based upon shifting political and social judgments, undermines the chances for consistent application of the Constitution from one generation to the next, a critical feature of its coherent interpretation. . . . In expounding the Constitution, the Court's role is to discern "principles sufficiently absolute to give them roots throughout the community and continuity over significant periods of time, and to lift them above the level of the pragmatic political judgments of a particular time and place." . . .

IV

We have held that in "order to justify the use of a suspect classification, a State must show that its purpose or interest is both constitutionally permissible and substantial, and that its use of the classification is 'necessary . . . to the accomplishment' of its purpose or the safeguarding of its interest." . . . The special admissions program purports to serve the purposes of: (i) "reducing the historic deficit of traditionally disfavored minorities in medical schools and in the medical profession"; (ii) countering the effects of societal discrimination; (iii) increasing the number of physicians who will practice in communities currently underserved; and (iv) obtaining the educational benefits that flow from an ethnically diverse student body. It is necessary to decide which, if any, of these purposes is substantial enough to support the use of a suspect classification.

A

If petitioner's purpose is to assure within its student body some specified percentage of a particular group merely because of its race or ethnic origin, such a preferential purpose must be rejected not as insubstantial but as facially invalid. Preferring members of any one group for no reason other than race or ethnic origin is discrimination for its own sake. This the Constitution forbids. . . .

B

. . . [T]he purpose of helping certain groups whom the faculty of the Davis Medical School perceived as victims of "societal discrimination" does not justify a classification that imposes disadvantages upon persons like respondent, who bear no responsibility for whatever harm the beneficiaries of the special admissions program are thought to have suffered. To hold otherwise would be to convert a remedy heretofore reserved for violations of legal rights into a privilege that all institutions throughout the Nation could grant at their pleasure to whatever groups are perceived as victims of societal discrimination. That is a step we have never approved. . . .

C

Petitioner identifies, as another purpose of its program, improving the delivery of health-care services to communities currently underserved. It may be assumed that in some situations a State's interest in facilitating the health care of its citizens is sufficiently compelling to support the use of a suspect classification. But there is virtually no evidence in the record indicating that petitioner's special admissions program is either needed or geared to promote that goal. . . .

D

The fourth goal asserted by petitioner is the attainment of a diverse student body. This clearly is a constitutionally permissible goal for an institution of higher education. Academic freedom, though not a specifically enumerated constitutional right, long has been viewed as a special concern of the First Amendment. . . .

. . . As the interest of diversity is compelling in the context of a university's admissions program, the question remains whether the program's racial classification is necessary to promote this interest. . . .

V

A

It may be assumed that the reservation of a specified number of seats in each class for individuals from the preferred ethnic groups would contribute to the attainment of considerable ethnic diversity in the student body. But petitioner's argument that this is the only effective means of serving the interest of diversity is seriously flawed. . . . Petitioner's special admissions program, focused *solely* on ethnic diversity, would hinder rather than further attainment of genuine diversity. . . .

The experience of other university admissions programs, which take race into account in achieving the educational diversity valued by the First Amendment, demonstrates that the assignment of a fixed number of places to a minority group is not a necessary means toward that end. . . .

B

In summary, it is evident that the Davis special admissions program involves the use of an explicit racial classification never before countenanced by this Court. It tells applicants who are not Negro, Asian, or Chicano that they are totally excluded from a specific percentage of the seats in an entering class. No matter how strong their qualifications, quantitative and extracurricular, including their own potential for contribution to educational diversity, they are never afforded the chance to compete with applicants from the preferred groups for the special admissions seats. At the same time, the preferred applicants have the opportunity to compete for every seat in the class.

The fatal flaw in petitioner's preferential program is its disregard of individual rights as guaranteed by the Fourteenth Amendment. . . . Such rights are not absolute. But when a State's distribution of benefits or imposition of burdens hinges on ancestry or the color of a person's skin or ancestry, that individual is entitled to a demonstration that the challenged classification is necessary to promote a substantial state interest. Petitioner has failed to carry this burden. For this reason, that portion of the California court's judgment holding petitioner's special admissions program invalid under the Fourteenth Amendment must be affirmed.

C

In enjoining petitioner from ever considering the race of any applicant, however, the courts below failed to recognize that the State has a substantial interest that legitimately may be served by a properly devised admissions program involving the competitive consideration of race and ethnic origin. For this reason, so much of the California court's judgment as enjoins petitioner from any consideration of the race of any applicant must be reversed.

Opinion of Mr. Justice Brennan, Mr. Justice White, Mr. Justice Marshall, and Mr. Justice Blackmun, concurring in the judgment in part and dissenting in part.

The Court today, in reversing in part the judgment of the Supreme Court of California, affirms the constitutional power of Federal and State Governments to act affirmatively to achieve equal opportunity for all. The difficulty of the issue presented — whether government may use race-conscious programs to redress the continuing effects of past discrimination — and the mature consideration which each of our Brethren has brought to it have resulted in many opinions, no single one speaking for the Court. But this should not and must not mask the central meaning of today's opinions: Government may take race into account when it acts not to demean or insult any racial group, but to remedy disadvantages cast on minorities by past racial prejudice, at least when appropriate findings have been made by judicial, legislative, or administrative bodies with competence to act in this area.

The Chief Justice and our Brothers Stewart, Rehnquist, and Stevens, have concluded that Title VI of the Civil Rights Act of 1964, . . . as amended, . . . prohibits programs such as that at the Davis Medical School. On this statutory theory alone, they would hold that respondent Allan Bakke's rights have been violated and that he must, therefore, be admitted to the Medical School. Our Brother Powell, reaching the Constitution, concludes that, although race may be taken into account in university admissions, the particular special admissions program used by petitioner, which resulted in the exclusion of respondent Bakke, was not shown to be necessary to achieve petitioner's stated goals. Accordingly, these Members of the Court form a majority of five affirming the judgment of the Supreme

Court of California insofar as it holds that respondent Bakke "is entitled to an order that he be admitted to the University." . . .

We agree with Mr. Justice Powell that, as applied to the case before us, Title VI goes no further in prohibiting the use of race than the Equal Protection Clause of the Fourteenth Amendment itself. We also agree that the effect of the California Supreme Court's affirmance of the judgment of the Superior Court of California would be to prohibit the University from establishing in the future affirmative action programs that take race into account. . . . Since we conclude that the affirmative admissions program at the Davis Medical School is constitutional, we would reverse the judgment below in all respects. Mr. Justice Powell agrees that some uses of race in university admissions are permissible and, therefore, he joins with us to make five votes reversing the judgment below insofar as it prohibits the University from establishing race-conscious programs in the future. . . .

II

. . . In our view, Title VI prohibits only those uses of racial criteria that would violate the Fourteenth Amendment if employed by a State or its agencies; it does not bar the preferential treatment of racial minorities as a means of remedying past societal discrimination to the extent that such action is consistent with the Fourteenth Amendment. The legislative history of Title VI, administrative regulations interpreting the statute, subsequent congressional and executive action, and the prior decisions of this Court compel this conclusion. None of these sources lends support to the proposition that Congress intended to bar all race-conscious efforts to extend the benefits of federally financed programs to minorities who have been historically excluded from the full benefits of American life. . . .

III

A

The assertion of human equality is closely associated with the proposition that differences in color or creed, birth or status, are neither significant nor relevant to the way in which persons should be treated. Nonetheless, the position that such factors must be "constitutionally an irrelevance" . . . summed up by the shorthand phrase "[o]ur Constitution is color-blind." *Plessy* v. *Ferguson* [1896] . . . has never been adopted by this Court as the proper meaning of the Equal Protection Clause. Indeed, we have expressly rejected this proposition on a number of occasions.

Our cases have always implied that an "overriding statutory purpose" . . . could be found that would justify racial classifications. . . .

We conclude, therefore, that racial classifications are not *per se* invalid under the Fourteenth Amendment. Accordingly, we turn to the problem of articulating what our role should be in reviewing state action that expressly classifies by race.

B

Respondent argues that racial classifications are always suspect and, consequently, that this Court should weigh the importance of the objectives served by Davis' special admissions program to see if they are compelling. . . .

Unquestionably we have held that a government practice or statute which restricts "fundamental rights" or which contains "suspect classifications" is to be subjected to "strict scrutiny" and can be justified only if it furthers a compelling government purpose and, even then, only if no less restrictive alternative is available. . . . But no fundamental right is involved here. . . . Nor do whites as a class have any of the "traditional indicia of suspectness: the class is not saddled with such disabilities, or subjected to such a history of purposeful unequal treatment, or relegated to such a position of political powerlessness as to command extraordinary protection from the majoritarian political process." . . .

On the other hand, the fact that this case does not fit neatly into our prior analytic framework for race cases does not mean that it should be analyzed by applying the very loose rational-basis standard of review that is the very least that is always applied in equal protection cases. " '[T]he mere recitation of a benign, compensatory purpose is not an automatic shield which protects against any inquiry into the actual purposes underlying a statutory scheme.' " . . . Instead, a number of considerations — developed in gender-discrimination cases but which carry even more force when applied to racial classifications — lead us to conclude that racial classifications designed to further remedial purposes " 'must serve important governmental objectives and must be substantially related to achievement of those objectives.' " . . .

First, race, like "gender-based classifications too often [has] been inexcusably utilized to stereotype and stigmatize politically powerless segments of society." . . . State programs designed ostensibly to ameliorate the effects of past racial discrimination obviously create the same hazard of stigma, since they may promote racial separatism and reinforce the views of those who believe that members of racial minorities are inherently incapable of succeeding on their own. . . .

Second, race, like gender and illegitimacy . . . is an immutable characteristic which its possessors are powerless to escape or set aside. While a classification is not *per se* invalid because it divides classes on the basis of an immutable characteristic . . . it is nevertheless true that such divisions are contrary to our deep belief that "legal burdens should bear some relationship to individual responsibility or wrongdoing" . . . and that advancement sanctioned, sponsored, or approved by the State should ideally be based on individual merit or achievement, or at the least on factors within the control of an individual. . . .

In sum, because of the significant risk that racial classifications established for ostensibly benign purposes can be misused, causing effects not unlike those created by invidious classifications, it is inappropriate to inquire only whether there is any conceivable basis that might sustain such a classification. Instead, to justify such a classification an important and articulated purpose for its use must be shown. In addition, any statute must be stricken that stigmatizes any group or that singles out those least well represented in the political process to bear the brunt of a benign program. Thus, our review under the Fourteenth Amendment should be strict — not " 'strict' in theory and fatal in fact," because it is stigma that causes fatality — but strict and searching nonetheless.

IV

Davis' articulated purpose of remedying the effects of past societal discrimination is, under our cases, sufficiently important to justify the use of race-conscious admissions programs where there is a sound basis for concluding that minority underrepresentation is substantial and chronic, and that the handicap of past discrimination is impeding access of minorities to the Medical School. . . .

A

. . . If it was reasonable to conclude — as we hold that it was — that the failure of minorities to qualify for admission at Davis under regular procedures was due principally to the effects of past discrimination, than there is a reasonable lieklihood that, but for pervasive racial discrimination, respondent would have failed to qualify for admission even in the absence of Davis' special admissions program.

Thus, our cases under Title VII of the Civil Rights Act have held that, in order to achieve minority participation in previously segregated areas of public life, Congress may require or authorize preferential treatment for those likely disadvantaged by societal racial discrimination. Such legislation has been sustained even without a requirement of findings of intentional racial discrimination by those required or authorized to accord preferential treatment, or a case-by-case determination that those to be benefited suffered from racial discrimination. These decisions compel the conclusion that States also may adopt race-conscious programs designed to overcome substantial, chronic minority underrepresentation where there is reason to believe that the evil addressed is a product of past racial discrimination. . . .

[Section B reviews the facts supporting the existence of discrimination and the underrepresentation of minorities in the Davis and other medical schools.]

C

The second prong of our test — whether the Davis program stigmatizes any discrete group or individual and whether race is reasonably used in light of the program's objectives — is clearly satisfied by the Davis program.

It is not even claimed that Davis' program in any way operates to stigmatize or single out any discrete and insular, or even any identifiable, nonminority group. Nor will harm comparable to that imposed upon racial minorities by exclusion or separation on grounds of race be the likely result of the program. It does not, for example, establish an exclusive preserve for minority students apart from and exclusive of whites. Rather, its purpose is to overcome the effects of segregation by bringing the races together. True, whites are excluded from participation in the special admissions program, but this fact only operates to reduce the number of whites to be admitted in the regular admissions program in order to permit admission of a reasonable percentage — less than their proportion of the California population — of otherwise underrepresented qualified minority applicants.

Nor was Bakke in any sense stamped as inferior by the Medical School's rejection of him. Indeed, it is conceded by all that he satisfied those criteria regarded by the school as generally relevant to academic performance better than most of the minority members who were admitted. Moreover, there is absolutely no basis for concluding that Bakke's rejection as a result of Davis' use of racial preference will affect him throughout his life in the same way as the segregation of the Negro school children in *Brown I* would have affected them. Unlike discrimination against racial minorities, the use of racial preferences for remedial purposes does not inflict a pervasive injury upon individual whites in the sense that wherever they go or whatever they do there is a significant likelihood that they will be treated as second-class citizens because of their color. This distinction does not mean that the exclusion of a white resulting from the preferential use of race is not sufficiently serious to require justification; but it does mean that the injury inflicted by such a policy is not distinguishable from disadvantages caused by a wide range of government actions, none of which has ever been thought impermissible for that reason alone.

In addition, there is simply no evidence that the Davis program discriminates intentionally or unintentionally against any minority group which it purports to benefit. The program does not establish a quota in the invidious sense of a ceiling on the number of minority applicants to be admitted. Nor can the program reasonably be regarded as stigmatizing the program's beneficiaries or their race as inferior. The Davis program does not simply advance less qualified applicants; rather, it compensates applicants, who it is uncontested are fully qualified to study medicine, for educational disadvantages which it was reasonable to conclude were a product of state-fostered discrimination. Once admitted, these students must satisfy the same degree requirements as regularly admitted students; they are taught by the same faculty in the same classes; and their performance is evaluated by the same standards by which regularly admitted students are judged. Under these circumstances, their performance and degrees must be regarded equally with the regularly admitted students with whom they compete for standing. Since minority graduates cannot justifiably be regarded as less well qualified than nonminority graduates by virtue of the special admissions program, there is no reasonable basis to conclude that minority graduates at schools using such programs would be stigmatized as inferior by the existence of such programs.

D

We disagree with the lower courts' conclusion that the Davis program's use of race was unreasonable in light of its objectives. First, as petitioner argues, there are no practical means by which it could achieve its ends in the foreseeable future without the use of race-conscious measures. With respect to any factor (such as poverty or family educational background) that may be used as a substitute for race as an indicator of past discrimination, whites greatly outnumber racial minorities simply because whites make up a far larger percentage of the total population and therefore far outnumber minorities in absolute terms at every socioeconomic level. . . .

Second, the Davis admissions program does not simply equate minority status with disadvantage. Rather, Davis considers on an individual basis each applicant's personal history to determine whether he or she has likely been disadvantaged by racial discrimination. The record makes clear that only minority applicants likely to have been isolated from the mainstream of American life are considered in the special program; other minority applicants are eligible only through the regular admissions program. . . .

V

Accordingly, we would reverse the judgment of the Supreme Court of California holding the Medical School's special admissions program unconstitutional and directing respondent's admission, as well as that portion of the judgment enjoining the Medical School from according any consideration to race in the admissions process.

Mr. Justice Marshall wrote a separate opinion.
Mr. Justice Blackmun wrote a separate opinion.

Mr. Justice Stevens, with whom the Chief Justice, Mr. Justice Stewart, and Mr. Justice Rehnquist join, concurring in the judgment in part and dissenting in part. . . .

Both petitioner and respondent have asked us to determine the legality of the University's admissions program by reference to the Constitution. Our settled practice, however, is to avoid the decision of a constitutional issue if a case can be fairly decided on a statutory ground. "If there is one doctrine more deeply rooted than any other in the process of constitutional adjudication, it is that we ought not to pass on questions of constitutionality . . . unless such adjudication is unavoidable." . . . The more important the issue, the more force there is to this doctrine. In this case, we are presented with a constitutional question of undoubted and unusual importance. Since, however, a dispositive statutory claim was raised at the very inception of this case, and squarely decided in the portion of the trial court judgment affirmed by the California Supreme Court, it is our plain duty to confront it. Only if petitioner should prevail on the statutory issue would it be necessary to decide whether the University's admissions program violated the Equal Protection Clause of the Fourteenth Amendment.

Section 601 of the Civil Rights Act of 1964 . . . provides:

> No person in the United States shall, on the ground of race, color, or national origin, be excluded from participation in, be denied the benefits of, or be subjected to discrimination under any program or activity receiving Federal financial assistance.

The University, through its special admissions policy, excluded Bakke from participation in its program of medical education because of his race. The University also acknowledges that it was, and still is, receiving federal financial assistance. The plain language of the statute therefore requires affirmance of the judgment below. A different result cannot be justified unless that language misstates the actual intent of the Congress that enacted the statute or the statute is not enforceable in a private action. Neither conclusion is warranted. . . .

. . . [I]t seems clear that the proponents of Title VI assumed that the Constitution itself required a colorblind standard on the part of government, but that does not mean that the legislation only codifies an existing constitutional prohibition. The statutory prohibition against discrimination in federally funded projects contained in § 601 is more than a simple paraphrasing of what the fifth or Fourteenth Amendment would require. . . .

In short, nothing in the legislative history justifies the conclusion that the broad language of § 601 should not be given its natural meaning. We are dealing with a distinct statutory prohibition, enacted at a particular time with particular concerns in mind; neither its language nor any prior interpretation suggests that its place in the Civil Rights Act, won after long debate, is simply that of a constitutional appendage. In unmistakable terms the Act prohibits the exclusion of individuals from federally funded programs because of their race. As succinctly phrased during the Senate debate, under Title VI it is not "permissible to say 'yes' to one person; but to say 'no' to another person, only because of the color of his skin." . . .

The University's special admissions program violated Title VI of the Civil Rights Act of 1964 by excluding Bakke from the Medical School because of his race. It is therefore our duty to affirm the judgment ordering Bakke admitted to the University.

Accordingly, I concur in the Court's judgment insofar as it affirms the judgment of the Supreme Court of California. To the extent that it purports to do anything else, I respectfully dissent.

How do the standards of judicial scrutiny differ in the Powell and Brennan opinions? Justice Powell wrote, "Racial and ethnic distinctions of any sort are inherently suspect and thus call for the most exacting judicial examination." Applying strict judicial scrutiny, Powell found no compelling justification for the use of racial quotas by the Davis Medical School. Powell reasoned that "The purpose of helping certain groups whom the faculty of the Davis Medical School perceived as victims of 'societal discrimination' does not justify a classification that imposes disadvantages upon persons like respondent [Bakke], who bear no responsibility for whatever harm the beneficiaries of the special admissions program are thought to have suffered." While Powell held that racial quotas are banned, he ruled that race may be taken into account in admissions programs because "the state has a substantial [i.e., compelling] interest that legitimately may be served by a properly devised admissions program involving the competitive consideration of race and ethnic origin."

The dissenting opinion of Justice Brennan supported the use of racial quotas in the Davis admissions program. Underlying Brennan's dissenting opinion was the finding that the classification under review was not "suspect," nor did it affect fundamental rights; therefore; strict judicial scrutiny, under which a compelling state interest has to be demonstrated to uphold the classification, was not required. Justice Brennan and his fellow dissenters used an intermediate standard of judicial scrutiny, which required more than the mere demonstration of a rational relationship between the classification and the goals sought but less than the demonstration of a compelling state interest to uphold the classification. The intermediate standard announced by Justice Brennan was that the classification "must serve important governmental objectives and be substantially related to achievement of those objectives." To uphold a racial classification, stated Brennan, "an important and articulated purpose for its use must be shown. In addition, any statute must be stricken that stigmatizes any group or that singles out those least well represented in the political process to bear the brunt of a benign program." Brennan concluded that the court's review should be "strict," but not at the level of strict judicial scrutiny, which, because it requires the demonstration of compelling state interests, is always fatal to the program under review.

Equal Protection of the Laws: Electoral Reapportionment

A development of profound significance to the political process has been the entrance of the federal judiciary into the sphere of legislative reapportionment. The Court has always attempted to avoid "political questions" that are highly controversial. Judicial intervention into the arena of electoral reapportionment was accompanied by a shift on the Supreme Court from a majority emphasizing self-restraint in such matters to one desiring positive judicial action.

What does the Constitution say about electoral apportionment? There is no explicit provision pertaining to representation in *state* legislatures, and regarding congressional districts, Article I provides only that each state shall have a number of representatives in proportion to its population and that every ten years this number may be changed in accordance with whatever directives Congress makes. Thus, the matter of congressional districting seemed to be solely within the jurisdiction of Congress, and by implication, the apportionment of state legislative districts would be the exclusive concern of state governments.

Gradually it became evident that leaving the redistricting up to Congress and state legislatures would not bring about equality of representation. In *Colegrove* v. *Green,* 328 U.S. 549 (1946), a strong appeal was made to the Supreme Court to change Congressional districting in Illinois that had resulted in giving a very unfair advantage to rural interests. For example, a congressional district in Chicago with a population of close to a million voters had the same representation in the House of Representatives as a southern Illinois rural district with a population of only about 100,000 voters. Regardless of such disparities, a plurality of the Supreme Court ruled that the issue of equal representation was not a matter of judicial concern and that it was a political question that should be left up to Congress to resolve. After holding in the *Colegrove* case that congressional districting was beyond judicial scrutiny, the Court later refused to intervene in the districting for elections to state legislatures. (See *South* v. *Peters,* 339 U.S. 276 [1950].)

In 1962 the judicial doctrine of self-restraint in the field of legislative reapportionment changed completely in the historic case of *Baker* v. *Carr* (1962). A civil action had been brought against the state of Tennessee to prohibit it from holding further elections under the provisions of a 1901 apportioning statute that based apportionment upon a census taken in the year 1900. All efforts to change the method of apportionment as the population of the state grew and shifted failed, resulting in what the Court called a "crazy-quilt" pattern of representation. For example, a relatively urban county with a population of approximately 37,000 voters had only twice as much representation as a rural county with a population of less that 3,000. There seemed to be no logic whatsoever in the patterns of representation from county to county. Counties with almost exactly the same number of voters had substantially different numbers of representatives in the state legislature. When the *Baker* case was initially brought before the Federal District Court in Tennessee, the action was dismissed for lack of jurisdiction on the basis of the *Colegrove* doctrine. The appellants had claimed that their rights under the Equal Protection of the Laws clause of the Fourteenth Amendment had been violated by the lack of equal representation in the state. In the opinion printed below, the Supreme Court overruled the district court decision, holding that apportionment of the Tennessee state legislature was a proper matter for judicial concern.

21
BAKER v. CARR
369 U.S. 186 (1962)

Mr. Justice Brennan delivered the opinion of the Court, saying in part:

This civil action was brought under 42 U.S.C. §§ 1983 and 1988 to redress the alleged deprivation of federal constitutional rights. The complaint, alleging that by means of a 1901 statute of Tennessee apportioning the members of the General Assembly among the state's ninety-five counties, "these plaintiffs and others similarly situated, are denied the equal protection of the laws accorded them by the Fourteenth Amendment to the Constitution of the United States by virtue of the debasement of their votes," was dismissed by a three-judge court. . . . The court held that it lacked jurisdiction of the subject matter and also that no claim was stated upon which relief could be granted. . . . We hold that the dismissal was in error, and remand the cause to the District Court for trial and further proceedings consistent with this opinion.

The General Assembly of Tennessee consists of the Senate with thirty-three members and the House of Representatives with ninety-nine members. . . .

Tennessee's standard for allocating legislative representation among her counties is the total number of qualified voters resident in the respective counties, subject only to minor qualifications. Decennial reapportionment in compliance with the constituted scheme was effected by the General Assembly each decade from 1871 to 1901. . . . In 1901 the General Assembly abandoned separate enumeration in favor of reliance upon the federal census and passed the Apportionment Act here in controversy. In the more than sixty years since that action, all proposals in both Houses of the General Assembly for reapportionment have failed to pass.

Between 1901 and 1961, Tennessee has experienced substantial growth and redistribution of her population. In 1901 the population was 2,020,616, of whom 487,380 were eligible to vote. The 1960 federal census reports the state's population at 3,567,089, of whom 2,092,891 are eligible to vote. The relative standings of the counties in terms of qualified voters have changed significantly. It is primarily the continued application of the 1901 Apportionment Act to this shifted and enlarged voting population which gives rise to the present controversy.

Indeed, the complaint alleges that the 1901 statute, even as of the time of its passage, "made no apportionment of Representatives and Senators in accordance with the constitutional formula . . . , but instead arbitrarily and capriciously apportioned representatives in the Senate and House without reference . . . to any logical or reasonable formula whatever." It is further alleged that "because of the population changes since 1900, and the failure of the legislature to reapportion itself since 1901," the 1901 statute became "unconstitutional and obsolete." Appellants also argue that, because of the composition of the legislature effected by the 1901 Apportionment Act, redress in the form of a state constitutional amendment to change the entire mechanism for reapportioning, or any other change short of that, is difficult or impossible. The complaint concludes that "these plaintiffs and others similarly situated, are denied the equal protection of the laws accorded them by the Fourteenth Amendment to the Constitution of the United States by virtue of the debasement of their votes." They seek a declaration that the 1901 statute is unconstitutional and an injunction restraining the appellees from acting to conduct any further elections under it. They also pray that unless and until the General Assembly enacts a valid reapportionment, the District Court should either decree a reapportionment by mathematical application of the Tennessee constitutional formulae to the most recent Federal Census figures, or direct the appellees to conduct legislative elections, primary and general, at large. They also pray for such other and further relief as may be appropriate.

THE DISTRICT COURT'S OPINION
AND ORDER OF DISMISSAL

Because we deal with this case on appeal from an order of dismissal granted on appellee's motions, precise identification of the issues presently confronting us demands clear exposition of the grounds upon which the District

Court rested in dismissing the case. The dismissal order recited that the court sustained the appellees' grounds "(1) that the Court lacks jurisdiction of the subject matter, and (2) that the complaint fails to state a claim upon which relief can be granted. . . ."

The court proceeded to explain its action as turning on the case's presenting a "question of the distribution of political strength for legislative purposes." For, "from a review of [numerous Supreme Court] . . . decisions there can be no doubt that the federal rule, as enunciated and applied by the Supreme Court, is that the federal courts, whether from a lack of jurisdiction or from the inappropriateness of the subject matter for judicial consideration, will not intervene in cases of this type to compel legislative reapportionment."

The court went on to express doubts as to the feasibility of the various possible remedies sought by the plaintiffs. Then it made clear that its dismissal reflected a view not of doubt that violation of constitutional rights was alleged, but of a court's impotence to correct that violation:

> With the plaintiff's argument that the legislature of Tennessee is guilty of a clear violation of the state constitution and of the rights of the plaintiffs the Court entirely agrees. It also agrees that the evil is a serious one which should be corrected without further delay. But even so the remedy in this situation clearly does not lie with the courts. It has long been recognized and is accepted doctrine that there are indeed some rights guaranteed by the Constitution for the violation of which the courts cannot give redress.

In light of the District Court's treatment of the case, we hold today only (a) that the court possessed jurisdiction of the subject matter; (b) that a justiciable cause of actions is stated upon which appellants would be entitled to appropriate relief; and (c) because appellees raise the issue before this Court, that the appellants have standing to challenge the Tennessee apportionment statutes. Beyond noting that we have no cause at this stage to doubt the District Court will be able to fashion relief if violations of constitutional rights are found, it is improper now to consider what remedy would be most appropriate if appellants prevail at the trial.

JURISDICTION OF THE SUBJECT MATTER

. . . Our conclusion, . . . that this cause presents no nonjusticiable "political question" settles the only possible doubt that it is a case or controversy [under Article 3].

Article 3 §2 of the federal Constitution provides that "the judicial Power shall extend to all Cases, in Law and Equity, arising under this Constitution, the Laws of the United States, and Treaties made, or which shall be made, under their Authority; . . . ." It is clear that the cause of action is one which "arises under" the federal Constitution. The complaint alleges that the 1901 statute effects an apportionment that deprives the appellants of the equal protection of the laws in violation of the Fourteenth Amendment. Dismissal of the complaint upon the ground of lack of jurisdiction of the subject matter would, therefore, be justified only if that claim were "so attenuated and unsubstantial as to be absolutely devoid of merit." . . . Since the District Court obviously and correctly did not deem the asserted federal constitutional claim unsubstantial and frivolous, it should not have dismissed the complaint for want of jurisdiction of the subject matter. And of course no further consideration of the merits of the claim is relevant to a determination of the court's jurisdiction of the subject matter.

An unbroken line of our precedents sustains the federal courts' jurisdiction of the subject matter of federal constitutional claims of this nature. . . .

The appellees refer to *Colegrove* v. *Green,* 328 U.S. 549, as authority that the District Court lacked jurisdiction of the subject matter. Appellees misconceive the holding of that case. The holding was precisely contrary to their reading of it. Seven members of the Court participated in the decision. Unlike many other cases in this field which have assumed without discussion that there was jurisdiction, all three opinions filed in *Colegrove* discussed the question. Two of the opinions expressing the views of four of the Justices, a majority, flatly held that there was jurisdiction of the subject matter. . . .

We hold that the District Court has jurisdiction of the subject matter of the federal constitutional claim asserted in the complaint.

STANDING

A federal court cannot "pronounce any statute, either of a state or of the United States, void, because irreconcilable with the Constitution, except as it is called upon to adjudge the legal rights of litigants in actual controversies." Have the appellants alleged such a personal stake in the outcome of the controversy as to assure that concrete adverseness which sharpens the presentation of issues upon which the court so largely depends for illumination of difficult constitutional questions? This is the gist of the question of standing. . . .

We hold that the appellants do have standing to maintain this suit. . . .

These appellants seek relief in order to protect or vindicate an interest of their own, and of those similarly situated. Their constitutional claim is, in substance, that the 1901 statute constitutes arbitrary and capricious state action, offensive to the Fourteenth Amendment in its irrational disregard of the standard of apportionment prescribed by the state's Constitution or of any standard, effecting a gross disproportion of representation to voting population. The injury which appellants assert is that this classification disfavors the voters in the counties in which they reside, placing them in a position of constitutionally unjustifiable inequality vis-à-vis voters in irrationally favored counties. A citizen's right to a vote free of arbitrary impairment by state action has been judicially recognized as a right secured by the Constitution, when such impairment resulted from dilution by a false tally, or by a refusal to count votes from arbitrarily selected precincts, or by a stuffing of the ballot box.

It would not be necessary to decide whether appellants' allegations of impairment of their votes by the 1901 apportionment will, ultimately, entitle them to any relief, in order to hold that they have standing to seek it. If such impairment does produce a legally cognizable injury, they are among those who have sustained it. They are entitled to a hearing and to the District Court's decision on their claims. "The very essence of civil liberty certainly consists in the right of every individual to claim the protection of the laws, whenever he receives an injury."

JUSTICIABILITY

In holding that the subject matter of this suit was not justiciable, the District Court relied on *Colegrove* v. *Green,* and subsequent per curiam cases. The court stated: "From a review of these decisions there can be no doubt that the federal rule . . . is that the federal courts . . . will not intervene in cases of this type to compel legislative reapportionment." We understand the District Court to have read the cited cases as compelling the conclusion that since the appellants sought to have a legislative apportionment held unconstitutional, their suit presented a "political question" and was therefore nonjusticiable. We hold that this challenge to an apportionment presents no nonjusticiable "political question." The cited cases do not hold the contrary.

Of course the mere fact that the suit seeks protection of a political right does not mean it presents a political question. Such an objection "is little more than a play upon words." Rather, it is argued that apportionment cases, whatever the actual wording of the complaint, can involve no federal constitutional right except one resting on the guaranty of a republican form of government, and that complaints based on that clause have been held to present political questions which are nonjusticiable.

We hold that the claim pleaded here neither rests upon nor implicates the Guaranty Clause and that its justiciability is therefore not foreclosed by our decisions of cases involving that clause. The District Court misinterpreted *Colegrove* v. *Green* and other decisions of this Court on which it relied. Appellants' claim that they are being denied equal protection is justiciable, and if "discrimination is sufficiently shown, the right to relief under the equal protection clause is not diminished by the fact the discrimination relates to political rights." To show why we reject the argument based on the Guaranty Clause, we must examine the authorities under it. But because there appears to be some uncertainty as to why those cases did present political questions, and specifically as to whether this apportionment case is like those cases, we deem it necessary first to consider the contours of the "political question" doctrine.

Our discussion, even at the price of extending this opinion, requires review of a number of political question cases, in order to expose the attributes of the doctrine — attributes which, in various settings, diverge, combine, appear, and disappear in seeming disorderliness. Since that review is undertaken solely to demonstrate that neither singly nor collectively do these cases support a conclusion that this apportionment case is nonjusticiable, we of course do not explore their implications in other contexts. That review reveals that in the Guaranty Clause cases and in the other "political question" cases, it is the relationship between the judiciary and the coordinate branches of the federal government, and not the federal judiciary's relationship to the states, which gives rise to the "political question."

We have said that "in determining whether a question falls within [the political question] category, the appropriateness under our system of government of attributing finality to the action of the political departments and also the lack of satisfactory criteria for a judicial determination are dominant considerations." The nonjusticiability of a political question is primarily a function of the separation of powers. Much confusion results from the capacity of the "political question" label to obscure the need for case-by-case inquiry. Deciding whether a matter has in any measure been committed by the Constitution to another branch of government, or whether the action of that branch exceeds whatever authority has been committed, is itself a delicate exercise in constitutional interpretation, and is a responsibility of this Court as ultimate interpreter of the Constitution. To demonstrate this requires no less than to analyze representative cases and to infer from them the analytical threads that make up the political question doctrine. We shall then show that none of those threads catches this case. . . .

We come, finally to the ultimate inquiry whether our precedents as to what constitutes a nonjusticiable "political question" bring the case before us under the umbrella of that doctrine. A natural beginning is to note whether any of the common characteristics which we have been able to identify and label descriptively are present. We find none: the question here is the consistency of state action with the federal Constitution. We have no question decided, or to be decided, by a political branch of government coequal with this Court. Nor do we risk embarrassment of our government abroad, or grave disturbance at home if we take issue with Tennessee as to the constitutionality of her action here challenged. Nor need the appellants, in order to succeed in this action, ask the Court to enter upon policy determinations for which judicially manageable standards are lacking. Judicial standards under the Equal Protection Clause are well developed and familiar, and it has been open to courts since the enactment of the Fourteenth Amendment to determine, if on the particular facts they must, that a discrimination reflects *no* policy, but simply arbitrary and capricious action. . . .

We conclude that the complaint's allegations of denial of equal protection present a justiciable constitutional cause of action upon which appellants are entitled to a trial and a decision. The right asserted is within the reach of judicial protection under the Fourteenth Amendment.

The judgment of the District Court is reversed and the cause is remanded for further proceedings consistent with this opinion.

Reversed and remanded.

Mr. Justice Whittaker did not participate in the decision of this case.

Mr. Justice Douglas, concurring, said in part:

While I join the opinion of the Court, and like the Court, do not reach the merits, a word of explanation is necessary. I put to one side the problems of "political" questions involving the distribution of power between this Court, the Congress, and the Chief Executive. We have here a phase of the recurring problem of the relation of the federal courts to state agencies. More particularly, the question is the extent to which a state may weight one person's vote more heavily than it does another's. . . .

It is . . . clear that by reason of the commands of the Constitution there are several qualifications that a state may not require.

Race, color, or previous condition of servitude are impermissible standards by reason of the Fifteenth Amendment. . . .

Sex is another impermissible standard by reason of the Nineteenth Amendment.

There is a third barrier to a state's freedom in prescribing qualifications of voters and that is the Equal Protection Clause of the Fourteenth Amendment, the provision invoked here. And so the question is, may a state weight the vote of one county or one district more heavily than it weights the vote in another?

The traditional test under the Equal Protection Clause has been whether a state has made "an invidious discrimination," as it does when it selects "a particular race or nationality for oppressive treatment."

I agree with my Brother Clark that if the allegations in the complaint can be sustained a case for relief is established. We are told that a single vote in Moore County, Tennessee, is worth nineteen votes in Hamilton County, that one vote in Stewart or in Chester County is worth nearly eight times a single vote in Shelby or Knox County. The opportunity to prove that an "invidious discrimination" exists should therefore be given the appellants. . . .

With the exceptions of *Colegrove* v. *Green,* 328 U.S. 549, *MacDougall* v. *Green,* 335 U.S. 281, *South* v. *Peters,* 339 U.S. 276, and the decisions they spawned, the Court has never thought that protection of voting rights was beyond judicial cognizance. Today's treatment of those cases removes the only impediment to judicial cognizance of the claims stated in the present complaint.

The justiciability of the present claims being established, any relief accorded can be fashioned in the light of well-known principles of equity.

Mr. Justice Clark, concurring, said in part:

One emerging from the rash of opinions with their accompanying clashing of views may well find himself suffering a mental blindness. The Court holds that the appellants have alleged a cause of action. However, it refuses to award relief here — although the facts are undisputed — and fails to give the District Court any guidance whatever. One dissenting opinion, bursting with words that go through so much and conclude with so little, condemns the majority action as "a massive repudiation of the experience of our whole past." Another describes the complaint as merely asserting conclusory allegations that Tennessee's apportionment is "incorrect," "arbitrary," "obsolete," and "unconstitutional." I believe it can be shown that this case is distinguishable from earlier cases dealing with the distribution of political power by a state, that a patent violation of the Equal Protection Clause of the United States Constitution has been shown, and that an appropriate remedy may be formulated. . . .

Although I find the Tennessee apportionment statute offends the Equal Protection Clause, I would not consider intervention by this Court into so delicate a field if there were any other relief available to the people of Tennessee. But the majority of the people of Tennessee have no "practical opportunities for exerting their political weight at the polls" to correct the existing "invidious discrimination." Tennessee has no initiative and referendum. I have searched diligently for other "practical opportunities" present under the law. I find none other than through the federal courts. The majority of the voters have been caught up in a legislative strait jacket. Tennessee has an "informed, civically militant electorate" and "an aroused popular conscience," but it does not sear "the conscience of the people's representatives." This is because the legislative policy has riveted the present seats in the Assembly to their respective constituencies, and by the votes of their incumbents a reapportionment of any kind is prevented. The people have been rebuffed at the hands of the Assembly; they have tried the constitutional convention route, but since the call must originate in the Assembly it, too, has been fruitless. They have tried Tennessee courts with the same result, and Governors have fought the tide only to flounder. It is said that there is recourse in Congress and perhaps that may be, but from a practical standpoint this is without substance. To date Congress has never undertaken such a task in any state. We therefore must conclude that the people of Tennessee are stymied and without judicial intervention will be saddled with the present discrimination in the affairs of their state government.

Finally, we must consider if there are any appropriate modes of effective judicial relief. The federal courts are, of course, not forums for political debate, nor should they resolve themselves into state constitutional conventions or legislative assemblies. Nor should their jurisdiction be exercised in the hope that such a declaration, as is made today, may have the direct effect of bringing on legislative action and relieving the courts of the problem of fashioning relief. To my mind this would be nothing less than blackjacking the Assembly into reapportioning the state. If judicial competence were lacking to fashion an effective decree, I would dismiss this appeal. However, like the Solicitor General of the United States, I see no such difficulty in the position of this case. One plan might be to start with the existing assembly districts, consolidate some of them, and award the seats thus released to those counties suffering the most egregious discrimination. Other possibilities are present and might be more effective. But the plan here suggested would at least release the strangle hold now on the Assembly and permit it to redistrict itself. . . .

In view of the detailed study that the Court has given this problem, it is unfortunate that a decision is not reached on the merits. The majority appears to hold, at least sub silentio, that an invidious discrimination is present, but it remands to the three-judge court for it to make what is certain to be that formal determination. It is true that Tennessee has not filed a formal answer. However, it has filed voluminous papers and made extended arguments supporting its position. At no time has it been able to contradict the appellants' factual claims; it has offered no rational explanation for the present apportionment; indeed, it has indicated that there are none known to it. As I have emphasized, the case proceeded to the point before the three-judge court that it was able to find an invidious discrimination factually present, and the state has not contested that holding here. In view of all this background I doubt if anything more can be offered or will be gained by the state on remand, other than time. Nevertheless, not being able to muster a court to dispose of the case on the merits, I concur in the opinion of the majority and acquiesce in the decision to remand. However, in fairness I do think that Tennessee is entitled to have my idea of what it faces on the record before us and the trial court some light as to how it might proceed.

As John Rutledge (later Chief Justice) said 175 years ago in the course of the Constitutional Convention, a chief function of the Court is to secure the national rights. Its decision today supports the proposition for which our forebears fought and many died, namely that "to be fully conformable to the principle of right, the form of government must be representative." That is the keystone upon which our government was founded and lacking which no republic can survive. It is well for this Court to practice self-restraint and discipline in constitutional adjudication, but never in its history have those principles received sanction where the national rights of so many have been so clearly infringed for so long a time. National respect for the courts is more enhanced through the forthright enforcement of those rights rather than by rendering them nugatory through the interposition of subterfuges. In my view the ultimate decision today is in the greatest tradition of this Court.

Mr. Justice Frankfurter, whom Mr. Justice Harlan joined, dissented, saying in part:

The Court today reverses a uniform course of decision established by a dozen cases, including one by which the very claim now sustained was unanimously rejected only five years ago. The impressive body of rulings thus cast aside reflected the equally uniform course of our political history regarding the relationship between population and legislative representation — a wholly different matter from denial of the franchise to individuals because of race, color, religion, or sex. Such a massive repudiation of the experience of our whole past in asserting destructively novel judicial power demands a detailed analysis of the role of this Court in our constitutional scheme. Disregard of inherent limits in the effective exercise of the Court's "judicial Power" not only presages the futility of judicial intervention in the essentially political conflict of forces by which the relation between population and representation has time out of mind been and now is determined. It may well impair the Court's position as the ultimate organ of "the supreme Law of the Land" in that vast range of legal problems, often strongly entangled in popular feeling, on which this Court must pronounce. The Court's authority — possessed neither of the purse nor the sword — ultimately rests on sustained public confidence in its moral sanction. Such feeling must be nourished by the Court's complete detachment, in fact and in appearance, from political entanglements and by abstention from injecting itself into the clash of political forces in political settlements.

A hypothetical claim resting on abstract assumptions is now for the first time made the basis for affording illusory relief for a particular evil even though it foreshadows deeper and more pervasive difficulties in consequence. The claim is hypothetical and the assumptions are abstract because the Court does not vouchsafe the lower courts — state and federal — guidelines for formulating specific, definite, wholly unprecedented remedies for the inevitable litigations that today's umbrageous disposition is bound to stimulate in connection with politically motivated reapportionments in so many states. In such a setting, to promulgate jurisdiction in the abstract is meaningless. It is devoid of reality as "a brooding omnipresence in the sky" for it conveys no intimation of what relief, if any, a District Court is capable of affording that would not invite legislatures to play ducks and drakes with the judiciary. For this Court to direct the District Court to enforce a claim to which the Court has over the years consistently found itself required to deny legal enforcement and at the same time to find it necessary to withhold any guidance to the lower court how to enforce this turnabout, new legal claim, manifests an odd — indeed an esoteric — conception of judicial propriety. One of the Court's supporting opinions, as elucidated by commentary, unwittingly affords a disheartening preview of the mathematical quagmire (apart from divers judicially inappropriate and elusive determinants), into which this Court today catapults the lower courts of the country without so much as adumbrating the basis for a legal calculus as a means of extrication. Even assuming the indispensable intellectual disinterestedness on the part of judges in such matters, they do not have accepted legal standards or criteria or even reliable analogies to draw upon for making judicial judgments. To charge courts with the task of accommodating the incommensurable factors of policy that underlie these mathematical puzzles is to attribute however flatteringly, omnicompetence to judges. The framers of the Constitution persistently rejected a proposal that embodied this assumption and Thomas Jefferson never entertained it.

Recent legislation, creating a district appropriately described as "an atrocity of ingenuity," is not unique. Considering the gross inequality among legislative electoral units within almost every state, the Court naturally shrinks from asserting that in districting at least substantial equality is a constitutional requirement enforceable by courts. Room continues to be allowed for weighting. This of course implies that geography, economics, urban-rural conflict, and all the other nonlegal factors which have throughout our history entered into political districting are to some extent not to be ruled out in the undefined vista now opened up by review in the federal courts of state reapportionments. To some extent — aye, there's the rub. In effect, today's decision empowers the courts of the country to devise what should constitute the proper composition of the legislatures of the fifty states. If state courts should for one reason or another find themselves unable to discharge this task, the duty of doing so is put on the federal courts or on this Court, if state views do not satisfy this Court's notion of what is proper districting.

We were soothingly told at the bar of this Court that we need not worry about the kind of remedy a court could effectively fashion once the abstract constitutional right to have courts pass on a statewide system of electoral districting is recognized as a matter of judicial rhetoric, because legislatures would heed the Court's admonition. This is not only an euphoric hope. It implies a sorry confession of judicial impotence in place of a frank acknowledgment that there is not under our Constitution a judicial remedy for every political mischief, for every undesirable exercise of legislative power. The framers carefully and with deliberate forethought refused so to enthrone the judiciary. In this situation, as in others of like nature, appeal for relief does not belong here. Appeal must be to an informed, civically militant electorate. In a democratic society like ours, relief must come through an aroused popular conscience that sears the conscience of the people's representatives. In any event there is nothing judicially more unseemly nor more self-defeating than for this Court to make in terrorem pronouncements, to indulge in merely empty rhetoric, sounding a word of promise to the ear, sure to be disappointing to the hope. . . .

Mr. Justice Harlan, whom Mr. Justice Frankfurter joined, dissented, saying in part:

The dissenting opinion of Mr. Justice Frankfurter, in which I join, demonstrates the abrupt departure the majority makes from judicial history by putting the federal courts into this area of state concerns — an area which, in this instance, the Tennessee state courts themselves have refused to enter.

It does not detract from his opinion to say that the panorama of judicial history it unfolds, though evincing a steadfast underlying principle of keeping the federal courts out of these domains, has a tendency, because of variants in expression, to becloud analysis in a given case. With due respect to the majority, I think that has happened here.

Once one cuts through the thicket of discussion devoted to "jurisdiction," "standing," "justiciability" and "political question," there emerges a straightforward issue which, in my view, is determinative of this case. Does the complaint disclose a violation of a federal constitutional right, in other words, a claim over which United States District Court would have jurisdiction . . . ? The majority opinion does not actually discuss this basic question, but, as one concurring Justice observes, seems to decide it "sub silentio." However, in my opinion, appellants' allegations, accepting all of them as true, do not, parsed down or as a whole, show an infringement by Tennessee of any rights assured by the Fourteenth Amendment. Accordingly, I believe the complaint should have been dismissed for "failure to state a claim upon which relief can be granted."

It is at once essential to recognize this case for what it is. The issue here relates not to a method of state electoral apportionment by which seats in the *federal* House of Representatives are allocated, but solely to the right of a state to fix the basis of representation in its *own* legislature. Until it is first decided to what extent that right is limited by the Federal Constitution, and whether what Tennessee has done or failed to do in this instance runs afoul of any such limitation, we need not reach the issues of "justiciability" or "political question" or any of the other considerations which in such cases as *Colegrove* v. *Green,* 328 U.S. 549, led the Court to decline to adjudicate a challenge to a state apportionment affecting seats in the federal House of Representatives, in the absence of a controlling Act of Congress.

The appellants' claim in this case ultimately rests entirely on the Equal

Protection Clause of the Fourteenth Amendment. It is asserted that Tennessee has violated the Equal Protection Clause by maintaining in effect a system of apportionment that grossly favors in legislative representation the rural sections of the state as against its urban communities. . . .

I can find nothing in the Equal Protection Clause or elsewhere in the federal Constitution which expressly or impliedly supports the view that state legislatures must be so structured as to reflect with approximate equality the voice of every voter. Not only is that proposition refuted by history, as shown by my Brother Frankfurter, but it strikes deep into the heart of our federal system. Its acceptance would require us to turn our backs on the regard which this Court has always shown for the judgment of state legislatures and courts on matters of basically local concern.

In the last analysis, what lies at the core of this controversy is a difference of opinion as to the function of representative government. It is surely beyond argument that those who have the responsibility for devising a system of representation may permissibly consider that factors other than bare numbers should be taken into account. The existence of the United States Senate is proof enough of that. To consider that we may ignore the Tennessee Legislature's judgment in this instance because that body was the product of an asymmetrical electoral apportionment would in effect be to assume the very conclusion here disputed. Hence we must accept the present form of the Tennessee Legislature as the embodiment of the state's choice, or, more realistically, its compromise, between competing political philosophies. The federal courts have not been empowered by the Equal Protection Clause to judge whether this resolution of the state's internal political conflict is desirable or undesirable, wise or unwise. . . .

. . . [R]educed to its essentials, the charge of arbitrariness and capriciousness rests entirely on the consistent refusal of the Tennessee Legislature over the past sixty years to alter a pattern of apportionment that was reasonable when conceived.

A federal District Court is asked to say that the passage of time has rendered the 1901 apportionment obsolete to the point where its continuance becomes vulnerable under the Fourteenth Amendment. But is not this matter one that involves a classic legislative judgment? Surely it lies within the province of a state legislature to conclude that an existing allocation of Senators and Representatives constitutes a desirable balance of geographical and demographical representation, or that in the interest of stability of government it would be best to defer for some further time the redistribution of seats in the state legislature.

Indeed, I would hardly think it unconstitutional if a state legislature's expressed reason for establishing or maintaining an electoral imbalance between its rural and urban population were to protect the state's agricultural interests from the sheer weight of numbers of those residing in its cities. . . .

In conclusion, it is appropriate to say that one need not agree, as a citizen, with what Tennessee has done or failed to do, in order to deprecate, as a judge, what the majority is doing today. Those observers of the Court who see it primarily as the last refuge for the correction of all inequality or injustice, no matter what its nature or source, will no doubt applaud this decision and its break with the past. Those who consider that continuing national respect for the Court's authority depends in large measure upon its wise exercise of self-restraint and discipline in constitutional adjudication, will view the decision with deep concern.

I would affirm.

After the *Baker* decision the Supreme Court on February 17, 1964, rendered additional decisions affecting Congressional apportionment. In *Wesberry* v. *Sanders,* 376 U.S. 1 (1964), the Court relied on Article I, Section 2 of the Constitution, which provides that Congressmen must be chosen "by the people of the several states," as a basis for holding that Congressional districts must be as nearly as possible equal in population. The *Baker* case was used as precedent.

Following the *Wesberry* decision the Supreme Court held, in a series of decisions in June 1964, that the Equal Protection Clause of the Fourteenth Amendment required the equal apportionment of *both* houses of state legislatures. Obviously such a decision could not be made regarding Congress because of constitutional specifications requiring that the Senate represent states as units, with two Senators for each state, regardless of population. The precedent-setting decision in June 1964 was *Reynolds* v. *Sims,* 377 U.S. 533 (1964). In holding that both houses of bicameral state legislatures must now be apportioned on a population basis, the Court nevertheless provided that some deviations might be permissible. In what can only be described as a mystical statement the Court held: "So long as the divergencies from a strict population standard are based on legitimate considerations incident to the effectuation of a rational state policy, some deviations from the equal-population principle are constitutionally permissible with respect to the apportionment of seats in either or both of the two houses of a bicameral state legislature." Thus political subdivisions of a state may be given some representation that is not directly related to population. But the Court made it abundantly clear that the states would not be permitted to stray very far from the equal-population principle.

In April, 1968, the Supreme Court extended its reapportionment doctrine by holding that a County Commissioner's Court in Texas, which was elected from single-member districts that were substantially unequal in population, violated the Equal Protection Clause of the Fourteenth Amendment. The Court held that since the County Commissioner's Court was a unit of local government with jurisdiction over the entire geographic area of the county, it was subject to the "one man — one vote" rule.

As a result of the *Baker, Reynolds,* and *Wesberry* decisions, in a majority of states attempts were made to equalize the populations of state and Congressional districts. Redistricting, however, was based upon 1960 census figures which were far out-of-date and inaccurate by the time of the 1970 census. In some cases, population variance between the largest and smallest district within a state even after redistricting was over 400,000 persons. The 1970 census figures are now being used as a basis for re-districting.

Without doubt, the Supreme Court's decisions affecting state legislatures as well as the requirements for equal populations in Congressional districts within states will have a profound effect upon the pattern of American politics. The long-felt power of the rural sections of the country will begin to fade. If the present trend toward the increment of *suburban* populations continues, these areas may begin to exercise important political power. In the final analysis the suburbs may be the biggest beneficiaries of equal apportionment. Therefore, although the reapportioned state legislatures may be more sympathetic to urban problems than their predecessors, there is no guarantee that urban issues will be emphasized unless a community of interest develops between the suburbs and the urban centers. Thus reapportionment will not necessarily bring about the renewed interest in the problems of the city hoped for by those who feel that in the past urban interests were lost in rural-dominated legislatures.

Are there any arguments that can be advanced against equal apportionment? Certainly it is important for any political system to take into account varied interests. The representation of equal numbers of people in different electoral districts may not by itself bring about this equality. As the suburbs and outlying areas grow in population it is entirely possible that with the advent of equal apportionment both the center city and many rural areas of the country will be underrepresented in relation to their importance. Public policy formulated by officials elected from constituencies whose boundaries are determined solely on the basis of equal population may not balance the interests of all sections of the country.

PART TWO

Political Parties, Electoral Behavior, and Interest Groups

CHAPTER 4

Political Parties and the Electorate

The political process involves the sources, distribution, and use of power in the state. All the institutions and processes of government relate to this area. The role of political parties and the electoral system in determining and controlling political power is examined in this chapter.

Constitutional Background

Political parties and interest groups have developed outside of the original constitutional framework to channel political power in the community, and for this reason they deserve special consideration from students of American government. The Constitution was designed to structure power relationships in such a way that the arbitrary exercise of political power by any one group or individual would be prevented. One important concept held by the framers of the Constitution was that faction, i.e., parties and interest groups, is inherently dangerous to political freedom and stable government. This is evident from *Federalist 10*.

22

James Madison

FEDERALIST 10

Among the numerous advantages promised by a well constructed Union, none deserves to be more accurately developed than its tendency to break and control the violence of faction. The friend of popular governments never finds himself so much alarmed for their character and fate as when he contemplates their propensity to this dangerous vice. He will not fail, therefore, to set a due value on any plan which, without violating the principles to which he is attached, provides a proper cure for it. The instability, injustice, and confusion, introduced into the public councils, have, in truth, been the mortal diseases under which popular governments have everywhere perished; as they continue to be the favorite and fruitful topics from which the adversaries to liberty derive their most specious declamations. The valuable improvements made by the American constitutions on the popular models, both ancient and modern, cannot certainly be too much admired; but it would be an unwarrantable partiality, to contend that they have as effectually obviated the danger on this side, as was wished and expected. Complaints are everywhere heard from our most considerate and virtuous citizens, equally the friends of public and private faith, and of public and personal liberty, that our governments are too unstable; that the public good is disregarded in the conflicts of rival parties; and that measures are too often decided, not according to the rules of justice, and the rights of the minor party, but by the superior force of an interested and overbearing majority. However anxiously we may wish that these complaints had no foundation, the evidence of known facts will not permit us to deny that they are in some degree true. It will be found, indeed, on a candid review of our situation, that some of the distresses under which we labor, have been erroneously charged on the operation of our governments; but it will be found, at the same time, that other causes will not alone account for many of our heaviest misfortunes; and, particularly, for that prevailing and increasing distrust of public engagements, and alarm for private rights, which are echoed from one end of the continent to the other. These must be chiefly, if not wholly, effects of the unsteadiness and injustice, with which a factious spirit has tainted our public administrations.

By a faction, I understand a number of citizens, whether amounting to a majority or minority of the whole, who are united and actuated by some common impulse of passion, or of interest, adverse to the rights of other citizens, or to the permanent and aggregate interest of the community.

There are two methods of curing the mischiefs of faction: The one, by removing its causes; the other, by controlling its effects.

There are again two methods of removing the causes of faction: the one, by destroying the liberty which is essential to its existence; the other, by giving to every citizen the same opinions, the same passions, and the same interests.

It could never be more truly said, than of the first remedy, that it was worse than the disease. Liberty is to faction what air is to fire, an aliment, without which it instantly expires. But it could not be a less folly to abolish liberty, which is essential to political life because it nourishes faction, than it would be to wish the annihilation of air, which is essential to animal life, because it imparts to fire its destructive agency.

The second expedient is as impracticable, as the first would be unwise. As long as the reason of man continues fallible, and he is at liberty to exercise it, different opinions will be formed. As long as the connection subsists between his reason and his self-love, his opinions and his passions will have a reciprocal influence on each other; and the former will be objects to which the latter will attach themselves. The diversity in the faculties of men, from which the rights of property originate, is not less an insuperable obstacle to a uniformity of interests. The protection of those faculties is the first object of government. From the protection of different and unequal faculties of acquiring property, the possession of different degrees and kinds of property immediately results; and from the influence of these on the sentiments and views of the respective proprietors, ensues a division of the society into different interests and parties.

The latent causes of faction are thus sown in the nature of man; and we see them everywhere brought into different degrees of activity, according to the different circumstances of civil society. A zeal for different opinions concerning religion, concerning government, and many other points, as well of speculation as of practice; an attachment to different leaders, ambitiously contending for preeminence and power; or to persons of other descriptions, whose fortunes have been interesting to the human passions, have, in turn, divided mankind into parties, inflamed them with mutual animosity, and rendered them much more disposed to vex and oppress each other, than to cooperate for their common good. So strong is this propensity of mankind, to fall into mutual animosities, that where no substantial occasion presents itself, the most frivolous and fanciful distinctions have been sufficient to kindle their unfriendly passions, and excite their most violent conflicts. But the most common and durable source of factions has been the various and unequal distribution of property. Those who hold, and those who are without property, have even formed distinct interests in society. Those who are creditors, and those who are debtors, fall under a like discrimination. A landed interest, a manufacturing interest, a mercantile interest, a moneyed interest, with many lesser interests, grow up of necessity in civilized nations, and divide them into different classes, actuated by different sentiments and views. The regulation of these various and interfering interests forms the principal task of modern legislation, and involves the spirit of party and faction in the necessary and ordinary operations of government.

No man is allowed to be a judge in his own cause; because his interest will certainly bias his judgment, and, not improbably, corrupt his integrity. With equal, nay, with greater reason, a body of men are unfit to be both judges and parties at the same time; yet what are many of the most important acts of legislation, but so many judicial determinations, not indeed concerning the rights of single persons, but concerning the rights of large bodies of citizens? And what are the different classes of legislators, but advocates and parties to the cause which they determine? Is a law proposed concerning private debts? It is a question to which the creditors are parties on one side, and the debtors on the other. Justice ought to hold the balance between them. Yet the parties are, and must be, themselves the judges; and the most numerous party, or, in other words, the most powerful faction, must be expected to prevail. Shall domestic manufactures be encouraged, and in what degree, by restrictions on foreign manufactures? are questions which would be differently decided by the landed and the manufacturing classes; and probably by neither with a sole regard to justice and the public good. . . .

It is in vain to say, that enlightened statesmen will be able to adjust these clashing interests, and render them all subservient to the public good. Enlightened statesmen will not always be at the helm; nor, in many cases, can such an adjustment be made at all, without taking into view indirect and remote considerations, which will rarely prevail over the immediate interest which one party may find in disregarding the rights of another, or the good of the whole.

The inference to which we are brought is, that the *causes* of faction cannot be removed; and that relief is only to be sought in the means of controlling its *effects*.

If a faction consists of less than a majority, relief is supplied by the republican principle, which enables the majority to defeat its sinister views, by regular vote. It may clog the administration, it may convulse the society; but it will be unable to execute and mask its violence under the forms of the constitution. When a majority is included in a faction, the form of popular government, on the other hand, enables it to sacrifice to its ruling passion or interest, both the public good and the rights of other citizens. To secure the public good, and private rights, against the danger of such a faction, and at the same time to preserve the spirit and the form of popular government, is then the great object to which our inquiries are directed. Let me add, that it is the great desideratum, by which along this form of government can be rescued from the opprobrium under which it has so long labored, and be recommended to the esteem and adoption of mankind.

By what means is this object attainable? Evidently by one of two only. Either the existence of the same passion or interest in a majority, at the same time must be prevented; or the majority, having such coexistent passion or interest, must be rendered, by their number and local situation, unable to concert and carry into effect schemes of oppression. If the impulse and the opportunity be suffered to coincide, we well know, that neither moral nor religious motives can be relied on as an adequate control. They are not found to be such on the injustice and violence of individuals, and lose their efficacy in proportion to the number combined together; that is, in proportion as their efficacy becomes needful.

From this view of the subject, it may be concluded, that a pure democracy, by which I mean a society consisting of a small number of citizens, who assemble and administer the government in person, can admit of no cure from the mischiefs of faction. A common passion or interest will, in almost every case, be felt by a majority of the whole; a communication and concert, results from the form of government itself; and there is nothing to check the inducements to sacrifice the weaker party, or an obnoxious individual. Hence it is, that such democracies have ever been spectacles of turbulence and contention; have ever been found incompatible with personal security, or the rights of property; and have, in general, been as short in their lives, as they have been violent in their deaths. Theoretic politicians, who have patronized this species of government, have erroneously supposed that by reducing mankind to a perfect equality in their political rights, they would, at the same time, be perfectly equalized and assimilated in their possessions, their opinions, and their passions.

A republic, by which I mean a government in which the scheme of representation takes place, opens a different prospect, and promises the cure for which we are seeking. Let us examine the points in which it varies from pure democracy, and we shall comprehend both the nature of the cure and the efficacy which it must derive from the union.

The two great points of difference, between a democracy and a republic, are, first, the delegation of the government, in the latter, to a small number of citizens elected by the rest; secondly, the greater number of citizens, and greater sphere of country, over which the latter may be extended.

The effect of the first difference is on the one hand, to refine and enlarge the public views, by passing them through the medium of a chosen body of citizens, whose wisdom may best discern the true interest in their country, and whose patriotism and love of justice, will be least likely to sacrifice it to temporary or partial considerations. Under such a regulation, it may well happen, that the public voice, pronounced by the representatives of the people, will be more consonant to the public good, than if pronounced by the people themselves, convened for the purpose. On the other hand, the effect may be inverted. Men of factious tempers, of local prejudices, or of sinister designs, may by intrigue, by corruption, or by other means, first obtain the suffrages, and then betray the interest of the people. The question resulting is, whether small or extensive republics are most favorable to the election of proper guardians of the public weal; and it is clearly decided in favor of the latter by two obvious considerations.

In the first place, it is to be remarked, that however small the republic may be, the representatives must be raised to a certain number, in order to guard against the cabals of a few; and that however large it may be, they must be limited to a certain number, in order to guard against the confusion of a multitude. Hence, the number of representatives in the two cases not being in proportion to that of the constituents, and being proportionally greatest in the small republic, it follows that if the proportion of fit characters be not less in the large than in the small republic, the former will present a greater option, and consequently a greater probability of a fit choice.

In the next place, as each representative will be chosen by a greater number of citizens in the large than in the small republic, it will be more difficult for unworthy candidates to practice with success the vicious arts, by which elections are too often carried; and the suffrages of the people being more free, will be more likely to center in men who possess the most attractive merit, and the most diffusive and established characters. . . .

The other point of difference is, the greater number of citizens, and extent of territory, which may be brought within the compass of republican, than of democratic government; and it is this circumstance principally which renders factious combinations less to be dreaded in the former, than in the latter. The smaller the society, the fewer probably will be the distinct parties and interests composing it; the fewer the distinct parties and interests, the more frequently will a majority be found of the same party; and the smaller the number of individuals composing a majority, and the smaller the compass within which they are placed, the more easily they will concert and execute their plans of oppression. Extend the sphere, and you take in a greater variety of parties and interests; you make it less probable that a majority of the whole will have a common motive to invade the rights of other citizens; or if such a common motive exists, it will be more difficult for all who feel it to discover their own strength, and to act in unison with each other. . . .

Hence, it clearly appears, that the same advantage, which a republic has over a democracy, in controlling the effects of faction, is enjoyed by a large over a small republic — is enjoyed by the union over the states composing it. Does this advantage consist in the substitution of representatives, whose enlightened views and virtuous sentiments render them superior to local prejudices, and to schemes of injustice? It will not be denied, that the representation of the union will be most likely to possess these requisite endowments. Does it consist in the greater security afforded by a greater variety of parties, against the event of any one party being able to outnumber and oppress the rest? In an equal degree does the increased variety of parties, comprised within the union, increase this security? Does it, in fine, consist in the greater obstacles opposed to the concert and accomplishment of the secret wishes of an unjust and interested majority? Here, again, the extent of the union gives it the most palpable advantage.

The influence of factious leaders may kindle a flame within their particular states, but will be unable to spread a general conflagration through the other states; a religious sect may degenerate into a political faction in a part of the confederacy; but the variety of sects dispersed over the entire face of it, must secure the national councils against any danger from that source; a rage for paper money, for an abolition of debts, for an equal division of property, or for any other improper or wicked project, will be less apt to pervade the whole body of the union, than a particular member of it; in the same proportion as such a malady is more likely to taint a particular county or district, than an entire state.

In the extent and proper structure of the union, therefore, we behold a republican remedy for the diseases most incident to republican government. And according to the degree of pleasure and pride we feel in being republicans, ought to be our zeal in cherishing the spirit, and supporting the character of Federalists.

The following selection is taken from E. E. Schattschneider's classic treatise, *Party Government*. In this material he examines both the implications of *Federalist 10* and counter-arguments to the propositions stated by Madison, with regard to political parties and interest groups.

23
E. E. Schattschneider

PARTY GOVERNMENT

The Convention at Philadelphia produced a constitution with a dual attitude: it was proparty in one sense and antiparty in another. The authors of the Constitution refused to suppress the parties by destroying the fundamental liberties in which parties originate. They or their immediate succes-

From *Party Government* by E. E. Schattschneider. Copyright 1942 by E. E. Schattschneider. Reprinted by permission of Holt, Rinehart and Winston.

sors accepted amendments that guaranteed civil rights and thus established a system of party tolerance, i.e., the right to agitate and to organize. This is the proparty aspect of the system. On the other hand, the authors of the Constitution set up an elaborate division and balance of powers within an intricate governmental structure designed to make parties ineffective. It was hoped that the parties would lose and exhaust themselves in futile attempts to fight their way through the labyrinthine framework of the government, much as an attacking army is expected to spend itself against the defensive works of a fortress. This is the antiparty part of the constitutional scheme. To quote Madison, the "great object" of the Constitution was "to preserve the public good and private rights against the danger of such a faction [party] and at the same time to preserve the spirit and form of popular government."

In Madison's mind the difference between an autocracy and a free republic seems to have been largely a matter of the precise point at which parties are stopped by the government. In an autocracy parties are controlled (suppressed) at the source; in a republic parties are tolerated but are invited to strangle themselves in the machinery of government. The result in either case is much the same, sooner or later the government checks the parties but *never do the parties control the government*. Madison was perfectly definite and unmistakable in his disapproval of party government as distinguished from party tolerance. In the opinion of Madison, parties were intrinsically bad, and the sole issue for discussion was the means by which bad parties might be prevented from becoming dangerous. What never seems to have occurred to the authors of the Constitution, however, is that parties might be *used* as beneficent instruments of popular government. It is at this point that the distinction between the modern and the antique attitude is made.

The offspring of this combination of ideas was a constitutional system having conflicting tendencies. The Constitution made the rise of parties inevitable yet was incompatible with party government. This scheme, in spite of its subtlety, involved a miscalculation. Political parties refused to be content with the role assigned to them. The vigor and enterprise of the parties have therefore made American political history the story of the unhappy marriage of the parties and the Constitution, a remarkable variation of the case of the irresistible force and the immovable object, which in this instance have been compelled to live together in a permanent partnership. . . .

THE RAW MATERIALS OF POLITICS

People who write about interests sometimes seem to assume that all interests are special and exclusive, setting up as a result of this assumption a dichotomy in which the interests on the one side are perpetually opposed to the public welfare on the other side. But there are common interests as well as special interests, and common interests resemble special interests in that they are apt to influence political behavior. The raw materials of politics are not all antisocial. Alongside of Madison's statement that differences in wealth are the most durable causes of faction there should be placed a corollary that the common possessions of the people are the most durable cause of unity. To assume that people have merely conflicting interests and nothing else is to invent a political nightmare that has only a superficial relation to reality. The body of agreement underlying the conflicts of a modern society ought to be sufficient to sustain the social order provided only that the common interests supporting this unity are mobilized. Moreover, not all differences of interest are durable causes of conflict. Nothing is apt to be more perishable than a political issue. In the democratic process, the nation moves from controversy to agreement to forgetfulness; politics is not a futile exercise like football, forever played back and forth over the same ground. The government creates and destroys interests at every turn.

There are, in addition, powerful factors inhibiting the unlimited pursuit of special aims by any organized minority. To assume that minorities will stop at nothing to get what they want is to postulate a degree of unanimity and concentration within these groups that does not often exist in real life. If every individual were capable of having only one interest to the exclusion of all others, it might be possible to form dangerous unions of monomaniacs who would go to great extremes to attain their objectives. In fact, however, people have many interests leading to a dispersion of drives certain to destroy some of the unanimity and concentration of any group. How many interests can an individual have? Enough to make it extremely unlikely that any two individuals will have the same combination of interests. Anyone who has ever tried to promote an association of people having some special interest in common will realize, first, that there are marked differences of enthusiasm within the group and, second, that interests compete with interests for the attention and enthusiasm of every individual. Every organized special interest consists of a group of busy, distracted individuals held together by the efforts of a handful of specialists and enthusiasts who sacrifice other matters in order to concentrate on one. The notion of resolute and unanimous minorities on the point of violence is largely the invention of paid lobbyists and press agents.

The result of the fact that every individual is torn by the diversity of his own interests, the fact that he is a member of many groups, is *the law of the imperfect political mobilization of interests*. That is, it has never been possible to mobilize any interest 100 percent. . . .

It is only another way of saying the same thing to state that conflicts of interests are not cumulative. If it were true that the dividing line in every conflict (or in all major conflicts) split the community identically in each case so that individuals who are opposed on one issue would be opposed to each other on all other issues also, while individuals who joined hands on one occasion would find themselves on the same side on all issues, always opposed to the same combination of antagonists, the cleavage created by the cumulative effect of these divisions would be fatal. But actually conflicts are not cumulative in this way. In real life the divisions are not so clearly marked, and the alignment of people according to interests requires an enormous shuffling back and forth from one side to the other, tending to dissipate the tensions created.

In view of the fact, therefore, (1) that there are many interests, including a great body of common interests, (2) that the government pursues a multiplicity of policies and creates and destroys interests in the process, (3) that each individual is capable of having many interests, (4) that interests cannot be mobilized perfectly, and (5) that conflicts among interests are not cumulative, it seems reasonable to suppose that the government is not the captive of blind forces from which there is no escape. There is nothing wrong about the raw materials of politics.

Functions and Types of Elections

Most people transmit their political desires to government through elections. Elections are a critical part of the democratic process, and the existence of *free* elections is a major difference between democracies and totalitarian or authoritarian forms of government. Because elections reflect popular attitudes toward governmental parties, policies, and personalities, it is useful to attempt to classify different types of elections on the basis of changes and trends that take place within the electorate. Every election is not the same. For example, the election of 1932 with the resulting Democratic landslide was profoundly different from the election of 1960, in which Kennedy won by less than 1 percent of the popular vote.

Members of the Survey Research Center at the University of Michigan, as well as V. O. Key, Jr., have developed a typology of elections that is useful in analyzing the electoral system. The most prevalent type of election can be classified as a "maintaining election," "one in which the pattern of partisan attachments prevailing in the preceding period persists and is the primary influence on the forces governing the vote." [1] Most elections fall into the maintaining category, a fact significant for the political system because such elections result in political continuity and reflect a lack of serious upheavals within the electorate and government. Maintaining elections result in the continuation of the majority political party.

At certain times in American history, what V. O. Key, Jr., has called "critical elections" take place. He discusses this type of election, which

---

[1] Angus Campbell, Philip E. Converse, Warren E. Miller, and Donald E. Stokes, *The American Voter* (New York: John Wiley & Sons, 1960), Chap. 19.

results in permanent realignment of the electorate and reflects basic changes in political attitudes.

Apart from maintaining and critical elections, a third type, in which only temporary shifts take place within the electorate, occurs, which can be called "deviating elections." For example, the Eisenhower victories of 1952 and 1956 were deviating elections for several reasons, including the personality of Eisenhower and the fact that voters could register their choice for President without changing their basic partisan loyalties at Congressional and state levels. Deviating elections, with reference to the office of President, are probable when popular figures are running for the office.

In "reinstating elections," a final category that can be added to a typology of elections, there is a return to normal voting patterns. Reinstating elections take place after deviating elections as a result of the demise of the temporary forces that caused the transitory shift in partisan choice. The election of 1960, in which most of the Democratic majority in the electorate returned to the fold and voted for John F. Kennedy,[2] has been classified as a reinstating election.

---

[2] See Philip E. Converse, Angus Campbell, Warren E. Miller, and Donald E. Stokes, "Stability and Change in 1960: A Reinstating Election," *The American Political Science Review,* vol. 55 (June 1961), pp. 269–80.

24

V. O. Key, Jr.

A THEORY OF CRITICAL ELECTIONS

Perhaps the basic differentiating characteristic of democratic order consists in the expression of effective choice by the mass of the people in elections. The electorate occupies, at least in the mystique of such orders, the position of the principal organ of governance; it acts through elections. An election itself is a formal act of collective decision that occurs in a stream of connected antecedent and subsequent behavior. Among democratic orders elections, so broadly defined, differ enormously in their nature, their meaning, and their consequences. Even within a single nation the reality of election differs greatly from time to time. A systematic comparative approach, with a focus on variations in the nature of elections would doubtless be fruitful

---

From V. O. Key, Jr., "A Theory of Critical Elections," *The Journal of Politics,* 17:1 (February 1955). Reprinted by permission.

in advancing understanding of the democratic governing process. In behavior antecedent to voting, elections differ in the proportions of the electorate psychologically involved, in the intensity of attitudes associated with campaign cleavages, in the nature of expectations about the consequences of the voting, in the impact of objective events relevant to individual political choice, in individual sense of effective connection with community decision, and in other ways. These and other antecedent variations affect the act of voting itself as well as subsequent behavior. An understanding of elections and, in turn, of the democratic process as a whole must rest partially on broad differentiations of the complexes of behavior that we call elections.

While this is not the occasion to develop a comprehensive typology of elections, the foregoing remarks provide an orientation for an attempt to formulate a concept of one type of election — based on American experience — which might be built into a more general theory of elections. Even the most fleeting inspection of American elections suggests the existence of a category of elections in which voters are, at least from impressionistic evidence, unusually deeply concerned, in which the extent of electoral involvement is relatively quite high, and in which the decisive results of the voting reveal a sharp alteration of the preexisting cleavage within the electorate. Moreover, and perhaps this is the truly differentiating characteristic of this sort of election, the realignment made manifest in the voting in such elections seems to persist for several succeeding elections. All these characteristics cumulate to the conception of an election type in which the depth and intensity of electoral involvement are high, in which more or less profound readjustments occur in the relations of power within the community, and in which new and durable electoral groupings are formed. These comments suppose, of course, the existence of other types of complexes of behavior centering about formal elections, the systematic isolation and identification of which, fortunately, are not essential for the present discussion.

I

The presidential election of 1928 in the New England states provides a specific case of the type of critical election that has been described in general terms. In that year Alfred E. Smith, the Democratic presidential candidate, made gains in all the New England states. The rise in Democratic strength was especially notable in Massachusetts and Rhode Island. When one probes below the surface of the gross election figures it becomes apparent that a sharp and durable realignment also occurred within the electorate, a fact reflective of the activation by the Democratic candidate of low-income, Catholic, urban voters of recent immigrant stock. In New England, at least, the Roosevelt revolution of 1932 was in large measure an Al Smith revolution of 1928, a characterization less applicable to the remainder of the country.

The intensity and extent of electoral concern before the voting of 1928 can only be surmised, but the durability of the realignment formed at the election can be determined by simple analyses of election statistics. An illustration of the new division thrust through the electorate by the campaign of 1928 is provided by the graphs in Figure A, which show the Democratic percentages of the presidential vote from 1916 through 1952 for the city of Somerville and the town of Ashfield in Massachusetts. Somerville, adjacent to Boston, had a population in 1930 of 104,000 of which 28 percent was foreign born and 41 percent was of foreign-born or mixed parentage. Roman Catholics constituted a large proportion of its relatively low-income population. Ashfield, a farming community in western Massachusetts with a 1930 population of 860, was predominantly native born (8.6 percent foreign born), chiefly rural-farm (66 percent), and principally Protestant.

The impressiveness of the differential impact of the election of 1928 on Somerville and Ashfield may be read from the graphs in Figure A. From 1920 the Democratic percentage in Somerville ascended steeply while the Democrats in Ashfield, few in 1920, became even less numerous in 1928. Inspection of the graphs also suggests that the great reshuffling of voters that occurred in 1928 was perhaps the final and decisive stage in a process that had been under way for some time. That antecedent process involved a relatively heavy support in 1924 for La Follette in those towns in which Smith was subsequently to find special favor. Hence, in Figure A, as in all the other charts, the 1924 figure is the percentage of the total accounted for by the votes of both the Democratic and Progressive candidates rather than the Democratic percentage of the two-party vote. This usage conveys a minimum impression of the size of the 1924–1928 Democratic gain but probably depicts the nature of the 1920–1928 trend.

For present purposes, the voting behavior of the two communities shown in Figure A after 1928 is of central relevance. The differences established between them in 1928 persisted even through 1952, although the two series fluctuated slightly in response to the particular influences of individual campaigns. The nature of the process of maintenance of the cleavage is, of course, not manifest from these data. Conceivably the impress of the events of 1928 on individual attitudes and loyalties formed partisan attachments of lasting nature. Yet it is doubtful that the new crystallization of 1928 projected itself through a quarter of a century solely from the momentum given it by such factors. More probably subsequent events operated to reenforce and to maintain the 1928 cleavage. Whatever the mechanism of its maintenance, the durability of the realignment is impressive.

Somerville and Ashfield may be regarded more or less as samples of major population groups within the electorate of Massachusetts. Since no sample survey data are available for 1928, about the only analysis feasible

Percent

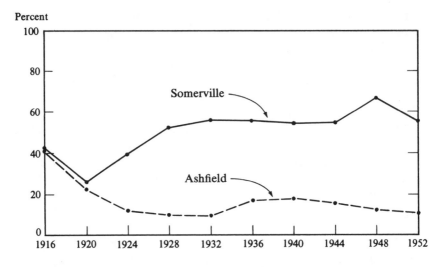

Figure A   Democratic Percentages of Major-Party Presidential Vote, Somerville and Ashfield, Massachusetts, 1916–1952

is inspection of election returns for geographic units contrasting in their population composition. Lest it be supposed, however, that the good citizens of Somerville and Ashfield were aberrants simply unlike the remainder of the people of the Commonwealth, examination of a large number of towns and cities is in order. In the interest of both compression and comprehensibility, a mass of data is telescoped into Figure B. The graphs in that figure compare over the period 1916–1952 the voting behavior of the 29 Massachusetts towns and cities having the sharpest Democratic increases, 1920–1928, with that of the 30 towns and cities having the most marked Democratic loss, 1920–1928. In other words, the figure averages out a great many Ashfields and Somervilles. The data of Figure B confirm the expectation that the pattern exhibited by the pair of voting units in Figure A represented only a single case of a much more general phenomenon. Yet by virtue of the coverage of the data in the figure, one gains a stronger impression of the difference in the character of the election of 1928 and the other elections recorded there. The cleavage confirmed by the 1928 returns persisted. At subsequent elections the voters shifted to and fro within the outlines of the broad division fixed in 1928.

Examination of the characteristics of the two groups of cities and towns of Figure B — those with the most marked Democratic gains, 1920–1928, and those with the widest movement in the opposite direction — reveals the expected sorts of differences. Urban, industrial, foreign-born, Catholic areas made up the bulk of the first group of towns, although an occasional rural Catholic community increased its Democratic vote markedly. The towns with a contrary movement tended to be rural, Protestant, native born. The new Democratic vote correlated quite closely with a 1930 vote on state enforcement of the national prohibition law.

Melancholy experience with the eccentricities of data, be they quantitative or otherwise, suggests the prudence of a check on the interpretation of 1928. Would the same method applied to any other election yield a similar result, i.e., the appearance of a more or less durable realignment? Perhaps there can be no doubt that the impact of the events of any election on many individuals forms lasting party loyalties; yet not often is the number so affected so great as to create a sharp realignment. On the other hand, some elections are characterized by a large-scale transfer of party affection that is quite short-term, a different sort of phenomenon from that which occurs in elections marked by broad and durable shifts in party strength. The difference is illustrated by the data on the election of 1932 in New Hampshire in Figure C. The voting records of the twenty-five towns with the widest Democratic gains from 1928 to 1932 are there traced from 1916 to 1952. Observe that Democratic strength in these towns shot up in 1932 but fairly quickly resumed about the same position in relation to other towns that it had occupied in 1928. It is also evident from the graph that this group of towns had on the whole been especially strongly repelled by the Democratic appeal of 1928. Probably the depression drove an appreciable number of hardened Republicans of these towns to vote for a change in 1932, but they gradually found their way back to the party of

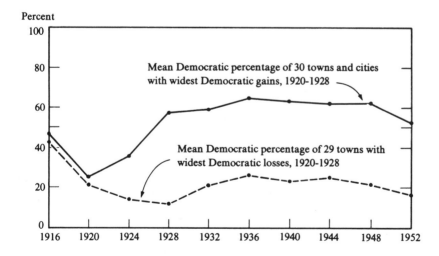

Figure B Persistence of Electoral Cleavage of 1928 in Massachusetts: Mean Democratic Percentage of Presidential Vote in Towns with Sharpest Democratic Gains, 1920–1928, and in Towns of Widest Democratic Losses, 1920–1928

their fathers. In any case, the figure reflects a type of behavior differing markedly from that of 1928. To the extent that 1932 resembled 1928 in the recrystallization of party lines, the proportions of new Democrats did not differ significantly among the groups of towns examined. In fact, what probably happened to a considerable extent in New England was that the 1928 election broke the electorate into two new groups that would have been formed in 1932 had there been no realignment in 1928.

The Massachusetts material has served both to explain the method of analysis and to present the case of a single state. Examinations of the election of 1928 in other New England states indicate that in each a pattern prevailed similar to that of Massachusetts. The total effect of the realignment differed, of course, from state to state. In Massachusetts and Rhode Island the number of people affected by the upheaval of 1928 was sufficient to form a new majority coalition. In Maine, New Hampshire, and Vermont the same sort of reshuffling of electors occurred, but the proportions affected were not sufficient to overturn the Republican combination, although the basis was laid in Maine and New Hampshire for later limited Democratic successes. To underpin these remarks the materials on Connecticut, Maine, New Hampshire, and Rhode Island are presented in Figure D. The data on Vermont, excluded for lack of space, form a pattern similar to that emerging from the analysis of the other states.

In the interpretation of all these 1928 analyses certain limitations of the technique need to be kept in mind. The data and the technique most

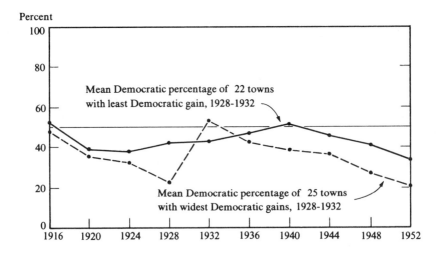

Figure C Impact of Election of 1932 in New Hampshire: Mean Democratic Percentage of Presidential Vote of Towns with Sharpest Democratic Gain, 1928–1932, Compared with Mean Vote of Towns at Opposite Extreme of 1928–1932 Change

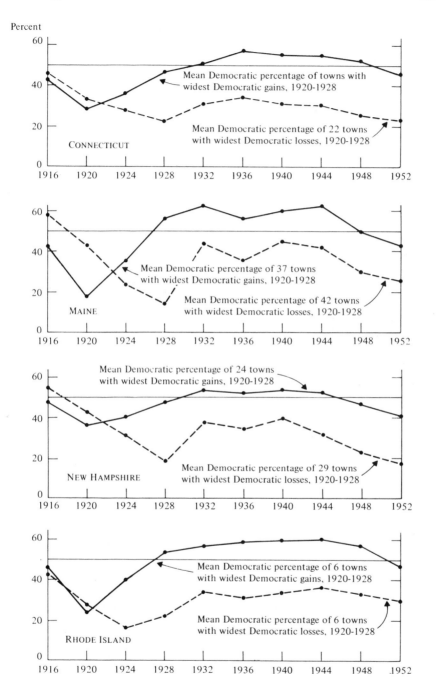

Figure D   Realignment of 1928 in Connecticut, Maine, New Hampshire, and Rhode Island

clearly reveal a shift when voters of different areas move in opposite directions. From 1928 to 1936 apparently a good deal of Democratic growth occurred in virtually all geographic units, a shift not shown up sharply by the technique. Hence, the discussion may fail adequately to indicate the place of 1928 as the crucial stage in a process of electoral change that began before and concluded after that year.

II

One of the difficulties with an ideal type is that no single actual case fits exactly its specifications. Moreover, in any system of categorization the greater the number of differentiating criteria for classes, the more nearly one tends to create a separate class for each instance. If taxonomic systems are to be of analytical utility, they must almost inevitably group together instances that are unlike at least in peripheral characteristics irrelevant to the purpose of the system. All of which serves to warn that an election is about to be classified as critical even though in some respects the behavior involved differed from that of the 1928 polling.

Central to our concept of critical elections is a realignment within the electorate both sharp and durable. With respect to these basic criteria the election of 1896 falls within the same category as that of 1928, although it differed in other respects. The persistence of the new division of 1896 was perhaps not so notable as that of 1928; yet the Democratic defeat was so demoralizing and so thorough that the party could make little headway in regrouping its forces until 1916. Perhaps the significant feature of the 1896 contest was that, at least in New England, it did not form a new division in which partisan lines became more nearly congruent with lines separating classes, religions, or other such social groups. Instead, the Republicans succeeded in drawing new support, in about the same degree, from all sorts of economic and social classes. The result was an electoral coalition formidable in its mass but which required both good fortune and skill in political management for its maintenance, given its latent internal contradictions.

If the 1896 election is described in our terms as a complex of behavior preceding and following the formal voting, an account of the action must include the panic of 1893. Bank failures, railroad receiverships, unemployment, strikes, Democratic championship of deflation and of the gold standard, and related matters created the setting for a Democratic setback in 1894. Only one of the eight New England Democratic Representatives survived the elections of 1894. The two 1892 Democratic governors fell by the wayside and in all the states the Democratic share of the gubernatorial vote fell sharply in 1894. The luckless William Jennings Bryan and the free-silver heresy perhaps did not contribute as much as is generally supposed to the 1892–1896 decline in New England Democratic strength;

New England Democrats moved in large numbers over to the Republican ranks in 1894.

The character of the 1892–1896 electoral shift is suggested by the data of Figure E, which presents an analysis of Connecticut and New Hampshire made by the technique used earlier in examining the election of 1928. The graphs make plain that in these states (and the other New England states show the same pattern) the rout of 1896 produced a basic realignment that persisted at least until 1916. The graphs in Figure E also make equally plain that the 1892–1896 realignment differed radically from that of 1928 in certain respects. In 1896 the net movement in all sorts of geographic units was toward the Republicans; towns differed not in the direction of their movement but only in the extent. Moreover, the persistence of the realignment of 1896 was about the same in those towns with the least Democratic loss from 1892 to 1896 as it was in those with the most marked decline in Democratic strength. Hence, the graphs differ from those on 1928 which took the form of opening scissors. Instead, the 1896

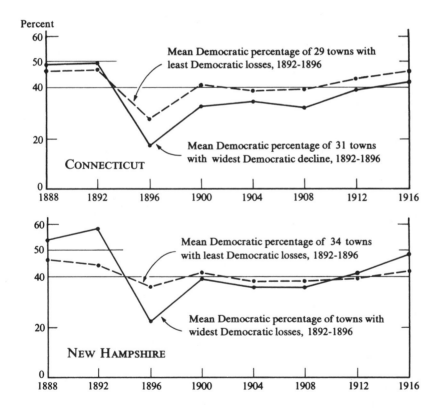

Figure E Realignment of 1896 in Connecticut and New Hampshire

realignment appears as a parallel movement of both groups to a lower plateau of Democratic strength.

If the election of 1896 had had a notable differential impact on geographically segregated social groups, the graphs in Figure E of towns at the extremes of the greatest and least 1892–1896 change would have taken the form of opening scissors as they did in 1928. While the election of 1896 is often pictured as a last-ditch fight between the haves and the have-nots, that understanding of the contest was, at least in New England, evidently restricted to planes of leadership and oratory. It did not extend to the voting actions of the electorate. These observations merit some buttressing, although the inference emerges clearly enough from Figure E.

Unfortunately the census authorities have ignored the opportunity to advance demographic inquiry by publishing data of consequence about New England towns. Not much information is available on the characteristics of the populations of these small geographic areas. Nevertheless, size of total population alone is a fair separator of towns according to politically significant characterstics. Classification of towns according to that criterion groups them roughly according to industrialization and probably generally also according to religion and national origin. Hence, with size of population of towns and cities as a basis, Table 1 contrasts the elections of 1896 and 1928 for different types of towns. Observe from the table that the mean shift between 1892 and 1896 was about the same for varying size groups of towns. Contrast this lack of association between size and political movement with the radically different 1920–1928 pattern which also appears in the table.

Table 1 makes clear that in 1896 the industrial cities, in their aggregate vote at least, moved toward the Republicans in about the same degree as did the rural farming communities. Some of the misinterpretations of the election of 1896 flow from a focus on that election in isolation rather than in comparison with the preceding election. In 1896, even in New England cities, the Democrats tended to be strongest in the poor, working-class, immigrant sections. Yet the same relation had existed, in a sharper form, in 1892. In 1896 the Republicans gained in the working-class wards, just as they did in the silk-stocking wards, over their 1892 vote. They were able to place the blame for unemployment upon the Democrats and to propagate successfully the doctrine that the Republican Party was the party of prosperity and the "full dinner pail." On the whole, the effect apparently was to reduce the degree of coincidence of class affiliation and partisan inclination. Nor was the election of 1896, in New England at least, a matter of heightened tension between city and country. Both city and country voters shifted in the same direction. Neither urban employers nor industrial workers could generate much enthusiasm for inflation and free trade; rather they joined in common cause. Instead of a sharpening of class

Table 1 Contrasts between Elections of 1896 and 1928 in Massachusetts: Shifts in Democratic Strength, 1892–1896 and 1920–1928, in Relation to Population Size of Towns

Population size group	Mean Democratic percentage 1892	1896	Mean change 1892–96	Mean Democratic percentage 1920	1928	Mean change 1920–28
1–999	34.0	14.7	−19.3	16.5	18.6	+ 2.1
2000–2999	38.8	18.3	−20.5	21.0	33.1	+12.1
10,000–14,999	46.7	26.9	−19.8	25.8	43.7	+17.9
50,000+	47.7	30.1	−17.6	29.5	55.7	+26.2

cleavages within New England the voting apparently reflected more a sectional antagonism and anxiety, shared by all classes, expressed in opposition to the dangers supposed to be threatening from the West.

Other contrasts between the patterns of electoral behavior of 1896 and 1928 could be cited but in terms of sharpness and durability of realignment both elections were of roughly the same type, at least in New England. In these respects they seem to differ from most other elections over a period of a half century, although it may well be that each round at the ballot boxes involves realignment within the electorate similar in kind but radically different in extent.

III

The discussion points toward the analytical utility of a system for the differentiation of elections. A concept of critical elections has been developed to cover a type of election in which there occurs a sharp and durable electoral realignment between parties, although the techniques employed do not yield any information of consequence about the mechanisms for the maintenance of a new alignment, once it is formed. Obviously any sort of system for the gross characterization of elections presents difficulties in application. The actual election rarely presents in pure form a case fitting completely any particular concept. Especially in a large and diverse electorate a single polling may encompass radically varying types of behavior among different categories of voters; yet a dominant characteristic often makes itself apparent. Despite such difficulties, the attempt to move toward a better understanding of elections in the terms here employed could provide a means for better integrating the study of electoral behavior with the analysis of political systems. In truth, a considerable proportion of the study of electoral behavior has only a tenuous relation to politics.

The sorts of questions here raised, when applied sufficiently broadly on a comparative basis and carried far enough, could lead to a consideration of basic problems of the nature of democratic orders. A question occurs, for example, about the character of the consequences for the political system of the temporal frequency of critical elections. What are the consequences for public administration, for the legislative process, for the operation of the economy of frequent serious upheavals within the electorate? What are the correlates of that pattern of behavior? And, for those disposed to raise such questions, what underlying changes might alter the situation? Or, when viewed from the contrary position, what consequences flow from an electorate which is disposed, in effect, to remain largely quiescent over considerable periods? Does a state of moving equilibrium reflect a pervasive satisfaction with the course of public policy? An indifference about matters political? In any case, what are the consequences for the public order? Further, what are the consequences when an electorate builds up habits and attachments, or faces situations, that make it impossible for it to render a decisive and clear-cut popular verdict that promises not to be upset by caprice at the next round of polling? What are the consequences of a situation that creates recurring, evenly balanced conflict over long periods? On the other hand, what characteristics of an electorate or what conditions permit sharp and decisive changes in the power structure from time to time? Such directions of speculation are suggested by a single criterion for the differentiation of elections. Further development of an electoral typology would probably point to useful speculation in a variety of directions.

Voting Behavior:
Rational or Irrational?

Parties are supposed to bridge the gap between the people and their government. Theoretically they are the primary vehicles for translating the wishes of the electorate into public policy, sharing this role with interest groups and other governmental instrumentalities in varying degrees. If parties are to perform this aspect of their job properly, the party system must be conducive to securing meaningful debate and action. Party organization and procedure profoundly affect the ability of parties to act in a democratically responsible manner. It should also be pointed out, however, that the electorate has a responsibility in the political process — the responsibility to act rationally, debate the issues of importance, and record a vote for one party or the other at election time. These, at least, are electoral norms traditionally discussed. But does the electorate act in this manner? Is it desirable to have 100 percent electoral participation considering the characteristics of voting behavior? What are the determinants of electoral behavior? These questions are discussed in the following selection.

25
Bernard R. Berelson, Paul F. Lazarsfeld, and William N. McPhee

DEMOCRATIC PRACTICE AND DEMOCRATIC THEORY

REQUIREMENTS FOR THE INDIVIDUAL

Perhaps the main impact of realistic research on contemporary politics has been to temper some of the requirements set by our traditional normative theory for the typical citizen. "Out of all this literature of political observation and analysis, which is relatively new," says Max Beloff, "there has come to exist a picture in our minds of the political scene which differs very considerably from that familiar to us from the classical texts of democratic politics."

Experienced observers have long known, of course, that the individual voter was not all that the theory of democracy requires of him. As Bryce put it:

> How little solidity and substance there is in the political or social beliefs of nineteen persons out of every twenty. These beliefs, when examined, mostly resolve themselves into two or three prejudices and aversions, two or three prepossessions for a particular party or section of a party, two or three phrases or catch-words suggesting or embodying arguments which the man who repeats them has not analyzed.

While our data [from the Elmira study] do not support such an extreme statement, they do reveal that certain requirements commonly assumed for the successful operation of democracy are not met by the behavior of the "average" citizen. The requirements, and our conclusions concerning them, are quickly reviewed.

Interest, Discussion, Motivation. The democratic citizen is expected to be interested and to participate in political affairs. His interest and participation can take such various forms as reading and listening to campaign materials, working for the candidate or the party, arguing politics, donating money, and voting. In Elmira the majority of the people vote, but in general they do not give evidence of sustained interest. Many vote without real involvement in the election, and even the party workers are not typically motivated by ideological concerns or plain civic duty.

If there is one characteristic for a democratic system (besides the ballot itself) that is theoretically required, it is the capacity for and the practice of discussion. "It is as true of the large as of the small society," says Lindsay, "that its health depends on the mutual understanding which discussion makes possible; and that discussion is the only possible instrument of its democratic government." How much participation in political discussion there is in the community, what it is, and among whom — these questions have been given answers . . . earlier. . . . In this instance there was little true discussion between the candidates, little in the newspaper commentary, little between the voters and the official party representatives, some within the electorate. On the grass roots level there was more talk than debate, and, at least inferentially, the talk had important effects upon voting, in reinforcing or activating the partisans if not in converting the opposition.

An assumption underlying the theory of democracy is that the citizenry has a strong motivation for participation in political life. But it is a curious quality of voting behavior that for large numbers of people motivation is weak if not almost absent. It is assumed that this motivation would gain its strength from the citizen's perception of the difference that alternative decisions made to him. Now when a person buys something or makes other decisions of daily life, there are direct and immediate consequences for him. But for the bulk of the American people the voting decision is not followed by any direct, immediate, visible personal consequences. Most voters, organized or unorganized, are not in a position to foresee the distant and indirect consequences for themselves, let alone the society. The ballot is cast, and for most people that is the end of it. If their side is defeated, "it doesn't really matter."

Knowledge. The democratic citizen is expected to be well informed about political affairs. He is supposed to know what the issues are, what their history is, what the relevant facts are, what alternatives are proposed, what the party stands for, what the likely consequences are. By such standards the voter falls short. Even when he has the motivation, he finds it difficult to make decisions on the basis of full information when the subject is relatively simple and proximate; how can he do so when it is complex and remote? The citizen is not highly informed on details of the campaign, nor does he avoid a certain misperception of the political situation when it is to his psychological advantage to do so. The electorate's perception of what goes on in the campaign is colored by emotional feeling toward one or the other issue, candidate, party, or social group.

Principle. The democratic citizen is supposed to cast his vote on the basis of principle — not fortuitously or frivolously or impulsively or habitually, but with reference to standards not only of his own interest but of the common good as well. Here, again, if this requirement is pushed at all strongly, it becomes an impossible demand on the democratic electorate.

Many voters vote not for principle in the usual sense but "for" a group to which they are attached — their group. The Catholic vote or the hereditary vote is explainable less as principle than as a traditional social allegiance. The ordinary voter, bewildered by the complexity of modern political problems, unable to determine clearly what the consequences are of alternative lines of action, remote from the arena, and incapable of bringing information to bear on principle, votes the way trusted people around him are voting. . . .

On the issues of the campaign there is a considerable amount of "don't know" — sometimes reflecting genuine indecision, more often meaning "don't care." Among those with opinions the partisans *agree* on most issues, criteria, expectations, and rules of the game. The supporters of the different sides disagree on only a few issues. Nor, for that matter, do the candidates themselves always join the issue sharply and clearly. The partisans do not agree overwhelmingly with their own party's position, or, rather, only the small minority of highly partisan do; the rest take a rather moderate position on the political consideration involved in an election.

Rationality. The democratic citizen is expected to exercise rational judgment in coming to his voting decision. He is expected to have arrived at his principles by reason and to have considered rationally the implications and alleged consequences of the alternative proposals of the contending parties. Political theorists and commentators have always exclaimed over the seeming contrast here between requirement and fulfillment. . . . The upshot of this is that the usual analogy between the voting "decision" and the more or less carefully calculated decisions of consumers or businessmen or courts, incidentally, may be quite incorrect. For many voters political preferences may better be considered analogous to cultural tastes — in music, literature, recreational activities, dress, ethics, speech, social behavior. Consider the parallels between political preferences and general cultural tastes. Both have their origin in ethnic, sectional, class, and family traditions. Both exhibit stability and resistance to change for individuals but flexibility and adjustment over generations for the society as a whole. Both seem to be matters of sentiment and disposition rather than "reasoned preferences." While both are responsive to changed conditions and unusual stimuli, they are relatively invulnerable to direct argumentation and vulnerable to indirect social influences. Both are characterized more by faith than by conviction and by wishful expectation rather than careful prediction or consequences. The preference for one party rather than another must be highly similar to the preference for one kind of literature or music rather than another, and the choice of the same political party every four years may be parallel to the choice of the same old standards of conduct in new social situations. In short, it appears that a sense of fitness is a more striking feature of political preference than reason and calculation.

REQUIREMENTS FOR THE SYSTEM

If the democratic system depended solely on the qualifications of the individual voter, then it seems remarkable that democracies have survived through the centuries. After examining the detailed data on how individuals misperceive political reality or respond to irrelevant social influences, one wonders how a democracy ever solves its political problems. But when one considers the data in a broader perspective — how huge segments of the society adapt to political conditions affecting them or how the political system adjusts itself to changing conditions over long periods of time — he cannot fail to be impressed with the total result. Where the rational citizen seems to abdicate, nevertheless angels seem to tread. . . .

That is the paradox. *Individual voters* today seem unable to satisfy the requirements for a democratic system of government outlined by political theorists. But the *system of democracy* does meet certain requirements for a going political organization. The individual members may not meet all the standards, but the whole nevertheless survives and grows. This suggests that where the classic theory is defective is in its concentration on the *individual citizen*. What are undervalued are certain collective properties that reside in the electorate as a whole and in the political and social system in which it functions.

The political philosophy we have inherited, then, has given more consideration to the virtues of the typical citizen of the democracy than to the working of the *system* as a whole. Moreover, when it dealt with the system, it mainly considered the single constitutive institutions of the system, not those general features necessary if the institutions are to work as required. For example, the rule of law, representative government, periodic elections, the party system, and the several freedoms of discussion, press, association, and assembly have all been examined by political philosophers seeking to clarify and to justify the idea of political democracy. But liberal democracy is more than a political system in which individual voters and political institutions operate. For political democracy to survive, other features are required: the intensity of conflict must be limited, the rate of change must be restrained, stability in the social and economic structure must be maintained, a pluralistic social organization must exist, and a basic consensus must bind together the contending parties.

Such features of the system of political democracy belong neither to the constitutive institutions nor to the individual voter. It might be said that they form the atmosphere or the environment in which both operate. In any case, such features have not been carefully considered by political philosophers, and it is on these broader properties of the democratic political system that more reflection and study by political theory is called for. In the most tentative fashion let us explore the values of the political system, as they involve the electorate, in the light of the foregoing considerations.

Underlying the paradox is an assumption that the population is homogeneous socially and should be homogeneous politically: that everybody is about the same in relevant social characteristics; that, if something is a political virtue (like interest in the election), then everyone should have it; that there is such a thing as "the" typical citizen on whom uniform requirements can be imposed. The tendency of classic democratic literature to work with an image of "the" voter was never justified. For, as we will attempt to illustrate here, some of the most important requirements that democratic values impose on a system require a voting population that is not homogeneous but heterogeneous in its political qualities.

The need for heterogeneity arises from the contradictory functions we expect our voting system to serve. We expect the political system to adjust itself and our affairs to changing conditions; yet we demand too that it display a high degree of stability. We expect the contending interests and parties to pursue their ends vigorously and the voters to care; yet, after the election is over, we expect reconciliation. We expect the voting outcome to serve what is best for the community; yet we do not want disinterested voting unattached to the purposes and interests of different segments of that community. We want voters to express their own free and self-determined choices; yet, for the good of the community, we would like voters to avail themselves of the best information and guidance available from the groups and leaders around them. We expect a high degree of rationality to prevail in the decision; but were all irrationality and mythology absent, and all ends pursued by the most coldly rational selection of political means, it is doubtful if the system would hold together.

In short, our electoral system calls for apparently incompatible properties — which, although they cannot all reside in each individual voter, can (and do) reside in a heterogeneous electorate. What seems to be required of the electorate as a whole is a *distribution* of qualities along important dimensions. We need some people who are active in a certain respect, others in the middle, and still others passive. The contradictory things we want from the total require that the parts be different. This can be illustrated by taking up a number of important dimensions by which an electorate might be characterized.

Involvement and Indifference. How could a mass democracy work if all the people were deeply involved in politics? Lack of interest by some people is not without its benefits, too. True, the highly interested voters vote more, and know more about the campaign, and read and listen more, and participate more; however, they are also less open to persuasion and less likely to change. Extreme interest goes with extreme partisanship and might culminate in rigid fanaticism that could destroy democratic processes if generalized throughout the community. Low affect toward the election — not caring much — underlies the resolution of many political problems; votes can be resolved into a two-party split instead of fragmented into many parties (the splinter parties of the left, for example, splinter because their advocates are *too* interested in politics). Low interest provides maneuvering room for political shifts necessary for a complex society in a period of rapid change. Compromise might be based upon sophisticated awareness of costs and returns — perhaps impossible to demand of a mass society — but it is more often induced by indifference. Some people are and should be highly interested in politics, but not everyone is or needs to be. Only the doctrinaire would deprecate the moderate indifference that facilitates compromise.

Hence, an important balance between action motivated by strong sentiments and action with little passion behind it is obtained by heterogeneity within the electorate. Balance of this sort is, in practice, met by a distribution of voters rather than by a homogeneous collection of "ideal" citizens.

Stability and Flexibility. A similar dimension along which an electorate might be characterized is stability-flexibility. The need for change and adaptation is clear, and the need for stability ought equally to be (especially from observation of current democratic practice in, say, certain Latin American countries). . . . [I]t may be that the very people who are most sensitive to changing social conditions are those most susceptible to political change. For, in either case, the people exposed to membership in overlapping strata, those whose former life-patterns are being broken up, those who are moving about socially or physically, those who are forming new families and new friendships — it is they who are open to adjustments of attitudes and tastes. They may be the least partisan and the least interested voters, but they perform a valuable function for the entire system. Here again is an instance in which an individual "inadequacy" provides a positive service for society: The campaign can be a reaffirming force for the settled majority and a creative force for the unsettled minority. There is stability on both sides and flexibility in the middle.

Progress and Conservation. Closely related to the question of stability is the question of past versus future orientation of the system. In America a progressive outlook is highly valued, but, at the same time, so is a conservative one. Here a balance between the two is easily found in the party system and in the distribution of voters themselves from extreme conservatives to extreme liberals. But a balance between the two is also achieved by a distribution of political dispositions through time. There are periods of great political agitation (i.e., campaigns) alternating with periods of political dormancy. Paradoxically, the former — the campaign period — is likely to be an instrument of conservatism, often even of historical regression. . . .

Again, then, a balance (between preservation of the past and receptivity to the future) seems to be required of a democratic electorate. The heterogeneous electorate in itself provides a balance between liberalism and conservatism; and so does the sequence of political events from periods of drifting change to abrupt rallies back to the loyalties of earlier years.

Consensus and Cleavage. . . . [T]here are required *social* consensus and cleavage — in effect pluralism — in politics. Such pluralism makes for enough consensus to hold the system together and enough cleavage to make it move. Too much consensus would be deadening and restrictive of liberty; too much cleavage would be destructive of the society as a whole. . . . Thus again a requirement we might place on an electoral system — balance between total political war between segments of the society and total political indifference to group interests of that society — translates into varied requirements for different individuals. With respect to group or bloc voting, as with other aspects of political behavior, it is perhaps not unfortunate that "some do and some do not."

Individualism and Collectivism. Lord Bryce pointed out the difficulties in a theory of democracy that assumes that each citizen must himself be capable of voting intelligently:

> Orthodox democratic theory assumes that every citizen has, or ought to have, thought out for himself certain opinions, i.e., ought to have a definite view, defensible by argument, of what the country needs, of what principles ought to be applied in governing it, of the man to whose hands the government ought to be entrusted. There are persons who talk, though certainly very few who act, as if they believed this theory, which may be compared to the theory of some ultra-Protestants that every good Christian has or ought to have . . . worked out for himself from the Bible a system of theology.

In the first place, however, the information available to the individual voter is not limited to that directly possessed by him. True, the individual casts his own personal ballot. But, as we have tried to indicate . . . that is perhaps the most individualized action he takes in an election. His vote is formed in the midst of his fellows in a sort of group decision — if, indeed, it may be called a decision at all — and the total information and knowledge possessed in the group's present and past generations can be made available for the group's choice. Here is where opinion-leading relationships, for example, play an active role.

Second, and probably more important, the individual voter may not have a great deal of detailed information, but he usually has picked up the crucial *general* information as part of his social learning itself. He may not know the parties' positions on the tariff, or who is for reciprocal trade treaties, or what are the differences on Asiatic policy, or how the parties split on civil rights, or how many security risks were exposed by whom. But he cannot live in an American community without knowing broadly where the parties stand. He has learned that the Republicans are more conservative and the Democrats more liberal — and he can locate his own sentiments and cast his vote accordingly. After all, he must vote for one or the other party, and, if he knows the big thing about the parties, he does not need to know all the little things. The basic role a party plays as an institution in American life is more important to his voting than a particular stand on a particular issue.

It would be unthinkable to try to maintain our present economic style of life without a complex system of delegating to others what we are not competent to do ourselves, without accepting and giving training to each other about what each is expected to do, without accepting our dependence on others in many spheres and taking responsibility for their dependence on us in some spheres. And, like it or not, to maintain our present political style of life, we may have to accept much the same interdependence with others in collective behavior. We have learned slowly in economic life that it is useful not to have everyone a butcher or a baker, any more than it is useful to have no one skilled in such activities. The same kind of division of labor — as repugnant as it may be in some respects to our individualistic tradition — is serving us well today in mass politics. There is an implicit division of political labor within the electorate.

The preceding selection discussed the role of apathy in a democratic political system and the necessity for a political division of labor. The authors suggested that apathy might be a positive force in making democracy work and not necessarily a negative quality of the electorate, nor an eroding trait of democratic politics. In the following selection voters speak for themselves about politics. Do their attitudes constitute a strong underpinning for effective democratic government, or do they reflect a dangerous alienation from politics?

26
Haynes Johnson

THE VOTERS SPEAK

Americans have always distrusted their political leaders, and belief in government's ineptness and corruption is an old national habit. But new factors distinguish political attitudes during the 1976 election year. People asked more questions, asserted themselves with less assurance, had more appreciation for the complexities of life, both theirs and their country's. They recognized their own limitations, as well as the politicians'.

"Sometimes I feel I could be as corrupt as the politicians are," a California man in his early forties said, "just as corrupt as the whole Watergate bunch — being manipulative and all. People are becoming more aware of that part of themselves. It scares me. That's the part of me I don't like, and I have to watch myself."

Personal judgments were given more tentatively. The martial, moralistic, or jingoistic words about communism or "Americanism" heard so often in other political years were notably absent. People articulated, with greater insights, their notions about what life in America was becoming — and whether they thought anything could be done to change it for the better through politics.

I recall two people out of many I interviewed — one was a Southerner:

The birth of Jesus starts with the scripture telling us the times were tough. They were numbering the people. Now people have never liked to be numbered. The first thing a sovereign does to show his complete mastery is to give you a number — when he puts you in prison, when he calls you into the army. We don't like numbers, with all they symbolize. And we're living in a society in which we're becoming permanently numbered.

The other was a Midwest businessman:

The question is asked: Well, why don't we just throw all the rascals out? Well, that's fine. And who are we going to get to take their places? Okay, why don't *I* run? Why don't *I* be a better practicing citizen? Well, I have a salary, but I don't have any money. To unseat our congressman would take half a million dollars. Where the hell's the money going to come from? If it comes from big business, I'm beholden to them. If it comes from labor unions, I'm beholden to them. It's not going to come from you and me and my friends at the Rotary Club. We seem to be stuck with

Selection from *In the Absence of Power* by Haynes Johnson. Copyright © 1980 by Haynes Johnson. Reprinted by permission of Viking Penguin, Inc.

the system, and the only alternative — and of course some people have been espousing this — is some sort of revolutionary process. I can't figure out an alternative other than something drastic. And I'm no revolutionary.

From that kind of thinking it wasn't hard to move into the increasing ranks of the nonvoters. Nonvoters tended to be well educated and well informed, and often young. They were the political future, and they usually could explain specifically why they were going to abstain. For many, their decision came after careful deliberation. Their explanations became familiar; they were the same everywhere: *No matter who's president, the real problems aren't going to be solved. . . . There's no major difference between either one; it's all personality. . . . Politics is corrupt. . . . The presidential candidates are always captives of hidden forces — business, labor, what have you. . . . And where do they get all that money to run on, anyway? . . . Promises are all you get, and the promises are never kept. . . . All they're in it for are power and glory. . . . They don't really care about people. . . . And even if they do believe what they say, they aren't going to be able to do anything when they get in office. . . .*

Beneath this litany of quick answers, two principal themes were expressed. One was skepticism about ever being able to know the facts. With all the massive outpouring of political rhetoric month after month, and all the conflicting claims coming from the candidates and the press, how could a citizen determine the truth? In the end, weren't they forced to take the candidates on faith? Look where faith got them in recent presidential elections. The other theme was related: the people saw politics and politicians as ever more hypocritical. The candidates' lavishly produced, studiedly casual television commercials, the synthetic speeches, the phony rallies, the unreality of it all — they were, in the vernacular, a turnoff. "I hate it, I hate it," said a young Southern woman, well educated, concerned about issues. "The bullshit. The secrecy. The manipulation. It just makes me ill. Everybody's negative about politics — and they have a reason to be."

On the West Coast, a group of residents sitting on a beach looking out across Tomales Point and the surrounding hills, covered with tall, dark pines, were talking about the election. A young woman was speaking: "It seems to me the most important thing a president can do concerns our economic foundation," said Elizabeth Whitney, who edited a small paper near Inverness, California. "The cost of living goes up, therefore workers want to get more money because they can't cope. So the cost of labor goes up, so the cost of living goes up. There's no way to stop it, and everybody's trying to figure out just how to stay in the same place. But I don't know if any president can turn any of it around. It has its own perpetual motion machine. I can't imagine if I had the power what I'd do first, and that seems to be the same way with the president. Who really knows what to do?"

Listening quietly was an older woman who lived nearby, in retirement with her husband. "I try to read and analyze the issues," Dorothy Johnstone said, "but I just get lost. Does everybody else? The more you know about something, the harder it is to know what you know. It's like what happens when you are bird-watching: you learn one bird, then you find that there are thousands of birds flying around that you haven't even noticed and don't know. I read all the League of Women Voters' material that comes in the house. I read *Skeptic* magazine. I read *Harper's*. I read the *Saturday Review*. I read — oh, well, I guess we'll survive regardless who's elected president."

These kinds of conversations made ridiculous all the talk about an "apathetic America." Apathy — indifference, and the absence of caring — wasn't a characteristic of the citizens you'd meet. They *were* concerned, but their problem was in finding political leadership.

What people were looking for was hard to define. The most popular model of a president seemed to be Harry Truman. Songs were sung about Old Harry — the blunt, decisive, plain-talking man of the Midwest who could plow a straight furrow and get his history and perspectives right. Politicians of both parties praised him. Presidential candidates tried to emulate him. He was a *real* leader: strong and compassionate. In fact, to me the great irony was that people seemed to be seeking the personal qualities they admired in Truman while rejecting the political reality that Truman and so many of his successors represented.

At the Truman Library, outside Independence, Missouri, you'd see crowds approaching the exhibits in an atmosphere of reverence. But what they saw and heard were hardly memorable — were, in fact, all the things people were now reacting against. *The glorification of the leader:* "Citizen, Statesman, Soldier," the legend under Harry's oil portrait read. *The rewards of political power:* "These swords and knives were given to the president by the royal families of Saudi Arabia and Iran," the inscription on a glass-enclosed case housing jewel-encrusted weapons informed you. *The paucity and cheapness of political rhetoric:* Tom Dewey, his voice droning on from a recording of the 1948 campaign, his tone insufferably pompous: "Let us move forward out of the desperate darkness of today into the bright light of tomorrow." Truman, speaking in that flat Missouri drawl, but far more vibrantly and self-assured, saying the choice was between the party of the people and the special interests, and adding: "We will win the election and make those Republicans like it. Don't you forget that. We'll do that because they're wrong and we're right."

No one you'd meet, in any part of the country, spoke of politics in such starkly partisan and simple terms. Farmers in Truman's home territory showed a shrewdness and sophistication far exceeding the level of Carter's or Ford's speeches — whether about foreign or domestic policy, about oil and the Middle East, wheat and the Soviet Union, productivity and the government — federal, state, and local. Gene Palmer, a farmer who lived in Platte City, just north of Truman's home, raised two subjects on a common theme when I talked to him — cynicism about government and political privilege:

> Two or three years ago when wheat was four or five dollars a bushel, the powers that be just panicked and predicted a dollar a loaf for bread. How horrible that was going to be! Well, today the farmer gets less than half of what he did then for wheat, and the cost of bread is higher. If every farmer that owns or controls wheat today could say, "Okay, I don't want two dollars and fifty cents for my wheat, I don't want five dollars, I don't want anything for my wheat. There'll be no charge. We don't want these farm products getting this high so just take this wheat free" — without a doubt in six months bakery products would cost more than they do today.
>
> In Kansas City, the residents of Jackson County were asked to approve some municipal revenue bonds to build those sports complexes we have out there. And we've got Mr. Lamar Hunt that's come in from Dallas, Texas, and brought us professional football games. But there's no way for the average person to go see a football game. The reason is, they have 'em all on season tickets and the tickets are held in very tight hands. The average person is never eligible, or ever given a chance, to buy season tickets even if he could afford to. The banks, all the major corporations, the utility companies, everybody in politics from the state level on down — they all have lots of tickets. The county court has one whole side of the stadium. And the public is paying whether they go or not. Every little guy that's got a three-bedroom house or any Goddam thing that's taxable, he's paying for it.[1]

People saw — or wanted to see — something special in Jimmy Carter. Certainly they were ready for something different. They sensed integrity and simplicity. He was critical, but caring. He was competent. He seemed able to address the real questions troubling people — power and powerlessness, size and functioning of government, energy and environment, equity for the small as well as the large. (He makes his own bed, they said in surprise after he stayed at someone's home on an early New England trip. Later it was Jimmy Carter carrying his own suit bag wherever he went. That these symbols of informality and unpretentiousness impressed people — and they did — showed possibly naïveté, but also how desperate

---

[1] This kind of thing is of course not restricted to Kansas City. Nothing shows more clearly the nature of Washington relationships — professional, social, political, and economic — than the scene on any Sunday at RFK Stadium (built by public funds) when the Redskins play: about fifteen thousand season-ticket holders — newspapers, law firms, advertising agencies, and political offices — control the fifty-five thousand seats. Entertained in the owners' box are presidents, Supreme Court justices, cabinet officers, members of Congress, editors, columnists, commentators, and wealthy Georgetown hostesses.

people were for a different presidential style.) And they also wanted to believe Carter was as capable a manager as his campaign made him out: zero-base budgeting (no one quite knew what it was, but supposedly it had worked in Georgia), make every program accountable, start fresh, shake things up, level with the people, cut out the pomp and artificial trappings of power.

People were willing to take a chance on a political novice. If they thought about it all, they knew that no president in the twentieth century had had such limited exposure to government — and especially to Washington — as Jimmy Carter.

Theodore Roosevelt came to the presidency after considerable national and international experience, and long exposure to Washington. Aside from family and political connections there, he had spent six years in Washington directing the fight against the spoils system while on the Civil Service Commission before becoming governor of New York, and then he was back in the capital as assistant secretary of the Navy and vice-president. William Howard Taft, too, grew up in politics. As the son of a cabinet officer he became solicitor general of the United States and then served in Teddy Roosevelt's cabinet. Woodrow Wilson's lifetime study of government and politics had been crowned by his governorship of New Jersey; his book on congressional government was still considered a classic half a century later. Even Warren G. Harding, probably the most ineffectual of presidents, was a Washington figure: he had served in the Senate and knew the city and its politics well. Calvin Coolidge had spent his life in politics before becoming vice-president, and then president. Herbert Hoover was perhaps as well prepared for the presidency as anyone — through his service in cabinet and subcabinet positions for several presidents. FDR, like his cousin Theodore, was an important figure in the capital before going back to New York politics and thence to the White House. Harry S Truman, a veteran senator; Dwight D. Eisenhower, the only nonprofessional politician in this group, nevertheless understood well the way power worked in Washington from his military service in the city dating back to the early 1930s; Kennedy and Nixon came to the Congress the same day, and thirteen years later competed for the presidency; LBJ had been congressional aide, congressman, senator, most powerful of Capitol Hill leaders, and vice-president; Ford had been in Congress a quarter of a century before becoming vice-president and then president.

The idea that Jimmy Carter, the only member of his family in two hundred years to go to college (his father was the only one to have gotten as far as the tenth grade; and few, it seems, ever left the state of Georgia) could become president was extraordinary by any measure. His election would signal a radical departure in the kind of person Americans chose as their president. In background and experience he would be different from any president any American had known. But by the time they voted in

1976, Americans already were moving in different directions. They were in the midst of a period of revolutionary change. As someone said to me, "The real revolution is how we're going to live our own lives." It was political change that was lagging behind others transforming the country.

The Role of Parties
in the Political Process

In the classical liberal democratic model of democracy political parties play a key role in bridging the gap between people and government. The purpose of parties is to develop meaningful programs and present choices to the electorate, and after the electorate has made its choice the parties are to implement programs in accordance with the wishes of the voters. The classical model of democracy can best be described as "government by discussion." Discussion proceeds in a sequential manner through three stages: (1) discussion within the parties on the formulation of issues that will be presented to the electorate; (2) discussion within the electorate of the party platforms that have been presented; (3) discussion within the legislature and the executive after the election to refine party programs in light of voter preferences. This model ideally presumes two-party government, a disciplined political party system, and a rational electorate. In the American political system, as the preceding selection indicates, the electorate does not always vote rationally in accordance with issue preferences. Moreover, as the following selection points out, a major development reaching fruition in the last decade is the decline in the role of political parties that may spell the "end of American party politics." If people cease to identify with political parties and no longer relate to government through parties then the usefulness of the electoral process as a vehicle of democratic participation is diminished.

27

Walter Dean Burnham

THE END OF AMERICAN PARTY POLITICS

American politics has clearly been falling apart in the past decade. We don't have to look hard for the evidence. Mr. Nixon is having as much difficulty controlling his fellow party members in Congress as any of his Democratic predecessors had in controlling theirs. John V. Lindsay, a year after he helped make Spiro Agnew a household word, had to run for mayor as a Liberal and an Independent with the aid of nationally prominent Democrats. Chicago in July of 1968 showed that for large numbers of its activists a major political party can become not just a disappointment, but positively repellent. Ticket-splitting has become widespread as never before, especially among the young; and George C. Wallace, whose third-party movement is the largest in recent American history, continues to demonstrate an unusually stable measure of support.

Vietnam and racial polarization have played large roles in this breakdown, to be sure; but the ultimate causes are rooted much deeper in our history. For some time we have been saying that we live in a "pluralist democracy." And no text on American politics would be complete without a few key code words such as "consensus," "incrementalism," "bargaining" and "process." Behind it all is a rather benign view of our politics, one that assumes that the complex diversity of the American social structure is filtered through the two major parties and buttressed by a consensus of middle-class values which produces an electoral politics of low intensity and gradual change. The interplay of interest groups and public officials determines policy in detail. The voter has some leverage on policy, but only in a most diffuse way; and, anyway, he tends to be a pretty apolitical animal, dominated either by familial or local tradition, on one hand, or by the charisma of attractive candidates on the other. All of this is a good thing, of course, since in an affluent time the politics of consensus rules out violence and polarization. It pulls together and supports the existing order of things.

There is no doubt that this description fits "politics as usual," in the

From W. D. Burnham, "The End of American Party Politics," published by permission of Transaction, Inc., from *Society* 7:2 (December 1969). Copyright © 1969 by Transaction, Inc.

United States, but to assume that it fits the whole of American electoral politics is a radical oversimplification. Yet even after these past years of turmoil, few efforts have been made to appraise the peculiar rhythms of American politics in a more realistic way. This article is an attempt to do so by focusing upon two very important and little celebrated aspects of the dynamics of our politics: the phenomena of critical realignments of the electorate and of decomposition of the party in our electoral politics.

As a whole and across time, the reality of American politics appears quite different from a simple vision of pluralist democracy. It is shot through with escalating tensions, periodic electoral convulsions, and repeated redefinitions of the rules and general outcomes of the political game. It has also been marked repeatedly by redefinitions — by no means always broadening ones — of those who are permitted to play. One other very basic characteristic of American party politics that emerges from an historical overview is the profound incapacity of established political leadership to adapt itself to the political demands produced by the losers in America's stormy socioeconomic life. As is well known, American political parties are not instruments of collective purpose, but of electoral success. One major implication of this is that, as organizations, parties are interested in control of offices but not of government in any larger sense. It follows that once successful routines are established or re-established for office-winning, very little motivation exists among party leaders to disturb the routines of the game. These routines are periodically upset, to be sure, but not by adaptive change within the party system. They are upset by overwhelming external force.

It has been recognized, at least since the publication of V. O. Key's "A Theory of Critical Elections" in 1955, that some elections in our history have been far more important than most in their long-range consequences for the political system. Such elections seem to "decide" clusters of substantive issues in a more clear-cut way than do most of the ordinary varieties. There is even a consensus among historians as to when these turning points in electoral politics took place. The first came in 1800 when Thomas Jefferson overthrew the Federalist hegemony established by Washington, Adams, and Hamilton. The second came in 1828 and in the years afterward, with the election of Andrew Jackson and the democratization of the presidency. The third, of course, was the election of Abraham Lincoln in 1860, an election that culminated a catastrophic polarization of the society as a whole and resulted in civil war. The fourth critical election was that of William McKinley in 1896; this brought to a close the "Civil War" party system and inaugurated a political alignment congenial to the dominance of industrial capitalism over the American political economy. Created in the crucible of one massive depression, this "System of 1896" endured until the collapse of the economy in a second. The election of Franklin D. Roosevelt in 1932 came last in this series, and brought a major realignment of electoral politics and policy-making structures into the now familiar "welfare-pluralist" mode.

Now that the country appears to have entered another period of political upheaval, it seems particularly important not only to identify the phenomena of periodic critical realignments in our electoral politics, but to integrate them into a larger — if still very modest — theory of stasis and movement in American politics. For the realignments focus attention on the dark side of our politics, those moments of tremendous stress and abrupt transformation that remind us that "politics as usual" in the United States is not politics as always, and that American political institutions and leadership, once defined or redefined in a "normal phase" seem themselves to contribute to the building of conditions that threaten their overthrow.

To underscore the relevance of critical elections to our own day, one has only to recall that in the past, fundamental realignments in voting behavior have always been signaled by the rise of significant third parties: the Anti-Masons in the 1820s, the Free Soilers in the 1840s and 1850s, the Populists in the 1890s, and the La Follette Progressives in the 1920s. We cannot know whether George Wallace's American Independent Party of 1968 fits into this series, but it is certain — as we shall see below — that the very foundations of American electoral politics have become quite suddenly fluid in the past few years, and that the mass base of our politics has become volatile to a degree unknown in the experience of all but the very oldest living Americans. The Wallace uprising is a major sign of this recent fluidity; but it hardly stands alone.

Third-party protests, perhaps by contrast with major-party bolts, point up the interplay in American politics between the inertia of "normal" established political routines and the pressures arising from the rapidity, unevenness and uncontrolled character of change in the country's dynamic socioeconomic system. All of the third parties prior to and including the 1968 Wallace movement constituted attacks by outsiders, who felt they were outsiders, against an elite frequently viewed in conspiratorial terms. The attacks were always made under the banner of high moralistic universals against an established political structure seen as corrupt, undemocratic, and manipulated by insiders for their own benefit and that of their supporters. All these parties were perceived by their activists as "movements" that would not only purify the corruption of the current political regime, but replace some of its most important parts. Moreover, they all telegraphed the basic clusters of issues that would dominate politics in the next electoral era: the completion of political democratization in the 1830s, slavery and sectionalism in the late 1840s and 1850s, the struggle between the industrialized and the colonial regions in the 1890s, and welfare liberalism vs. laissez-faire in the 1920s and 1930s. One may well view the American Independent Party in such a context.

The periodic recurrence of third-party forerunners of realignment — and realignments themselves, for that matter — are significantly related to dominant peculiarities of polity and society in the United States. They point to an electorate especially vulnerable to breaking apart, and to a political system in which the sense of common nationhood may be much more nearly skin-deep than is usually appreciated. If there is any evolutionary scale of political modernization at all, the persistence of deep fault lines in our electoral politics suggests pretty strongly that the United States remains a "new nation" to this day in some important political respects. The periodic recurrence of these tensions may also imply that — as dynamically developed as our economic system is — no convincing evidence of political development in the United States can be found after the 1860s.

Nation-wide critical realignments can only take place around clusters of issues of the most fundamental importance. The most profound of these issues have been cast up in the course of the transition of our Lockeian-liberal commonwealth from an agrarian to an industrial state. The last two major realignments — those of 1893–1896 and 1928–1936 — involved the two great transitional crises of American industrial-capitalism, the economic collapses of 1893 and 1929. The second of these modern realignments produced, of course, the broad coalition on which the New Deal's welfare-pluralist policy was ultimately based. But the first is of immediate concern to us here. For the 1896 adaptation of electoral politics to the imperatives of industrial-capitalism involved a set of developments that stand in the sharpest possible contrast to those occurring elsewhere in the Western world at about the same time. Moreover, they set in motion new patterns of behavior in electoral politics that were never entirely overcome even during the New Deal period, and which, as we shall see, have resumed their forward march during the past decade.

As a case in point, let me briefly sketch the political evolution of Pennsylvania — one of the most industrially developed areas on earth — during the 1890–1932 period. There was in this state a pre-existing, indeed, preindustrial, pattern of two-party competition, one that had been forged in the Jacksonian era and decisively amended, though not abolished, during the Civil War. Then came the realignment of the 1890s, which, like those of earlier times, was an abrupt process. In the five annual elections from 1888 through November 1892, the Democrats' mean percentage of the total two-party vote was 46.7 percent, while for the five elections beginning in February 1894 it dropped to a mean of 37.8 percent. Moreover, the greatest and most permanent Republican gains during this depression decade occurred where they counted most, numerically: in the metropolitan areas of Philadelphia and Pittsburgh.

The cumulative effect of this realignment and its aftermath was to convert Pennsylvania into a thoroughly one-party state, in which conflict over the basic political issues was duly transferred to the Republican primary after it was established in 1908. By the 1920s this peculiar process had been completed and the Democratic party had become so weakened that, as often as not, the party's nominees for major office were selected by the Republican leadership. But whether so selected or not, their general-election prospects were dismal: of the 80 state-wide contests held from 1894 through 1931, a candidate running with Democratic party endorsement won just one. Moreover, with a highly ephemeral exception of Theodore Roosevelt's bolt from the Republican party in 1912, no third parties emerged as general-election substitutes for the ruined Democrats.

The political simplicity which had thus emerged in this industrial heartland of the Northeast by the 1920s was the more extraordinary in that it occurred in an area whose socioeconomic division of labor was as complex and its level of development as high as any in the world. In most other regions of advanced industrialization the emergence of corporate capitalism was associated with the development of mass political parties with high structural cohesion and explicit collective purposes with respect to the control of policy and government. These parties expressed deep conflicts over the direction of public policy, but they also brought about the democratic revolution of Europe, for electoral participation tended to rise along with them. Precisely the opposite occurred in Pennsylvania and, with marginal and short-lived exceptions, the nation. It is no exaggeration to say that the political response to the collectivizing thrust of industrialism in this American state was the elimination of organized partisan combat, an extremely severe decline in electoral participation, the emergence of a Republican "coalition of the whole" and — by no means coincidentally — a highly efficient insulation of the controlling industrial-financial elite from effective or sustained countervailing pressures.

IRRELEVANT RADICALISM

The reasons for the increasing solidity of this "system of 1896" in Pennsylvania are no doubt complex. Clearly, for example, the introduction of the direct primary as an alternative to the general election, which was thereby emptied of any but ritualistic significance, helped to undermine the minority Democrats more and more decisively by destroying their monopoly of opposition. But nationally as well the Democratic party in and after the 1890s was virtually invisible to Pennsylvania voters as a usable opposition. For with the ascendency of the agrarian Populist William Jennings Bryan, the Democratic party was transformed into a vehicle for colonial, periphery-oriented dissent against the industrial-metropolitan center, leaving the Republicans as sole spokesmen for the latter.

This is a paradox that pervades American political history, but it was sharpest in the years around the turn of the century. The United States was so vast that it had little need of economic colonies abroad; in fact it had two major colonial regions within its own borders, the postbellum South and the West. The only kinds of attacks that could be made effective on a nation-wide basis against the emergent industrialist hegemony — the only attacks that, given the ethnic heterogeneity and extremely rudimentary political socialization of much of the country's industrial working class, could come within striking distance of achieving a popular majority — came out of these colonial areas. Thus "radical" protest in major-party terms came to be associated with the neo-Jacksonian demands of agrarian small-holders and small-town society already confronted by obsolescence. The Democratic party from 1896 to 1932, and in many respects much later, was the national vehicle for these struggles.

The net effect of this was to produce a condition in which — especially, but not entirely on the presidential level — the more economically advanced a state was, the more heavy were its normal Republican majorities likely to be. The nostalgic agrarian-individualist appeals of the national Democratic leadership tended to present the voters of this industrial state with a choice that was not a choice: between an essentially backward-looking provincial party articulating interests in opposition to those of the industrial North and East as a whole, and a "modernizing" party whose doctrines included enthusiastic acceptance of and co-operation with the dominant economic interests of region and nation. Not only did this partitioning of the political universe entail normal and often huge Republican majorities in an economically advanced state like Pennsylvania, but the survival of national two-party competition on such a basis helped to ensure that no local reorganization of electoral politics along class lines could effectively occur even within such a state. Such a voting universe had a tendency toward both enormous inbuilt stability and increasing entrenchment in the decades after its creation. Probably no force less overwhelming than the post-1929 collapse of the national economic system would have sufficed to dislodge it. Without such a shock, who can say how, or indeed whether, the "System of 1896" would have come to an end in Pennsylvania and the nation? To ask such a question is to raise yet another. For there is no doubt that in Pennsylvania, as elsewhere, the combination of trauma in 1929–1933 and Roosevelt's creative leadership provided the means for overthrowing the old order and for reversing dramatically the depoliticization of electoral politics which had come close to perfection under it. Yet might it not be the case that the dominant pattern of political adaptation to industrialism in the United States has worked to eliminate, by one means or another, the links provided by political parties between voters and rulers? In other words, was the post-1929 reversal permanent or only a transitory phase in our political evolution? And if transitory, what bearing would this fact have on the possible recurrence of critical realignments in the future?

WITHERING AWAY OF THE PARTIES

The question requires us to turn our attention to the second major dynamic of American electoral politics during this century: the phenomenon of electoral disaggregation, of the breakdown of party loyalty, which in many respects must be seen as the permanent legacy of the fourth party system of 1896–1932. One of the most conspicuous developments of this era, most notably during the 1900–1920 period, was a whole network of changes in the rules of the political game. This is not the place for a thorough treatment and documentation of these peculiarities. One can only mention here some major changes in the rules of the game, and note that one would have no difficulty in arguing that their primary latent function was to ease the transition from a preindustrial universe of competitive, highly organized mass politics to a depoliticized world marked by drastic shrinkage in participation or political leverage by the lower orders of the population. The major changes surely include the following:

1.   The introduction of the Australian ballot, which was designed to purify elections but also eliminated a significant function of the older political machines, the printing and distribution of ballots, and eased a transition from party voting to candidate voting.
2.   The introduction of the direct primary, which at once stripped the minority party of its monopoly of opposition and weakened the control of party leaders over nominating processes, and again hastened preoccupation of the electorate with candidates rather than parties.
3.   The movement toward nonpartisan local elections, often accompanied by a drive to eliminate local bases of representation such as wards in favor of at-large elections, which produced — as Samuel Hays points out — a shift of political power from the grass roots to city-wide cosmopolitan elites.
4.   The expulsion of almost all blacks, and a very large part of the poor-white population as well, from the Southern electorate by a series of legal and extralegal measures such as the poll tax.
5.   The introduction of personal registration requirements the burden of which, in faithful compliance with dominant middle-class values, was placed on the individual rather than on public authority, but which effectively disenfranchised large numbers of the poor.

BREAKDOWN OF PARTY LOYALTY

Associated with these and other changes in the rules of the game was a profound transformation in voting behavior. There was an impressive growth in the numbers of political independents and ticket-splitters, a growth accompanied by a sea-change among party elites from what Richard Jensen has termed the "militarist" (or ward boss) campaign style to the "mercantilist" (or advertising-packaging) style. Aside from noting that the transition was largely completed as early as 1916, and hence that the practice of "the selling of the president" goes back far earlier than we usually think, these changes too must be left for fuller exposition elsewhere.

Critical realignments, as we have argued, are an indispensable part of a stability-disruption dialectic which has the deepest roots in American political history. Realigning sequences are associated with all sorts of aberrations from the normal workings of American party politics, in the events leading up to nominations, the nature and style of election campaigning and the final outcome at the polls. This is not surprising, since they arise out of the collision of profound transitional crisis in the socio-economic system with the immobility of a nondeveloped political system.

At the same time, it seems clear that for realignment to fulfill some of its most essential tension-management functions, for it to be a forum by which the electorate can participate in durable "constitution making," it is essential that political parties not fall below a certain level of coherence and appeal in the electorate. It is obvious that the greater the electoral disaggregation the less effective will be "normal" party politics as an instrument of countervailing influence in an industrial order. Thus, a number of indices of disaggregation significantly declined during the 1930s as the Democratic Party remobilized parts of American society under the stimulus of the New Deal. In view of the fact that political parties during the 1930s and 1940s were once again called upon to assist in a redrawing of the map of American politics and policy-making, this regeneration of partisan voting in the 1932–1952 era is hardly surprising. More than that, regeneration was necessary if even the limited collective purposes of the new majority coalition were to be realized.

Even so, the New Deal realignment was far more diffuse, protracted, and incomplete than any of its predecessors, a fact of which the more advanced New Dealers were only too keenly aware. It is hard to avoid the impression that one contributing element in this peculiarity of our last realignment was the much higher level of electoral disaggregation in the 1930s and 1940s than had existed at any time prior to the realignment of the 1890s. If one assumes that the end result of a long-term trend toward electoral disaggregation is the complete elimination of political parties as foci that shape voting behavior, then the possibility of critical realignment would, by definition, be eliminated as well. Every election would be dominated by TV packaging, candidate charisma, real or manufactured, and short-term, ad hoc influences. Every election, therefore, would have become deviating or realigning by definition, and American national politics would come to resemble the formless gubernatorial primaries that V. O. Key described in his classic *Southern Politics*.

The New Deal clearly arrested and reversed, to a degree, the march toward electoral disaggregation. But it did so only for the period in which the issues generated by economic scarcity remained central, and the generation traumatized by the collapse of 1929 remained numerically preponderant in the electorate. Since 1952, electoral disaggregation has resumed, in many measurable dimensions, and with redoubled force. The data on this point are overwhelming. Let us examine a few of them.

A primary aspect of electoral disaggregation, of course, is the "pulling apart" over time of the percentages for the same party but at different levels of election: this is the phenomenon of split-ticket voting. Recombining and reorganizing the data found in two tables of Milton Cummings' excellent study, *Congressmen and the Electorate,* and extending the series back and forward in time, we may examine the relationship between presidential and congressional elections during this century.

Such an array captures both the initial upward thrust of disaggregation in the second decade of this century, the peaking in the middle to late 1920s, the recession beginning in 1932, and especially the post-1952 resumption of the upward trend.

Other evidence points precisely in the same direction. It has generally been accepted in survey-research work that generalized partisan identification shows far more stability over time than does actual voting behavior, since the latter is subject to short-term factors associated with each election. What is not so widely understood is that this glacial measure of party identification has suddenly become quite volatile during the 1960s, and particularly during the last half of the decade. In the first place, as both Gallup and Survey Research Center data confirm, the proportion of independents underwent a sudden shift upward around 1966: while from 1940 to 1965 independents constituted about 20 percent to 22 percent of the electorate, they increased to 29 percent in 1966. At the present time, they outnumber Republicans by 30 percent to 28 percent.

Second, there is a clear unbroken progression in the share that independents have of the total vote along age lines. The younger the age group, the larger the number of independents in it, so that among the 21–29 year olds, according to the most recent Gallup findings this year, 42 percent are independents — an increase of about 10 percent over the first half of the decade, and representing greater numbers of people than identify with either major party. When one reviews the June 1969 Gallup survey of college students, the share is larger still — 44 percent. Associated with this quantitative increase in independents seems to be a major qualitative change as well. Examining the data for the 1950s, the authors of *The American Voter* could well argue that independents tended to have lower political awareness and political involvement in general than did identifiers (particularly strong identifiers) of either major party. But the current concentration of independents in the population suggests that this may no longer be the case. They are clearly and disproportionately found not only among the young, and especially among the college young, but also among

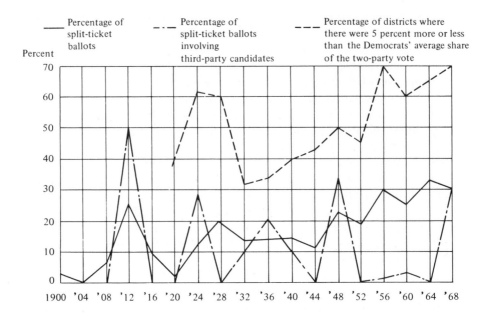

Figure A The Emergent Independent Majority, 1900–1968. Third-party candidates often inspire voters to split their tickets, but the overall trend has been for voters to ignore party labels.

men, those adults with a college background, people in the professional-managerial strata and, of course, among those with higher incomes. Such groups tend to include those people whose sense of political involvement and efficacy is far higher than that of the population as a whole. Even in the case of the two most conspicuous exceptions to this — the pile-up of independent identifiers in the youngest age group and in the South — it can be persuasively argued that this distribution does not reflect low political awareness and involvement but the reverse: a sudden, in some instances almost violent, increase in both awareness and involvement among southerners and young adults, with the former being associated both with the heavy increase in southern turnout in 1968 and the large Wallace vote polled there.

Third, one can turn to two sets of evidence found in the Survey Research Center's election studies. If the proportion of strong party identifiers over time is examined, the same pattern of long-term inertial stability and recent abrupt change can be seen. From 1952 through 1964, the proportion of strong Democratic and Republican party identifiers fluctuated in a narrow range between 36 percent and 40 percent, with a steep downward trend in strong Republican identifiers between 1960 and 1964 being matched by a moderate increase in strong Democratic identifiers. Then in

1966 the proportion of strong identifiers abruptly declined to 28 percent, with the defectors overwhelmingly concentrated among former Democrats. This is almost certainly connected, as is the increase of independent identifiers, with the Vietnam fiasco. While we do not as yet have the 1968 SRC data, the distribution of identifications reported by Gallup suggests the strong probability that this abrupt decline in party loyalty has not been reversed very much since. It is enough here to observe that while the ratio between strong identifiers and independents prior to 1966 was pretty stably fixed at between 1.6 to 1 and 2 to 1 in favor of the former, it is now evidently less than 1 to 1. Both Chicago and Wallace last year were the acting out of these changes in the arena of "popular theater."

Finally, both survey and election data reveal a decline in two other major indices of the relevance of party to voting behavior: split-ticket voting and the choice of the same party's candidates for President across time.

It is evident that the 1960s have been an era of increasingly rapid liquidation of pre-existing party commitments by individual voters. There is no evidence anywhere to support Kevin Phillips's hypothesis regarding an emergent Republican majority — assuming that such a majority would involve increases in voter identification with the party. More than that, one might well ask whether, if this process of liquidation is indeed a preliminary to realignment, the latter may not take the form of a third-party movement of truly massive and durable proportions.

The evidence lends some credence to the view that American electoral politics is undergoing a long-term transition into routines designed only to fill offices and symbolically affirm "the American way." There also seem to be tendencies for our political parties gradually to evaporate as broad and active intermediaries between the people and their rulers, even as they may well continue to maintain enough organizational strength to screen out the unacceptable or the radical at the nominating stage. It is certain that the significance of party as link between government and the governed has now come once again into serious question. Bathed in the warm glow of diffused affluence, vexed in spirit but enriched economically by our imperial military and space commitments, confronted by the gradually unfolding consequences of social change as vast as it is unplanned, what need have Americans of political parties? More precisely, why do they need parties whose structures, processes, and leadership cadres seem to grow more remote and irrelevant to each new crisis?

FUTURE POLITICS

It seems evident enough that if this long-term trend toward a politics without parties continues, the policy consequences must be profound. One can put the matter with the utmost simplicity: political parties, with all their

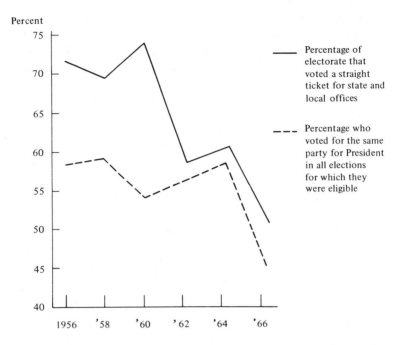

Figure B   The Decline of Party Loyalty, 1956–1966

well-known human and structural shortcomings, are the only devices thus far invented by the wit of Western man that can, with some effectiveness, generate countervailing collective power on behalf of the many individually powerless against the relatively few who are individually or organizationally powerful. Their disappearance as active intermediaries, if not as preliminary screening devices, would only entail the unchallenged ascendancy of the already powerful, unless new structures of collective power were somehow developed to replace them, and unless conditions in America's social structure and political culture came to be such that they could be effectively used. Yet neither of these contingencies, despite recent publicity for the term "participatory democracy," is likely to occur under immediately conceivable circumstances in the United States. It is much more probable that the next chapter of our political history will resemble the metapolitical world of the 1920s.

But, it may be asked, may not a future realignment serve to recrystallize and revitalize political parties in the American system?

The present condition of America contains a number of what Marxists call "internal contradictions," some of which might provide the leverage for a future critical realignment if sufficiently sharp dislocations in everyday life should occur. One of the most important of these, surely, is the conversion — largely through technological change — of the American social stratification system from the older capitalist mixture of upper or "owning" classes, dependent white-collar middle classes, and proletarians into a mixture described recently by David Apter: the technologically competent, the technologically obsolescent, and the technologically superfluous. It is arguable, in fact, that the history of the Kennedy-Johnson Administrations on the domestic front could be written in terms of a coalition of the top and bottom of this Apter-ite mix against the middle, and the 1968 election as the first stage of a "counterrevolution" of these middle strata against the pressures from both of the other two. Yet the inchoate results of 1968 raise some doubts, to say the least, that it can yet be described as part of a realigning sequence: there was great volatility in this election, but also a remarkable and unexpectedly large element of continuity and voter stability.

It is not hard to find evidence of cumulative social disaster in our metropolitan areas. We went to war with Japan in 1941 over a destruction inflicted on us far less devastating in scope and intensity than that endured by any large American city today. But the destruction came suddenly, as a sharp blow, from a foreign power; while the urban destruction of today has matured as a result of our own internal social and political processes, and it has been unfolding gradually for decades. We have consequently learned somehow to adapt to it piecemeal, as best we can, without changing our lives or our values very greatly. Critical realignments, however, also seem to require sharp, sudden blows as a precondition for their emergence. If we think of realignment as arising from the spreading internal disarray in this country, we should also probably attempt to imagine what kinds of events could produce a sudden, sharp, and general escalation in social tensions and threatened deprivations of property, status or values.

Conceivably, ghetto and student upheavals could prove enough in an age of mass communications to create a true critical realignment, but one may doubt it. Student and ghetto rebellions appear to be too narrowly defined socially to have a direct impact on the daily lives of the "vast middle," and thus produce transformations in voting behavior that would be both sweeping and permanent. For what happens in times of critical realignment is nothing less than an intense, if temporary, quasi revolutionizing of the vast middle class, a class normally content to be traditionalists or passive-participants in electoral politics.

Yet, even if students and ghetto blacks could do the trick, if they could even begin, with the aid of elements of the technological elite, a process of electoral realignment left-ward, what would be the likely consequences? What would the quasi revolutionizing of an insecure, largely urban middle class caught in a brutal squeeze from the top and the bottom of the social system look like? There are already premonitory evidences: the Wallace vote in both southern and nonsouthern areas, as well as an unexpected durability in his postelection appeal; the mayoral elections in Los Angeles and Minneapolis this year, and not least, Lindsay's narrow squeak into a second term as mayor of New York City. To the extent that the "great middle" becomes politically mobilized and self-conscious, it moves toward what has been called "urban populism," a stance of organized hostility to blacks, student radicals, and cosmopolitan liberal elites. The "great middle" remains, after all, the chief defender of the old-time Lockeian faith; both its material and cultural interests are bound up in this defense. If it should become at all mobilized as a major and cohesive political force in today's conditions, it would do so in the name of a restoration of the ancient truths by force if necessary. A realignment that directly involved this kind of mobilization — as it surely would, should it occur — would very likely have sinister overtones unprecedented in our political history.

Are we left, then, with a choice between the stagnation implicit in the disaggregative trends we have outlined here and convulsive disruption? Is there something basic to the American political system, and extending to its electoral politics, which rules out a middle ground between drift and mastery?

The fact that these questions were raised by Walter Lippmann more than half a century ago — and have indeed been raised in one form or other in every era of major transitional crisis over the past century — is alone enough to suggest an affirmative answer. The phenomena we have described here provide evidence of a partly quantitative sort which seems to point in the same direction. For electoral disaggregation is the negation of party. Further, it is — or rather, reflects — the negation of structural and behavioral conditions in politics under which linkages between the bottom, the middle, and the top can exist and produce the effective carrying out of collective power. Critical realignments are evidence not of the presence of such linkages or conditions in the normal state of American electoral politics, but precisely of their absence. Correspondingly, they are not manifestations of democratic accountability, but infrequent and hazardous substitutes for it.

Taken together, both of these phenomena generate support for the inference that American politics in its normal state is the negation of the public order itself, as that term is understood in politically developed nations. We do not have government in our domestic affairs so much as "nonrule." We do not have political parties in the contemporary sense of that term as understood elsewhere in the Western world; we have anti-parties instead. Power centrifuges rather than power concentrators, they have been immensely important not as vehicles of social transformation but for its prevention through political means.

The entire setting of the critical realignment phenomenon bears witness to a deep-seated dialectic within the American political system. From the beginning, the American socioeconomic system has developed and transformed itself with an energy and thrust that has no parallel in modern history. The political system, from parties to policy structures, has seen no such development. Indeed, it has shown astonishingly little substantive transformation over time in its methods of operation. In essence, the political system of this "fragment society" remains based today on the same Lockeian formulation that, as Louis Hartz points out, has dominated its entire history. It is predicated upon the maintenance of a high wall of separation between politics and government on one side and the socioeconomic system on the other. It depends for its effective working on the failure of anything approximating internal sovereignty in the European sense to emerge here.

The Lockeian cultural monolith, however, is based upon a social assumption that has come repeatedly into collision with reality. The assumption, of course, is not only that the autonomy of socioeconomic life from political direction is the prescribed fundamental law for the United States, but that this autonomous development will proceed with enough smoothness, uniformity and generally distributed benefits that it will be entirely compatible with the usual functioning of our antique political structures. Yet the high (though far from impermeable) wall of separation between politics and society is periodically threatened with inundations. As the socioeconomic system develops in the context of unchanging institutions of electoral politics and policy formation, dysfunctions become more and more visible. Whole classes, regions or other major sectors of the population are injured or faced with an imminent threat of injury. Finally the triggering event occurs, critical realignments follow, the universe of policy and of electoral coalitions is broadly redefined, and the tensions generated by the crisis receive some resolution. Thus it can be argued that critical realignment as a periodically recurring phenomenon is as centrally related to the workings of such a system as is the archaic and increasingly rudimentary structure of the major parties themselves.

PARTY VS. SURVIVAL

One is finally left with the sense that the twentieth-century decomposition of partisan links in our electoral system also corresponds closely with the contemporary survival needs of what Samuel P. Huntington has called the American "Tudor polity." Electoral disaggregation and the concentration of certain forms of power in the hands of economic, technological, and administrative elites are functional for the short-term survival of nonrule in the United States. They may even somehow be related to the gradual emergence of internal sovereignty in this country — though to be sure under not very promising auspices for participatory democracy of any kind. Were such a development to occur, it would not necessarily entail the disappearance or complete suppression of subgroup tensions or violence in American social life, or of group bargaining and pluralism in the policy process. It might even be associated with increases in both. But it would, after all, reflect the ultimate sociopolitical consequences of the persistence of Lockeian individualism into an era of Big Organization: oligarchy at the top, inertia and spasms of self-defense in the middle, and fragmentation at the base. One may well doubt whether political parties or critical realignments need have much place in such a political universe.

Political Campaigning

V. O. Key, Jr., in *The Responsible Electorate* (Cambridge Mass.: The Belknap Press of Harvard University Press, 1966), suggests that the voice of the people is not capable of being manipulated by skillful politicians, nor is it apathetic. Rather, he suggests the sanguine view that individuals are indeed aware of government decisions affecting their lives and are capable of rendering rational judgments on the actions of political leaders. At the same time Key points out that voter rationality depends upon the rationality of political campaigns, although he argues that in many instances voters are clever enough to see through political propaganda. Joe McGinniss describes in his book *The Selling of the President 1968* how public relations experts and political propagandists view the electorate and also demonstrates how these views affected the management of President Nixon's campaign in 1968. Readers should ask themselves how a rational democratic electorate can be maintained if the political leadership holds voters in such low esteem.

28

Joe McGinniss

THE SELLING
OF THE PRESIDENT
1968

Politics, in a sense, has always been a con game.

The American voter, insisting upon his belief in a higher order, clings to his religion, which promises another, better life; and defends passionately the illusion that the men he chooses to lead him are of finer nature than he.

It has been traditional that the successful politician honor this illusion. To succeed today, he must embellish it. Particularly if he wants to be President.

"Potential presidents are measured against an ideal that's a combination of leading man, God, father, hero, pope, king, with maybe just a touch of the avenging Furies thrown in," an adviser to Richard Nixon wrote in a memorandum late in 1967. Then, perhaps aware that Nixon qualified only as father, he discussed improvements that would have to be made — not upon Nixon himself, but upon the image of him which was received by the voter.

That there is a difference between the individual and his image is human nature. Or American nature, at least. That the difference is exaggerated and exploited electronically is the reason for this book.

Advertising, in many ways, is a con game, too. Human beings do not need new automobiles every third year; a color television set brings little enrichment of the human experience; a higher or lower hemline no expansion of consciousness, no increase in the capacity to love.

It is not surprising, then, that politicians and advertising men should have discovered one another. And, once they recognized that the citizen did not so much vote for a candidate as make a psychological purchase of him, not surprising that they began to work together.

The voter, as reluctant to face political reality as any other kind, was hardly an unwilling victim. "The deeper problems connected with advertising," Daniel Boorstin has written in *The Image,* "come less from the unscrupulousness of our 'deceivers' than from our pleasure in being deceived, less from the desire to seduce than from the desire to be seduced. . . .

From Joe McGinniss, *The Selling of the President 1968,* Chapter 2. Copyright © 1969, by Joemac, Inc. Reprinted by permission of Simon & Schuster, a Division of Gulf & Western Corporation.

"In the last half-century we have misled ourselves . . . about men . . . and how much greatness can be found among them. . . . We have become so accustomed to our illusions that we mistake them for reality. We demand them. And we demand that there be always more of them, bigger and better and more vivid."

The presidency seems the ultimate extension of our error.

Advertising agencies have tried openly to sell presidents since 1952. When Dwight Eisenhower ran for reelection in 1956, the agency of Batton, Barton, Durstine and Osborn, which had been on a retainer throughout his first four years, accepted his campaign as a regular account. Leonard Hall, national Republican chairman, said: "You sell your candidates and your programs the way a business sells its products."

The only change over the past twelve years has been that, as technical sophistication has increased, so has circumspection. The ad men were removed from the parlor but were given a suite upstairs.

What Boorstin says of advertising: "It has meant a reshaping of our very concept of truth," is particularly true of advertising on TV.

With the coming of television, and the knowledge of how it could be used to seduce voters, the old political values disappeared. Something new, murky, undefined started to rise from the mists. "In all countries," Marshall McLuhan writes, "the party system has folded like the organization chart. Policies and issues are useless for election purposes, since they are too specialized and hot. The shaping of a candidate's integral image has taken the place of discussing conflicting points of view."

Americans have never quite digested television. The mystique which should fade grows stronger. We make celebrities not only of the men who cause events but of the men who read reports of them aloud.

The televised image can become as real to the housewife as her husband, and much more attractive. Hugh Downs is a better breakfast companion, Merv Griffin cozier to snuggle with on the couch.

Television, in fact, has given status to the "celebrity" which few real men attain. And the "celebrity" here is the one described by Boorstin: "Neither good nor bad, great nor petty . . . the human pseudo-event . . . fabricated on purpose to satisfy our exaggerated expectations of human greatness."

This is, perhaps, where the twentieth century and its pursuit of illusion have been leading us. "In the last half-century," Boorstin writes, "the old heroic human mold has been broken. A new mold has been made, so that marketable human models — modern 'heroes' — could be mass-produced, to satisfy the market, and without any hitches. The qualities which now commonly make a man or woman into a 'nationally advertised' brand are in fact a new category of human emptiness."

The television celebrity is a vessel. An inoffensive container in which someone else's knowledge, insight, compassion, or wit can be presented.

And we respond like the child on Christmas morning who ignores the gift to play with the wrapping paper.

Television seems particularly useful to the politician who can be charming but lacks ideas. Print is for ideas. Newspapermen write not about people but policies; the paragraphs can be slid around like blocks. Everyone is colored gray. Columnists — and commentators in the more polysyllabic magazines — concentrate on ideology. They do not care what a man sounds like; only how he thinks. For the candidate who does not, such exposure can be embarrassing. He needs another way to reach the people.

On television it matters less that he does not have ideas. His personality is what the viewers want to share. He need be neither statesman nor crusader, he must only show up on time. Success and failure are easily measured: How often is he invited back? Often enough and he reaches his goal — to advance from "politician" to "celebrity," a status jump bestowed by grateful viewers who feel that finally they have been given the basis for making a choice.

The TV candidate, then, is measured not against his predecessors — not against a standard of performance established by two centuries of democracy — but against Mike Douglas. How well does he handle himself? Does he mumble, does he twitch, does he make me laugh? Do I feel warm inside?

Style becomes substance. The medium is the massage and the masseur gets the votes.

In office, too, the ability to project electronically is essential. We were willing to forgive John Kennedy his Bay of Pigs; we followed without question the perilous course on which he led us when missiles were found in Cuba; we even tolerated his calling of reserves for the sake of a bluff about Berlin.

We forgave, followed, and accepted because we liked the way he looked. And he had a pretty wife. Camelot was fun, even for the peasants, as long as it was televised to their huts.

Then came Lyndon Johnson, heavy and gross, and he was forgiven nothing. He might have survived the sniping of the displaced intellectuals had he only been able to charm. But no one taught him how. Johnson was syrupy. He stuck to the lens. There was no place for him in our culture.

"The success of any TV performer depends on his achieving a low-pressure style of presentation," McLuhan has written. The harder a man tries, the better he must hide it. Television demands gentle wit, irony, understatement: the qualities of Eugene McCarthy. The TV politician cannot make a speech; he must engage in intimate conversation. He must never press. He should suggest, not state; request, not demand. Nonchalance is the key word. Carefully studied nonchalance.

Warmth and sincerity are desirable but must be handled with care. Unfiltered, they can be fatal. Television did great harm to Hubert Humphrey. His excesses — talking too long and too fervently, which were merely annoying in an auditorium — became lethal in a television studio. The performer must talk to one person at a time. He is brought into the living room. He is a guest. It is improper for him to shout. Humphrey vomited on the rug.

It would be extremely unwise for the TV politician to admit such knowledge of his medium. The necessary nonchalance should carry beyond his appearance while *on* the show; it should rule his attitude *toward* it. He should express distaste for television; suspicion that there is something "phony" about it. This guarantees him good press, because newspaper reporters, bitter over their loss of prestige to the television men, are certain to stress anti-television remarks. Thus, the sophisticated candidate, while analyzing his own on-the-air technique as carefully as a golf pro studies his swing, will state frequently that there is no place for "public relations gimmicks" or "those show business guys" in his campaign. Most of the television men working for him will be unbothered by such remarks. They are willing to accept anonymity, even scorn, as long as the pay is good.

Into this milieu came Richard Nixon: grumpy, cold, and aloof. He would claim privately that he lost elections because the American voter was an adolescent whom he tried to treat as an adult. Perhaps. But if he treated the voter as an adult, it was as an adult he did not want for a neighbor.

This might have been excused had he been a man of genuine vision. An explorer of the spirit. Martin Luther King, for instance, got by without being one of the boys. But Richard Nixon did not strike people that way. He had, in Richard Rovere's words, "an advertising man's approach to his work," acting as if he believed "policies [were] products to be sold the public — this one today, that one tomorrow, depending on the discounts and the state of the market."

So his enemies had him on two counts: his personality, and the convictions — or lack of such — which lay behind. They worked him over heavily on both.

Norman Mailer remembered him as "a church usher, of the variety who would twist a boy's ear after removing him from church."

McLuhan watched him debate Kennedy and thought he resembled "the railway lawyer who signs leases that are not in the best interests of the folks in the little town."

But Nixon survived, despite his flaws, because he was tough and smart, and — some said — dirty when he had to be. Also, because there was nothing else he knew. A man to whom politics is all there is in life will almost always beat one to whom it is only an occupation.

He nearly became President in 1960, and that year it would not have been by default. He failed because he was too few of the things a President had to be — and because he had no press to lie for him and did not know how to use television to lie about himself.

It was just Nixon and John Kennedy and they sat down together in a television studio and a little red light began to glow and Richard Nixon was finished. Television would be blamed but for all the wrong reasons.

They would say it was makeup and lighting, but Nixon's problem went deeper than that. His problem was himself. Not what he said but the man he was. The camera portrayed him clearly. America took its Richard Nixon straight and did not like the taste.

The content of the programs made little difference. Except for startling lapses, content seldom does. What mattered was the image the viewers received, though few observers at the time caught the point.

McLuhan read Theodore White's *The Making of the President* book and was appalled at the section on the debates. "White offers statistics on the number of sets in American homes and the number of hours of daily use of these sets, but not one clue as to the nature of the TV image or its effects on candidates or viewers. White considers the 'content' of the debates and the deportment of the debaters, but it never occurs to him to ask why TV would inevitably be a disaster for a sharp intense image like Nixon's and a boon for the blurry, shaggy texture of Kennedy." In McLuhan's opinion: "Without TV, Nixon had it made."

What the camera showed was Richard Nixon's hunger. He lost, and bitter, confused, he blamed it on his beard.

He made another, lesser thrust in 1962, and that failed, too. He showed the world a little piece of his heart the morning after and then he moved East to brood. They did not want him, the hell with them. He was going to Wall Street and get rich.

He was afraid of television. He knew his soul was hard to find. Beyond that, he considered it a gimmick; its use in politics offended him. It had not been part of the game when he had learned to play, he could see no reason to bring it in now. He half suspected it was an eastern liberal trick: one more way to make him look silly. It offended his sense of dignity, one of the truest senses he had.

So his decision to use it to become President in 1968 was not easy. So much of him argued against it. But in his Wall Street years, Richard Nixon had traveled to the darkest places inside himself and come back numbed. He was, as in the Graham Greene title, a burnt-out case. All feeling was behind him; the machine inside had proved his hardiest part. He would run for President again and if he would have to learn television to run well, then he would learn it.

America still saw him as the 1960 Nixon. If he were to come at the people again, as candidate, it would have to be as something new; not this scarred, discarded figure from their past.

He spoke to men who thought him mellowed. They detected growth, a new stability, a sense of direction that had been lacking. He would return with fresh perspective, a more unselfish urgency.

His problem was how to let the nation know. He could not do it through the press. He knew what to expect from them, which was the same as he had always gotten. He would have to circumvent them. Distract them with coffee and doughnuts and smiles from his staff and tell his story another way.

Television was the only answer, despite its sins against him in the past. But not just any kind of television. An uncommitted camera could do irreparable harm. His television would have to be controlled. He would need experts. They would have to find the proper settings for him, or if they could not be found, manufacture them. These would have to be men of keen judgment and flawless taste. He was, after all, Richard Nixon, and there were certain things he could not do. Wearing love beads was one. He would need men of dignity. Who believed in him and shared his vision. But more importantly, men who knew television as a weapon: from broadest concept to most technical detail. This would be Richard Nixon, the leader, returning from exile. Perhaps not beloved, but respected. Firm but not harsh; just but compassionate. With flashes of warmth spaced evenly throughout.

Nixon gathered about himself a group of young men attuned to the political uses of television. They arrived at his side by different routes. One, William Gavin, was a thirty-one-year-old English teacher in a suburban high school outside Philadelphia in 1967, when he wrote Richard Nixon a letter urging him to run for President and base his campaign on TV. Gavin wrote on stationery borrowed from the University of Pennsylvania because he thought Nixon would pay more attention if the letter seemed to be from a college professor.

> Dear Mr. Nixon:
> May I offer two suggestions concerning your plans for 1968?
> 1. Run. You can win. Nothing can happen to you, politically speaking, that is worse than what has happened to you. Ortega y Gasset in his *The Revolt of the Masses* says: "These ideas are the only genuine ideas: the ideas of the shipwrecked. All the rest is rhetoric, posturing, farce. He who does not really feel himself lost, is lost without remission . . ." You, in effect, are "lost"; that is why you are the only political figure with a vision to see things the way they are and not as Leftist or Rightist kooks would have them be. Run. You will win.
> 2. A tip for television: instead of those wooden performances beloved by politicians, instead of a glamorboy technique, instead of safety, be bold. Why not have live press conferences as your campaign on television? People will see you daring all, asking and answering questions from reporters, and not simply answering phony "questions" made up by your staff. This would be dynamic; it would be daring. Instead of the medium

using you, you would be using the medium. Go on "live" and risk all. It is the only way to convince people of the truth: that you are beyond rhetoric, that you can face reality, unlike your opponents, who will rely on public relations. Television hurt you because you were not yourself; it didn't hurt the "real" Nixon. The real Nixon can revolutionize the use of television by dynamically going "live" and answering everything, the loaded and the unloaded question. Invite your opponents to this kind of a debate.

Good luck, and I know you can win if you see yourself for what you are; a man who had been beaten, humiliated, hated, but who can still see the truth.

A Nixon staff member had lunch with Gavin a couple of times after the letter was received and hired him.

William Gavin was brought to the White House as a speech writer in January of 1969.

Harry Treleaven, hired as creative director of advertising in the fall of 1967, immediately went to work on the more serious of Nixon's personality problems. One was his lack of humor.

"Can be corrected to a degree," Treleaven wrote, "but let's not be too obvious about it. Romney's cornball attempts have hurt him. If we're going to be witty, let a pro write the words."

Treleaven also worried about Nixon's lack of warmth, but decided that "he can be helped greatly in this respect by how he is handled. . . . Give him words to say that will show his *emotional* involvement in the issues. . . . Buchanan wrote about RFK talking about the starving children in Recife. *That's* what we have to inject. . . .

"He should be presented in some kind of 'situation' rather than cold in a studio. The situation should look unstaged even if it's not."

Some of the most effective ideas belonged to Raymond K. Price, a former editorial writer for the *New York Herald Tribune,* who became Nixon's best and most prominent speech writer in the campaign. Price later composed much of the inaugural address.

In 1967, he began with the assumption that, "The natural human use of reason is to support prejudice, not to arrive at opinions." Which led to the conclusion that rational arguments would "only be effective if we can get the people to make the *emotional* leap, or what theologians call [the] 'leap of faith.' "

Price suggested attacking the "personal factors" rather than the "historical factors" which were the basis of the low opinion so many people had of Richard Nixon.

"These tend to be more a gut reaction," Price wrote, "unarticulated, non-analytical, a product of the particular chemistry between the voter and the *image* of the candidate. *We have to be very clear on this point: that the response is to the image, not to the man. . . .* It's not what's *there* that counts, it's what's projected — and carrying it one step further, it's not

what *he* projects but rather what the voter receives. It's not the man we
have to change, but rather the *received impression.* And this impression
often depends more on the medium and its use than it does on the candidate himself."

So there would not have to be a "new Nixon." Simply a new approach
to television.

"What, then, does this mean in terms of our uses of time and of
media?" Price wrote.

"For one thing, it means investing whatever time RN needs in order
to work out firmly in his own mind that vision of the nation's future that
he wants to be identified with. This is crucial. . . ."

So, at the age of fifty-four, after twenty years in public life, Richard
Nixon was still felt *by his own staff* to be in need of time to "work out firmly
in his own mind that vision of the nation's future that he wants to be identified with."

"Secondly," Price wrote, "it suggests that we take the time and the
money to experiment, in a controlled manner, with film and television techniques, with particular emphasis on pinpointing those *controlled* uses of the
television medium that can *best* convey the *image* we want to get across. . . ."

"The TV medium itself introduces an element of distortion, in terms
of its effect on the candidate and of the often subliminal ways in which the
image is received. And it inevitably is going to convey a partial image —
thus ours is the task of finding how to control its use so the part that gets
across is the part we want to have gotten across. . . .

"Voters are basically lazy, basically uninterested in making an *effort*
to understand what we're talking about . . . ," Price wrote. "Reason requires
a high degree of discipline, of concentration; impression is easier. Reason
pushes the viewer back, it assaults him, it demands that he agree or disagree; impression can envelop him, invite him in, without making an intellectual demand. . . . When we argue with him we demand that he make the
effort of replying. We seek to engage his intellect, and for most people this
is the most difficult work of all. The emotions are more easily roused, closer
to the surface, more malleable. . . ."

So, for the New Hampshire primary, Price recommended "saturation
with a film, in which the candidate can be shown better than he can be
shown in person because it can be edited, so only the best moments are
shown; then a quick parading of the candidate in the flesh so that the guy
they've gotten intimately acquainted with on the screen takes on a living
presence — not saying anything, just being seen. . . .

"[Nixon] has to come across as a person larger than life, the stuff of
legend. People are stirred by the legend, including the living legend, not
by the man himself. It's the aura that surrounds the charismatic figure
more than it is the figure itself, that draws the followers. Our task is to
build that aura. . . .

"So let's not be afraid of television gimmicks . . . get the voters to like the guy and the battle's two-thirds won."

So this was how they went into it. Trying, with one hand, to build the illusion that Richard Nixon, in addition to his attributes of mind and heart, considered, in the words of Patrick J. Buchanan, a speech writer, "communicating with the people . . . one of the great joys of seeking the Presidency"; while with the other they shielded him, controlled him, and controlled the atmosphere around him. It was as if they were building not a President but an Astrodome, where the wind would never blow, the temperature never rise or fall, and the ball never bounce erratically on the artificial grass.

They could do this, and succeed, because of the special nature of the man. There was, apparently, something in Richard Nixon's character which sought this shelter. Something which craved regulation, which flourished best in the darkness, behind clichés, behind phalanxes of antiseptic advisers. Some part of him that could breathe freely only inside a hotel suite that cost a hundred dollars a day.

And it worked. As he moved serenely through his primary campaign, there was new cadence to Richard Nixon's speech and motion; new confidence in his heart. And, a new image of him on the television screen.

TV both reflected and contributed to his strength. Because he was winning he looked like a winner on the screen. Because he was suddenly projecting well on the medium he had feared, he went about his other tasks with assurance. The one fed upon the other, building to an astonishing peak in August as the Republican convention began and he emerged from his regal isolation, traveling to Miami not so much to be nominated as coronated. On live, but controlled, TV.

The entrance of the professional public relations man into politics, the extensive use of television to "sell" the candidate, all of which began in 1952, has changed the landscape of presidential politics. The advertising of presidential candidates has changed little over the years, because their public relations advisers basically take the same approach to the campaign and the electorate. The images of candidates are to be shaped to optimize their appeal to the voters. The loss of elections is now blamed as much on media advisers as on the candidates and their public policy stances. Joe McGinniss, in the preceding selection, puts this idea in its most cynical form in his comment on President Nixon's campaign in 1960: "He nearly became President in 1960, and that year it would not have been by default. He failed because he was too few of the things that a President had to be — and because he had no press to lie for him and did not know how to use television to lie about himself." Nixon's defeat in 1960 is often said to have been caused by deficiencies in his popular image, including his *physical* appearance in the first television debate with John F. Kennedy. Thus, his television advisers in 1968 were very careful to structure the television environment in such a way as to project a favorable Nixon image.

The McGinniss description of the 1968 election could, with very few changes, have been applied to the 1976 and 1980 presidential elections. The candidates were different, but the public relations advisers took the same approach to selling them to the public. On the whole, the emphasis was on *images,* not issues. One seeks in vain through the verbiage of the 1976 and 1980 presidential campaigns to find many concrete statements on public policy. And, as is always the case, what public issues were highlighted were largely selected on the basis of their supposed appeal to the electorate.

Long before the 1976 presidential campaigns got under way Jimmy Carter had become a media event, if not a media creation. Hundreds of newspaper and magazine articles had portrayed him as an exciting new face on the political scene, which had helped him (admittedly with a highly effective political organization) to gain widespread support in the presidential primaries throughout the nation. People felt that they "knew" Jimmy Carter. The popular image of Carter raised expectations to a point where people were bound to be disappointed. The 1980 election reflected widespread cynicism about the role of government, perhaps in part the result of disbelief in the continuous media hype of the candidates as persons who would solve the nation's problems.

Presidential Campaigns and the Press

Timothy Crouse's book, *The Boys on the Bus,* an account of the inner workings and personalities of the press corps in a presidential campaign, has become a classic of political literature.[1] The book is one of many absorbing accounts of the ill-fated McGovern campaign of 1972. McGovern has faded from the national political scene, but presidential campaigns and press behavior continue to exhibit the same characteristics that were written about the press and McGovern at that time. A presidential campaign is a frenzied, harrowing, and at the same time, exalted, experience for all of those who participate in it — the candidates, their staffs, and the press that follows the candidates around by bus or plane. Hundreds of thousands of miles are traversed by the presidential party and the accompanying press, and by the time of the November election, the common experiences of all concerned bind the participants together in many ways. The political reporters who follow a successful presidential candidate often become members of the White House Press Corps to

---

[1] See Timothy Crouse, *The Boys on the Bus* (New York: Random House, 1972).

cover "their" candidate, who is now in the Oval Office. The following selection portrays the atmosphere of the McGovern campaign from the vantage point of the political reporters assigned to the candidate.

29

Timothy Crouse

COVERING A PRESIDENTIAL CAMPAIGN

The reporters attached to George McGovern had a very limited usefulness as political observers, by and large, for what they knew best was not the American electorate but the tiny community of the press plane, a totally abnormal world that combined the incestuousness of a New England hamlet with the giddiness of a mid-ocean gala and the physical rigors of the Long March.

There were two press planes, actually — the Dakota Queen II (named for the B–24 McGovern had piloted during World War II) and the Zoo Plane (etymology uncertain.) [1] Both were United Airlines 727's with all the "tourist" seats replaced by "first class" armchairs. The Dakota Queen II carried the Senator (who usually remained in his curtained-off working space at the front of the plane), the major staffers (who had an office complete with telephones, typewriters, and mimeograph machines in the rear of the plane) and the journalistic heavies — the network correspondents, the man on duty for each of the wires, the reporters from the big dailies, newsmagazines and chains, and *both* of the *New York Times*-men. Many days, they spent five or six hours in the air.

The atmosphere aboard the Dakota Queen II was informal but businesslike. The reporters with deadlines looming banged away at their portables; the others milled in the aisles, talking shop with each other and the staff, drinking, and sifting through the latest barrel of rumors. Every so often, McGovern wandered back to the press section, and the reporters piled up around him like ants on a crumb; small talk was made, pleasantries exchanged, nothing momentous emerged. After McGovern left, the

---

From *The Boys on the Bus* by Timothy Crouse. Copyright © 1973 by Timothy Crouse. Reprinted by permission of Random House, Inc.

[1] Since Presidential campaigns first took flight, the second (or third) plane has always been known as the Zoo Plane. Apparently, this name derives from the large numbers of TV technicians who ride the second plane and who are considered slightly less than human by the print journalists.

reporters who had been at the fringes of the group hopped from seat to seat, trying to piece together the conversation. Sometimes, on long, mellow night flights, some of the reporters sang hymns or danced to a tape recorder in the rear compartment, but usually the Dakota Queen II remained staid.

The Zoo Plane carried the lesser staffers, the backup men from the networks and wires, the reporters from small papers, the cameramen and technicians, the bulk of the Secret Service and the occasional *persona non grata* like Bob Novak or Joe Alsop.

("Put him on the Zoo," Mankiewicz snapped one night upon learning of Alsop's imminent arrival. "I don't want to see him on the Senator's plane, I don't want him anywhere near there."

"Why not?" asked Polly Hackett, the press aide.

"Because I'm liable to punch him in the nose, that's why," said Mankiewicz.)

A whole status system grew up around the two planes. The heavies — the men at the top of the pecking order — had permanent seats on the Dakota Queen II; therefore, these seats became symbols of journalistic glory. To sit with *The New York Times* and the Washington *Post* meant that you had arrived. To be banished to the Zoo Plane meant social disgrace. Reporters *begged* Polly Hackett not to send them to the Zoo Plane. A man like Adam Clymer would rather have traveled by dogsled. But more and more heavies showed up as the campaign progressed, so a number of reporters were bumped from the Dakota Queen II. Some took it badly and worried so incessantly about missing something on the No. 1 plane that they were unable to concentrate on their work. What made this all the more absurd was the fact that the Zoo Plane was ten times as much fun as the Dakota Queen II; the difference between the Senator's plane and the Zoo was the difference between Lent and Mardi Gras.

The Zoo Plane had the look and air of the poorest but wildest frat house on a Southern campus. There were posters and campaign totems everywhere — a cardboard skeleton labeled "Ms. Boney Maroney," a dandruff ad onto which had been pasted a picture of George McGovern with confetti in his hair, a Roosevelt and Garner poster, Polaroid snapshots of all the regulars, orange and black streamers for Halloween and, taped to the sides of the overhead racks, keys from hotels in every other city in America. Seven hundred fourteen keys, all of which were mass mailed at the end of the trip.

The excitement of riding the Zoo Plane sprang from the fact that all rules had been totally suspended. As the plane took off on the first flight of the morning, half the reporters crowded into the galleys, mixing themselves Bloody Marys from the endless supplies of free booze. The cameramen were up front, letting loose spools of film, apples, oranges — anything that would careen wildly down the aisle of a plane that was climbing at 45 degrees. Meanwhile, as the FASTEN SEAT BELT signs still flashed their warning, other reporters worked their way up the aisle to fetch their own breakfasts and make more drinks. A Bach organ toccata swelled from the speakers in the front of the plane. The Rolling Stones blared from the rear. The stewardesses had long since given up trying to control the situation. They were just happy to be along for the ride. Three of them were McGovern supporters. The fourth, slightly more old-fashioned, had a thing for Secret Service men and entertained no less than eighteen of them before the campaign ended.

You could do anything you wanted on the Zoo Plane; it was like smashing china at Tivoli. The network technicians were the most uncontrollably manic people on the plane, and with good reason — they were making upwards of $1,500 a week. They had constant wars with aerosol cans that shot long, sticky filaments of plastic. And it was the TV technicians who held one of the crew one night while a drunken lady journalist stripped him down to his boxer shorts which were badly ripped in the rear. The rest of the crew locked the wretched man out of the cockpit until just before landing.

There were drugs on the plane, too, pot, hash, MDA, cocaine. And those who indulged in such stimulants swore that there was no greater thrill than standing in the cockpit as the plane came in for a landing, listening to the crackle of the radio, surrounded by green and orange dials, watching the bright blue lights of the runway rush up at the window as the powerful engines cut back. Then a United Airlines liaison man who called himself the Hippy Dippy Weatherman would launch into his jive weather report over the PA system: "Hey, baby, it's seventy-one degrees down here in L.A. — that's *sixty-nine* plus two!" Every night, the pilots played to an overflow crowd in the cockpit.

The plane always taxied to a carefully staked-out corner of the runway. After each flight, the campaign began anew. The arrivals were strangely like reunions. The Zoo Plane always landed first, and the TV crews stampeded for the taildoor, rushed out and set up their cameras. Then the Dakota Queen II landed, slowly rolled up beside the Zoo, and let down its rear door so that the reporters could disembark. There were greetings, new stories, fresh rumors, a curious delight at seeing these familiar faces in a new city.

Everyone would crowd around the front ramp of the plane in the drizzle, or sleet, or darkness, to await McGovern. Gordon Weil would rush down the ramp first, carrying the Senator's attaché case. After a pause, McGovern would appear at the top of the ramp with Eleanor, wave, make a statement and submit to questions while all the reporters held their Sonys above their heads to catch his words. Finally, Dougherty would cut off the questions: "That's it, that's enough. The Senator is late." Everyone would dash for the buses, which were waiting in a row. Then the motorcade would start off, with motorcycles roaring and police sirens screaming, and the buses would slice through the traffic of some great city; nobody would admit it, but it was more fun than riding a fire engine. There was all the noise, speed, pomp, and license that only a Presidential candidate could generate, and it was these things that gave the press the energy to survive the eighteen-hour days.

As the campaign unfolded, loose pairings emerged. Stout and Fischer. Naughton and Kneeland. Witcover and Mears. Adam Clymer and Bruce Morton, both Harvard men, both affecting disenchantment with the campaign. Morton claimed that he intended to vote for Benjamin Spock. At rallies, they stood together at the edge of the crowd taking shots at McGovern's performance. Frank Reynolds of ABC, on the other hand, found a friend in George McGovern, for they had similar problems with their teenage sons.

Other, romantic, pairings formed. These casual affairs produced at least three cases of the clap and one lawsuit — a stewardess, finding out on the last day of the campaign that her paramour was married, sued him for "illegal acts committed over the state of Iowa." The few serious affairs produced frustration. The men were invariably married,[2] if not to a woman then to the paper. There were inevitable arguments. *He* wanted them to go to *his* room, in case he got a call-back. *She* insisted on going to *her* room, in case *her* editor called. Eventually they would settle the quarrel, arrive at the room, and then he would suddenly remember he had to get the "overnight," the last handout of the day. He would run off to get it, find something he had to file, and return two hours later, barely able to keep his eyes open.

"My God," one of the veterans said of campaign romances, "all those tired men. It must be dreadful for the women."

The campaign lurched along in ten-day cycles. Every week and a half, just as everyone on the plane was coming down with the flu and beginning to go crazy with boredom from listening to the standard speech, McGovern would return to Washington for a day. Most of the men would troop off to see their wives with mingled feelings of guilt, dread, and longing. "There's no way to win," said one of them. "Even if you're not screwing around, she thinks you're screwing around." At the very least, their wives were jealous of the freedom, the excitement, the sheer fun of the campaign. The men often felt badly about their neglected wives, or guilty because they had not thought to buy anything for the kids and so were forced to take them hotel soap for the third time; and the kids were growing disenchanted with Camay from the Sherman House. Some of the reporters were hopelessly torn between their professional duties and situations that cried out for them to be with their families; one man's wife had

---

[2] Which gave rise to the West-of-the-Potomac-Rule: "Nothing that happens West of the Potomac is ever talked about East of the Potomac." The penalty for violating this rule, I was repeatedly warned, is lynching.

suffered a miscarriage, another's daughter was dying of an incurable disease, and a third had a mentally disturbed son. And the campaign served as a kind of Foreign Legion for more than one man who wanted to escape from a shaky marriage or forget about a broken home.

Even the men with solid marriages suffered. Jim Doyle, for instance, believed that you couldn't survive the demands of the campaign if you didn't have a healthy family life to replenish your wasted spirits. One Saturday night, he tried to skip a rally in Spokane in order to get back to his family a few hours sooner. The *Star* told him he couldn't afford to miss the rally; something might happen to McGovern. He flew back with everyone else on the red-eye flight, getting home at 6 A.M. He woke his wife and they agreed that he would get up at 9 A.M. "But my daughters didn't wake me until ten," he said, "because I was out on my ass. Then they gave me a pitch about Was the job *that* important to me that I was never home? And I told them, 'Well, we have to eat, I have to make a living.' But they know that was bullshit. And I realized that my wife had put the girls up to it as a joke, but I also knew that they were all really pissed at me and jealous of my time, and I didn't blame them for being pissed."

Doyle had breakfast with his wife and daughters, and they chatted and laughed all morning. Being a family of football fans, they watched the football game at one o'clock. At two o'clock, Doyle left to rejoin George McGovern, who was starting off on another ten-day swing.

If you stayed away from the campaign for any period of time and then came on again, the first thing that struck you was the shocking physical deterioration of the press corps. During the summer, the reporters had looked fairly healthy. Now their skin was pasty and greenish, they had ugly dark pouches under their glazed eyes, and their bodies had become bloated with the regimen of nonstop drinking and five or six starchy airplane meals every day. Toward the end, they began to suffer from a fiendish combination of fatigue and anxiety. They had arrived at the last two weeks, when the public finally wanted to read about the campaign — front-page play every day! — and they were so tired that it nearly killed them to pound out a decent piece.

The reporters were trying desperately to write well, but it sometimes took them five minutes to think of the answer to a simple question. At filing time, everyone would suddenly become jittery and manic — smoking, crumpling papers, biting fingernails, shouting into phones, cruising on the last dregs of nervous energy — and then they would lapse back into catatonia. To do a decent job, they often had to stay up all night to finish a long piece, and there was no way to catch up on sleep. They were coming down to the wire — they had to save a few volts of energy to grind out long pre- and post-election articles. Yet all they could feel was numbness. McGovern, too, was pushing himself to the limits of his strength, pulling out all the stops on Vietnam and the Watergate affair, but through the haze of exhaustion all of his speeches sounded like one long echo of the same speech. The men had to force themselves to listen for new themes, new accusations.

During the last week, the press bus looked like a Black Maria sent out to round up winos; half the reporters were passed out with their mouths wide open and their notebooks fallen in their laps. When they were awake, they often wandered like zombies. On one of the last days of the campaign, Jules Witcover walked from the Biltmore Hotel to a rally in midtown Manhattan and had to be repeatedly stopped from sleepwalking into traffic against the red light. Bill Greider, perhaps the most exhausted man on the plane, had a strange habit of placing his arms by his sides, as if wearing an imaginary strait jacket, and walking around in circles. Toward the end, the only thing that stimulated Greider's adrenal glands was martial music, and he recorded the high school bands at every rally. Later, when he needed a shot of energy in the pressroom, he would turn up his Sony all the way and bang away at his Olivetti as "Onward Christian Soldiers" or "Happy Days" blasted out of the speaker.

The exhaustion of the final week drew the press together in a strange, almost mystic bond. It was as if the massed weight of fatigue had dragged everyone down into the same dream, where all emotions were electric but somehow inappropriate, and nobody could quite remember why all these people were flying all over America. The scheduling grew increasingly surreal — nobody could explain the long trips to Waco or Corpus Christi or Little Rock, deep in the hostile South. Why not Guam? Toward the end, an eerie serenity descended on McGovern, and he began to act like a man who was not only about to be elected, but beatified as well. Had he actually deluded himself into thinking he would win, or had he merely made his peace with defeat? The reporters couldn't figure him out, but their natural cynicism gradually turned into a kind of sentimental admiration. They liked him, and as his defeat became more and more certain, they felt it was safe to show their affection. They also began to realize how much they liked the way of life, the womblike protection of the plane, and how sorry they would be to leave it. They were tired, cross, and so overworked that they could not stand another second of the campaign, and yet they wanted it to go on forever. . . .

CHAPTER 5

Interest Groups

Interest groups are vital cogs in the wheels of the democratic process. Although *Federalist 10* suggests that one major purpose of the separation of powers system is to break and control the "evil effects" of faction, modern political theorists take a much more sanguine view of the role that political interest groups as well as parties play in government. No longer are interest groups defined as being opposed to the "public interest." They are vital channels through which particular publics participate in the governmental process. This chapter examines the nature of interest groups and shows how they function.

The Nature and Functions of Interest Groups

Group theory has been the keystone of democratic political theory for several decades. The essence of group theory is that in the democratic process interest groups interact naturally and properly to produce public policy. In American political thought, the origins of this theory can be found in the theory of concurrent majority in John C. Calhoun's *Disquisition on Government.*

It is very useful to discuss the operation of interest groups within the framework of what can best be described as a concurrent majority system. In contemporary usage the phrase "concurrent majority" means a system in which major government policy decisions must be approved by the dominant interest groups directly affected. The word *concurrent* suggests that each group involved must give its consent before policy can be enacted. Thus a concurrent majority is a majority of each group considered separately. If we take as an example an area such as agricultural policy, in which three or four major private interest groups can be identified, we can say that the concurrent majority is reached when each group affected gives its approval before agricultural policy is passed. The extent to which such a system of concurrent majority is actually functioning is a matter that has not been fully clarified by empirical research. Nevertheless, it does seem tenable to conclude that in many major areas of public policy, it is necessary at least to achieve a concurrent majority of the *major* or *dominant* interests affected.

The *theory* of concurrent majority originated with John C. Calhoun. Calhoun, born in 1781, had a distinguished career in public service at both the national and state levels. The idea of concurrent majority evolved from the concept of state nullification of federal law. Under this states' rights doctrine, states would be able to veto any national action. The purpose of this procedure was theoretically to protect states in a minority from encroachment by a national majority that could act through Congress, the President, and even the Supreme Court. Those who favored this procedure had little faith in the separation of powers doctrine as an effective device to prevent the arbitrary exercise of national power. At the end of his career Calhoun decided to incorporate his earlier views on state nullification into a more substantial theoretical treatise in political science; thus he wrote his famous *Disquisition on Government* (New York: D. Appleton & Co., 1853) in the decade between 1840 and 1850. He attempted to develop a general theory of constitutional (limited) government, the primary mechanism of which would be the ability of the major interest groups (states in Calhoun's time) to veto legislation adverse to their interests. Students should overlook some of the theoretical inconsistencies in Calhoun and concentrate upon the basic justification he advances for substituting his system of concurrent majority for the separation of powers device. Under the latter, group interests are not necessarily taken into account, for national laws can be passed on the basis of a numerical majority. And even though this majority may reflect the interests of some groups, it will not necessarily reflect the interests of all groups affected. Calhoun argued that a system in which the major interest groups can dominate the policy process is really more in accord with constitutional democracy than the system established in our Constitution and supported in *Federalist 10.*

The group theory of John C. Calhoun has been updated and carried over into modern political science by several writers, one of the most important being David B. Truman. David Truman's selection, taken from *The Governmental Process* (1951), contains (1) a definition of the term "interest group" and (2) a brief outline of the frame of reference within which the operations of interest groups should be considered. A fairly articulate interest group theory of the governmental process is sketched by Truman. It will become evident to the student of American government that interest groups, like political parties, form an integral part of our political system. Further, interest group theory suggests an entirely new way of looking at government.

30

David B. Truman

THE GOVERNMENTAL PROCESS

INTEREST GROUPS

Interest group refers to any group that, on the basis of one or more shared attitudes, makes certain claims upon other groups in the society for the establishment, maintenance, or enhancement of forms of behavior that are implied by the shared attitudes. . . . [F]rom interaction in groups arise certain common habits of response, which may be called norms, or shared attitudes. These afford the participants frames of reference for interpreting and evaluating events and behaviors. In this respect all groups are interest groups because they are shared-attitude groups. In some groups at various points in time, however, a second kind of common response emerges, in addition to the frame of reference. These are shared attitudes toward what is needed or wanted in a given situation, as demands or claims upon other groups in the society. The term "interest group" will be reserved here for those groups that exhibit both aspects of the shared attitudes. . . .

Definition of the interest group in this fashion . . . permits the identification of various potential as well as existing interest groups. That is, it invites examination of an interest whether or not it is found at the moment as one of the characteristics of a particular organized group. Although no group that makes claims upon other groups in society will be found without an interest or interests, it is possible to examine interests that are not at a particular point in time the basis of interactions among individuals, but that may become such. . . .

GROUPS AND GOVERNMENT:
DIFFICULTIES IN A GROUP INTERPRETATION
OF POLITICS

Since we are engaged in an effort to develop a conception of the political process in the United States that will account adequately for the role of groups, particularly interest groups, it will be appropriate to take account of some of the factors that have been regarded as obstacles to such a conception and that have caused such groups to be neglected in many explanations of the dynamics of government. Perhaps the most important practical reason for this neglect is that the significance of groups has only fairly recently been forced to the attention of political scientists by the tremendous growth in the number of formally organized groups in the United States within the last few decades. It is difficult and unnecessary to attempt to date the beginning of such attention, but Herring in 1929, in his groundbreaking book, *Group Representation Before Congress,* testified to the novelty of the observations he reported when he stated: "There has developed in this government an extra-legal machinery of as integral and of as influential a nature as the system of party government that has long been an essential part of the government. . . ." Some implications of this development are not wholly compatible with some of the proverbial notions about representative government held by specialists as well as laymen. . . . This apparent incompatibility has obstructed the inclusion of group behaviors in an objective description of the governmental process.

More specifically, it is usually argued that any attempt at the interpretation of politics in terms of group patterns inevitably "leaves something out" or "destroys something essential" about the processes of "our" government. On closer examination, we find this argument suggesting that two "things" are certain to be ignored: the individual, and a sort of totally inclusive unity designated by such terms as "society" and "the state."

The argument that the individual is ignored in any interpretation of politics as based upon groups seems to assume a differentiation or conflict between "the individual" and some such collectivity as the group. . . .

Such assumptions need not present any difficulties in the development of a group interpretation of politics, because they are essentially unwarranted. They simply do not square with . . . evidence concerning group affiliations and individual behavior. . . . We do not, in fact, find individuals otherwise than in groups; complete isolation in space and time is so rare as to be an almost hypothetical situation. It is equally demonstrable that the characteristics of any interest group, including the activities by which we identify it, are governed by the attitudes and the circumstances that gave rise to the interactions of which it consists. There are variable factors, and, although the role played by a particular individual may be quite different in a lynch mob from that of the same individual in a meeting of the church deacons, the attitudes and behaviors involved in both are as much a part of his personality as is his treatment of his family. "The individual" and "the group" are at most merely convenient ways of classifying behavior, two ways of approaching the same phenomena, not different things.

The persistence among nonspecialists of the notion of an inherent conflict between "the individual" and "the group" or "society" is understandable in view of the doctrines of individualism that have underlain various political and economic conflicts over the past three centuries. The notion persists also because it harmonizes with a view of the isolated and independent individual as the "cause" of complicated human events. The personification of events, quite apart from any ethical considerations, is a kind of shorthand convenient in everyday speech and, like supernatural explanations of natural phenomena, has a comforting simplicity. Explanations that take into account multiple causes, including group affiliations, are difficult. The "explanation" of a national complex like the Soviet Union wholly in terms of a Stalin or the "description" of the intricacies of the American government entirely in terms of a Roosevelt is quick and easy. . . .

The second major difficulty allegedly inherent in any attempt at a group interpretation of the political process is that such an explanation inevitably must ignore some greater unity designated as society or the state. . . .

Many of those who place particular emphasis upon this difficulty assume explicitly or implicitly that there is an interest of the nation as a whole, universally and invariably held and standing apart from and superior to those of the various groups included within it. This assumption is close to the popular dogmas of democratic government based on the familiar notion that if only people are free and have access to "the facts," they will all want the same thing in any political situation. It is no derogation of democratic preferences to state that such an assertion flies in the face of all that we know of the behavior of men in a complex society. Were it in fact true, not only the interest group but even the political party should properly be viewed as an abnormality. The differing experiences and perceptions of men not only encourage individuality but also . . . inevitably result in differing attitudes and conflicting group affiliations. "There are," says Bentley in his discussion of this error of the social whole, "always some parts of the nation to be found arrayed against other arts." [From *The Process of Government* (1908).] Even in war, when a totally inclusive interest should be apparent if it is ever going to be, we always find pacifists, conscientious objectors, spies, and subversives, who reflect interests opposed to those of "the nation as a whole."

There is a political significance in assertions of a totally inclusive interest within a nation. Particularly in times of crisis, such as an international war, such claims are a tremendously useful promotional device by means of which a particularly extensive group or league of groups tries to reduce or eliminate opposing interests. Such is the pain attendant upon not "belonging" to one's "own" group that if a normal person can be convinced that he is the lone dissenter to an otherwise universally accepted agreement, he usually will conform. This pressure accounts at least in part for the number of prewar pacifists who, when the United States entered World War II, accepted the draft or volunteered. Assertion of an inclusive "national" or "public interest" is an effective device in many less critical situations as well. In themselves, these claims are part of the data of politics. However, they do not describe any actual or possible political situation within a complex modern nation. In developing a group interpretation of politics, therefore, we do not need to account for a totally inclusive interest, because one does not exist.

Denying the existence of an interest of the nation as a whole does not completely dispose of the difficulty raised by those who insist that a group interpretation must omit "the state." We cannot deny the obvious fact that we are examining a going political system that is supported or at least accepted by a large proportion of the society. We cannot account for such a system by adding up in some fashion the National Association of Manufacturers, the Congress of Industrial Organizations, the American Farm Bureau Federation, The American Legion, and other groups that come to mind when "lobbies" and "pressure groups" are mentioned. Even if the political parties are added to the list, the result could properly be designated as "a view which seems hardly compatible with the relative stability of the political system. . . ." Were such the exclusive ingredients of the political process in the United States, the entire system would have torn itself apart long since.

If these various organized interest groups more or less consistently reconcile their differences, adjust, and accept compromises, we must acknowledge that we are dealing with a system that is not accounted for by the "sum" of the organized interest groups in the society. We must go further to explain the operation of such ideals or traditions as constitutionalism, civil liberties, representative responsibility, and the like. These are not, however, a sort of disembodied metaphysical influence, like Mr. Justice Holmes's "brooding ominipresence." We know of the existence of such factors only from the behavior and the habitual interactions of men. If they exist in this fashion, they are interests. We can account for their operation and for the system by recognizing such interests as representing what . . . we called potential interest groups in the "becoming" stage of activity. "It is certainly true," as Bently has made clear, "that we must accept a . . . group of this kind as an interest group itself." It makes no difference that we cannot find the home office and the executive secretary of such a group. Organization in this formal sense, as we have seen, represents merely a stage or degree of interaction that may or may not be significant at any particular point in time. Its absence does not mean that these interests do not exist, that the familiar "pressure groups" do not operate as if such potential groups were organized and active, or that these interests may not move from the potential to the organized stage of activity.

It thus appears that the two major difficulties supposedly obstacles to a group interpretation of the political process are not insuperable. We can employ the fact of individuality and we can account for the existence of the state without doing violence to the evidence available from the observed behaviors of men and groups. . . .

INTEREST GROUPS AND
THE NATURE OF THE STATE

Men, wherever they are observed, are creatures participating in those established patterns of interaction that we call groups. Excepting perhaps the most casual and transitory, these continuing interactions, like all such interpersonal relationships, involve power. This power is exhibited in two closely interdependent ways. In the first place, the group exerts power over its members; an individual's group affiliations largely determine his attitudes, values, and the frames of reference in terms of which he interprets his experiences. For a measure of conformity to the norms of the group is the price of acceptance within it. . . . In the second place, the group, if it is or becomes an interest group, which any group in society may be, exerts power over other groups in the society when it successfully imposes claims upon them.

Many interest groups, probably an increasing proportion in the United States, are politicized. That is, either from the outset or from time to time in the course of their development they make their claims through or upon the institutions of government. Both the forms and functions of government in turn are a reflection of the activities and claims of such groups. . . .

The institutions of government are centers of interest-based power; their connections with interest groups may be latent or overt and their activities range in political character from the routinized and widely accepted to the unstable and highly controversial. In order to make claims, political interest groups will seek access to the key points of decision within these institutions. Such points are scattered throughout the structure, including not only the formally established branches of government but also the political parties in their various forms and the relationships between governmental units and other interest groups.

The extent to which a group achieves effective access to the institutions of government is the resultant of a complex of interdependent factors. For the sake of simplicity these may be classified in three somewhat overlapping categories: (1) factors relating to a group's strategic position in the society; (2) factors associated with the internal characteristics of the group; and (3) factors peculiar to the governmental institutions themselves. In the first category are: the group's status or prestige in the society, affecting the ease with which it commands deference from those outside its bounds; the standing it and its activities have when measured against the widely held but largely unorganized interests or "rules of the game"; the extent to which government officials are formally or informally "members" of the group; and the usefulness of the group as a source of technical and political knowledge. The second category includes: the degree and appropriateness of the group's organization; the degree of cohesion it can achieve in a given situation, especially in the light of competing group demands upon its membership; the skills of the leadership; and the group's resources in numbers and money. In the third category are: the operating structure of the government institutions, since such established features involve relatively fixed advantages and handicaps; and the effects of the group life of particular units or branches of the government. . . .

A characteristic feature of the governmental system in the United States is that it contains a multiplicity of points of access. The federal system establishes decentralized and more or less independent centers of power, vantage points from which to secure privileged access to the national government. Both a sign and a cause of the strength of the constituent units in the federal scheme is the peculiar character of our party system, which has strengthened parochial relationships, especially those of national legislators. National parties, and to a lesser degree those in the states, tend to be poorly cohesive leagues of locally based organizations rather than unified and inclusive structures. Staggered terms for executive officials and various types of legislators accentuate differences in the effective electorates that participate in choosing these officers. Each of these different, often opposite, localized patterns (constituencies) is a channel of independent access to the larger party aggregation and to the formal government. Thus, especially at the national level, the party is an electing-device and only in limited measure an integrated means of policy determination. Within the Congress, furthermore, controls are diffused among committee chairmen and other leaders in both chambers. The variety of these points of access is further supported by relationships stemming from the constitutional doctrine of separation of powers, from related checks and balances, and at the state and local level from the common practice of choosing an array of executive officials by popular election. At the federal level the formal simplicity of the executive branch has been complicated by a Supreme Court decision that has placed a number of administrative agencies beyond the removal power of the President. The position of these units, however, differs only in degree from that of many that are constitutionally within the Executive Branch. In consequence of alternative lines of access available through the legislature and the Executive and of divided channels for the control of administrative policy, many nominally executive agencies are at various times virtually independent of the Chief Executive.

. . . Within limits, therefore, organized interest groups, gravitating toward responsive points of decision, may play one segment of the structure against another as circumstances and strategic considerations permit. The total pattern of government over a period of time thus presents a protean complex of crisscrossing relationships that change in strength and direction with alternations in the power and standing of interests, organized and unorganized.

From Truman's definition *any* group, organized or unorganized, that has a shared attitude toward goals and methods for achieving them should be classified as an interest group. Truman is essentiálly saying that, since people generally function as members of groups, it is more useful and accurate for the political observer to view the governmental process as the interaction of political interest groups. If one accepts the sociologist's assumption that men act and interact only as members of groups, then it is imperative that the governmental process be viewed as one of interest group interaction.

Within the framework of Truman's definition it is possible to identify both *public* and *private* interest groups. In the political process, governmental groups sometimes act as interest groups in the same sense as private organizations. In many public policies, governmental groups may have more at stake than private organizations. Thus administrative agencies, for example, may lobby as vigorously as their private counterparts to advance their own interests.

Theodore Lowi refers to group theory as "interest group liberalism." The following selection is taken from his well-known book *The End of Liberalism* (1969), in which he severely criticizes group theory and its pervasive influence upon governmental decision makers. In reading the following selection, remember that the author does not use the term "liberal" in its ordinary sense. The political "liberal" in Lowi's terminology is much like the "economic Liberal" of the early 19th century. Just as economic liberalism preached that the public good emerged automatically from the free clash of private interests, the political liberal (in Lowi's terms) supports group theory which holds that the public interest in government is automatically achieved through the interaction of pressure groups.

31
Theodore J. Lowi

THE END OF LIBERALISM: THE INDICTMENT

The corruption of modern democratic government began with the emergence of interest-group liberalism as the public philosophy. Its corrupting influence takes at least four important forms, four counts, therefore, of an indictment for which most of the foregoing chapters are mere documenta-

Reprinted from *The End of Liberalism* by Theodore J. Lowi, with the permission of W. W. Norton & Company, Inc. Copyright © 1969 by W. W. Norton & Company, Inc.

tion. Also to be indicted, on at least three counts, is the philosophic component of the ideology, pluralism.

SUMMATION I: FOUR COUNTS
AGAINST THE IDEOLOGY

1. Interest-group liberalism as public philosophy corrupts democratic government because it deranges and confuses expectations about democratic institutions. Liberalism promotes popular decision-making but derogates from the decisions so made by misapplying the notion to the implementation as well as the formulation of policy. It derogates from the processes by treating all values in the process as equivalent interests. It derogates from democratic rights by allowing their exercise in foreign policy, and by assuming they are being exercised when access is provided. Liberal practices reveal a basic disrespect for democracy. Liberal leaders do not wield the authority of democratic government with the resoluteness of men certain of the legitimacy of their positions, the integrity of their institutions, or the justness of the programs they serve.

2. Interest-group liberalism renders government impotent. Liberal governments cannot plan. Liberals are copious in plans but irresolute in planning. Nineteenth-century liberalism was standard without plans. This was an anachronism in the modern state. But twentieth-century liberalism turned out to be plans without standards. As an anachronism it, too, ought to pass. But doctrines are not organisms. They die only in combat over the minds of men, and no doctrine yet exists capable of doing the job. All the popular alternatives are so very irrelevant, helping to explain the longevity of interest-group liberalism. Barry Goldwater most recently proved the irrelevance of one. The *embourgeoisement* of American unions suggests the irrelevance of others.

The Departments of Agriculture, Commerce, and Labor provide illustrations, but hardly exhaust illustrations, of such impotence. Here clearly one sees how liberalism has become a doctrine whose means are its ends, whose combatants are its clientele, whose standards are not even those of the mob but worse, are those the bargainers can fashion to fit the bargain. Delegation of power has become alienation of public domain — the gift of sovereignty to private satrapies. The political barriers to withdrawal of delegation are high enough. But liberalism reinforces these through the rhetoric of justification and often even permanent legal reinforcement: Public corporations — justified, oddly, as efficient planning instruments — permanently alienate rights of central coordination to the directors and to those who own the corporation bonds. Or, as Walter Adams finds, the "most pervasive method . . . for alienating public domain is the certificate of convenience and necessity, or some variation thereof in the form of an exclusive franchise, license or permit. . . . [G]overnment has become increasingly careless and subservient in issuing them. The net result is a general legalization of private monopoly. . . ." While the best examples still are probably the 10 self-governing systems of agriculture policy, these are obviously only a small proportion of all the barriers the interest-group liberal ideology has erected to democratic use of government.

3. Interest-group liberalism demoralizes government, because liberal governments cannot achieve justice. The question of justice has engaged the best minds for almost as long as there have been notions of state and politics, certainly ever since Plato defined the ideal as one in which republic and justice were synonymous. And since that time philosophers have been unable to agree on what justice is. But outside the ideal, in the realms of actual government and citizenship, the problem is much simpler. We do not have to define justice at all in order to weight and assess justice in government, because in the case of liberal policies we are prevented by what the law would call a "jurisdictional fact." In the famous jurisdictional case of *Marbury* v. *Madison* Chief Justice Marshall held that even if all the Justices hated President Jefferson for refusing to accept Marbury and the other "midnight judges" appointed by Adams, there was nothing they could do. They had no authority to judge President Jefferson's action one way or another because the Supreme Court did not possess such jurisdiction over the President. In much the same way, there is something about liberalism that prevents us from raising the question of justice at all, no matter what definition of justice is used.

Liberal governments cannot achieve justice because their policies lack the *sine qua non* of justice — that quality without which a consideration of justice cannot even be initiated. Considerations of the justice in or achieved by an action cannot be made unless a deliberate and conscious attempt was made by the actor to derive his action from a general rule or moral principle governing such a class of acts. One can speak personally of good rules and bad rules, but a homily or a sentiment, like liberal legislation, is not a rule at all. The best rule is one which is relevant to the decision or action in question and is general in the sense that those involved with it have no direct control over its operation. A general rule is, hence, *a priori*. Any governing regime that makes a virtue of avoiding such rules puts itself totally outside the context of justice.

Take the homely example of the bull and the china shop. Suppose it was an op art shop and that we consider op worthy only of the junk pile. That being the case, the bull did us a great service, the more so because it was something we always dreamed of doing but were prevented by law from entering and breaking. But however much we may be pleased, we cannot judge the act. We can only like or dislike the consequences. The consequences are haphazard; the bull cannot have intended them. The act was a thoughtless, animal act which bears absolutely no relation to any aesthetic principle. We don't judge the bull. We only celebrate our good fortune. Without the general rule, the bull can reenact his scenes of creative destruction daily and still not be capable of achieving, in this case, aesthetic justice. The whole idea of justice is absurd.

The general rule ought to be a legislative rule because the United States espouses the ideal of representative democracy. However, that is merely an extrinsic feature of the rule. All that counts is the character of the rule itself. Without the rule we can only like or dislike the consequences of the governmental action. In the question of whether justice is achieved, a government without good rules, and without acts carefully derived therefrom, is merely a big bull in an immense china shop.

4. Finally, interest-group liberalism corrupts democratic government in the degree to which it weakens the capacity of governments to live by democratic formalisms. Liberalism weakens democratic institutions by opposing formal procedure with informal bargaining. Liberalism derogates from democracy by derogating from all formality in favor of informality. Formalism is constraining; playing it "by the book" is a role often unpopular in American war films and sports films precisely because it can dramatize personal rigidity and the plight of the individual in collective situations. Because of the impersonality of formal procedures, there is inevitably a separation in the real world between the forms and the realities, and this kind of separation gives rise to cynicism, for informality means that some will escape their collective fate better than others. There has as a consequence always been a certain amount of cynicism toward public objects in the United States, and this may be to the good, since a little cynicism is the father of healthy sophistication. However, when the informal is elevated to a positive virtue, and hard-won access becomes a share of official authority, cynicism becomes distrust. It ends in reluctance to submit one's fate to the governmental process under any condition, as is the case in the United States in the mid-1960s.

Public officials more and more frequently find their fates paradoxical and their treatment at the hands of the public fickle and unjust when in fact they are only reaping the results of their own behavior, including their direct and informal treatment of the public and the institutions through which they serve the public. The more government operates by the spreading of access, the more public order seems to suffer. The more public men pursue their constituencies, the more they seem to find their constituencies alienated. Liberalism has promoted concentration of democratic authority but deconcentration of democratic power. Liberalism has opposed privilege in policy formulation only to foster it, quite systematically, in the implementation of policy. Liberalism has consistently failed to recognize, in short, that in a democracy forms are important. In a medieval monarchy all formalisms were at court. Democracy proves, for better or worse, that the masses like that sort of thing too.

Another homely parable may help. In the good old days, everyone in the big city knew that traffic tickets could be fixed. Not everyone could get his ticket fixed, but nonetheless a man who honestly paid his ticket suffered in some degree a dual loss: his money, and his self-esteem for having so little access. Cynicism was widespread, violations were many, but perhaps it did not matter, for there were so few automobiles. Suppose, however, that as the automobile population increased a certain city faced a traffic crisis and the system of ticket fixing came into ill repute. Suppose a mayor, victorious on the Traffic Ticket, decided that, rather than eliminate fixing by universalizing enforcement, he would instead reform the system by universalizing the privileges of ticket fixing. One can imagine how the system would work. One can imagine that some sense of equality would prevail, because everyone could be made almost equally free to bargain with the ticket administrators. But one would find it difficult to imagine how this would make the total city government more legitimate. Meanwhile, the purpose of the ticket would soon have been destroyed.

Traffic regulation, fortunately, was not so reformed. But many other government activities were. The operative principles of interest-group liberalism possess the mentality of a world of universalized ticket fixing: Destroy privilege by universalizing it. Reduce conflict by yielding to it. Redistribute power by the maxim of each according to his claim. Reserve an official place for every major structure of power. Achieve order by worshipping the processes (as distinguished from the forms and the procedures) by which order is presumed to be established.

If these operative principles will achieve equilibrium — and such is far from proven — that is all they will achieve. Democracy will have disappeared, because all of these maxims are founded upon profound lack of confidence in democracy. Democracy fails when it lacks confidence in its own authority.

Democratic forms were supposed to precede and accompany the formulation of policies so that policies could be implemented authoritatively and firmly. Democracy is indeed a form of absolutism, but ours was fairly well contrived to be an absolutist government under the strong control of consent-building prior to taking authoritative action in law. Interest-group liberalism fights the absolutism of democracy but succeeds only in taking away its authoritativeness. Whether it is called "creative federalism" by President Johnson, "cooperation" by the farmers, "local autonomy" by the Republicans, or "participatory democracy" by the New Left, the interest-group liberal effort does not create democratic power but rather negates it.

The following discussion by V. O. Key, Jr., concentrates on private pressure groups and the extent to which they are links between public opinion
and government. One interesting conclusion is that the elites of interest
groups are not able to influence their members' attitudes to anywhere
near the degree commonly thought possible. Pressure group participation
in government more often than not reflects highly limited participation by
the active elements of the groups. Public policy is often hammered out by
very small numbers of individuals both in the government and in the private sphere. Political leaders can never stray too far beyond the boundaries of consent, but these are often very broad.

32
V. O. Key, Jr.

PRESSURE GROUPS

Pressure groups occupy a prominent place in analyses of American politics. In a regime characterized by official deference to public opinion and
by adherence to the doctrine of freedom of association, private organizations may be regarded as links that connect the citizen and government.
They are differentiated in both composition and function from political
parties. Ordinarily they concern themselves with only a narrow range of
policies, those related to the peculiar interests of the group membership.
Their aim is primarily to influence the content of public policy rather than
the results of elections. Those groups with a mass membership, though,
may oppose or support particular candidates; in that case they are treated
as groups with power to affect election results and, thereby, with capacity
to pressure party leaders, legislators, and others in official position to act
in accord with their wishes. . . .

PUZZLES OF PRESSURE POLITICS

. . . [There are] a series of puzzles as we seek to describe the role of pressure groups as links between opinion and government. Clearly the model
of the lobbyist who speaks for a united following, determined in its aims

and prepared to reward its friends and punish its enemies at the polls, does not often fit reality. Nor is it probable that the unassisted effort of pressure organizations to mold public opinion in support of their position has a large effect upon mass opinion. Yet legislators listen respectfully to the representations of the spokesmen of private groups, which in turn spend millions of dollars every year in propagandizing the public. Leaders of private groups articulate the concerns of substantial numbers of persons, even though they may not have succeeded in indoctrinating completely the members of their own groups. All this activity must have some functional significance in the political system. The problem is to identify its functions in a manner that seems to make sense. In this endeavor a distinction of utility is that made . . . between mass-membership organizations and nonmass organizations, which far outnumber the former.

Representation of Mass-Membership Groups. Only the spokesmen for mass-membership organizations can give the appearance of representing voters in sufficient numbers to impress (or intimidate) government. The influence of nonmass groups, which often have only a few hundred or a few thousand members, must rest upon something other than the threat of electoral retribution. As has been seen, the reality of the behavior of members of mass organizations is that in the short run they are not manipulable in large numbers by their leaders. Their party identification anchors many of them to a partisan position, and over the longer run they seem to be moved from party to party in presidential elections by the influences that affect all types and classes of people.

The spokesmen of mass-membership groups also labor under the handicap that they may be made to appear to be unrepresentative of the opinions of their members. When the president of an organization announces to a Congressional committee that he speaks for several million people, the odds are that a substantial proportion of his members can be shown to have no opinion or even to express views contrary to those voiced by their spokesmen. This divergency is often explained as a wicked betrayal of the membership or as a deliberate departure from the mass mandate. Yet it is not unlikely that another type of explanation more often fits the facts. Opinions, as we have seen in many contexts, do not fall into blacks and whites. It may be the nature of mass groups that attachment to the positions voiced by the peak spokesmen varies with attachment to and involvement in the group. At the leadership level the group position is voiced in its purest and most uncompromising form. A substantial layer of group activists subscribes to the official line, but among those with less involvement the faith wins less general acceptance. At the periphery of the group, though, the departure from the official line may be more a matter of indifference than of dissent. Leadership policy is often pictured as the consequence of interaction between leadership and group member-ship, which may be only partially true. Leaders may be more accurately regarded as dedicated souls who bid for group support of their position. Almost invariably they receive something less than universal acquiescence. This may be especially true in mass organizations in which political en-deavor is to a degree a side issue — as, for example, in trade unions and farm organizations. As one traces attitudes and opinions across the strata of group membership, the clarity of position and the extremeness of posi-tion become more marked at the level of high involvement and activism.

If it is more or less the nature of mass organizations to encompass a spectrum of opinion rather than a single hue, much of the discussion of the representativeness of group leadership may be beside the point. However that may be, circumstances surrounding the leadership elements of mass organizations place them, in their work of influencing government, in a position not entirely dissimilar to that of leaders of nonmass groups. They must rely in large measure on means not unlike those that must be em-ployed by groups with only the smallest membership. The world of pres-sure politics becomes more a politics among the activists than a politics that involves many people. Yet politics among the activists occurs in a context of concern about public opinion, a concern that colors the mode of action if not invariably its substance.

Arenas of Decision and Norms of Action. The maneuvers of pressure-group politics thus come ordinarily to occur among those highly involved and immediately concerned about public policy; the connection of these maneuvers with public opinion and even with the opinions of mass-mem-bership organizations tends to be tenuous. Many questions of policy are fought out within vaguely bounded arenas in which the activists concerned are clustered. A major factor in the determination of the balance of forces within each arena is party control of the relevant governmental apparatus. Included among the participants in each issue-cluster of activists are the spokesmen for the pressure groups concerned, the members of the House and Senate committees with jurisdiction, and the officials of the adminis-trative departments and agencies concerned. In the alliances of pressure politics those between administrative agencies and private groups are often extremely significant in the determination of courses of action. The cluster of concerned activists may include highly interested persons, firms, and organizations scattered over the country, though the boundaries delimit-ing those concerned vary from question to question, from arena to arena. In short, pressure politics among the activists takes something of the form that it would take if there were no elections or no concern about the na-ture of public opinion; that is, those immediately concerned make them-selves heard in the process of decision.

In the give and take among the activists, norms and values with foundations in public opinion are conditioning factors. The broad values of the society determine to a degree who will be heard, who can play the game. Those who claim to speak for groups that advocate causes outside the range of consensus may be given short shrift. Some groups advocating perfectly respectable causes may be heard with less deference than others. Subtle standards define what David Truman calls "access" to the decision makers. To some extent this is a party matter: an AFL-CIO delegation does not expect to be heard with much sympathy by a committee dominated by right-wing Republicans. The reality of access, too, may provide an index to the tacit standards in definition of those interests regarded as having a legitimate concern about public policy. The spokesmen of groups both large and small are often heard with respect, not because they wield power, but because they are perceived as the representatives of interests entitled to be heard and to be accorded consideration as a matter of right.

Within the range of the permissible, the process of politics among the activists is governed to some extent by the expectation that all entitled to play the game shall get a fair deal (or at least a fair hearing before their noses are rubbed in the dirt). Doubtless these practices parallel a fairly widespread set of attitudes within the population generally. Probably those attitudes could be characterized as a disposition to let every group — big business and labor unions as well — have its say, but that such groups should not be permitted to dominate the government. In the implementation of these attitudes the legalism of American legislators plays a role. Frequently Congressional committeemen regard themselves as engaged in a judicial role of hearing the evidence and of arriving at decisions based on some sort of standards of equity.

Rituals of the Activists. The maneuvers of group spokesmen, be they spokesmen for mass or nonmass organizations, are often accompanied by rituals in obeisance to the doctrine that public opinion governs. The belief often seems to be that Congressmen will be impressed by a demonstration that public opinion demands the proposed line of action or inaction. Hence, groups organize publicity campaigns and turn up sheaves of editorials in support of their position. They stimulate people to write or to wire their Congressmen; if the labor of stimulation is too arduous, they begin to sign to telegrams names chosen at random from the telephone directory. They solicit the endorsement of other organizations for their position. They lobby the American Legion and the General Federation of Women's Clubs for allies willing to permit their names to be used. On occasion they buy the support of individuals who happen to hold official positions in other organizations. They form fraudulent organizations with impressive letterheads to advance the cause. They attempt to anticipate and to soften the opposition of organizations that might be opposed to their position. Groups of similar ideological orientation tend to "run" together or to form constellations in confederation for mutual advantage.

All these maneuvers we have labeled "rituals"; that is, they are on the order of the dance of the rainmakers. They may be too brutal a characterization, for sometimes these campaigns have their effects — just as rain sometimes follows the rainmakers' dance. Yet the data make it fairly clear that most of these campaigns do not affect the opinion of many people and even clearer that they have small effect by way of punitive or approbative feedback in the vote. Their function in the political process is difficult to divine. The fact that organizations engage in these practices, though, is in itself a tribute to the importance of public opinion. To some extent, too, these opinion campaigns are not so much directed to mass opinion as to other activists who do not speak for many people either but have access to the arena of decision-making and perhaps have a viewpoint entitled to consideration. In another direction widespread publicity, by its creation of the illusion of mass support, may legitimize a position taken by a legislator. If a legislator votes for a measure that seems to arouse diverse support, his vote is not so likely to appear to be a concession to a special interest.

Barnums among the Businessmen. An additional explanation that apparently accounts for a good deal of group activity is simply that businessmen (who finance most of the campaigns of public education by pressure groups) are soft touches for publicity men. The advertising and public-relations men have demonstrated that they can sell goods; they proceed on the assumption that the business of obtaining changes in public policy is analogous to selling soap. They succeed in separating businessmen from large sums of money to propagate causes, often in a manner that sooner or later produces a boomerang effect.

Professional bureaucrats of the continuing and well-established organizations practice restraint in their public-relations campaigns. They need to gain the confidence of Congressmen and other officials with whom they also need to be able to speak the next time they meet. The fly-by-night organization or the business group that falls into the clutches of an unscrupulous public relations firm is more likely to indulge in the fantastic public relations and pressure campaign. Thus the National Tax Equality Association raised some $600,000 to finance a campaign against the tax exemptions of cooperatives, the most important of which are farm coops. Contributions came from concerns as scattered as the Central Power & Light Co., of Corpus Christi, Texas; Fairmont Foods Co., of Omaha, Nebraska; Central Hudson Gas Electric Corporation, of Poughkeepsie, New York; and the Rheem Manufacturing Co., of San Francisco. The late

Representative Reed, of New York, who was not one to attack business lightly, declared:

> Mr. Speaker, an unscrupulous racket, known as the National Tax Equality Association, has been in operation for some time, directing its vicious propaganda against the farm co-operatives. To get contributions from businessmen, this racketeering organization has propagandized businessmen with false statements to the effect that if farm co-operatives were taxed and not exempted the revenue to the government would mount annually to over $800,000,000. [The treasury estimate was in the neighborhood of $20,000,000.] This is, of course, absolutely false and nothing more nor less than getting money under false pretenses. . . . This outfit of racketeers known as the Tax Equality Association has led honest businessmen to believe that their contributions were deductible from gross income as ordinary and necessary business expense with reference to their Federal income-tax return.

The Tax Equality Association provided its subscribers with the following form letter to send to their Congressmen:

> Dear Mr. Congressman: You raised my income taxes. Now I hear you are going to do it again. But you still let billions in business and profits escape. How come you raise my taxes, but let co-ops, mutuals, and other profit-making corporations get off scot free, or nearly so? I want a straight answer — and I want these businesses fully taxed before you increase my or anyone else's income taxes again.

Letters so phrased are not well designed to produce favorable Congressional response. The ineptness of this sort of campaign creates no little curiosity about the political judgment of solvent businessmen who put their money or their corporation's money into the support of obviously stupidly managed endeavors.

Autonomous Actors or Links? This review of the activities of pressure groups may raise doubts about the validity of the conception of these groups as links between public opinion and government. The reality seems to be that the conception applies with greater accuracy to some groups than to others. Certainly group spokesmen may represent a shade of opinion to government even though not all their own members share the views they express. Yet to a considerable degree the work of the spokesmen of private groups, both large and small, proceeds without extensive involvement of either the membership or a wider public. Their operations as they seek to influence legislation and administration, though, occur in a milieu of concern about opinion, either actual or latent. That concern also disposes decision makers to attend to shades of opinion and preference relevant to decision though not necessarily of great electoral strength — a disposition of no mean importance in the promotion of the equitable treatment of people in a democratic order. The chances are that the effects of organized groups on public opinion occur mainly over the long run rather than in short-run maneuvers concerned with particular congressional votes. Moreover, group success may be governed more by the general balance of partisan strength than by the results of group endeavors to win friends in the mass public. An industry reputed to be led by swindlers may not expect the most cordial reception from legislative committees, especially at times when the balance of strength is not friendly to any kind of business. If the industry can modify its public image, a task that requires time, its position as it maneuvers on particulars (about which few of the public can ever know anything) may be less unhappy. That modification may be better attained by performance than by propaganda.

Case Studies in Pressure Group Politics

Administrative agencies often are the focal point of government policy-making, and therefore pressure groups concentrate upon the bureaucracy in order to achieve their objectives. Public policy often emerges from administrative agency-pressure group interaction, for together such an alliance of public and private interest is very difficult to overcome. The following selection illustrates the way in which such a combination of interests has developed in the defense policy field, causing concern to proponents of greater presidential and Congressional control independent of the Pentagon and private contractors' interests. The selection was written in 1961 after President Eisenhower's warning to the nation in his final address that a military-industrial complex had developed which threatened to take over control of defense and armaments policy. Although many of the individuals and some of the agencies mentioned are no longer in or part of government, the military-industrial complex continues to challenge the civilian arm of government for control over armaments policy. The selection describes an intermixture of public and private interests that continues to exist.

33

THE "MILITARY LOBBY": ITS IMPACT ON CONGRESS AND THE NATION

What led President Eisenhower, on the eve of his retirement, to warn the nation of "unwarranted influence" by what he called "the military-industrial complex"?

What is this complex, what is the nature and extent of its influence, and how is it exercised?

What dangers — if any — are implicit in the situation described by the former President?

These were the principal questions raised by the President's parting words (for text, see below). In an attempt to answer them, *Congressional Quarterly* culled the record of presidential press conferences, Congressional hearings, and other public documents. In addition, extensive off-the-record interviews were conducted with members of Congress, representatives of defense contractors, former government officials, and other persons with pertinent information. Results of this survey of fact and opinion are summarized on the following pages.

EISENHOWER'S WARNING

In his final address to the Nation on January 17 [1961] President Eisenhower noted that the United States has been compelled to "create a permanent armaments industry of vast proportions" and to maintain a defense establishment employing 3.5 million persons and spending huge sums. He continued as follows:

This conjunction of an immense military establishment and a large arms industry is new in American experience. The total influence — economic, political, even spiritual — is felt in every city, every state house, every office of the federal government. We recognize the imperative need for this development. Yet we must not fail to comprehend its grave implications. Our toil, resources and livelihood are all involved; so is the very structure of our society.

In the councils of government, we must guard against the acquisition of

---

From the Congressional Quarterly, March 24, 1961. Copyright © 1961 by the Congressional Quarterly Service. Reprinted by permission. This article appeared in the *Congressional Record,* March 26, 1961, pp. 4557 ff.

unwarranted influence, whether sought or unsought, by the military-industrial complex. The potential for the disastrous rise of misplaced power exists and will persist. We must never let the weight of this combination endanger our liberties or democratic processes. We should take nothing for granted. Only an alert and knowledgeable citizenry can compel the proper meshing of the huge industrial and military machinery of defense with our peaceful methods and goals, so that security and liberty may prosper together.

EISENHOWER'S VIEWS

The President's warning of January 17 [1961] was his first public reference to a "military-industrial complex." But the concept was in the making for eight years, during which the President had touched on most of the major components of his final declaration. These were the principal elements of his thinking, as seen by his associates and partially reflected in the record:

National survival, he stated in 1953 and repeatedly thereafter, rested on "security with solvency." To achieve this required maximum effort to counter the inherent tendency of federal expenditures in general, and defense spending in particular, to rise. The key to success lay in "balance" — not, as he said April 25, 1958, during his battle with Congress over reorganization, in "overindulging sentimental attachments to outmoded military machines and concepts," nor, as he put it January 27, 1960, in heeding the "noisy trumpeting about dazzling military schemes or untrustworthy programs."

Ranged against this view, the President realized, was a host of special interests — the armed services and their civilian allies in business and in Congress. Beginning in 1953, when he cut the Air Force budget by $5 billion, the services had repeatedly carried their fight for more funds to Congress and the press. (More than one member had called him to say they were changing their votes in response to local pressures generated by the Pentagon.) "Obviously political and financial considerations" rather than "strict military needs" were influencing the situation, he said June 3, 1959. If such forces were allowed to prevail, he said March 11, 1959, "everybody with any sense knows that we are finally going to a garrison state."

Revered by the nation as its chief military hero, and respected as its Commander in Chief, the President was confident of his ability to "put need above pressure-group inducement, before local argument, before every kind of any pressure except that that America needs," as he put it February 11, 1960. The star-studded brass of the Pentagon awed him not a bit; "there are too many of these generals who have all sorts of ideas," he said February 3, 1960. Knowing how they "operated," however, he feared that his successor — whether Nixon or Kennedy — would be unable to withstand their pressures.

This, according to a close associate, was what impelled the President to speak out as he prepared to leave office. Deeply committed to the goal of disarmament, he was sensitive to the counterinfluence of the "military-industrial complex." The extent of his concern was indicated when, at his final press conference, January 18, he described the impact of widespread advertising by missile manufacturers as "almost an insidious penetration of our own minds that the only thing this country is engaged in is weaponry and missiles." This, he said, was something "we just can't afford."

BACKGROUND

Defense spending reached its postwar low of $11.1 billion in fiscal 1948. By 1953, the cold war and a hot war in Korea had boosted spending to its post war high of $43.7 billion. President Eisenhower cut that to $35.5 billion in 1955; thereafter, defense outlays climbed each year, to reach a projected $42.9 billion in fiscal 1962. At no time during his eight years in office did military spending amount to less than one-half of the federal budget or less than 8 percent of the nation's gross national product. All told, the armed services spent $313 billion during the eight years, fiscal 1954–1961; when the costs of military aid, atomic energy, and stockpiling are added, that total mounts to $354 billion.

There is no yardstick by which to measure with precision the economic impact of these expenditures, but there is no question that it has been considerable. According to a 1960 study by the Defense Procurement Subcommittee of the Joint Economic Committee, there were 38 million procurement transactions with a dollar volume of $228 billion from 1950 through 1959. Few areas of the economy were untouched by these purchases of goods and services.

The largest portion of defense spending, however, is allocated to the development, production, and deployment of major weapons systems. In fiscal 1960, when military prime contract awards of $10,000 or more totaled $21 billion, $15.4 billion or 73.4 percent of the total went to 100 companies (or their subsidiaries) of which sixty-five were engaged primarily in "research, development, test or production of aircraft, missiles, or electronics." . . .

Despite the heavy concentration of prime contract awards among a small number of companies (in 1960 five companies accounted for 25 percent of the dollar volume, twenty-one companies for 50 percent), extensive subcontracting helps to spread procurement expenditures, employment and profits throughout the country — although not as evenly as some states would like it. In addition, some 1.5 million members of the armed services and almost 1 million civilian employees of the Defense Department are spread throughout the fifty states, with payrolls that totaled $11.4 billion in fiscal 1960. Another $650 million was paid to more than one million members of the National Guard and other Reserve groups. . . .

A further indication of the extent of defense-related activities is the wide distribution of facilities. From lists furnished by the military services, Atomic Energy Commission, and National Aeronautics and Space Administration, CQ determined the location of 738 separate installations by Congressional district. According to this list, there are one or more installations in 282 of the country's 437 districts. . . .

Taken together, these data suggest the sweeping extent of the defense establishment and its economic impact, and provide the background against which to examine the concept of a "military-industrial complex."

HÉBERT PROBE

In mid-1959, the House Armed Services Special Investigations Subcommittee, headed by Representative F. Edward Hébert, Democrat of Louisiana, questioned seventy-five witnesses over twenty-five days regarding the employment of retired officers by defense industries. The public, and Hébert as the hearings began, was alarmed by reports "about the alleged conduct of some military men who depart the ranks of defense for lush places on the payrolls of defense contractors." As it turned out, no real evidence of misconduct was produced. But the hearings shed considerable light on the ramifications of military-industrial relations.

Retired Officers. More than 1,400 retired officers in the rank of major or higher — including 261 of general or flag rank — were found to be employed by the top 100 defense contractors. The company employing the largest number (187, including twenty-seven retired generals and admirals) was General Dynamics Corp., headed by former Secretary of the Army Frank Pace, which also received the biggest defense orders of any company in 1960. Duties of these officers, according to the testimony of their employers, encompassed a wide range of technical, management, and "representation" functions. But in no case, it appeared, was the officer involved in "selling" or the negotiation of defense contracts.

"Influence." With little variation, retired officers told the Hébert subcommittee that they were "has-beens" without influence upon the decisions of their former colleagues still on active duty. None had experienced "pressure" of this kind while still in the service; if any retired officers had asked him for a favor, "I would throw them out on their ear," said Lt. Gen. C. S. Irvine (retired), director of planning for Avco Corp. No one, however, took issue with the statement of Vice Adm. H. G. Rickover that the former jobs of retired officers often were filled "by people who are their dear friends, or even by people whom they have been influential in appointing, and naturally they will be listened to."

Illustrative of this point was the testimony of Adm. William M. Fechteler (retired), former Chief of Naval Operations and a consultant to General Electric Atomic Products Division. He told of arranging appointments for a GE vice-president: "I took him in to see Mr. Gates, the Secretary of the Navy. I took him in to see Admiral Burke. He had not met Admiral Burke before. And then I made appointments with him with the Chief of the Bureau of Ships. But I did not accompany him there, because those are materiel bureaus which make contracts. And I studiously avoid even being in the room when anybody talks about a contract."

Entertainment. Two instances of entertainment by defense contractors came before the Hébert subcommittee. George Bunker, chairman of the Martin Co., acknowledged that his firm had entertained at least twenty-six active-duty officers at a weekend retreat in the Bahamas. Bunker denied there was any impropriety involved, saying "a man could neither operate nor compete effectively unless he had a close personal relationship." But spokesmen for the Secretaries of the three services agreed that such chumminess "doesn't look well" and could not be condoned.

The second case concerned an invitation to a "small off-the-record party" to discuss the plans and problems of the Air Research and Development Command with its newly promoted Chief, Lt. Gen. Bernard S. Schriever. The invitation, sent to Representative Hébert and nine other members of Congress (all but two of whom were members of the Armed Services or Appropriations Committees), was issued by three Air Force contractors: Aerojet-General President Dan A. Kimball (onetime Secretary of the Navy), General Dynamics' Pace, and Martin's Bunker. All three men defended the propriety of the proposed party (which was called off because of the "publicity") as, being in Pace's words, "a means of advancing the interests of the United States of America."

Advertising. Shortly before the Hébert hearings began, a major controversy developed in and out of Congress over the respective merits of two competing antiaircraft missile systems — the Army's Nike-Hercules and the Air Force's Bomarc. Advertisements extolling the virtues of the two systems were inserted in Washington, D.C., newspapers by their prime contractors — Western Electric Co. and Boeing Airplane Co., respectively — while the issue was before Congress. Questioned by the Hébert subcommittee about the timing and purpose of the ads, spokesmen for the companies insisted that they were parts of long-term "information" programs.

However, Boeing's Harold Mansfield acknowledged that his company was fighting against a "campaign" of "misinformation" about the Bomarc, while Western Electric's W. M. Reynolds said the Nike ads had been suggested to the company by the Army. Both companies also acknowledged discussing proposed cutbacks in the Nike and Bomarc programs with members of Congress from areas where employment would be affected. Said Mansfield: "Many of the most important decisions in the defense of our country are not made by military technicians. They are made in the Congress of the United States. And the Bomarc-Nike decision is one such decision."

Associations. Also questioned by the Hébert subcommittee were representatives of six organizations engaged in promoting the mutual interests of the armed services and their contractors in national security matters. All headquartered in Washington, they are:

Association of the U.S. Army, with about 63,000 members (including military personnel on active duty) and 1958 income of $290,000, of which $143,000 was revenue from advertising in *Army* magazine. One of its aims: "To foster public understanding and support of the U.S. Army." Executive vice president: Lt. Gen. W. L. Weible, USA (retired). Among those on its advisory board: Donald Douglas, Jr., president of Douglas Aircraft Co.; Frank Pace, chairman of General Dynamics Corp.; Senators John J. Sparkman, Democrat, of Alabama, and Strom Thurmond, Democrat, of South Carolina.

Navy League, with about 38,000 members (no active duty personnel) and 1958 income of $179,000 plus $32,000 from advertising in *Navy — The Magazine of Sea Power*. Self-description: "The civilian arm of the Navy." President: Frank Gard Jameson. Among those on its advisory council: Dan Kimball, president of Aerojet-General and former Secretary of the Navy; Adm. Robert B. Carney (retired), chairman of Bath Iron Works Shipbuilding Corp., and former Chief of Naval Operations.

Air Force Association, with about 60,000 members (including about 30,000 Air Force personnel) and 1958 income of $1.2 million, including $527,000 from advertising in *Air Force and Space Digest*. Its aim: "To support the achievement of such airpower as is necessary" for national security. Executive director: James H. Straubel. Among its directors: 14 employees of defense contractors, including Lt. Gen. James H. Doolittle, USAF (retired) of Space Technology Laboratories.

American Ordnance Association, formerly the Army Ordnance Association, with about 42,000 members and 1958 income of $474,000, of which subscriptions and advertisements in the magazine *Ordnance* furnished $253,000. Its aim: "Armament preparedness." Executive vice president: Col. Leo A. Codd, USAR (retired).

Aerospace Industries Association, formerly the Aircraft Industries Association, a trade association with 79 member companies and 1958 income of $1.4 million in dues ranging up to $75,000 per member. Its aim: To promote the manufacture and sale of "aircraft and astronautical vehicles of every nature and description." President: Gen. Orval R. Cook, USAF (retired).

National Security Industrial Association, formerly the Navy Industrial Association, with 502 member companies and 1958 income $238,000, mostly from dues. Its aim: "To establish a close working relationship between industrial concerns" and national security agencies. Executive director: Capt. R. N. McFarlane, USN (retired).

According to the testimony of their representatives, none of these groups had anything to do with procurement; all were ignorant of any "pressure" in behalf of one or another manufacturer. The three service groups acknowledged their interest in building up grass roots support for the respective branches of the armed forces; they also maintained that they were fully independent of the services they represented, although the testimony showed that, for the most part, Army, Navy, and Air Force doctrines and weapon systems received enthusiastic support in their respective publications.

All of the groups insisted that their primary function was to inform and educate. Only the Aerospace Industries Association has registered under the lobby law, but General Cook said "we believe we do not operate according to the classic definition of a lobbyist. . . . We don't even dream of buying any influence of any kind." Asked whether the best interests of the industry would be served by an increase or decrease in defense spending, Cook said: "From a selfish point of view, the best interest of the industry would be served by an increase, of course, but from a patriotic and national point of view, it might not be."

Peter J. Schenck, then president of the Air Force Association and an official of Raytheon Corp., described the basis for close military-industrial relations as follows: "The day is past when the military requirement for a major weapons system is set up by the military and passed on to industry to build the hardware. Today it is more likely that the military requirement is the result of joint participation of military and industrial personnel, and it is not unusual for industry's contribution to be a key factor. Indeed there are highly placed military men who sincerely feel that industry currently is setting the pace in the research and development of new weapons systems."

Conclusion

In its report filed January 18, 1960, the Hébert subcommittee said it was "impressed by several obvious inconsistencies in testimony" relating to the influence enjoyed by retired officers in the employment of defense contractors. Said the report: "The better grade and more expensive influence is a very subtle thing when being successfully applied. . . . The 'coincidence' of contract and personal contacts with firms represented by retired officers and retired civilian officials sometimes raises serious doubts as to the complete objectivity of some of these decisions." The subcommittee proposed, among other steps, a much tighter law regarding "sales" to the government by retired personnel; the House later passed a watered-down version of the proposal. (1959 Almanac, p. 727; 1960 Almanac, p. 279.)

ROLE OF CONGRESS

Charged with the responsibility of appropriating more than $40 billion each year for defense — and in the process deciding how to meet the conflicting claims of competing services for a larger share of the pie — Congress is up to its ears in the military-industrial issue. Collectively, the record shows, the members strive to sift fact from fancy, and to point up and root out instances of waste and duplication in the defense program. The record also shows that, individually, the members are zealous in representing the interests of their districts and states. Here are some examples:

"Fair Share." Documenting his case with facts and figures, Representative Hechler, Democrat, of West Virginia, told the House on June 1, 1959: "I am firmly against the kind of logrolling which would subject our defense program to narrowly sectional or selfish pulling and hauling. But I am getting pretty hot under the collar about the way my state of West Virginia is shortchanged in Army, Navy, and Air Force installations. I am going to stand up on my hind legs and roar until West Virginia gets the fair treatment she deserves." (Hechler plans to resume his campaign shortly.)

In the same vein, members of the New York delegation, led by Senators Kenneth B. Keating, Republican, and Jacob K. Javits, Republican, have long complained about the overconcentration of prime contract awards placed with California firms. Asking only for a "fair share," they want defense procurement officials to consider "the strategic and economic desirability of allocating purchases to different geographic areas" of the country. . . .

Installations. The opening, expansion, cutback, or closing of any military installation is of vital interest to the Member whose area is affected. In recent years, with reductions in the size of the Army and other changes in the composition of defense forces, there have been more closings than openings, and the affected members have been quick to take issue. Some recent instances: Senator Albert Gore, Democrat, of Tennessee, said February 15 that he had written Secretary of the Air Force Eugene M. Zuckert about reports that Stewart Air Force Base at Smyrna, Tennessee, might be closed, and had been assured that "as of now no change is contemplated which should cause any concern."

Senator Olin D. Johnston, Democrat, of South Carolina, after calling on President Kennedy February 20, said he had been assured that careful consideration would be given to the future of Fort Jackson at Columbia,

South Carolina, and Donaldson Air Force Base at Greenville, South Carolina.

Representative Samuel S. Stratton, Democrat, of New York, said March 3 that he had wired Secretary Zuckert about reports of a plan to transfer certain operations from Griffiss Air Force Base at Rome, New York. Said Stratton: "It is fantastic to learn that one more defense department is considering recommendations which would have the effect of increasing unemployment in upstate New York, already hard hit by lay-offs."

Representative Emanuel Celler, Democrat, of New York, said March 6 that Secretary of Defense Robert S. McNamara had assured him he had no knowledge "of any plans or proposals to shut down the operations" at the Brooklyn Navy Yard.

Procurement. Decisions to begin, accelerate, reduce, or stop production of various weapons and weapon systems are also of major interest to members in whose districts or states the manufacturers involved are located. Here are examples of Representatives at work:

When the House Appropriations Committee chopped the Air Force's 1959 request for the Bomarc by $162.7 million, Representative Don Magnuson, Democrat, of Washington, charged that few members were aware of "the incredible lengths to which the adherents of the Nike defense system have gone in their attempt to discredit the Bomarc. . . . Of course, this is Army inspired." (Contractor for Bomarc was Boeing Airplane Co., headquartered in Seattle, Washington.)

Also in 1959, Representative John R. Foley, Democrat, of Maryland, offered an amendment to the defense bill to add $10 million to Air Force funds to buy 10 F–27 transports from the Fairchild Aircraft Co. of Hagerstown, Maryland, in Foley's district. This failed, but the Senate obliged with $11 million. When House conferees refused to go along, Senator J. Glenn Beall, Republican, of Maryland, begged the Senate to insist, saying that, of the $4 billion to be spent on aircraft, "all we ask for Fairchild is $11 million."

Recent reports that the Pentagon was thinking of cutting back the B–70 program led Representative Edgar W. Hiestand, Republican, of California, to write Secretary McNamara February 27 to assure him of "the strong congressional support for this valued program." North American Aviation, Inc., prime contractor for the B–70, is located in Heistand's district.

Reserves. The well-known solicitude shown by Congress for the National Guard and other Reserve forces reflects to some degree a widespread local interest in the payrolls, armories, and other benefits involved, as well as effective work by the National Guard Association and the Reserve Officers Association. Among the forty Reserve officers in Congress are . . . [four]

generals: Howard W. Cannon, Democrat, of Nevada, brigadier general, USAFR; Strom Thurmond, Democrat, of South Carolina, major general, USAR; and Representatives James Roosevelt, Democrat, of California, brigadier general, USMCR; and Robert L. F. Sikes, Democrat, of Florida, brigadier general, USAR; Cannon and Thurmond are members of the Armed Services Committee; Sikes, of the Defense Appropriations Subcommittee. . . .

President Eisenhower made no headway whatsoever in his three-year campaign to reduce National Guard and Army Reserve manpower levels to "conform to the changing character and missions" of the active forces; Congress responded with a mandatory floor of 400,000 for the Guard, and funds to maintain both the Guard and the Reserve at full strength. These actions, said the President in his final budget message, "are unnecessarily costing the American people over $80 million annually and have been too long based on other than strictly military needs." Even at the lower strengths he again proposed, the Reserves would cost "well over $1 billion in 1962," he said.

Summing up the cumulative impact of these varied expressions of Congressional interest, Representative Jamie L. Whitten, Democrat, of Mississippi, a member of the House Appropriations Defense Subcommittee, testified as follows January 29, 1960, before the Joint Economic Committee's Defense Procurement Subcommittee:

> I am convinced defense is only one of the factors that enter into our determinations for defense spending. The others are pump priming, spreading the immediate benefits of defense spending, taking care of all services, giving all defense contractors a fair share, spreading the military bases to include all sections, etc. There is no state in the Union and hardly a district in a state which doesn't have defense spending, contracting, or a defense establishment. We see the effect in public and Congressional insistence on continuing contracts, or operating military bases, though the need has expired.

CASE OF THE ZEUS

The confluence of service, contractor, and Congressional pressures is illustrated by the current revival of a campaign to launch production of the Army's Nike-Zeus anti-missile system, although final tests are more than a year away. Congress added $137 million to the budget in 1958 to start production, but the President refused to spend it; in his final budget, providing about $287 million for further development of Nike-Zeus, he said, "funds should not be committed to production until development tests are satisfactorily completed." Subsequently, these things happened.

On February 1 the magazine *Army* appeared with seven articles lauding the Nike-Zeus — four of them by Army commanders on active duty.

Also in the issue: full-page advertisements by Western Electric Co., prime contractor for Nike-Zeus, and eight of its major subcontractors, together with a map showing how much of the $410 million contract was being spent in each of thirty-seven states (but $111 million in California, $110 million in New Jersey). The general message: It's time to start production.

On February 2, Senator Thurmond told the Senate that "we must start production of the Nike-Zeus now." Extolling the "experienced Army-industry team" that developed the system, he argued that "by spending money now to provide a capability for the production of components in quantity, we will save money in the long run." Rising to support his arguments were Senators B. Everett Jordon, Democrat, of North Carolina, and Frank Carlson, Republican, of Kansas. (*Army's* map showed spending of $36 million in North Carolina and $8.5 million in Kansas.)

On February 7, Representative George P. Miller, Democrat, of California, urged every Member of the House to "read the current issue of *Army* magazine" and to "support immediate action for limited component production of the Nike-Zeus system." Miller, a member of the Science and Astronautics Committee, said this could be done, "with the addition of less than $175 million to the present Army budget."

On February 13, Representative Daniel J. Flood, Democrat, of Pennsylvania, gave the House substantially the same speech delivered February 2 by Senator Thurmond, and also concluded that "we must start production of the Nike-Zeus now." Flood appended an article on the subject published by the Sperry Rand Corp , a subcontractor for Nike-Zeus. (*Army's* figure for spending in Pennsylvania: $10 million.)

On February 23, Representative John W. McCormack, Democrat, of Massachusetts, House majority leader, asked every Member to read Flood's "prescient address" of February 13. McCormack's conclusion: "Close the gap in our military posture; muzzle the mad-dog missile threat of the Soviet Union; loose the Zeus through America's magnificent production lines now." (*Army's* figure for Massachusetts: $1.5 million.)

On March 6, the press reported that President Kennedy was expected to approve a Defense Department compromise plan calling for an additional $100 million to $200 million to start tooling up. Eventual costs were estimated at from $5 billion to $20 billion.

EXTENT OF INFLUENCE

Proponents of the Nike-Zeus, it should be noted, base their case squarely on the national interest — the touchstone of debate, pro and con, concerning the merits of every proposal made in the name of defense. It is never clear, however, where the national interest begins and self-interest leaves off.

All of the persons questioned by CQ agreed that an element of self-interest pervades relationships among the services, their contractors and members of Congress. There was no consensus, however, regarding the extent to which decisions affecting the national interest are influenced by the self-interest of persons and organizations involved. Here is the gist of these views.

The Services. Locked in competition for larger shares of a defense budget that has not kept pace with the soaring costs of new weapon systems, the services toil constantly to "sell" their particular doctrines, programs, and requirements to the public, industry, and Congress. Recent examples: television programs on the Navy's Polaris and "The New Marine," an Army-Industry Liaison Seminar in New Orleans, an Air Force tour of Strategic Air Command headquarters in Omaha for 35 new Members of Congress.

The services are especially careful of their relations with Congress, particularly with members of the Armed Services and Appropriations Committees. When a senior member of the House Armed Services Committee complained of rumors that a Marine Corps installation might be removed from his district, the Commandant came in person to assure him that no change would be made "so long as I am in the job." A junior committee member, on learning that an unsolicited Army training center was to be located in his district, concluded that "someone" in the Pentagon was looking out for his interests.

There is some truth, all agree, in Representative Whitten's statement to the Defense Procurement Subcommittee that "you can look at some of our key people in the key places in Congress and go see how many military establishments are in their districts." One oft-cited example: the state of Georgia, home of the chairmen of both Senate and House Armed Services Committees. (To the proposal that a new Air Force installation be placed in Georgia, one brave General is credited with replying that "one more base would sink the state.")

But Congressmen accustomed to the prevalence of "logrolling" in many other areas see nothing sinister in this situation. The services are generally credited with being "correct" in their dealings with members; none of those questioned by CQ complained of "pressure" by the services.

The Contractors. For many of the major defense contractors, their only client of any importance is the United States government and the bulk of their business is obtained through negotiated contracts with one or more of the armed services. It is a highly competitive field, by all accounts, in which a considerable premium is placed on "good personal relations" with the client. Even those companies doing business exclusively with one service will be found supporting all three service sounding boards: the Air Force Association, Navy League, and Association of the U.S. Army. Entertainment practices vary widely throughout the industry, but no one denies that personal friendships play an important part in shaping working relationships between client and vendor. Two episodes serve to illustrate the point.

In one "competition" for a new weapon system, Navy technicians decided to throw out one proposal on grounds it was based on faulty data. Warned by a Navy friend of the impending decision, the contractor promptly went to the admiral in charge and persuaded him to order a thirty-day delay to permit all bidders to submit additional data. (The well-informed contractor failed to win in the end, however.)

An Air Force "competition" for a new missile ended with a top-level decision to award the contract to Company A. Learning of this, the president of Company B went straight to the Secretary and persuaded him to order a complete review of the decision. Result: the contract went to Company B.

Sometimes helped and sometimes hurt by such manifestations of "influence," contractors generally accept it as "part of the game," recognizing that to some degree the outcome reflects a tendency on the part of all three services to take care of companies with whom they have been doing business for some time, before admitting any "outsiders." (Some companies have nevertheless managed to secure important prime contracts from all three services.)

Defense contractors vary in their attitudes toward relations with Congress. Small, new companies, trying to gain a foothold in the defense business, are quick to seek the aid of their Congressmen; established contractors recognize that such intercession may backfire, especially in an attempt to reverse an essentially technical decision by the services. As the Hébert hearings demonstrated, however, contractors are not at all reluctant to solicit the aid of interested members when (as in the Nike-Bomarc dispute) it is in the mutual interest of all concerned.

Congress. As the elected representatives of their states and districts, members of Congress take a keen political interest in the economic impact of defense activities in their areas, and are the first to admit it. But few believe that such considerations exert any significant influence over the course of defense spending or the shape of national strategy. The major complaint of some members is their lack of influence!

Certain members of the Armed Services Committees admit seeking the assignment because of large military installations and defense industries in their states or districts. Others consider themselves fortunate that they do not have such activities — and the local pressures that go along with them — in their own areas. Recognizing that changing military requirements may produce a "boom and bust" effect on any given community, they try to dissuade local enthusiasts who clamor for a new installation.

Outsiders detect a Navy bias in the makeup of the House Armed Services Committee and to a lesser extent, the Senate Armed Services Committee. (Of the former's thirty-seven members, twenty-five come from coastal states.) Committee members acknowledge that some of their colleagues reflect a service point of view (ten members of the House Committee are active reservists) and that the Navy's position is amply represented; they also contend, however, that there is a minimum of service-oriented partisanship in the work of the Committees.

As for dealings with contractors, most members express doubt concerning both the desirability and feasibility of intervening in procurement decisions. One Senator who did go to bat for one of his constituents (to no avail) found himself under fire from a competitor in the same state. His conclusion: it doesn't pay to get involved.

PROS AND CONS

Does the evidence support President Eisenhower's warning against "the acquisition of unwarranted influence, whether sought or unsought, by the military-industrial complex"? The answer varies with the individual.

"There is no question that the services and their contractors have an interest in maintaining a high degree of tension in the country," says a senior member of the House Defense Appropriations Subcommittee. But he foresees no threat to the democratic process, although admitting the need to guard against overly intimate relations between soldier, salesman, and legislator.

"There is a real danger that we may go the way of prewar Japan and Germany," says one member of the House Armed Services Committee, who objects to the presence of reserve officers on the Committee and sees the appointment of industrialists to top Defense Department posts as a bad practice.

"I don't know what Eisenhower was talking about," says a former Defense Department official. Strong civilian control over the military services can be maintained, he believes, by the selection of a sufficient number of able presidential appointees, regardless of their industrial background.

"The trouble is that national security has become popular — and the record of Congressional appropriations proves it," says a former Eisenhower associate. He sees the military-industrial complex as a "floating power" largely free of any restraint.

Several of those questioned by CQ ascribed the President's concern to over-preoccupation with the budget. Believing that the nation needs and can afford an even larger defense effort, they were inclined to dismiss his warning as misdirected. This point of view was reflected in *Air Force* magazine, which characterized reaction to the President's statement as a "flap" and deplored the "small wave of learned essays rehashing all of the irresponsible charges and insinuations that have been bandied around in Congressional hearings for the past few years." The great danger, it concluded, was that "an exercise of misdirected caution . . . could menace national security."

The first moves of the Kennedy Administration suggest little sympathy with the Eisenhower viewpoint. Orders have been placed for large numbers of additional transport planes. Steps have been taken to speed up defense purchases and "spread the business" in the interests of stimulating the lagging economy. Other proposals under consideration would add substantially to defense spending in the future.

At the same time, the new administration stands pledged to seek an agreement with the Soviets on banning nuclear tests and to pursue the goal of arms control. As yet, the chances of achieving either appear to be so remote as to preclude serious consideration of the possible opposition to any agreement by a "military-industrial complex." It may be worth noting, however, that the American Ordnance Assn. is calling for the "immediate resumption . . . of nuclear tests for both small and large weapons," and that *Ordnance* magazine argues that until the communist "goal of world dominion . . . is abandoned, there can be no lessening of our armament preparedness."

The Politics of Oil

Oil and politics have always been intertwined, both in the international and the domestic spheres. Given the predominant economic position of the oil industry, and its vast wealth, it is surprising that it does not exert more influence in the political system. Even Louisiana Senator Russell Long, chairman of the Senate Finance Committee and an outspoken advocate of oil interests, recognized in 1980 that a windfall profits tax on the oil industry was inevitable. The industry was reaping huge profits due to decontrol, and even its strong allies in government knew that it was strategically necessary to have such a tax to appease public opinion. While the oil industry won an important battle in Washington in securing decontrol, there was no doubt in the minds of industry leaders that Washington would continue to take a strong interest in oil that would affect profits in the future. The following selection describes how the oil industry has buttressed its position by strengthening its lobbying efforts.

34

Richard Halloran

THE CAPITAL'S DIVERSE OIL LOBBYISTS: MUCH CRITICIZED, OFTEN EFFECTIVE

WASHINGTON, Aug. 8 — It's known on Capitol Hill, sometimes admiringly and sometimes begrudgingly, as the Slick and Smiley Show.

William T. Slick Jr. is a senior vice president of Exxon U.S.A., and he is in charge of Government and public affairs at the company's Houston headquarters. His colleague, Donald E. Smiley, is a vice president of the parent Exxon Corporation and is in charge of its Washington office.

Together, Mr. Slick and Mr. Smiley lead a squad of oil lobbyists that is widely considered among the most effective in Washington. "They really get out and lobby," an admiring competitor said. Mr. Smiley quietly agreed: "Yes, we do."

Not everyone in Washington admires Exxon's lobbying prowess, of course. Notable among the nonadmirers is the President of the United States. In news conferences and speeches, President Carter has repeatedly assailed the entire "oil lobby" — of which the giant Exxon is but a small part — for opposing his proposed "windfall" profits tax and other energy measures.

Immediately after he proposed the tax last April, President Carter predicted that the oil lobby would be "all over Capitol Hill like a chicken on a June bug." More recently, he criticized what he called "the enormous power of a well-organized special interest" for trying to thwart his efforts.

In the babel of voices and causes that is Washington, Mr. Smiley and Mr. Slick and scores of other oil lobbyists are competing mainly for access to influential people, the assurance that they will return their calls, hear them out and take their point of view seriously.

By most accounts, that access and trust comes from providing reliable information to Congressmen and their staffs, who are deluged with an endless variety of complicated problems. Especially useful information would include an accurate assessment of how proposed legislation would affect a Congressman's home district. The lobbyist works his influence by playing what is known as "constituent politics."

Campaign contributions — from business political action committees, for example — still exist. But, according to several lobbyists, contributions have become less important because of recent Federal election campaign restrictions. However, a contribution does help open a door, the lobbyists acknowledge.

Mr. Smiley and his staff of six collect political intelligence on legislative and executive-branch actions that will likely affect Exxon or the oil industry and pass it along to New York or Houston, together with their recommendations on what Exxon should do.

In Houston, Mr. Slick assembles specialists to analyze that intelligence, to research and write position papers and to plan Exxon's strategy on the issue at hand. That work, in turn, is passed back to Mr. Smiley in Washington, where his lobbyists seek out members of Congress, Administration officials, and, in particular, their staffs, to expound the views on the world's largest oil company.

"Exxon is unique," another lobbyist said. "They can get together a task force of 10 people, do a position paper, fly it up from Houston overnight, and send an expert to explain it."

Those in the oil lobby, however, vigorously dispute the portrait that some of their critics paint of a vast monolith, a powerful conspiracy, a mysterious legion of insidious lobbyists. It all depends, the oil people contend, on whose side the lobbyists take: When they are against you, they are sinister, when they are for you, as President Harry S. Truman once said, "we would call them citizens appearing in the public interest."

ONE VOICE OR MANY?

"There is no oil lobby; there are dozens of oil lobbies," a long-time lobbyist here asserted. A senior official at the Department of Energy agreed. "There's nothing monolithic about the oil lobby," he said. "Out there, it's a sea of constantly changing alliances."

The most pronounced difference is between the large international oil companies, known as the "majors," and the smaller "independents."

"That's been a definite improvement over the last five years," the spokesman for one independent oil company said. "We've finally established the difference between the small producers, and Exxon and Texaco and all those big guys."

In Washington, the majors like Texaco Inc. and the Standard Oil Company of California are regarded as industry oriented because they are affected by anything that happens to oil. By contrast, companies like Ashland Oil Inc. are considered issue oriented. Ashland's executives tend to be uninterested in the windfall profits tax because their company has little domestic crude oil to be taxed.

Among the independents, it can be a free-for-all. They run the gamut of explorers, producers, pipeline operators and truckers, jobbers and refiners. Their broadest trade group is the Independent Petroleum Association of America, which has 5,100 members in 33 states. But there are dozens of smaller, more specific associations, like the National Oil Jobbers Council.

There are basic differences in tactics among the oil companies and associations. Some prefer that their own people do the lobbying; others hire Washington firms with good contacts in the Administration and particularly on Capitol Hill. Some company men typically look on the Washington lobbyists as "hired guns," out for themselves, while the Washington firms deprecate the company men as "bureaucrats," who do not understand the political scene.

Whether company people or freelance specialists, many oil lobbyists scoff at reports of their enormous influence. "The terror and the power of the oil lobby is the biggest myth in this country," said Lloyd N. Unsell, executive vice president of the Independent Petroleum Association. To help prove his point, he has pulled together a two-page list of important bills passed over the last 25 years that the oil lobby has failed to stop. Other oil men note that for 20 years the industry has been unable to overcome objections to new refineries.

As for mystery, Charles H. Sandler, the vice president for government affairs at the American Petroleum Institute, said: "Some lobbyists like to foster the myth that their work is mysterious. I suspect that the degree of mystery is in direct relation to the fees they charge out-of-town clients."

According to Mr. Sandler, lobbying is not arcane, "but a hard, nuts-and-bolts job." His organization, the mainstream trade association for the oil industry (it has 277 corporate and 7,300 individual members), provides research and analysis that lobbyists use in their campaigns to influence members of Congress and Administration officials.

Top-flight lobbyists can clear as much as $100,000 or more a year for their efforts, while salaries for most company lobbyists range between $20,000 and $80,000. Those in consulting and legal firms charge fees of $300 a day and up. Nobody knows the overall cost of oil lobbying, which includes Washington operations, public relations, advertising and campaigns to involve shareholders and employees. The lobbying laws do not require extensive reports, but the fact that it runs into hundreds of millions of dollars seems safe to say.

CHANGING TARGETS

Whom do the lobbyists lobby? That has changed in recent years. With the increase in American dependence on imported oil and the rise in strength of the Organization of Petroleum Exporting Countries, the focus of power in oil has shifted from the individual states and Houston to the Federal Government in Washington. Here, Congress is the primary target of lobbying, although the Administration gets its share.

Oil executives, in their private moments, said they have little hope of rolling back the laws and regulations that govern their industry. They lobby to make the regulations less restrictive and the taxes less onerous. "It's hard to think of any legislation that was intended to make our work easier, or the tax load lighter," a company lobbyist said.

The consensus among lobbyists and Government officials is that the independents are more effective than the big companies in lobbying. In this day of "participatory democracy," there are more of them.

"When the call goes out to Texas," one official said, "the sky gets dark with Lear jets if they don't like what's going on here."

A longtime lobbyist said the "independents come to town to do it for themselves." In his view, they get attention because "a 50-year-old millionaire in his 10-gallon hat and his boots is a far more interesting, captivating and effective human being."

And those who do not descend on Washington from the oilfields send telegrams that come in "like a cloud of locusts," said an official who has been on the receiving end.

Mr. Unsell, who heads the Independent Petroleum Association's Washington office, estimates that 1,200 to 1,500 independents have been involved in the legislative process over the last five years.

About 90 independent producers came to Washington last month to lobby against the windfall profits tax in the House Ways and Means Committee. They lost. The committee not only passed the proposal sent up by the President, but also toughened it. On the House floor, however, the lobbyists were able to dilute the measure somewhat.

In September, Mr. Unsell said, he planned to call up 75 or 80 independents to talk to every senator when the tax bill gets to the floor. "If it's super bad," he said, "we'll get a group in here to try to improve it first — and then beat it."

SUBGROUPS SPRING UP

In an organization the size of the Independent Petroleum Association, however, the common denominator is sometimes too low to satisfy all members. Two offshoots, the Domestic Wildcatters Association in Houston, and the Small Producers for Energy Independence, in Wichita, Kan., have sprung up to represent narrower interests.

Two independent Houston oilmen, Jack Warner and Alan King, set up the Domestic Wildcatters and got in touch with Representative Charles Wilson, Democrat of Texas. He introduced them and other oilmen to Democrats from the North and East who had not met oilmen before. "It was enormously effective," said a lobbyist.

In Wichita, a group of oilmen from Kansas, Colorado and Oklahoma led by Don Slawson and Robert Baren formed the Small Producers and hired as their lobbyist a prominent Washington lawyer, Harry C. McPherson Jr., who was once an aide to Lyndon B. Johnson when he was a senator and, later, President, and an adviser to Senator Edmund S. Muskie, the Maine Democrat who remains a power in his party.

They won a fight over the oil-depletion allowance a couple of years ago after hiring Robert Nathan Associates to make an elaborate study on the cost of oil. Mr. Nathan testified before Congressional committees four times, and five oilmen from Kansas made the rounds with the study to see 100 senators and representatives and their staffs. They won the final vote in the Senate, 41 to 40.

Last year, the two groups decided to join forces and set up the Council of Active Independent Oil and Gas Producers with Richard A. Kline as their lobbyist. Mr. Kline had been a political fund raiser for Senator Muskie and Senator Henry M. Jackson, Democrat of Washington and chairman of the Committee on Energy and Natural Resources.

Still another group of independents is the Domestic Petroleum Council, whose lobbyist is J. D. Williams. His name is on every list of the top five oil lobbyists in Washington. A colleague calls him "a good-ole boy with a steel-trap mind."

Mr. Williams was an aide to the late Senator Robert S. Kerr, Democrat of Oklahoma, one-time chairman of the Kerr-McGee Corporation and Governor of Oklahoma. Mr. Williams is considered so knowledgeable that White House staff members call him for advice, even though the President has assailed oil lobbyists.

NONCOMPANY LOBBYISTS

Of Washington's noncompany lobbyists who represent either independents or majors here, Tom C. Korologos is among the most influential. Mr. Korologos, a White House liaison officer with Congress during the Nixon and Ford Administrations, "knows everyone on Capitol Hill," according to a colleague. Another said: "He is respected by Democrats and Republicans alike."

Mr. Korologos is vice president of a firm headed by William Timmons, also of the Nixon and Ford White House Congressional liaison staffs. Their oil clients include the Standard Oil Company (Indiana) and the American Petroleum Institute.

Another name on every list is Thomas Hale Boggs Jr., son of the late Representative T. Hale Boggs, Democrat of Louisiana and majority leader, and Corrine C. Boggs, the successor to her husband's seat in Congress. Mr. Boggs's law firm represents the Marathon Oil Company, the Association of Oil Pipelines, the state of Louisiana, the Independent U.S. Tanker Owners Committee and other pipelines. Most recently he was in the news on another front — as an architect of the Chrysler Corporation's request for $1 billion in Federal aid.

It is not uncommon for oil companies to look to former senators and representatives to carry their flag. The Pennzoil Company of Houston, has retained the law firm of Smathers, Symington & Herlong, Mr. Smathers being a former Senator from Florida and Mr. Symington a former Representative from Missouri.

ACTIVE CHAIRMEN

Among the lobbyists, Mr. Smiley of Exxon is often mentioned as being effective. Even a White House official acknowledged his influence: "He is as good a lobbyist as I've found in this town. He's discreet, trustworthy, and he has a good sense of who needs to talk to whom."

Mr. Smiley, 47, a philosophical man who likes to quote Will Durant, brushed off the compliment lightly: "Bill Slick and I have been walking those halls together for a lot of years." Mr. Slick, 56, is that relatively rare Ivy Leaguer in the oil business, having been with Exxon ever since he graduated from Brown University in 1948.

Shell's lobbyists also reflect the changing times. Two are women; Sharon Lee Bonitt, who works the Senate side, and Barbara Jo Pease, assigned to the House; while a third is a black, L. H. Wells, who also works on the House side.

Beyond the lobbyists posted here, the presidents and other senior executives of the major oil companies often lobby in person. The president of the Standard Oil Company (Ohio), Alton W. Whitehouse Jr., is even registered as a lobbyist.

Officials at the Department of Energy say that company presidents often call Energy Secretary James R. Schlesinger, or come to the department to brief senior officials on their views. The same is true on Capitol Hill.

But oil executives have been singularly unsuccessful in getting through to the White House. John E. Swearingen, chairman of Standard of Indiana and the current chairman of the A.P.I., said: "I've had a request in for a meeting with the President of the United States since last November but have had no answer."

Oilmen here note that Thornton F. Bradshaw, president of the Atlantic Richfield Company, was the only oil executive invited to Camp David to meet with the President during the recent domestic summit conferences there.

The Individual as Lobbyist

An important premise of group theory is that individuals do not count in the political process except as they operate through interest groups. The example of Ralph Nader might suggest the contrary, because there is little doubt that on an individual basis he has been able to gain many concessions from government in areas in which he is interested, such as automobile safety. Although he represents "consumer" interests, only in recent years has he attempted to organize his support in any formal way; originally he operated largely alone. Although Congressmen may have thought that a potential interest group was behind him and therefore they should pay attention to his demands, the fact is that until recently he stood alone against powerful private interests and was able to persuade Congressional committees and administrative agencies to enact policies more protective of the public interest as he conceived it. Richard Armstrong reviews Nader's activities and illustrates his influence upon the political process.

35

Richard Armstrong

THE PASSION THAT RULES
RALPH NADER

On a recent visit to Marymount College in Arlington, Virginia, Ralph Nader arrived at the school gymnasium an hour late. But he then proceeded to pacify an overflowing crowd of restless students — and earn a lecture fee of $2,500 — by denouncing America's big corporations in venomous language. Afterward one question from the audience brought a rousing and spontaneous burst of applause. When, the questioner asked, did he plan to run for President?

A slightly more measured assessment of the Nader phenomenon came from Bess Myerson, New York City's commissioner of consumer affairs, when she introduced him as star witness at a recent hearing on deceptive advertising. "Mr. Nader," she said, "is a remarkable man who, in the last six years, has done more as a private citizen for our country and its people than most public officials do in a lifetime."

The remarkable thing about this tribute is that it is literally true. In the seven years since he moved to Washington from Winsted, Connecticut

— without funds and with a narrow base of expert knowledge in a single subject, automobile safety — Nader has created a flourishing nationwide movement, known as consumerism. He is chiefly responsible for the passage of at least six major laws, imposing new federal safety standards on automobiles, meat and poultry products, gas pipelines, coal mining, and radiation emissions from electronic devices. His investigations have led to a strenuous renovation of both the Federal Trade Commission and the Food and Drug Administration. And if the quality and convenience of American life do not seem dramatically improved after all that furious crusading, Nader can point to at least one quite tangible result. Last year, for the first time in nine years, traffic fatalities in the United States declined, to 55,300 from 56,400 in 1969. Unless the decline was a fluke (and officials at the Highway Traffic Safety Administration do not think it was), then for those 1,100 living Americans, whoever they may be, Nader can be said to have performed the ultimate public service.

MORE THAN TEN KREMLINS

And yet, despite all this, it is easy to conclude after a conversation with Nader that he is not primarily interested in protecting consumers. The passion that rules in him — and he is a passionate man — is aimed at smashing utterly the target of his hatred, which is corporate power. He thinks, and says quite bluntly, that a great many corporate executives belong in prison — for defrauding the consumer with shoddy merchandise, poisoning the food supply with chemical additives, and willfully manufacturing unsafe products that will maim or kill the buyer. In his words, the law should "pierce the corporate veil" so that individual executives could be jailed when their companies misbehaved. He emphasizes that he is talking not just about "fly-by-night hucksters" but the top management of "blue-chip business firms."

The lawyers who provide legal cover for all these criminal acts are, to Nader, nothing but "high-priced prostitutes." As for the advertising profession, Nader recently served up the following indictment: "Madison Avenue is engaged in an epidemic campaign of marketing fraud. It has done more to subvert and destroy the market system in this country than ten Kremlins ever dreamed of." With the certainty of the visionary, Nader would sweep away that shattered market system and replace it by various eccentric devices of his own, such as a government rating system for every consumer product.

If, on the one hand, Nader has advanced the cause of consumer protection by his skillful marshaling of facts in support of specific reforms, he has, on the other hand, made reform more difficult through his habit of coating his facts with invective and assigning the worst possible motives to almost everybody but himself. By some peculiar logic of his own, he has cast the consumer and the corporation as bitter enemies, and he seems to think that no reform is worth its salt unless business greets it with a maximum of suspicion, hostility, and fear.

Nader is a strange apparition in the well-tailored world of the Washington lawyer. His suits hang awkwardly off his lanky frame, all of them apparently gray and cut about a half size too large. His big brown eyes in their deep sockets have a permanent expression of hurt defiance, and before a crowd he blinks them nervously. The eyes, the bony face, and a small, set chin give him, at thirty-seven, the look of an underfed waif.

Nobody has been able to explain the deep personal anger that erupts when Nader begins to speak about corporations. He himself simply denies that he is anti-business. "People who make that charge are escalating the abstraction," he told an interviewer recently, his long hands clasped together, his brown eyes flashing. "They don't dare face the issues." But anger of some kind is unmistakably there. It seems to spring out of some profound alienation from the comfortable world he sees around him, and perhaps dates back to his early days in the conservative little town of Winsted, where he was something of an oddball, the son of a Lebanese immigrant, the boy who read the Congressional Record. He recalls proudly that his father, who kept a restaurant and assailed customers with his political views, "forecast the corporate takeover of the regulatory agencies back in the 1930s." Princeton and Harvard Law School trained Nader's brilliant mind, but their social graces never touched his inner core. There seems something of the desert in him still, the ghost of some harsh prophet from his ancestral Lebanon.

According to one old friend, Nader has always had a conspiratorial view of the world, and when General Motors put private detectives on his trail in 1965 just before the publication of *Unsafe at Any Speed* that view was strongly reinforced. "He thought somebody was following him around," says the friend, "and then, by gosh, somebody *was* following him around." Apparently, at the time, Nader was convinced that GM planned to have him bumped off. He still moves about Washington in great secrecy from one rendezvous to the next.

THE FIFTH BRANCH OF GOVERNMENT

In his role as scourge of the regulatory agencies, Nader is aggressive and ill-mannered as a matter of calculated policy. "Rattle off a few facts so they will know you can't be bluffed," he tells his teams of young investigators setting out to interview government officials. "Get on the offensive and stay there." Says Lowell Dodge, who runs Nader's Auto Safety Center: "If somebody is messing up, Ralph wants to embarrass them."

But Nader can be an engaging fellow when he chooses. He takes care to maintain good relations with Washington journalists — parceling out news tips with an even hand — and many of them pay him the ultimate tribute of calling him the best reporter they know. To these men he seems to serve as a sort of ghost of conscience past, a reminder of investigations not pursued and stables left uncleansed. Both reporters and professional politicians find him extremely useful. "Nader has become the fifth branch of government, if you count the press as fourth," says a Senate aide who has worked with Nader often in drafting legislation. "He knows all the newspaper deadlines and how to get in touch with anybody any time. By his own hard work he has developed a network of sources in every arm of government. And believe me, no Senator turns down those calls from Ralph. He will say he's got some stuff and it's good, and the Senator can take the credit. Any afternoon he's in town you still see him trudging along the corridors here with a stack of documents under his arm, keeping up his contacts."

What Nader gets out of the intercourse is power — not the trappings but the substance — more of it by now than most of the Senators and Congressmen on whom he calls. When an important bill is pending he is quite capable of playing rough, threatening to denounce a Representative to the press unless he goes along on a key amendment. "Does Ralph like power?" The Senate aide laughed at such a naive question. "Good gracious, yes. He loves it." Compared to other powerful men in Washington, Nader enjoys a rare freedom of action, flourishing as a sort of freebooter who is able to pick his targets at will, unconstrained by an electorate or any judgment but his own. "You will find sensitive people around town who are saying it's time to take a second look at this guy," says the Senate aide. "There are people who wonder whether he ought to be the final arbiter of safety in autos or in the food supply. Nader has something the companies don't have — credibility — especially with the press. There is a danger that people will be afraid to go up against him for that reason alone."

REGRETS TO DAVID SUSSKIND

By any measure, Nader's power is still growing. He remains absolute master of his own movement, but he is no longer alone. "When I think of all the lean years Ralph spent knocking on doors — " says Theodore Jacobs, who was Nader's classmate at both Princeton and Harvard Law School and now serves as a sort of chief of staff. Jacobs had just concluded a telephone call that, from his end, had consisted only of various expressions of regret. "That was Susskind. He's got a new show, he wants Ralph, and I had to turn him down. Ralph hates New York — all that traffic and pollution — and I can't get him up there unless it's imperative. I spend a lot of my time saying no. Among other problems, he's got two people on his tail right now who are writing full-length biographies. He has to husband his time. He's down for the *Today* show next Tuesday, but that's right here in town. If there is an important bill pending in committee and they need some input, he'll be there. He'll duck anything else for that."

Jacobs presides, loosely, over a modern suite of offices in downtown Washington housing the Center for the Study of Responsive Law. This is home base for the seven most senior of Nader's "raiders" and is one of the three organizations through which Nader now operates. The other two are located a few blocks away: the five-man Auto Safety Center and the Public Interest Research Group, staffed by twelve bright young graduates of top law schools, three of them women. In addition, there are the summertime student raiders, who this year will number about fifty, only one-quarter as many as last year. The program is being cut back, Jacobs explains, because the students are a mixed blessing, requiring a good deal of nursemaiding by the full-time staff. "But we still think it's useful for the regulatory agencies to see a fresh batch of faces wafting through."

One of the center's main functions is to handle a flood of crank calls. "No, I'm afraid Mr. Nader isn't here," says the young girl at the switchboard. "Can you tell me what it's about?" After a protracted conversation, she explains with a grin: "He said it was something so big he didn't dare put a word on paper. No name either, but still he wants to speak to Ralph." Nader drops by for a few minutes every day or so, and the other raiders emulate his casual example; by the switchboard, message boxes improvised out of brown paper are filled to overflowing with notices of calls never returned.

The Center for the Study of Responsive Law is tax-exempt, supported by well-known foundations, such as Field, Carnegie, and Stern, and by wealthy benefactors such as Midas muffler heir Gordon Sherman and Robert Townsend, author of *Up the Organization*. (Townsend gave $150,000.) On a budget of $300,000 a year, the center is able to pay its raiders a stipend of up to $15,000 each. "A far cry from five years ago," says one of the veteran raiders, Harrison Wellford, thirty-one, "when Ralph was being trailed by GM gumshoes and we would meet at night at the Crystal City hamburger joint on Connecticut Avenue to compare notes. We'd work our heads off and then get gunned down by someone from Covington & Burling [a large Washington law firm] who had been on an issue for a corporate client for ten years."

Consumers Union is the biggest single donor to the Auto Safety Center, which operates on a slender budget of $30,000 a year. The Public Interest Research Group, or PIRG as it is called, is Nader's own nonprofit law firm, and he pays all the bills out of his own pocket, including the stipends of $4,500 a year to the twelve young lawyers. It is an irony that must warm Nader's heart that the money comes out of the $270,000 he netted in the settlement of his lawsuit against GM for invasion of privacy. Since PIRG's budget is $170,000 a year, Nader is obviously going through his windfall at an unsustainable clip.

CONSCIOUSNESS III DOESN'T GIVE A DAMN

Nader calls his own organization "a big joke really, a drop in the bucket compared to the size of the problem." It is in his nature to conceive of the enemy as being enormous, pervasive, and exceedingly powerful. "How many public-interest lawyers would it take to oversee the Pentagon? A hundred? Multiply that by the number of departments and agencies. This country needs 50,000 full-time citizens, including 10,000 public-interest lawyers. And I could get that many applicants if I had the money." Last month Nader began a campaign to raise $750,000 from students in two states, Connecticut and Ohio, where the money would be used to set up Nader-like centers for investigating state and local government. Students in two other states, Oregon and Minnesota, have voted to donate $3 each from their college activities funds to finance similar organizations. Nader hopes that one plan or another will spread across the country.

To the young, Nader is a hero of great stature. Thousands of students in law, medicine, engineering, and every other field want to "conform their careers and their ideals," as he puts it, by going to work for him. They are the mass base of his movement, and he is able to pick and choose among them for his staff. (They say on campus that getting a job with Nader is "tougher than getting into Yale Law School.") And yet this appeal is in many ways hard to fathom. Nader has no use at all for the "counterculture," and he abhors drugs. "There's a conflict between living life on a level of feeling on the one hand and Ralph's product ethic on the other," admits Lowell Dodge. "To produce, to have an impact — that's what Ralph admires. Consciousness III doesn't give a damn about the FTC. Ralph does." Dodge thinks Nader is growing ever stronger on campus as revolutionary ideas begin to fade. "There's more interest in change *within* the system, and Ralph is the most effective example of an agent for change."

Nader hectors students mercilessly about their public duties, about their "anemic imaginations," about their "thousands of hours on the beach or playing cards." And they seem to love it. "Suppose students would engage in one of history's greatest acts of sacrifice and go without Coke and tobacco and alcohol, on which they spend $250 each a year?" he asked a student audience at Town Hall in New York. "They could develop the most powerful lobby in the country. Write to us! We'll tell you how to do it." Hands dived for pens as he called out his address in Washington.

It is possible to question, nevertheless, whether this enthusiasm would survive a close association with Nader. Although most of the members of his full-time staff plan to stay in public-interest legal work, many of them talk with enthusiasm about the day when they will be leaving Nader. One reason, of course, is money. "On $4,500 a year, it's tough," says Christopher White, one of the young lawyers at the Public Interest Research Group. And then these young people are blither spirits than Nader and have a spontaneity and graciousness he lacks. Although they refrain from criticizing him directly, the picture that emerges is of a boss at least as dictatorial as any they would find in a private law firm. "The emphasis is on production," one of them says. "Ralph thinks that if a brief is 90 percent right, it's a waste of time to polish it." Nader tells them that a work week of 100 hours is "about right." He lectures them about smoking, refuses to ride in their Volkswagens, and never has time to waste socializing. Lowell Dodge got a call from Nader last Christmas Eve, but only because Nader had a question to ask about work in progress.

NOTCHES ON NADER'S GUN

The Automobile. An auto-safety enthusiast while at Princeton and Harvard Law School, Nader went to Washington in 1964 to work on his pet subject as an aide to Daniel Patrick Moynihan, then Assistant Secretary of Labor, who happened to be interested in a field far removed from his assigned duties. Bored with office routine, Nader quit the following year and wrote *Unsafe at Any Speed* in ten weeks. During the Senate hearings on auto safety, he came out a clear winner in a much-publicized confrontation with James Roche, president (now chairman) of General Motors. The publicity assured passage of the Motor Vehicle Safety Act of 1966, establishing a government agency to set mandatory vehicle-safety standards, of which there are now thirty-four.

Unsanitary Meat. For his second campaign, Nader found ready-made evidence in a study done by the Department of Agriculture of state-regulated packing plants, considered to be in intrastate commerce and so not covered by federal law. Many of the plants were filthy and rodent infested, but apparently nobody of any consequence had ever bothered to read the study's report. Nader did. The result was the Wholesome Meat Act of 1967, giving states the option of bringing their inspection programs up to federal standards or having them supplanted by federal inspection. In 1968 the provisions of the act were applied to poultry products.

Federal Trade Commission. A team of student raiders assigned by Nader to the FTC in 1968 found one official at the agency literally asleep on the job, others frequenting nearby saloons during working hours, and still others who seldom bothered to come to work at all. President Nixon commissioned a study of the FTC by an American Bar Association panel, which confirmed the major findings of the Nader report: low morale, lack of planning, preoccupation with trivial cases and timidity in pursuing important ones. Outcome: new faces and new vigor at the FTC.

Food and Drug Administration. Student raiders studying the FDA in the summer of 1969 compiled evidence on two important regulatory blunders: approval of cyclamates and monosodium glutamate for unrestricted use in the food supply. Alerted by the raiders, the news media covered both stories with unrestrained enthusiasm until the FDA banned cyclamates

from soft drinks and manufacturers voluntarily stopped putting monosodium glutamate in baby food. In December, President Nixon fired the
three top officials at the FDA.

Other Doings. Legislation inspired by Nader: Natural Gas Pipeline Safety
Act (1968), Radiation Control for Health and Safety Act (1968), Coal
Mine Health and Safety Act (1969), Comprehensive Occupational Safety
and Health Act (1970). Published reports: *The Chemical Feast* (on the
FDA); *The Interstate Commerce Omission* (it recommends abolishing the
ICC); *Vanishing Air* (a critical look at air-pollution-control laws and industry compliance); *What to Do with Your Bad Car* ("an action manual
for lemon owners"); *One Life — One Physician* (on the medical profession). Reports in progress on: the Department of Agriculture, nursing
homes, water pollution, Du Pont, First National City Bank of New York,
the Washington law firm of Covington & Burling, land-use policies in California, supermarkets, and "brown lung" disease in the textile industry.

The warmth and empathy so important to the young are not to be
found in any relationship with Nader. Robert Townsend's daughter Claire,
a pretty blonde student at Princeton, says with unblushing candor that she
became a raider last summer partly because "I had a terrible crush on
Ralph. All the girls have crushes on Ralph." But Nader apparently never
has crushes on them. He still lives monklike in a rented room. His most
pronounced concession to cravings of the flesh comes in appeasing a vora-
cious though picky appetite. He is leery of most meats but often tops off a
meal with two desserts. It is somehow typical of the man that when the
soon-to-be-famous blonde detective tried to pick him up, back during his
fight with GM, she found him in a supermarket buying a package of
cookies.

TRYING TO FIND
FREE ENTERPRISE

What young people admire in Nader is a dark and uncompromising idealism, coupled with a system of New Left economics that he is able to shore
up with all sorts of impressive-sounding facts. They think he has got the
goods on "the system." And he is completely free of any humdrum sense of
proportion. A conversation with Nader makes the consumer society sound
as gory as a battlefield: motorists "skewered like shish kebab on non-
collapsible steering wheels"; babies burned to death by flammable fabrics
improperly labeled; a little girl decapitated because a glove-compartment
door popped open in a low-speed collision; "thousands of people poisoned
and killed every year through the irresponsible use of pesticides and chemicals."

The corporate criminals responsible for this slaughter always go unpunished. "If we were as lenient toward individual crime as we are toward big-business crime we would empty the prisons, dissolve the police forces, and subsidize the criminals." The regulatory agencies are "chatteled to business and indifferent to the public," and Congress is "an anachronism, although a good investment for corporations." As for the market economy, it is rapidly being destroyed by the same corporate executives who are always "extolling it at stockholder meetings."

"Where is the free-enterprise system?" Nader asks, a sly smile lighting up his face. "I'm trying to find it. Is it the oil oligopoly, protected by import quotas? The shared monopolies in consumer products? The securities market, that bastion of capitalism operating on fixed commissions and now provided with socialized insurance? They call me a radical for trying to restore power to the consumer, but businessmen are the true radicals in this country. They are taking us deeper and deeper into corporate socialism — corporate power using government power to protect it from competition."

DOWN TO ZERO PROFITS

Nader is not exactly the first social critic to be astonished at the functions — and malfunctions — of a market economy, and to render them in overtones of darkest evil. But sinister tales of this sort, while they go down well enough with college crowds, throw no light at all on the issues Nader claims to want to face. It is true enough that unless consumers themselves are concerned about product safety, corporations have no particular bias in its favor. This is due, however, not to corporate depravity but rather to the economics of the case: an extra margin of safety is an invisible benefit that usually increases costs. When products, automobiles for example, are too complicated for consumers to make independent judgments as to safety, government must usually set standards if there are to be any — and it is a measure not just of business power but also of consumer indifference that safety standards for autos came so late.

Government must also counter the ceaseless efforts of corporations to escape from the rigors of competition through the acquisition of monopoly power, through tariff protection, import quotas, and the like. Granted that government hasn't done a very good job of this. All the same, most corporate executives, obliged to immerse themselves daily in what feels very much like competition, would be surprised to learn from Nader how free of it they are supposed to have become.

Given Nader's own diagnosis, it might be thought that he has been spending his time battling restraints on trade, but this is far from the case. He has instead been devoting his considerable ingenuity to devising new schemes for regulating and "popularizing" business, by such means as a federal charter for all corporations, "which would be like a constitution for a country," publication of corporate tax returns, and the election of public members to corporate boards. He would require an attack on pollution "with maximum use of known technology and down to zero profits."

Nader denies any desire to take the country into socialism, and in this he is apparently sincere. One of his raiders, Mark Green, told *The New York Times* recently that when Nader thinks of socialism "he doesn't think of Lenin but of Paul Rand Dixon," former Chairman of the FTC and, in Nader's mind, the quintessential bureaucrat. Yet Nader seems never to have grasped that when he talks about operating on "zero profits" he is talking not about a market economy but about a confiscatory, state-imposed system that would inevitably bring in train a host of other controls.

In his "consumer democracy" of the future, as he outlines it, everybody could order business around. Tightly controlled from above by the federal government, business would be policed at the local level by what would amount to consumer soviets. Nader thinks it will be easy to organize them, by handing out application forms in the parking lots of shopping centers. "Then collectively you can bargain with the owners of the center. You can say, 'Here are 18,000 families. We want a one-room office where we can have our staff within the center that will serve as a liaison between us and you. And we're going to develop certain conditions of our continuing patronage on a mass basis.' It might take the form of banning detergents with phosphates, improving service under a warranty, or holding down prices." Nader's product-rating system, including a telephone data bank for easy reference, would force manufacturers, he says, to abandon their present policy of "severe protective imitation" for one of "competition on price and quality." (Nobody has been able to explain just how such a system would make the millions of decisions the market makes now, many of them involving subjective judgments as to quality or value.)

While otherwise holding business in low esteem, Nader seems to have a blind faith in instant technology, insisting that if corporations are given tough enough deadlines, on antipollution devices or on proving the safety of food additives, they will somehow manage to comply. While it is true that some corporations plead ignorance as a convenient alibi for doing nothing about pollution, it is also true that feasible systems have not yet been developed to control a number of crucial pollutants, including sulphur dioxide. On the question of food additives, James Grant, deputy commissioner of the Food and Drug Administration says, "Scientific advances solve problems but also raise new questions. We can prove that certain chemicals are unsafe, but we can never prove, once and for all, that *anything* in the food supply is safe. We frequently are obliged to make absolute decisions on the basis of partial knowledge. If I have one criticism to level at the consumer advocates, it's that they're unwilling to take scientific uncertainty into account."

DOES SEARS, ROEBUCK CHEAT?

Economics, clearly, is not Nader's strong suit. He seems to think of figures as weapons, to be tossed around for maximum effect. To cite one of his current favorite examples of business fraud, he says that the orange-juice industry is watering its product by 10 percent, and thus bilking the public out of $150 million a year. And he adds: "You may wish to compare that with what bank robbers took last year in their second most successful performance to date: $8 million." Nader says he arrived at the 10 percent figure on the basis of "insider information." He applied it to total sales of the citrus industry and, lo, another "statistic" on business fraud. Even if the industry were watering, which it strenuously denies, it does not follow that the public is being gypped out of $150 million. On a watering job of that scale, the price would reflect the water content, and if water were eliminated the price would have to go up.

Another of Nader's current favorite targets is Sears, Roebuck & Co. "Nobody thinks Sears, Roebuck cheats people. But they charge interest from the date the sales contract is signed rather than from the date of delivery — a few pennies, millions of times a year." But Sears no longer has ownership or use of the merchandise once the contract is signed, and could not, for example, apply any price increase that might subsequently be decided upon. The contract is perfectly open and aboveboard and should be considered in the context of the total transaction, price versus values received.

Nader quotes and endorses an estimate by Senator Philip Hart of Michigan that the whole gamut of business fraud and gouging, from shoddy merchandise to monopoly pricing, costs the consumer some $200 billion a year, "or 25 percent of all personal income." That utterly fantastic figure is also more than four times as large as all corporate profits in 1970. For a clipping of that magnitude to be possible, even theoretically, it would have to run as a sort of inflationary factor through the whole economy — wages as well as prices — and thus the argument becomes something of a wash, but a grossly misleading one all the same.

Like reformers before him, Nader is extremely reluctant to admit that any progress at all has been made in any area of consumer protection, even where he has helped write new legislation. "Very little progress, really," he sums it up. "It's a push-and-shove situation." He still refers to the nation's meat supply as "often diseased or putrescent, contaminated by rodent hairs and other assorted debris, its true condition disguised by chemical additives." This is the identical language he used three years ago to arouse Congress and propel passage of the Wholesale Meat Act. Since then the Department of Agriculture has declared 289 packing plants "potentially hazardous to human health," and has told state authorities to clean them up or shut them down. The department says "much remains to be done" to eliminate unsanitary conditions — but perhaps not as much as Nader seems to think. Similarly, despite the thirty-four automobile safety standards enforced by law and 701 recall campaigns, Nader says that "the changes are purely cosmetic."

SHOCK WAVES AT THE AGENCIES

The most impressive documents to come out of the Nader movement are the reports on the regulatory agencies. In most respects they are detailed and thoughtful, written with surprising skill by various groups of amateurs working under Nader's direction. And they have sent shock waves through Washington's bureaucracy. Since their publication, agency awareness of the public interest has greatly increased, and a certain distance has crept into the previously cozy relations between the regulators and the regulated. That distance, however, is still not nearly great enough to please Nader, who wants industry policed with eternal suspicion. "Sharpness" is one word he uses to describe the proper attitude. Jail terms for executives, he says, would be far more effective than the voluntary compliance on which the agencies now mostly rely. "Jail is a great stigma to a businessman, and even a short sentence is a real deterrent," explains James Turner, who wrote the FDA report. "You would get maximum compliance with a minimum of prosecutions."

That may well be so. But in the atmosphere of hostility that would result, regulation might actually be less effective than at present. The agencies can now make sweeping judgments — that a rate is "discriminatory" or a trade practice "deceptive" — on the basis of a simple hearing. "If criminal penalties were involved, our statutes would be interpreted in a much less flexible way," says Robert Pitofsky, the new head of FTC's Bureau of Consumer Protection. Most regulatory matters are exceedingly complex, and the agencies have trusted the industries concerned to furnish the data. If this system were replaced by a program of independent government research on countless topics, the sums expended could be huge enough to dent the federal budget. "It has to be a cooperative effort," argues Administrator Douglas Toms of the National Highway Traffic Safety Administration, which sets auto safety standards. "We're not going to get anywhere with an ugly, persistent confrontation, where the two sides try to outshout each other. We'd be pitting a tiny government agency against the worldwide auto industry."

At the FDA, a new leadership is attempting to stay on cordial terms with the $125 billion food industry while attacking the two key problems documented in great detail in the Nader report, *The Chemical Feast*. First, the FDA is undertaking a comprehensive review of the hundreds of chemicals added to the food supply as preservatives, colorings, or flavorings.

"None of these chemicals, perhaps, has been put to the most rigorous testing that present-day science could muster," admits Deputy Commissioner Grant, one of the new men at the agency. Second, the FDA has also acted on mounting evidence that many prepared foods are deficient in nutritional values, and is now setting guidelines for their fortification with vitamins and minerals. "In many ways the FDA was a bar to progress," says Grant, "and we are attempting to turn that around."

CONFESSIONAL FOR SINNERS

Among the agencies Nader has investigated, the FTC comes closest to the tough, pro-consumer point of view that he is pushing for. Under its new leadership the FTC has filed a flurry of complaints on deceptive advertising, and in a number of these cases it has gone far beyond the traditional cease-and-desist order (known around the FTC as "go and sin no more"). To the dismay of the advertising profession, the FTC now seeks what it calls "affirmative disclosure" — that is, an admission in future advertising, for a specific period, that previous ads were deceptive. Howard Bell, president of the American Advertising Federation, says this amounts to "public flogging."

"Somebody is going to take us to court on affirmative disclosure, and they should," Pitofsky cheerfully admits. "It is a substantial expansion of FTC power." The FTC is also insisting that claims be based on evidence. "We're not after something that 'tastes better.' " Pitofsky says. "That's just puffery. But if you say it's twice as fast or 50 percent stronger, we will take that to mean faster or stronger than your competitor's product, and it better be so."

By swinging to "a fairly stiff enforcement of the law," as Pitofsky puts it, the FTC hopes to encourage self-regulation by industry. "Voluntary compliance comes when companies see that they are better off cleaning house themselves than letting government do it for them." And that is what seems to be happening. Warning of "the regulatory tidal wave which threatens to envelop us," the American Advertising Federation is trying to establish a National Advertising Review Board, which would set standards for ads, seek vountary compliance with the standards, and refer ads it finds deceptive to the FTC for action.

In all this unaccustomed bustle, the agencies are, of course, just doing what they were supposed to be doing all along. To say only that, however, is to ignore the extraordinary difficulty of the regulatory function when there is no counterpressure to the steady, case-by-case intervention of skilled lawyers with specific and valuable corporate interests to protect. Congress, like the agencies, responds to the pressure applied — it's a case of "who's banging on the door," in Nader's words. Yet the pressures applied by individual corporations in individual cases can work to subvert the larger interests of the business community as a whole. "Intriguingly enough," says the FDA's Grant, "the overwhelming majority of the food industry believes that it is better off with a strong FDA, because all get balanced treatment." It is Nader's accomplishment, and no small one, that he has given the agencies the other constituency they need, the public. "Until we came along," says Nader, "the people at the agencies had forgotten what citizens looked like."

Nader will bend all of his lobbying skill this year to persuade Congress to pass a bill that would give the consumer permanent representation before regulatory bodies. The consumer agency to be established by the bill would, in fact, attempt to do just the sort of thing that Nader is doing now, but with the help of government funds and powers. A number of other consumer bills have broad support this year, including regulation of warranties and power for the FTC to seek preliminary injunctions against deceptive advertising. But Nader says, "I'd trade them all for the consumer agency."

THE PROBLEM OF MAINTAINING CLOUT

But can a movement like consumerism, powerful and yet amorphous, really be institutionalized? Certainly the passion and craft of a Nader cannot be. Nor would the director of a consumer agency enjoy Nader's complete freedom of action. A Senate aide who helped draft the bill predicts that the new office might "have its time in the sun, like the Peace Corps or OEO. Then it will carve out a rather cautious domain of its own and become part of the bureaucracy."

That being so, there will still be opportunities for Nader, always provided that he can stay in the sun himself. His support is volatile, a matter of vague tides of public opinion. "His problem is maintaining clout," says Douglas Toms, the Traffic Safety Administrator. "He has a strange kind of constituency, people with a burr under their saddle for one reason or another. He has to constantly find vehicles to keep him in the public eye." Financing will continue to be a problem. Nader himself is well aware of all these difficulties. He says that a basic error of reform movements is expecting to succeed. "You will never succeed. All you're trying to do is reduce problems to the level of tolerability."

Nader's answer to that question about the presidency is: "I find that I am less and less interested in who is going to become President. A far more interesting question is, who's going to be the next president of General Motors?" Despite any such disclaimers, it is easy to imagine the movement going political and Nader running in some future year as, say, a candidate for the United States Senate from Connecticut. Nader might do well in politics, as a sort of latter-day Estes Kefauver. A recent Harris survey revealed that 69 percent of the people think "it's good to have critics like

Nader to keep industry on its toes," while only 5 percent think he is "a troublemaker who is against the free enterprise system." This is the sort of public response that most politicians, including presidents, yearn for in vain.

Judging Nader on the basis of the specific reforms he has brought about, it would be hard to disagree with this public verdict. There has been some cost, however, and this cannot be measured. He has visited his own suspicions and fears upon a whole society, and in the end his hyperbole may prove to be a dangerous weapon. But this year at least, the public apparently expects its crusaders to be twice as fast and 50 percent stronger.

PART THREE

National Governmental Institutions

CHAPTER 6

The Presidency

The American presidency is the only unique political institution that the United States has contributed to the world. It developed first in this country and later was imitated, usually unsuccessfully, in many nations. In no country and at no time has the institution of the presidency achieved the status and power that it possesses in the United States. This chapter will analyze the basis, nature, and implications of the power of this great American institution.

Constitutional Background: Single v. Plural Executive

The change that has taken place in the presidency since the office was established in 1789 is dramatic and significant. The framers of the Constitution were primarily concerned with the control of the arbitrary exercise of power by the legislature; thus they were willing to give the President broad power since he was not to be popularly elected and would be constantly under attack by the coordinate legislative branch. Although the framers were not afraid of establishing a vigorous presidency, there was a great deal of opposition to a potentially strong executive at the time the Constitution was drafted. In the *Federalist 70* Alexander Hamilton attempts to persuade the people of the desirability of a strong presidential office, and, while persuading, he sets forth the essential constitutional basis of the office.

36

Alexander Hamilton

FEDERALIST 70

There is an idea, which is not without its advocates, that a vigorous executive is inconsistent with the genius of republican government. The enlightened well-wishers to this species of government must at least hope that the supposition is destitute of foundation; since they can never admit its truth, without, at the same time, admitting the condemnation of their own principles. Energy in the executive is a leading character in the definition of good government. It is essential to the protection of the community against foreign attacks; it is not less essential to the steady administration of the laws, to the protection of property against those irregular and high-handed combinations, which sometimes interrupt the ordinary course of justice, to the security of liberty against the enterprises and assaults of ambition, of faction, and of anarchy. Every man, the least conversant in Roman story, knows how often that republic was obliged to take refuge in the absolute power of a single man, under the formidable title of dictator, as well as against the intrigues of ambitious individuals, who aspired to the tyranny, and the seditions of whole classes of the community, whose conduct threatened the existence of all government, as against the invasions of external enemies, who menaced the conquest and destruction of Rome.

There can be no need, however, to multiply arguments or examples on this head. A feeble executive implies a feeble execution of the government. A feeble execution is but another phrase for a bad execution; and a government ill executed, whatever it may be in theory, must be, in practice, a bad government.

Taking it for granted, therefore, that all men of sense will agree in the necessity of an energetic executive, it will only remain to inquire, what are the ingredients which constitute this energy? How far can they be combined with those other ingredients, which constitute safety in the republican sense? And how far does this combination characterize the plan which has been reported by the convention?

The ingredients which constitute energy in the executive are: unity; duration; and adequate provision for its support; competent powers.

The ingredients which constitute safety in the republican sense are: a due dependence on the people; a due responsibility.

Those politicians and statesmen, who have been the most celebrated for the soundness of their principles, and for the justness of their views, have declared in favor of a single executive, and a numerous legislature.

They have, with great propriety, considered energy as the most necessary qualification of the former, and have regarded this as most applicable to power in a single hand; while they have, with equal propriety, considered the latter as best adapted to deliberation and wisdom, and best calculated to conciliate the confidence of the people, and to secure their privileges and interests.

That unity is conducive to energy will not be disputed. Decision, activity, secrecy, and dispatch, will generally characterize the proceedings of one man, in a much more eminent degree than the proceedings of any greater number; and in proportion as the number is increased, these qualities will be diminished.

This unity may be destroyed in two ways; either by vesting the power in two or more magistrates, of equal dignity and authority; or by vesting it ostensibly in one man, subject, in whole or in part, to the control and co-operation of others, in the capacity of counsellors to him. . . .

The experience of other nations will afford little instruction on this head. As far, however, as it teaches anything, it teaches us not to be enamoured of plurality in the executive. . . .

Wherever two or more persons are engaged in any common enterprise or pursuit, there is always danger of difference of opinion. If it be a public trust of office, in which they are clothed with equal dignity and authority, there is peculiar danger of personal emulation and even animosity. From either, and especially from all these causes, the most bitter dissentions are apt to spring. Whenever these happen, they lessen the respectability, weaken the authority, and distract the plans and operations of those whom they divide. If they should unfortunately assail the supreme executive magistracy of a country, consisting of a plurality of persons, they might impede or frustrate the most important measures of the government, in the most critical emergencies of the state. And what is still worse, they might split the community into violent and irreconcilable factions, adhering differently to the different individuals who composed the magistracy. . . .

Upon the principles of a free government, inconveniences from the source just mentioned, must necessarily be submitted to in the formation of the legislature; but it is unnecessary, and therefore unwise, to introduce them into the constitution of the executive. It is here, too, that they may be most pernicious. In the legislature, promptitude of decision is oftener an evil than a benefit. The differences of opinion, and the jarrings of parties in that department of the government, though they may sometimes obstruct salutary plans, yet often promote deliberation and circumspection; and serve to check excesses in the majority. When a resolution, too, is once taken, the opposition must be at an end. That resolution is a law, and resistance to it punishable. But no favorable circumstances palliate, or atone for the disadvantages of dissention in the executive department. Here they are pure and unmixed. There is no point at which they cease to operate. They serve to embarrass and weaken the execution of the plan or measure to which they relate, from the first step to the final conclusion of it. They constantly counteract those qualities in the executive, which are the most necessary ingredients in its composition — vigor and expedition; and this without any counterbalancing good. In the conduct of war, in which the energy of the executive is the bulwark of the national security, everything would be to be apprehended from its plurality.

It must be confessed, that these observations apply with principal weight to the first case supposed, that is, to a plurality of magistrates of equal dignity and authority, a scheme, the advocates for which are not likely to form a numerous sect; but they apply, though not with equal, yet with considerable weight, to the project of a council, whose concurrence is made constitutionally necessary to the operations of the ostensible executive. An artful cabal in that council would be able to distract and to enervate the whole system of administration. If no such cabal should exist, the mere diversity of views and opinions would alone be sufficient to tincture the exercise of the executive authority with the spirit of habitual feebleness and dilatoriness.

But one of the weightiest objections to a plurality in the executive, and which lies as much against the last as the first plan, is, that it tends to conceal faults, and destroy responsibility. . . . It often becomes impossible, amidst mutual accusations, to determine on whom the blame or the punishment of a pernicious measure . . . ought really to fall. It is shifted from one to another with so much dexterity, and under such plausible appearances, that the public opinion is left in suspense about the real author. . . .

A little consideration will satisfy us, that the species of security sought for in the multiplication of the executive, is unattainable. Numbers must be so great as to render combination difficult; or they are rather a source of danger than of security. The united credit and influence of several individuals must be more formidable to liberty than the credit and influence of either of them separately. When power, therefore, is placed in the hands of so small a number of men, as to admit of their interests and views being easily combined in a common enterprise, by an artful leader, it becomes more liable to abuse, and more dangerous when abused, than if it be lodged in the hands of one man; who, from the very circumstances of his being alone, will be more narrowly watched and more readily suspected, and who cannot unite so great a mass of influence as when he is associated with others. . . .

I will only add, that prior to the appearance of the constitution, I rarely met with an intelligent man from any of the states, who did not admit as the result of experience, that the unity of the executive of this state was one of the best of the distinguishing features of our constitution.

The Nature of The Presidency:
Power and Persuasion

What is the position of the presidential office today? There is little doubt that it has expanded far beyond the expectations of the framers of the Constitution. The presidency is the only governmental branch with the necessary unity and energy to meet many of the most crucial problems of twentieth-century government in the United States; people have turned to the President in times of crisis to supply the central direction necessary for survival. In the next selection Clinton Rossiter, one of the leading American scholars of the presidency, gives his view of the role of the office.

37

Clinton Rossiter

THE PRESIDENCY —
FOCUS OF LEADERSHIP

No American can contemplate the presidency . . . without a feeling of solemnity and humility — solemnity in the face of a historically unique concentration of power and prestige, humility in the thought that he has had a part in the choice of a man to wield the power and enjoy the prestige.

Perhaps the most rewarding way to grasp the significance of this great office is to consider it as a focus of democratic leadership. Free men, too, have need of leaders. Indeed, it may well be argued that one of the decisive forces in the shaping of American democracy has been the extraordinary capacity of the presidency for strong, able, popular leadership. If this has been true of our past, it will certainly be true of our future, and we should therefore do our best to grasp the quality of this leadership. Let us do this by answering the essential question: For what men and groups does the President provide leadership?

First, the President is *leader of the Executive Branch*. To the extent that our federal civil servants have need of common guidance, he alone is in a position to provide it. We cannot savor the fullness of the President's

---

duties unless we recall that he is held primarily accountable for the ethics, loyalty, efficiency, frugality, and responsiveness to the public's wishes of the two and one-third million Americans in the national administration.

Both the Constitution and Congress have recognized his power to guide the day-to-day activities of the Executive Branch, strained and restrained though his leadership may often be in practice. From the Constitution, explicitly or implicitly, he receives the twin powers of appointment and removal, as well as the primary duty, which no law or plan or circumstances can ever take away from him, to "take care that the laws be faithfully executed."

From Congress, through such legislative mandates as the Budget and Accounting Act of 1921 and the succession of Reorganization Acts, the President has received further acknowledgment of his administrative leadership. Although independent agencies such as the Interstate Commerce Commission and the National Labor Relations Board operate by design outside his immediate area of responsibility, most of the government's administrative tasks are still carried on within the fuzzy-edged pyramid that has the President at its lonely peak; the laws that are executed daily in his name and under his general supervision are numbered in the hundreds.

Many observers, to be sure, have argued strenuously that we should not ask too much of the President as administrative leader, lest we burden him with impossible detail, or give too much to him, lest we inject political considerations too forcefully into the steady business of the civil service. Still, he cannot ignore the blunt mandate of the Constitution, and we should not forget the wisdom that lies behind it. The President has no more important tasks than to set a high personal example of integrity and industry for all who serve the nation, and to transmit a clear lead downward through his chief lieutenants to all who help shape the policies by which we live.

Next, the President is *leader of the forces of peace and war*. Although authority in the field of foreign relations is shared constitutionally among three organs — president, Congress, and, for two special purposes, the Senate — his position is paramount, if not indeed dominant. Constitution, laws, customs, the practice of other nations and the logic of history have combined to place the President in a dominant position. Secrecy, dispatch, unity, continuity, and access to information — the ingredients of successful diplomacy — are properties of his office, and Congress, needless to add, possesses none of them. Leadership in foreign affairs flows today from the President — or it does not flow at all.

The Constitution designates him specifically as "Commander in Chief of the Army and Navy of the United States." In peace and war he is the supreme commander of the armed forces, the living guarantee of the American belief in "the supremacy of the civil over military authority."

In time of peace he raises, trains, supervises and deploys the forces that Congress is willing to maintain. With the aid of the Secretary of Defense, the Joint Chiefs of Staff and the National Security Council — all of whom are his personal choices — he looks constantly to the state of the nation's defenses. He is never for one day allowed to forget that he will be held accountable by the people, Congress and history for the nation's readiness to meet an enemy assault.

In time of war his power to command the forces swells out of all proportion to his other powers. All major decisions of strategy, and many of tactics as well, are his alone to make or to approve. Lincoln and Franklin Roosevelt, each in his own way and time, showed how far the power of military command can be driven by a President anxious to have his generals and admirals get on with the war.

But this, the power of command, is only a fraction of the vast responsibility the modern President draws from the Commander in Chief clause. We need only think back to three of Franklin D. Roosevelt's actions in World War II — the creation and staffing of a whole array of emergency boards and offices, the seizure and operation of more than sixty strike-bound or strike-threatened plants and industries, and the forced evacuation of 70,000 American citizens of Japanese descent from the West Coast — to understand how deeply the President's authority can cut into the lives and liberties of the American people in time of war. We may well tremble in contemplation of the kind of leadership he would be forced to exert in a total war with the absolute weapon.

The President's duties are not all purely executive in nature. He is also intimately associated, by Constitution and custom, with the legislative process, and we may therefore consider him as *leader of Congress*. Congress has its full share of strong men, but the complexity of the problems it is asked to solve by a people who still assume that all problems are solvable has made external leadership a requisite of effective operation.

The President alone is in a political, constitutional, and practical position to provide such leadership, and he is therefore expected, within the limits of propriety, to guide Congress in much of its lawmaking activity. Indeed, since Congress is no longer minded or organized to guide itself, the refusal or inability of the President to serve as a kind of prime minister results in weak and disorganized government. His tasks as leader of Congress are difficult and delicate, yet he must bend to them steadily or be judged a failure. The president who will not give his best thoughts to leading Congress, more so the president who is temperamentally or politically unfitted to "get along with Congress," is now rightly considered a national liability.

The lives of Jackson, Lincoln, Wilson, and the two Roosevelts should be enough to remind us that the President draws much of his real power from his position as *leader of his party*. By playing the grand politician with unashamed zest, the first of these men gave his epic administration a unique sense of cohesion, the second rallied doubting Republican leaders and their followings to the cause of the Union, and the other three achieved genuine triumphs as catalysts of Congressional action. That gifted amateur, Dwight D. Eisenhower, has also played the role for every drop of drama and power in it. He has demonstrated repeatedly what close observers of the presidency know well: that its incumbent must devote an hour or two of every working day to the profession of Chief Democrat or Chief Republican.

It troubles many good people, not entirely without reason, to watch the president dabbling in politics, distributing loaves and fishes, smiling on party hacks, and endorsing candidates he knows to be unfit for anything but immediate delivery to the county jail. Yet if he is to persuade Congress, if he is to achieve a loyal and cohesive administration, if he is to be elected in the first place (and reelected in the second), he must put his hand firmly to the plow of politics. The President is inevitably the nation's No. 1 political boss.

Yet he is, at the same time, if not in the same breath, *leader of public opinion*. While he acts as political chieftain of some, he serves as moral spokesman for all. It took the line of Presidents some time to sense the nation's need for a clear voice, but since the day when Andrew Jackson thundered against the Nullifiers of South Carolina, no effective president has doubted his prerogative to speak the people's mind on the great issues of his time, to serve, in Wilson's words, as "the spokesman for the real sentiment and purpose of the country."

Sometimes, of course, it is no easy thing, even for the most sensitive and large-minded Presidents, to know the real sentiment of the people or to be bold enough to state it in defiance of loudly voiced contrary opinion. Yet the President who senses the popular mood and spots new tides even before they start to run, who practices shrewd economy in his appearances as spokesman for the nation, who is conscious of his unique power to compel discussion on his own terms and who talks the language of Christian morality and the American tradition, can shout down any other voice or chorus of voices in the land. The President is the American people's one authentic trumpet, and he has no higher duty than to give a clear and certain sound.

The President is easily the most influential leader of opinion in this country principally because he is, among all his other jobs, our Chief of State. He is, that is to say, the ceremonial head of the government of the United States, the *leader of the rituals of American democracy*. The long catalogue of public duties that the Queen discharges in England and the Governor General in Canada is the President's responsibility in this country, and the catalogue is even longer because he is not a king, or even the agent of one, and is therefore expected to go through some rather undignified paces by a people who think of him as a combination of scoutmaster, Delphic oracle, hero of the silver screen, and father of the multitudes.

The role of Chief of State may often seem trivial, yet it cannot be neglected by a President who proposes to stay in favor and, more to the point, in touch with the people, the ultimate support of all his claims to leadership. And whether or not he enjoys this role, no President can fail to realize that his many powers are invigorated, indeed are given a new dimension of authority, because he is the symbol of our sovereignty, continuity and grandeur as a people.

When he asks a senator to lunch in order to enlist his support for a pet project, when he thumps his desk and reminds the antagonists in a labor dispute of the larger interests of the American people, when he orders a general to cease caviling or else be removed from his command, the senator and the disputants and the general are well aware — especially if the scene is laid in the White House — that they are dealing with no ordinary head of government. The framers of the Constitution took a momentous step when they fused the dignity of a king and the power of a prime minister in one elective office — when they made the President a national leader in the mystical as well as the practical sense.

Finally, the President has been endowed — whether we or our friends abroad like it or not — with a global role as *a leader of the free nations.* His leadership in this area is not that of a dominant executive. The power he exercises is in a way comparable to that which he holds as a leader of Congress. Senators and congressmen can, if they choose, ignore the President's leadership with relative impunity. So, too, can our friends abroad; the action of Britain and France in the Middle East is a case in point. But so long as the United States remains the richest and most powerful member of any coalition it may enter, then its President's words and deeds will have a direct bearing on the freedom and stability of a great many other countries.

Having engaged in this piecemeal analysis of the categories of Presidential leadership, we must now fit the pieces back together into a seamless unity. For that, after all, is what the presidency is, and I hope this exercise in political taxonomy has not obscured the paramount fact that this focus of democratic leadership is a single office filled by a single man.

The President is not one kind of leader one part of the day, another kind in another part — leader of the bureaucracy in the morning, of the armed forces at lunch, of Congress in the afternoon, of the people in the evening. He exerts every kind of leadership every moment of the day, and every kind feeds upon and into all the others. He is a more exalted leader of ritual because he can guide opinion, a more forceful leader in diplomacy because he commands the armed forces personally, a more effective leader of Congress because he sits at the top of his party. The conflicting demands of these categories of leadership give him trouble at times, but in the end all unite to make him a leader without any equal in the history of democracy.

I think it important to note the qualification: "the history of democracy." For what I have been talking about here is not the Fuehrerprinzip of Hitler or the "cult of personality," but the leadership of free men. The presidency, like every other instrument of power we have created for our use, operates within a grand and durable pattern of private liberty and public morality, which means that the president can lead successfully only when he honors the pattern — by working toward ends to which a "persistent and undoubted" majority of the people has given support, and by selecting means that are fair, dignified and familiar.

The President, that is to say, can lead us only in the direction we are accustomed to travel. He cannot lead the gentlemen of Congress to abdicate their functions; he cannot order our civil servants to be corrupt and slothful; he cannot even command our generals to bring off a coup d'état. And surely he cannot lead public opinion in a direction for which public opinion is not prepared — a truth to which our strongest Presidents would make the most convincing witnesses. The leadership of free men must honor their freedom. The power of the presidency can move as a mighty host only with the grain of liberty and morality.

The President, then, must provide a steady focus of leadership — of administrators, ambassadors, generals, congressmen, party chieftains, people and men of good will everywhere. In a constitutional system compounded of diversity and antagonism, the presidency looms up as the countervailing force of unity and harmony. In a society ridden by centrifugal forces, it is the only point of reference we all have in common. The relentless progress of this continental republic has made the presidency our truly national political institution.

There are those, to be sure, who would reserve this role to Congress, but, as the least aggressive of our Presidents, Calvin Coolidge, once testified, "It is because in their hours of timidity the Congress becomes subservient to the importunities of organized minorities that the President comes more and more to stand as the champion of the rights of the whole country." The more Congress becomes, in Burke's phrase, "a confused and scuffling bustle of local agency" the more the presidency must become a clear beacon of national purpose.

It has been such a beacon at most great moments in our history. In this great moment, too, we may be confident it will burn brightly.

The constitutional and statutory *authority* of the President is indeed extraordinary. However, it is important to point out that the actual power of the president depends upon his political abilities. The President must act within the framework of a complex and diversified political constituency. He can use the authority of his office to buttress his strength, but this alone is not sufficient. Somehow he must be able to persuade those with whom he deals to follow him; otherwise, he will be weak and ineffective.

38
Richard E. Neustadt

PRESIDENTIAL POWER

In the United States we like to "rate" a President. We measure him as "weak" or "strong" and call what we are measuring his "leadership." We do not wait until a man is dead; we rate him from the moment he takes office. We are quite right to do so. His office has become the focal point of politics and policy in our political system. Our commentators and our politicians make a speciality of taking the man's measurements. The rest of us join in when we feel "government" impinging on our private lives. In the third quarter of the twentieth century millions of us have that feeling often.

. . . Although we all make judgments about presidential leadership, we often base our judgments upon images of office that are far removed from the reality. We also use those images when we tell one another whom to choose as President. But it is risky to appraise a man in office or to choose a man for office on false premises about the nature of his job. When the job is the presidency of the United States the risk becomes excessive. . . .

We deal here with the President himself and with his influence on governmental action. In institutional terms the presidency now includes 2,000 men and women. The President is only one of them. But *his* performance scarcely can be measured without focusing on *him*. In terms of party, or of country, or the West, so-called, his leadership involves far more than governmental action. But the sharpening of spirit and of values and of purposes is not done in a vacuum. Although governmental action may not be the whole of leadership, all else is nurtured by it and gains meaning from it. Yet if we treat the presidency as the President, we cannot measure him as though he were the government. Not action as an outcome but his impact on the outcome is the measure of the man. His strength or weakness, then, turns on his personal capacity to influence the conduct of the men who make up government. His influence becomes the mark of leadership. To rate a President according to these rules, one looks into the man's own capabilities as seeker and as wielder of effective influence upon the other men involved in governing the country. . . .

"Presidential" . . . means nothing but the President. "Power" means *his* influence. It helps to have these meanings settled at the start.

From Richard E. Neustadt, *Presidential Power,* pp. 1–2, 6–8, 186–187. Reprinted by permission of John Wiley & Sons, Inc. Copyright © 1960 by John Wiley & Sons, Inc.

There are two ways to study "presidential power." One way is to focus on the tactics, so to speak, of influencing certain men in given situations: how to get a bill through Congress, how to settle strikes, how to quiet Cabinet feuds, or how to stop a Suez. The other way is to step back from tactics on those "givens" and to deal with influence in more strategic terms: what is its nature and what are its sources? What can *this* man accomplish to improve the prospect that he will have influence when he wants it? Strategically, the question is not how he masters Congress in a peculiar instance, but what he does to boost his chance for mastery in any instance, looking toward tomorrow from today. The second of these two ways has been chosen for this [selection]. . . .

In form all Presidents are leaders, nowadays. In fact this guarantees no more than that they will be clerks. Everybody now expects the man inside the White House to do something about everything. Laws and customs now reflect acceptance of him as the Great Initiator, an acceptance quite as widespread at the Capitol as at his end of Pennsylvania Avenue. But such acceptance does not signify that all the rest of government is at his feet. It merely signifies that other men have found it practically impossible to do *their* jobs without assurance of initiatives from him. Service for themselves, not power for the President, has brought them to accept his leadership in form. They find his actions useful in their business. The transformation of his routine obligations testifies to their dependence on an active White House. A President, these days, is an invaluable clerk. His services are in demand all over Washington. His influence, however, is a very different matter. Laws and customs tell us little about leadership in fact.

Why have our Presidents been honored with this clerkship? The answer is that no one else's services suffice. Our Constitution, our traditions, and our politics provide no better source for the initiatives a President can take. Executive officials need decisions, and political protection, and a referee for fights. Where are these to come from but the White House? Congressmen need an agenda from outside, something with high status to respond to or react against. What provides it better than the program of the President? Party politicians need a record to defend in the next national campaign. How can it be made except by "their" Administration? Private persons with a public ax to grind may need a helping hand or they may need a grinding stone. In either case who gives more satisfaction than a President? And outside the United States, in every country where our policies and postures influence home politics, there will be people needing just the "right" thing said and done or just the "wrong" thing stopped in *Washington.* What symbolizes Washington more nearly than the White House?

A modern President is bound to face demands for aid and service from five more or less distinguishable sources: from Executive officialdom, from Congress, from his partisans, from citizens at large, and from abroad. The presidency's clerkship is expressive of these pressures. In effect they are constituency pressures and each President has five sets of constituents. The five are not distinguished by their membership; membership is obviously an overlapping matter. And taken one by one they do not match the man's electorate; one of them, indeed, is outside his electorate. They are distinguished, rather, by their different claims upon him. Initiatives are what they want, for five distinctive reasons. Since government and politics have offered no alternative, our laws and customs turn those wants into his obligations.

Why, then, is the President not guaranteed an influence commensurate with services performed? Constituent relations are relations of dependence. Everyone with any share in governing this country will belong to one (or two, or three) of his "constituencies." Since everyone depends on him why is he not assured of everyone's support? The answer is that no one else sits where he sits, or sees quite as he sees; no one else feels the full weight of his obligations. Those obligations are a tribute to his unique place in our political system. But just because it is unique they fall on him alone. *The same conditions that promote his leadership in form preclude a guarantee of leadership in fact.* No man or group at either end of Pennsylvania Avenue shares his peculiar status in our government and politics. That is why his services are in demand. By the same token, though, the obligations of all other men are different from his own. His Cabinet officers have departmental duties and constituents. His legislative leaders head *Congressional* parties, one in either House. His national party organization stands apart from his official family. His political allies in the states need not face Washington, or one another. The private groups that seek him out are not compelled to govern. And friends abroad are not compelled to run in our elections. Lacking his position and prerogatives, these men cannot regard his obligations as their own. They have their jobs to do; none is the same as his. As they perceive their duty they may find it right to follow him, in fact, or they may not. Whether they will feel obliged *on their responsibility* to do what he wants done demains an open question. . . .

There is reason to suppose that in the years immediately ahead the power problems of a President will remain what they have been in the decades just behind us. If so there will be equal need for presidential expertise of the peculiar sort . . . that has [been] stressed [i.e., political skill]. Indeed, the need is likely to be greater. The President himself and with him the whole government are likely to be more than ever at the mercy of his personal approach.

What may the sixties do to politics and policy and to the place of presidents in our political system? The sixties may destroy them as we know them; that goes without saying. But barring deep depression or unlimited war, a total transformation is the least of likelihoods. Without catastrophes of those dimensions nothing in our past experience suggests that we shall see either consensus of the sort available to F.D.R. in 1933 and 1942, or popular demand for institutional adjustments likely to assist a President. Lacking popular demand, the natural conservatism of established institutions will keep Congress and the party organizations quite resistant to reforms that could give him a clear advantage over them. Four-year terms for congressmen and senators might do it, if the new terms ran with his. What will occasion a demand for that? As for crisis consensus it is probably beyond the reach of the next President. We may have priced ourselves out of the market for "productive" crises on the pattern Roosevelt knew — productive in the sense of strengthening his chances for sustained support *within* the system. Judging from the fifties, neither limited war nor limited depression is productive in those terms. Anything unlimited will probably break the system.

In the absence of productive crises, and assuming that we manage to avoid destructive ones, nothing now foreseeable suggests that our next President will have assured support from any quarter. There is no use expecting it from the bureaucracy unless it is displayed on Capitol Hill. Assured support will not be found in Congress unless contemplation of their own electorates keeps a majority of members constantly aligned with him. In the sixties it is to be doubted . . . that pressure from electors will move the same majority of men in either House toward consistent backing for the President. Instead the chances are that he will gain majorities, when and if he does so, by ad hoc coalition-building, issue after issue. In that respect the sixties will be reminiscent of the fifties; indeed, a closer parallel may well be in the late forties. As for "party discipline" in English terms — the favorite cure-all of political scientists since Woodrow Wilson was a youth — the first preliminary is a party link between the White House and the leadership on both sides of the Capitol. But even this preliminary has been lacking in eight of the fifteen years since the Second World War. If ballot-splitting should continue through the sixties it will soon be "un-American" for President and Congress to belong to the same party.

Even if the trend were now reversed, there is no short-run prospect that behind each party label we would find assembled a sufficiently like-minded bloc of voters, similarly aligned in states and districts all across the country, to negate the massive barriers our institutions and traditions have erected against "discipline" on anything like the British scale. This does not mean that a reversal of the ballot-splitting trend would be without significance. If the White House and the legislative leadership were linked by party ties again, a real advantage would accrue to both. Their opportunities for mutually productive bargaining would be enhanced. The policy results might surprise critics of our system. Bargaining "within the family" has a rather different quality than bargaining with members of the rival clan. But we would still be a long way from "party government." Bargaining, not "discipline," would still remain the key to Congressional action on a President's behalf. The critical distinctions between presidential party and Congressional party are not likely to be lost in the term of the next President.

The Presidential Establishment

The expansion of the Executive Office of the President is a major development of the modern presidency. Created in 1939 by an executive order of President Roosevelt under the reorganization authority granted to him by Congress, the Executive Office has expanded over the years and now occupies a pivotal position in government. The Executive Office was devised originally to act as a staff arm of the presidency. It was to consist of his closest personal advisors, as well as a small number of agencies, such as the Bureau of the Budget (now the Office of Management and Budget) and was to function as an aid to him in carrying out his presidential responsibilities.

The Executive Office was not to be an independent bureaucracy but was to be accountable to the President and to act in accordance with his wishes. However, the tremendous expansion that has occurred in the Executive Office has raised the question of whether or not it has become an "invisible presidency," not accountable to anyone within or without government. The relationships between President Nixon and the Executive Office, particularly, raised this question. President Nixon's emphasis upon managerial techniques led him to expand very significantly the number of agencies within the Executive Office. Moreover, he delegated to his personal staff a wide range of responsibilities over which he failed to exercise continuous supervision. Ehrlichman and Haldeman, before they resigned because of their involvement in events surrounding the Watergate affairs, ruthlessly wielded power around Washington in the name of the President. It was the lack of presidential supervision over his own staff that may have accounted for the Watergate break-in in the first place, as well as other questionable activities, including the burglary of Daniel Ellsberg's psychiatrist's office and the solicitation of unreported funds during the 1972 presidential election year.

President Carter came into office with a promise to reduce the presidential bureaucracy, a promise that he made in conjunction with another to reorganize the regular bureaucracy of the federal government. Both of these promises had a ring of great familiarity, as they had been part of the campaigns of many prior Presidents. Carter in particular wanted to reinstate the Cabinet as a major policy-making group that would act as a collegial body advising the President directly. He wanted to reverse the flow of power from the Cabinet to the presidential bureaucracy, reinstating Cabinet secretaries as the primary spokespersons for presidential policy in the areas under their jurisdiction. President Carter soon found, like Presidents before him, however, that Cabinet government does not work to the advantage of the President. The only bureaucracy the President can trust is the presidential bureaucracy. Cabinet secretaries tend to develop their own power bases and soon become independent of, and even antagonistic to, the President. By the summer of 1979 Carter fully recognized the strains on his leadership being produced by a weak presidential bureaucracy and by antagonistic cabinet secretaries. He fired HEW Secretary Joseph A. Califano, Jr., and Treasury Secretary W. Michael Blumenthal, both of whom had flouted the White House staff by going their own ways. At the same time, Carter strengthened the presidential bureaucracy by centralizing responsibility in the White House in the hands of his principal adviser, Hamilton Jordan, whom he made chief of the White House staff. Carter's initial promises to decentralize power and reduce the size of the presidential bureaucracy failed. In the following selection Thomas E. Cronin examines the politics, structure, and responsibilities of the presidential establishment.

39

Thomas E. Cronin

THE SWELLING OF THE PRESIDENCY: CAN ANYONE REVERSE THE TIDE?

In 1939 President Franklin D. Roosevelt created the Executive Office of the President. In his executive order, Roosevelt stated that "in no event shall the Administrative Assistants to the President be interposed between the President and the head of any department or agency."

More than forty years later, the size and importance of the White House staff and the Executive Office of the President have been controversial precisely because they seem to be frequently interposed between president and heads of departments and agencies. In campaigning for the presidency in 1976, Jimmy Carter had pledged to reduce the size of the presidential establishment by 30 percent. Further he claimed he would reverse the flow of power away from the White House staffers and back to his cabinet heads. Two and a half years later, however, he had fired about half his cabinet secretaries and strengthened the hand of his chief White House aides. And though he had tried to reduce somewhat the number of

Copyright © 1981 by Thomas E. Cronin. For a book length treatment of many of these problems, see Thomas E. Cronin, *The State of the Presidency*, 2nd Ed. (Little, Brown and Company, 1980).

White House aides by one means or another, the size and importance of the presidential establishment was just as great as it had been in the Nixon and Ford years.

Why has the presidential bureaucracy become a problem? Many analysts feel it is too bloated and too top-heavy with aides, counselors, and advisers who invariably intrude themselves between the president and the department heads — thereby breaking FDR's old promise.

A few months after Carter was in office, the White House staff had grown to nearly 700 aides — although perhaps as many as 175 of these were "on loan" from other governmental departments to assist with energy program planning, appointments and the sizeable increase of mail pouring into the Carter White House (see Table 1). In addition to the White House staff there were about 17 support agencies in the Executive Office, such as the National Security Office and the Office of Management and Budget.

Table 1   Expanding the White House Staff

Year	President	Full time employees	Employees temporarily detailed to the White House from outside agencies	Total
1937	Franklin D. Roosevelt	45	112 (June 30)	157
1947	Harry S Truman	190	27 (June 30)	217
1957	Dwight D. Eisenhower	364	59 (June 30)	423
1967	Lyndon B. Johnson	251	246 (June 30)	497
1972	Richard M. Nixon	550	34 (June 30)	584
1975	Gerald R. Ford	533	27 (June 30)	560
1977	Jimmy Carter	480	175 (April 30)	655
1980[a]	Jimmy Carter	488	75 (est.) (June 30)	570 (est.)

[a] SOURCE: Dom Bonafede, "The Mystery of the Executive Office Budget," *National Journal,* June 16, 1979, p. 1006.

Plainly, the cabinet has lost power and the Executive Office has grown in status, in size, and in powers. In light of experience, should Roosevelt's promise be revised? Can the performance of the Executive Office be made to conform to Roosevelt's promise? To Carter's campaign pledges? Can the presidential establishment really be cut back?

After he was elected, some of Carter's aides discounted the importance of staff cutbacks. Improved delivery of services, better public understanding, and fixing accountability are more important than reducing numbers and costs. And the 30 percent cutback was "an arbitrary figure . . . it was for us to have a target at the start of the transition," according to White House press secretary Jody Powell.

We have heard many plans and promises about government reorganization before. President Nixon was genuinely worried that the presidency had "grown like Topsy" so that it weakened rather than strengthened his ability to manage the federal government. Nixon proposed a sweeping consolidation of Cabinet Departments into four functionally oriented super-departments — Community Development, Natural Resources, Human Resources, and Economic Affairs — and at one point wanted to cut the White House workforce in half. But he did not prevent one of the largest expansions of the presidency in history, nor the aggrandizement of power in his White House that contributed to his isolation and downfall. Rather than assisting the President, Nixon's aides often became assistant presidents.

Nixon had little success in these efforts. The Office of the President increased 13 percent during the Eisenhower and Kennedy years, and another 13 percent under LBJ. But it rose approximately another 25 percent under Nixon. Many of President Nixon's cabinet members say they had difficulty in seeing the President. One joked that "Nixon should have told me I was being appointed to a secret mission when I was made Secretary of Commerce." It was said of another that he had to take the public tour of the White House to get in.

Unchecked growth of the White House establishment and its battalion of "faceless ministers" continued to grow even under Gerald Ford. Mr. Ford had always promised to curb bureaucratic growth. His favorite motto was " A government big enough to give you everything you want is a government big enough to take from you everything you have." But Ford was unsuccessful in reversing the trend. Midway through his brief presidential term, one account indicated there were about seventy-five more White House aides on his staff than when Richard Nixon departed.

The expansion of the presidency, it should be emphasized, was by no means only a phenomenon of the Nixon-Ford years. The number of employees directly under the President has been growing steadily since the New Deal days, when only a few dozen people served in the White House entourage at a cost of less than a few hundred thousand dollars annually.

According to the traditional civics textbook picture, the executive branch is more or less neatly divided into Cabinet departments and their secretaries, agencies and their heads, and the president. A more contemporary view takes note of a few prominent presidential aides, and refers to them as the "White House staff." Neither view adequately recognizes the large and growing coterie surrounding the president, which comprises dozens of assistants, hundreds of presidential advisers, and thousands of members of an institutional amalgam called the Executive Office of the President. The men and women in these categories all fall directly under a president in organizational charts — not under the Cabinet departments — and may best be considered by the term the Presidential Establishment. See Figure 1.

In the mid-1970s the Presidential Establishment embraced nearly a score of support staffs (the White House Office, National Security Council, Office of Management and Budget, etc.) and advisory office (Council of

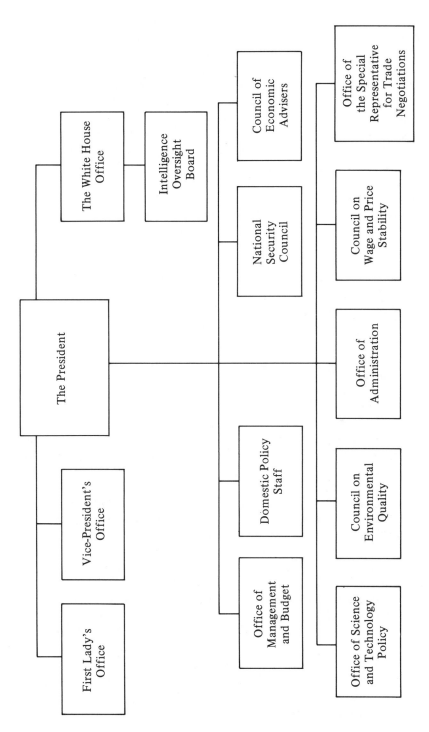

Figure 1   The Presidential Establishment, 1981

Economic Advisors, Office of Science and Technology Policy, Office of Telecommunications Policy, etc.). It spawned a vast proliferation of ranks and titles to go with its proliferation of functions (Counsel to the President, Assistant to the President, Special Consultant, Director, Staff Director, etc.). "The White House now has enough people with fancy titles to populate a Gilbert and Sullivan comic opera," Congressman Morris Udall once observed.

Official figures on the size of the Presidential Establishment, and standard body counts vary widely, depending on exactly who is included, but by one frequently used reckoning, between two to two and a half thousand people work directly for the President of the United States. Payroll and maintenance costs for this staff run to several hundred million dollars annually. Salary alone for the 488 White House aides in 1980 was estimated at over 22 million dollars.

Under President Nixon, there was a systematic bureaucratization of the Presidential Establishment, in which more new councils and offices were established and more specialization, division of labor, and layers of staffing added than at any time except during World War II. Among the major Nixon additions were the Council of Environmental Quality, the Council on International Economic Policy, the Office of Consumer Affairs, and the Domestic Council. Nixon aide John Ehrlichman wanted the Domestic Council as a base from which to control domestic policy and bypass the Office of Management and Budget as well as the domestic department heads. This may not have been the formal intent exactly, but it was plainly the result.

President Nixon in 1973 moved a number of trusted domestic-policy assistants from the White House rolls and dispersed them to key sub-Cabinet posts across the span of government, virtually setting up White House outposts throughout the Cabinet departments. One of Nixon's most important staffing actions, after his landslide victory in 1972, was to set up formally a second office, with space and a staff in the White House, for Treasury Secretary George Shultz, as chairman of yet another new presidential body, the Council on Economic Policy. With Shultz as over-secretary of economic affairs, and John Ehrlichman as over-secretary for domestic affairs, Nixon attempted to accomplish the cabinet consolidation that Congress had denied him a year earlier. This super-cabinet was dismantled almost immediately with the Watergate-pressured resignations of Haldeman and Ehrlichman.

President Ford made few changes in the organizational structure of the Executive Office that he inherited from Nixon. He established the Nixon-proposed Council on Wage and Price Stability and a few other councils and boards, most notably an Economic Policy Board that served as a kind of National Security Council and staff for major economic issues. He also allowed the Congress to establish the Office of Science and Technology Policy. Ford continued the Nixon practice of double appointments, such as Kissinger as Secretary of State and head of the National Security Council, and William Simon as Secretary of Treasury and chief spokesman for the White House-based Economic Policy Board.

Carter pledged to cut the White House staff and its importance, and in his first year he earnestly tried to act upon this pledge. He reduced the White House staff by over one hundred persons, but he did so merely by transferring most of the administrative personnel to a newly created Office of Administration within the Executive Office of the President. In fact, many, if not most, of these aides did not even move from their regular offices. They were already located in the Old Executive Office Building, and there they remained. What was labeled a "reduction" was simply a rejuggling of the organizational boxes. Representative Clarence E. Miller of Ohio, who keeps tabs on the Carter White House, declared in 1979 that "It appears we are fooling the American people," and he called the Carter reductions "really a shuffling of the deck." White House reporters who studied the growth of the payroll at the White House say appropriations for the White House Office have jumped from $8.3 million in 1971 to a proposed $18.2 million for 1980.

Early in 1980 I had an opportunity to meet with Carter's staff director at the White House, a Mr. Alonzo McDonald. McDonald was a former managing director of McKinsey & Company, the management-consultant firm. He was brought to the Carter White House to reduce the chaos that developed under the decidedly unmanagerial Hamilton Jordon, then the chief of staff. After being in the White House for less than a year, McDonald told me: "Frankly, I would increase the size of the White House staff. It requires more staff. We need larger groups for congressional relations, for dealing with important interest groups; they deserve to be listened to and I now feel that these kinds of staffs can't be cut, they actually should be larger." What did he think, then, of Jimmy Carter's 1976 pledge to cut the White House staff? He diplomatically avoided answering that one.

Carter probably talked more about reorganizing the bureaucracy and the executive branch than any recent president. Yet, after about two years in office he seemed to have given up. One of his early reorganization aides later summed up Carter's problem as a reorganizer this way:

> For Carter, reorganization was an end in itself, unconnected with the higher purposes of government. He never really linked it together with other policy goals. He gave it up after the first couple of years. Perhaps it was because the rest of government resisted because policy ends and reorganization ends were never discussed or dealt with in any coherent way. Carter, to repeat, had kind of an engineer's notion that organization itself was a policy area. (Personal interview with the writer, February 1980.)

However the names and numbers have changed recently, or may be shifted about in the near future, the Presidential Establishment has not declined in terms of functions, power, or prerogatives; in fact, it has grown.

Does it matter? A number of political analysts have argued recently that it does, and I agree with them. To be sure, the debate about the size of the White House establishment is less important than the purposes to which it is put. But size and purposes are hard to separate. Perhaps the most disturbing aspect of the expansion of the Presidential Establishment is that it has become a powerful inner sanctum of government, isolated from traditional, constitutional checks and balances. It has become common practice for anonymous, unelected, and unratified aides to negotiate sensitive international commitments that are free from congressional oversight. Other aides in the Presidential Establishment wield fiscal authority over billions of dollars in funds that Congress appropriates yet a President refuses to spend, or that Congress assigns to one purpose and the administration routinely redirects to another — all with no semblance of public scrutiny. Such exercises of power pose an important, perhaps vital, question of governmental philosophy: Should a political system that has made a virtue of periodic electoral accountability accord an ever-increasing policy-making role to White House counselors who are neither confirmed by the U.S. Senate nor, because of the doctrine of "executive privilege," subject to questioning by Congress?

Another disquieting aspect of the growth of the Presidential Establishment is that the increase of its powers has been largely at the expense of the traditional sources of executive power and policy-making — the Cabinet members and their departments. When I asked a former Kennedy-Johnson Cabinet member a while ago what he would like to do if he ever returned to government, he said he would rather be a presidential assistant than a Cabinet member. And this is an increasingly familiar assessment of the relative influence of the two levels of the executive branch. In Carter's White House, it was pretty clear from the very beginning that Stuart Eisenstadt, the domestic issues advisor, Hamilton Jordan, the virtual Chief of Staff, and Zbigniew Brzezinski, the National Security Council aide were among the most powerful members of the Carter administration. Their influence increased the longer Carter kept them.

The Presidential Establishment has become, in effect, a whole layer of government between the President and the Cabinet, and it often stands above the Cabinet in terms of influence with the President. In spite of the exalted position that Cabinet members hold in textbooks and protocol, a number of Cabinet members in recent administrations have complained that they could not even get the President's ear except through a presidential assistant. In his book *Who Owns America?*, former Secretary of the Interior Walter Hickel recounts his combat with a dozen different presidential functionaries and tells how he needed clearance from them before he could get to talk to the President, or how he frequently had to deal with the assistants themselves because the President was "too busy." During an earlier administration, President Eisenhower's chief assistant, Sherman Adams, was said to have told two Cabinet members who could not resolve a matter of mutual concern: "Either make up your mind or else tell me and I will do it. We must not bother the President with this. He is trying to keep the world from war." Several of President Kennedy's Cabinet members regularly battled with White House aides who blocked them from seeing the President. And McGeorge Bundy, as Kennedy's chief assistant for national security affairs, simply side-stepped the State Department in one major area of department communications. He had all important incoming State Department cables transmitted simultaneously to his office in the White House, part of an absorption of traditional State Department functions that visibly continues to this day.

Carter began his presidency by holding weekly Cabinet meetings — two and three hours in length — every Monday morning. He was the first President in recent years to try to get the Cabinet working, talking, and arguing about wide-ranging issues. His intent was not to turn his Cabinet into a parliamentary decision-making collegium, but to establish a team of advisors who could assist and advise him on matters above and beyond the narrow functions of their departments. It was also a recognition by Carter that so many of the problems for a President and for Cabinet members are interdepartmental in character.

Did Carter's Cabinet system work? One White House aide who attended some of these sessions told a *New York Times* reporter that most of the Cabinet members "just sit there, go through their little recitations of what's happening in their departments and nod agreeably when the President speaks." Said another: "These [weekly] meetings . . . are essentially a waste of everybody's time, including the President's."

By his third year, Carter had pretty much given up on his Cabinet experiment. He had fired just about half of his Cabinet in the summer of 1978, and he had grown accustomed to relying more heavily than ever on his own proximate White House aides. To his credit, he tried to use the Cabinet more responsibly than his immediate predecessors. He even held more than 60 Cabinet meetings during his first two years. Most of the cabinet meetings had no agendas. The President raised issues that were on his mind, and then solicited the views of those around the table, both on the subjects he had raised and on other matters they thought appropriate. Some of the meetings were criticized as nothing less than adult versions of a grade-school "show-and-tell" session. As the months wore on, several of his Cabinet members, especially Joseph Califano, Michael Blumenthal, Brock Adams, and Andrew Young made their differences of views with the President a public matter. Many of them, from the vantage point of the White House, seemed to be going into business for themselves. Carter and his aides worried about this, and with the tough 1980 elections in mind they decided to "clean house."

When the Carter Administration is studied in the years to come, the verdict will probably be that the Cabinet failure of his first two years or so was caused more by the President and his aides than by the members of his Cabinet. If Carter had been more experienced in the ways of Washington, if he had been a stronger, more effective coalition builder, he might have molded these talented individuals into a positive force in his Administration. If he had been more popular in the country as a whole, higher in the polls, he would have had greater respect from his Cabinet officers — and they, in turn, would have probably tried fewer end-runs around him in pursuit of their own particular interests.

Perhaps the more things change, the more they stay the same — as the old saying goes.

In a speech in 1971, Senator Ernest Hollings of South Carolina plaintively noted the lowering of Cabinet status. "It used to be," he said, "that if I had a problem with food stamps, I went to see the Secretary of Agriculture, whose department had jurisdiction over that problem. Not anymore. Now, if I want to learn the policy, I must go to the White House to consult John Price [a special assistant]. If I want the latest on textiles, I won't get it from the Secretary of Commerce, who has the authority and responsibility. No, I am forced to go to the White House and see Mr. Peter Flanigan. I shouldn't feel too badly. Secretary Stans [Maurice Stans, then Secretary of Commerce] has to do the same thing."

If Cabinet members individually have been downgraded in influence, the Cabinet as a council of government has become somewhat of a relic, replaced by more specialized policy clusters that as often as not are presided over by White House staffers. The Cabinet's decline has taken place over several administrations. John Kennedy started out his term intending to use the Cabinet as a major policy-making body, but Postmaster General J. Edward Day noted, "After the first two or three meetings, one had the distinct impression that the President felt that decisions on major matters were not made — or even influenced — at Cabinet sessions, and that discussion there was a waste of time. . . . When members spoke up to suggest or to discuss major administration policy, the President would listen with thinly disguised impatience and then postpone or otherwise bypass the question."

President Eisenhower held weekly well-structured Cabinet meetings. Johnson, however, was disenchanted with the Cabinet as a body and characteristically held Cabinet sessions only when the press talked about how the Cabinet was withering away. Under Nixon, the Cabinet was almost never convened at all. Former Nixon counsel John Dean suggested, "I would like to see a more dominant Cabinet. The Nixon Cabinet was totally controllable by the White House staff. A strong Cabinet member should be able to tell a White House staffer, 'Buzz off' or 'Have the President call me himself and I'll tell him why I'm doing what I am.' " Nixon aide John Ehrlichman was very blunt in his description of Nixon's relationship with the

Cabinet, "The Cabinet officers are tied closely to the executive, or to put it in extreme terms, when he says jump, they only ask, 'How high?' "

President Ford met with his Cabinet about once a month, using it as a discussion group, not a decision-making body. Ford's Cabinet members have reported that little was accomplished at these sessions and rarely if ever did any arguments take place.

As the Presidential Establishment has taken over policy-making and even some operational functions from the Cabinet departments, the departments have been undercut continuously and the cost has been heavy. These intrusions can cripple the capacity of Cabinet officials to present policy alternatives, and they diminish self-confidence, morale, and initiative within the departments. George Ball, a former undersecretary of state, noted the effects on the State Department: "Able men, with proper pride in their professional skills, will not long tolerate such votes of no-confidence, so it should be no surprise that they are leaving the career service, and making way for mediocrity with the result that, as time goes on it may be hopelessly difficult to restore the Department. . . ."

The irony of this accretion of numbers and functions to the Presidential Establishment is that the presidency has been increasingly afflicted with the very ills of the traditional departments that expansion was intended to remedy. The presidency has become a large, complex bureaucracy itself, rapidly acquiring many dubious characteristics of large bureaucracies in the process: layering, overspecialization, communication gaps, interoffice rivalries, inadequate coordination, and an impulse to become consumed with short-term, urgent operational concerns at the expense of thinking systematically about the consequences of varying sets of policies and priorities and about important long-range problems.

White House aides, in assuming more and more responsibility for the management of government programs, inevitably lose the detachment and objectivity that is so essential for evaluating new ideas. Can a lieutenant vigorously engaged in implementing the presidential will admit the possibility that what the President wants is wrong or not working? Yet a President is increasingly dependent on the judgment of these same staff members, since he seldom sees some of his Cabinet members.

WHY HAS THE PRESIDENCY GROWN BIGGER AND BIGGER?

There is no single villain or systematically organized conspiracy promoting this expansion. A variety of factors is at work. The most significant is the expansion of the role of the presidency itself — an expansion that for the most part has taken place during national emergencies. It should be noted, too, that the business of government has dramatically increased and that the rise of the White House staff is a result of the same forces that have seen a tripling of Congress's staff and a marked increase in law clerks and aides to Supreme Court members. The public and Congress in recent decades have both tended to look to the President for the decisions that were needed in those emergencies. The Great Depression and World War II in particular brought sizeable increases in presidential staffs. And once in place, many stayed on, even after the emergencies that brought them had faded. Smaller national crises have occasioned expansion in the White House entourage, too. After the Russians successfully orbited Sputnik in 1957, President Eisenhower added several science advisors. After the Bay of Pigs, President Kennedy enlarged his national security staff.

Considerable growth in the Presidential Establishment, especially in the post World War II years, stems directly from the belief that critical societal problems require wise men be assigned to the White House to alert the President to appropriate solutions and to serve as the agents for implementing these solutions. Congress has frequently acted on the basis of this belief, legislating the creation of the National Security Council, the Council of Economic Advisors, and the Council on Environmental Quality, among others. Congress has also increased the chores of the presidency by making it a statutory responsibility for the President to prepare more and more reports on critical social areas — annual economic and manpower reports, a biennial report on national growth, etc.

President Nixon responded to a number of troublesome problems that defy easy relegation to any one department — problems like international trade and drug abuse —by setting up special offices in the Executive Office with sweeping authority and sizeable staffs. Once established, these units rarely get dislodged. And an era of permanent crisis ensures a continuing accumulation of such bodies.

Another reason for the growth of the Presidential Establishment is that occupants of the White House frequently distrust members of the permanent government. Nixon aides, for example, viewed most civil servants not only as Democratic but as wholly unsympathetic to such Nixon objectives as decentralization, revenue-sharing, and the curtailment of several Great Society programs. Departmental bureaucracies are viewed from the White House as independent, unresponsive, unfamiliar, and inaccessible. They are suspected again and again of placing congressional, special-interest, or their own priorities ahead of those communicated to them from the White House. Even the President's own Cabinet members soon become viewed in the same light; one of the strengths of Cabinet members, namely their capacity to make a compelling case for their programs, has proved to be their chief liability with presidents.

Presidents may want this type of advocacy initially, but they soon grow weary and wary of it. Not long ago, one White House aide accused a former labor secretary of trying to "out-Meany Meany." Efforts by former Interior Secretary Hickel to advance certain environmental programs and by departing Housing and Urban Development Secretary George Romney to promote innovative housing construction methods not only were unwelcome but after a while were viewed with considerable displeasure and suspicion at the White House.

Hickel writes poignantly of coming to this recognition during his final meeting with President Nixon, in the course of which the President frequently referred to him as an "adversary." "Initially," writes Hickel, "I considered that a compliment because, to me, an adversary is a valuable asset. It was only after the President had used the term many times and with a disapproving inflection that I realized he considered an adversary an enemy. I could not understand why he would consider me an enemy."

Not only have recent Presidents been suspicious about the depth of the loyalty of those in their Cabinets, but also they invariably become concerned about the possibility that sensitive administration secrets may leak out through the departmental bureaucracies; this is another reason why Presidents have come to rely more on their own personal staff and advisory groups.

Still another reason that more and more portfolios have been given to the presidency is that new federal programs frequently concern more than one federal agency, and it seems reasonable that someone at a higher level is needed to fashion a consistent policy and to reconcile conflicts. Attempts by Cabinet members themselves to solve sensitive jurisdictional questions frequently result in bitter squabbling. At times, too, Cabinet members themselves have recommended that these multidepartmental issues be settled at the White House. Sometimes new presidential appointees insist that new offices for program coordination be assigned directly under the President. Ironically, such was the plea of George McGovern, for example, when President Kennedy offered him the post of director of the Food-for-Peace program in 1961. Later, in his own campaign for the White House, McGovern attacked the buildup of the Presidential Establishment; but back in 1961 he wanted visibility (and no doubt celebrity status), and he successfully argued against his being located outside the White House — in either the State Department or the Department of Agriculture. President Kennedy and his then campaign manager Robert Kennedy felt indebted to McGovern because of his efforts in assisting the Kennedy campaign in South Dakota. Accordingly, McGovern was granted not only a berth in the Executive Office of the President but also the much-coveted title of Special Assistant to the President.

The Presidential Establishment has also been enlarged by the representation of interest groups within its fold. Even a partial listing of staff specializations that have been grafted onto the White House in recent years reveals how interest-group brokerage has become added to the more traditional staff activities of counseling and administration. These specializations form a veritable index of American society: budget and management, national security, economics, congressional matters, science and technology, drug abuse prevention, telecommunications, consumers, national goals, intergovernmental relations, environment, domestic policy, international economics, military affairs, civil rights, disarmament, labor relations, District of Columbia, cultural affairs, education, foreign trade and tariffs, the aged, health and nutrition, physical fitness, volunteerism, intellectuals, Blacks, youth, women, Wall Street, governors, mayors, "ethnics," regulatory agencies and related industry, state party chairmen.

Both President Ford and President Carter, in their efforts to "keep the door of the White House open," maintained a fairly large staff called the Public Liaison Office. William Baroody, Jr., ran Ford's office. Margaret "Midge" Costanza and later Anne Wexler served as Carter's top aides for this operation. Their staffs were constantly meeting with ethnic groups, special interest organizations, and with everyone from poet Allen Ginsberg, who wanted to talk about his philosophy on food, to groups opposed to the B-1 bomber and the 1980 Olympic boycott. Critics contend that this kind of White House staff is unnecessary, too much of an on-going campaign unit, or merely a staff that engages in "stroking" people who want to say they have taken their cause to the White House. White House aides, of course, claim that ensuring access to the White House for nearly every interest is a requirement of an open presidency.

One of the more fascinating elements in the growth of the Presidential Establishment is the development, particularly under the current administration, of a huge public-relations apparatus. More than 100 presidential aides are now engaged in various forms of press-agentry or public relations, busily selling and reselling the President. This activity — sometimes cynically called the politics of symbolism — is devoted to the particular occupant of the White House, but inevitably, it affects the presidency itself, expanding public expectations about the presidency.

Last, but by no means least, Congress, which has grown increasingly critical of the burgeoning power of the presidency, must itself take some blame for the expansion of the White House. Divided within itself, and often ill-equipped or simply disinclined to make some of the nation's toughest political decisions in recent decades, Congress often has abdicated significant authority to the presidency. In late 1972 Congress almost passed a grant of authority to the President that would have given him the right to determine which programs to cut whenever the budget went beyond the $250 billion ceiling limit — a bill which, in effect, would have handed over to the President some of Congress's long-cherished "power of the purse." Fortunately, Congress could not agree on how to yield this precious power to the executive. In April 1977 Congress restored to President Carter wide latitude to propose abolishing or consolidating or modifying organizational bodies within and outside of the departments.

Fortunately, Congress is now making better use of its own General Accounting Office and Congressional Research Service for chores that too often were assigned to the President. It might also establish in each of its houses special committees on Executive Office operations. Most congressional committees are organized to deal with areas such as labor, agriculture, armed services, or education, paralleling the organization of the Cabinet. What we need now are committees designed explicitly to oversee the White House, to probe how much it costs to run the White House, to probe the size and quality of White House staff arrangements, and to periodically review what might better be removed from the White House and decentralized to the Cabinet secretaries. Can the task of overseeing presidential operations be dispersed among dozens of committees and subcommittees, each of which can look at only small segments of the Presidential Establishment? Since Truman, presidents have had staffs to oversee and lobby the Congress; Congress might want to reciprocate.

While the number of functionaries is the most tangible and dramatic measure of the White House's expansion, its increasing absorption of governmental functions is more disturbing. The Carter Administration has already forewarned us of a slow and incremental approach to reorganization, stressing that delivery of services and fixing of accountability are more important than reductions in size and cost of the bureaucracy. The Carter Administration must also understand the dangers inherent in a Presidential Establishment that has become swollen in functions as well as in numbers. The next White House occupant may consider cutting his staff or consolidating a number of agencies, but it is yet another thing to reduce the accumulated prerogatives and responsibilities of the presidency.

It is incumbent upon the president-elect not only to criticize the swelling government and its inefficiencies, but also to move to deflate this swelling in the areas where it most needs to be deflated — at home, in the White House, and in the Executive Office of the President. But there is always a remaining doubt that attempts to reorganize and reduce the presidential bureaucracy will not succeed, and the forces that buttress the large presidential establishment will remain unchanged.

Presidential Character and Style

The preceding selections in this chapter have focused upon the institutional aspects of the presidency, and the constitutional and political responsibilities of the office. Richard Neustadt does focus upon certain personal dimensions of the power equation, the ability to persuade, but he does not deal with presidential character outside of the power context. The following selection is taken from one of the most important and innovative of the recent books dealing with the presidency, in which the author, James David Barber, presents the thesis that it is the *total character* of the person who occupies the White House that is the determinant of presidential performance. As he states, "The presidency is much more than an institution." It is not only the focus of the emotional involvement of most people in politics, but also occupied by an emotional person. How that person is able to come to grips with his feelings and emotions often shapes his orientation toward issues and the way in which he makes decisions. From the very beginning the office was thought of in highly personal terms, for the framers of the Constitution, in part at least, built the office around the character of George Washington who virtually everyone at the time thought would be the first occupant of the office. And evolution of the office since 1787 has added to its personal quotient. James David Barber provides a framework for the analysis of presidential character and its effect upon performance in the White House.

40

James David Barber

THE PRESIDENTIAL CHARACTER

When a citizen votes for a presidential candidate he makes, in effect, a prediction. He chooses from among the contenders the one he thinks (or feels, or guesses) would be the best President. He operates in a situation of immense uncertainty. If he has a long voting history, he can recall time and time again when he guessed wrong. He listens to the commentators, the politicians, and his friends, then adds it all up in some rough way to produce his prediction and his vote. Earlier in the game, his anticipations have been taken into account, either directly in the polls and primaries or indirectly in the minds of politicians who want to nominate someone he will like. But he must choose in the midst of a cloud of confusion, a rain of phony advertising, a storm of sermons, a hail of complex issues, a fog of charisma and boredom, and a thunder of accusation and defense. In the face of this chaos, a great many citizens fall back on the past, vote their old allegiances, and let it go at that. Nevertheless, the citizen's vote says that on balance he expects Mr. X would outshine Mr. Y in the presidency.

From James David Barber, *The Presidential Character,* 2d ed. © 1977 by James David Barber. Published by Prentice-Hall, Inc., Englewood Cliffs, New Jersey. Reprinted by permission. This selection was originally entitled, "Presidential Character and How to Foresee It."

This [book] is meant to help citizens and those who advise them cut through the confusion and get at some clear criteria for choosing Presidents. To understand what actual Presidents do and what potential Presidents might do, the first need is to see the man whole — not as some abstract embodiment of civic virtue, some scorecard of issue stands, or some reflection of a faction, but as a human being like the rest of us, a person trying to cope with a difficult environment. To that task he brings his own character, his own view of the world, his own political style. None of that is new for him. If we can see the pattern he has set for his political life we can, I contend, estimate much better his pattern as he confronts the stresses and chances of the presidency.

The presidency is a peculiar office. The founding fathers left it extraordinarily loose in definition, partly because they trusted George Washington to invent a tradition as he went along. It is an institution made a piece at a time by successive men in the White House. Jefferson reached out to Congress to put together the beginnings of political parties; Jackson's dramatic force extended electoral partisanship to its mass base; Lincoln vastly expanded the administrative reach of the office, Wilson and the Roosevelts showed its rhetorical possibilities — in fact every President's mind and demeanor has left its mark on a heritage still in lively development.

But the presidency is much more than an institution. It is a focus of feelings. In general, popular feelings about politics are low-key, shallow, casual. For example, the vast majority of Americans knows virtually nothing of what Congress is doing and cares less. The presidency is different. The Presidency is the focus for the most intense and persistent emotions in the American polity. The President is a symbolic leader, the one figure who draws together the people's hopes and fears for the political future. On top of all his routine duties, he has to carry that off — or fail.

Our emotional attachment to Presidents shows up when one dies in office. People were not just disappointed or worried when President Kennedy was killed; people wept at the loss of a man most had never even met. Kennedy was young and charismatic — but history shows that whenever a President dies in office, heroic Lincoln or debased Harding, McKinley or Garfield, the same wave of deep emotion sweeps across the country. On the other hand, the death of an ex-President brings forth no such intense emotional reaction.

The President is the first political figure children are aware of (later they add Congress, the Court, and others, as "helpers" of the President). With some exceptions among children in deprived circumstances, the President is seen as a "benevolent leader," one who nurtures, sustains, and inspires the citizenry. Presidents regularly show up among "most admired" contemporaries and forebears, and the President is the "best known" (in the sense of sheer name recognition) person in the country. At inauguration time, even Presidents elected by close margins are supported by much larger majorities than the election returns show, for people rally round as he actually assumes office. There is a similar reaction when the people see their President threatened by crisis: if he takes action, there is a favorable spurt in the Gallup poll whether he succeeds or fails.

Obviously the President gets more attention in schoolbooks, press, and television than any other politician. He is one of very few who can make news by doing good things. *His* emotional state is a matter of continual public commentary, as is the manner in which his personal and official families conduct themselves. The media bring across the President not as some neutral administrator or corporate executive to be assessed by his production, but as a special being with mysterious dimensions.

We have no king. The sentiments English children — and adults — direct to the Queen have no place to go in our system but to the President. Whatever his talents — Coolidge-type or Roosevelt-type — the President is the only available object for such national-religious-monarchical sentiments as Americans possess.

The President helps people make sense of politics. Congress is a tangle of committees, the bureaucracy is a maze of agencies. The president is one man trying to do a job — a picture much more understandable to the mass of people who find themselves in the same boat. Furthermore, he is the top man. He ought to know what is going on and set it right. So when the economy goes sour, or war drags on, or domestic violence erupts, the President is available to take the blame. Then when things go right, it seems the President must have had a hand in it. Indeed, the flow of political life is marked off by Presidents: the "Eisenhower Era," the "Kennedy Years."

What all this means is that the President's *main* responsibilities reach far beyond administering the Executive Branch or commanding the armed forces. The White House is first and foremost a place of public leadership. That inevitably brings to bear on the President intense moral, sentimental, and quasi-religious pressures which can, if he lets them, distort his own thinking and feeling. If there is such a thing as extraordinary sanity, it is needed nowhere so much as in the White House.

Who the President is at a given time can make a profound difference in the whole thrust and direction of national politics. Since we have only one President at a time, we can never prove this by comparison, but even the most superficial speculation confirms the commonsense view that the man himself weighs heavily among other historical factors. A Wilson reelected in 1920, a Hoover in 1932, a John F. Kennedy in 1964 would, it seems very likely, have guided the body politic along rather different paths from those their actual successors chose. Or try to imagine a Theodore Roosevelt ensconced behind today's "bully pulpit" of a presidency, or Lyndon Johnson as President in the age of McKinley. Only someone mesmerized by the lures of historical inevitability can suppose that it would have little or no difference to government policy had Alf Landon replaced FDR in 1936, had Dewey beaten Truman in 1948, or Adlai Stevenson reigned through the 1950s. Not only would these alternative Presidents have advocated different policies — they would have approached the office from very different psychological angles. It stretches credibility to think that Eugene McCarthy would have run the institution the way Lyndon Johnson did.

The burden of this book is that the crucial differences can be anticipated by an understanding of a potential President's character, his world view, and his style. This kind of prediction is not easy; well-informed observers often have guessed wrong as they watched a man step toward the White House. One thinks of Woodrow Wilson, the scholar who would bring reason to politics; of Herbert Hoover, the Great Engineer who would organize chaos into progress; of Franklin D. Roosevelt, that champion of the balanced budget; of Harry Truman, whom the office would surely overwhelm; of Dwight D. Eisenhower, militant crusader; of John F. Kennedy, who would lead beyond moralisms to achievements; of Lyndon B. Johnson, the Southern conservative; and of Richard M. Nixon, conciliator. Spotting the errors is easy. Predicting with even approximate accuracy is going to require some sharp tools and close attention in their use. But the experiment is worth it because the question is critical and because it lends itself to correction by evidence.

My argument comes in layers.

First, a President's personality is an important shaper of his presidential behavior on nontrivial matters.

Second, presidential personality is patterned. His character, world view, and style fit together in a dynamic package understandable in psychological terms.

Third, a President's personality interacts with the power situation he faces and the national "climate of expectations" dominant at the time he serves. The tuning, the resonance — or lack of it — between these external factors and his personality sets in motion the dynamics of his presidency.

Fourth, the best way to predict a President's character, world view, and style is to see how they were put together in the first place. That happened in his early life, culminating in his first independent political success.

But the core of the argument . . . is that presidential character — the basic stance a man takes toward his presidential experience — comes in four varieties. The most important thing to know about a President or candidate is where he fits among these types, defined according to (a) how active he is and (b) whether or not he gives the impression he enjoys his political life.

Let me spell out these concepts briefly before getting down to cases.

PERSONALITY SHAPES PERFORMANCE

I am not about to argue that once you know a President's personality you know everything. But as the cases will demonstrate, the degree and quality of a President's emotional involvement in an issue are powerful influences on how he defines the issue itself, how much attention he pays to it, which facts and persons he sees as relevant to its resolution, and, finally, what principles and purposes he associates with the issue. Every story of presidential decision-making is really two stories: an outer one in which a rational man calculates and an inner one in which an emotional man feels. The two are forever connected. Any real President is one whole man and his deeds reflect his wholeness.

As for personality, it is a matter of tendencies. It is not that one President "has" some basic characteristic that another President does not "have." That old way of treating a trait as a possession, like a rock in a basket, ignores the universality of aggressiveness, compliancy, detachment, and other human drives. We all have all of them, but in different amounts and in different combinations.

THE PATTERN OF CHARACTER, WORLD VIEW, AND STYLE

The most visible part of the pattern is style. *Style is the President's habitual way of performing his three political roles: rhetoric, personal relations, and homework.* Not to be confused with "stylishness," charisma, or appearance, style is how the President goes about doing what the office requires him to do — to speak, directly or through media, to large audiences; to deal face to face with other politicians, individually and in small, relatively private groups; and to read, write, and calculate by himself in order to manage the endless flow of details that stream onto his desk. No President can escape doing at least some of each. But there are marked differences in stylistic emphasis from President to President. The *balance* among the three style elements varies; one President may put most of himself into rhetoric, another may stress close, informal dealing, while still another may devote his energies mainly to study and cogitation. Beyond the balance, we want to see each President's peculiar habits of style, his mode of coping with and adapting to these presidential demands. For example, I think both Calvin Coolidge and John F. Kennedy were primarily rhetoricians, but they went about it in contrasting ways.

A President's *world view consists of his primary, politically relevant beliefs, particularly his conceptions of social causality, human nature, and the central moral conflicts of the time.* This is how he sees the world and his lasting opinions about what he sees. Style is his way of acting; world view is his way of seeing. Like the rest of us, a President develops over a lifetime certain conceptions of reality — how things work in politics, what people are like, what the main purposes are. These assumptions or conceptions help him make sense of his world, give some semblance of order to the chaos of existence. Perhaps most important: a man's world view affects what he pays attention to, and a great deal of politics is about paying attention. The name of the game for many politicians is not so much "Do this, do that" as it is "Look here!"

"Character" comes from the Greek word for engraving; in one sense it is what life has marked into a man's being. As used here, *character is the way the President orients himself toward life* — not for the moment, but enduringly. Character is the person's stance as he confronts experience. And at the core of character, a man confronts himself. The President's fundamental self-esteem is his prime personal resource; to defend and advance that, he will sacrifice much else he values. Down there in the privacy of his heart, does he find himself superb, or ordinary, or debased, or in some intermediate range? No President has been utterly paralyzed by self-doubt and none has been utterly free of midnight self-mockery. In between, the real Presidents move out on life from positions of relative strength or weakness. Equally important are the criteria by which they judge themselves. A President who rates himself by the standard of achievement, for instance, may be little affected by losses of affection.

Character, world view, and style are abstractions from the reality of the whole individual. In every case they form an integrated pattern: the man develops a combination which makes psychological sense for him, a dynamic arrangement of motives, beliefs, and habits in the service of his need for self-esteem.

THE POWER SITUATION
AND "CLIMATE OF EXPECTATIONS"

Presidential character resonates with the political situation the President faces. It adapts him as he tries to adapt it. The support he has from the public and interest groups, the party balance in Congress, the thrust of Supreme Court opinion together set the basic power situation he must deal with. An activist President may run smack into a brick wall of resistance, then pull back and wait for a better moment. On the other hand, a President who sees himself as a quiet caretaker may not try to exploit even the most favorable power situation. So it is the relationship between President and the political configuration that makes the system tick.

Even before public opinion polls, the President's real or supposed popularity was a large factor in his performance. Besides the power mix in Washington, the President has to deal with a national climate of expectations, the predominant needs thrust up to him by the people. There are at least three recurrent themes around which these needs are focused.

People look to the President for *reassurance,* a feeling that things will be all right, that the President will take care of his people. The psychological request is for a surcease of anxiety. Obviously, modern life in America involves considerable doses of fear, tension, anxiety, worry; from time to time, the public mood calls for a rest, a time of peace, a breathing space, a "return to normalcy."

Another theme is the demand for a *sense of progress and action.* The President ought to do something to direct the nation's course — or at least be in there pitching for the people. The President is looked to as a take-charge man, a doer, a turner of the wheels, a producer of progress — even if that means some sacrifice of serenity.

A third type of climate of expectations is the public need for a sense of *legitimacy* from, and in, the presidency. The President should be a master politician who is above politics. He should have a right to his place and a rightful way of acting in it. The respectability — even religiosity — of the office has to be protected by a man who presents himself as defender of the faith. There is more to this than dignity, more than propriety. The President is expected to personify our betterness in an inspiring way, to express in what he does and is (not just in what he says) a moral idealism which, in much of the public mind, is the very opposite of "politics."

Over time the climate of expectations shifts and changes. Wars, depressions, and other national events contribute to that change, but there also is a rough cycle, from an emphasis on action (which begins to look too "political") to an emphasis on legitimacy (the moral uplift of which creates its own strains) to an emphasis on reassurance and rest (which comes to seem like drift) and back to action again. One need not be astrological about it. The point is that the climate of expectations at any given time is the political air the President has to breathe. Relating to this climate is a large part of his task.

PREDICTING PRESIDENTS

The best way to predict a President's character, world view, and style is to see how he constructed them in the first place. Especially in the early stages, life is experimental; consciously or not, a person tries out various ways of defining and maintaining and raising self-esteem. He looks to his environment for clues as to who he is and how well he is doing. These lessons of life slowly sink in: certain self-images and evaluations, certain ways of looking at the world, certain styles of action get confirmed by his experience and he gradually adopts them as his own. If we can see that process of development, we can understand the product. The features to note are those bearing on presidential performance.

Experimental development continues all the way to death; we will not blind ourselves to midlife changes, particularly in the full-scale prediction case, that of Richard Nixon. But it is often much easier to see the basic patterns in early life histories. Later on a whole host of distractions — especially the image-making all politicians learn to practice — clouds the picture.

In general, character has its *main* development in childhood, world view in adolescence, style in early adulthood. The stance toward life I call character grows out of the child's experiments in relating to parents, brothers and sisters, and peers at play and in school, as well as to his own body and the objects around it. Slowly the child defines an orientation toward experience; once established, that tends to last despite much subsequent contradiction. By adolescence, the child has been hearing and seeing how people make their worlds meaningful, and now he is moved to relate himself — his own meanings — to those around him. His focus of attention shifts toward the future; he senses that decisions about his fate are coming and he looks into the premises for those decisions. Thoughts about the way the world works and how one might work in it, about what people are like and how one might be like them or not, and about the values people share and how one might share in them too — these are typical concerns for the post-child, pre-adult mind of the adolescent.

These themes come together strongly in early adulthood, when the person moves from contemplation to responsible action and adopts a style. In most biographical accounts this period stands out in stark clarity — the time of emergence, the time the young man found himself. I call it his first independent political success. It was then he moved beyond the detailed guidance of his family; then his self-esteem was dramatically boosted; then he came forth as a person to be reckoned with by other people. The *way* he did that is profoundly important to him. Typically he grasps that style and hangs onto it. Much later, coming into the presidency, something in him remembers this earlier victory and re-emphasizes the style that made it happen.

Character provides the main thrust and broad direction — but it does not *determine,* in any fixed sense, world view and style. The story of development does not end with the end of childhood. Thereafter, the culture one grows in and the ways that culture is translated by parents and peers shapes the meanings one makes of his character. The going world view gets learned and that learning helps channel character forces. Thus it will not necessarily be true that compulsive characters have reactionary beliefs, or that compliant characters believe in compromise. Similarly for style: historical accidents play a large part in furnishing special opportunities for action — and in blocking off alternatives. For example, however much anger a young man may feel, that anger will not be expressed in rhetoric unless and until his life situation provides a platform and an audience. Style thus has a stature and independence of its own. Those who would reduce all explanation to character neglect these highly significant later channelings. For beyond the root is the branch, above the foundation the superstructure, and starts do not prescribe finishes.

FOUR TYPES OF PRESIDENTIAL CHARACTER

The five concepts — character, world view, style, power situation, and climate of expectations — run through the accounts of Presidents in the chapters to follow, which cluster the Presidents since Theodore Roosevelt into four types. This is the fundamental scheme of the study. It offers a way to move past the complexities to the main contrasts and comparisons.

The first baseline in defining presidential types is *activity-passivity*. How much energy does the man invest in his presidency? Lyndon Johnson went at his day like a human cyclone, coming to rest long after the sun went down. Calvin Coolidge often slept eleven hours a night and still needed a nap in the middle of the day. In between the Presidents array themselves on the high or low side of the activity line.

The second baseline is *positive-negative affect* toward one's activity — that is, how he feels about what he does. Relatively speaking, does he seem to experience his political life as happy or sad, enjoyable or discouraging, positive or negative in its main effect. The feeling I am after here is not grim satisfaction in a job well done, not some philosophical conclusion. The idea is this: is he someone who, on the surfaces we can see, gives forth the feeling that he has *fun* in political life? Franklin Roosevelt's Secretary of War, Henry L. Stimson wrote that the Roosevelts "not only understood the *use* of power, they knew the *enjoyment* of power, too. . . . Whether a man is burdened by power or enjoys power; whether he is trapped by responsibility or made free by it; whether he is moved by other people and outer forces or moves them — that is the essence of leadership."

The positive-negative baseline, then, is a general symptom of the fit between the man and his experience, a kind of register of *felt* satisfaction.

Why might we expect these two simple dimensions to outline the main character types? Because they stand for two central features of anyone's orientation toward life. In nearly every study of personality, some form of the active-passive contrast is critical; the general tendency to act or be acted upon is evident in such concepts as dominance-submission, extraversion-introversion, aggression-timidity, attack-defense, fight-flight, engagement-withdrawal, approach-avoidance. In everyday life we sense quickly the general energy output of the people we deal with. Similarly we catch on fairly quickly to the affect dimension — whether the person seems to be optimistic or pessimistic, hopeful or skeptical, happy or sad. The two baselines are clear and they are also independent of one another: all of us know people who are very active but seem discouraged, others who are quite passive but seem happy, and so forth. The activity baseline refers to what one does, the affect baseline to how one feels about what he does.

Both are crude clues to character. They are leads into four basic character patterns long familiar in psychological research. In summary form, these are the main configurations:

Active-positive: There is a congruence, a consistency, between much activity and the enjoyment of it, indicating relatively high self-esteem and relative success in relating to the environment. The man shows an orientation toward productiveness as a value and an ability to use his styles flexibly, adaptively, suiting the dance to the music. He sees himself as developing over time toward relatively well defined personal goals — growing toward his image of himself as he might yet be. There is an emphasis on rational mastery, on using the brain to move the feet. This may get him into trouble; he may fail to take account of the irrational in politics. Not everyone he deals with sees things his way and he may find it hard to understand why.

Active-negative: The contradiction here is between relatively intense effort and relatively low emotional reward for that effort. The activity has a compulsive quality, as if the man were trying to make up for something or to escape from anxiety into hard work. He seems ambitious, striving upward, power-seeking. His stance toward the environment is aggressive and he has a persistent problem in managing his aggressive feelings. His self-image is vague and discontinuous. Life is a hard struggle to achieve and hold power, hampered by the condemnations of a perfectionistic conscience. Active-negative types pour energy into the political system, but it is an energy distorted from within.

Passive-positive: This is the receptive, compliant, other-directed character whose life is a search for affection as a reward for being agreeable and cooperative rather than personally assertive. The contradiction is between low self-esteem (on grounds of being unlovable, unattractive) and a superficial optimism. A hopeful attitude helps dispel doubt and elicits encouragement from others. Passive-positive types help soften the harsh edges of politics. But their dependence and the fragility of their hopes and enjoyments make disappointment in politics likely.

Passive-negative: The factors are consistent — but how are we to account for the man's *political* role-taking? Why is someone who does little in politics and enjoys it less there at all? The answer lies in the passive-negative's character-rooted orientation toward doing dutiful service; this compensates for low self-esteem based on a sense of uselessness. Passive-negative types are in politics because they think they ought to be. They may be well adapted to certain nonpolitical roles, but they lack the experience and flexibility to perform effectively as political leaders. Their tendency is to withdraw, to escape from the conflict and uncertainty of politics by emphasizing vague principles (especially prohibitions) and procedural arrangements. They become guardians of the right and proper way, above the sordid politicking of lesser men.

Active-positive Presidents want most to achieve results. Active-negatives aim to get and keep power. Passive-positives are after love. Passive-negatives emphasize their civic virtue. The relation of activity to enjoyment in a President thus tends to outline a cluster of characteristics, to set apart the adapted from the compulsive, compliant, and withdrawn types.

The first four Presidents of the United States, conveniently, ran through this gamut of character types. (Remember, we are talking about tendencies, broad directions; no individual man exactly fits a category.) George Washington — clearly the most important President in the pantheon — established the fundamental legitimacy of an American government at a time when this was a matter in considerable question. Washington's dignity, judiciousness, his aloof air of reserve and dedication to duty fit the passive-negative or withdrawing type best. Washington did not seek innovation, he sought stability. He longed to retire to Mount Vernon, but fortunately was persuaded to stay on through a second term, in which, by rising above the political conflict between Hamilton and Jefferson and inspiring confidence in his own integrity, he gave the nation time to develop the organized means for peaceful change.

John Adams followed, a dour New England Puritan, much given to work and worry, an impatient and irascible man — an active-negative President, a compulsive type. Adams was far more partisan than Washington; the survival of the system through his presidency demonstrated that the nation could tolerate, for a time, domination by one of its nascent political parties. As President, an angry Adams brought the United States to the brink of war with France, and presided over the new nation's first experiment in political repression: the Alien and Sedition Acts, forbidding, among other things, unlawful combinations "with intent to oppose any measure or measures of the government of the United States," or "any false, scandalous, and malicious writing or writings against the United States, or the President of the United States, with intent to defame . . . or to bring them or either of them, into contempt or disrepute."

Then came Jefferson. He too had his troubles and failures — in the design of national defense, for example. As for his presidential character (only one element in success or failure), Jefferson was clearly active-positive. A child of the Enlightenment, he applied his reason to organizing connections with Congress aimed at strengthening the more popular forces. A man of catholic interests and delightful humor, Jefferson combined a clear and open vision of what the country could be with a profound political sense, expressed in his famous phrase, "Every difference of opinion is not a difference of principle."

The fourth president was James Madison, "Little Jemmy," the constitutional philosopher thrown into the White House at a time of great international turmoil. Madison comes closest to the passive-positive, or compliant, type; he suffered from irresolution, tried to compromise his way out, and gave in too readily to the "warhawks" urging combat with Britain. The nation drifted into war, and Madison wound up ineptly commanding his collection of amateur generals in the streets of Washington. General Jackson's victory at New Orleans saved the Madison administration's historical reputation; but he left the presidency with the United States close to bankruptcy and secession.

These four Presidents — like all Presidents — were persons trying to cope with the roles they had won by using the equipment they had built over a lifetime. The President is not some shapeless organism in a flood of novelties, but a man with a memory in a system with a history. Like all of us, he draws on his past to shape his future. The pathetic hope that the White House will turn a Caligula into a Marcus Aurelius is as naive as the fear that ultimate power inevitably corrupts. The problem is to understand — and to state understandably — what in the personal past foreshadows the presidential future.

Perhaps because of the emphasis on the importance of presidential character, highlighted by the publication in 1972 of James David Barber's book, *The Presidential Character: Predicting Performance in the White House,* and the subsequent actions of President Richard M. Nixon, which seemed to bear out perfectly Barber's prediction that he would be an "active-negative" president, the "character" of presidential candidate Jimmy Carter, and subsequently, of President Carter came under close scrutiny from all quarters. The relative openness of the Carter candidacy and presidency, his willingness to grant interviews and to reveal candidly his views and the influences upon his life, served to encourage assessment of the Carter character. To some his style in the White House seemed rigid and inflexible, while to others he exhibited an open and positive approach toward his job. Searching inquiries were made on his humor or lack of it. Exhibitions of temper were duly reported in the press. After the President had been in office for several months, the *New York Times* reported that he was demanding, humorless, often rigid and arrogant, blaming rather than praising his staff. In response, presidential press secretary Jody Powell issued a strong denial, citing the article as totally inaccurate. Amateurish psychoanalysis of character is a risky venture at best. But the trend largely started by Barber could not be reversed, and it continued during and after the presidential campaign of 1980, as assessments were made of the impact of character upon future performance.

The way in which President Nixon handled the Watergate affair was shaped in part, if not entirely, by his character. In April 1974, President Nixon released transcripts of Oval Office discussions about Watergate and related matters. The President released the transcripts to the public in a last ditch attempt to gain support. He gave the original tapes of the conversations to the House Judiciary Committee. Instead of producing the kind of favorable public reaction that the President inscrutably expected, the transcripts caused a public outcry of unprecedented proportions and a rapid withdrawal of what little support the President had in Congress before the text of the transcripts was revealed.

The Nixon transcripts were bad enough for the President, but even worse were transcripts of the same tapes that were released in July 1974 by the House Judiciary Committee that revealed discrepancies, alterations and omissions in the White House version of Oval Office conversations. The Committee account pictured a president actively involved in the Watergate coverup. Finally, after the Supreme Court ruling in *United States* v. *Richard M. Nixon* (see Selection 43, Chapter 6), President Nixon was essentially forced to reveal to the public the fact that he had been involved in the Watergate cover-up only six days after the break-in occurred. The following selection contains portions of the Nixon transcripts and part of the June 23, 1972, tape released by President Nixon before his resignation on August 9, 1974. There are no meaningful differences between the White House and the House Judiciary Committee on what was said in the following selections. Each speaker is identified by an initial: the President (**P.**), White House counsel John Dean (**D.**), Presidential advisers H. R. Haldeman (**H.**) and John Ehrlichman (**E.**), and former Attorney General John Mitchell (**M.**).

In reading the transcripts students should attempt to assess the ways in which the transcripts support or detract from the conclusions of Barber regarding the importance of presidential character. Barber classified Nixon as "active-negative." Do the tapes support this conclusion?

41

THE NIXON TRANSCRIPTS

JUNE 23, 1972

H. You know the Democratic break-in thing, we're back in the problem area because the FBI is not under control . . . the way to handle this now is for us to have Walters call Pat Gray and just say, "stay to hell out of this — this is, ah, business here we don't want you to go any further on it."

P. What about Pat Gray — you mean Pat Gray doesn't want to?

H. Pat does want to. He doesn't know how to, and he doesn't have, he doesn't have any basis for doing it. . . .

H. And you seem to think the thing to do is get them to stop?

P. Right, fine. . . .

P. Play it tough. That's the way they play it and that's the way we are going to play it. . . .

P. When you get in [to the CIA] people say, "Look, the problem is that this will open the whole Bay of Pigs thing, and the President just feels that ah," without going into the details — don't, don't lie to them to the extent to say there is no involvement, but just say this is a comedy of errors . . . they should call the FBI in and (unintelligible) don't go any further into this case period!

SEPTEMBER 15, 1972

This transcript begins as Haldeman and Ehrlichman enter the Oval Office.

P. Hi, how are you? You had quite a day today didn't you? You got Watergate on the way didn't you?

D. We tried.

H. How did it all end up?

D. Ah, I think we can say well at this point. The press is playing it just as we expect.

H. Whitewash?

D. No, not yet — the story right now —

P. It is a big story.

H. Five indicted plus the WH former guy and all that.

D. Plus two White House fellows.

H. That is good that takes the edge off whitewash really that was the thing Mitchell kept saying that to people in the country [Watergate defendants G. Gordon] Liddy and [Howard] Hunt were big men. Maybe that is good.

P. How did [Mitchell's successor as head of CRP, Clark] MacGregor handle himself?

D. I think very well. He had a good statement which said that the Grand Jury had met and that it was now time to realize that some apologies may be due.

H. Fat chance . . .

P. Just remember, all the trouble we're taking, we'll have a chance to get back one day. How are you doing on your other investigations?

H. What has happened on the bug?

P. What bug?

D. The second bug there was a bug found in the telephone of one of the men at the [Democratic National Committee].

P. You don't think it was left over from the other time?

D. Absolutely not, the Bureau has checked and re-checked the whole place after that night. The man had specifically checked and rechecked the telephone and it was not there.

P. What the hell do you think was involved?

D. I think DNC was planted.

P. You think they did it?

D. Uh huh.

P. (Expletive deleted) — do they really want to believe that we planted that?

H. Did they get anything on the finger prints?

D. No, nothing at all — either on the telephone or on the bug. The FBI has unleashed a full investigation . . . at the DNC starting with [Democratic chairman Lawrence] O'Brien right now.

H. (Laughter.) Using the same crew —

D. The same crew — the Washington Field Office.

P. What kind of questions are they asking him?

D. Anything they can think of because O'Brien is charging them with failing to find all the bugs.

H. Good, that will make them mad.

D. So [acting FBI Director L. Patrick] Gray is pissed and his people are pissed off. So maybe they will move in because their reputation is on the line. I think that is a good development.

P. I think that is a good development because it makes it look so (adjective deleted) funny. Am I wrong?

D. No, no, sir. It looks silly. If we can find that the DNC planted that, the whole story will reverse.

After a few minutes, the meeting is interrupted by a telephone call from John Mitchell. Only the President's side of the conversation is recorded. The Mitchell talk ends this way:

P. Well I tell you just don't let this keep you or your colleagues from concentrating on the big game. This thing is just one of those side issues and a month later everybody looks back and wonders what all the shooting was about. OK, John. Good night. Get a good night's sleep. And don't bug anybody without asking me. OK? Yeah. Thank you.

D. Three months ago I would have had trouble predicting there would be a day when this would be forgotten, but I think I can say that 54 days from now nothing is going to come crashing down to our surprise.

P. That what?

D. Nothing is going to come crashing down to our surprise.

P. Oh well, this is a can of worms as you know a lot of this stuff that went on. And the people who worked this way are awfully embarrassed. But the way you have handled all this seems to me has been very skillful putting your fingers in the leaks that have sprung here and sprung there . . . We are all in it together. This is a war. We take a few shots and it will be over. We will give them a few shots and it will be over . . . Don't worry. I wouldn't want to be on the other side right now. Would you?

D. Along that line, one of the things I've tried to do, I have begun to keep notes on a lot of people who are emerging as less than our friends because this will be over some day and we shouldn't forget the way some of them have treated us.

P. I want the most comprehensive notes on all those who tried to do us in. They didn't have to do it. If we had had a very close election and they were playing the other side I would understand this. No — they were doing this quite deliberately and they are asking for it and they are going to get it. We have not used the power in this first four years as you know. We have never used it. We have not used the Bureau and we have not used the Justice Department but things are going to change now. And they are either going to do it right or go.

D. What an exciting prospect.

P. Thanks. It has to be done. We have been (adjective deleted) fools for us to come into this election campaign and not do anything with regard to the Democratic Senators who are running, et cetera. And who the hell are they after? They are after us. It is absolutely ridiculous. It is not going to be that way any more.

H. Really, it is ironic that we have gone to extremes. You and your damn regulations. Everybody worries about not picking up a hotel bill.

D. I think you can be proud of the White House staff. It really has had no problems of that sort. And I love this [General Accounting Office] audit that is going on now. I think they have some suspicion that even a cursory investigation is going to discover something here. I don't think they can find a thing. I learned today, incidentally, and have not confirmed it, that the GAO auditor who is down here is here at the Speaker of the House's request.

P. That surprises me.

H. Well, (expletive deleted) the Speaker of the House. Maybe we better put a little heat on him.

P. I think so too.

H. Because he has a lot worse problems than he is going to find down here.

D. That's right.

H. That is the kind of thing that, you know, we really ought to do is call the Speaker and say, "I regret to say your calling the GAO down here because of what it is going to cause us to do to you."

P. Why don't you see if [Presidential aide Bryce] Harlow will tell him that.

H. Because he wouldn't do it — he would just be pleasant and call him Mr. Speaker . . .

P. You really can't sit and worry about it all the time. The worst may happen but it may not. So you just try to button it up as well as you can and hope for the best, and remember basically the damn business is unfortunately trying to cut our losses.

D. Certainly that is right and certainly it has had no effect on you.

H. No, it has been kept away from the White House and of course completely from the President.

FEBRUARY 28, 1973

The President meets with Dean in the Oval Office. The conversation turns to the planned hearings by the Senate Watergate Committee:

D. I would suspect if we are going to get any insight to what that Committee is going to do, it is going to be through [GOP Sen. Edward] Gurney. I don't know about [GOP Sen. Lowell] Weicker . . .

P. Weicker, I think the line to Weicker is through [Pat] Gray. Gray has to shape up here and handle himself well too. Do you think he will?

D. I do. I think Pat has had it tough. He goes up this morning as you know. He is ready. He is very comfortable in all of the decisions he has made, and I think he will be good.

P. But he is close to Weicker — that is what I meant.

D. Yes, he is.

P. And so, Gray . . .

D. He has a lead in there — yes.

P. One amusing thing about the Gray thing, and I knew this would come. They say Gray is a political crony and a personal crony of the President's. Did you know that I have never seen him socially?

D. Is that correct? No, I didn't.

P. I think he has been to a couple White House events, but I have never seen him separately.

D. The press has got him meeting you at a social function. And, back in 1947, (inaudible) is something I have read.

P. Maybe at a [Adm. Arthur] Radford party or something like that. That's all. I don't know. But Gray is somebody that I know only — He was Radford's assistant, used to attend [National Security Council] meetings. He has never been a social friend. Edgar Hoover, on the other hand, I have seen socially at least a hundred times. He and I were very close friends.

D. This is curious the way the press —

P. (expletive deleted) — Hoover was my crony. He was closer to me than Johnson, actually, although Johnson used him more. But as for Pat Gray, (expletive deleted) I never saw him.

D. While it might have been a lot of blue chips to the late Director, I think we would have been a lot better off during this whole Watergate thing if he had been alive. Because he knew how to handle that Bureau — knew how to keep them in bounds.

P. Well, Hoover performed. He would have fought. That was the point. He would have defied a few people. He would have scared them to death. He has a file on everybody.

Later, the President speculates about the motives of the Democrats on the Watergate committee:

P. I frankly say that I would rather they would be partisan — rather than for them to have a façade of fairness and all the rest. [Sam] Ervin always talks about his being a great Constitutional lawyer. (expletive deleted) He's got [Howard] Baker totally toppled over to him. Ervin works harder than most of our Southern gentlemen. They are great politicians. They are just more clever than the minority . . .

D. I am convinced that he has shown that he is merely a puppet for Kennedy in this whole thing. The fine hand of the Kennedys' is behind this whole hearing . . .

P. Uh, huh.

D. He has kept this quiet and constant pressure on this thing. I think this fellow Sam Dash, who has been selected Counsel, is a Kennedy choice. I think this is also something we will be able to quietly and slowly document. Leak this to the press, and the parts and cast become much more apparent.

P. Yes, I guess the Kennedy crowd is just laying in the bushes waiting to make their move. I had forgotten, by the way, we talk about Johnson using the FBI. Did your friends tell you what Bobby did?

D. I haven't heard but I wouldn't be —

P. Johnson believed that Bobby bugged him.

D. That wouldn't surprise me.

P. Bobby was a ruthless (characterization omitted). But the FBI does blatantly tell you that — or [former FBI assistant director William] Sullivan told you about the New Jersey thing. He did use a bug up there for intelligence work. (inaudible)

Dean informs the President that William Sullivan has information that the agency bugged Mr. Nixon during his 1968 campaign. The President is intrigued. Dean suggests that another former FBI official, Mark Felt, could make the details of that bugging operation public. This prompts the President to reminisce about Whittaker Chambers, who was the chief witness against Alger Hiss in the celebrated investigation that Mr. Nixon helped conduct when he was a young congressman:

P. Let's face it. Suppose Felt comes out now and unwraps. What does it do to him?

D. He can't do it.

P. How about (unintelligible)? Who is going to hire him? Let's face it — the guy who goes out — he couldn't do it unless he had a guarantee from somebody like TIME Magazine who would say look we will give you a job for life. Then what do they do? He would go to a job at LIFE, and everyone would treat him like a pariah. He is in a very dangerous situation. These guys you know — the informers. Look what it did to Chambers. Chambers informed because he didn't give (expletive deleted). But then one of the most brilliant writers according to [Time Inc. president] Jim Shepley we have ever seen in this country — and I am not referring to the Communist issue — greatest writer of his time — about 30 years ago, probably TIME's best writer of the century — they finished him. Either way, the informer is not one in our society. Either way, that is the one thing people can't survive. They say no civilized (characterization deleted) informs.

The conversation moves on to the subject of news leaks and then to a discussion of White House strategy regarding the investigation of the Watergate break-in:

D. I have got to say one thing. There has never been a leak out of my office. There never will be a leak out of my office. I wouldn't begin to know how to leak and I don't want to learn how you leak . . .

P. This happens all the time. Well, you can follow these characters to their Gethsemane. I feel for those poor guys in jail, particularly for Hunt with his wife dead.

D. Well there is every indication they are hanging in tough right now.

P. What the hell do they expect though? Do they expect clemency in a reasonable time? What would you advise on that?

D. I think it is one of those things we will have to watch very closely. For example —

P. You couldn't do it, say, in six months.

D. No, you couldn't. This thing may become so political as a result of these hearings that it is a vendetta. This judge [John Sirica] may go off the deep end in sentencing, and make it so absurd that it's clearly injustice that they have been heavily —

P. Is there any kind of appeal left?

D. Right. Liddy and [former CRP security chief James] McCord, who sat through the trial, will both be on appeal and there is no telling how long that will last. It is one of these things we will just have to watch.

P. . . . But the President should not become involved in any part of this case. Do you agree with that?

D. I agree totally, sir. Absolutely. That doesn't mean that quietly we are not going to be working around the office. You can rest assured that we are not going to be sitting quietly.

P. I don't know what we can do. The people who are most disturbed about this (unintelligible) are the (adjective deleted) Republicans. A lot of these Congressmen, financial contributors, et cetera, are highly moral. The Democrats are just sort of saying, "(expletive deleted) fun and games!"

D. Well, hopefully we can give them [political prankster Donald] Segretti.

P. (Expletive deleted) He was such a dumb figure, I don't see how our boys could have gone for him. But, nevertheless, they did. It was really juvenile! But, nevertheless, what the hell did he do? What in the (characterization deleted) did he do? Shouldn't we be trying to get intelligence? Weren't they trying to get intelligence from us?

The President pauses to consider the state of the Democratic Party:

P. . . . all this business is a battle and they are going to wage the battle. A lot of them have enormous frustrations about those elections, state of their party, etc. And their party has its problems. We think we have had problems, look at some of theirs. [Democratic chairman Robert] Strauss has had people and all the actors, and they haven't done that well you know.

D. Well, I was — we have come a long road on this thing now. I had thought it was an impossible task to hold together until after the election until things started falling out, but we have made it this far and I am convinced we are going to make it the whole road and put this thing in the funny pages of the history books rather than anything serious because actually —

P. It will be somewhat serious but the main thing, of course, is also the isolation of the President.

D. Absolutely! Totally true!

P. Because that, fortunately, is totally true.

D. I know that sir!

P. (expletive deleted) Of course, I am not dumb and I will never forget when I heard about this (adjective deleted) forced entry and bugging. I thought, what in the hell is this? What is the matter with these people? Are they crazy? I thought they were nuts! A prank! But it wasn't! It wasn't very funny. I think that our Democratic friends know that, too. They know what the hell it was. They don't think we'd be involved in such.

D. I think they do too.

P. Maybe they don't. They don't think I would be involved in such stuff. They think I have people capable of it. And they are correct, in that [former adviser Charles] Colson would do anything . . . now I will not talk to you again until you have something to report to me.

D. Alright, sir.

P. But I think it is very important that you have these talks with our good friend [Attorney General Richard] Kleindienst.

D. That will be done.

P. Tell him we have to get these things worked out. We have to work together on this thing. I would build him up. He is the man who can make the difference. Also point out to him what we have. (expletive deleted) Colson's got (characterization deleted), but I really, really — this stuff here — let's forget this. But let's remember this was not done by the White House. This was done by the Committee to Re-Elect, and Mitchell was the Chairman, correct?

D. That's correct!

P. And Kleindienst owes Mitchell everything. Mitchell wanted him for Attorney General. Wanted him for Deputy, and here he is. Now (expletive deleted). Baker's got to realize this, and that if he allows this thing to get out of hand he is going to potentially ruin John Mitchell. He won't. Mitchell won't allow himself to be ruined. He will put on his big stone face. But I hope he does and he will. There is no question what they are after. What the Committee is after is somebody at the White House. They would like to get Haldeman or Colson, Ehrlichman.

D. Or possibly Dean. — You know, I am a small fish.

MARCH 13, 1973

The President and Dean confer again in the Oval Office. They discuss to what extent White House personnel should cooperate with the Federal prosecutors and the grand jury investigating Watergate:

D. Well, then you will get a barrage of questions probably, on will you supply — will Mr. Haldeman and Mr. Ehrlichman and Mr. Dean go up to the Committee and testify?

P. No, absolutely not.

D. Mr. Colson?

P. No. Absolutely not. It isn't a question of not — [Presidential press secretary Ronald] Ziegler or somebody had said that we in our executive privilege statement it was interpreted as meaning that we would not furnish information and all that. We said we will furnish information, but we are not going to be called to testify. That is the position. Dean and all the rest will grant you information. Won't you?

D. Yes. Indeed I will.

P. My feeling, John, is that I better hit it now rather than just let it build up where we are afraid of these questions and everybody, etc., and let Ziegler go out there and bob and weave around. I know the easy thing is to bug out, but it is not . . .

D. You're right. I was afraid. For the sake of debate, but I was having reservations. It is a bullet biter and you just have to do it. These questions are just not going to go away. Now the other thing that we talked about in the past, and I still have the same problem, is to have a "here it all is" approach. If we do that . . .

P. And let it all hang out.

D. And let it all hang out. Let's with a Segretti — etc.

P. We have passed that point.

D. Plus the fact, they are not going to believe the truth! That is the incredible thing!

The President and his counsel return to the question of the FBI bugging the Nixon campaign in 1968. Dean suggests that such a revelation would discredit the Democrats and help L. Patrick Gray in his confirmation hearings as the new director of the FBI:

D. . . . Let's say in the Gray hearings — where everything is cast that we are the political people and they are not — that Hoover was above reproach, which is just not accurate, total (expletive omitted). The person who would destroy Hoover's image is going to be this man Bill Sullivan. Also it is going to tarnish quite severely . . .

P. Some of the FBI.

D. . . . some of the FBI. And a former President. He is going to lay it out, and just all hell is going to break loose once he does it. It is going to change the atmosphere of the Gray hearings and it is going to change the atmosphere of the whole Watergate hearings. Now the risk . . .

P. How will it change?

D. Because it will put them in context of where government institutes were used in the past for the most flagrant political purposes.

P. How can that help us?

D. How does it help us?

P. I am being the devil's advocate . . .

D. I appreciate what you are doing. It is a red herring. It is what the public already believes. I think the people would react: (expletive deleted), more of that stuff! They are all bad down there! Because it is a one way street right now . . .

P. Do you think the press would use it? They may not play it.

D. It would be difficult not to. Ah, it would be difficult not to.

Getting back to the grand-jury investigation of Watergate, the two men discuss one of their most serious concerns — the testimony of Hugh Sloan, former deputy treasurer of the Committee to Re-elect the President:

P. Who is going to be the first witness up there?

D. Sloan.

P. Unfortunate.

D. No doubt about it —

P. He's scared?

D. He's scared, he's weak. He has a compulsion to cleanse his soul by confession. We are giving him a lot of stroking. Funny thing is this fellow goes down to the Court House here before [Judge John] Sirica, testifies as honestly as he can testify, and Sirica looks around and called him a liar. He just said — Sloan just can't win! So [Nixon personal attorney Herbert] Kalmbach has been dealing with Sloan. Sloan is like a child. Kalmbach has done a lot of that. The person who will have a greater problem as a result of Sloan's testimony is Kalmbach and [former CRP finance director Maurice] Stans. So they are working closely with him to make sure that he settles down . . .

P. Mitchell is now studying, is he?

D. He is studying. Sloan will be the worst witness. I think [former CRP deputy director Jeb Stuart] Magruder will be a good witness. This fellow, [campaign aide Herbert L.] Porter, will be a good witness. They have already been through Grand Jury . . . They did well . . .

P. None will be witnesses.

D. They won't be witnesses?

P. Hell, no. They will make statements. That will be the line which I think we have to get across to Ziegler in all his briefings where he is constantly saying we will provide information. That is not the question. It is how it is to be furnished. We will not furnish it in a formal session. That would be a breakdown of the privilege. Period. Do you agree with that?

D. I agree. I agree. I have always thought that's the bottom line, and I think that is the good thing that is happening in the Gray hearings right now. If they send a letter down with specific questions, I send back written interrogatories sworn. He knows, the lawyer, that you can handle written interrogatories, where cross examination is another ball game.

P. That's right.

The discussion continues on targets of the grand-jury investigation:

P. Let's face it, I think they are really after Haldeman.

D. Haldeman and Mitchell.

P. Colson is not a big enough name for them. He really isn't. He is, you know, he is on the government side, but Colson's name doesn't bother them so much. They are after Haldeman and after Mitchell. Don't you think so?

D. Sure . . .

P. In any event, Haldeman's problem is [Presidential appointments secretary Dwight] Chapin isn't it?

D. Bob's problem is circumstantial.

P. Why is that? Let's look at the circumstantial. I don't know, Bob didn't know any of those people like the Hunts and all that bunch. Colson did, but Bob didn't. OK?

D. That's right.

P. Now where the hell, or how much Chapin knew I will be (expletive deleted) if I know.

D. Chapin didn't know anything about the Watergate.

P. Don't you think so?

D. Absolutely not.

P. [Haldeman aide Gordon] Strachan?

D. Yes.

P. He knew?

D. Yes.

P. About the Watergate?

D. Yes.

P. Well, then, he probably told Bob. He may not have.

D. He was judicious in what he relayed, but Strachan is as tough as nails. He can go in and stonewall, and say, "I don't know anything about what you are talking about." He has already done it twice you know, in interviews.

P. I guess he should, shouldn't he? I suppose we can't call that justice, can we?

D. Well, it is a personal loyalty to him. He doesn't want it any other way. He didn't have to be told. He didn't have to be asked. It just is something that he found was the way he wanted to handle the situation.

P. But he knew? He knew about Watergate? Strachan did?

D. Yes.

P. I will be damned! Well that is the problem in Bob's case. Not Chapin then, but Strachan. Strachan worked for him, didn't he?

D. Yes. They would have one hell of a time proving that Strachan had knowledge of it, though.

P. Who knew better? Magruder?

D. Magruder and Liddy.

P. Oh, I see. The other weak link for Bob is Magruder. He hired him et cetera.

D. That applies to Mitchell, too.

P. Mitchell — Magruder. Where do you see Colson coming into it?

D. . . . I think that Chuck had knowledge that something was going on over there, but he didn't have any knowledge of the details of the specifics of the whole thing.

P. There must have been an indication of the fact that we had poor pickings. Because naturally anybody, either Chuck or Bob, were always reporting to me about what was going on. If they ever got any information they would certainly have told me that we got some information, but they never had a thing to report. What was the matter? Did they never get anything out of the damn thing?

D. I don't think they ever got anything, sir.

P. A dry hole?

D. That's right.

P. (Expletive deleted)

D. Well, they were just really getting started.

P. Yeah. Bob one time said something to me about something, this or that or something, about the fact we got some information about this, or that or the other but I think it was something about the Convention, I think it was about the convention problems they were planning something. I assume that must have been [Clark] MacGregor — not MacGregor, but Segretti.

D. No, Segretti wasn't involved in the intelligence gathering piece of it at all.

P. Oh, he wasn't? Who the hell was gathering intelligence?

D. That was Liddy and his outfit.

P. Apart from Watergate?

D. That's right. Well you see Watergate was part of intelligence gathering, and this was their first thing. What happened is —

P. That was such a stupid thing!

D. It was incredible — that's right. That was Hunt.

P. To think Mitchell and Bob would have allowed — would have allowed — this kind of operation to be in the campaign committee!

P. . . . (Unintelligible) to think that Mitchell and Bob would allow, would have allowed this kind of operation to be in the Committee.

D. I don't think he knew it was there.

P. I don't think that Mitchell knew about this sort of thing.

P. You kidding?

D. I don't —

P. You don't think Mitchell knew about this thing?

D. Oh, no, no! Don't misunderstand me. I don't think that he knew the people. I think he knew that Liddy was out intelligence gathering. I don't think he knew that Liddy would use a fellow like [James] McCord, (expletive removed), who worked for the Committee. I can't believe that.

P. Hunt?

D. I don't think Mitchell knew about Hunt either.

P. Well Mitchell thought, well, gee, and I hired this fellow and I told him to gather intelligence. Maybe Magruder says the same thing.

D. Magruder says — as he did in the trial — well, of course, my name has been dragged in as the guy who sent Liddy over there, which is an interesting thing. Well what happened they said is that Magruder asked — he wanted to hire my deputy over there as Deputy Counsel and I said, "No way. I can't give him up."

P. Was Liddy your deputy?

D. No, Liddy never worked for me . . .

P. How the hell does Liddy stand up so well?

D. He's a strange man . . .

P. Strange or strong?

D. Strange and strong. His loyalty is — I think it is just beyond the pale . . .

P. He hates the other side too, doesn't he?

D. Oh, absolutely! He is strong. He really is.

MARCH 17, 1973

At this session, Dean and the President discuss two items that are only indirectly related to Watergate: (1) the activities of "dirty tricks" specialist Donald Segretti and (2) the break-in at the office of Daniel Ellsberg's psychiatrist. The President leads off:

P. Now on the Segretti thing, I think you've just got to — [Dwight] Chapin, all of them have just got to take the heat. Look, you've got to admit the facts, John, and —

D. That's right.

P. And that's our — and that's that. And [Herbert] Kalmbach paid him. And (unintelligible) a lot of people. I just think on Segretti, no matter how bad it is. It isn't nearly as bad as people think it was. Espionage, sabotage?

D. The intent, when Segretti was hired, was nothing evil nothing vicious, nothing bad, nothing. Not espionage, not sabotage. It was pranksterism that got out of hand and we know that. And I think we can lay our story out there. I have no problem with the Segretti thing. It's just not that serious. The other potential problem is Ehrlichman's and this is —

P. In connection with Hunt?

D. In connection with Hunt and Liddy both.

P. They worked for him?

D. They — these fellows had to be some idiots as we've learned after the fact. They went out and went into Dr. Ellsberg's doctor's office and they had, they were geared up with all this CIA equipment — cameras and the like. Well they turned the stuff back in to the CIA some point in time and left film in the camera. CIA has not put this together, and they don't know what it all means right now. But it wouldn't take a very sharp investigator very long because you've got pictures in the CIA files that they had to turn over to (unintelligible).

P. What in the world — what in the name of God was Ehrlichman having something (unintelligible) in the Ellsberg (unintelligible)?

D. They were trying to — this was a part of an operation that — in connection with the Pentagon papers. They were — the whole thing — they wanted to get Ellsberg's psychiatric records for some reason. I don't know.

P. This is the first I ever heard of this. I, I (unintelligible) care about Ellsberg was not our problem.

D. That's right.

P. (Expletive deleted) . . .

MARCH 20, 1973

As the effort to "contain" the scandal loses ground, the President decides to ask Dean for a formal report on his "investigation" of White House involvement in Watergate. They discuss the report over the telephone:

P. See, for example, I was even thinking if you could even talk to Cabinet, the leaders, you know, just orally and say, "I have looked into this, and this is that," so that people get sort of a feeling that — your own people have got to be reassured.

D. Uh, huh . . .

P. Could you do that?

D. Well, I think I can but I don't think you would want to make that decision until we have about a —

P. No, I want to know. I want to know where all the bodies are first.

D. And then, once you decide after that, we can program it any way you want to do it.

P. Yeah. Because I think, for example, you could do it orally, even if you don't want to make the written statement. You could do it orally before the Cabinet, the leaders and the rest. Lay it all out. You see, I would not be present. You just lay it all out and I just — See what I mean?

D. Uh, huh . . .

P. What I mean is we need something to answer somebody, answer things, you know they say, "What are you basing this on," I can say, "Well, my counsel has advised me that" — Is that possible or not, or are —

D. Well, you know there is that — and there is always the FBI report which we have probably not relied upon enough. There is not one scintilla of evidence.

P. I know. But I mean, can't you say that? Or do you want to put it out?

D. Ah, it could be said, and it is something we haven't really emphasized.

MARCH 21, 1973

The most significant of all the transcripts records the meeting in the Oval Office between the President, Dean and Haldeman at which Dean lays out some of the unpleasant facts about Watergate and its aftermath:

D. The reason that I thought we ought to talk this morning is because in our conversations, I have the impression that you don't know everything I know and it makes it very difficult for you to make judgments that only you can make on some of these things and I thought that —

P. In other words, I have to know why you feel that we shouldn't unravel something?

D. Let me give you my overall first.

P. In other words, your judgment as to where it stands, and where we will go.

D. I think that there is no doubt about the seriousness of the problem we've got. We have a cancer within, close to the Presidency, that is growing. It is growing daily. It's compounded, growing geometrically now, because it compounds itself. That will be clear if I, you know, explain some of the details of why it is. Basically, it is because (1) we are being blackmailed; (2) people are going to start perjuring themselves very quickly that have not had to perjure themselves to protect other people in the line. And there is no assurance —

P. That that won't bust?

D. That that won't bust.

Dean proceeds to describe the beginnings of the Watergate affair. The original aim of the CRP, he says, was to set up "a perfectly legitimate campaign intelligence operation." The task was assigned to Gordon Liddy, who drew up "a million-dollar plan that was the most incredible thing I have ever laid my eyes on." When the plan was presented to John Mitchell, says Dean, he "just sat there puffing and laughing . . . so Liddy was told to go back to the drawing board and come up with something realistic." The second plan included bugging, and Dean says he thought that even this undertaking had been "turned off" by Mitchell. But yet a third plan followed, and it led to the break-in at Democratic National Committee headquarters:

D. . . . Apparently after they had initially broken in and bugged the DNC they were getting information. The information was coming over here to [Gordon] Strachan and some of it was given to Haldeman, there is no doubt about it.

P. Did he know where it was coming from?

D. I don't really know if he would.

P. Not necessarily?

D. Not necessarily. Strachan knew it. There is no doubt about it, and whether Strachan — I have never come to press these people on these points because it hurts them to give up that next inch, so I had to piece things together. Strachan was aware of receiving information, reporting to Bob. At one point Bob even gave instructions to change their capabilities from Muskie to McGovern, and passed this back through Strachan to [Jeb] Magruder and apparently to Liddy. And Liddy was starting to make arrangements to go in and bug . . . McGovern . . .

P. They had never bugged Muskie, though, did they?

D. No, they hadn't, but they had infiltrated it by a secretary.

P. By a secretary?

D. By a secretary and a chauffeur. There is nothing illegal about that. So the information was coming over here and then I, finally, after —. The next point in time that I became aware of anything was on June 17th when I got the word that there had been this break-in at the DNC and somebody from our Committee had been caught in the DNC. And I said, "Oh, (expletive deleted)." You know, eventually putting the pieces together —

P. You knew what it was.

D. I knew who it was. So I called Liddy on Monday morning and said, "First, Gordon, I want to know whether anybody in the White House was involved in this." And he said, "No, they weren't." I said, "Well I want to know how in (adjective deleted) name this happened." He said, "Well, I was pushed without mercy by Magruder to get in there and to get more information. That the information was not satisfactory. That Magruder said, 'The White House is not happy with what we are getting.'"

P. The White House?

D. The White House. Yeah!

P. Who do you think was pushing him?

D. Well, I think it was probably Strachan thinking that Bob wanted things, because I have seen that happen on other occasions where things were said to have been of very prime importance when they really weren't.

P. Why at that point in time I wonder? I am just trying to think. We had just finished the Moscow trip. The Democrats had just nominated McGovern. I mean, (expletive deleted), what in the hell were these people doing? I can see their doing it earlier. I can see the pressures, but I don't see why all the pressure was on then.

D. I don't know, other than the fact that they might have been looking for information about the conventions.

P. That's right.

D. Because, I understand that after the fact that there was a plan to bug Larry O'Brien's suite down in Florida. So Liddy told me that this is what had happened and this is why it had happened.

P. Where did he learn . . . there were plans to bug Larry O'Brien's suite?

D. From Magruder, long after the fact.

P. Magruder is (unintelligible)

D. Yeah. Magruder is totally knowledgeable on the whole thing.

P. Yeah.

D. Alright now, we have gone through the trial. I don't know if Mitchell has perjured himself in the Grand Jury or not.

P. Who?

D. Mitchell, I don't know how much knowledge he actually had. I know that Magruder has perjured himself in the Grand Jury. I know that Porter has perjured himself in the Grand Jury.

P. Who is Porter? (unintelligible)

D. He is one of Magruder's deputies. They set up this scenario which they ran by me. They said, "How about this?" I said, "I don't know. If this is what you are going to hang on, fine."

P. What did they say in the Grand Jury?

D. They said, as they said before the trial in the Grand Jury, that Liddy had come over as Counsel and we knew he had these capacities to do legitimate intelligence. We had no idea what he was doing. He was given an authorization of $250,000 to collect information, because our surrogates were out on the road. They had no protection, and we had information that there were going to be demonstrations against them, and that we had to have a plan as to what liabilities they were going to be confronted with and Liddy was charged with doing this. We had no knowledge that he was going to bug the DNC.

P. The point is, that is not true?

D. That's right.

P. Magruder did know it was going to take place?

D. Magruder gave the instructions to be back in the DNC.

P. He did?

D. Yes.

P. You know that?

D. Yes.

P. I see. OK.

D. I honestly believe that no one over here knew that. I know that as God is my maker, I had no knowledge that they were going to do this.

P. Bob didn't either, or wouldn't have known that either. You are not the issue involved. Had Bob known, he would be.

D. Bob — I don't believe he specifically knew that they were going in there . . .

P. Did Strachan know?

D. I think Strachan did know.

P. (unintelligible) Going back into the DNC — Hunt, etc. — this is not understandable! . . .

D. . . . this could have been disastrous on the electorate if all hell had broken loose. I worked on a theory of containment —

P. Sure.

D. To try to hold it right where it was.

P. Right.

D. There is no doubt that I was totally aware of what the Bureau was doing at all times. I was totally aware of what the Grand Jury was doing. I knew what witnesses were going to be called. I knew what they were asked, and I had to.

P. Why did [Assistant Attorney General Henry] Petersen play the game so straight with us?

D. Because Petersen is a soldier. He kept me informed. He told me when we had problems, where we had problems and the like. He believes in you and he believes in this Administration. This Administration has made him. I don't think he has done anything improper, but he did make sure that the investigation was narrowed down to the very, very fine criminal thing which was a break for us . . .

Next Dean turns to the payments that have been made to the Watergate burglars:

D. . . . Liddy said if they all got counsel instantly and said we will ride this thing out. Alright, then they started making demands. "We have to have attorneys' fees. We don't have any money ourselves, and you are asking us to take this through the election." Alright, so arrangements were made through Mitchell, initiating it. And I was present in discussions where these guys had to be taken care of. Their attorneys' fees had to be done. [Herbert] Kalmbach was brought in. Kalmbach raised some cash.

P. They put that under the cover of a Cuban Committee, I suppose?

D. Well, they had a Cuban Committee and they had — some of it was given to Hunt's lawyer, who in turn passed it out. You know, when Hunt's wife was flying to Chicago with $10,000 she was actually, I understand after the fact now, was going to pass that money to one of the Cubans — to meet him in Chicago and pass it to somebody there.

P. (unintelligible) but I would certainly keep that cover for whatever it is worth.

D. That's the most troublesome post-thing because (1) Bob is involved in that; (2) John is involved in that; (3) I am involved in that; (4) Mitchell is involved in that. And that is an obstruction of justice.

P. In other words the bad it does. You were taking care of witnesses. How did Bob get in it?

D. Well, they ran out of money over there. Bob had $350,000 in a safe over here that was really set aside for polling purposes. And there was no other source of money, so they came over and said you all have got to give us some money. I had to go to Bob and say, "Bob, they need some money over there." He said "What for." So I had to tell him what it was for because he wasn't just about to send money over there willy-nilly. And John was involved in those discussions. And then we decided there was no price too high to pay to let this thing blow up in front of the election.

P. I think we should be able to handle that issue pretty well. May be some lawsuits.

D. I think we can too. Here is what is happening right now. What sort of brings matters to the (unintelligible). One, this is going to be a continual blackmail operation by Hunt and Liddy and the Cubans. No doubt about it. And McCord, who is another one involved. McCord has asked for nothing. McCord did ask to meet with somebody, with [former CRP agent] Jack Caulfield who is his old friend who had gotten him hired over there. And when Caulfield had him hired, he was a perfectly legitimate security man. And he wanted to talk about commutation, and things like that. And as you know Colson has talked indirectly to Hunt about commutation. All of these things are bad, in that they are problems, they are promises, they are commitments. They are the very sort of thing that the Senate is going to be looking most for. I don't think they can find them, frankly.

P. Pretty hard.

D. Pretty hard. Damn hard. It's all cash.

P. Pretty hard I mean as far as the witnesses are concerned.

D. Alright, now, the blackmail is continuing. Hunt called one of the lawyers from the Re-Election Committee on last Friday to leave it with him over the weekend. The guy came in to see me to give a message directly to me. From Hunt to me . . . Hunt has now made a direct threat against Ehrlichman. As a result of this, this is his blackmail. He says, "I will bring John Ehrlichman down to his knees and put him in jail. I have done enough seamy things for he and [White house aide Bud] Krogh, they'll never survive it."

P. Was he talking about Ellsberg?

D. Ellsberg, and apparently some other things. I don't know the full extent of it.

P. I don't know about anything else.

D. I don't know either, and I hate to learn some of these things. So that is that situation. Now, where are the soft points? How many people know about this? Well, let me go one step further in this whole thing. The Cubans that were used in the Watergate were also the same Cubans that Hunt and Liddy used for this California Ellsberg thing, for the break-in out there. So they are aware of that. How high their knowledge is, is something else. Hunt and Liddy, of course, are totally aware of it, of the fact that it is right out of the White House.

P. I don't know what the hell we did that for!

D. I don't know either.

P. What in the (expletive deleted) caused this? (unintelligible)

D. Mr. President, there have been a couple of things around here that I have gotten wind of. At one time there was a desire to do a second story job on the Brookings Institute where they had the Pentagon papers. Now I flew to California because I was told that John had instructed it and he said, "I really hadn't. It is a mis-impression, but for (expletive deleted), turn it off." So I did. I came back and turned it off. The risk is minimal and the pain is fantastic. It is something with a (unintelligible) risk and no gain. It is just not worth it. But — who knows about all this now? You've got the Cubans' lawyer, a man by the name of Rothblatt, who is a no good, publicity seeking (characterization deleted), to be very frank with you. He has had to be pruned down and tuned off. He was canned by his own people because they didn't trust him. He didn't want them to plead guilty. He wants to represent them before the Senate. So F. Lee Bailey, who was a partner of one of the men representing McCord, got in and cooled Rothblatt down. So that means that F. Lee Bailey has knowledge. Hunt's lawyer, a man by the name of Bittmann, who is an excellent criminal lawyer from the Democratic era of Bobby Kennedy, he's got knowledge.

P. He's got some knowledge?

D. Well, all the direct knowledge that Hunt and Liddy have, as well as all the hearsay they have. You have these two lawyers over at the Re-Election Committee who did an investigation to find out the facts. Slowly, they got the whole picture. They are solid.

P. But they know?

D. But they know. You've got, then, an awful lot of the principals involved who know. Some people's wives know. Mrs. Hunt was the savviest woman in the world. She had the whole picture together.

P. Did she?

D. Yes. Apparently, she was the pillar of strength in that family before the death.

P. Great sadness. As a matter of fact, there was a discussion with somebody about Hunt's problem on account of his wife and I said, of course commutation could be considered on the basis of his wife's death, and that is the only conversation I ever had in that light.

D. Right.

D. So that is it. That is the extent of the knowledge. So where are the soft spots on this? Well, first of all, there is the problem of the continued blackmail which will not only go on now, but it will go on while these people are in prison, and it will compound the obstruction of justice situation. It will cost money. It is dangerous. People around here are not pros at this sort of thing. This is the sort of thing Mafia people can do: washing money, getting clean money, and things like that. We just don't know about those things . . .

P. That's right.

D. It is a tough thing to know how to do.

P. Maybe it takes a gang to do that . . . How much money do you need?

D. I would say these people are going to cost a million dollars over the next two years.

P. We could get that. On the money, if you need the money you could get that. You could get a million dollars. You could get it in cash. I know where it could be gotten. It is not easy, but it could be done. But the question is who the hell would handle it? Any ideas on that?

D. That's right. Well, I think that is something that Mitchell ought to be charged with.

P. I would think so too.

D. And get some pros to help him . . .

D. Let me continue a little bit right here now. When I say this is a growing cancer, I say if for reasons like this. Bud Krogh, in his testimony before the Grand Jury, was forced to perjure himself. He is haunted by it. Bud said, "I have not had a pleasant day on my job." He said, "I told my wife all about this. The curtain may ring down one of these days, and I may have to face the music, which I am perfectly willing to do."

P. What did he perjure himself on, John?

D. Did he know the Cubans? He did.

P. He said he didn't?

D. That is right. They didn't press him hard.

P. He might be able to — I am just trying to think. Perjury is an awful hard rap to prove . . .

D. Well, so that is one perjury. Mitchell and Magruder are potential perjurers. There is always the possibility of any one of these individuals blowing. Hunt. Liddy. Liddy is in jail right now, serving his time and having a good time right now. I think Liddy in his own bizarre way the strongest of all of them. So there is that possibility.

P. Your major guy to keep under control is Hunt?

D. That is right.

P. I think. Does he know a lot?

D. He knows so much. He could sink Chuck Colson. Apparently he is quite distressed with Colson. He thinks Colson has abandoned him. Colson was to meet with him when he was out there after, you know, he had left the White House. He met with him through his lawyer. Hunt raised the question he wanted money. Colson's lawyer told him Colson wasn't doing anything with money. Hunt took offense with that immediately, and felt Colson had abandoned him.

P. Just looking at the immediate problem, don't you think you have to handle Hunt's financial situation damn soon?

D. I think that is — I talked with Mitchell about that last night and —

P. It seems to me we have to keep the cap on the bottle that much, or we don't have any options.

D. That's right.

P. Either that or it all blows right now?

D. That's the question . . . What really bothers me is this growing situation. As I say, it is growing because of the continued need to provide support for the Watergate people who are going to hold us up for everything we've got, and the need for some people to perjure themselves as they go down the road here. If this thing ever blows, then we are in a cover up situation. I think it would be extremely damaging to you and the —

P. Sure. The whole concept of Administration justice. Which we cannot have!

D. That is what really troubles me. For example, what happens if it starts breaking, and they do find a criminal case against a Haldeman, a Dean, a Mitchell, an Ehrlichman? That is —

P. If it really comes down to that, we would have to (unintelligible) some of the men.

D. That's right. I am coming down to what I really think, is that Bob and John and John Mitchell and I can sit down and spend a day, or however long, to figure out one, how this can be carved away from you, so that it does not damage you or the Presidency. It just can't! You are not involved in it and it is something you shouldn't —

P. That is true!

D. I know, sir. I can just tell from our conversation that these are things that you have no knowledge of.

P. You certainly can! Buggings, etc! Let me say I am keenly aware of the fact Colson, et al., were doing their best to get information as we went along. But they all knew very well they were supposed to comply with the law. There was no question about that! You feel that really the trigger man was really Colson on this then?

D. No. He was one of us. He was just in the chain. He helped push the thing . . .

P. Let's come back to this problem. What are your feelings yourself, John? You know what they are all saying. What are your feelings about the chances?

D. I am not confident that we can ride through this. I think there are soft spots.

P. You used to be —

D. I am not comfortable for this reason. I have noticed of recent — since the publicity has increased on this thing again, with the Gray hearings, that everybody is now starting to watch after their behind. Everyone is getting their own counsel. More counsel are getting involved. How do I protect my ass?

P. They are scared . . .

P. So what you really come to is what we do. Let's suppose that you and Haldeman and Ehrlichman and Mitchell say we can't hold this? What then are you going to say? What are you going to put out after it? Complete disclosure, isn't that the best way to do it?

D. Well, one way to do it is —

P. That would be my view —

D. One way to do it is for you to tell the Attorney General that you finally know. Really, this is the first time you are getting all the pieces together.

P. Ask for another Grand Jury?

D. Ask for another Grand Jury. The way it should be done though, is a way — for example, I think that we could avoid criminal liability for countless people and the ones that did get it could be minimal.

P. How?

D. Well . . . You know, some people could be granted immunity.

P. Like Magruder?

D. Yeah. To come forward. But some people are going to have to go to jail. That is the long and short of it, also.

P. Who? Let's talk about —

D. Alright. I think I could. For one.

P. You go to jail?

D. That's right.

P. Oh, hell no! I can't see how you can.

D. Well, because —

P. I can't see how. Let me say I can't see how a legal case could be made against you, John.

D. It would be tough but, you know, I can see people pointing fingers. You know, to get it out of their own, put me in an impossible position. Just really give me a (unintelligible).

P. Oh, no! Let me say I got the impression here — but just looking at it from a cold legal standpoint: you are a lawyer, you were a counsel — doing what you did as counsel. You were not — What would you go to jail for?

D. The obstruction of justice.

P. The obstruction of justice?

D. That is the only one that bothers me.

P. Well, I don't know. I think that one. I feel it could be cut off at the pass, maybe, the obstruction of justice . . . Let me put it this way: let us suppose that you get the million bucks, and you get the proper way to handle it. You could hold that side?

D. Uh, huh.

P. It would seem to me that would be worthwhile.

D. Well, that's one problem.

P. I know you have a problem here. You have the problem with Hunt and his clemency.

D. That's right. And you are going to have a clemency problem with the others. They all are going to expect to be out and that may put you in a position that is just untenable at some point. You know, the Watergate Hearings just over, Hunt now demanding clemency or he is going to blow. And politically, it's impossible for you to do it. You know, after everybody —

P. That's right!

D. I am not sure that you will ever be able to deliver on the clemency. It may be just too hot.

P. You can't do it politically until after the '74 elections, that's for sure. Your point is that even then you couldn't do it.

D. That's right. It may further involve you in a way you should not be involved in this.

P. No — it is wrong, that's for sure.

Dean and the President take stock of some grim options:

P. Suppose the worst — that Bob is indicted and Ehrlichman is indicted. And I must say, we just better then try to tough it through. You get the point.

D. That's right.

P. If they, for example, say let's cut our losses and you say we are going to go down the road to see if we can cut our losses and no more blackmail and all the rest. And then the thing blows cutting Bob and the rest to pieces. You would never recover from that, John.

D. That's right.

P. It is better to fight it out. Then you see that's the other thing. It's better to fight it out and not let people testify, and so forth. And now, on the other hand, we realize that we have these weaknesses . . . in terms of blackmail.

D. There are two routes. One is to figure out how to cut the losses and minimize the human impact and get you up and out and away from it in any way. In a way it would never come back to haunt you. That is one general alternative. The other is to go down the road, just hunker down, fight it at every corner, every turn, don't let people testify — cover it up is what we really are talking about. Just keep it buried, and just hope that we can do it, hope that we make good decisions at the right time, keep our heads cool, we make the right moves.

P. And just take the heat?

D. And just take the heat.

P. Now with the second line of attack. You can discuss this (unintelligible) the way you want to. Still consider my scheme of having you brief the Cabinet, just in very general terms and the leaders in very general terms and maybe some very general statement with regard to my investigation. Answer questions, basically on the basis of what they told you, not what you know. Haldeman is not involved. Ehrlichman is not involved.

D. If we go that route Sir, I can give a show we can sell them just like we were selling Wheaties on our position. There's no —

P. The problem that you have are these mine fields down the road. I think the most difficult problem are the guys who are going to jail. I think you are right about that.

D. I agree.

P. Now. And also the fact that we are not going to be able to give them clemency.

D. That's right. How long will they take? How long will they sit there? I don't know. We don't know what they will be sentenced to. There's always a chance —

P. Thirty years, isn't it?

D. It could be. You know, they haven't announced yet, but it —

P. Top is thirty years, isn't it?

D. It is even higher than that. It is about fifty years. It all —

P. So ridiculous!

D. And what is so incredible is, he is (unintelligible)

P. People break and enter, etc., and get two years. No weapons! No results! What the hell are they talking about?

Turning to the Ellsberg burglary, Dean, the President, and Haldeman, who has joined them, search for a way to explain the affair:

D. You might put it on a national security grounds basis.

H. It absolutely was.

D. And say that this was —

H. (unintelligible) — CIA —

D. Ah —

H. Seriously.

P. National Security. We had to get information for national security . . .

D. Then the question is, why didn't the CIA do it or why didn't the FBI do it?

P. Because we had to do it on a confidential basis.

H. Because we were checking them.

P. Neither could be trusted.

H. It has basically never been proven. There was reason to question their position.

P. With the bombing thing coming out and everything coming out, the whole thing was national security.

D. I think we could get by on that.

P. On that one I think we should simply say this was a national security investigation that was conducted.

Next the three men discuss the tactics used by Charles Colson to keep the seven Watergate burglary defendants in line:

H. What's he planning on, money?

D. Money and —

H. Really?

P. It's about $120,000. That's what, Bob. That would be easy. It is not easy to deliver, but it is easy to get . . .

H. If the case is just that way, then the thing to do if the thing cranks out.

P. If, for example, you say look we are not going to continue to — let's say, frankly, on the assumption that if we continue to cut our losses, we are not going to win. But in the end, we are going to be bled to death. And in the end, it is all going to come out anyway. Then you get the worst of both worlds. We are going to lose, and people are going to —

H. And look like dopes!

P. And in effect, look like a cover-up. So that we can't do. Now the other line, however, if you take that line, that we are not going to continue to cut our losses, that means then we have to look square in the eye as to what the hell those losses are, and see which people can — so we can avoid criminal liability. Right?

D. Right.

P. And that means keeping it off you. Herb has started this Justice thing. We've got to keep it off Herb. You have to keep it, naturally, off of Bob, off Chapin, if possible, Strachan, right?

D. Uh, huh.

P. And Mitchell. Right?

D. Uh, huh.

H. And Magruder, if you can.

P. John Dean's point is that if Magruder goes down, he will pull everybody with him.

H. That's my view. Yep, I think Jeb, I don't think he wants to. And I think he even would try not to, but I don't think he is able not to.

D. I don't think he is strong enough.

P. Another way to do it then Bob, and John realizes this, is to continue to try to cut our losses. Now we have to take a look at that course of action. First it is going to require approximately a million dollars to take care of the jackasses who are in jail. That can be arranged. That could be arranged. But you realize that after we are gone, and assuming we can expend this money, then they are going to crack and it would be an unseemly story. Frankly, all the people aren't going to care that much.

D. That's right.

P. People won't care, but people are going to be talking about it, there is no question. And the second thing is, we are not going to be able to deliver on any of a clemency thing. You know Colson has gone around on this clemency thing with Hunt and the rest?

D. Hunt is now talking about being out by Christmas.

H. This year?

D. This year. He was told by [CRP attorney Paul] O'Brien, who is my conveyor of doom back and forth, that hell, he would be lucky if he were out a year from now, or after Ervin's hearings were over. He said how in the Lord's name could you be commuted that quickly? He said, "Well, that is my commitment from Colson."

H. By Christmas of this year?

D. Yeah.

H. See that, really, that is verbal evil. Colson is — That is your fatal flaw in Chuck. He is an operator in expediency, and he will pay at the time and where he is to accomplish whatever he is there to do. And that, and that's — I would believe that he has made that commitment if Hunt says he has. I would believe he is capable of saying that.

P. The only thing we could do with him would be to parole him like the (unintelligible) situation. But you couldn't buy clemency.

D. Kleindienst has now got control of the Parole Board, and he said to tell me we could pull Paroles off now where we couldn't before. So —

H. Kleindienst always tells you that, but I never believe it.

P. Paroles — let the (unintelligible) worry about that. Parole, in appearance, etc., is something I think in Hunt's case, you could do Hunt, but you couldn't do the others. You understand.

The other defendants in the break-in seem to be cooperating with the White House. But Howard Hunt is a serious problem:

D. [The others are] going to stonewall it, as it now stands. Excepting Hunt. That's why his threat.

H. It's Hunt opportunity.

P. That's why for your immediate things you have no choice but to come up with the $120,000, or whatever it is. Right?

D. That's right.

P. Would you agree that that's the prime thing that you damn well better get that done?

D. Obviously he ought to be given some signal anyway . . .

P. Well look, what is it you need on that? When — I am not familiar with the money situation . . .

D. . . . You have to wash the money. You can get a $100,000 out of a bank, and it all comes in serialized bills.

P. I understand.

D. And that means you have to go to Vegas with it or a bookmaker in New York City. I have learned all these things after the fact. I will be in great shape for the next time around.

H. (Expletive deleted)?

Presidential Transition: Forming a New Administration

The change from one presidential administration to another, called the "presidential transition," is never easy. It is usually characterized by "muddling through" on the part of the president-elect, his staff, new Cabinet officials, and the transition team.[1] There are poignant moments for the outgoing administration, which are counterbalanced by times of elation and frenzy for the incoming administration. In the following selection Henry Kissinger describes his experiences with a presidential transition from the vantage point of his position as the president-elect's newly appointed Assistant for National Security Affairs.

[1] The term "to muddle through" is chiefly British. It is defined by the American Heritage Dictionary as meaning "to push on to a successful conclusion in a disorganized way."

42
Henry Kissinger

PERIOD OF INNOCENCE:
THE TRANSITION

GETTING ACQUAINTED

The period immediately after an electoral victory is a moment of charmed innocence. The President-elect is liberated from the harrowing uncertainty, the physical and psychological battering, of his struggle for the great prize. For the first time in months and perhaps in years, he can turn to issues of substance. He and his entourage share the exhilaration of imminent authority but are not yet buffeted by its ambiguities and pressures. His advisers are suddenly catapulted from obscurity into the limelight. Their every word and action are now analyzed by journalists, diplomats, and foreign intelligence services as a clue to future policy. Usually such scrutiny is vain; the entourage of a candidate have no time to address the problem of governance; nor have they been selected for their mastery of issues. And after the election is over they are soon consumed by the practical problems of organizing a new administration.

So it was with me. One of the most delicate tasks of a new appointee is how to handle the transition with one's predecessors. I stayed out of Washington as much as possible. Walt Rostow, President Johnson's security adviser, gave me an office in the Executive Office Building next door to the White House and suggested generously that I begin following the daily cables. I thought this unwise since I had no staff to help me assess the information they contained.

My feelings toward Johnson and Rostow were warm and friendly; soon after my appointment I called on them to pay my respects. I had met President Johnson a few times but had never worked for him directly. In 1967, I had conducted a negotiation for him with the North Vietnamese through two French intermediaries. In that connection, I had attended a meeting he held in the Cabinet Room with his senior advisers. I was impressed and oddly touched by this hulking, powerful man, so domineering and yet so insecure, so overwhelming and yet so vulnerable. It was President Johnson's tragedy that he became identified with a national misadventure that was already long in the making by the time he took office and in the field of foreign policy for which his finely tuned political antennae proved worthless. President Johnson did not take naturally to international relations. One never had the impression that he would think about the topic spontaneously — while shaving, for example. He did not trust his own judgment; he therefore relied on advisers, most of whom he had not appointed and whose way of thinking was not really congenial to him. Many of these advisers were themselves without bearings amidst the upheavals of the 1960s. Some of them were growing restless with the consequences of their own recommendations and began to work against policies which they themselves had designed.

No President had striven so desperately for approbation, and none since Andrew Johnson had been more viciously attacked. LBJ had labored for a special place in history; his legislative accomplishments and authentic humanitarianism will in time earn it for him. But the very qualities of compromise and consultation on which his domestic political successes were based proved disastrous in foreign policy. Too tough for the liberal wing of his party, too hesitant for its more conservative elements, Lyndon Johnson could never mount an international enterprise that commanded the wholehearted support of either his party or the nation. He took advice that he thought better informed than his more elemental instincts, finally cutting himself off from all constituencies as well as from his emotional roots.

When I called on him in the Oval Office, President Johnson was in a melancholy mood. For the outgoing, the transition (as I later learned) is a somber time. The surface appurtenances of power still exist; the bureaucracy continues to produce the paperwork for executive decision. But authority is slipping away. Decisions of which officials disapprove will be delayed in implementation; foreign governments go through the motions of diplomacy but reserve their best efforts and their real attention for the new team. And yet so familiar has the exercise of power become that its loss is sensed only dimly and intermittently. Days go by in which one carries out one's duties as if one's actions still matter.

So it was with President Johnson. The walls of the Oval Office in his day were lined with television sets and news tickers noisily disgorging their copy. It was strange to see the most powerful leader in the world, with instant access to all the information of our intelligence services, jumping up periodically to see what the news ticker was revealing.

He launched into a long soliloquy about the war in Vietnam. He urged that we apply military pressure and at the same time pursue serious negotiations; he did not describe precisely what he had in mind for either course. He advised me to ensure that the bureaucracy was loyal; he had been destroyed, in part, he thought, by systematic leaking. "I have one piece of advice to give you, Professor," he said, and I leaned forward to profit from the distilled wisdom of decades of public service. "Read the columnists," he added, "and if they call a member of your staff thoughtful, dedicated, or any other friendly adjective, fire him immediately. He is your leaker." I left the Oval Office determined to do my utmost to spare the new Administration the heartache and isolation of Johnson's waning days.

The transition period leaves little time for such reflections, however. My immediate problem was more mundane: to establish my relationship with the advisers who had been with Nixon during the campaign and to recruit a staff.

It would have required superhuman qualities of tolerance for some in the Nixon team not to resent an outsider who seemed to have the best of all worlds: what they considered the glamorous aura of a Harvard professor and Rockefeller associate, and association with the President-elect after his victory. I had, after all, not been merely absent from the election struggle; I had been in the mainstream of those who had either been hostile to Nixon or disdained him. One of the most painful tasks of a new President is to cull from the entourage that helped him into office the men and women who can assist him in running it. This leads to almost unavoidable rivalry between those who have borne up the President-elect during his journey to election and the newcomers who appear to the old guard as interlopers reaping the fruits of their labors. Newcomers there must be because the qualities of a campaign aide are different from those of a policymaker. It takes a very special personality to join a Presidential aspirant early in a campaign when the odds against success are usually overwhelming. Campaign chores are highly technical and some are demeaning: the preparation of schedules, the "advancing" of rallies and meetings, the endless wooing of delegates or media representatives. A candidate's staffers are selected — or volunteer — on the basis of loyalty and endurance; they provide emotional support in an inherently anxious situation. With the firmest resolve or best intentions few can predict what they will do or stand for when the elusive goal of high office is finally reached; their performance in the campaign offers no clue to their capabilities in the Executive Branch.

This was a particular problem for the Nixon staff. The loyal few who had remained with Nixon after his defeat for the governorship of California in 1962 exemplified an almost perverse dedication and faith. According to all conventional wisdom, Nixon's political career was finished. His dogged pursuit of the Presidency was turning into a national joke (LBJ ridiculed him as a "chronic campaigner"). There were no early or obvious rewards — even the attention of those who bet on long odds — in sticking with so unlikely an aspirant. Only congenital outsiders would hazard everything on so improbable an enterprise. Such men and women were almost certain to feel beleaguered; they inherently lacked the ability to reach out.

Nor did this attitude lack a basis in fact; paranoia need not be unjustified to be real. When Nixon moved to New York in 1962, he was shunned by the people whose respect he might have expected as a former Vice President of the United States who had come within an eyelash of election as President. He was never invited by what he considered the "best" families. This rankled and compounded his already strong tendency to see himself beset by enemies. His associates shared his sense of isolation and resentment. The Nixon team drew the wagons around itself from the beginning; it was besieged in mind long before it was besieged in fact.

This fortress mentality, which was to have such a corrosive effect on the entire Administration, showed itself in many ways. The team was temperamentally unable, for instance, to exploit the opportunities of Washington's social life for oiling the wheels of national politics. Washington is a one-industry town where the work is a way of life. Everyone at the higher levels of government meets constantly in the interminable conferences by which government runs itself; they then encounter the same people in the evening together with a sprinkling of senior journalists, socially adept and powerful members of Congress, and the few members of the permanent Washington Establishment. To all practical purposes there is no topic of conversation except government, and that generally in Washington means not the national purpose but the relationship to one another of the key personalities in the Administration of the day: who, at any given point, is "up" and who is "down."

The criteria of this social life are brutal. They are geared substantially to power, its exercise and its decline. A person is accepted as soon as he enters the charmed circles of the holders of power. With the rarest exceptions, he is dropped when his position ends, his column is discontinued, or he is retired from Congress. There is no need to expend effort to crash this charmed circle; membership — or at least its availability — is nearly automatic; but so is the ultimate exclusion. In Washington the appearance of power is therefore almost as important as the reality of it; in fact, the appearance is frequently its essential reality. Since the topic of who is "up" and who is "down" is all-consuming, struggles result sometimes about nothing more than abstract bureaucratic designations.

Precisely because the official life is so formal, social life provides a mechanism for measuring intangibles and understanding nuances. Moods can be gauged by newspapermen and ambassadors and senior civil servants that are not discernible at formal meetings. It is at their dinner parties and receptions that the relationships are created without which the machinery of government would soon stalemate itself. The disdain of the Nixon entourage for this side of Washington complicated its actions and deprived it of the sensitivity to respond to brewing domestic anxieties.

I, too, it must be said, was ignorant of the ways of Washington or government when I proclaimed at the press conference announcing my new position that I would have no dealings with the press. As soon as my appointment was announced senior members of the press began calling to look me over. I was no little awed by the famous men whom I had read or listened to for years and whom I now was meeting at first hand. I saw

Walter Lippmann, James ("Scotty") Reston, and Joseph Alsop — of whom Reston and Alsop were to become personal friends. (Lippmann fell ill soon afterward.) Lippmann urged upon me the necessity of bringing American commitments into line with our resources, especially in Indochina and the Middle East. Reston talked to me with avuncular goodwill tinged with Calvinist skepticism, then and after, about the imperfectibility of man. Joe Alsop interviewed me with the attitude that his criteria for my suitability for high office would be more severe than Nixon's. He gave me to understand that his knowledge of the Indochina problem far exceeded that of any neophyte Presidential Assistant. I had the impression that he had suspended judgment about the wisdom of the President's choice and that I would remain on probation for some time to come.

The editors of *Newsweek* invited me to meet with them. Pedantically I explained once again the incompatibility between my position and any worthwhile briefing of the press. They greeted this information with the amused tolerance reserved for amateurs or victims.

I soon found how naive my attitude was. One of the most important functions of the Presidential Assistant is to explain the President's policies and purposes. I learned that I could not ignore the media and I began to see journalists, though at first almost always at their initiative. I experienced the symbiotic relationship in Washington between media and government. Much as the journalist may resent it, he performs a partly governmental function. He is the one person in town who can be reasonably sure that everyone who matters listens to him or hears him. Officials seek him out to bring their pet projects to general attention, to settle scores, or to reverse a decision that went against them. Whatever the official's motive, it cannot be disinterested. At a minimum he seeks to put himself in his best light. For the experienced Washington observer careful reading of the press or listening to the key commentators provides invaluable intelligence concerning the cross-currents of bureaucracy, or the subterranean gathering of pent-up political forces.

The journalist has comparably interested motives in his contacts with the official. He must woo and flatter the official because without his goodwill he will be deprived of information. But he cannot let himself be seduced — the secret dream of most officials — or he will lose his objectivity. A love-hate relationship is almost inevitable. Officials are tempted to believe that social relationships lay the groundwork for compassionate treatment; journalists often prove their "objectivity" by attacking precisely those who shower them with attention. If both sides are realistic and mature they will establish a mutual respect. The official will recognize that not seduction but the journalist's personal integrity is the ultimate guarantee of fairness. The journalist will accept that to the official duty is paramount, and that its requirements are not always identical with providing scoops. If both the makers of policy and its interpreters can respect each other's vital function, the resulting working relationship can be one of the strongest guarantees of a free society.

I soon discovered also that another of my original ideas could not survive. I had thought I could continue teaching at Harvard until just before Inauguration. It was impossible. I had to educate myself on my duties; I had to set up the machinery of analysis and planning promised by the President-elect during his campaign. Some of my education was supplied by consulting many men and women who had been prominent in the Eisenhower, Kennedy, and Johnson administrations. For the entire postwar period foreign policy had been ennobled by a group of distinguished men who, having established their eminence in other fields, devoted themselves to public service. Dean Acheson, David K. E. Bruce, Ellsworth Bunker, Averell Harriman, John McCloy, Robert Lovett, Douglas Dillon, among others, represented a unique pool of talent — an aristocracy dedicated to the service of this nation on behalf of principles beyond partisanship. Free peoples owe them gratitude for their achievements; Presidents and Secretaries of State have been sustained by their matter-of-fact patriotism and freely tendered wisdom. While I was in office they were always available for counsel without preconditions; nor was there ever fear that they would use governmental information for personal or political advantage. Unfortunately, when I came into office they were all in their seventies. My generation had men equal to them in intelligence; but none had yet been sufficiently tested to develop the selflessness and integrity that characterized their predecessors. As the older group leaves public office, they take with them one of the steadying and guiding factors in our foreign policy.

The member of this group whom I saw most frequently in the transition period was John McCloy; later, when I moved to Washington, Dean Acheson and David Bruce became close friends and advisers. With the body of a wrestler and a bullet head, John McCloy seemed more like a jovial gnome than a preeminent New York lawyer and perennial counselor of Presidents and Secretaries of State. On the surface, his influence was hard to account for. He had never served at the Cabinet level; the positions he had held were important but not decisive. He could be time-consuming with his penchant for anecdotes; his intelligence was balanced rather than penetrating. But high officials always face perplexing choices. Presidents and Secretaries of State found in John McCloy a reliable pilot through treacherous shoals. He rarely supplied solutions to difficult problems, but he never failed to provide the psychological and moral reassurance that made solutions possible. On my first day back in the office from an unsuccessful negotiation in the Middle East in 1975, I asked John McCloy to see me. He came, as requested, without a murmur. Only weeks later did I learn that it had been his eightieth birthday and that he had given up a family celebration, never dreaming of suggesting a twenty-four-hour postponement. He was always available. He was ever wise.

When I started choosing staff, frictions with the Nixon team developed immediately. By custom the responsibility for selecting the National Security Council staff fell to the President's national security adviser. As the first Presidential appointee in the foreign policy area I had the advantage of being able to begin recruiting early. As a White House assistant I was not limited by departmental or civil service practices. Thus, unrestrained by bureaucratic limitations and with the President-elect's charter to build a new organization from the ground up, I was determined to recruit the ablest and strongest individuals I could find.

While I hold strong opinions I have always felt it essential to test them against men and women of intelligence and character; those who stood up to me earned my respect and often became my closest associates. If my staff was to be of decisive influence in guiding interdepartmental planning, it had to substitute in quality for what it lacked in numbers. Indeed, its small size could be an advantage, since we could avoid the endless internal negotiations that stultify larger organizations. So I looked for younger men and women and promoted them rapidly, reasoning that someone well along in his career would have reached his level of performance and would be unlikely to do much better. on my staff than in his present position. I recruited professional officers from the Foreign Service, the Defense Department, and the intelligence community, both to gain the benefit of their experience and to help guide me through the bureaucratic maze; I hired talented people from the academic world. For balance, I strove for representatives of as many different points of view as possible.

I took the position that I would abide by security objections but would accept no other criterion than quality. Peter Flanigan, a Nixon associate responsible for political appointments (who later became a good friend), sent me six names of people who had been promised political appointments. After interviewing some of them, I rejected all. In at least two cases Haldeman challenged my staff selections on grounds of security, which turned out to be more a matter of liberal convictions or a propensity to talk to journalists. In both cases I overruled Haldeman.

Nixon invariably supported me. He had his private doubts and later, as public pressures began to mount, he came to regard my staff with disquiet. He suspected some of my colleagues of disliking him, which was correct, and of fueling the debate with leaks, for which there was never any evidence. But during the transition period Nixon backed my choices. He did so because he treated foreign policy differently from the domestic area. In domestic politics, he had used — and would use again — rough tactics and relied on some odd associates. To be fair, Nixon remained convinced to the end that in the domestic area he was following traditional practice for which a hypocritical Establishment, following an incomprehensible double standard, condemned only him. But foreign policy he regarded as something apart. Where the basic national interest and the security and progress of the free world were concerned his touchstone was to do what was right, not expedient, whatever the conventional practice, and when necessary against the conventional wisdom. Only in the rarest cases did he permit partisan interests to infringe on foreign policy decisions.

Though some of my personnel choices proved in the end unwise, the dedication and ability of my staff contributed fundamentally to the foreign policy successes of the first Nixon Administration. The core members — Winston Lord, Lawrence Eagleburger, Helmut Sonnenfeldt, William Hyland, Harold Saunders, Peter Rodman, and Alexander Haig — remained with me through all vicissitudes and became close friends as well. The high quality of this team was an important reason for the growing influence of the office of the President's national security adviser, and the viability of my office became crucial since Richard Nixon appointed a Cabinet of able, astute, and willful men that were never able to operate effectively as a team.

Presidential Power and Executive Privilege

On July 24, 1974, the Supreme Court in *United States* v. *Richard M. Nixon* rendered a historic decision interpreting the meaning of the separation of powers. President Nixon had attempted to claim executive privilege in refusing to obey a district court order to turn over tape recordings and other data involving White House conversations pertaining to the Watergate coverup. Special Watergate Prosecutor Leon Jaworski had successfully sought from District Court Judge John Sirica a subpoena directing the President to produce the tapes and documents, to be used as evidence in the trial of six former Nixon aides who were accused of conspiring to conceal the burglary in 1972 of the Democratic National Headquarters in the Watergate complex. The court held unanimously (Justice Rehnquist, one of Nixon's four appointees to the court, disqualified himself) that the President is subject to the judicial process, and cannot claim executive privilege in refusing to turn over the subpoenaed material on the general grounds that the material contained "confidential conversations between a President and his close advisors that it would be inconsistent with the public interest to produce." The court stated that although the separation of powers requires that each branch give deference to the others, only the courts have the power to say what the law is with respect to the claim of executive privilege. The proper scope of judicial power in a particular case and controversy cannot in any way be subject to presidential control.

UNITED STATES v. RICHARD M. NIXON
418 U.S. 683 (1974)

Mr. Chief Justice Burger delivered the opinion of the Court:

These cases present for review the denial of a motion, filed on behalf of the President of the United States, in the case of *United States* v. *Mitchell et al.* (D.C. Crim. No. 74–110), to quash a third party subpoena duces tecum [requires the party who is summoned to appear in court to bring some document or piece of evidence to be used or inspected by the court] issued by the United States District Court for the District of Columbia, pursuant to Fed. Rule Crim. Proc. 17 (C). The subpoena directed the President to produce certain tape recordings and documents relating to his conversations with aides and advisors. The Court rejected the President's claims of absolute executive privilege, of lack of jurisdiction, and of failure to satisfy the requirements of Rule 17 (C) [that the evidence sought must be specific, relevant to the case, and admissible in court]. The President appealed to the Court of Appeals. We granted the United States petition for certiorari before judgment, and also the President's responsive cross-petition for certiorari before judgment, because of the public importance of the issues presented and the need for their prompt resolution.

On March 1, 1974, a grand jury of the United States District Court for the District of Columbia returned an indictment charging seven named individuals with various offenses, including conspiracy to defraud the United States and to obstruct justice. Although he was not designated as such in the indictment, the grand jury named the President, among others, as an unindicted co-conspirator. On April 18, 1974, upon motion of the special prosecutor . . . a subpoena duces tecum was issued pursuant to Rule 17 (C) to the President by the United States District Court and made returnable on May 2, 1974. This subpoena required the production, in advance of the September 9 trial date, of certain tapes, memoranda, papers, transcripts, or other writings relating to certain precisely identified meetings between the President and others. The Special Prosecutor was able to fix the time, place, and persons present at these discussions because the White House daily logs and appointment records had been delivered to him.

On April 30, 1974, the President publicly released edited transcripts of forty-three conversations; portions of twenty conversations subject to subpoena in the present case were included. On May 1, 1974, the President's counsel filed a "special appearance" and a motion to quash the subpoena, under Rule 17 (C). This motion was accompanied by a formal claim of privilege. At a subsequent hearing, further motions to expunge the grand jury's action naming the President as an unindicted co-conspirator and for protective orders against the disclosure of that information were filed or raised orally by counsel for the President.

On May 20, 1974, the District Court denied the motion to quash and the motions to expunge and for protective orders. It further ordered "the President or any subordinate officer, official or employee with custody or control of the documents or objects subpoenaed," to deliver to the District Court, on or before May 31, 1974, the originals of all subpoenaed items, as well as an index and analysis of those items, together with tape copies of those portions of the subpoenaed recordings for which transcripts had been released to the public by the President on April 30. . . .

The District Court held that the judiciary, not the President, was the final arbiter of a claim of executive privilege. The court concluded that, under the circumstances of this case, the presumptive privilege was overcome by the Special Prosecutor's prima facie "demonstration of need sufficiently compelling to warrant judicial examination in chambers. . . ."

THE CLAIM OF PRIVILEGE

A

Having determined that the requirements of Rule 17 (e) were satisfied, we turn to the claim that the subpoena should be quashed because it demands "confidential conversations between a President and his close advisors that it would be inconsistent with the public interest to produce." . . . The first contention is a broad claim that the separation of powers doctrine precludes judicial review of a president's claim of privilege. The second contention is that if he does not prevail on the claim of absolute privilege, the Court should hold as a matter of constitutional law that the privilege prevails over the subpoena duces tecum.

In the performance of assigned constitutional duties each branch of the Government must initially interpret the Constitution, and the interpretation of its powers by any branch is due great respect from the others.

The President's counsel, as we have noted, reads the Constitution as providing an absolute privilege of confidentiality for all presidential communications. Many decisions of this Court, however, have unequivocally reaffirmed the holding of *Marbury* v. *Madison,* 1 Cranch 137 (1803), that "it is emphatically the province and duty of the Judicial department to say what the law is." . . .

No holding of the Court has defined the scope of judicial power specifically relating to the enforcement of a subpoena for confidential presidential communications for use in a criminal prosecution, but other exercises of powers by the executive branch and the legislative branch have been found invalid as in conflict with the Constitution. . . .

Our system of government "requires that Federal courts on occasion interpret the Constitution in a manner at variance with the construction given the document by another branch." . . .

Notwithstanding the deference each branch must accord the others, the "judicial power of the United States" vested in the Federal courts by Art. 111, Section 1, of the Constitution can no more be shared with the executive branch than the chief executive, for example, can share with the judiciary the veto power, or the Congress share with the judiciary the power to override a presidential veto. Any other conclusion would be contrary to the basic concept of separation of powers and the checks and balances that flow from the scheme of a tripartite Government. [See] the Federalist, No. 47, . . . We therefore reaffirm that it is "emphatically the province and the duty" of this court "to say what the law is" with respect to the claim of privilege presented in this case. *Marbury* v. *Madison,* supra, ...

B

In support of his claim of absolute privilege, the President's counsel urges two grounds one of which is common to all governments and one of which is peculiar to our system of separation of powers. The first ground is the valid need for protection of communications between high government officials and those who advise and assist them in the performance of their manifold duties; the importance of this confidentiality is too plain to require further discussion. Human experience teaches that those who expect public dissemination of their remarks may well temper candor with a concern for appearances and for their own interests to the detriment of the decision-making process. Whatever the nature of the privilege of confidentiality of presidential communications in the exercise of Art. 8 powers, the privilege can be said to derive from the supremacy of each branch within its own assigned area of constitutional duties. Certain powers and privileges flow from the nature of enumerated powers; the protection of the confidentiality of presidential communications has similar constitutional underpinnings.

The second ground asserted by the President's counsel in support of the claim of absolute privilege rests on the doctrine of separation of powers. Here it is argued that the independence of the executive branch within its own sphere, Humphrey's *Executor* v. *United States,* 295 U.S. 602, 629–630 (1935): *Kilbourn* v. *Thompson,* 103 U.S. 168, 190–191 (1880), insulates a President from a judicial subpoena in an ongoing criminal prosecution, and thereby protects confidential presidential communications.

However, neither the doctrine of separation of powers, nor the need for confidentiality of high level communications, without more, can sustain an absolute unqualified presidential privilege of immunity from judicial process under all circumstances. The President's need for complete candor and objectivity from advisors calls for great deference from the courts. However, when the privilege depends solely on the broad, undifferentiated claim of public interest in the confidentiality of such conversations, a confrontation with other values arises. Absent a claim of need to protect military, diplomatic, or sensitive national security secrets, we find it difficult to accept the argument that even the very important interest in confidentiality of presidential communications is significantly diminished by production of such material for in camera inspection [in the judge's chambers] with all the protection that a District Court will be obliged to provide.

The impediment that an absolute, unqualified privilege would place in the way of the primary constitutional duty of the judicial branch to do justice in criminal prosecutions would plainly conflict with the function of the courts under Art. III. In designing the structure of our government and dividing and allocating the sovereign power among three coequal branches, the framers of the Constitution sought to provide a comprehensive system, but the separate powers were not intended to operate with absolute independence.

"While the Constitution diffuses power the better to secure liberty, it also contemplates that practice will integrate the dispersed powers into a workable Government. It enjoins upon its branches separateness but interdependence, autonomy but reciprocity. *Youngstown Sheet & Tube Co.* v. *Sawyer,* 343 U.S. 579, 635 (1952) (Jackson, J., concurring)."

To read the Art. II powers of the President as providing an absolute privilege as against a subpoena essential to enforcement of criminal statutes on no more than a generalized claim of the public interest in confidentiality of nonmilitary and nondiplomatic discussions would upset the constitutional balance of "a workable government" and gravely impair the role of the courts under Art. III.

C

Since we conclude that the legitimate needs of the judicial process may outweigh presidential privilege, it is necessary to resolve those competing interests in a manner that preserves the essential functions of each branch. The right and indeed the duty to resolve that question does not free the judiciary from according high respect to the representations made on behalf of the President. *United States* v. *Burr,* 25 Fed. Cas. 187, 190, 191–192 (No. 14,694) (1807).

The expectation of a president to the confidentiality of his conversations and correspondence, like the claim of confidentiality of judicial deliberations, for example, has all the values to which we accord deference for the privacy of all citizens and added to those values the necessity for protection of the public interest in candid, objective, and even blunt or harsh opinions in presidential decision-making. A president and those who assist him must be free to explore alternatives in the process of shaping policies and making decisions and to do so in a way many would be unwilling to express except privately. These are the considerations justifying a presumptive privilege for presidential communications. The privilege is fundamental to the operation of government and inextricably rooted in the separation of powers under the Constitution. In *Nixon* v. *Sirica,* 487 F. 2d 700 (1973), the Court of Appeals held that such presidential communications are "presumptively privileged," id., at 717, and this position is accepted by both parties in the present litigation.

We agree with Mr. Chief Justice Marshall's observation, therefore, that "in no case of this kind would a Court be required to proceed against the President as against an ordinary individual." *United States* v. *Burr,* 25 Fed. Cas. 187, 191 (No. 14,694) (CCD Va. 1807).

But this presumptive privilege must be considered in light of our historic commitment to the rule of law. This is nowhere more profoundly manifest than in our view that "the twofold aim [of criminal justice] is that guilt shall not escape or innocence suffer." *Berger* v. *United States,* 295 U.S. 18, 88 (1935). We have elected to employ an adversary system of criminal justice in which the parties contest all issues before a court of law. The need to develop all relevant facts in the adversary system is both fundamental and comprehensive. The ends of criminal justice would be defeated if judgments were to be founded on a partial or speculative presentation of the facts. The very integrity of the judicial system and public confidence in the system depend on full disclosure of all the facts, within the framework of the rules of evidence.

To ensure that justice is done, it is imperative to the function of courts that compulsory process be available for the production of evidence needed either by the prosecution or by the defense.

Only recently the Court restated the ancient proposition of law, albeit in the context of a grand jury inquiry rather than a trial,

" 'That the public . . . has a right to every man's evidence' except for those persons protected by a constitutional, common law, or statutory privilege, *United States* v. *Bryan,* 339 U.S., at 331 (1949); *Blackmer* v. *United States,* 284 U.S. 421, 438, *Branzburg* v. *United States,* 408 U.S. 665, 638 (1972)."

The privileges referred to by the Court are designed to protect weighty and legitimate competing interests. Thus, the Fifth Amendment to the Constitution provides that no man "shall be compelled in any criminal case to be a witness against himself."

And, generally, an attorney or a priest may not be required to disclose what has been revealed in professional confidence. These and other interests are recognized in law by privileges against forced disclosure, established in the Constitution, by statute, or at common law. Whatever their origins, these exceptions to the demand for every man's evidence are not lightly created nor expansively construed, for they are in derogation of the search for truth.

In this case the President challenges a subpoena served on him as a third party requiring the production of materials for use in a criminal prosecution on the claim that he has a privilege against disclosure of confidential communications. He does not place his claim of privilege on the ground they are military or diplomatic secrets. As to these areas of Art. II duties the courts have traditionally shown the utmost deference to presidential responsibilities. In *C. & S. Air Lines* v. *Waterman Steamship Corp.,* 333 U.S. 103, 111 (1948), dealing with presidential authority involving foreign policy considerations, the Court said:

"The President, both as commander-in-chief and as the nation's organ for foreign affairs, has available intelligence services whose reports are not and ought not to be published to the world. It would be intolerable that courts, without the relevant information, should review and perhaps nullify actions of the executive taken on information properly held secret." Id., at 111.

In *United States* v. *Reynolds,* 345 U.S. 1 (1952), dealing with a claimant's demand for evidence in a damage case against the government the Court said:

"It may be possible to satisfy the Court, from all the circumstances of the case, that there is a reasonable danger that compulsion of the evidence will expose military matters which, in the interest of national security, should not be divulged. When this is the case, the occasion for the privilege is appropriate, and the Court should not jeopardize the security which the privilege is meant to protect by insisting upon an examination of the evidence, even by the judge alone, in chambers."

No case of the Court, however, has extended this high degree of deference to a President's generalized interest in confidentiality. Nowhere in the Constitution as we have noted earlier, is there any explicit reference to a privilege of confidentiality, yet to the extent this interest relates to the effective discharge of a President's powers, it is constitutionally based.

The right to the production of all evidence at a criminal trial similarly has constitutional dimensions. The Sixth Amendment explicitly confers upon every defendant in a criminal trial the right "to be confronted with the witnesses against him" and "to have compulsory process for obtaining witnesses in his favor." Moreover, the Fifth Amendment also guarantees that no person shall be deprived of liberty without due process of law. It is the manifest duty of the courts to vindicate those guarantees and to accomplish that it is essential that all relevant and admissible evidence be produced.

In this case we must weigh the importance of the general privilege of confidentiality of presidential communications in performance of his responsibilities against the inroads of such a privilege on the fair administration of criminal justice. The interest in preserving confidentiality is weighty indeed and entitled to great respect. However we cannot conclude that advisors will be moved to temper the candor of their remarks by the infrequent occasions of disclosure because of the possibility that such conversations will be called for in the context of a criminal prosecution.

On the other hand, the allowance of the privilege to withhold evidence that is demonstrably relevant in a criminal trial would cut deeply into the guarantee of due process of law and gravely impair the basic function of the courts. A President's acknowledged need for confidentiality in the communications of his office is general in nature, whereas the constitutional need for production of relevant evidence in a criminal proceeding is specific and central to the fair adjudication of a particular criminal case in the administration of justice.

Without access to specific facts a criminal prosecution may be totally frustrated. The President's broad interest in confidentiality of communications will not be vitiated by disclosure of a limited number of conversations preliminarily shown to have some bearing on the pending criminal cases.

We conclude that when the ground for asserting privilege as to subpoenaed materials sought for use in a criminal trial is based only on the generalized interest in confidentiality, it cannot prevail over the fundamental demands of due process of law in the fair administration of criminal justice. The generalized assertion of privilege must yield to the demonstrated, specific need for evidence in a pending criminal trial.

D

We have earlier determined that the District Court did not err in authorizing the issuance of the subpoena. If a President concludes that compliance with a subpoena would be injurious to the public interest he may properly, as was done here, invoke a claim of privilege on the return of the subpoena. Upon receiving a claim of privilege from the chief executive, it became the further duty of the District Court to treat the subpoenaed material as presumptively privileged and to require the Special Prosecutor to demonstrate that the presidential material was "essential to the justice of the [pending criminal] case." *United States* v. *Burr,* supra, at 192. Here the District Court treated the material as presumptively privileged, proceeded to find that the Special Prosecutor had made a sufficient showing to rebut the presumption and ordered an in camera examination of the subpoenaed material.

On the basis of our examination of the record we are unable to conclude that the District Court erred in ordering the inspection. Accordingly we affirm the order of the District Court that subpoenaed materials be transmitted to that court. We now turn to the important quesion of the District Court's responsibilities in conducting the in camera examination of presidential materials or communications delivered under the compulsion of the subpoena duces tecum.

E

Enforcement of the subpoena duces tecum was stayed pending this Court's resolution of the issues raised by the petitions for certiorari. Those issues now having been disposed of, the matter of implementation will rest with the district court. "[T]he guard, furnished to [The President] to protect him from being harassed by vexations and unnecessary subpoenas, is to be looked for in the conduct of the [District] Court after the subpoenas have issued; not in any circumstances which is to precede their being issued." *United States* v. *Burr,* supra, at 34. Statements that meet the test of admissibility and relevance must be isolated; all other material must be excised. At this stage, the District Court is not limited to representations of the Special Prosecutor as to the evidence sought by the subpoena; the material will be available to the District Court. It is elementary that in camera inspection of evidence is always a procedure calling for scrupulous protection against any release or publication of material not found by the Court, at that stage, probably admissible in evidence and relevant to the issues of the trial for which it is sought. That being true of an ordinary situation, it is obvious that the District Court has a very heavy responsibility to see to it that presidential conversations which are either not relevant or not admissible, are accorded that high degree of respect due the President of the United States. Mr. Chief Justice Marshall sitting as a trial judge in the Burr case, supra, was extraordinarily careful to point out that:

". . . [I]n no case of this kind would a court be required to proceed against the President as against an ordinary individual." *United States* v. *Burr,* 25 Fed. Cases 187, 191 (No. 14,694).

Marshall's statement cannot be read to mean in any sense that a president is above the law, but relates to the singularly unique role under Art. II of a President's communications and activities related to the performance of duties under that Article. Moreover, a President's communications and activities encompass a vastly wider range of sensitive material than would be true of any "ordinary individual." It is therefore necessary in the public interest to afford presidential confidentiality the greatest protection consistent with the fair administration of justice. The need for confidentiality even as to idle conversations with associates in which casual reference might be made concerning political leaders within the country or foreign statesmen is too obvious to call for further treatment. We have no doubt that the District Judge will at all times accord to presidential records that high degree of deference suggested in *United States* v. *Burr,* supra, and will discharge his responsibility to see to it that until released to the Special Prosecutor no in camera material is revealed to anyone. This burden applies with even greater force to excised material; once the decision is made to excise, the material is restored to its privileged status and should be returned under seal to its lawful custodian.

Since the matter came before the Court during the pendency of a criminal prosecution, and on representations that time is of the essence, the mandate shall issue forthwith.

Affirmed.

Mr. Justice Rehnquist took no part in the consideration or decision of these cases.

Judging the Presidency

The presidency, standing as it does at the focal point of our political system and drawing into its vortex the expectations of the American people about government performance, virtually guarantees that presidents will strive to excel in their performance in the White House. In particular, presidents who view the office as the center of political activity and the major source of policy initiative hope to be judged as among the great presidents of history. Before Watergate Richard Nixon, who viewed the presidency as an active-conservative force, hoped to take his place among the great presidents in American history. Presidential "greatness" is almost surely an aspiration of Jimmy Carter.

Running for the position of great president may have an important effect upon performance in the White House. All candidates for greatness are well aware that historians will judge them on the basis of what they have accomplished, the decisions they have made, and the actions they have taken that exhibit leadership. Sometimes Presidents feel that the appearance of leadership is as important as the real thing. Style may be substituted for substance. Above all, a President seeking greatness will always strive to aggrandize the presidency in word and deed. This means raising the level of popular expectation about what the president can do to meet and solve national problems, and at the same time demanding support for unilateral presidential actions that may circumvent the carefully constructed constitutional processes of separation of powers and checks and balances. Many "great" Presidents have not paid enough attention to constitutional niceties nor respected the coequal role in the governmental process of Congress and the Supreme Court. In the following selection Nelson Polsby argues that while presidential performance may be enhanced because of aspirations to achieve greatness, it is more common for such strivings to produce difficulties and reduce effective leadership.

44

Nelson W. Polsby

AGAINST PRESIDENTIAL GREATNESS

Until election day is past, candidates for President campaign among their fellow citizens with the simple end in view of being elected. Once they are inaugurated, however, Presidents frequently yearn for an even higher office — a niche in the pantheon of "great" Presidents. Membership in this exclusive society is, on the whole, not to be achieved through sheer popularity. Was there ever a more popular President than Dwight D. Eisenhower? Yet we all "know" he was not a "great" President, nor even a "near great" one.

How do we know this? Essentially I think the answer is: we know it because historians tell us so. In each generation, or possibly over a shorter span, a consensus arises among the authors of political and historical texts about how well various Presidents met the alleged needs of their times. These opinions are in turn the distillate of writings of journalists and other leading opinion-makers who were contemporaries of the various Presidents, filtered through the ideological predispositions of the current batch of history writers.

This means that running for great President is a chancy business, since the admissions committee is small and self-conscious, somewhat shifty-eyed, and possibly even harder to please than, let us say, the wonderful folks who guard the lily-white portals of the Chevy Chase Club. Some Presidents are smart enough to take out a little insurance. Surely that was one extremely good reason for John Kennedy to invite Arthur Schlesinger, Jr., to join his White House staff and to encourage him to keep notes. Schlesinger's father, also a distinguished historian, was after all the author of two well-publicized surveys of historians — in 1949 and 1962 — that ranked Presidents for overall greatness.

Lyndon Johnson and, evidently, Richard Nixon, pursued somewhat different strategies. Apparently neither found a court historian wholly to his liking — though after an unsatisfactory experience with Eric Goldman, perhaps Johnson found Doris Kearns more tractable and useful for somewhat similar purposes. Both recent Presidents caused their administrations to engage in what might be called over-documentation of their official activ-

From Nelson W. Polsby, "Against Presidential Greatness." Reprinted from *Commentary,* January 1977, by permission; all rights reserved.

ities. Johnson hauled tons of stuff down to his museum in Texas where a staff composed "his" memoirs at leisure. One assumes the Nixon tapes, had they remained undiscovered, would have been employed to some such similar end.

In general, authorized ex-presidential memoirs are pretty awful to read, and nobody takes them seriously as history. At best they can be self-revelatory, and hence grist for the analyst's mill, but they are mostly stale, dull, self-serving documents. By common repute the best ex-presidential memoir ever written was that of Ulysses S. Grant. It was about his Civil War service, not his presidency, and so it is probably too much to expect that it would have saved Grant's presidency from the adverse judgment of "history."

We must conclude that writing memoirs may be a respectable way to fatten the exchequer of an ex-President, but that it is of negligible value in running for great president. Hiring, or charming, a court historian is a somewhat better investment, and especially if, by calculation or misfortune, the court historian's account appears after the death of the President in question. Reflective readers may find it slightly loony that Presidents would want to control what people think of them after they have died, but the desire to leave an admiring posterity is surely not all that unusual among Americans. Moreover, among those Americans who land in the White House one can frequently discern an above-average desire to control the rest of the world, future generations, if possible, included.

What is it that historians like to see on the record when they make their ratings? It is impossible to speak with assurance for all future generations of historians. Fads and cross-currents make it difficult even to read the contemporary scene in a perfectly straightforward way. Nevertheless, over the near term, I think it is fair to say that the predominant sentiments of historians about Presidents have been shaped by the experience of the New Deal, a longish episode in which presidential leadership was generally perceived to have saved the country not merely in the sense of restoring a modicum of prosperity to the economy, but more fundamentally rescuing the political system from profound malaise and instability.

The evidence that the New Deal actually did either of these things is, as a matter of fact, rather thin. But I shall not argue that attentiveness to evidence is a strong point of the gatekeepers of presidential greatness. They do, however, appear very much to admire Presidents who adopt an activist, aggrandizing, constitutional posture toward presidential power. As the senior Schlesinger wrote: "Mediocre Presidents believed in negative government, in self-subordination to the legislative power." My view is that this reflects a New Deal-tutored preference for a particular sort of political structure rather than a statement of constitutional principles about which there can be no two opinions.

William Howard Taft, later a notably activist Chief Justice, put the classic case for the passive presidency when he wrote:

> The true view of the executive function is, as I conceive it, that the President can exercise no power which cannot be fairly and reasonably traced to some specific grant of power or justly implied and included within such express grant as proper and necessary to its exercise. Such specific grant must be either in the federal Constitution or in an act of Congress passed in pursuance thereof. There is no undefined residuum of power which he can exercise because it seems to him to be in the public interest. ...

Poor Taft! That sort of argument got him low marks for presidential greatness, and especially since he evidently acted on his beliefs. Says James David Barber, author of the recent study of *The Presidential Character,* ". . . he was from the start a genial, agreeable, friendly, compliant person, much in need of affection. . . ."

Whereas the senior Arthur Schlesinger's 1962 survey rated Taft an "average" sixteenth, between McKinley and Van Buren on the all-time hit parade, Theodore Roosevelt, Taft's friend and patron, comes in a "near great" seventh, just below Andrew Jackson on the list. Roosevelt's theory of the presidency undoubtedly helped him in the sweepstakes. He said:

> I declined to adopt the view that what was imperatively necessary for the Nation could not be done by the President unless he could find some specific authorization to do it. My belief was that it was not only his right but his duty to do anything that the needs of the Nation demanded unless such action was forbidden by the Constitution or by the laws. Under this interpretation of executive power I did and caused to be done many things not previously done by the President and the heads of the departments. I did not usurp power, but I did greatly broaden the use of executive power. In other words, I acted for the public welfare, I acted for the common well-being of all our people, whenever and in whatever manner was necessary, unless prevented by direct constitutional or legislative prohibition. ...

The beginnings of this conflict in constitutional interpretation and practice have been traced back to the founding of the Republic. In those early years, Leonard White found:

> The Federalists emphasized the necessity for power in government and for energy in the executive branch. The Republicans emphasized the liberties of the citizen and the primacy of representative assemblies. The latter accused their opponents of sympathy to monarchy and hostility to republican institutions. ... Hamilton ... insisted on the necessity for executive leadership of an otherwise drifting legislature; Jefferson thought the people's representatives would readily find their way if left alone to educate each other by free discussion and compromise. ... By 1792 Jefferson thought the executive power had swallowed up the legislative branch; in 1798 Hamilton thought the legislative branch had so curtailed executive power that an able man could find no useful place in the government.

In the present era there is no real conflict at the theoretical level. The last sitting President even half-heartedly to argue against a self-aggrandizing presidency was Eisenhower. To be sure, a few voices — notably Eugene McCarthy's — could be heard proposing structural limitations on presidential powers in the dark days of Vietnam, but the resonance of his argument has faded quickly.

Even the remarkable shenanigans of the Nixon years seem only slightly to have diminished the enthusiasm of opinion leaders for strong Presidents. Theodore Sorensen has gone so far as to advance the comforting view that we have nothing to fear from a strong President because Nixon was not in fact a strong President. In the light of such ingenuity one can only conclude that even today the mantle of presidential greatness is available only to those Presidents who subscribe to a constitutional theory affording the widest scope for presidential action.

Does the historical record suggest any other helpful hints to the aspiring presidential great? Indeed it does. Crises are good for presidential reputations. Over the short run, as countless public-opinion surveys have shown, a small crisis in foreign affairs followed by a small show of presidential decisiveness is always good for a boost in the President's ratings. These ratings, moreover, are evidently indifferent to the efficacy of the presidential decision; triumph or fiasco, it makes little short-run difference.

Presidential greatness, however, is not decided over the short run. Yet the things that mass publics like today are frequently attractive to historians when painted on a larger canvas. Our three "greatest" presidents were reputedly Washington, Lincoln, and Franklin Roosevelt. The service of all three is intimately associated with three incidents in American history when the entire polity was engaged in total war.

Total war — that is, war engaging some major fraction of the gross national product in its prosecution — creates vastly different conditions of psychological mobilization than the nagging, running sores of limited wars, which, in time, invariably become extremely unpopular. Lyndon Johnson was one President who showed awareness of the irony implicit in the popularity risks of restricting, as well as pursuing, a limited war.

To those scrupulous souls who shrink from manufacturing a war of total mobilization in the service of their future reputations, is there anything left to be said? Surely lessons can be drawn equally from our least successful as well as our most successful Presidents. Harding, Grant, and, one surmises, Nixon, lurk somewhere near the bottom of the heap. The smell of very large-scale scandal (not the small potatoes of the Truman era) attaches to the administration of each.

Assuming, for the sake of argument, that Presidents want to run an administration untainted by scandal, can they do it? Considering the scale of operations of the United States government, the general absence of cor-

ruption in the conduct of its business is an admirable achievement. One
doubts that if some illegal and greedy scheme were discovered somewhere
in the vast labyrinth of the executive bureaucracies, the President would be
held strictly to account. One doubts it unless one of three conditions obtains:
the President, once apprised of the scandal, failed to act promptly to set
things right, or, second, trusted friends and close associates of the President
were involved, or, worse yet, the President himself were involved.

Only Richard Nixon, it will be observed, with his well-known penchant for presidential firsts, hits the jackpot on this list of no-no's. Neither
Harding nor Grant escaped blame for the criminal acts of others close to
them, but both are commonly held to have been themselves free of wrongdoing.

A final arena in which Presidents achieve greatness is in the legislative
record. Normally, what is required is a flurry of action, like FDR's hundred
days, or Woodrow Wilson's first term. A kindly fate can sweep a new
President into office along with a heavy congressional majority of his own
party. With a little more luck there can be a feeling abroad in the land that
something must be done. Whereupon, for a little while at least, the President and Congress together do something. Great strides in the enactment of
public policy are commonly made in this fashion. And it is now settled
custom that the President gets the long-run credit.

Thus many of the factors that go into presidential greatness appear to
boil down to being in the right place at the right time. Much of the rest
consists of having others put the right construction on ambiguous acts. Understandably, quite a lot of White House effort consequently goes into
cultivating favorable notice for the incumbent. And here, at this point, a
worm begins to emerge from the apple. The scenery, cosmetics, and sound
effects that go into good public relations, unless strongly resisted, can begin
to overwhelm more substantive concerns. The aspiration to presidential
greatness, which under ideal circumstances can provide an incentive for
good presidential behavior, under less than ideal circumstances leads to a
great variety of difficulties. For fear of being found out and downgraded,
there is the temptation to deny failure, to refuse to readjust course when a
program or a proposal doesn't work out. There is the temptation to hoard
credit rather than share it with the agencies that actually do the work and
produce the results. There is the temptation to export responsibility away
from the White House for the honest shortfalls of programs, thus transmitting to the government at large an expectation that loyalty upward will be
rewarded with disloyalty down. There is the temptation to offer false hopes
and to proclaim spurious accomplishments to the public at large.

As Henry Fairlie and others point out, a presidency that inflates expectations can rarely deliver. Worse yet, such a presidency gives up a
precious opportunity to perform essential tasks of civic education, to help
ordinary people see both the limitations and the possibilities of democratic

government. George Reedy and others have observed that a presidency made of overblown rhetoric and excessive pretension can lose touch with the realities of politics, can waste its resources on trivialities, can fail, consequently, to grasp opportunities to govern well.

This, such as it is, is the case against the pursuit of presidential greatness. It is a case based upon a hope that there can be something approximating a restoration of democratic manners in the presidency. There are, however, good reasons to suppose that such a restoration will be hard to accomplish.

Part of the problem is structural. The complex demands of modern governmental decision-making require that Presidents receive plenty of help. They need advice, information, criticism, feedback. They also need people to take care of the endless round of chores that fall to a President's lot: press secretaries, congressional liaison, managers of paper work and the traffic of visitors. Presidents also need to be able to trust the help they are getting, to be able to feel that what is being said and done in their behalf does genuinely place presidential interests first. From these requirements comes the need for an entourage of people whose careers in the limelight are solely the product of presidential favor. And from this entourage invariably comes what I suppose could be called the First Circle of presidential Moonies.

These are the people who "sleep a little better at night," as Jack Valenti so memorably said, because the charisma of their chief powers the machinery of government. During the day, we can be sure, they wear sunglasses to keep from being dazzled by "that special grace" (as members of John Kennedy's entourage frequently put it).

Anybody who doubts Kennedy's impact to this day on his successors should look again at the "great" debates of 1960 and 1976. For his encounter with Richard Nixon, Kennedy was stuffed like a Christmas goose with small discrete facts. In the course of the debates, out they came, two and three at a time. By all accounts, Kennedy "won" the 1960 encounter, albeit by nearly as small a margin as he won the election itself.

This evidently established a standard presidential-candidate debating style which the candidates of 1976 dutifully aped: neither risked the variety of facial expressions that did Nixon in, both spouted facts — not all of them true or relevant — rather than risk explaining their points of view.

It is probably foolish to expect some sort of civic enlightenment to come from debates. They are, rather, as near as our society gets to a trial by ordeal. The debater's central task is neither to inform nor to enlighten, but rather to survive, to avoid saying something that newspaper and television commentators will fix upon as an error or that will require an endless round of "clarifications" and become the "issue" of the following week or two. No wonder both Ford and Carter stood like tethered goats for the twenty-seven-minutes' silence that interrupted their first debate. To have been there at all no doubt temporarily exhausted their capacity to take risks.

The needs of White House staff to bask in reflected glory, plus risk-aversion in the face of the work habits of the mass media, are a potent combination tending to sustain a President's interest in President-worship. Moreover, the mystique of the presidency can be useful politically, vesting the visit in the rose garden, the invitation to breakfast, even a beseeching telephone call to Capitol Hill, with an added value that can spell the difference between political victory and defeat. And of course a President may simply grow fond of being coddled.

Added to these are the powerful factors in the world and in the American political system that have brought the President to the forefront: the increased importance of foreign affairs in the life of the nation, an area in which the President has no serious constitutional rival; the creation and proliferation of federal bureaucracies, all of them subject to presidential influence and supervision; the growth of the mass media with their focus upon the personalities at the center of our national politics, and the decline of political parties as a countervailing force. No wonder the entire political system seems President-preoccupied.

Against this formidable array of forces a plea for modesty of presidential aims, for prudence and moderation in the choice of instruments, for a scaling-down of promises and claims of achievement, seems unlikely to attract widespread agreement, least of all from Presidents and their entourages bent on making their mark on History.

CHAPTER 7

The Bureaucracy

American bureaucracy today is an important fourth branch of the government. Too frequently the administrative branch is lumped under the heading of the "Executive" and is considered to be subordinate to the President. But the following selections will reveal that the bureaucracy is often autonomous, acting outside of the control of Congress, the President, and even the judiciary. This fact raises an important problem for our constitutional democracy: How can the bureaucracy be kept responsible if it does not fit into the constitutional framework that was designed to guarantee limited and responsible government?

Constitutional Background

While the constitution carefully outlined the responsibilities and powers of the President, Congress, and to a lesser extent the Supreme Court, it did not mention the bureaucracy. The position of the bureaucracy in the separation of powers scheme developed by custom and statutory law, rather than by explicit constitutional provisions. The following selection makes it clear that although the constitution did not provide for an administrative branch, it did have bearing upon the development of the bureaucracy. Perhaps the most important result of constitutional bureaucracy is that the administrative agencies have become pawns in the constant power struggle between the President and Congress.

45

Peter Woll

CONSTITUTIONAL DEMOCRACY
AND BUREAUCRATIC POWER

The administrative branch today stands at the very center of our governmental process; it is the keystone of the structure. And administrative agencies exercise legislative and judicial as well as executive functions — a fact that is often overlooked. . . .

How should we view American bureaucracy? Ultimately, the power of government comes to rest in the administrative branch. Agencies are given the responsibility of making concrete decisions carrying out vague policy initiated in Congress or by the President. The agencies can offer expert advice, closely attuned to the most interested pressure groups, and they often not only determine the policies that the legislature and executive recommend in the first place, but also decisively affect the policy-making process. Usually it is felt that the bureaucracy is politically "neutral," completely under the domination of the President, Congress, or the courts. We will see that this is not entirely the case, and that the President and Congress have only sporadic control over the administrative process.

The bureaucracy is a semi-autonomous branch of the government, often dominating Congress, exercising strong influence on the President, and only infrequently subject to review by the courts. If our constitutional democracy is to be fully analyzed, we must focus attention upon the administrative branch. What is the nature of public administration? How are administration and politics intertwined? How are administrative constituencies determined? What is the relationship between agencies and their constituencies? What role should the President assume in relation to the administrative branch? How far should Congress go in controlling agencies which in fact tend to dominate the legislative process? Should judicial review be expanded? What are the conditions of judicial review? How do administrative agencies perform judicial functions, and how do these activities affect the ability of courts to oversee their actions? These questions confront us with what is called the problem of administrative responsibility: that is, how can we control the activities of the administrative branch? In order to approach an understanding of this difficult problem, it is necessary to appreciate the nature of the administrative process and how it interacts with other branches of the government and with the general public. It is also important to understand the nature of our constitutional system, and the political context within which agencies function.

We operate within the framework of a constitutional democracy. This means, first, that the government is to be limited by the separation of powers and Bill of Rights. Another component of the system, federalism, is designed in theory to provide states with a certain amount of authority when it is not implied at the national level. Our separation of powers, the system of checks and balances, and the federal system help to explain some of the differences between administrative organization here and in other countries. But the Constitution does not explicitly provide for the administrative branch, which has become a new fourth branch of government. This raises the question of how to control the bureaucracy when there are no clear constitutional limits upon it. The second aspect of our system, democracy, is of course implied in the Constitution itself, but has expanded greatly since it was adopted. We are confronted, very broadly speaking, first with the problem of constitutional limitation, and secondly with the problem of democratic participation in the activities of the bureaucracy. The bureaucracy must be accommodated within the framework of our system of constitutional democracy. This is the crux of the problem of administrative responsibility.

Even though the Constitution does not explicitly provide for the bureaucracy, it has had a profound impact upon the structure, functions, and general place that the bureaucracy occupies in government. The administrative process was incorporated into the constitutional system under the heading of "The Executive Branch." But the concept of "administration" at the time of the adoption of the Constitution was a very simple one, involving the "mere execution" of "executive details," to use the phrases of Hamilton in *The Federalist*. The idea, at that time, was simply that the President as Chief Executive would be able to control the Executive Branch in carrying out the mandates of Congress. In *Federalist 72*, after defining administration in this very narrow way, Hamilton stated:

> . . . The persons, therefore, to whose immediate management the different administrative matters are committed ought to be considered as Assistants or Deputies of the Chief Magistrate, and on this account, they ought to derive their offices from his appointment, at least from his nomination, and ought to be subject to his superintendence.

It was clear that Hamilton felt the President would be responsible for administrative action as long as he was in office. This fact later turned up in what can be called the "presidential supremacy" school of thought, which held and still holds that the President is *constitutionally* responsible for the administrative branch, and that Congress should delegate to him all necessary authority for this purpose. Nevertheless, whatever the framers of the

Constitution might have planned if they could have foreseen the nature of bureaucratic development, the fact is that the system they constructed in many ways supported bureaucratic organization and functions independent of the President. The role they assigned to Congress in relation to administration assured this result, as did the general position of Congress in the governmental system as a check or balance to the power of the President. Congress has a great deal of authority over the administrative process.

If we compare the powers of Congress and the President over the bureaucracy it becomes clear that they both have important constitutional responsibility. Congress retains primary control over the organization of the bureaucracy. It alone creates and destroys agencies, and determines whether they are to be located within the executive branch or outside it. This has enabled Congress to create a large number of *independent* agencies beyond presidential control. Congress has the authority to control appropriations and may thus exercise a great deal of power over the administrative arm, although increasingly the Bureau of the Budget and the President have the initial, and more often than not the final say over the budget. Congress also has the authority to define the jurisdiction of agencies. Finally, the Constitution gives to the legislature the power to interfere in high level presidential appointments, which must be "by and with the advice and consent of the Senate."

Congress may extend the sharing of the appointive power when it sets up new agencies. It may delegate to the President pervasive authority to control the bureaucracy. But one of the most important elements of the separation of powers is the electoral system, which gives to Congress a constituency which is different from and even conflicting with that of the President. This means that Congress often decides to set up agencies beyond presidential purview. Only rarely will it grant the President any kind of final authority to structure the bureaucracy. During World War II, on the basis of the War Powers Act, the President had the authority to reorganize the administrative branch. Today he has the same authority, provided that Congress does not veto presidential proposals within a certain time limit. In refusing to give the President permanent reorganization authority, Congress is jealously guarding one of its important prerogatives.

Turning to the constitutional authority of the President over the bureaucracy, it is somewhat puzzling to see that it gives him a relatively small role. He appoints certain officials by and with the advice and consent of the Senate. He has directive power over agencies that are placed within his jurisdiction by Congress. His control over patronage, once so important, has diminished sharply under the merit system. The President is Commander-in-Chief of all military forces, which puts him in a controlling position over the Defense Department and agencies involved in military matters. In the area of international relations, the President is by constitutional authority the

"Chief Diplomat," to use Rossiter's phrase. This means that he appoints Ambassadors (by and with the advice and consent of the Senate), and generally directs national activities in the international arena — a crucially important executive function. But regardless of the apparent intentions of some of the framers of the Constitution as expressed by Hamilton in *The Federalist,* and in spite of the predominance of the presidency in military and foreign affairs, the fact remains that we seek in vain for explicit constitutional authorization for the President to be "Chief Administrator."

This is not to say that the President does not have an important responsibility to act as chief of the bureaucracy, merely that there is no constitutional mandate for this. As our system evolved, the President was given more and more responsibility until he became, in practice, Chief Administrator. At the same time the constitutional system has often impeded progress in this direction. The President's Committee on Administrative Management in 1937, and later the Hoover Commissions of 1949 and 1955, called upon Congress to initiate a series of reforms increasing presidential authority over the administrative branch. It was felt that this was necessary to make democracy work. The President is the only official elected nationally, and if the administration is to be held democratically accountable, he alone can stand as its representative. But meaningful control from the White House requires that the President have a comprehensive program which encompasses the activities of the bureaucracy. He must be informed as to what they are doing, and be able to control them. He must understand the complex responsibilities of the bureaucracy. Moreover, he must be able to call on sufficient political support to balance the support which the agencies draw from private clientele groups and congressional committees. This has frequently proven a difficult and often impossible task for the President. He may have the *authority* to control the bureaucracy in many areas, but not enough *power.*

On the basis of the Constitution, Congress feels it quite proper that when it delegates legislative authority to administrative agencies it can relatively often place these groups outside the control of the President. For example, in the case of the Interstate Commerce Commission . . . Congress has delegated final authority to that agency to control railroad mergers and other aspects of transportation activity, without giving the President the right to veto. The President may feel that a particular merger is undesirable because it is in violation of the antitrust laws, but the Interstate Commerce Commission is likely to feel differently. In such a situation, the President can do nothing because he does not have the *legal authority* to take any action. If he could muster enough political support to exercise influence over the ICC, he would be able to control it, but the absence of legal authority is an important factor in such cases and diminishes presidential power. Moreover, the ICC draws strong support from the railroad industry, which has been able to counterbalance the political support possessed by the President and other groups that have wished to control it. Analogous situations exist with respect to other regulatory agencies.

Besides the problem of congressional and presidential control over the bureaucracy, there is the question of judicial review of administrative decisions. The rule of law is a central element in our Constitution. The rule of law means that decisions judicial in nature should be handled by common law courts, because of their expertise in rendering due process of law. When administrative agencies engage in adjudication their decisions should be subject to judicial review — at least, they should if one supports the idea of the supremacy of law. Judicial decisions are supposed to be rendered on an independent and impartial basis, through the use of tested procedures, in order to arrive at the accurate determination of the truth. Administrative adjudication should not be subject to presidential or congressional control, which would mean political determination of decisions that should be rendered in an objective manner. The idea of the rule of law, derived from the common law and adopted within the framework of our constitutional system, in theory limits legislative and executive control over the bureaucracy.

The nature of our constitutional system poses very serious difficulties to the development of a system of administrative responsibility. The Constitution postulates that the functions of government must be separated into different branches with differing constituencies and separate authority. The idea is that the departments should oppose each other, thereby preventing the arbitrary exercise of political power. Any combination of functions was considered to lead inevitably to arbitrary government. This is a debatable point, but the result of the Constitution is quite clear. The administrative process, on the other hand, often combines various functions of government in the same hands. Attempts are made, of course, to separate those who exercise judicial functions from these in the prosecuting arms of the agencies. But the fact remains that there is a far greater combination of functions in the administrative process than can be accommodated by strict adherence to the Constitution.

It has often been proposed, as a means of alleviating what may be considered the bad effects of combined powers in administrative agencies, to draw a line of control from the original branches of the government to those parts of the bureaucracy exercising similar functions. Congress would control the legislative activities of the agencies, the President the executive aspects, and the courts the judicial functions. This would maintain the symmetry of the constitutional system. But this solution is not feasible, because other parts of the Constitution, giving different authority to these three branches make symmetrical control of this kind almost impossible. The three branches of the government are not willing to give up whatever powers they may have over administrative agencies. For example, Congress is not willing to give the President complete control over all executive functions, nor to give the courts the authority to review all the decisions of the agencies. At present, judicial review takes place only if Congress authorizes it, except in those rare instances where constitutional issues are involved.

Another aspect of the problem of control is reflected in the apparent paradox that the three branches do not always use to the fullest extent their authority to regulate the bureaucracy, even though they wish to retain their power to do so. The courts, for example, have exercised considerable self-restraint in their review of administrative decisions. They are not willing to use all their power over the bureaucracy. Similarly, both Congress and the President will often limit their dealings with the administrative branch for political and practical reasons.

In the final analysis, we are left with a bureaucratic system that has been fragmented by the Constitution, and in which administrative discretion is inevitable. The bureaucracy reflects the general fragmentation of our political system. It is often the battleground for the three branches of government, and for outside pressure groups which seek to control it for their own purposes.

The Bureaucracy and Congress: Friends or Foes?

More often than not, the powerful chairmen of congressional committees consider administrative agencies to be their allies, not their enemies. After all, the agencies are supposed to implement congressional programs. Each agency is directly under the jurisdiction of specific authorization and appropriations committees on Capitol Hill. The chairmen of these committees exercise a great deal of informal power over the agencies, for to most bureaucrats, Congress is the keystone of the Washington establishment. The senior members of Congress that control the committees possess political clout and expertise that most senior bureaucrats find useful in their constant battle for political survival. And, conversely, members of Congress seeking electoral support and power on Capitol Hill find it useful to have the support of agencies that possess a great deal of independent power of their own. Agencies carefully cultivate political constituencies that, in addition to their expertise, can be of enormous aid to power-seekers in Congress.

While the relationship between Congress and the bureaucracy is more one of collusion than conflict, agencies that do not have on balance important political support are vulnerable to congressional attack. Agencies must constantly seek a balance of political support over opposition. They must maintain the backing of their Capitol Hill sponsors, particularly the chairmen of the committees that control their funds and authority. If an agency cannot keep a balance of political support in Congress its appropriations and powers may be reduced, and there is even the possibility that a weakened agency may be eliminated. However, the outright abolition of an agency is rare and has occurred only a few times in history.

The importance of political support for administrative agencies is demonstrated by the Federal Trade Commission, which has battled for survival in an atmosphere of congressional hostility. The consumer constituency of the FTC has never been a match for the business interests that are within the agency's jurisdiction. During most of the history of the FTC since its creation in 1914 consumer interests were dormant. The lack of a powerful consumer constituency meant that the agency did not vigorously pursue its mandate to act in the public interest to regulate business advertising and prevent restraints of trade under the anti-trust laws. The political underpinning of the agency that led to its creation in 1914 soon dissipated during the laissez faire era of the 1920s. While the FTC was somewhat reinvigorated during the New Deal of Franklin Roosevelt, which resulted in a vast, general expansion of the federal bureaucracy, the agency for the most part remained a relatively passive regulator.

The rise of the consumer movement and its growing power on Capitol Hill in the 1970s led to a resurgence of the FTC. In 1974 Congress delegated to the agency the authority to write consumer-protection trade rules that would govern entire industries. Although the FTC had engaged in such rule-making in the past, its authority to do so was in doubt before Congress unequivocally spelled it out in legislation. The agency was further strengthened by President Carter's appointment of Michael Pertschuk to be its chairman in April 1977. Pertschuk had been a powerful Capitol Hill staffer who, as chief counsel of the Senate Commerce Committee, helped to enact the legislation increasing the FTC's powers. Pertschuk had been Warren Magnuson's principal aide and was largely responsible for establishing the Washington senator as a leading Capitol Hill advocate of consumer causes. As chairman of the FTC, Perschuk now had a chance to wear publicly the consumer-advocate mantle. He found, however, that the mood of the country was increasingly beginning to favor deregulation over regulation. That mood was reflected on Capitol Hill. Pertschuk's active stance as the chairman of the FTC caused a backlash in the business community and in Congress that threatened to cripple the agency. The following selection reveals that agency power must be based upon maintaining a balance of political support and that in the quest for political backing Congress cannot be ignored.

46

Robert Sherrill

JOUSTING ON THE HILL: SKEWERING THE CONSUMER'S DEFENDER

Congress seems determined to cripple further the Federal Trade Commission, Washington's best-known "consumer protection" agency. Many consumers won't care if this happens because they don't have even a vague notion of what the FTC is or does. Recent polls revealed that eight out of 10 Americans are in that benighted condition.

With a budget of about $60 million — enough to run the Pentagon for about 15 minutes — and, until recently, a history of timidity and inaction, the FTC is one of Washington's smallest regulatory agencies. Lately, though, the FTC has been doing that for which it was created: fighting the concentration of economic power and investigating "unfair or deceptive" business practices. Under a string of dynamic leaders and armed with a revision of its own power, the new commission has taken on such giants as the funeral and the "kid vid" industries.

Unfortunately Congress, which is, after all, responsible for the existence of the FTC, doesn't like the new commission. Some members claim that federal agencies should assume the role of arbitrator, not advocate; others contend that the FTC has been overzealous in its pursuit of deceptive business practices. Congressman Bill Frenzel, a Minnesota Republican, calls the FTC "a king-sized cancer on our economy." Senator John C. Danforth, a Missouri Republican with strong pro-business sentiments, says the FTC is "out of control."

In fact, many congressmen appear to be most concerned with their campaign coffers, which are largely taken care of by business "political action committees." The feeling on Capitol Hill runs so strong that the FTC's present chairman, Michael Pertschuk, sometimes arouses vicious personal attacks. An official of Formica Corporation described him as "a complete socialist" and "one of the most dangerous men in America."

Such responses might be almost funny if they were not merely the latest notation in a long history of abuse.

In 1912–1913 Congress, investigating the Money Trust, decided there was a dangerous concentration of economic power in America that should be broken up. In the spirit of reform it passed the Federal Reserve Act of

1913, the Clayton Antitrust Act of 1914, and the Federal Trade Commission Act of 1914.

None of these acts has reduced even slightly the concentration of economic power in America. Indeed, it has grown more intense. The largest 500 firms today account for more than 80 percent of all the manufacturing and mining assets in the country, an increase of more than 20 percent in the last two decades. The reforms of 1913–1914 were long ago mummified. The Federal Reserve Board became practically a tool of the major banks. The Clayton Antitrust Act has been treated by succeeding administrations as a quaint relic of an almost forgotten populist era. And, for most of its life, the Federal Trade Commission has been only a bad joke.

On paper, of course, Congress intended to give the FTC great authority. The legislation empowered the commission to take legal action against monopolies and cartels (a power it shared with the Justice Department) and to stamp out unfair and deceptive business practices. In short, it was supposed to police the commercial world in such a way that honest businesses would not be placed at a disadvantage with unscrupulous competitors and that consumers would not be cheated.

But having given these pious marching orders, Washington's politicians promptly abandoned the FTC. Not only did it receive little encouragement, but it was not allowed to show any independent inclination to fulfill its congressional mandate. When the FTC tried to break up interlocking corporate directorates, when it issued a comprehensive study of the international oil cartel and pushed for antitrust action, when it tried to force conglomerates to issue line-of-business reports on their income (a tremendous aid in the FTC's antitrust efforts), the FTC was smothered by political opposition. For most of its 66 years the FTC has gotten no moral support from Congress; it has gotten virtually none from the executive branch. And, until recently, the agency was sodden internally with despair, lack of talent, and conflict of interest. It was what journalist David Burnham called "a patronage dumping ground for friends of powerful Southern Democrats."

So passed its first half century. Frustrated in all major efforts, reduced to the listless pursuit of trivia, it was generally considered to be the most useless regulatory agency in Washington: timid, lazy, inept, indifferent, and totally intimidated by big business.

Year after year, the FTC churned out hundreds of inconsequential rulings relating to such matters as the price of fruit pies in Salt Lake City, the operation of gift shops in the Virgin Islands, the mislabeling of weasel coats in New York City, and the attempt of a bubblegum manufacturer to monopolize baseball picture cards. Commonly, prosecution of cases of mislabeling, false advertising, and deceitful practices would be dragged out by the FTC for so many years that they just fell apart and died — the witnesses scattered, the evidence misplaced, and often the accused company itself gone into bankruptcy. It took the old FTC, as Jean Carper, columnist and co-author of *Eating May Be Hazardous to Your Health,* once pointed out, "13 years to make Geritol stop claiming it cured 'tired blood' and 30 years to make Holland Furnace Company salesmen stop faking explosions in people's basements."

Then one of Washington's rare miracles occurred: A bureaucratic corpse, electrified by criticism, began to stir.

The first criticism came from Ralph Nader's investigators who, in 1969, issued a ferocious exposé showing that the FTC was staffed by political hacks who strenuously avoided fighting the frauds of big business. Though the Nader report was taken seriously, the Washington establishment accepted it with reservations because most of the investigators were recent law-school graduates suspected of being hyped on the then-new consumer movement. President Nixon asked for a second opinion from the American Bar Association. Instead of discrediting Nader, the ABA concluded that the FTC was so worthless that "if change does not occur, there will be no substantial purpose" in keeping the agency alive.

Thus forced into a put-up or shut-up position, Nixon for once put up. He first appointed Casper Weinberger, California's director of finance, to take over the FTC and begin a "complete reorganization." Weinberger had hardly begun the job, however, when Nixon pulled him out and transferred him elsewhere in the bureaucracy. Next Nixon appointed as chairman Miles Kirkpatrick, the Philadelphia lawyer who had headed the ABA investigation of the FTC. Kirkpatrick also took his assignment seriously. Suddenly the FTC was leveling charges of deceptive promotion against such sanctified outposts of capitalism as the Coca-Cola Company, McDonald's Hamburgers, Reader's Digest, and Procter & Gamble. The FTC was even so bold as to suggest that Wonder Bread really wasn't doing anything wonderful enough to build strong bodies 12 ways. In its fresh heretical frenzy, the FTC insisted that manufacturers of electric razors, air conditioners, and automobiles send evidence of the accuracy of their advertisements.

Even more startling, the FTC began to show imagination. It thought up a new system for balancing false advertisements: Instead of merely ordering manufacturers to quit lying about their products, the FTC demanded that they place *corrective* ads in which they acknowledged that their previous claims had been false.

Many of Nixon's big money supporters were furious. Herbert Klein, Nixon's director of communications, announced that the White House felt the FTC was going "too far" in its zeal to protect consumers, and shortly thereafter Kirkpatrick was persuaded to step down. He had lasted three years. His successor, Lewis A. Engman, who had recently served as assistant director of the White House Domestic Council, was greeted by consumer groups with deep suspicion. They thought he would probably represent Nixon's interests in protecting big business from regulation.

Instead, Engman proved to be an independent, fairly gutsy fellow who carried on the reforms begun by Kirkpatrick and started some of his own.

The most important new power given Engman was the Magnuson-Moss Act of 1974. Previously, the FTC had been restricted to policing the conduct of individual companies. If Company X was caught in deceptive practices, the FTC could move against it — but all the other companies in the industry, even if they were equally guilty, might escape until a later day of judgment. Such a time-consuming company-by-company process left the FTC incapable of achieving sweeping reforms. The Magnuson-Moss Act, among other things, enabled the FTC to make industry-wide rules.

Armed with that authority, Engman launched 11 rule-making investigations into questionable activities involving vocational schools, mobile-home dealers, food advertisers, prescription-drug marketers, over-the counter drug marketers, hearing-aid companies, health spas, and the funeral industry.

The next FTC head, Calvin Collier, followed Engman's lead. In a single year he initiated four other industry-wide rule-making investigations into such things as the practices of used-car dealers and eyeglass hucksters. By the end of 1976, the FTC had more than 750 investigations underway. It was also breaking up some illegally interlocking directorates, and it was slowly nursing along an antitrust suit filed in 1973 against eight major oil companies.

At 35, Collier was the youngest chairman in FTC history. Critics of the agency — noting that by January 1977 the FTC had replaced one out of every 10 lawyers on its staff with recruits from that year's class and that 20 percent of the young newcomers were Phi Beta Kappas — began to complain that business was being victimized by smart-alecky kids. The criticisms were especially ominous because they came from executives of such giants as Kellogg, General Foods, General Motors, Exxon, and Sears — all of whom had recently been hit by FTC action.

This was the situation that prevailed when, in April 1977, Michael Pertschuk, then 44 years old, was sworn in as the new chairman. The future was murky. The FTC was again under intense fire from *Fortune*'s 500 on down. It was again being accused of going too far, of carrying out vendettas against business. Some influential conservatives were again urging the ultimate reform — abolition of the agency.

Pertschuk's appointment did little to soothe them. Son of a wealthy furrier, educated at private prep schools and at Yale, Pertschuk had flourished on Capitol Hill during its most pro-consumer era. For more than a dozen years he had served as chief counsel of the Senate Commerce Committee, and for many of those years he was thought by some to be as influential as the committee's chairman, Senator Warren Magnuson. Pertschuk was known to be one of the few persons in Washington with Ralph Nader's private phone number, and it was not difficult to see the results of that friendship in the legislation Pertschuk helped write: on health warnings for cigarette labeling, no-fault insurance, auto safety, truth-in-packaging — a list that is, in the words of Senator Magnuson, "as long as your arm."

Still, despite his do-gooder credentials, many business lobbyists knew Pertschuk to be "a reasonable, practical, sensible problem solver," as one of Washington's corporate lawyers described him to the *New York Times*. Fanatics don't get to be chief counsel of the Senate Commerce Committee. He was a consummate wheeler-dealer when it came to bringing opposing parties together in the drafting of legislation. One of the oft-told stories around Washington was how he got Ralph Nader and Lloyd N. Cutler, lawyer for the auto industry, to cooperate on a Commerce Committee report. He put Nader in one room and Cutler in another, eventually persuading these vigorous opponents to redraft the report in such a way that Congress would pass the National Traffic and Motor Vehicle Safety Act.

At the time Pertschuk was sworn in, his friends and enemies did agree on one thing: Under his leadership the FTC would surely have an easier time with Congress than it had had under its recent Republican management. The logic of the prediction was simple enough: With the White House once again occupied by a Democrat, the President's nominee would be more kindly treated by a Democratic Congress, especially when he was Congress's own protégé.

Ironically, the results were just the opposite. The partisanship on which Pertschuk might have depended for his strength in earlier eras was fast disappearing from Washington. Party leaders — which is to say, party fund raisers — no longer had the influence they once held. The public treasury (for presidential candidates) and business "political action committees" (for congressmen) had replaced the old-style party fund raisers. With most politicians getting their money independently, their loyalty to the party machine declined sharply. The appointee of a Democratic President could no longer automatically expect friendship from a nominally Democratic Congress. The once-reliable Pennsylvania Avenue marriage was being broken up by money from special-interest groups.

In 1974, when many of the pro-consumer laws were being rushed through Congress, there were only 89 corporate political action committees spreading money around. But four years later, just as Pertschuk was taking on his new job, the Federal Election Commission reported the existence of 784 corporate political action committees and 451 trade and professional action organizations. These groups — each of which is permitted to spend up to a total of $10,000 in primary and general elections — were becoming the big source of campaign funds for congressional candidates. Political committees linked with the American Medical Association, for example, gave more than $4.9 million to House and Senate candidates between 1974 and 1978.

Pertschuk, for all his political sophistication, apparently did not realize the profound change these moneyed groups were making. He seemed oblivious to the massive army that was already arrayed against further FTC regulations. He walked into his new job spouting the most quixotic plans for turning the FTC into what he boldly called "the best public-interest law firm in the country." In an interview with *U.S. News & World Report,* he implied that he might even get the FTC to make advertisers toe the line according to some politically ordained "national policy." If the "national policy" was to save energy, he said, the FTC might outlaw "an automobile ad that touted a car for its large size, quick starts, and power — while obscuring its poor fuel efficiency. . . ." He hinted that, to boost competition, the FTC might impose a ceiling on how much some giant corporations could spend for advertising.

Even before he was sworn in, he was vowing to crack down on the $600 million "kid vid" industry, the portion of the television advertising industry specializing in appeals to children — a group that too often, said Pertschuk, "manipulates sounds and symbols to exploit the vulnerability of a child's mind." He said it was unfair to go on television and fast-talk a six-year-old into eating sugar-laden foods that might ruin his teeth and health. Kellogg and colleagues accepted these comments as a declaration of war.

Between rhetorical outbursts, Pertschuk plunged into the varied rule-making activities he inherited from his Republican predecessors. But he did so with such enthusiasm that the Republican origins of the proposed rules were forgotten. Pertschuk alone got the blame for the trouble the FTC was causing business. He became the target — the symbolic, pre-eminent villain in a town where it had become quite faddish, even among liberals, to be against government regulation. At a White House Christmas party in 1979, one of the Senate's tougher members sidled up to Congressman Bob Eckhardt, chairman of a consumer protection subcommittee and very much a supporter of Pertschuk, to say cheerily: "We're going to get your boy next year."

The irony of the current get-Pertschuk movement — or to be more exact, the latest get-the-FTC movement, for there are four other members of the commission who must be considered, as they have generally given Pertschuk strong support — is that he could be classified as a white knight only by comparison with Washington's usual run of flaccid bureaucrats. By the standards of any real reformer, Pertschuk's knightly color would have to be gray.

The changes Pertschuk's FTC has ordered various industries to make in their conduct — or that it has said it *may* order them to make — are quite ordinary. They are such casual reforms, in fact, that one reads through the list with amazement that such changes hadn't been imposed long ago.

One is also dumbfounded to discover that of the 18 rule-making proceedings begun as a result of the Magnuson-Moss Act, only four have been completed. The commission has proceeded with excruciating caution. For example, it spent seven years of the most painstaking investigation and heard 327 witnesses before handing down its rules for reforming the funeral industry.

Here, in brief, are the four industry-wide rulings passed by the FTC:

1. Funeral directors were ordered to itemize price information rather than give "package" prices, and quote prices over the phone so that bereaved customers can shop around for the cheapest funeral. Directors were also ordered not to deceive people into thinking they had to get their dead embalmed if in fact they didn't have to, or buy a coffin for a cremation if that wasn't necessary. In short, funeral merchants were told they shouldn't take advantage of grieving people to sell a $2,500 funeral — the average price these days for the package — when they really would have preferred to buy one for $600.
2. Vocational schools were ordered to provide students with an escape clause and a rebate plan. No longer would some unsuspecting ghetto kid be locked into paying for a "guaranteed employment" computer course that he couldn't possibly complete.
3, State laws that prohibited advertising by optometrists were struck down. Also, doctors were ordered to give prescriptions to their customers so that they could do comparison buying. (That one rule has reportedly saved consumers $500 million since 1978.)
4. Manufacturers of home insulation were ordered to stop making unsubstantiated claims of energy-saving performances and to start telling consumers exactly what they could expect from their product in the way of R-value — the measure of insulating power.

Obviously, those four rules fall far short of being revolutionary. Pertschuk says the four rules show "judiciousness and restraint." Indeed, they are so restrained as to hardly qualify as reform. They are no more than housekeeping regulations that would, in the long haul, help the affected industries as much as they helped the public.

But the response of industry was predictably excessive. Even *proposed* investigations by the FTC prompted hysteria. When the commission announced that it was going to look into charges that Sunkist Growers Incorporated was suppressing competition, Sunkist wailed that it was being picked on, that federal law specifically exempted government regulation of cooperatives. (Sunkist is quite correct in that, but the law was aimed at assisting the *little* co-ops; it was decidedly not written for a giant that controls 60–80 percent of the western lemon and orange market.)

Used-car dealers said that the FTC had no right even to consider forcing them to inspect and list the defects of the 20 million used cars

Americans buy each year; insurance companies were outraged when the FTC began investigating charges that consumers were being cheated of billions of dollars in the interest paid on their policies.

Big business did more than complain. Either by lawsuits or by legislation, it succeeded in getting all four rules to be put on hold. The FTC was stopped dead in its tracks — at least momentarily.

Legislation, as everyone knows, is written with money. A team of reporters from the *Philadelphia Inquirer* discovered that industries under investigation by the FTC had pumped more than $5 million into congressional races in 1978; the tally for 1980 is, of course, still far from over but it is expected to be at least as generous.

The money seems to have been profitably invested. Congress passed legislation to significantly stunt the agency's independence — the House favoring a draconian one-house veto power over FTC rules, the Senate choosing a more gentlemanly two-house overriding process. Both House and Senate also singled out specific rule-making proceedings — children's TV ads, funeral pricing, etc. — that they insist the agency back away from. (To be sure, the FTC could have done worse. Before the Senate vote a top agency official had said, "We can't count on more than 10 percent of their members." In fact the FTC got the support of 13 percent.)

As of this writing the conference committee has not put the prohibitions into a compromise package. But the general congressional message is already plain, and it has had its desired effect. The bounce has gone out of the commission once again.

Pertschuk no longer sounds much like a militant reformer. Compromise is in the air. Now he soothes congressional critics by conceding that some of his staff may have been a little too zealous and he claims that these zealots "are no longer with" the FTC. He tells conservatives that he is "not unsympathetic with the motivation for a legislative veto," though he does not think it would work. He insists that both he and his commission are, at bottom, full of "institutional humility."

Such a shift in attitude on his part, though perhaps politically smart, makes consumer advocates very uneasy. Nancy Drabble, a staff attorney at Nader's Congress Watch, says, "Our concern is that the FTC may become scared, that it may go back to being the little old lady of Pennsylvania Avenue."

That would be a tragedy. For the FTC is finally beginning to be useful. Recently Arthur F. Burns, the former chairman of the Federal Reserve Board, asked Pertschuk: "The Federal Trade Commission has been around for a good many years. What major contributions has it made to creating or maintaining a healthy competitive environment in this country? Or, to put the same question another way, if the commission were abolished today, would we have a very different world?"

Pertschuk replied accurately, "I would have to say that the commission cannot claim any great credit for reshaping the structure of this economy."

If Congress and its business buddies have their way, the FTC's valiant battle to change that situation will have been for nothing.

The Bureaucracy as a Check on the President

The final staff report of the Senate Watergate Committee in 1974 recommended the dilution of White House powers by giving more independence to the permanent agencies of the bureaucracy, in particular the Justice Department, the Federal Bureau of Investigation, the Internal Revenue Service, and the Central Intelligence Agency. Essentially the report recommended strengthening the bureaucracy as a check upon the President. Before Watergate, and dating back to the New Deal, the trend in public administration was toward increasing executive power over administrative agencies rather than diminishing it. One of the principal recommendations of the President's Committee on Administrative Management in 1937, the Hoover Commissions of 1949 and 1955, and later management-oriented study groups, was that the independence of the bureaucracy constituted a major barrier in the path of efficient government. These groups recommended eliminating administrative independence and centralizing control over the bureaucracy in the White House. A major rethinking of the proper role of the bureaucracy in relation to the President occurred as the result of Watergate. The following selection discusses the role of the bureaucracy as a check upon the President in light of the events of Watergate.

47

Peter Woll and Rochelle Jones

THE BUREAUCRACY: A BRAKE
ON PRESIDENTIAL POWER

The Watergate hearings have intensified the debate over the growth — and proper limits — of presidential power. Among many concerned people in and out of government the feeling is that Richard Nixon was making an unprecedented attempt to concentrate political power in the White House. For evidence the critics point to Nixon's attempt to dismantle the Office of Economic Opportunity, an office created by Congress, his impoundment of funds appropriated by Congress for water pollution, highways and other programs, and his repeated disregard of congressional resolutions on the war in Southeast Asia. Only after he was pushed to the wall by congressional action that threatened to cut off funds for the entire federal government if he did not stop the bombing of Cambodia, did he agree to an August 15th deadline for a bombing halt. In a recent series of articles in the *New York Times* Henry Steele Commager said that the United States is closer to one-man rule than at any time in its history.

While there is no doubt that Nixon frequently thwarts the will and intent of Congress, it does not necessarily mean we are on the verge of one-man rule. Nixon apparently would like to retitle the federal government "U.S. Government, Inc.; President: Richard M. Nixon," but the federal bureaucracy, composed of the Cabinet, independent regulatory commissions and administrative agencies, puts important limits on the power of the President. Under the Nixon Administration the bureaucracy is turning into a vital although little noticed safeguard of the democratic system.

The bureaucracy, sometimes with Congress but often by itself, has frequently been able to resist and ignore presidential commands. Whether the President is FDR or Richard M. Nixon, bureaucratic frustration of White House policies is a fact of life. Furthermore, the bureaucracy often carries out its own policies which are at times the exact opposite of White House directives. A classic case occurred during the India-Pakistan war in 1971 when the State Department supported India while the White House backed Pakistan. The State Department's behind-the-scenes maneuvering in support

From Peter Woll and Rochelle Jones, "Against One-Man Rule: Bureaucratic Defense in Dept.," *The Nation* (September 17, 1973), pp. 229–232. Reprinted by permission.

of India prompted Henry Kissinger's famous enraged order "to tilt" toward Pakistan.

In a system marked by a weak Congress and a Supreme Court that is increasingly taking its direction from Nixon appointees, the bureaucracy is turning into the crucial check on presidential power. Under the Constitution Nixon is chief executive, but this does not mean he has legal authority or political power to control the bureaucracy. On the contrary, the bureaucracy has become a fourth branch of government, separate and independent of the President, Congress and the courts. There are limits to bureaucratic discretion, but these are set as much by Congress and the courts as by the President. Decisions of independent regulatory commissions may be overturned under certain circumstances by the courts. And while the administrative agencies created by Congress are delegated considerable discretionary authority, this authority must be exercised with broad guidelines that are set by the legislature. It is precisely this accountability of the bureaucracy to the courts and Congress that helps it to be a powerful constraint on Presidential power. For example, in *State Highway Commission of Missouri* v. *Volpe* (*1973*) the Eighth Circuit Court of Appeals ruled that the Secretary of Transportation could not legally follow Nixon's directives and impound highway funds. The court held that Congress had clearly specified in the Federal Highway Act that appropriated funds were to be apportioned among the states. In effect, the court was saying that the Department of Transportation, a Cabinet department presumably under presidential control, must comply with the intent of Congress, as it is interpreted by the court, instead of following the orders of the President.

Ultimately the bureaucracy curbs the President because it has independent sources of political power. Nixon's attempt to cut back governmental programs and reduce spending conflicts with the vested interests of powerful groups in and out of government. Like Congress and the President, administrative agencies and regulatory commissions have constituencies that are relied on for political support. The Defense Department needs the armaments industry, Agriculture the farmers, Labor the AFL-CIO, the ICC the railroads and truckers, and the Food and Drug Administration the giant pharmaceutical companies.

Because the bureaucracy depends on the political support of these allies for its continued existence, and because this alliance survives the four or eight years a President is in office, the bureaucracy is apt to prefer its interests over the wishes of the President. This is not new. On numerous occasions, for instance, the independent regulatory agencies have adopted policies that directly opposed the programs of the President. In the early 1960s both the Interstate Commerce Commission and Civil Aeronautics Board ignored White House directives in approving railroad and airline mergers that reduced competition.

Outside political support enables agencies to act independently. The regulatory agencies have been able to resist, for the most part, attempts by presidents from Franklin D. Roosevelt to Richard Nixon to organize and bring them under presidential supervision. A number of presidents on a number of occasions have tried to transfer the regulatory functions of the Interstate Commerce Commission to a Cabinet department like the Department of Transportation, which is more capable of being controlled by the White House. But the railroads' support for the ICC has been felt in and reflected by Congress, and the ICC has retained its separate identity. With the help of equally strong support from their allies, other agencies have defeated attempts, most recently by Nixon, to reorganize them. In 1971 Nixon proposed a major reorganization of the Executive Branch that would have meant a major shift of authority. The Department of Agriculture, for example, would have lost control over a variety of programs to a proposed super Department of Natural Resources. But the Department of Agriculture rallied its constituency behind it, and the reorganization plan languished in Congress.

Agencies that lack independent political support in Congress and are not supported by private pressure groups are apt to be swayed by the President. There is a big difference between the Department of Transportation and the Department of State. The former is supported by a wide range of groups, from proponents of federal airport subsidies to groups connected with aviation safety, urban transit, highway safety, and the Coast Guard. The latter is without Congressional and interest group backing. When Nixon tried to create a "super-Cabinet" at the start of his second term, Secretary of Transportation Claude S. Brinegar announced loudly and repeatedly that he was not going to be subordinate to the super-Cabinet Secretary James Lynn, Secretary of the Department of Housing and Urban Development, who had been named his superior by Nixon. But Secretary of State William Rogers was upstaged from the very start of the Nixon Administration by Henry Kissinger. Kissinger has usurped the major foreign policy-making responsibilities of the State Department while serving as an unofficial ambassador at large and roving emissary to foreign governments, a pleasant duty that is traditionally the prerogative of the Secretary of State. Secretary of State John Foster Dulles played such a role in the Eisenhower administration. But this is possible only if the Secretary of State enjoys the confidence of the President as Dulles did. If he doesn't, the Secretary of State will be a mere figurehead in the foreign policy field because the State Department is exceedingly vulnerable to domination by the White House. Its lack of domestic allies enables it to win very little support from Congress. When Sen. Joseph McCarthy launched his witch hunt after subversives in government, he wisely tackled the State Department first. As long as he was battling the State Department, he was safe. When he turned on the Department of the Army with its close links to a powerful domestic constituency and hence to key Congressional committees, his downfall was imminent.

In addition to its political support the bureaucracy contains the President in other ways. The President has minimal influence within the bureaucracy because of its size, complexity, wide-ranging responsibilities and continuity. More than one-half of the 3 million civilian employees of the federal government work for the Defense Department, for one good example. Tens of thousands of them are in key policy-making positions. All recent Secretaries of Defense, with the possible exception of McNamara, have had difficulty keeping up with day-to-day shifts in policy that are the result of decisions made by subordinates. Obviously Nixon cannot keep up with the operations of this mammoth department. And this is true in every large department of government. The president must delegate authority, and by doing so tends to lose control. Admittedly Nixon has made a strong attempt to change this. Before Watergate heightened the debate over the limits of presidential power, Washington civil servants were operating in an atmosphere that was permeated with fear. Since the Watergate hearings started, however, bureaucrats have resumed their traditional independent stance.

Moreover, since Nixon can't know what is going on in every nook of the federal bureaucracy, he must rely on the information that is provided by it for his decision making. By carefully controlling the information that reaches the President, the bureaucracy can control his decision making. This is not necessarily Machiavellian. Very often administrators, even subordinate administrators, are the only ones who possess the background and arcane knowledge to fill in the details of vague Congressional legislation. The strength of the bureaucracy is magnified when the President and Congress must come to it for the necessary information and technical skills to formulate and implement public policy. In a highly technical and increasingly specialized society the power of bureaucracy grows because the bureaucracy is the domain of the specialist, while the Congress and President are necessarily generalists.

The use of bureaucratic expertise in congressional policy making will be facilitated through the Office of Technological Assessment (OTA), being formed under the sponsorship of Sen. Edward Kennedy (D., Mass.). The OTA, created by legislation in 1972, is a way of challenging the present power of the Office of Management and Budget to prevent agencies from going directly to Congress with policy-making proposals. Such administrative inputs to the legislative process must first be cleared by the OMB. But the OTA is authorized to use the technical resources of the bureaucracy to draft policies that reflect the priorities of Congress. With these outside sources of information Congress will be able to challenge the President in a way previously impossible. Because Congress will be relying on information that comes from the bureaucracy, the bureaucracy will have vastly increased influence in the policy-making process. And since agency personnel assigned to the OTA will be working for Congress, not the President, they can give substantial help in developing programs that may directly contradict the programs of the President. A new bureaucratic check on the President is emerging.

Presidents come and go; the bureaucracy stays. Even if the President's only concern were the control of the bureaucracy, he would find this extremely difficult to accomplish in eight years. Obviously the President has many other pressing concerns besides the bureaucracy. At the beginning of his first term he is concerned with making a good impression. With the election mandate behind him and the congressional honeymoon ahead of him, the president wants to charge ahead, to do great things which, if they don't win him a place in the history books, may at least win him a second term in office. But such great plans can be abruptly halted by the bureaucracy. The newly elected President can find that many top bureaucrats who were appointed by the previous President are entrenched in power, protected by civil service regulations or terms of office that are set by statutes. The President is reduced to watching helplessly as the bureaucracy stymies his key programs. By the start of his second term the President may decide to make a determined effort to control the bureaucracy in a final, valiant attempt to push through his program.

And in fact, Nixon tried exactly that, finding that it is easy to try to curb the bureaucracy but exceedingly difficult to succeed. Nixon created a super-Cabinet last January in an attempt to centralize power in the White House; it was a dismal failure. It never functioned as it was supposed to. Agencies ignored it and did as they pleased or bypassed it and went directly to the President. Nixon finally junked the super-Cabinet four months after it was established.

In opposing presidential programs, the bureaucracy relies heavily on informal contacts with Congress. The White House may, and often does, try to muzzle administrators, but the bureaucracy has ways of getting necessary information to key Congressmen. Information flows back and forth among bureaucrats and Congressmen over the phone, at casual meetings and cocktail parties. Pressure groups also channel information from the agencies to Congressional committees.

For example, the President can order the Department of Agriculture to eliminate or reduce various agricultural programs, but these orders are likely to fail eventually because of the strong support for the department in Congress and among various agricultural interest groups. The department might have to go along with the President temporarily, but it would not have to wait long for congressional support to back up its policy favoring maintenance of such programs. This happened in 1972 when the Department of Agriculture abolished several key programs at the request of Nixon. An angry Congress overwhelmingly voted to restore the programs.

Many agencies are closer to Congress than to the President. The Securities and Exchange Commission (SEC) is a good example of an agency that has stronger ties to the House and Senate than to the White House. Rep.

John Moss (D., Calif.), chairman of the House Subcommittee on Commerce and Finance, and Sen. Harrison Williams (D., N.J.), chairman of the Securities Subcommittee of the Senate Banking Committee, deal directly with the SEC on a continuous basis. The SEC supplies these legislators with information, and they, in turn, prod the agency to implement the policy positions that they favor. With the help of a strong professional staff, these men are directly involved in the regulation of the securities industry. Of course, the White House can wield a certain amount of power, as it did when it influenced the SEC staff to withhold important information on the financial dealings of financier Robert Vesco because the information might embarrass the Committee for the Re-election of the President. But this influence is sporadic and limited to specific issues, while Congress deals with the SEC and other agencies on an almost daily basis.

Nixon can exert some control over the bureaucracy through his power of appointment. The President directly controls the appointment of more than 2,000 top-level bureaucrats. These positions were filled during Nixon's first term with people considered "reliable." After the 1972 election all of these appointees were required to submit their resignations. Many have been fired, producing great disillusionment throughout the ranks. As a result of the insensitive behavior of Nixon's staff, the White House faced enormous difficulty in recruiting new people, and many positions remain vacant in the top echelons of departments and agencies.

Nixon has been appointing former White House aides and CRP employees as an elite corps of "agents," numbering more than 100, to departments, independent regulatory commissions and agencies to find out what is going on and to carry out the Nixon philosophy. Such agents have been installed at the Under Secretary level in Treasury, Interior, Transportation and HEW. At lower levels agents were placed in Commerce (25), Interior (13), Agriculture (17), Treasury (11), the Environmental Protection Agency (20), Veterans Administration (11), FAA (5), and FTC (9). Nixon has filled twenty-eight of the thirty-eight positions on six major regulatory commissions and named the chairmen of all six. White House clearance has been required of many staff appointments. This attempt to control the independent regulatory commissions prompted the House Interstate and Foreign Commerce Committee to begin an investigation of what its chairman, Harley O. Staggers (D., W. Va.), considers inappropriate White House pressure.

For a short time Nixon's appointees can undoubtedly influence administrative policy making. But Nixon has failed more often than he has succeeded in changing the direction of the bureaucracy through the appointment process. He has created anxiety, frustration and disillusionment, and impeded independent policy making by the bureaucrats in those limited number of agencies where he has placed his agents.

In the case of the independent regulatory commissions the President may be able to stack them in his favor, but this is only a temporary impediment to the commissions' inherent ability to limit presidential power. Nixon's appointees will constitute a major limitation on the next President. From the standpoint of the presidency, the influence of one President on Regulatory agencies through appointments can lay the groundwork for future agency resistance to a new President. Similarly, the expansion of the bureaucracy in line with the philosophy of a President who believes in an activist government, such as FDR, limits future Presidents who believe in a concept of limited governmental intervention. Thus the appointment process is a two-edged sword, working against presidential power in the long run while giving short-term advantage.

Many of Nixon's appointees, even in his elite corps, were given jobs as a political payoff for their loyalty to him and their work in his campaigns. These strictly political types have been put in showcase jobs in many cases, often as assistants to top-echelon people, consultants, and in public affairs jobs. Even "deputy administrators" are often phony jobs with an impressive title but little clout. Moreover, most political types know little or nothing about the agencies they are appointed to. They cannot rival the top-grade permanent civil servants in policy making. And while the political appointees often have short stays in their jobs, the civil servants tend to be permanent employees. In the final analysis the expertise, continuity and political ties of the permanent civil service severely limit the ability of any President to alter bureaucratic practices through his appointments.

The courts can help the bureaucracy in imposing limits on the President. In recent years, an active judiciary has forced administrative agencies to adhere closely to congressional intent, as defined by the courts, reinforcing the ability of the bureaucracy to resist presidential control. Within the last few months the courts declared *ultra vires* Nixon's actions to impound funds that would be appropriated to administrative agencies under normal circumstances. The courts also preserved, at least temporarily, the Office of Economic Opportunity which was in the process of being dismantled under orders from Nixon.

The Watergate affair clearly reveals the value of a semi-autonomous bureaucracy. A President who could direct the activities of all administrative agencies would threaten our constitutional system. If the White House had been able to use the FBI and CIA as it had planned, a far-flung political intelligence operation would now be operating in a way that would undermine basic guarantees of our constitutional system, such as the Fourth Amendment guarantees against unreasonable searches and seizures. It was because J. Edgar Hoover and the FBI resisted that the efforts of the White House to set up a secret police operation with the approval of Nixon were stymied. Asst. Atty. Gen. Henry Petersen, a career attorney, refused to go along with Ehrlichman's improper requests. Richard Helms and General Walters of the CIA likewise maintained their independence under pressure by Haldeman and Ehrlichman. And it seems evident that a number of career professionals at the FBI leaked information to the press in order to frustrate what they saw as a move to corrupt the bureau.

At the same time, however, bureaucrats need to be imbued with the values of our constitutional democracy because, for the most part, the limits on them are those they impose upon themselves. It is ironic that the independence of the FBI and J. Edgar Hoover, so often criticized as a potential threat to responsible government, turned out under the Nixon Administration to be a bulwark of freedom. Perhaps, in the final analysis, we are saved from tyranny by the pluralism of our system and even its inefficiency. The pluralistic and independent bureaucracy, although often inefficient and yielding to special-interest group pressure, helps to preserve the balance of powers among the branches of government that is necessary for the preservation of our system of constitutional democracy.

The incentives and powers of the bureaucracy to check the President, so clearly exhibited during the Nixon years, are characteristic of all presidential administrations. In the twentieth century virtually every President has come into office with a grand design to increase administrative efficiency by streamlining the organization of the federal bureaucracy and by making the administrative branch accountable to the White House. While Presidents may be hopeful as they enter office that they can accomplish this task, they soon learn that the bureaucracy is an independent force, buttressed by Congress and private pressure groups, that defies presidential attempts to change it. Congress and the bureaucracy have forged a highly incestuous relationship that resents outside intrusions. And in addition to congressional support, agencies often have the support of powerful pressure groups that back administrators in return for favorable consideration of their interests.

As President Carter took over the reins of government in the spring of 1977 he immediately confronted the reality of an independent bureaucracy. He had promised sweeping reorganization of the bureaucracy, and there was a definite anti-bureaucratic atmosphere in the White House that reminded some old-timers of the early Nixon years. Would President Carter be any more successful in dealing with the administrative branch than President Nixon had been before him? The following selection discusses, in the context of history and the political realities of Washington, President Carter's confrontation with the bureaucracy.

48

Rochelle Jones and Peter Woll

PRESIDENT CARTER v.
THE BUREAUCRACY:
THE INTEREST VESTED IN CHAOS

"I think that it is generally agreed that there should be a systematic reorganization and reassembling of its [the government's] parts so as to secure greater efficiency and effect considerable savings in expense."
— President Woodrow Wilson, 1914

"For many years we have all known that the executive and administrative departments of the Government in Washington are a higgledy-piggledy patchwork of duplicative responsibilities and overlapping powers."
— President Franklin Roosevelt, 1937

"The time has come to match our structure to our purposes — to look with fresh eye, and to organize the Government by conscious, comprehensive design to meet the new needs of a new era."
— President Richard Nixon, 1971

"It's time for us to take a new look at our government, to eliminate waste, to release our civil servants from bureaucratic chaos, to provide tough management. . . ."
— Presidential nominee Carter, 1976

A lot of people who thought last November that a vote for Carter was a vote to clean up the mess in Washington are in for a disappointment.

As presidential nominee, Carter campaigned on a platform of government reorganization, attacking the bloat and waste in the federal bureaucracy and pledging to reduce the number of executive branch agencies from 1,900 to 200. An electorate, disenchanted with grandiose federal programs and the large-scale bureaucracies that administer them, saw in him a political outsider whose very lack of ties to Washington would enable him to take on the federal bureaucrats and win.

But it is one thing for a presidential nominee to promise reorganization

From Rochelle Jones and Peter Woll, "Carter vs. the Bureaucracy," *The Nation* (April 2, 1977). Reprinted by permission. This selection was originally entitled, "Carter vs. the Bureaucrats: The Interest Vested in Chaos."

and quite another for a President to carry it out. Such attempts are bound
to unite the Washington political establishment against the President, even
while it superficially supports his goals.

The opposition is not based on disagreement with President Carter's
premises; the waste and inefficiency created by a hodgepodge of government
agencies are too well documented. The federal bureaucracy consists of eleven
Cabinet departments, forty-four independent agencies and some 1,240 advisory boards, committees, commissions and councils, with more added annually. In fact, President Carter has already established four new advisory
bodies — the Commission on Mental Health, the U.S. Circuit Judiciary
Nomination Commission, the Committee on Selection of the Director of the
Federal Bureau of Investigation and the Advisory Board on Ambassadorial
Appointments.

There are some 228 separate health programs, 156 separate income
security and social service programs and eighty-three separate housing programs. Functionally similar programs are scattered throughout the various
Cabinet departments. Education, for instance, is nominally the responsibility
of the Department of Health, Education and Welfare, but the Department
of Agriculture operates its own graduate school and the Department of
Defense oversees a far-flung school system for the children of military personnel abroad. The regulations issued by federal agencies and programs fill
60,000 pages of fine print a year in the *Federal Register* and the paperwork
they stipulate is so extensive that the state of Maryland not long ago declined
a $60,000 HEW grant because it would cost at least that much to apply.

Thus, everyone agrees in the abstract that government reorganization
would be desirable, but while the electorate perceives it as relief from an
overburdening government, politicians, political appointees and top career
civil servants see it as a threat to power and status. They are for reorganization — but of somebody else's program or agency.

Every American President in this century has taken office pledging wholesale reorganization of the federal bureaucracy, and each of them has had to
settle for piecemeal reform at best. Meanwhile, the bureaucracy has continued to grow.

Theodore Roosevelt established the pattern in 1905 when he appointed
the Keep Commission, the first presidential commission on government organization, to study the efficiency of the Cabinet departments. Its recommendations, like those of its successors, were defeated by Congress and a
recalcitrant Cabinet. (It was William McAdoo who, as Secretary of the
Treasury in the Wilson administration, reportedly "kicked like a steer" at
even the suggestion that health services and the building of post offices be
taken away from his department.)

During the 1930s public concern over the how and why of government organization reached its peak. Congress succumbed to this pressure long enough to pass the Economy Act of 1932, which permitted the President to reorganize the executive branch unless his proposals were vetoed by either branch of Congress within sixty days. It was the first in a series of such acts, enacted over the next twenty years, culminating in the Reorganization Act of 1949. Hoover submitted a sweeping reorganization plan to Congress in late 1932, but his recommendations were rejected by a heavily Democratic House of Representatives.

The presidential election that year had been dominated by two issues: government organization and the economy. Franklin Roosevelt joined the issues by calling for a reorganization of the government so that federal expenditures could be reduced and the budget balanced. He promised to secure in advance the cooperation of potential Cabinet appointees and at his first press conference as president named reorganization as one of his top priorities.

However, he waited until the end of his first term to appoint his Committee on Administrative Management popularly called the Brownlow Committee. Roosevelt by then saw reorganization through the eyes of the president, who is always responsible for, but never fully in control of, the bureaucracy. At one point, for example, he learned from a newspaper story that the Navy planned to undertake a $2 billion shipbuilding program. Roosevelt, recalling the incident, said, "Here I am, the Commander in Chief of the Navy having to read about that for the first time in the press. Do you know what I said to that? . . . I said: 'Jesus Chr-rist!' "

The Brownlow Committee made recommendations designed to insure Presidential control of the bureaucracy. Roosevelt then waited until after his landslide re-election and the election of an overwhelmingly Democratic Congress in 1937 to ask for authority to implement the recommendations. Even so, his request met tough opposition. Secretary of Interior Harold Ickes wrote, "I do not believe that I have seen so much hysteria over any proposed piece of legislation since the World War and the attempt of President Wilson to force the ratification of the League of Nations." Congress finally approved a narrowly circumscribed version of Roosevelt's original request. Roosevelt's only real achievement under the act was the creation of the Executive Office of the President, including the Bureau of the Budget.

Richard Nixon, the most anti-bureaucratic of Presidents, tried the most sweeping reforms. He proposed merging a number of existing Cabinet departments into four super departments — Community Development, Natural Resources, Human Resources and Economic Affairs. The proposal was thoroughly logical but totally impractical, given the political reality. After some cursory Congressional hearings, the proposals were forgotten — even by Nixon.

He was more successful in reorganizing the Executive Office of the President. After a tough struggle with Congress, he abolished the Bureau of the Budget, which had operated by statute, and created in its place the Office of Management and Budget, which operated under presidential directive. He created the Domestic Council and other staff agencies, hoping that a new presidential bureaucracy would counterbalance and control the existing bureaucracy. But he lost touch with his own organization as it expanded, and in the end both bureaucracies were beyond his control. In fact, the Washington bureaucracy grew the most under Nixon, the president who most desired to control it. Between 1969 and 1972 there was a net increase of eighty agencies, many of them in the presidential bureaucracy.

That being the capsule history of bureaucratic reform, one may expect Mr. Carter to find that Congress will fight to preserve the status quo and the bureaucrats — career civil servants and Cabinet officers — will oppose any diminution of their authority. Congress and the federal bureaucracy have established a highly effective relationship in this area. Bureaucrats intent on resisting attempts to dismantle agencies and programs under their control find allies on Capitol Hill among the chairmen of Congressional committees and subcommittees that control their authorizations and appropriations. The civil servants obviously need the Congressmen to keep their agencies and programs alive and funded. The Congressmen, less obviously, need the civil servants whose expert knowledge of their areas helps to build the Congressmen's legislative reputations. Each needs the other to survive in Washington. The result is exemplified in the career of Rep. Jamie Whitten (D., Miss.), chairman of the House Appropriations Subcommittee on Agriculture. Whitten has been called the Permanent Secretary of Agriculture, a nickname earned by his long-time advocacy of funds for farm programs sponsored by the department. In turn, the civil servants who run Agriculture, administration after administration, provide Whitten with inside information that helps him to maintain his reputation among fellow Congressmen as an expert on agriculture policy.

Virtually every Cabinet department and administrative agency of any consequence is backed by powerful members of Congress. For example, Sen. Warren Magnuson (D., Wash.), chairman of the Commerce Committee, permitted the transfer of the Federal Aviation Administration into the Department of Transportation only on condition that the FAA retain its separate identity. Even the smaller, more obscure agencies have loyal supporters. The American Battle Monuments Commission was criticized on national television earlier this year by a Congressman who felt that its mere existence demonstrated the need for government reorganization. But when representatives of the commission appeared before a House Appropriations Subcommittee a few days later to make their annual request for funds, the chairman, Rep. Edward Boland (D., Mass.), had nothing but praise for the efficiency and quality of the commission's work.

Congressmen have strong incentives to preserve, even tacitly to encourage, the present hodgepodge of overlapping jurisdictions among agencies and departments. The wider the responsibility is diffused throughout the executive branch, the greater the number of Congressional committees and subcommittees that can legitimately claim jurisdiction. Then, when an issue like energy captures national attention, nearly every Congressman has an opportunity to be personally involved. During the first nine months of the 94th Congress, energy-related hearings were held by twelve committees and twenty-five subcommittees in the Senate and seventeen committees and thirty-five subcommittees in the House of Representatives. The Federal Energy Administration alone testified at forty-six Senate hearings, fifty-eight House hearings and eight joint Congressional hearings in 1975.

In addition to the support of Congressmen, the federal bureaucracy can count on the support of Congressional staff, particularly committee staff. The tremendous growth in staff — a 44.2 percent increase between 1970 and 1975 — has created a Congressional bureaucracy which often has a vested interest in supporting its counterparts in the federal bureaucracy. When the FEA was due to expire in 1976, the eighteen staff members of the Energy and Power Subcommittee of the House Interstate and Foreign Commerce Committee automatically backed its extension. Their jobs depended largely on the continuation of the FEA.

Some reorganization is possible if the power structure of existing Congressional committees is not threatened. The creation of both the Departments of Housing and Urban Development and of Transportation, for instance, left the committee systems intact. However, former Undersecretary of the Interior John Whitaker recently stated that Congressional jurisdictional disputes blocked the creation of a unified energy department in the Nixon administration. For similar reasons, President Carter's proposed Department of Energy is likely to win quicker approval in the Senate than in the House. Senate committees were reorganized this year and jurisdiction over energy was consolidated in the Energy and Natural Resources Committee. Its chairman, Sen. Henry Jackson (D., Wash.), has enthusiastically endorsed the new department. Jurisdiction in the House remains scattered through numerous committees.

The federal bureaucracy does not always need to turn to its Congressional allies for support. Cabinet officials and federal bureaucrats are often capable of opposing on their own Presidential interference in their departments. Over the years the Cabinet departments have evolved their own special views on policy which reflect a blend of special and bureaucratic interests, and these positions are jealously guarded against Presidential encroachment. J. Edgar Hoover is the paradigm of bureaucratic resistance. The FBI was untouchable while Hoover was alive, and remains so to a large extent today because of his influence. Most bureaucrats, however, prefer to work quietly behind the scenes. Public resistance and outright opposition are usually left to Cabinet secretaries.

Most Cabinet officials, in fact, are chosen with the concurrence of groups having a special interest in the departments they will head. That is particularly true at departments like Labor, Agriculture and Commerce that serve a well-defined constituency. Peter Brennan, for instance, was head of the New York State Building and Construction Trades Council before he became Secretary of Labor. Such Cabinet officials represent first the interests of their departments and the groups their departments serve; the interests of the President and the public at large come second.

Even when Presidents attempt to circumvent the special-interest groups by making an "outside" appointment, they soon find their appointees adopting the viewpoint of the department. Walter J. Hickel, a millionaire with close ties to the oil industry, seemed an unlikely environmentalist when he was tapped for the post of Secretary of the Interior by Nixon. In fact, as Governor of Alaska he had favored the economic development of public lands in the state. Hickel, however, compiled an outstanding record on conservation issues at the Interior Department.

President Carter clearly sought the approval of the vested interests — labor, business, conservation, agriculture — served by the departments when he picked his Cabinet officials. In many instances he selected people who already had an ingrained interest in protecting their departments because they were part of the establishment served by the department. Secretary of Defense Harold Brown was Secretary of the Air Force in the Johnson administration. Secretary of Health, Education and Welfare Joseph Califano created many of its programs as Lyndon Johnson's deputy and alter ego for domestic affairs. Secretary of Transportation Brock Adams represented for twelve years a Congressional District in which Boeing Aircraft is the major employer. Secretary of the Treasury Michael Blumenthal was chairman of the board, president and chief executive officer of the Bendix Corporation. Others in the Cabinet, including some of the fresh faces promised by Carter, have strong ties to their constituencies. Secretary of the Interior Cecil Andrus, when Governor of Idaho, fought alongside conservationists to preserve the scenic and wild rivers of that state. Secretary of Agriculture Bob Bergland is a farmer and former member of the House Agriculture Committee. Secretary of Commerce Juanita Kreps was a member of the Board of Governors of the New York Stock Exchange, Inc., and served on the board of directors of several corporations, including the J. C. Penney Company.

Moreover, President Carter has promised to give his Cabinet officials unprecedented autonomy in running their departments. He has repeatedly said his Cabinet secretaries will not be dictated to by White House staff. In the Carter administration the Cabinet has not only the incentive to resist any reorganization but also a power base from which to do so.

And, in fact, several Cabinet secretaries have already begun to preserve and protect their departments from presidential tampering. Brown said shortly after his nomination that he could not envision reducing the defense budget by the $5 billion promised by Carter during the campaign. Califano has stated that he did not become Secretary of the Department of Health, Education and Welfare to preside over its dismemberment. While Andrus reluctantly agreed to relinquish to the proposed Energy Department the authority to establish production goals for gas, oil and coal produced under federal leases, he refused to cede Interior's power to lease the land in the first place.

Under President Carter paper reorganizations of the executive branch and cosmetic reforms of the federal bureaucracy may be possible, as they have been in the past. But substantive changes are as unlikely now as they were seventy-two years ago when Theodore Roosevelt resolved to improve the government's efficiency. The real power in Washington, as President after President has discovered to his dismay, is not located in the Oval Office. It is held by the politicians and their aides, the top career civil servants and the political appointees. The arms of this political establishment will continue to support and protect one another, held together by a network of mutual self-interest, professional ties, and a shared belief that "this is the way it's done in Washington."

CHAPTER 8

Congress

The United States Congress, exercising supreme legislative power, was at the beginning of the nineteenth century the most powerful political institution in the national government. It was feared by the framers of the Constitution, who felt that unless it was closely guarded and limited it would easily dominate both the presidency and the Supreme Court. Its powers were carefully enumerated, and it was made a bicameral body. This latter provision not only secured representation of different interests but also limited the power of the legislature which, when hobbled by two houses often working against each other, could not act as swiftly and forcefully as a single body could. Although still important, the power and prestige of Congress have declined while the powers of the President and the Supreme Court, not to mention those of the vast governmental bureaucracy, have increased. Congressional power, its basis, and the factors influencing the current position of Congress vis-à-vis coordinate governmental departments are discussed in this chapter.

Constitutional Background: Representation of Popular, Group, and National Interests

Article I, Section 1 of the Constitution states that "all legislative powers herein granted shall be vested in a Congress of the United States, which shall consist of a Senate and House of Representatives." Section 8 specifically enumerates Congressional powers, and provides that Congress shall have power "to make all laws which shall be necessary and proper for carrying into execution the foregoing powers, and all other powers vested by this Constitution in the government of the United States, or in any department or officer thereof."

Apart from delineating the powers of Congress, Article I provides that the House shall represent the people, and the Senate the states through appointment of members by the state legislatures. The representative function of Congress is written into the Constitution, and at the time of the framing of the Constitution much discussion centered on the nature of representation and what constituted adequate representation in a national legislative body. Further, relating in part to the question of representation, the framers of the Constitution had to determine what the appropriate tasks for each branch of the legislature were, and to what extent certain legislative activities should be within the exclusive or initial jurisdiction of the House or the Senate. All these questions depended to some extent upon the conceptualization the framers had of the House as representative of popular interests on a short-term basis and the Senate as a reflection of conservative interests on a long-term basis. These selections from *The Federalist* indicate the thinking of the framers about the House of Representatives and the Senate.

49

James Madison

FEDERALIST 53

... No man can be a competent legislator who does not add to an upright intention and a sound judgment a certain degree of knowledge of the subjects on which he is to legislate. A part of this knowledge may be acquired by means of information, which lie within the compass of men in private, as well as public stations. Another part can only be attained, or at least thoroughly attained, by actual experience in the station which requires the use of it. The period of service ought, therefore, in all such cases, to bear some proportion to the extent of practical knowledge requisite to the due performance of the service. . . .

In a single state the requisite knowledge relates to the existing laws, which are uniform throughout the state, and with which all the citizens are more or less conversant. . . . The great theater of the United States presents a very different scene. The laws are so far from being uniform that they vary in every state; whilst the public affairs of the union are spread throughout a very extensive region, and are extremely diversified by the local affairs connected with them, and can with difficulty be correctly learnt in any other place than in the central councils, to which a knowledge of them will be brought by representatives of every part of the empire. Yet some knowledge of the affairs, and even of the laws of all the states, ought to be possessed by the members from each of the states. . . .

A branch of knowledge which belongs to the acquirements of a federal representative, and which has not been mentioned, is that of foreign affairs. In regulating our own commerce he ought to be not only acquainted with the treaties between the United States and other nations, but also with the commercial policy and laws of other nations. He ought not to be altogether ignorant of the law of nations; for that, as far as it is a proper object of municipal legislation, is submitted to the federal government. And although the House of Representatives is not immediately to participate in foreign negotiations and arrangements, yet from the necessary connection between the several branches of public affairs, those particular subjects will frequently deserve attention in the ordinary course of legislation, and will sometimes demand particular legislative sanction and cooperation. Some portion of this knowledge may, no doubt, be acquired in a man's closet; but some of it also can only be acquired to best effect, by a practical attention to the subject, during the period of actual service in the legislature. . . .

FEDERALIST 56

The . . . charge against the House of Representatives is, that it will be too small to possess a due knowledge of the interests of its constituents.

As this objection evidently proceeds from a comparison of the proposed number of representatives, with the great extent of the United States, the number of their inhabitants, and the diversity of their interests, without taking into view, at the same time, the circumstances which will distinguish the Congress from other legislative bodies, the best answer that can be given to it, will be a brief explanation of these peculiarities.

It is a sound and important principle that the representative ought to be acquainted with the interests and circumstances of his constituents. But this principle can extend no farther than to those circumstances and interests to which the authority and care of the representative relate. An ignorance of a variety of minute and particular objects, which do not lie within the compass of legislation, is consistent with every attribute necessary to a due performance of the legislative trust. In determining the extent of information required in the exercise of a particular authority, recourse then must be had to the objects within the purview of that authority.

What are to be the objects of federal legislation? Those which are of most importance, and which seem most to require knowledge, are commerce, taxation, and the militia.

A proper regulation of commerce requires much information, as has been elsewhere remarked; but as far as this information relates to the laws, and local situation of each individual state, a very few representatives would be sufficient vehicles of it to the federal councils.

Taxation will consist, in great measure, of duties which will be involved in the regulation of commerce. So far the preceding remark is applicable to this object. As far as it may consist of internal collections, a more diffusive knowledge of the circumstances of the state may be necessary. But will not this also be possessed in sufficient degree by a very few intelligent men, diffusively elected within the state? . . .

With regard to the regulation of the militia there are scarcely any circumstances in reference to which local knowledge can be said to be necessary. . . . The art of war teaches general principles of organization, movement, and discipline, which apply universally.

The attentive reader will discern that the reasoning here used, to prove the sufficiency of a moderate number of representatives, does not, in any respect, contradict what was urged on another occasion, with regard to the extensive information which the representatives ought to possess, and the time that might be necessary for acquiring it. . . .

FEDERALIST 57

... The House of Representatives is so constituted as to support in the members an habitual recollection of their dependence on the people. Before the sentiments impressed on their minds by the mode of their elevation, can be effaced by the exercise of power, they will be compelled to anticipate the moment when their power is to cease, when their exercise of it is to be reviewed, and when they must descend to the level from which they were raised; there for ever to remain unless a faithful discharge of their trust shall have established their title to a renewal of it.

I will add, as a ... circumstance in the situation of the House of Representatives, restraining them from oppressive measures, that they can make no law which will not have its full operation on themselves and their friends, as well as on the great mass of the society. This has always been deemed one of the strongest bonds by which human policy can connect the rulers and the people together. It creates between them that communion of interest, and sympathy of sentiments, of which few governments have furnished examples; but without which every government degenerates into tyranny. If it be asked, what is to restrain the House of Representatives from making legal discriminations in favor of themselves, and a particular class of the society? I answer, the genius of the whole system; the nature of just and constitutional laws; and, above all, the vigilant and manly spirit which actuates the people of America; a spirit which nourishes freedom, and in return is nourished by it.

If this spirit shall ever be so far debased as to tolerate a law not obligatory on the legislature, as well as on the people, the people will be prepared to tolerate anything but liberty.

Such will be the relation between the House of Representatives and their constituents. Duty, gratitude, interest, ambition itself, are the cords by which they will be bound to fidelity and sympathy with the great mass of the people. It is possible that these may all be insufficient to control the caprice and wickedness of men. But are they not all that government will admit, and that human prudence can devise? Are they not the genuine, and the characteristic means, by which republican government provides for the liberty and happiness of the people? ...

FEDERALIST 58

... In this review of the constitution of the House of Representatives ... one observation ... I must be permitted to add ... as claiming, in my judgment, a very serious attention. It is, that in all legislative assemblies, the greater the number composing them may be, the fewer will be the men who will in fact direct their proceedings. In the first place, the more numerous any assembly may be, of whatever characters composed, the greater is known to be the ascendancy of passion over reason. In the next place, the larger the number, the greater will be the proportion of members of limited information and of weak capacities. Now it is precisely on characters of this description that the eloquence and address of the few are known to act with all their force. In the ancient republics, where the whole body of the people assembled in person, a single orator, or an artful statesman, was generally seen to rule with as complete a sway as if a sceptre had been placed in his single hands. On the same principle, the more multitudinous a representative assembly may be rendered, the more it will partake of the infirmities incident to collective meetings of the people. Ignorance will be the dupe of cunning; and passion the slave of sophistry and declamation. The people can never err more than in supposing, that by multiplying their representatives beyond a certain list, they strengthen the barrier against the government of a few. Experience will for ever admonish them, that, on the contrary, after securing a sufficient number for the purposes of safety, of local information, and of diffusive sympathy with the whole society, they will counteract their own views by every addition to their representatives. The countenance of the government may become more democratic; but the soul that animates it will be more oligarchic. The machine will be enlarged, but the fewer, and often the more secret, will be the springs by which its motions are directed. . . .

FEDERALIST 62

Having examined the constitution of the House of Representatives . . . I enter next on the examination of the Senate.

The heads under which this member of the government may be considered are — I. The qualifications of senators; II. The appointment of them by the state legislatures; III. The equality of representation in the Senate; IV. The number of senators, and the term for which they are to be elected; V. The powers vested in the Senate.

I

The qualifications proposed for senators, as distinguished from those of representatives, consist in a more advanced age and a longer period of citizenship. A senator must be thirty years of age at least; as a representative must be twenty-five. And the former must have been a citizen nine years; as seven years are required for the latter. The propriety of these distinctions is explained by the nature of the senatorial trust; which, requiring greater extent of information and stability of character, requires at the same time, that the senator should have reached a period of life most likely to supply these advantages. . . .

II

It is equally unnecessary to dilate on the appointment of senators by the state legislators. Among the various modes which might have been devised for constituting this branch of the government, that which has been proposed by the convention is probably the most congenial with the public opinion. It is recommended by the double advantage of favoring a select appointment, and of giving to the state governments such an agency in the formation of the federal government, as must secure the authority of the former, and may form a convenient link between the two systems.

III

The equality of representation in the Senate is another point, which, being evidently the result of compromise between the opposite pretensions of the large and the small states, does not call for much discussion. If indeed it be right, that among a people thoroughly incorporated into one nation, every district ought to have a *proportional* share in the government: and that among independent and sovereign states bound together by a simple league, the parties, however unequal in size, ought to have an *equal* share in the common councils, it does not appear to be without some reason, that in a compound republic, partaking both of the national and federal character, the government ought to be founded on a mixture of the principles of proportional [as found in the House of Representatives] and equal representation [in the Senate]. . . .

. . . [T]he equal vote allowed to each state, is at once a constitutional recognition of the portion of sovereignty remaining in the individual states, and an instrument for preserving that residuary sovereignty. So far the equality ought to be no less acceptable to the large than to the small states; since they are not less solicitous to guard by every possible expedient against an improper consolidation of the states into one simple republic.

Another advantage accruing from this ingredient in the constitution of the Senate is, the additional impediment it must prove against improper acts of legislation. No law or resolution can now be passed without the concurrence, first, of a majority of the people, and then, of a majority of the states. It must be acknowledged that this complicated check on legislation may, in some instances, be injurious as well as beneficial; and that the peculiar defense which it involves in favor of the smaller states, would be more rational, if any interests common to them, and distinct from those of the other states, would otherwise be exposed to peculiar danger. But as the larger states will always be able, by their power over the supplies, to defeat unreasonable exertions of this prerogative of the lesser states; and as the facility and excess of law-making seem to be the diseases to which our governments are most liable, it is not impossible, that this part of the constitution may be more convenient in practice than it appears to many in contemplation.

IV

The number of senators, and the duration of their appointment, come next to be considered. In order to form an accurate judgment on both these points, it will be proper to inquire into the purposes which are to be answered by the Senate; and, in order to ascertain these, it will be necessary to review the inconveniences which a republic must suffer from the want of such an institution.

First. It is a misfortune incident to republican government, though in a less degree than to other governments, that those who administer it may forget their obligations to their constituents, and prove unfaithful to their important trust. In this point of view, a senate, as a second branch of the legislative assembly, distinct from, and dividing the power with, a first, must be in all cases a salutary check on the government. It doubles the security to the people by requiring the concurrence of two distinct bodies in schemes of usurpation or perfidy, where the ambition or corruption of one would otherwise be sufficient. . . . [A]s the improbability of sinister combinations will be in proportion to the dissimilarity in the genius of the two bodies, it must be politic to distinguish them from each other by every circumstance which will consist with a due harmony in all proper measures, and with the genuine principles of republican government.

Second. The necessity of a senate is not less indicated by the propensity of all single and numerous assemblies, to yield to the impulse of sudden and violent passions, and to be seduced by factious leaders into intemperate and pernicious resolutions. Examples on this subject might be cited without number; and from proceedings within the United States, as well as from the history of other nations. But a position that will not be contradicted need not be proved. All that need be remarked is, that a body which is to correct this infirmity ought itself to be free from it, and consequently ought to be less numerous. It ought, moreover, to possess great firmness, and consequently ought to hold its authority by a tenure of considerable duration.

Third. Another defect to be supplied by a senate lies in a want of due acquaintance with the objects and principles of legislation. It is not possible that an assembly of men, called, for the most part, from pursuits of a private nature, continued in appointments for a short time, and led by no permanent motive to devote the intervals of public occupation to a study of the laws, the affairs, and the comprehensive interests of their country, should, if left wholly to themselves, escape a variety of important errors in the exercise of their legislative trust. . . .

Fourth. The mutability in the public councils, arising from a rapid succession of new members, however qualified they may be, points out, in the strongest manner, the necessity of some stable institution in the government. Every new election in the states is found to change one-half of the representatives. From this change of men must proceed a change of opinions; and from a change of opinions, a change of measures. But a continual change even of good measures is inconsistent with every rule of prudence, and every prospect of success. . . .

FEDERALIST 63

A *fifth* desideratum, illustrating the utility of a senate, is the want of a due sense of national character. Without a select and stable member of the government, the esteem of foreign powers will not only be forfeited by an unenlightened and variable policy . . . ; but the national councils will not possess that sensibility to the opinion of the world, which is perhaps not less necessary in order to merit, than it is to obtain, its respect and confidence. . . .

I add, as a *sixth* defect, the want in some important cases of a due responsibility in the government to the people, arising from that frequency of elections, which in other cases produces this responsibility. . . .

Responsibility, in order to be reasonable, must be limited to objects within the power of the responsible party, and in order to be effectual, must relate to operations of that power, of which a ready and proper judgment can be formed by the constituents. The objects of government may be divided into two general classes; the one depending on measures, which have singly an immediate and sensible operation; the other depending on a succession of well chosen and well connected measures, which have a gradual and perhaps unobserved operation. The importance of the latter description to the collective and permanent welfare of every country, needs no explanation. And yet it is evident that an assembly elected for so short a term as to be unable to provide more than one or two links in a chain of measures, on which the general welfare may essentially depend, ought not to be answerable for the final result, any more than a steward or tenant, engaged for one year, could be justly made to answer for plans or improvements, which could not be accomplished in less than half a dozen years. Nor is it possible for the people to estimate the *share* of influence, which their annual assemblies may respectively have on events resulting from the mixed transactions of several years. It is sufficiently difficult, at any rate, to preserve a personal responsibility in the members of a *numerous* body, for such acts of the body as have an immediate, detached, and palpable operation on its constituents.

The proper remedy for this defect must be an additional body in the legislative department, which, having sufficient permanency to provide for such objects as require a continued attention, and a train of measures, may be justly and effectually answerable for the attainment of those objects.

Thus far I have considered the circumstances, which point out the necessity of a well constructed senate, only as they relate to the representatives of the people. To a people as little blinded by prejudice, or corrupted by flattery, as those whom I address, I shall not scruple to add, that such an institution may be sometimes necessary, as a defense to the people against their own temporary errors and delusions. As the cool and deliberate sense of the community ought, in all governments, and actually will, in all free governments, ultimately prevail over the views of its rulers; so there are particular moments in public affairs, when the people, stimulated by some irregular passion, or some illicit advantage, or misled by the artful misrepresentations of interested men, may call for measures which they themselves will afterwards be the most ready to lament and condemn. In these critical moments, how salutary will be the interference of some temperate and respectable body of citizens, in order to check the misguided career, and to suspend the blow meditated by the people against themselves, until reason, justice and truth can regain their authority over the public mind? What bitter anguish would not the people of Athens have often avoided, if their government had contained so provident a safeguard against the tyranny of their own passions? Popular liberty might then have escaped the indelible reproach of decreeing to the same citizens the hemlock on one day, and statues on the next.

It may be suggested that a people spread over an extensive region cannot, like the crowded inhabitants of a small district, be subject to the infection of violent passions; or to the danger of combining in the pursuit of unjust measures. I am far from denying that this is a distinction of peculiar importance. I have, on the contrary, endeavored in a former paper to show that it is one of the principal recommendations of a confederated republic. At the same time this advantage ought not to be considered as superseding the use of auxiliary precautions. It may even be remarked that the same extended situation, which will exempt the people of America from some of the dangers incident to lesser republics, will expose them to the inconveniency of remaining for a longer time under the influence of those misrepresentations which the combined industry of interested men may succeed in distributing among them. . . .

Committee Chairmen as Part of the Washington Establishment

In 1885 Woodrow Wilson was able to state categorically in his famous work *Congressional Government:*

> The leaders of the House are the chairmen of the principal Standing Committees. Indeed, to be exactly accurate, the House has as many leaders as there are subjects of legislation; for there are as many Standing Committees as there are leading classes of legislation, and in the consideration of every topic of business the House is guided by a special leader in the person of the chairman of the Standing Committee, charged with the superintendence of measures of the particular class to which that topic belongs. It is this multiplicity of leaders, this many-headed leadership, which makes the organization of the House too complex to afford uninformed people and unskilled observers any easy clue to its methods of rule. For the chairmen of the Standing Committees do not constitute a cooperative body like a ministry. They do not consult and concur in the adoption of homogeneous and mutually helpful measures; there is no thought of acting in concert. Each Committee goes its own way at its own pace. It is impossible to discover any unity or method in the disconnected and therefore unsystematic, confused, and desultory action of the House, or any common purpose in the measures which its Committees from time to time recommend.

With regard to the Senate he noted:

> It has those same radical defects of organization which weaken the House. Its functions also, like those of the House, are segregated in the prerogatives of numerous Standing Committees. In this regard Congress is all of a piece. There is in the Senate no more opportunity than exists in the House for gaining such recognized party leadership as would be likely to enlarge a man by giving him a sense of power, and to steady and sober him by filling him with a grave sense of responsibility. So far as its organization controls it, the Senate . . . proceedings bear most of the characteristic features of committee rule.

The Legislative Reorganization Act of 1946 was designed to streamline Congressional committee structure and provide committees and individual Congressmen with increased expert staff; however, although the number of standing committees was reduced, subcommittees have increased so that the net numerical reduction is not as great as was originally intended. Further, because Congress still conducts its business through committees: (1) the senior members of the party with the majority in Congress dominate the formulation of public policy through the seniority rule; (2) policy formulation is fragmented with each committee maintaining relative dominance over policy areas within its jurisdiction; (3) stemming from this fragmentation, party control is weakened, especially when the President attempts to assume legislative dominance.

Although Congress is often pictured as powerless in confrontation with the executive branch, the fact is that the chairmen of powerful congressional committees often dominate administrative agencies over which they have jurisdiction. They are an important part of the broad Washington establishment. This is particularly true of the chairmen of appropriations committees and subcommittees, for they are able to wield far more influence over the bureaucracy because of their control of the purse strings than the chairmen of other committees. The appropriations committees have a direct weapon — money — that they can wield against administrative adversaries. And, the chairmen of all committees have seniority that often exceeds that of the bureaucrats with whom they are dealing. The secretaries and assistant secretaries of executive departments are political appointments who rarely stay in government more than two years, whereas powerful congressmen have been around for one or more decades. This gives the congressmen expertise that the political levels of the bureaucracy often lack. Political appointees in the bureaucracy must rely upon their professional staff in order to match the expertise of senior congressmen. The power of the chairmen of the appropriations committees often leads them to interfere directly in administrative operations. They become in effect part of the bureaucracy, often dominating it and determining what programs it will implement. The constant interaction between committee chairmen and agencies results in "government without passing laws," to use the phrase of Michael W. Kirst. (See Michael W. Kirst, *Government Without Passing Laws,* Capitol Hill: University of North Carolina Press, 1969.) The following selection deals with this process of legislative influence, and describes how one senior Southern congressman established himself as the "permanent secretary of agriculture." [1]

---

[1] The selection deals with Mississippi Congressman Jamie Whitten, who has moved into the most powerful position in the House of Representatives since the piece was written — the chairmanship of the Appropriations Committee. At the same time he has retained his position as Chairman of the Appropriations Subcommittee on Agriculture.

50

Nick Kotz

JAMIE WHITTEN,
PERMANENT SECRETARY
OF AGRICULTURE

With the sensitive instincts of a successful career bureaucrat, Dr. George Irving scanned the list of states scheduled for the National Nutrition Survey, which was to measure the extent of hunger in America. Halfway down the column his glance froze, and he quickly dialed Congressman Jamie Whitten, the man known in Washington as the "permanent secretary of agriculture."

"Mr. Chairman, they've got Mississippi on that malnutrition study list, and I thought you'd want to know about it," dutifully reported Irving, Administrator of the Agriculture Department's Agricultural Research Service.

For the better part of eighteen years as chairman of the House Appropriations Subcommittee on Agriculture, dapper Jamie L. Whitten has held an iron hand over the budget of the Department of Agriculture (USDA). The entire 107,000-man department is tuned in to the Mississippi legislator's every whim.

"George, we're not going to have another smear campaign against Mississippi, are we?" declared Whitten to his informant. "You boys should be thinking about a *national* survey — and do some studies in Watts and Hough and Harlem!"

Dr. Irving alerted the government's food aid network. "Mr. Whitten wants Mississippi taken off that list," he told Department of Agriculture food administrator Rodney Leonard.

Leonard, in turn, called Dr. George Silver, a Deputy Assistant Secretary of Health, Education, and Welfare, who was responsible for the joint USDA-HEW malnutrition survey.

"Jamie Whitten's found out Mississippi is on the list and is raising hell. I think we'd better drop it," Leonard said.

Silver, recalling HEW Secretary Wilbur Cohen's order to "avoid unnecessary political friction" in choosing the sample states for the hunger survey, called Dr. Arnold Schaefer, the project chief.

"Mississippi's out — politics!" Silver said curtly.

Back at the Department of Agriculture, food administrator Leonard

From Nick Kotz, *Let Them Eat Promises: The Politics of Hunger in America.* © 1969 by Nick Kotz. Published by Prentice-Hall, Inc., Englewood Cliffs, New Jersey.

snapped at Jamie Whitten's informant, "You couldn't have killed the project any better if you had planned it!"

Thus, in August, 1967, the Johnson Administration's first meaningful attempt to ascertain the facts about hunger in Mississippi was stopped cold by an executive department's fear of one congressman. This kind of bureaucratic-congressional maneuvering, exercised between the lines of the law, is little understood, seldom given public scrutiny, and far too infrequently challenged. In the quiet process of hidden power, a bureaucrat in the Agriculture Department reacts more quickly to a raised eyebrow from Jamie Whitten than to a direct order from the Secretary himself. Time after time, a few words from Jamie Whitten can harden into gospel at the Department of Agriculture. Indeed, a casual Whitten statement may be so magnified, as it is whispered from official to official, that the response is more subservient than even the Congressman had in mind.

The stocky, 59-year-old Congressman is not shy about his meteoric rise from a country store in Tallahatchie County to a key position in the nation's capital. And his record is impressive — trial lawyer and state legislator at 21, district attorney for five counties at 23, U.S. Congressman at 31 (in 1941), and chairman of an appropriations subcommittee at 36. His steely self-confidence, studied informality, and carefully conservative clothes suggest anything but the stereotype of country-lawyer-come-to-Washington. Only the beginning of a paunch detracts from a physical sense of strength and energy that radiates from Jamie Whitten.

For all his dynamic presence, Whitten has a way of confounding a listener — or potential critic — with silky Southern rhetoric. It is a test of mental agility to remember the original course of a conversation, as one high USDA official noted: "When you check on things with him, Whitten can go all around the barn with you. Often-times you don't fully understand what he meant. So you latch onto the most obvious point you can find and act on that."

With his implicit power, Whitten doesn't *have* to threaten or be specific. In fact, as George Irving pointed out about his conversation with the Congressman that led to dropping Mississippi from the national hunger survey, "He wasn't saying 'don't go to Mississippi,' he was just suggesting that we think about other places."

Bureaucratic officials who are familiar with Whitten's oblique way of expressing his ideas know also that the Mississippian can rattle off complicated economic statistics and arguments with precise logic and organized thought.

Whitten legally holds the power of the purse, and he exercises it shrewdly. His appropriations subcommittee doles out funds for every item in the Agriculture Department's $7 billion budget, and it does not take long for Washington bureaucrats to realize that the chairman's wrath can destroy precious projects and throw hundreds of people out of jobs.

"He's got the most phenomenal information and total recall," one Agriculture official says of Whitten. "Once you fully understand his do's and don't's and establish rapport with him, life is a whole lot easier!"

Jamie Whitten's considerable power is enhanced by his scholarship. He is a conscientious student of every line of the Agriculture budget, and his hawk's-eye is legendary among Department officials. They, in turn, anticipate his scrutiny by checking planned moves with him, thus extending to him a virtual veto on the most minute details. "A suggestion, that's all you have to have in this business," admitted Rodney Leonard.

The key to this phenomenal power — which goes beyond that of budget control — lies in Whitten's network of informants within the Department, and his skill directing their activities and operations. Executive branch officials learn to protect their own jobs, adjusting their loyalties to the legislative branch in a way the Founding Fathers may not have envisioned when they devised their splendid system of checks and balances. Bureaucratic allies of a particular congressman may be able to inject that congressman's political views (or their own) into laws or programs sponsored by the Administration without the consent, or even the knowledge, of the Department head. Secretaries of Agriculture come and go, but Jamie Whitten remains, a product of Mississippi's political oligarchy and the seniority system in Congress.

In theory, an appropriations subcommittee only considers requests for funds to finance programs already approved by Congress. Thus, Whitten shares some power with Bob Poage (D-Tex.), chairman of the House Agriculture Committee. In actuality, a skillful chairman such as Whitten can control policy, alter the original authorizing legislation, and wind up virtually controlling the administration of a department.

In addition to Chairman Whitten, the Agriculture Appropriations Subcommittee has seven members: Democrats William H. Natcher of Kentucky, W. R. Hull, Jr., of Missouri, George Shipley of Illinois, and Frank Evans of Colorado, and Republicans Odin Langen of Minnesota, Robert H. Michel of Illinois, and Jack Edwards of Alabama. Because a majority of these members share Whitten's outlook on agriculture and his arch-conservative view of social action, the chairman's will becomes the subcommittee's will. As chairman, he also has a hold over staff appointments.

Much of Whitten's power derives from the system within the House of Representatives. Once a subcommittee makes a decision, the full House Appropriations Committee almost always backs it up. This is particularly true with agriculture appropriations, because House Appropriations Chairman George Mahon (D-Tex.) shares Whitten's views on farm policy, welfare spending, and racial issues. For years, Whitten has been in absolute control of all bills before his subcommittee, from the first markup session to the final House vote. "The lines in my face would be deeper except for you" Mahon inscribed on his own portrait in the Mississippian's office.

The House at large rarely has challenged Agriculture budgets because most non-farmbloc members find the subject too complex or dull and rarely take the trouble to inform themselves about it. If some members, or the public, are roused to the point where a challenge develops, the House's committee chairmen generally pull together to defeat the move. Committee members follow to ensure that they will have the chairman's support for their own pet bills — and to keep sacrosanct the whole system of mutual support and protection.

If a challenge happens to get out of hand, the first commandment of a subcommittee chairman is "Never let yourself in for a battle on the House floor if there is any chance for defeat." Part of the power of chairman stems from his apparent invincibility — and the image must be preserved! Therefore, Whitten went along with the Nixon Administration's full budget request for food aid in 1969, knowing there was sufficient pressure for a much bigger appropriation. Whitten responded here only to the politics of the issue, not the substance, for he still complained to Senator George McGovern that hunger was not a problem, that "Nigras won't work" if you give them free food, and that McGovern was promoting revolution by continuing to seek free food stamps for the poorest Americans.

Where agriculture legislation is concerned, Whitten must share power in some measure with Senator Spessard Holland, a Florida Democrat who chairs the Senate Appropriations Subcommittee on Agriculture. Holland is a blunt man who insists that Section 32 funds — food dollars from customs receipts — should be held in reserve to be used at the proper time to boost prices for his state's citrus, vegetable, and beef industries. When Whitten and Holland act in unison — as they often do — the results are predictable. After the School Lunch Act was liberalized in 1964, they managed to refuse funding free school lunches for more than two years. The Johnson administration had sought only $2–3 million to help some of the estimated 5 million poor children who got no benefits from the lunch program, but all the funds were held back in committee until Senator Philip Hart (D-Mich.) threatened to take the fight to the floor.

Jamie Whitten's power is greater than Holland's, however, not only because appropriations usually originate in the House, but also because in the smaller body of the Senate there is less hesitation to overturn subcommittee decisions than in the tradition-bound House of Representatives. The House system, therefore, assures more *inherent* power for its subcommittee chairmen, and Jamie Whitten has been vigorous and skillful in pursuing it.

GETTING ALONG WITH WHITTEN

Even the Secretary himself feels he must bend to the power of the "permanent secretary." When a delegation headed by Richard Boone of the Citizens' Crusade Against Poverty had asked Orville Freeman to provide free stamps and commodities to help the hungry in Mississippi, the Secretary told them: "I've got to get along with two people in Washington — the President and Jamie Whitten. How can you help me with Whitten?"

Just back from a study of hunger in Mississippi in April, 1967, Dr. Robert Coles and three other doctors also found out about Whitten's influence when they appealed to Orville Freeman. They walked into the Secretary's office feeling that they would be welcomed as helpful, authoritative reporters of the facts, and they left feeling that they had been tagged as troublemakers.

"We were told that we and all the hungry children we had examined and all the other hungry Americans would have to reckon with Mr. Jamie L. Whitten, as indeed must the Secretary of Agriculture, whose funds come to him through the kindness of the same Mr. Whitten. We were told of the problems that the Agriculture Department has with Congress, and we left feeling we ought to weigh those problems as somehow of the same order as the problems we had met in the South — and that we know from our work elsewhere existed all over the country," recalled Coles.

Whitten's power goes beyond the secretary to the presidency itself. In the last year of his administration, President Johnson steadily refused to adopt proposals for broadened food aid that were drafted within his administration. Johnson was then trying to get his income surtax bill through the Congress, and he needed the support of Whitten and the rest of the small group of Southern hierarchs. Johnson declined to risk possible loss of critical votes on the war- and inflation-related surtax.

When Senator Jacob Javits (R-N.Y.) asked Agriculture Secretary Freeman, "What are you afraid of in Mississippi?" (at a July, 1967, hearing on hunger in Mississippi), he wanted to know why Freeman would not modify the food program to reach more of the hungry in Mississippi and elsewhere. The only response he got was ex-marine Freeman's outthrust jaw and a growl that he was not afraid of anyone and would not be intimidated.

Nevertheless, faced with Jamie Whitten's power over his department, and fed information by a Whitten-conscious bureaucracy, Freeman had failed for two years to take measures to feed more of the hungry poor in America. Moreover, the Secretary had stubbornly refused to acknowledge the chasm between his department's efforts and the real needs of the hungry.

From Freeman on down, every Agriculture Department official knew that hunger spelled "hound dog" to Jamie Whitten.

"You've got to understand how Jamie feels about 'hound dog' projects," a career official explained. (In Southern country jargon, a "hound dog" is always hanging around, useless, waiting to be thrown scraps.) Years before, the chairman had killed a small pilot project to teach unemployed Southern Negroes how to drive tractors. "Now, that's a 'hound dog' project, and I don't want to see any more of them," he had said.

Whitten's opposition to any program resembling social welfare — or aid to Negroes — contributed to the failure of War on Poverty programs for rural America. When President Johnson signed an executive order, giving the Agriculture Department responsibility for coordinating the rural war on poverty, Secretary Freeman created a Rural Community Development Service (RCDS) to give the Department a focal point for helping the poor. It was designed to coordinate programs meeting all the needs of the rural poor — housing, education, water, food — not only within the Agriculture Department, but throughout the federal government.

Within a year, the Rural Community Development Service was dead. "Whitten thought the Service smacked of social experimentation and civil rights," a Department of Agriculture official said. In addition, Whitten's brother-in-law, one of many cronies who have filled Agriculture jobs over the years, had clashed with Robert G. Lewis, the idealistic Wisconsin progressive who headed the program. Whitten simply cut off the funds and pigeonholed the coordinating powers of RCDS by placing the responsibility with the docile, conservative Farmers Home Administration. Freeman never fought the issue. There were too many other matters, other appropriations, that were more important to him, so the embryonic effort to coordinate rural poverty programs through the Department of Agriculture ended as little more than a passing idea.

(By assigning the broad rural poverty responsibility to the Department of Agriculture, President Johnson, like President Nixon after him, indicated either a great naïveté about the Department or a lack of seriousness in his proposals. The four congressional committees with which Agriculture must deal undoubtedly are the least receptive of any in Congress to attempts to provide meaningful help to the hard-core rural poor.)

Jamie Whitten has wielded that kind of influence since the mid-1940s, when he killed an emerging Agriculture study that tried to anticipate the social and economic problems of Negro GI's returning from World War II to the feudal cotton South. At that time, the Mississippi Congressman was the youngest chairman of an appropriations subcommittee. By opposing all studies exploring the effects of a changing agriculture upon people, Whitten helped ensure that Agriculture's farm policy would never include serious consideration of the effects of its programs on sharecroppers or farm workers. Whitten and the other powerful Southern congressmen who share his views ensure that the Department would focus only on the cotton planter and his crop. As a result, farm policies that have consistently ignored their toll on millions of black poor have contributed to a rural-urban migration, to a civil rights revolution, and to the ruin of many Americans.

There is no doubt as to the motives of Whitten and the other congressmen who run the Agriculture Department. Testifying on the proposed food stamp law before the Senate Agriculture Committee in 1964, one Department official boldly suggested that it would not help those with little or no income. Committee Chairman Allen J. Ellender (D-La.) indignantly dismissed this complaint against the bill, revealing clearly his own legislative intent.

"I know that in my state we had a number of fishermen who were unable to catch fish," retorted Ellender. "Do you expect the government, because they cannot catch fish, to feed them until the fish are there? In other words, this food stamp program is not to be considered a program just simply to feed people because they cannot get work. This is not what it is supposed to be."

SURPLUS SERFS

What the food stamp program was "supposed to be" was a substitute for a free commodity program that had outlived its usefulness — to Southern plantation owners. Surplus commodities — barely enough to live on — were distributed in the winter when work ceased on the Mississippi plantation of Senator James Eastland (D-Miss.) and on the huge Texas ranches. In the spring, when the $3-a-day planting jobs opened up, the food aid ended. The federal government eased the planter's responsibility by keeping his workers alive during the winter, then permitted the counties that administered the program to withdraw that meager support during planting season — forcing the workers to accept near-starvation wages for survival. When the rural serfs were no longer needed, having been slowly replaced by machines, even that support vanished as the government stopped free commodities in favor of food stamps, which the poorest rural people could not afford. As counties throughout the nation changed from commodities to food stamps, participation fell off by 40 percent; more than 1 million persons, including 100,000 in Mississippi, were forced to drop out of the food program. Whispers of "planned starvation" emerged from the economic crisis of 1967, when the combination of production cutbacks in cotton, automated machinery, and the end of free commodities left the Deep South with thousands of blacks who were unneeded — and hungry. The decisions of the white supremacists in Congress, supported by the subservient Department of Agriculture, contributed to that result.

Whitten's decisions are not always understood by the uninitiated. With his wily ability to juggle figures and cloud ideas, Whitten convinces officials unfamiliar with his technique (and lacking intimate knowledge of the facts) that he is quite a reasonable man — especially when the conversation turns to hunger and the food programs. As he tells it, he was a pioneer on the nutrition issue.

In 1950, he fought for funds for a Department of Agriculture cookbook, and he warned the House it had better concern itself with human as well as animal health. To this day, Whitten insists that the Agriculture

Department keep the book in print; he sends a free copy to newlyweds in his district.

The subcommittee chairman also denies that he paralyzed Freeman on the hunger issue: "I *helped* the Secretary by making two points with him," Whitten insists. "I told him he had to charge people what they were accustomed to paying for food stamps because that's what the law says. And I pointed out to him that the law forbids selling food stamps and distributing commodities in the same counties." By making these two helpful points, Whitten blocked the most feasible emergency measures.

"Why, I gave him more money for those food programs than he could spend!" said Whitten.

Actually, the hopelessly inadequate $45 million for food programs Whitten "gave" to Freeman was fought, bought, and paid for by the administration and congressional liberals; this was what was left after Whitten and Holland whittled down the original $100 million, three-year authorization won by liberals on the House floor.

Whitten's explanations of food programs may have appeared perfectly reasonable to Freeman, Sargent Shriver, and many members of Congress, but their total impact was to stop any reform that would get food to the hungry. His own strongly held view is that the food programs should serve the farm programs, not vice versa, and his actions over the years have halted any kind of aid the Agriculture Department might have directed toward the poor. In the early 1960s, when the Kennedy Administration was momentarily concerned for the poor of Appalachia, Agriculture found a way to provide housing grants to aid the hardest-core poor; but once Whitten discovered the grant program in operation, he killed all further appropriations for it.

A few years later, a new cotton program provided advance payments to cotton farmers for withdrawing some of their acreage from production. Sharecroppers, who provided most of the cotton labor force, were supposed to receive their "share" of government payments for idle land. With Whitten's inspiration or blessing, Agriculture adopted a regulation permitting the plantation owner to deduct from the sharecropper's government payments the amount he claimed was owed for the sharecropper's rent, farming expenses, etc. Under the feudal system of the plantation, however, the sharecropper *never* had any legal guarantee that he would receive his fair share of profit for the crop he produced. Blacks who declined to turn over their checks were kicked off hundreds of plantations. The Agriculture Department did not halt the practice.

One of Whitten's sharecropper constituents, trying desperately to find food for her family, gave her own intuitive view of her congressman's attitudes: "He's probably with the bossman's side, don't you know. He's with them. No one's with us but ourselves, and no matter how many of us there are, we don't have what they have."

WINE FOR MISSISSIPPI

Although much of the legislation he favors has enriched American agricultural business with government funds, Whitten's stock answer to any proposed liberalization of the Department of Agriculture food programs is that they are "food programs, not welfare programs." He is adamant about suggestions that food programs be moved to the more liberal Department of Health, Education, and Welfare, "Who'll see to it that [funds for food] don't go for frivolity and wine?" he asks.

Whitten's views on welfare, so strongly felt through the Department of Agriculture, are shared by many Americans. Yet when viewed against the background of Tallahatchie County and its social history, these views, and their interpretations through Agriculture programs, take on a different meaning. Since hunger means poverty, and poverty in Mississippi usually means black, any expanded aid to the hungry means one more threat to the socio-economic order in which the black worker has always been held in absolute dependency upon crumbs from the plantation owner.

The 100,000 or more black Mississippi farm workers who suddenly found themselves with nothing to hold onto in the winter of 1967 were little concerned with frivolity and wine. They had lost their sole supply of food, as Mississippi counties switched over from the inadequate but free surplus commodities to a food stamp program the poor could not afford. "No work, no money, and now, no food," was their outcry, and they desperately sought a reduction in the price of stamps at the very moment when Jamie Whitten was starting his annual review of the Department of Agriculture's budget, with its accompanying discourses on the nature of the poor man. He had heard, the chairman said, that "organized groups" sought to make food stamps free to the poor.

"This is one of the things you always run into," he said to Secretary Freeman. "You make stamps available at 30 percent discount; then they want them at 50, then 75. Now, I have heard reports that some of the organized minority groups are insisting they be provided free of charge. When you start giving people something for nothing, just giving them all they want for nothing, I wonder if you don't destroy character more than you might improve nutrition. I think more and more American people are coming to that conclusion."

They built a lot of character in Mississippi that winter, where the disruption caused by the abrupt changeover to food stamps contributed to the kind of wholesale destitution not seen in this country since the Great Depression.

But the chairman did not seem to think his black constituents were learning the character lesson well enough when it came to the school lunch and new school breakfast programs. Out of work and out of money, few Mississippi Negroes could afford to give their children 25 cents a day for a

school lunch, and few schools provided the free lunches that the law technically required for the poor. Agriculture officials virtually begged that the
special school lunch assistance budget be raised from $2 million to $10 million annually to give meals to an added 360,000 children in poor areas.
Whitten expressed concern only about the impact of civil rights sanctions
as he slashed the request by two-thirds.

When another project — a requested million dollars for a pilot school
breakfast program to help the neediest youngsters — came up, Whitten's
patience wore thin. "Do you contemplate having a pilot dinner program —
evening meals — called supper where I grew up?" Whitten asked sarcas-
tically.

When Agriculture Department officials explained that "a hungry child
in the morning is not able to take full advantage of the schooling that is
offered," Whitten wanted to know why the government should be supplying
what the family should have supplied before the child left home.

"We all recognize that the type of home from which some children
come affects them in many, many ways, but there is a problem always as to
whether the federal government should start doing everything for the citizens. You may end up with a certain class of people doing nothing to help
themselves. To strike a happy medium is always a real problem."

In this case, Whitten struck it by cutting all $6.5 million requested for
breakfast funds from the budget.

Each time a group of doctors, team of reporters, or other investigators
produced firsthand reports of hunger in the South, Whitten launched his own
"investigation" and announced that parental neglect is largely responsible
for any problems. In 1968, when the drive for a bigger food program began
to gather steam nationally, Whitten sent out the FBI to disprove the evidence
of the problem. The FBI men, who are assigned to the House Appropriations Committee, in effect intimidated people who had provided evidence of
hunger.

When a private group investigating hunger, the Citizens' Board of Inquiry, reported after a lengthy investigation that "we have found concrete
evidence of chronic hunger and malnutrition in every part of the United
States where we have held hearings or conducted hearings," even the Pentagon rallied to the defense of Jamie Whitten's system. The Pentagon-financed
Institute for Defense Analyses published an attack on the book *Hunger
USA*,[1] which contained the Board of Inquiry report. The author of the
defense document, Dr. Herbert Pollack, took the position that ignorance
was at the root of any hunger problems in the United States — the same position taken by Whitten and his congressional allies.

The Mississippi Congressman demands that the poor, if they are to get
any benefits, must prove they are hungry on a case-by-case basis. "The

---

[1] Citizen's Board of Inquiry. *Hunger USA* (Boston: Beacon Press, 1968).

doctors have not submitted any names," he wrote one concerned Northern lady, assuring her that he would be "most sympathetic and helpful in trying to work this matter out."

Time after time, Whitten has requested names and addresses of the poor who complain of ill-treatment in his home state. Yet in Jamie Whitten's home county, the thought of having their names known strikes terror among those who have had dealings with the local officials.

A news team from television's Public Broadcast Laboratory (PBL), interviewing a black housewife in Whitten's home town of Charleston, felt the danger involved in "naming names." As Mrs. Metcalf began to explain why the food stamp and school lunch programs were not helping her family, a task force of sedans and panel trucks began to cruise back and forth on the U.S. highway about fifty yards from her plantation shack. Suddenly the trucks lunged off the highway into the shack's front yard, surrounding the television crew's two station wagons. A rifle or shotgun was mounted in the rear window of each truck.

"You're trespassing. Git!" growled the plantation manager as he pushed his way past the TV reporter and ordered Mrs. Metcalf to get outside the shack if she knew what was good for her.

"You were trespassing when you crossed the Mississippi state line," shouted Deputy Sheriff Buck Shaw as he ordered the PBL crew to clear out.

In an attempt to ensure Mrs. Metcalf's safety from the local "law," the reporter phoned Congressman Whitten in Washington.

"You remember when Martin Luther King went through my town!" the Congressman answered. "You read the *Wall Street Journal*? It said that he went through there and everybody turned out to look at him. And as soon as he left, they just turned over and went back to sleep. I just know, I live down there and I know. Good God, Chicago, Washington, Detroit. Every one of them would give any amount of money if they could go to sleep feeling as safe — both races — as my folks will!"

It wasn't so peaceful about three o'clock that afternoon with those hard-eyed men threatening Mrs. Metcalf, the reporter explained.

"I suspect Deputy Shaw's like I am," Whitten snapped. "They recognized when you crossed that state line you had no good intention in your mind. I'm no kingfish. I just know my people and my people get along. Unfortunately, you folks and the folks up here don't know how to get along. I bet you money if I ran tomorrow, and nobody voted except the colored people, I'd get the majority. I grew up where five or six of my closest neighbors were Negroes. We played together as kids. We swapped vegetables. Why, I grew up hugging my Momma, and my Momma hugging them."

There were as many Negroes as whites at his father's funeral, Whitten asserts — and he keeps on his desk a yellowed 1936 newspaper editorial that praised District Attorney Jamie Whitten for successfully prosecuting the white man who burned some Mississippi Negroes to death.

Against Whitten's statements about how he is respected by Negroes and would get their vote, about how close his relationship and understanding with Negroes has been, about how quiet and peaceful life is in Charleston, another point of view appeared, as one of his black constituents spoke on the same subject — rambling much as Jamie Whitten does. An eloquent, middle-aged woman told Dr. Robert Coles about the plantation owner for whom her husband works, about his wife, about food, and about life in America:

> He [the plantation owner] doesn't want us trying to vote and like that — and first I'd like to feed my kids, before I go trying to vote.
>
> His wife — the boss man's — she'll come over here sometimes and give me some extra grits and once or twice in the year some good bacon. She tells me we get along fine down here and I says "yes" to her. What else would I be saying, I ask you?
>
> But it's no good. The kids aren't eating enough, and you'd have to be wrong in the head, pure crazy to say they are. Sometimes we talk of leaving; but you know it's just no good up there either, we hear. They eat better, but they have bad things up there I hear, rats as big as raccoons I hear, and they bit my sister's kid real bad.
>
> It's no kind of country to be proud of, with all this going on — the colored people still having it so bad, and the kids being sick and there's nothing you can do about it.[2]

AFFECTION, NOT CASH

Whitten's affection for black constituents like this woman does not extend to federal measures to assist their lot in life. Of the 24,081 residents of Tallahatchie County, 18,000 have family incomes less than $3,000 a year, and 15,197 make less than $2,000. Of these thousands legally defined as poor, only 2,367 qualify for public assistance, and 6,710 receive food stamps. Only a few blocks from Whitten's own white frame home, Negroes live in shacks without toilets, running water, electricity — or food.

Whitten and his fellow white Mississippians point with great pride to the economic progress their state has made in recent years. Improved farming methods, conversion of marginal cropland to timber and other uses, and a strong soil bank program have greatly enriched the commercial farmer in Mississippi. Other government programs, including state tax inducements, have promoted wide industrialization, and rural white workers have found a new affluence in the hundreds of factories and small shops that have sprung up.

But the new farming has eliminated thousands of jobs for Negro plantation workers while the segregated social system denies them factory jobs. The able-bodied usually head north, leaving the very young, the very old,

---

[2] Robert Coles and Harry Hughe, "We Need Help," *New Republic,* March 8, 1969.

and the unskilled to cope with "progress." The rural black does not share in the new prosperity of Mississippi, and some Negroes are worse off than at any time since the Depression. Indeed, in many parts of the Deep South the black man is literally being starved out by the new prosperity.

Perhaps the white Southern politician is no more to blame than are whites anywhere. But the white in the South could not afford to see the truth of the Negro's suffering, because to feel that truth would have shattered a whole way of life.

Jamie Whitten truly believes in his own fairness, his idea of good works, and the imagined affection he receives from Negroes back home. For fifty-nine years, he has anesthetized his soul to the human misery and indignity only a few yards from his own home and has refused to believe that the responsibility for that indignity lies on his white shoulders. His belief in the basic laziness, indifference, and unworthiness of the black poor is as strong as his belief in the virtues of a way of life that for three centuries has denied these same black poor any avenues of pursuing ambition, self-respect, or a better future for their children.

That Jamie Whitten should suffer from blindness to human need is one thing. But that he can use this blindness as an excuse to limit the destiny of millions of Americans is another matter, one which should concern anyone who believes in the basic strengths of this country's constitutional guarantees. The checks and balances of a reasonable democratic republic have gone completely awry when a huge bureaucracy and the top officials of an Administration base their actions concerning deepest human need on their fearful perception of what one rather limited man seems to want.

The system of seniority and temerity that gives a man such as Jamie Whitten such awesome power must come under more serious public scrutiny if the American system of government is ever to establish itself on the basis of moral concern about the individual human being.

Congressmen and the Electoral Connection

Throughout the 1970s public opinion polls consistently revealed that Congress was held in low esteem by the American people. The book *Who Runs Congress?* published by the Ralph Nader Congress Project reflected and at the same time helped to crystallize public disenchantment with Capitol Hill.[1] The book emphasized the need for citizens to take on Congress to prevent a further flagging of the institution. In his introduction, Ralph Nader summarized the contents of the book by stating that "the

---

[1] Mark J. Green et al. (ed.), *Who Runs Congress?* (New York: Bantam/Grossman, 1972).

people have indeed abdicated their power, their money, and their democratic birthright to Congress. As a result, without the participation of the
people, Congress has surrendered its enormous authority and resources
to special interest groups, waste, insensitivity, ignorance, and bureaucracy." [2] The 1972 theme of the Nader project that Congress was in crisis
continues to be accepted by the vast majority of people.

While Ralph Nader and his colleagues feel that the major cause of
the demise of Congress is its detachment from the people, Richard Fenno
in the following selection adopts a different viewpoint. He feels that people
fault the *institution* of Congress, not their individual representatives on
Capitol Hill. In fact, he points out that there is a close connection between
legislators and constituents, and often, a feeling of affection by voters for
their representatives. Fenno feels that we apply different standards in
judging individual members of Congress than we do in assessing the
institution, being far more lenient in the former than the latter case. The
individual is judged for his personality, style, and representativeness, while
the institution is judged by its ability to recognize and solve the nation's
problems. But, the institution cannot be thought of apart from the members that compose it. It is they who have given it its unique character. It
is the individual member who, more often than not, has supported a decentralized and fragmented legislature because of the members' incentive to
achieve personal power and status on Capitol Hill.

---

[2] Ibid. p. 1.

51

Richard F. Fenno, Jr.

IF, AS RALPH NADER SAYS, CONGRESS IS "THE BROKEN BRANCH," HOW COME WE LOVE OUR CONGRESSMEN SO MUCH?

Off and on during the past two years, I accompanied ten members of the
House of Representatives as they traveled around in their home districts. In
every one of those districts I heard a common theme, one that I had not

---

From Richard F. Fenno, Jr., "If, As Ralph Nader Says, Congress Is 'The
Broken Branch,' How Come We Love Our Congressmen So Much?" Originally written as part of an editorial project entitled "The Role of Congress: A Study of the
Legislative Branch," © 1972 by Time, Inc., and Richard F. Fenno, Jr. Reprinted by
permission.

expected. Invariably, the representative I was with — young or old, liberal or conservative, Northerner, Southerner, Easterner, or Westerner, Democrat or Republican — was described as "the best congressman in the United States." Having heard it so often, I now accept the description as fact. I am even prepared to believe the same thing (though I cannot claim to have heard it with my own ears) of the members of the Senate. Each of our 435 representatives and 100 senators is, indeed, "the best congressman in the United States." Which is to say that each enjoys a great deal of support and approbation among his or her constituents. Judging by the election returns, this isn't much of an exaggeration. In the recent election, 96 percent of all House incumbents who ran were reelected; and 85 percent of all Senate incumbents who ran were reelected. These convincing figures are close to the average reelection rates of incumbents for the past ten elections. We do, it appears, love our congressmen.

On the other hand, it seems equally clear that we do not love our Congress. Louis Harris reported in 1970 that only one-quarter of the electorate gave Congress a positive rating on its job performance — while nearly two-thirds expressed themselves negatively on the subject. And we would not be here tonight if there were not considerable concern — dramatized recently by the critical Nader project — for the performance of Congress as an institution. On the evidence, we seem to approve of our legislators a good deal more than we do our legislature. And therein hangs something of a puzzle. If our congressmen are so good, how can our Congress be so bad? If it is the individuals that make up the institution, why should there be such a disparity in our judgments? What follows are a few reflections on this puzzle.

A first answer is that we apply different standards of judgment, those that we apply to the individual being less demanding than those we apply to the institution. For the individual, our standard is one of representativeness — of personal style and policy views. Stylistically, we ask that our legislator display a sense of identity with us so that we, in turn, can identify with him or her — via personal visits to the district, concern for local projects and individual "cases," and media contact of all sorts, for example. On the policy side, we ask only that his general policy stance does not get too frequently out of line with ours. And, if he should become a national leader in some policy area of interest to us, so much the better. These standards are admittedly vague. But because they are locally defined and locally applied, they are consistent and manageable enough so that legislators can devise rules of thumb to meet them. What is more, by their performance they help shape the standards, thereby making them easier to meet. Thus they win constituent recognition as "the best in the United States." And thus they establish the core relationship for a representative democracy.

For the institution, however, our standards emphasize efforts to solve national problems — a far less tractable task than the one we (and he) set for the individual. Given the inevitable existence of unsolved problems, we are destined to be unhappy with congressional performance. The individual legislator knows when he has met our standards of representativeness; he is re-elected. But no such definitive measure of legislative success exists. And, precisely because Congress is the most familiar and most human of our national institutions, lacking the distant majesty of the Presidency and the Court, it is the easy and natural target of our criticism. We have met our problem solvers, and they are us.

Furthermore, such standards as we do use for judging the institutional performance of Congress are applied inconsistently. In 1963, when public dissatisfaction was as great as in 1970, Congress was criticized for being obstructionist, dilatory and insufficiently cooperative with regard to the Kennedy programs. Two years later, Congress got its highest performance rating of the decade when it cooperated completely with the executive in rushing the Great Society program into law. But by the late 1960s and early 1970s the standard of judgment had changed radically — from cooperation to counterbalance in Congressional relations with the Executive. Whereas, in 1963, Harris had found "little in the way of public response to the time-honored claim that the Legislative Branch is . . . the guardian against excessive Executive power," by 1968 he found that three-quarters of the electorate wanted Congress to act as the watchdog of the Executive and not to cooperate so readily with it. The easy passage of the Tonkin Resolution reflects the cooperative standards set in the earlier period; its repeal reflects the counterbalancing standards of the recent period. Today we are concerned about Ralph Nader's "broken branch" which, we hear, has lost — and must reclaim from the Executive — its prerogatives in areas such as war-making and spending control. To some degree, then, our judgments on Congress are negative because we change our minds frequently concerning the kind of Congress we want. A Congress whose main job is to cooperate with the Executive would look quite different from one whose main job is to counterbalance the Executive.

Beneath the differences in our standards of judgment, however, lies a deeper dynamic of the political system. Senators and representatives, for their own reasons, spend a good deal more of their time and energy polishing and worrying about their individual performance than they do working at the institution's performance. Though it is, of course, true that their individual activity is related to institutional activity, their first-order concerns are individual, not institutional. Foremost is their desire for reelection. Most members of Congress like their job, want to keep it, and know that there are people back home who want to take it away from them. So they work long and hard at winning reelection. Even those who are safest want election margins large enough to discourage opposition back home and/or to help them float further political ambitions. No matter what other personal goals representatives and senators wish to accomplish — increased influence in

Washington and helping to make good public policy are the most common — reelection is a necessary means to those ends.

We cannot criticize these priorities — not in a representative system. If we believe the representative should mirror constituency opinion, we must acknowledge that it requires considerable effort for him to find out what should be mirrored. If we believe a representative should be free to vote his judgment, he will have to cultivate his constituents assiduously before they will trust him with such freedom. Either way we will look favorably on his efforts. We come to love our legislators, in the *second* place, because they so ardently sue for our affections.

As a courtship technique, moreover, they re-enforce our unfavorable judgments about the institution. Every representative with whom I traveled criticized the Congress and portrayed himself, by contrast, as a fighter against its manifest evils. Members run *for* Congress by running *against* Congress. They refurbish their individual reputations as "the best congressman in the United States" by attacking the collective reputation of the Congress of the United States. Small wonder the voters feel so much more warmly disposed and so much less fickle toward the individuals than toward the institution.

One case in point: the House decision to grant President Nixon a spending ceiling plus authority to cut previously appropriated funds to maintain that ceiling. One-half the representatives I was with blasted the House for being so spineless that it gave away its power of the purse to the President. The other half blasted the House for being so spineless in exercising its power of the purse that the President had been forced to act. Both groups spoke to supportive audiences; and each man enhanced his individual reputation by attacking the institution. Only by raising both questions, however, could one see the whole picture. Once the President forced the issue, how come the House didn't stand up to him and protect its crucial institutional power over the purse strings? On the other hand, if economic experts agreed that a spending ceiling was called for, how come the House didn't enact it and make the necessary budget cuts in the first place? The answer to the first question lies in the proximity of their reelection battles, which re-enforced the tendency of all representatives to think in individualistic rather than institutional terms. The answer to the second question lies in the total absence of institutional machinery whereby the House (or, indeed, Congress) can make overall spending decisions.

Mention of the institutional mechanisms of Congress leads us to a *third* explanation for our prevailing pattern of judgments. When members of Congress think institutionally — as, of course they must — they think in terms of a structure that will be most congenial to the pursuit of their individual concerns — for reelection, for influence, or for policy. Since each individual has been independently designated "the best in the United States," each has an equal status and an equal claim to influence within the structure. For these reasons, the members naturally think in terms of a very fragmented, decentralized institution, providing a maximum of opportunity for individual performance, individual influence, and individual credit.

The 100-member Senate more completely fits this description than the 435-member House. The smaller body permits a more freewheeling and creative individualism. But both chambers tend strongly in this direction, and representatives as well as senators chafe against centralizing mechanisms. Neither body is organized in hierarchical — or even in well-coordinated — patterns of decision-making. Agreements are reached by some fairly subtle forms of mutual adjustment—by negotiation, bargaining, and compromise. And interpersonal relations — of respect, confidence, trust — are crucial building blocks. The members of Congress, in pursuit of their individual desires, have thus created an institution that is internally quite complex. Its structure and processes are, therefore, very difficult to grasp from the outside.

In order to play out some aspects of the original puzzle, however, we must make the effort. And the committee system, the epitome of fragmentation and decentralization, is a good place to start. The performance of Congress as an institution is very largely the performance of its committees. The Nader project's "broken branch" description is mostly a committee-centered description because that is where the countervailing combination of congressional expertise and political skill resides. To strengthen Congress means to strengthen its committees. To love Congress means to love its committees. Certainly when we have not loved our Congress, we have heaped our displeasure upon its committees. The major legislative reorganizations, of 1946 and 1970, were committee-centered reforms — centering on committee jurisdictions, committee democracy, and committee staff support. Other continuing criticisms — of the seniority rule for selecting committee chairmen, for example — have centered on the committees.

Like Congress as a whole, committees must be understood first in terms of what they do for the individual member. To begin with, committees are relatively more important to the individual House member than to the individual senator. The representative's career inside Congress is very closely tied to his committee. For the only way such a large body can function is to divide into highly specialized and independent committees. Policy-making activity funnels through these committees; so does the legislative activity and influence of the individual legislator. While the Senate has a set of committees paralleling those of the House, a committee assignment is nowhere near as constraining for the career of the individual senator. The Senate is more loosely organized, senators sit on many more committees and subcommittees than representatives, and they have easy access to the work of committees of which they are not members. Senators, too, can command and utilize national publicity to gain influence beyond the confines of their committee. Whereas House committees act as funnels for individual activity, Senate committees act as facilitators of individual activity. The difference in functions is considerable — which is why committee chairmen are a good deal more important in the House than in the Senate and why the first modifications of the seniority rule should have come in the House rather than the Senate. My examples will come from the House.

Given the great importance of his committee to the career of the House member, it follows that we will want to know how each committee can affect such careers. . . .

Where a committee's members are especially interested in pyramiding their individual influence, they will act so as to maintain the influence of their committee (and, hence, their personal influence) within the House. They will adopt procedures that enhance the operating independence of the committee. They will work hard to remain relatively independent of the Executive Branch. And they will try to underpin that independence with such resources as specialized expertise, internal cohesion, and the respect of their House colleagues. Ways and Means and Appropriations are committees of this sort. By contrast, where a committee's members are especially interested in getting in on nationally controversial policy action, they will not be much concerned about the independent influence of their committee. They will want to ally themselves closely with any and all groups outside the committee who share their policy views. They want to help enact what they individually regard as good public policy; and if that means ratifying policies shaped elsewhere — in the Executive Branch particularly — so be it. And, since their institutional independence is not a value for them, they make no special effort to acquire such underpinnings as expertise, cohesion, or chamber respect. Education and Labor and Foreign Affairs are committees of this sort.

These two types of committees display quite different strengths in their performance. Those of the first type are especially influential. Ways and Means probably makes a greater independent contribution to policy making than any other House committee. Appropriations probably exerts a more influential overview of executive branch activities than any other House committee. The price they pay, however, is a certain decrease in their responsiveness to noncommittee forces — as complaints about the closed rule on tax bills and executive hearings on appropriations bills will attest. Committees of the second type are especially responsive to noncommittee forces and provide easy conduits for outside influence in policymaking. Education and Labor was probably more receptive to President Johnson's Great Society policies than any other House committee; it successfully passed the largest part of that program. Foreign Affairs has probably remained as thoroughly responsive to Executive Branch policies, in foreign aid for instance, as any House committee. The price they pay, however, is a certain decrease in their influence — as complaints about the rubber-stamp Education and

Labor Committee and about the impotent Foreign Affairs Committee will attest. In terms of the earlier discussions of institutional performance standards, our hopes for a cooperative Congress lie more with the latter type of committee; our hopes for a counterbalancing Congress lie more with the former.

So, committees differ. And they differ to an important degree according to the desires of their members. This ought to make us wary of blanket descriptions. Within the House, Foreign Affairs may look like a broken branch, but Ways and Means does not. And, across chambers, Senate Foreign Relations (where member incentives are stronger) is a good deal more potent than House Foreign Affairs. With the two Appropriations committees, the reverse is the case. It is not just that "the broken branch" is an undiscriminating, hence inaccurate, description. It is also that blanket descriptions lead to blanket prescriptions. And it just might be that the wisest course of congressional reform would be to identify existing nodes of committee strength and nourish them rather than to prescribe, as we usually do, reforms in equal dosages for all committees.

One lesson of the analysis should be that member incentives must exist to support any kind of committee activity. Where incentives vary, it may be silly to prescribe the same functions and resources for all committees. The Reorganization Act of 1946 mandated all committees to exercise "continuous watchfulness" over the executive branch — in the absence of any supporting incentive system. We have gotten overview activity only where random individuals have found an incentive for doing so — not by most committees and certainly not continuously. Similarly, I suspect that our current interest in exhorting all committees to acquire more information with which to combat the executive may be misplaced. Information is relatively easy to come by — and some committees have a lot of it. What is hard to come by is the incentive to use it, not to mention the time and the trust necessary to make it useful. I am not suggesting a set of reforms but rather a somewhat different strategy of committee reforms — less wholesale, more retail.

Since the best-known target of wholesale committee reform is the seniority rule, it deserves special comment. If our attacks on the rule have any substance to them, if they are anything other than symbolic, the complaint must be that some or all committee chairmen are not doing a good job. But we can only find out whether this is so by conducting a committee-by-committee examination. Paradoxically, our discussions of the seniority rule tend to steer us away from such a retail examination by mounting very broad, across-the-board kinds of arguments against chairmen as a class — arguments about their old age, their conservatism, their national unrepresentativeness. Such arguments produce great cartoon copy, easy editorial broadsides, and sitting-duck targets for our congressmen on the stump. But we ought not to let the arguments themselves, nor the Pavlovian public reactions induced by our cartoonists, editorial writers, and representatives, pass for good institutional analysis. Rather, they have diverted us from that task.

More crucial to a committee's performance than the selection of its chairman is his working relationship with the other committee members. Does he agree with his members on the functions of the committee? Does he act to facilitate the achievement of their individual concerns? Do they approve of his performance as chairman? Where there is real disagreement between chairman and members, close analysis may lead us to fault the members and not the chairman. If so, we should be focusing our criticisms on the members. If the fault lies with the chairman, a majority of the members have the power to bring him to heel. They need not kill the king; they can constitutionalize the monarchy. While outsiders have been crying "off with his head," the members of several committees have been quietly and effectively constitutionalizing the monarchy. Education and Labor, Post Office, and Interior are recent examples where dissatisfied committee majorities have subjected their chairmen to majority control. Where this has not been done, it is probably due to member satisfaction, member timidity, member disinterest, or member incompetence. And the time we spend railing against the seniority rule might be better spent finding out, for each congressional committee, just which of these is the case. If, as a final possibility, a chairman and his members are united in opposition to the majority part or to the rest of us, the seniority rule is not the problem. More to the point, as I suspect is usually the case, the reasons and the ways individual members get sorted onto the various committees is the critical factor. In sum, I am not saying that the seniority rule is a good thing. I am saying that, for committee performance, it is not a very important thing.

What has all this got to do with the original puzzle — that we love our congressmen so much more than our Congress? We began with a few explanatory guesses. Our standards of judgment for individual performance are more easily met; the individual member works harder winning approval for himself than for his institution; and Congress is a complex institution, difficult for us to understand. The more we try to understand Congress — as we did briefly with the committee system — the more we are forced to peel back the institutional layers until we reach the individual member. At that point, it becomes hard to separate, as we normally do, our judgments about congressmen and Congress. The more we come to see institutional performance as influenced by the desires of the individual member, the more the original puzzle ought to resolve itself. For as the independence of our judgments decreases, the disparity between them ought to grow smaller. But if we are to hold this perspective on Congress, we shall need to understand the close individual-institution relationship — chamber by chamber, party by party, committee by committee, legislator by legislator.

This is not a counsel of despair. It is a counsel of sharper focus and a more discriminating eye. It counsels the mass media, for example, to forego "broken branch" type generalizations about Congress in favor of examining a committee in depth, or to forego broad criticism of the seniority rule for a close look at a committee chairman. It counsels the rest of us to focus more on the individual member and to fix the terms of our dialogue with him more aggressively. It counsels us to fix terms that will force him to think more institutionally and which will hold him more accountable for the performance of the institution. "Who Runs Congress," asks the title of the Nader report, "the President, Big Business or You?" From the perspective of this paper, it is none of these. It is the members who run Congress. And we get pretty much the kind of Congress they want. We shall get a different kind of Congress when we elect different kinds of congressmen or when we start applying different standards of judgment to old congressmen. Whether or not we ought to have a different kind of Congress is still another, much larger, puzzle.

The previous selection defines one dimension of the relationship between congressmen and their constituencies. A commonly held assumption about members of Congress is that their primary incentive is to engage in activities that strengthen their prospects for reelection. David Mayhew, one proponent of this theory, argues in his book *Congress: The Electoral Connection* that both the formal and informal organizations of Congress are oriented principally toward the reelection of its members. For example, the dispersion of committees, which numbered close to 300 in the 96th Congress (1979–1980), maximizes the opportunities of committee chairmen to use their power to distribute benefits directly to their districts and states and to take positions on issues that will be appealing to their constituents. Moreover, the weak party structure of Capitol Hill allows individual members to go their own ways in dealing with their diverse constituencies. Unified congressional parties, argues Mayhew, would not allow congressmen the necessary flexibility to advertise, claim credit, and take positions to gain electoral support. In the following selection Mayhew illustrates the kinds of activities congressmen engage in to maximize their electoral support.

52

David Mayhew

CONGRESS:
THE ELECTORAL CONNECTION

Whether they are safe or marginal, cautious or audacious, congressmen must constantly engage in activities related to reelection. There will be differences in emphasis, but all members share the root need to do things — indeed, to do things day in and day out during their terms. The next step here is to present a typology, a short list of the *kinds* of activities congressmen find it electorally useful to engage in. The case will be that there are three basic kinds of activities. It will be important to lay them out with some care, . . .

One activity is *advertising,* defined here as any effort to disseminate one's name among constituents in such a fashion as to create a favorable image but in messages having little or no issue content. A successful congressman builds what amounts to a brand name, which may have a generalized electoral value for other politicians in the same family. The personal qualities to emphasize are experience, knowledge, responsiveness, concern, sincerity, independence, and the like. Just getting one's name across is difficult enough; only about half the electorate, if asked, can supply their House members' names. It helps a congressman to be known. "In the main, recognition carries a positive valence; to be perceived at all is to be perceived favorably." A vital advantage enjoyed by House incumbents is that they are much better known among voters than their November challengers. They are better known because they spend a great deal of time, energy, and money trying to make themselves better known. There are standard routines — frequent visits to the constituency, nonpolitical speeches to home audiences, the sending out of infant care booklets and letters of condolence and congratulation. Of 158 House members questioned . . . 121 said that they regularly sent newsletters to their constituents; 48 wrote separate news or opinion columns for newspapers; 82 regularly reported to their constituencies by radio or television; 89 regularly sent out mail questionnaires. Some routines are less standard. Congressman George E. Shipley (D., Ill.) claims to have met personally about half his constituents (i.e. some 200,000 people). For over twenty years Congressman Charles C. Diggs, Jr. (D., Mich.) has run a radio program

featuring himself as a "combination disc jockey–commentator and minister." Congressman Daniel J. Flood (D., Pa.) is "famous for appearing un-
announced and often uninvited at wedding anniversaries and other events."
Anniversaries and other events aside, congressional advertising is done
largely at public expense. Use of the franking privilege has mushroomed
in recent years; in early 1973 one estimate predicted that House and Senate
members would send out about 476 million pieces of mail in the year 1974,
at a public cost of $38.1 million — or about 900,000 pieces per member
with a subsidy of $70,000 per member. By far the heaviest mailroom traffic
comes in Octobers of even-numbered years. There are some differences between House and Senate members in the ways they go about getting their
names across. House members are free to blanket their constituencies with
mailings for all boxholders; senators are not. But senators find it easier to
appear on national television — for example, in short reaction statements
on the nightly news shows. Advertising is a staple congressional activity,
and there is no end to it. For each member there are always new voters to
be apprised of his worthiness and old voters to be reminded of it.

A second activity may be called *credit claiming,* defined here as acting
so as to generate a belief in a relevant political actor (or actors) that one
is personally responsible for causing the government, or some unit thereof,
to do something that the actor (or actors) considers desirable. The political
logic of this, from the congressman's point of view, is that an actor who
believes that a member can make pleasing things happen will no doubt wish
to keep him in office so that he can make pleasing things happen in the
future. The emphasis here is on individual accomplishment (rather than,
say, party or governmental accomplishment) and on the congressman as
doer (rather than as, say, expounder of constituency views). Credit claiming is highly important to congressmen, with the consequence that much of
congressional life is a relentless search for opportunities to engage in it.

Where can credit be found? If there were only one congressman rather
than 535, the answer would in principle be simple enough. Credit (or
blame) would attach in Downsian fashion to the doings of the government
as a whole. But there are 535. Hence it becomes necessary for each congressman to try to peel off pieces of governmental accomplishment for
which he can believably generate a sense of responsibility. For the average
congressman the staple way of doing this is to traffic in what may be called
"particularized benefits." Particularized governmental benefits, as the term
will be used here, have two properties: (1) Each benefit is given out to a
specific individual, group, or geographical constituency, the recipient unit
being of a scale that allows a single congressman to be recognized (by relevant political actors and other congressmen) as the claimant for the benefit
(other congressmen being perceived as indifferent or hostile). (2) Each
benefit is given out in apparently ad hoc fashion (unlike, say, social security checks) with a congressman apparently having a hand in the alloca-

tion. A particularized benefit can normally be regarded as a member of a class. That is, a benefit given out to an individual, group, or constituency can normally be looked upon by congressmen as one of a class of similar benefits given out to sizable numbers of individuals, groups, or constituencies. Hence the impression can arise that a congressman is getting "his share" of whatever it is the government is offering. (The classes may be vaguely defined. Some state legislatures deal in what their members call "local legislation.")

In sheer volume the bulk of particularized benefits come under the heading of "casework" — the thousands of favors congressional offices perform for supplicants in ways that normally do not require legislative action. High school students ask for essay materials, soldiers for emergency leaves, pensioners for location of missing checks, local governments for grant information, and on and on. Each office has skilled professionals who can play the bureaucracy like an organ — pushing the right pedals to produce the desired effects. But many benefits require new legislation, or at least they require important allocative decisions on matters covered by existent legislation. Here the congressman fills the traditional role of supplier of goods to the home district. It is a believable role; when a member claims credit for a benefit on the order of a dam, he may well receive it. Shiny construction projects seem especially useful. . . .

The third activity congressmen engage in may be called *position taking,* defined here as the public enunciation of a judgmental statement on anything likely to be of interest to political actors. The statement may take the form of a roll call vote. The most important classes of judgmental statements are those prescribing American governmental ends (a vote cast against the war; a statement that "the war should be ended immediately") or governmental means (a statement that "the way to end the war is to take it to the United Nations"). The judgments may be implicit rather than explicit, as in: "I will support the president on this matter." But judgments may range far beyond these classes to take in implicit or explicit statements on what almost anybody should do or how he should do it: "The great Polish scientist Copernicus has been unjustly neglected"; "The way for Israel to achieve peace is to give up the Sinai." The congressman as position taker is a speaker rather than a doer. The electoral requirement is not that he make pleasing things happen but that he make pleasing judgmental statements. The position itself is the political commodity. Especially on matters where governmental responsibility is widely diffused it is not surprising that political actors should fall back on positions as tests of incumbent virtue. For voters ignorant of congressional processes the recourse is an easy one. The following comment [by a Congressman] is highly revealing: "Recently, I went home and began to talk about the ———— act. I was pleased to have sponsored that bill, but it soon dawned on me that the point wasn't getting through at all. What was getting through was that the act might be a help to people. I changed the emphasis: I didn't mention my role particularly, but stressed my support of the legislation."

The ways in which positions can be registered are numerous and often imaginative. There are floor addresses ranging from weighty orations to mass-produced "nationality day statements." There are speeches before home groups, television appearances, letters, newsletters, press releases, ghostwritten books, *Playboy* articles, even interviews with political scientists. On occasion congressmen generate what amount to petitions; whether or not to sign the 1956 Southern Manifesto defying school desegregation rulings was an important decision for southern members. Outside the roll call process the congressman is usually able to tailor his positions to suit his audiences. A solid censensus in the constituency calls for ringing declarations. . . .

Probably the best position-taking strategy for most congressmen at most times is to be conservative — to cling to their own positions of the past where possible and to reach for new ones with great caution where necessary. Yet in an earlier discussion of strategy the suggestion was made that it might be rational for members in electoral danger to resort to innovation. The form of innovation available is entrepreneurial position taking, its logic being that for a member facing defeat with his old array of positions it makes good sense to gamble on some new ones. It may be that congressional marginals fulfill an important function here as issue pioneers — experimenters who test out new issues and thereby show other politicians which ones are usable. An example of such a pioneer is Senator Warren Magnuson (D., Wash.), who responded to a surprisingly narrow victory in 1962 by reaching for a reputation in the area of consumer affairs. Another example is Senator Ernest Hollings (D., S.C.), a servant of a shaky and racially heterogeneous southern constituency who launched "hunger" as an issue in 1969 — at once pointing to a problem and giving it a useful nonracial definition. One of the most successful issue entrepreneurs of recent decades was the late Senator Joseph McCarthy (R., Wis.); it was all there — the close primary in 1946, the fear of defeat in 1952, the desperate casting about for an issue, the famous 1950 dinner at the Colony Restaurant where suggestions were tendered, the decision that "Communism" might just do the trick.

The effect of position taking on electoral behavior is about as hard to measure as the effect of credit claiming. Once again there is a variance problem; congressmen do not differ very much among themselves in the methods they use or the skills they display in attuning themselves to their diverse constituencies. All of them, after all, are professional politicians. . . .

There can be no doubt that congressmen believe positions make a difference. An important consequence of this belief is their custom of watching each other's elections to try to figure out what positions are salable. Nothing is more important in Capitol Hill politics than the shared conviction that election returns have proven a point. . . .

These, then, are the three kinds of electorally oriented activities congressmen engage in — advertising, credit claiming, and position taking. . . .

David Mayhew's thesis, part of which is presented in the preceding selection, is that the Washington activities of congressmen are, with few exceptions, geared toward reelection. In contrast, Richard Fenno argues that the Washington careers of congressmen may or may not be related to reelection. In his early work on Congress, Fenno pointed out that the *incentives* of members of Congress fall generally into three categories: (1) reelection, (2) internal power and influence on Capitol Hill, and (3) good public policy. While the incentives of congressmen cannot always be placed neatly into one of these categories, Fenno's research suggested that the behavior of members *in Congress* tends to be dominated by one of these incentives.[1]

Committee selection, in particular, is made to advance reelection, increase power and status on Capitol Hill, or make a good public policy. For example, such committees as Interior and Insular Affairs in the House serve the reelection incentives of its members by channeling specific benefits, such as water and conservation projects, into their districts. Members seeking influence in the House prefer such committees as Ways and Means and Appropriations, both of which reflect the role of the House in the constitutional system and represent it in the outside world. Congressmen on the Ways and Means and the Appropriations Committees, particularly the chairmen and ranking minority members, can use their positions effectively to bolster their reputations for power in the House. "Good public policy" committees are those that are used to reflect ideological viewpoints, such as the House Education and Labor Committee, rather than to give particular benefits to constituents or to augment internal influence.

Generally, as congressmen gain seniority, their Washington careers become separated from their constituency activities. If they have built an effective organization within their constituency, they are free to pursue goals on Capitol Hill that are not specifically for the purpose of gaining votes. In the following selection Richard Fenno discusses the linkage between the constituency and Washington activities of congressmen.

---

[1] Richard F. Fenno, Jr. *Congressmen in Committees* (Boston: Little, Brown and Co., 1973).

53
Richard F. Fenno, Jr.

HOME STYLE AND WASHINGTON CAREER

... When we speak of constituency careers, we speak primarily of the pursuit of the goal of reelection. When we speak of Washington careers, we speak primarily of the pursuit of the goals of influence in the House and the making of good public policy. Thus the intertwining of careers is, at bottom, an intertwining of member goals.

So long as they are in the expansionist stage of their constituency careers, House members will be especially attentive to their home base. They will pursue the goal of reelection with single-minded intensity and will allocate their resources disproportionately to that end. ... [F]irst-term members go home more frequently, place a larger proportion of their staff in the district, and more often leave their families at home than do their senior colleagues. Building a reelection constituency at home and providing continuous access to as much of that constituency as possible requires time and energy. Inevitably, these are resources that might otherwise be allocated to efforts in Washington. "The trouble is," said one member near the end of his second term,

> I haven't been a congressman yet. The first two years, I spent all of my time getting myself reelected. That last two years, I spent getting myself a district so that I could get reelected. So I won't be a congressman until next year.

By being "a congressman" he means pursuing goals above and beyond that of reelection (i.e., power in the House and good public policy).

In a House member's first years, the opportunities for gaining inside power and policy influence are limited. Time and energy and staff can be allocated to home without an acute sense of conflict. At rates that vary from congressman to congressman, however, the chances to have some institutional or legislative effect improve. As members stretch to avail themselves of the opportunity, they may begin to experience some allocative strain. It requires time and energy to develop a successful career in Washington just as it does to develop a successful career in the district. Because it may not be possible to allocate these resources to House and home, each to an optimal degree, members may have to make allocative and goal choices.

A four-term congressman with a person-to-person home style described the dilemma of choice:

> I'm beginning to be a little concerned about my political future. I can feel myself getting into what I guess is a natural and inevitable condition — the gradual erosion of my local orientation. I'm not as enthused about tending my constituency relations as I used to be and I'm not paying them the attention I should be. There's a natural tension between being a good representative and taking an interest in government. I'm getting into some heady things in Washington, and I want to make an input into the government. It's making me a poorer representative than I was. I find myself avoiding the personal collisions that arise in the constituency — turning away from that one last handshake, not bothering to go to that one last meeting. I find myself forgetting people's names. And I find myself caring less about it than I used to. Right now, it's just a feeling I have. In eight years I have still to come home less than forty weekends a year. This is my thirty-sixth trip this year. What was it Arthur Rubinstein said? "If I miss one practice, I notice it. If I miss two practices, my teacher notices it. If I miss a week of practice, my audience notices it." I'm at stage one right now — or maybe stage one and stage two. But I'm beginning to feel that I could be defeated before long. And I'm not going to change. I don't want the status. I want to contribute to government.

The onset of a Washington career is altering his personal goals and his established home style. He is worried about the costs of the change; but he is willing to accept some loss of reelection support in exchange for his increased influence in Congress.

This dilemma faces every member of Congress. It is built into the twin requirements that Congress be a representative and a legislative institution. Some members believe they can achieve reelection at home together with influence or policy in Washington without sacrificing either. During Congressman O's first year as a subcommittee chairman, I asked him whether his new position would make it more difficult to tend to district matters. He replied,

> If you mean, am I getting Potomac fever, the answer is, no. If you mean, has the change in my official duties here made me a better congressman, the answer is, yes. If you mean has it taken away from my activity in the constituency, the answer is no.

Congressman O, we recall, has been going home less; but he has been increasing the number and the activity of his district staff. Although he speaks confidently of his allocative solution, he is not unaware of potential problems. "My staff operation runs by itself. They don't need me. Maybe I should worry about that. You aren't going back and say I'm ripe for the plucking are you? I don't think I am."

A three-term member responded very positively when I paraphrased the worries of the congressman friend of his who had quoted Arthur Rubinstein:

> You can do your job in Washington and in your district if you know how. My quarrel with [the people like him] of this world is that they don't learn to be good politicians before they get to Congress. They get there because some people are sitting around the table one day and ask them to do it. They're smart, but they don't learn to organize a district. Once you learn to do that, it's much easier to do your job in Washington.

This member, however, has not yet tasted the inside influence of his friend. Moreover, he does not always talk with such assurance. His district is not so well organized that he has reduced his personal attentiveness to it.

> Ralph Krug [the congressman in the adjacent district] tells me I spoil my constituents. He says, "You've been elected twice; you know your district; once a month is enough to come home." But that's not my philosophy. Maybe it will be someday. . . . My lack of confidence is still a pressure which brings me home. This is my political base. Washington is not my political base. I feel I have to come home to get nourished, to see for myself what's going on. It's my security blanket — coming home.

For now, he feels no competing pulls; but he is not unaware of his friend's dilemma.

Members pose the dilemma with varying degrees of immediacy. No matter how confident members may be of their ability to pursue their Washington and their constituency careers simultaneously, however, they all recognize the potentiality of conflict and worry about coping with it. It is our guess that the conflict between the reelection goal on the one hand and the power or policy goals on the other hand becomes most acute for members as they near the peak of influence internally. For, at this stage of their Washington career, the resource requirements of the Washington job make it nearly impossible to meet established expectations of attentiveness at home. Individuals who want nothing from their Washington careers except the status of being a member of Congress will never pursue any other goal except reelection. For these people, the dilemma of which we speak is minimal. Our concern is with those individuals who find, sooner or later, that they wish to pursue a mix of goals in which reelection must be weighed along with power or policy.

One formula for managing a mix of goals that gives heavy weight to a Washington career is to make one's influence in Washington the centerpiece of home style. The member says, in effect, "I can't come home to present myself in person as much as I once did, because I'm so busy tending to the nation's business; but my seniority, my influence, my effectiveness in Washington is of great benefit to you." He asks his supportive constituents to adopt a new set of expectations, one that would put less of a premium on access. Furthermore, he asks these constituents to remain sufficiently intense in their support to discourage challengers — especially those who will promise access. All members do some of this when they explain their Washington activity — especially in connection with "explaining power." And, where possible, they quote from favorable national commentary in their campaign literature. But [very few Congressmen] have made Washington influence the central element of [their] home style.

One difficulty of completely adopting such a home style is that the powerful Washington legislator can actually get pretty far out of touch with his supportive constituents back home. One of the more senior members of [Congress], and a leader of his committee, recounted the case when his preoccupation with an internal legislative impasse affecting Israel caused him to neglect the crucial Jewish element of his primary constituency — a group "who contribute two-thirds of my money." A member of the committee staff had devised an amendment to break the deadlock.

> Peter Tompkins looked at it and said to me, "Why don't we sponsor it?" So we put it forward, and it became known as the Crowder-Tompkins Amendment. I did it because I respected the staff man who suggested it and because I wanted to get something through that was reasonable. Well, a member of the committee called people back home and said, "Crowder is selling out." All hell broke loose. I started getting calls at two and three in the morning from my friends asking me what I was doing. So I went back home and discussed the issue with them. When I walked into the room, it made me feel sad and shocked to feel their hostility. They wanted me to know that they would clobber me if they thought I was selling out. Two hours later, we walked out friends again. I dropped the Crowder-Tompkins Amendment. That's the only little flare up I've ever had with the Jewish community. But it reminded me of their sensitivity to anything that smacks of discrimination.

The congressman survived. But he would not have needed so forceful a reminder of his strongest supporters' concerns were he nearer the beginning of his constituency career. But, of course, neither would he have been a committee leader, and neither would the imperatives of a House career bulked so large in his mix of goals.

Another way to manage conflicting reelection and Washington career goals might be to use one's Washington influence to alter support patterns at home. That is, instead of acting — as is the normal case — to reenforce home support, to keep what he had "last time," the congressman might act to displace that old support with compensating new support. He might even accomplish this inadvertently, should his pursuit of power or policy attract, willy-nilly, constituents who welcome his new mix of goals. The very Washington activity that left him out of touch with previously supportive constituents might put him in touch with newly supportive ones. A newly acquired position of influence in a particular policy area or a new reputation as an effective legislator might produce such a feedback effect. . . .

... [There is] a tendency for successful home styles to harden over time and to place stylistic constraints on the congressman's subsequent behavior. The pursuit of a Washington career helps us explain this constituency phenomenon. That is, to the degree that a congressman pursues power or policy goals in the House, he will have that much less time or energy to devote to the consideration of alternative home styles. His predisposition to "do what we did last time" at home will be further strengthened by his growing preoccupation with Washington matters. Indeed, the speed with which a congressman begins to develop a Washington career will affect the speed with which his home style solidifies....

In all of this speculation about career linkages, we have assumed that most members of Congress develop, over time, a mix of personal goals. We particularly assume that most members will trade off some of their personal commitment to reelection in order to satisfy a personal desire for institutional or policy influence. It is our observation ... that House members do, in fact, exhibit varying degrees of commitment to reelection. All want reelection in the abstract, but not all will pay any price to achieve it; nor will all pay the same price....

One senior member contemplated retirement in the face of an adverse redistricting but, because he had the prospect of a committee chairmanship, he decided to run and hope for the best. He wanted reelection because he wanted continued influence; but he was unwilling to put his present influence in jeopardy by pursuing reelection with the same intensity that marked his earlier constituency career. As he put it,

> Ten years ago, I whipped another redistricting. And I did it by neglecting my congressional duties.... Today I don't have the time, and I'm not going to neglect my duties.... If I do what is necessary to get reelected and thus become chairman of the committee, I will lose the respect and confidence of my fellow committee members because of being absent from the hearings and, occasionally, the votes.

He did not work hard at reelection, and he won by his narrowest margin ever. But he succeeded in sustaining a mix of personal goals very different from an earlier one....

The congressman's home activities are more difficult and taxing than we have previously recognized. Under the best of circumstances, the tension involved in maintaining constituency contact and achieving legislative competence is considerable. Members cannot be in two places at once, and the growth of a Washington career exacerbates the problem. But, more than that, the demands in both places have grown recently. The legislative workload and the demand for legislative expertise are steadily increasing. So is the problem of maintaining meaningful contact with their several constituencies. Years ago, House members returned home for months at a time to live among their supportive constituencies, soak up the home atmosphere, absorb local problems at first hand. Today, they race home for a day, a weekend, a week at a time. [Few] maintain a family home in their district. [Many] stay with relatives or friends or in barely furnished rooms when they are at home. The citizen demand for access, for communication, and for the establishment of trust is as great as ever. So members go home. But the quality of their contact has suffered. "It's like a one-night stand in a singles bar." It is harder to sustain a genuine two-way communication than it once was. House member worries about the home relationship — great under any circumstances, but greater now — contribute to the strain and frustration of the job. Some cope; but others retire. It may be those members who cannot stand the heat of the home relationship who are getting out of the House kitchen. If so, people prepared to be more attentive to home . . . are likely to replace them.

The interplay between home careers and Washington careers continues even as House members leave Congress. For, in retirement or in defeat, they still face a choice — to return home or to remain in Washington. The subject of postcongressional careers is too vast to be treated here. But students of home politics can find, in these choices, indications of the depth and durability of home attachments in the face of influential Washington careers. It is conventional wisdom in the nation's capital that senators and representatives "get Potomac fever" and that "they don't go back to Pocatello" when their legislative careers end. Having pursued the goals of power and policy in Washington with increasing success, they prefer, it is said, to continue their Washington career in some nonlegislative job rather than to go back home. In such a choice, perhaps, we might find the ultimate displacement of the constituency career with the Washington career.

An examination of the place of residence of 370 individuals who left the House between 1954 and 1974, and who were alive in 1974, sheds considerable doubt on this Washington wisdom. It appears that most House members do, indeed, "go back to Pocatello." Of the 370 former members studied, 253 (68 percent) resided in their home states in 1974; 91 lived in the Washington, D.C., area; and 26 resided someplace else. Of those 344 who chose either Washington or home, therefore, nearly three-quarters chose home. This simple fact underscores the very great strength of the home attachments we have described in this book.

No cross section of living former members will tell us for sure how many members lingered in Washington for a while before eventually returning home. Only a careful tracing of all individual cases, therefore, will give us a full and accurate description of the Washington-home choice. Even so, among the former members most likely to be attracted to Washington — those who left Congress from 1970 to 1974 — only 37 percent have chosen to remain there. A cursory glance at all those who have chosen to prolong their Washington careers, however, tells us what we might expect — that they have already had longer congressional careers than those who returned home. Our data also tell us that these members are younger than those who choose to return home. Thus, we speculate, the success of a member's previous career in Congress and the prospect that he or she still has time to capitalize on that success in the Washington community are positive inducements to stay. And these inducements seem unaffected by the manner of his or her leaving Congress — whether by electoral defeat (for renomination or reelection) or retirement. Those who were defeated, however, had shorter congressional careers and were younger than those who had voluntarily retired.

Congressional Staff: The Surrogates of Power

Both the committee and personal staffs of Capitol Hill are important forces in the legislative process. Astute senators and congressmen know that their effectiveness in Congress largely depends upon the caliber of their staff. Each member of Congress has a personal staff; and the committee chairmen control staffs that are usually far greater in number than those in congressional and senatorial offices.

Although an embryo congressional staff began to develop in the nineteenth century, the origins of today's professional staff are found in the Legislative Reorganization Act of 1946, which increased the staffs of committees and their members. More important than the actual numbers of professional aides provided by the Act was the fact that Congress, for the first time, officially recognized the need for expert assistance, not only to cope with the increasingly complex problems confronting government but also to counterbalance the growing dominance of a highly expert executive branch.

Since the passage of the Legislative Reorganization Act in 1946 there has been a vast increase in congressional staff to approximately 14,000 aides in 1981. The greatest increment in staff occurred during the period from 1970 to 1980, as subcommittees expanded at an unprecedented rate. Moreover, as committee staffs grew, members who were not committee chairmen, noting how effective chairmen used their staffs to boost their power on Capitol Hill, demanded more personal staff. Over 10,000 professional staffers now serve in the offices of members, and approximately 4000 are employed by the close to 300 committees and subcommittees of Congress.

To what extent does congressional staff constitute an invisible government, exercising power and responsibility that the Constitution has delegated to the elected members of Congress? While senators and congressmen nominally exert control over their staffs, in actual fact, staffers often control their bosses. The time constraints upon members alone make it impossible for them to exercise more than cursory control of staff, and usually, this increases their dependence upon staff. Members rely upon their aides to set their daily schedules, keep them abreast of important issues, and determine what should be on their legislative agenda. Members often become the surrogates of the staffers, rather than vice versa.

An absorbing account of the role of the staff on Capitol Hill is presented by Eric Redman, who, fresh from college with a Rhodes Scholarship ahead of him, was employed temporarily as a junior aide by Senator Warren Magnuson, at that time chairman of the Commerce Committee. No one could have been a more junior staffer than Redman, yet he was able to operate effectively as Magnuson's surrogate in securing the passage of a National Health Service Corps bill by the Senate, and indirectly, by the House.

In this selection Redman describes some of the lessons he learned as a beginner on Capitol Hill. He attempted first to get the National Health Service Corps proposal passed, not as legislation but through the appropriations process. Magnuson was the chairman of the HEW appropriations subcommittee, which could earmark money for the doctor service corps that Redman wanted to have included under the umbrella appropriation for the Public Health Service in HEW. The appropriations route was an especially attractive strategy, not only because it would avoid the cumbersome, risky, and slow legislative process, but also because Magnuson had clear jurisdiction over HEW appropriations but not over legislation for the department. Each committee chairman has tight control over legislation falling under his jurisdiction. Redman, even as a beginner, knew that his strategy, if it worked, would be an easy way to give credit to Magnuson for the new program. Above all, as a loyal staffer, Redman did not want his, and by extension, Magnuson's proposal to be "stolen" by other senators and staffers. He wanted to assure that Magnuson would get full credit for the plan, to keep the proposal on Magnuson's turf — at all costs.

54
Eric Redman

BEGINNER'S LESSONS

Confronted with a National Health Service Corps scheme that purported to strengthen the system of private practice, a sufficiently paranoid member of the American Medical Association might have recognized it immediately as the Trojan Horse of socialized medicine. In Senator Magnuson's office, however, the Corps proposal seemed singularly undramatic at first, and we hardly pursued it with the zeal one would expect of conspirators. In fact, we agreed from the first that the NHSC should not be as grand in scale as it might be in philosophy; even [Dr. Abe] Bergman [a consultant to Magnuson] did not want it to begin as a massive new program, for he doubted any single approach could solve the complex "doctor distribution" problem. So we settled for what we hoped would be a small but imaginative experiment: an NHSC in which several dozen Public Health Service doctors would run a handful of health-care projects in a few selected communities scattered throughout the United States. If this limited program proved successful, we reasoned, Senator Magnuson could eventually persuade Congress to expand it.

One reason our plans were so modest was that our initial strategy called for Magnuson to create the NHSC without any new legislation. Legislation would have been "best," of course, in the sense that legislation alone could give visibility, coherence, and an unambiguous mission to the new Corps. But an NHSC bill, unlike earlier Bergman-inspired legislation, would not fall within the jurisdiction of the Senate Commerce Committee, where Magnuson, as Chairman, could pass virtually any bill he liked. Instead, such a bill would automatically go to the Committee on Labor and Public Welfare, which considers all health legislation in the Senate — and Magnuson was not a member of that Committee. Nor did Magnuson sit on the Senate Armed Services Committee, which might ask to review the bill no matter how carefully we tried to skirt the draft law. So the one thing we knew for certain was that we didn't want to establish the NHSC through new legislation; this reinforced the seeming wisdom of aiming for a small NHSC.

Fortunately, Magnuson could create the Corps without writing a bill — or so we thought. Through the HEW Appropriations Subcommittee, the Senator controlled HEW's funds and the funds of its relevant subdivision, the Public Health Service. Our initial strategy, therefore, was simple: Magnuson would merely add a few million dollars to the HEW Appropriation bill and "earmark" the money (i.e., specify its use, in the bill or in the accompanying Report) for an NHSC-type experiment under Public Health Service auspices. Since the total HEW Appropriation involved approximately $20 billion, and since Congress habitually adds a few hundred million dollars to the President's annual budget request for HEW, a small increase for the NHSC might go unnoticed, or at least cause little controversy.

We knew Magnuson would have no difficulty earmarking the funds; the question was whether HEW would cooperate thereafter. The whole strategy hinged on HEW's willingness to play along: if the Department was inclined to balk, it could refuse to spend the money, on the ground that the Public Health Service law did not explicitly authorize any program like the NHSC. But if, on the other hand, HEW did want to establish the Corps, it could quietly agree with Senator Magnuson that, yes, the law *could* be interpreted broadly as allowing this new experiment.

Obviously, we needed to reach an understanding with the Department of Health, Education and Welfare. This would have been true even with a less covert strategy, however, because in practice hostile Departments can effectively scuttle even the firmest of Congressional directives. Moreover, I had been taught in college (and consequently insisted to Bergman) that a prerequisite of "good" public administration is that the Executive Branch, with all its expertise, participate in designing the programs it will eventually have to administer. Whenever I passed the vast HEW Building at the foot of Capitol Hill, I couldn't help thinking that somewhere within than labyrinth there must be people who understood the "doctor distribution" problem better than Bergman and I did (particularly since all *I* knew was what Bergman had told me).

We anticipated that HEW would want to cooperate. First of all, the Department would be stupid not to "play ball" with Magnuson, the Chairman of the HEW Appropriations Subcommittee. But more important, we thought HEW would like the Corps proposal itself. Top HEW officials were already feuding publicly with the White House, asserting the need for new health programs but checked by fiscal and policy constraints from the President and the Office of Management and Budget (OMB). Dr. Roger O. Egeberg, the Assistant Secretary of HEW for Health and Scientific Affairs (and hence the "nation's number one doctor"), charged openly that the men on Pennsylvania Avenue were "callous," "indifferent," or "insensitive" to America's health-care problems. Egeberg's criticism received widespread coverage in the news, not only as one of the first indications of dissension within the Nixon Administration, but also as evidence that Egeberg himself was not the docile yes-man observers had once thought. Nixon's first choice for the post Egeberg occupied had, after all, been the reform-minded Dr. John M. Knowles, but that nomination had provoked such an outcry from the American Medical Association (AMA) that Nixon had withdrawn it and substituted Egeberg, a seemingly innocuous academic administrator whom the AMA could accept. Nixon's capitulation to the AMA had seemed to indicate that no one in the Administration (least of all Egeberg himself) would challenge the status quo of American medicine — but now Egeberg was proving that judgment premature.

In addition to Egeberg's growing independence, the historical "alliance" between HEW and Congress encouraged us to seek the Department's cooperation in making plans for the NHSC. Throughout the 1950's and early 1960's,[1] Congress had consistently provided more funds for HEW than the President had requested, and the increases had been engineered through more or less open collusion between HEW officials and the Chairmen of the HEW Appropriations Subcommittees in the House and Senate.

---

[1] President Eisenhower established HEW in 1953. In the mid-1960's, for a number of reasons (including the Vietnam war), HEW funding remained relatively stable.

Magnuson continued this pattern when he became Chairman in 1969, adding a standard $300 million to the Fiscal 1970 HEW Appropriation, but President Nixon promptly vetoed the entire bill. The veto (Nixon's first, and televised live to the nation) meant more work for Magnuson — he and his Subcommittee had to rewrite the whole appropriation during the Christmas holidays — but it stung HEW more severely. Speculation grew that HEW would seek to reforge its traditional alliance with Congress in order to resist Presidential "downgrading" of its programs — a classic textbook response for any out-of-favor Department, and one that HEW particularly had followed in the past.

Under the circumstances, we didn't hesitate to ask HEW's help in creating the National Health Service Corps, nor did the Department's initial reaction disappoint us. When we requested technical assistance, for example, in drafting the earmarking provision and in determining how much money to allot the proposed Corps, HEW promptly agreed to send us some of its top talent — a young doctor and a young lawyer from the Department's operating division, the Health Services and Mental Health Administration (HSMHA).

In order to elicit maximum cooperation from the HSMHA doctor and lawyer, Bergman and I carefully staged our first meeting to impress upon them the control Magnuson exercised over their Department's money. We picked as a conference site the cavernous hearing room of the HEW Appropriations Subcommittee in the New Senate Office Building, and in case the significance of the chamber should escape our visitors, we deliberately invited a fifth participant: Harley Dirks, the chief clerk of the Subcommittee and hence Magnuson's top aide in deciding the size and distribution of HEW's funds. Not a subtle show of power, perhaps, but one not easily dismissed.

We needn't have worried. Our doctor and lawyer readily endorsed the NHSC concept; in fact, they insisted, people in HSMHA had long been eager for just such a program. HEW welcomed innovative proposals for better health care, they said, but the White House and the OMB blocked the Department's own initiatives. Conspiring with Congress, however, could bring fast results; perhaps after we had set up the NHSC (an easy matter, they suggested), we could undertake some more substantial tasks together. The only caveat entered in this optimistic discussion was the lawyer's cautious remark, just before leaving, that the legality of our earmarking strategy was unclear; if the PHS lacked authority for patient care, Magnuson could not create that authority simply by giving the agency more money. Perhaps, the lawyer added, specific authorizing legislation might be needed, in which case the earmarking strategy wouldn't work. But this was only a possibility, and the lawyer promised to consult his books and produce a definitive answer.

With the technical details "farmed out" to the HSMHA doctor and lawyer, we began to consider the more rarefied politics of our earmarking strategy. We decided the next step was to visit Dr. Egeberg himself, the unexpected new advocate of innovative health-care programs. And we knew the most important person to include as a member of our delegation was again Harley Dirks.

Dirks is in many ways a legendary man on Capitol Hill. Rumor has it that he was once a shoe salesman in Othello, Washington, a drowsy little farm town in the dry Columbia Basin. A more likely version is that Dirks *owned* a shoe store in Othello, and if he occasionally fitted the customers himself, it was not because he lacked grander dreams. Othello is miles from anywhere, an oasis of sorts in prairielike Eastern Washington, and its isolation — even from Seattle — cannot be adequately expressed in a mileage number on a road map. Othello was so slow, and Dirks so fast, that soon he found himself owning a host of its businesses and one of its banks — or so the story goes — despite the fact that he spent much of his time catching trout, shooting pheasant, and siring offspring. For whatever reason, Dirks eventually felt the urge to move on, and to a man of his imagination that did not mean bundling up the family and heading for Walla Walla. Instead, he worked for Senator Magnuson in the 1962 campaign and then followed him back to Washington, D.C.

Dirks became a "clerk" on the Appropriations Committee at a time when Magnuson handled the funds of HUD, NASA, and the many independent agencies and regulatory commissions. When Magnuson switched to the HEW Appropriations post, Dirks went with him, simply moving his pipe rack to a new office and confronting a new set of figures. At first, his nominal superior was the "Chief Clerk" of the Subcommittee, an irascible Southerner who had served under chairmen now almost forgotten on Capitol Hill. Before long, however, Dirks moved in behind the Chief Clerk's desk (his own had become an unworkable mountain of papers), and within a few months the Chief Clerk stopped coming to work altogether. Dirks redecorated the staid office with oils he had painted, and as a quiet joke he arrayed on his new desk much "authoritative" academic works as *The Power of the Purse* and *The Politics of the Budgetary Process.* He had neither the time nor the need to read books about appropriations; he ran a Subcommittee that appropriated nearly $40 billion each year (an amount second only to the Defense Department's).[2]

Like other Appropriations Committee clerks, Dirks is unknown to the public and to much of the Washington press corps. Tourists do not call at his office (although Senators and Secretaries do), and at appropriations hearings members of the audience sometimes whisper, "Who is that man

---

[2] When trust fund expenditures are included, the HEW appropriation totals some $80 billion, an amount in excess of the regular Defense Department appropriation.

sitting next to the Chairman?" That Dirks carries his power so judiciously says much about his fierce loyalty to Senator Magnuson, his sole constituent. Magnuson relies on Dirks heavily, not simply because he is loyal, or because a chairman has little choice, but also because Dirks is thorough, alert, and discreet. The only outsider, in fact, who has ever sensed Dirks's true influence was an academic researcher who interviewed him in connection with a study attempting to correlate appropriations figures with Senators' backgrounds; amused, Dirks simply jotted down for his visitor his own prediction of dollar amounts, by program, in an appropriations bill the Senators themselves had not yet even discussed. When the bill finally passed, Dirks's projections corresponded uncannily with the approved figures.

Dirks's anonymity does not extend to the Department of Health, Education and Welfare. Bergman and I witnessed a revealing, if somewhat comic, demonstration of this as we walked with Harley down HEW's long corridors on our way to discuss the earmarking strategy with Dr. Egeberg. From one doorway after another, men and women emerged to intone respectfully, "Good morning, Mr. Dirks," or "Hello, Harley!" and so on down the list of ingratiating pleasantries. Bergman and I felt obscure and incidental, as if we were Secret Service escorts; Dirks, for his part, smiled and waved like a Presidential candidate. It was hard to imagine him ever going back to Othello.

Even Dr. Egeberg, when we arrived, seemed sensitive to Dirks's presence. He welcomed us warmly and ushered us immediately into his inner office, hastily summoning aides and ordering coffee. A huge, bald man in his late sixties, Egeberg sported a jaunty yellow BULLSHIT button on his lapel. Hardly giving us time to sit down (much less to broach the subject of our visit), he launched into an animated monologue, designed (I supposed) to establish his credentials as a critic of the President and Presidential health policies.

"I had an appointment to see the President a month or so ago," he began, "because I wanted him to add a hundred and fifty million dollars to our budget for training more doctors. I was sitting outside the door to the Oval Office, waiting, when John Ehrlichman [the President's top aide for domestic affairs] came up and asked, 'This visit doesn't have anything to do with money, does it?' I said, 'Of course it has to do with money — we need a hundred and fifty million dollars to train more doctors.' 'Oh, well,' Ehrlichman said, 'if it has to do with money, we'll have to reprogram this appointment. No one can discuss money matters with the President unless George Shultz [Nixon's fiscal adviser] is here.'

"Now, I've called every single week since," Egeberg concluded, "and I still haven't been able to get the appointment 'reprogrammed.' And the hell of it is, I *know* the President of the AMA can walk in and see Nixon anytime he wants!"

The anecdote suggested Egeberg might cooperate with us; so did his eagerness in turning to Harley to ask why we had come (evidently he hadn't been briefed). Harley, adopting the role of silent sage, nodded to indicate that I should explain our plan. Somewhat nervously (this was the "nation's number one doctor"), I told Egeberg what we hoped to establish: a National Health Service Corps, within the Public Health Service, created solely through an earmarking of funds in the HEW Appropriation. Would Egeberg and the Department help?

Egeberg responded without hesitation. "I've always wanted a program like that," he said, "but I can't come right out and ask for it myself. I've got certain problems down *there,* you know [he motioned toward the White House]. But if *Maggie* proposed it," he went on, in mock conspiratorial tones, "and if he provided the *money* for it, well then I'd *have* to set it up, wouldn't I?

"We need a new mission for the Public Health Service," he continued, after exchanging broad smiles with Dirks, "and in fact, I've got a committee looking at the problem right now. I think the answer has got to be some kind of doctor corps. So let's hear your plan."

The plan we agreed upon, after a brief discussion, was simple. Egeberg's staff would write some questions, based on the HSMHA doctor-lawyer team's research, and give them to Magnuson so that he could "spontaneously" ask Egeberg about an NHSC when the doctor came to testify during the HEW Appropriation hearings in June. Magnuson would describe his idea briefly, then ask Egeberg (for example), "if Congress provided you with three million dollars for this type of program, staffed with Public Health Service doctors, how would you spend it?" Egeberg would then reply, "Well, Mr. Chairman, of course the Department has not *asked* for any such program, but if you and the Committee feel so strongly about it that you provide three million dollars, I guess this is what we would have to do. . . ." Then Egeberg would outline the details of the hypothetical Corps, prompted occasionally by carefully prearranged questions from Magnuson. The exchange, printed in the hearing record and in the Report accompanying the appropriation, would serve both to define the "Congressional intent" behind the NHSC (since no legislation would be available for this purpose) and to create the impression that Magnuson had "forced" the new program upon a reluctant but ultimately pliable HEW officialdom. The scheme was so clever that we wondered if Magnuson and Egeberg would be able to keep straight faces while reciting their lines.

After chuckling over the impending "drama" in the hearing room, Egeberg rose and walked us to the door. As we left, I mentioned to him the HSMHA lawyer's warning that the strategy might prove impossible for legal reasons. Egeberg replied that he hoped the lawyer was wrong, and that if not, we could still count on the services of HEW's General Counsel in drafting any legislation we might need. "Let's keep in touch," he added, and bade us goodbye.

I had to admit, as we walked away, that I felt better about our enlisting Egeberg as an ally than I had before the visit. My misgivings had stemmed from my only previous exposure to him, at a press conference in 1969 when HEW announced a partial ban on cyclamate sweeteners, which had just been found to cause cancer in rats. In later weeks, the cyclamate "ban" became the object of Washington humor, but the press conference had been tense (and held on a Saturday for a deliberate reason: the stock market would be closed). "This is going to be ten times worse than when Thalidomide hit," confided a White House aide I knew, and HEW Secretary Robert Finch, who had spoken first, gripped the podium tightly; sweat showed all over his face. Yet Dr. Egeberg, speaking next, treated the issue nonchalantly from the first, pointing out that everything — cyclamates, the Pill, cigarettes — had its advantages and disadvantages from a health standpoint. This attitude had surprised the press corps, and reinforced my distasteful image of Egeberg, an image I had picked up during the earlier "Knowles Affair."

Now, however, I found I liked Egeberg. I could even interpret sympathetically his position on cyclamates, something I had judged too quickly in any event. I could see why Magnuson liked Egeberg too, almost alone of the HEW officials he confronted each year (the indecisive Finch had become "Secretary Flinch" in Magnuson's vocabulary). What struck me most about Egeberg was his good nature and his obviously good intentions. Climbing into a cab for a brief ride back to Capitol Hill, I confided all this to Bergman and Harley Dirks.

Harley looked at me and grinned. "Wait and see," he admonished. "You like him because he's barking at the White House, but he's barking because the White House keeps him on a very short leash."

Redman's initial optimism was soon dashed when it became clear that HEW was not going to cooperate with his strategy. He soon found that the Washington power establishment, with the key committee chairmen of Capitol Hill at the apex, was far more complicated and sensitive than he ever could have imagined. Eventually, "Magnuson's" and "Redman's" National Health Service Corps bill was passed by both the House and the Senate, but only after intricate and often frustrating political maneuvering to enlist the aid of the powerful committee chairmen in the Senate and the House who had jurisdiction over the proposal. Just as Magnuson's staff claimed credit for their senator, the staffs of Senator Ralph Yarborough, chairman of the key Committee on Labor and Public Welfare (now called the Labor and Human Resources Committee) and its Health Subcommittee, proclaimed that *their* senator was responsible for the bill. On the House side, the bill was credited to Congressman Paul Rogers of West Palm Beach, Florida, who, as acting chairman of the Health Subcommittee skillfully guided the legislation through numerous obstacles to a floor victory.

Successful congressional careers are built upon good staff work. While staff tends to be more an attribute of power in the Senate than in the House, politically astute congressmen know that they, too, can build their Capitol Hill power and status through a talented and adroit staff. The following selection describes how deft and aggressive staffwork placed a freshman congressman in the public eye at the same time it boosted his status on Capitol Hill.

55
Rochelle Jones and Peter Woll

STAFF: THE SURROGATES OF POWER

Maguire was swept into office in the post-Watergate elections of 1974. He is an unlikely Congressman for the seventh district in northern New Jersey. He is a Democrat in a district that went two to one for Nixon in 1972 and voted predominantly for Ford in 1976. He is an urban affairs specialist in a district that takes in some of the most beautiful and affluent suburbs in the country. Maguire, however, had two things going for him — the nationwide revulsion against the Watergate capers and an aging incumbent who was no match for his aggressive campaigning. Like most of the freshmen who took office that year, Maguire had no patience with the old "go along to get along" ways of the House. Maguire was used to getting ahead, not along. After studying economics on a Woodrow Wilson fellowship and earning a Ph.D. in politics at Harvard, Maguire worked at the United Nations and from there had gone on to the Ford Foundation. At thirty-five, Maguire was ready to make his mark in Congress.

Maguire saw things differently than most of the older members of the House and a lot of the newer ones as well. Having served on staffs at the UN and the Ford Foundation, he knew the importance of good staff work. At freshman orientation in December a senior Congressman told the incoming class, "The greatest contribution any of us can make to the welfare of America is to return here in two years. That's what you should concentrate on. Don't waste money hiring staff. Anything you need you can get through the DSG [the Democratic Study Group] or the committee. The sole purpose of your staff is to answer the mail." The older members of the House nodded sagely, but while Maguire listened politely, he didn't take the Congressman's advice. And as it happened, Maguire's staff ended up doing everything but answering the mail.

Maguire, in fact, chose to do exactly the opposite of what the Congressman advised. At the outset he hired Bob Kerr, a young political scientist from the University of Pittsburgh, as his administrative assistant. Kerr, having worked previously for Senator Hubert Humphrey, had decidedly Senate notions about the proper role for staff. The combination of Maguire's personality and Kerr's experience shaped subsequent happenings.

Maguire was both smart and brash, and he had come to Congress at a propitious time. That winter a sense of excitement was abroad in Washington and especially in the House. The changes wrought by the internal reforms of the 1970s were having their effect. Some of the stodginess of an earlier era in the House had been swept away. Moreover, the House still felt a kind of residual collective pride in the highly praised performance of its Judiciary Committee as it handled the articles of impeachment that summer against Richard Nixon. As a result, some of the debilitating feeling of inferiority to the Senate from which the House habitually suffers had worn away temporarily. And in general the nation was no longer morbidly glued to the national soap opera of Richard Nixon's demise. The long nightmare was ended. The nation was ready to get on with the business at hand.

The freshmen Congressmen arriving in Washington that winter believed they represented the first of a new generation of post-Watergate politicians. They were serious and idealistic. Starry-eyed, some of the veterans thought. Many had campaigned heavily for political reforms and owed their election to promises to change the system. The election had been heavily chronicled by the national media, and the media were watching over the shoulders of the incumbents to see if these notions of reform would be accepted. The House leaders were more willing to listen, more open to the freshmen's ideas than they had ever been. There was a sense of changing seasons when they came in December that had nothing to do with the plummeting temperatures which heralded the arrival of the Washington winter.

Andy Maguire correctly sensed that in this atmosphere he could play the power and status game in a new way. Instead of moving up through the committee hierarchy, hopscotching from a low-ranking committee to a high-ranking committee and waiting for subcommittee chairmanships to open up, which would ordinarily take years, he would force the establishment to let him in immediately. The way to do that, he rightly reasoned, was to become a national figure in some important area. As a nationally recognized figure he would be able to command the attention of the leadership. Maguire and his staff set about creating a national image for him. The energy crisis provided an opportunity, and the national press unwittingly became the means.

The freshmen were something of a novelty to the media, which paid substantial attention to their initial comings and goings. Maguire, however, realized he needed to differentiate himself from the rest of the newcomers if his strategy was to work. The press is notoriously fickle, and Maguire knew that if he were going to keep its interest, he eventually had to do something that would be newsworthy. Press interest in the freshmen would last only so long.

The Ford administration's energy program created the ideal setting. One of the centerpieces was a gasoline tax which would raise the price of gas at the pump. Neither Al Ullman, chairman of the Ways and Means Committee, nor John Dingell, chairman of the Energy and Power Sub-committee, came out against it. Maguire seized the opportunity to become the spokesman for the consumers. Together with five other newly elected Congressmen, Maguire put together an alternate program and held a press conference to announce the freshman energy coalition. The press conference attracted a number of key reporters and Maguire was on his way.

Maguire's press secretary was young and inexperienced, and his naiveté proved to be a decided asset. An experienced press secretary, more knowledgeable about the workings of the press, would have known that the national media would not have the slightest interest in the pronouncements of the 435th member of Congress. But Gary Sardo, who had no experience as a press secretary, was blissfully unaware of that fact. He was also, in the words of a fellow staff member, "obstinate as hell, totally charming and able to talk endlessly." He turned out to be as bold and brash as his boss.

Soon the staffs at such papers as the *New York Times* and on such programs as "Today" and "Not for Women Only" were receiving phone calls from Sardo. At the start they were nonplussed. Why, they wondered in amazement, would anybody imagine they would be interested in a freshman Congressman from, of all places, New Jersey? They became increasingly befuddled as the phone calls kept up. Sardo was completely undaunted by refusals. Eventually skepticism gave way to grudging admiration of Sardo's tenacity. He simply did not give up or go away. It took ten phone calls to the "Op Ed" page of the *New York Times* to place the article that Maguire had written, but in the end the editor accepted it. It took three months of badgering before Sardo placed Maguire on the "Today" show, but he got on.

"We were a group of zealots and generally regarded that way," said an aide, recalling that time. " 'Brash,' 'abrasive,' and 'aggressive' were favored adjectives in the press."

Meanwhile, Maguire's staff were focusing all of their attention on energy. Everything else was shoved to a corner of their desks. The district office staff back in Bergen County screamed at the Washington staff daily as the routine work of a Congressman's office piled up behind more statements on energy policy. Even the mail went unanswered for months at a time. One day as Maguire strolled into the office from the floor, he chided Kerr. Another Congressman had just told him that his office answered mail within two days. "Why can't we have a two-day turnaround?" he said. Kerr asked if he wanted the staff to answer mail or work on energy. Maguire shrugged his shoulders and wandered away. It was the first and last time anyone in the office heard Maguire complain about the mail.

Maguire had managed to assemble a large staff for a first-term Congressman by finding people who were willing to work long hours for hideously low salaries, but even so they could accomplish only so much in the course of a twelve-hour work day. Maguire knew he could not have everything, and he deliberately chose for them to spend their time to establish him as a spokesman on energy. He might not be picked as Congressman of the Year by his constituents, but he could make headlines in the *Washington Post*.

Moreover, the strategy was working. Outside of Congress Maguire was being recognized as an energy expert. Maguire took the toughest possible stands on energy. If Ford or Ullman or Dingell took one position, Maguire took the exact opposite. The reporters who covered the Hill for the Washington *Star* and *Post* came to realize that Maguire could be counted on for an articulate and highly quotable reaction to the energy proposals that were floating around the administration and Congress. They also realized that Maguire always knew the ins and outs of issues. Sardo managed to break through the initial resistance of the media through sheer force of personality. Their attitude was, as a Maguire aide described it, "Let's hear what this nutty guy has to say." Once they started listening, Maguire became that favorite thing — a good source. The "Today" show, which had initially laughed at Sardo's attempts to place Maguire, invited him back three times in a year. And Maguire's frequent appearances there were something more senior Congressmen could easily envy. The press was beginning to trust the young Congressman from New Jersey. An aide said, "In the Senate you are automatically assumed to have credibility until you blow it. In the House you must establish it. So we did." The press began to see Andrew Maguire as the person to talk to on energy issues. Press coverage inevitably engenders press coverage. The more press a Congressman can get, the more he tends to be sought out by the press.

The press helped to build up Maguire's reputation inside the House. It was not just the sheer volume of press clippings he was accumulating, although that obviously added to his visibility. More important, it was the kinds of press he was getting. Newspapers such as the *New York Times* and the *Washington Post,* whose opinions carried weight with members of Congress, were taking Maguire seriously. And the Op Ed piece in the *New York Times* was a brilliant stratagem on the part of Maguire's staff. Other Congressmen, who were not privy to the effort which had preceded its acceptance, were impressed. As a young man in a hurry, Maguire had no time to waste. Since he was unwilling to put in the time on the inside that would ordinarily be required, he sought to build his expertise, a necessary prerequisite of power in the House, off the Hill.

Not all Congressmen were pleased by the attention which Maguire was getting and by his use of staff. Some were hostile outright. Others were merely affronted by his unwillingness to play the game in the old way. Once when Maguire brought an aide to sit beside him in a committee hearing, a Congressman asked, "Has that man been elected by the people?" But Maguire was able to deflect a lot of criticism by always doing his homework, always being prepared. He might speak out more than freshmen Congressmen were supposed to do even in 1975, but at least when he did, he had something of consequence to say.

The initial payoff was Maguire's reassignment to the Interstate and Foreign Commerce Committee. Maguire had sought that committee in the beginning but had been appointed to the Banking Committee instead. When Congressman John Jarman of Oklahoma switched parties, a vacancy was created among the Democrats. Maguire reapplied, as did Larry McDonald of Georgia, a self-proclaimed member of the John Birch Society. Ordinarily McDonald would have been able to claim the seat because of his seniority. But the leadership was anxious to keep McDonald, who had a regrettable tendency, from their viewpoint, to go his own way, off the committee. Maguire, having demonstrated with the help of his friends in the press a potential for leadership in energy policy, was the logical choice. He might not always support the party position but unlike McDonald he was considered a responsible dissenter. Through hard-headed bargaining, Maguire was able to get himself assigned to the Energy Subcommittee of the Interstate and Foreign Commerce Committee also.

Within a year of his election Maguire's staff had been able to accomplish for him what other Congressmen spend a decade or more doing. They built an image for him. They made other Congressmen take him seriously. And they had gotten him on the right committees. Maguire had emerged as a comer. Without an aggressive, dynamic staff that was incapable of taking no for an answer, Maguire would have been languishing in obscurity on the Banking Committee, still waiting, as political scientist Richard Fenno would say, to become a Congressman. . . .

A Day in the United States Senate

The environments of the Senate and the House differ rather significantly. Election to the United States Senate means that one has arrived politically. With the exception of the White House, the Senate is the most prestigious body in Washington. Rarely does a senator resign to take another post, as did Maine Senator Edmund Muskie in 1980 to become Secretary of State, considered to be the highest ranking job in the Cabinet. Senators are statesmen in their own right, and they often act as sovereign bodies. They may be involved in international as well as national politics. The six-year term of office and the broad constituencies of senators make them less directly dependent upon the people, and as the framers of the Constitution intended, more capable of independent, deliberative action than members of the House.

Although the Senate is no longer dominated by an inner club of senior members, as described by William S. White in *The Citadel* in 1956, a spirit of collegiality prevails and some past traditions do linger. Norms of hard work, expertise, courtesy, and respect for the institution and its ways continue to characterize those senators who have achieved power and status in the body. A long apprenticeship is no longer required of junior senators before they can make their voice heard on Capitol Hill, but it still behooves them to respect the informal rules governing the way in which the Senate operates.

In the following selection, Elizabeth Drew, Washington correspondent for *The New Yorker* magazine and a freelance writer on politics, describes a day in the life of Senator John Culver of Iowa. Culver first arrived at Capitol Hill in 1964, when he was elected to the House. He was an influential member of the Democratic Study Group and was a leading proponent of House reform. He ran for the Senate in 1974 and won with 52 percent of the vote. He became an active member of the Senate, leading his Democratic colleagues on a number of issues, including arms control and the SALT treaty. As a member of the Armed Services Committee he developed a reputation for hard work, expertise, and an aggressive stance on reviewing defense expenditures that did not always conform to the hawkish views of the committee. He did not hesitate to fight what he considered to be unwarranted increases in defense expenditures. He was an active chairman of the Research and Development Subcommittee of Armed Services. In another policy sphere, he was a member of the Environment and Public Works Committee and chairman of its Resource Protections Subcommittee, which he used to sponsor the endangered-species legislation for which he was the floor-manager.

While Culver was building his profile in the Senate, he faced difficult reelection prospects in 1980 in a state that was shifting to the Republican party. To what extent is the senator's day, described in the following selection and largely devoted to floor-managing his endangered-species bill, helpful to reelection? Is Culver striving for power and status in the Senate and in the broader world of Washington? Is the senator's visibility on Capitol Hill useful to him back home?

56
Elizabeth Drew

A DAY IN THE LIFE
OF A UNITED STATES SENATOR

Wednesday, July 19th: Culver has gone to the White House for the eight-o'clock breakfast meeting on lifting the embargo on the sale of arms to Turkey (he asked the President to what extent the policy of lifting the embargo, in the interests of strengthening NATO, had anticipated a negative reaction in Greece, which could have consequences that would weaken NATO); at nine-thirty, he met on the Senate steps with 4-H Clubs from three counties in Iowa; at nine-forty-five, he met with Charles Stevenson to go over some questions he had on the material, which he had read early this morning, for the press conference on Soviet civil defense; and then he met with George Jacobson and Kathi Korpon on amendments that will come up today on the endangered-species bill.

Now, at ten o'clock, the Senate resumes debate on the bill. S. I. Hayakawa, Republican of California, offers a minor amendment, which Culver accepts, in accordance with his policy of accepting as many as he can in order to build a consensus behind the bill. Representatives of the Fish and Wildlife Service are stationed in the Vice President's Capitol Hill office, off the Senate floor, and amendments that Culver is giving consideration to accepting are sent out to them for their opinion. He turns the floor over to Wallop so that Wallop can engage Hayakawa in a colloquy to establish the legislative history of the amendment. Culver is giving Wallop a larger role than the majority manager usually affords the minority — also in the interest of building a consensus.

Shortly before ten-thirty, Culver leaves the floor to go to the Dirksen Office Building for his press conference on Soviet civil defense. Just before the press conference begins, he goes over again with Charles Stevenson the points he wants to stress. A fair number of newspaper reporters are here, along with reporters from two television networks and one television station in Iowa. Culver enters the room and sits behind a table that has several microphones on it. He is wearing a navy-blue suit, a blue shirt, and a navy-blue tie with small white dots. He reads a statement explaining that "for the past two years I have sought an official but unclassified assessment of Soviet civil defense which could be made available for a better-informed public debate on this issue." The report he has received, and is releasing today, he says, "represents the first comprehensive and authoritative analysis of this crucial topic in unclassified form." He says that "the study indicates that the Soviet civil-defense system, while representing a significant national effort, is by no means sufficiently effective to encourage the Soviets to risk starting a nuclear war."

He continues, "While crediting the Soviet Union with a major, ongoing civil-defense program, this report demonstrates that those efforts are not sufficient to prevent millions of casualties and massive industrial damage in the event of a nuclear war. In short, Soviet programs are not enough to tip the strategic balance against us." He is addressing himself to recent alarms that the Soviets are engaged in a new civil-defense effort of sufficient proportions that the strategic balance might indeed be tipped, and to arguments that therefore the United States should also engage in a new, enlarged civil-defense program. Now, also addressing himself to the arguments of critics of SALT, and pursuing his goal, about which he spoke to me earlier, of achieving more understanding in both the United States and the Soviet Union concerning the consequences of a nuclear exchange, he says, "Despite the widespread claims that Soviet leaders might launch a nuclear attack because they expect to suffer only moderate damage and few casualties — and we hear that suggested today in a number of quarters — the professional judgment of our intelligence community is that they would not be emboldened to expose themselves and their country to a higher risk of nuclear attack. Even under the 'worst case' assumptions of this study, nuclear war would be a disaster for the Soviet Union." He takes questions, and answers earnestly and with a large number of facts. He says that the estimates of each side's losses in a nuclear attack vary with the targeting plan and the warning time — that the Soviet Union could lose well over a hundred million people, but that figure could be cut by more than fifty per cent if it had two to three days' warning. "I guess the bottom line in all this," he says, "is that even in the worst case the casualties would be awesome."

When one of the reporters questions his conclusions, Culver becomes annoyed. "We do have a great deal of speculation. It's rampant," he says, referring to the alarms about the nature of the Soviet threat. His voice rises. "We don't need to panic," he says. "There is no surge planning. Since they can't have high confidence — and that's what this report is about — the Soviet Union would not be emboldened to risk a nuclear war." Culver is getting involved, and he just keeps going, making his argument, ranging into the way he thinks about the whole subject. He may have a bill pending on the Senate floor, but now he gives this his all, takes the opportunity to present his case. He says, "We talk so much about military doctrine — that General So-and-So says this, that General So-and-So says that. Soldiers in every country all the time talk about victory. They're not paid to talk about defeat. They are trained with the can-do spirit, and the can-do spirit can lead to nuclear war — holocaust, believe it or not." The passion has come to the surface again. "The political leadership on both sides believe that nuclear war would be a disaster," he says. "Now, whether the troops have got the message is another question." Addressing himself to his questioner, he continues, "The Soviet civil-defense effort, I beg your pardon, is not the coördinated, effective system that some so-called experts have claimed, according to the judgment of the people who wrote this report." He goes on — as he did with me in his office, as he did with the constituents in Des Moines — about both sides having civil-defense signs in their subways, both sides having pamphlets. He says, "If you just like to embrace rumor and innuendo and fear, fine. Some people make a life-time career of it."

He then tries to turn to someone else, but the reporter follows up with a question based on a statement by a Soviet general.

"I could probably provide you with some statements by our highest military or some article they've written," Culver replies. "In that context, everyone's talking about, quote, winning a war, unquote."

He goes on for a while, talking about Soviet history. "I'm not min-imizing their effort, and it may be comfortable to characterize my position as 'weak on civil defense,' " he says, "but what I want to do is to get objective information before the public."

In answer to a question about whether he thinks that the United States should proceed to spend substantially increased funds on civil defense over the next few years, Culver says, "I think that we're just going to have to carefully look at it and review it." He adds that he thinks this is an area that should be explored in future SALT talks. "It seems to me that before we all pour a lot of money along this line," he says, "why don't we get together and try to agree, in the spirit of the A.B.M. agreement" — in 1972, the United States and the Soviet Union agreed to limit substantially their deployment of anti-ballistic missiles — "and try to find a way to minimize the threat." This is how he argued in opposing construction of a military base on Diego Garcia, and later there were talks on demilitarizing the Indian Ocean; this is how he argued about conventional-arms sales, and later there were talks on that subject. However fruitful the talks may or may not be, Culver considers such efforts worth a try.

Culver concludes the press conference at eleven-fifteen.

In an anteroom, Don Brownlee is waiting with a tape-recording ma-chine, so that Culver can record "actualities" to send out to the Iowa radio stations. As Brownlee holds a microphone, Culver reads two excerpts from his statement. Charles Stevenson tells Culver that he has some questions about provisions that Culver backed which might come up in the House-Senate conference on the military-procurement bill this afternoon — ques-tions about which provisions he might want to trade for what. "We'll have to talk about that more, Charlie," Culver says.

When Culver returns to the Senate floor, an amendment by Nelson is pending. This one would limit projects that could be exempted to those for which "a substantial and irretrievable commitment of resources had been made." Culver speaks in opposition, saying that the amendment "does have some superficial appeal" but could have undesirable results — that it could have the effect of discouraging agencies from confronting the problem until a project was well along. He does an imitation, in a prissy voice, of an imagined, unrealistic statement by a representative of the Fish and Wildlife Service in the course of a discussion over whether a project should proceed. He draws an analogy — perhaps because of what he was dealing with in his press conference — between such discussions and the bargaining over SALT. "This amendment could have the force and effect of accelerating the move toward construction," he says. "This amendment says the only way you can have any hope for receiving an exemption is to get in there and build." He cites Nelson's proposed language — "a substantial and irretrievable commitment of resources." He bellows, "What on earth is that? Is there a lawyer in the house? Substantial to whom? Irretrievable to whom?" He returns to the defense analogy, referring now to the current controversy over whether and what sort of a mobile-missile system should be built. "We may have to dig a hole where the Furbish lousewort lives," he says, and he goes on to say that we should not get into a situation where it would be like saying to the Defense Department, " 'Go ahead and build the damn thing, and if you build it enough to spend thirty million dollars, then we will tell you you should not have done it in the first place.' " Nelson's amendment is defeated by a vote of twenty-five to seventy.

During the roll call, Culver goes over to the Republican side to confer with Scott.

Now Scott offers an amendment to exempt a project that might prevent the recurrence of a natural disaster, and Culver accepts it. Scott previously referred several times in the debate to a flood in Virginia that took the lives of four people, and yesterday afternoon Culver decided to try to reach agreement with him on an amendment to cover natural disasters. Next, he accepts an amendment by Scott to provide that five rather than all seven members of the interagency committee will constitute a quorum. Culver's hope is that if he accommodates Scott, Scott may reciprocate by withholding some of the several amendments he still has pending. "It's like a negotiating situation," Culver has explained to me. "You have twelve amendments, but there are only three or four you care about." Scott, however, is unpredictable. And though Scott has little influence within the Senate, Culver still has to be concerned that, as the day goes on, the Senate might accept something that Scott proposes or an atmosphere might be created in which some surprise amendment would be adopted. When Senate sessions go on until late in the day or into the evening, matters can get increasingly out of hand: tempers rise, a few drinks may have been consumed, and a certain "what the hell?" attitude can take over. "Late in the day gets to be the silly season," Culver has explained to me. "It gets harder and harder to control what happens."

For that reason, Culver has persuaded Scott to bring up now the amendment that Culver most fears: the one to require a majority vote, rather than a vote of five of the seven members, of the interagency committee in granting an exemption. He is worried that his proposal is vulnerable here. And he is concerned that if the number of votes required to exempt a project should be reduced to a simple majority many more projects might be exempted. Scott was not enthusiastic about offering the amendment at this point, but Culver has talked him into it. The theory behind having Scott bring up the amendment now is that it is better to have such a proposal come up in the morning — a time when many senators are in committee meetings or in their offices and are more distracted than usual from the business that is taking place on the floor. Also, Culver figures that most of his colleagues will assume that at this point, especially after a long day of taking up amendments — and major ones — yesterday, only routine, "housekeeping" amendments are being considered, and that they will pay less attention to the issue, be less eager to join the fray, than they might be later on.

These are the sorts of calculations that managers of bills must make. Culver figures, further, that if an amendment is to be offered on the voting of the new committee he would prefer that it be offered by Scott. And, by a prior arrangement that Culver has made with Nelson, Nelson will ask for a roll-call vote on the amendment. Scott does not want a roll call on it. Culver's idea is to beat the amendment, and beat it good, burying the issue in the Senate once and for all, and also putting him in a position to tell a Senate-House conference on the bill that the proposal was resoundingly defeated in the Senate. "It's a judgment call," Culver has said, explaining to me the considerations behind whether or not to put something to a roll-call vote. Sometimes, as happened when Stennis, as chairman of the Armed Services Committee and floor manager of the military-procurement bill, accepted Culver's amendment on aircraft carriers, a senator will decide not to press for a roll-call vote, to — as Culver puts it — "God, take it and run."

So now Scott calls up his amendment to require that the votes of only four of the seven members of the interagency committee are necessary in order to exempt a project. Culver, speaking in opposition to the amendment, offers some precedents for requiring a "super-majority" vote. Culver wasn't sure there were any precedents, but his staff has been imaginative: he uses the example of jury trials in criminal cases — which require unanimity — and he cites the Senate rule that a filibuster can be cut off only by the votes of sixty members, or three-fifths, of the Senate. Scott's amendment is defeated on a roll-call vote, twenty-three to sixty-nine.

Now Culver accepts a number of other amendments offered by Republicans. He has told me, "You can take a couple of amendments you know you are going to drop in a spittoon on the way to the conference." Nelson had some other amendments, too, but by one-thirty he and the environmentalists backing him have decided to give up.

Off the Senate floor, a Democratic senator talks to me about Culver. "He's doing a real good job of managing the bill," the senator says. "It's a controversial issue; he's picking his way through the amendments, and working some out, and fighting and defeating others, and establishing his control over the floor. That's very important: others will follow your lead if they feel that you're being sensible and you have control."

This afternoon, Culver — he has skipped lunch again — works to keep that control. He quickly moves against a senator who has asked for more time than was permitted under the unanimous-consent agreement and who wants to offer a non-germane amendment.

While another senator is speaking, Culver leaves the floor briefly; he has received a card of the sort that visitors send in when they want to see senators, this one telling him that a delegation of forty-one Catholics from Dubuque would like to see him. (He has turned down a number of other requests today to meet with people off the Senate floor.) He goes over to the Rotunda of the Capitol and meets with the group for five minutes, explaining to them that he is managing a bill on the Senate floor, and adding, "I figured if I didn't come out to see you, you'd fire me, but if I don't get back in there the Majority Leader will fire me."

When Culver returns to the Senate, Wallop is sitting next to Scott's seat, in the second-to-last row, talking to Scott, and Culver goes back to join them. After he accepted Scott's amendments this morning, Culver told him that he hoped that that would take care of matters and that Scott would offer no further amendments. Scott said then that he wanted to go back to his office and look over his other amendments. This afternoon, he returned to say that he had four more he wanted to offer, and Culver asked Wallop to go back and talk to Scott and see what he could do. Now Culver finds that they haven't got very far; Scott is insisting that either he be allowed to offer four amendments or he will ultimately offer twelve. Culver has asked for a quorum call — a device used from time to time during a debate in order to gain time to get a senator to the floor, or to regroup, or to work out an amendment, or to negotiate — and the clerk calls the roll, slowly. At one point during the negotiations, Culver puts his head in his hands, seeming very weary.

Finally, at five minutes to three, Culver comes back to his desk and asks that the quorum call be ended. He has talked Scott into offering just one more amendment. Now Scott offers one providing that if the National Security Council determines that any interference with a critical military installation on behalf of an endangered species "would have an adverse effect on the security of the United States," it is authorized to notify the interagency committee in writing and that "the committee shall give immediate consideration to such determination." In the preceding negotiations, Culver has succeeded in getting Scott to modify this amendment; in its original form, it would have allowed the National Security Council to grant an automatic exemption, and it would have been invoked to prevent an adverse effect on any installation, not just one deemed essential to the national security. Culver's objections were that anything might be found adverse to an installation and that granting an automatic exemption was contrary to the spirit of the bill.

Now Scott says, "Suppose a bird or some endangered species was in front of an intercontinental ballistic missile. They could not release that missile." He goes on to say that he thinks "any commander worth his salt" would go ahead and fire the missile, but that, under the Endangered Species Act, the commander would then "be subject to a fine of twenty thousand dollars and imprisonment for up to a year."

Culver, who appears to be struggling to keep a straight face, commends Scott, saying that his amendment "is extremely important and is acceptable."

Then, just as the debate is nearing its end, the Senate sets aside the endangered-species bill to take up the Quiet Communities Act of 1978 — the noise-control bill that Culver had talked about in Des Moines, and that he must also manage. Culver is waiting for a certain senator to reach the floor to offer an amendment to the endangered-species bill, and he knows that the noise-control bill is noncontroversial and will take little time, so he and Byrd have decided to bring it up now. Arrangements of this sort are made from time to time, both to accommodate senators and to move legislation along. After Culver reads a statement explaining the provisions of the noise-control bill, it is adopted by voice vote, and the Senate returns to the endangered-species bill, and the last pending amendment is offered and withdrawn.

Now Wallop and Culver commend each other, and their own staffs, on the work on the bill, a few other senators make brief statements, and the roll is called on final passage.

It is clear that the bill will pass, so during the roll call Culver leaves the floor. Don Brownlee has asked him to meet on a grassy spot in front of the Capitol with Dean Norland, a television correspondent from Cedar Rapids. Norland has to have his film at the airport by four o'clock in order to get it on tonight's news.

It is one of those hot, humid Washington summer afternoons. "Hi, Dean," Culver says to Norland. "Can we do this before your subject melts?"

Norland asks him what this bill will do for Iowa, and makes specific reference to the problem of the Dubuque bridge and the Higgins' eye clam.

Culver explains that the bill would require a consultation process. He stands with his hands folded in front of him, and has his somber look; he talks firmly and with composure. There is no sign of how hot and tired he is. The bill, he says, "represents a responsible and rational balance of competing needs, with a strong presumption in favor, whenever there is doubt, of the endangered species." He talks a bit longer, says, "Thank you, Dean, 'preciate it," and then says, "I think I'll go see how my vote is."

On the way back, he glances at his schedule card and notices that he was to meet a constituent for a handshake at three o'clock. He asks Brownlee, "What happened to that constituent?" Brownlee isn't sure. Culver reads a memorandum Brownlee has given him about phone calls that have come in for him: James Schlesinger, the Secretary of Energy, has called him, and so has Patricia Harris, the Secretary of Housing and Urban Development.

When Culver reaches the Senate floor, the roll call is just about completed, and in a few moments Adlai Stevenson, who is presiding, gives the final tally. "On this vote," he says, "the yeas are ninety-four and the nays are three." Culver allows himself a smile of satisfaction, but quickly suppresses it and accepts the congratulations of his colleagues.

It is now shortly after four, and, after going into the cloakroom to talk with some of his colleagues and unwind for a few minutes, Culver goes to the President's Room, a small room behind the Senate floor, to meet Bill Griffee, an Iowa state representative from Nashua, who has been attempting to obtain funds from the Department of Energy to revitalize an old power-dam system. "What would you like me to do at this stage, Bill?" Culver asks.

Griffee replies, "I would like you to keep track of the people in the Department of Energy." Jim Larew, who has accompanied Griffee here, takes notes. Griffee continues, "It just helps if they know a United States senator is darned interested."

Culver offers to make calls when Griffee thinks it would be helpful, and Griffee asks whether he has any objections if when he talks to the press he says that he has spoken with Senator Culver about this project. Culver says, "No, that's all right," and he adds, "I'm not familiar with all the feelings about the project." Don Brownlee takes a picture of the two men standing together.

It is now four-twenty. Jim Larew gives Culver a memorandum from Mike Naylor, Culver's legislative director, telling him that tomorrow the Administration will announce its position on product-liability insurance for small businesses, and that it will fall short of what Culver has proposed. He suggests that Culver get ready to respond to the Administration's announcement, and asks whether, if Culver does not have time to receive a briefing on it this afternoon — he doesn't — Naylor may tell Commerce Department staff members that Culver has asked that Naylor be briefed on the details. Culver writes "Yes" on the memorandum. An aide sends word that today the Agriculture Appropriations Subcommittee has approved one hundred million dollars for Culver's soil-conservation, clean-water program. Brownlee gives him a note saying that a certain part of the military-procurement bill is coming up in conference at four-thirty. Culver decides that if it is important enough one of his colleagues will send word asking him to come.

Now Culver proceeds to the Radio and Television Gallery to talk about the endangered-species bill. This is routine for major figures in a legislative battle. Culver goes into a room containing a set that consists of a mock office. He sits at a desk, with rows of maroon-bound volumes of the *Congressional Record* behind him. There are blue drapes on either side, and Culver pops a cigar that he has been smoking — the cigar is one small way to relieve the tension — on a shelf behind one of the drapes. ABC and CBS are here, and so are several radio reporters.

The first question is "Senator Culver, why did you find it necessary to weaken this act?"

Culver replies carefully — and evenly, under the circumstances — "I don't think we've weakened this act. I think we effected a compromise that would enable it to continue at all. Our subcommittee's hearings indicated that either it would be compromised or it wouldn't be reauthorized at all or it would be emasculated." He explains the bill. This is his best opportunity to explain publicly what it is about. He hasn't had lunch, and he's very tired — he hasn't stopped going all day — but now he states clearly and with energy why the bill was necessary. He draws on his capacity for discipline one more time. He tells how the inflexibility of the existing law had inhibited the Fish and Wildlife Service in carrying it out, and says, "So if you're really concerned about endangered species you've got to be concerned about inflexibility in the law." He stresses the point that through the requirement for five out of seven votes in the committee "the presumption is heavily in favor of the species."

A reporter says that he has had trouble with his tape recorder, and asks Culver if he will explain it all again.

Culver's eyes roll upward, but he coöperates. Then he says, "I hope what we've done is get out ahead of this problem a little bit."

He takes a few more questions, and ends the press conference and retrieves his cigar.

Over coffee in the Senate dining room, Culver talks about the day and goes over some of the messages he has been given. A State Department official is trying to reach him in connection with the proposal to lift the embargo on the sale of arms to Turkey; Howard Metzenbaum is trying to reach him in connection with a torts bill that is pending before the Judiciary Committee. Culver looks at a memorandum about the torts bill. "Doesn't it all just defy belief?" he says to me.

It is now six o'clock. The Senate has taken up the authorization bill for the Department of Housing and Urban Development and is still in session. Later, Culver will go to a fund-raiser for a friend of his who is running for attorney general of Iowa. Tomorrow, he is scheduled to go at eight o'clock to a breakfast seminar on SALT; and then attend a hearing of the Environmental Pollution Subcommittee; and meet with Dr. Norman Borlaug, who is from Iowa, and who received a Nobel Peace Prize for his development of high-yield grain (the "green revolution"); and then meet with Josy Gittler about bills pending before his Juvenile Delinquency Subcommittee; and then have lunch with his two daughters who are in Washington (this weekend, he will go back to McGregor); and then attend the House-Senate conference on the military-procurement bill and also a meeting of the Environment and Public Works Committee on a bill that is part of the President's economic stimulus program (these two meetings will overlap); and meet with a constituent for a handshake; and, of course, go to the Senate floor to vote.

CHAPTER 9

The Judiciary

An independent judicial system is an important part of constitutional government. The United States Supreme Court was created with this view, and its members were given life tenure and guaranteed compensation to maintain their independence. However, Congress was given power to structure the entire subordinate judicial system, including control over the appellate jurisdiction of the Supreme Court. Regardless of any initial lack of power and various attempts made by and through Congress to curb its power, the Supreme Court today occupies a predominant position in the governmental system. The evolution of the Court, its present powers, and their implications are analyzed in this chapter, along with selected problems in the administration of justice.

Constitutional Background: Judicial Independence and Judicial Review

The Supreme Court and the judicial system play important roles in the intricate separation-of-powers scheme. Through judicial review, both legislative and executive decisions may be overruled by the courts for a number of reasons. To some extent, then, the judiciary acts as a check upon arbitrary action by governmental departments and agencies. The intent of the framers of the Constitution regarding the role of the judiciary, particularly the Supreme Court, in our governmental system is examined in *Federalist 78.*

57

Alexander Hamilton

FEDERALIST 78

We proceed now to an examination of the judiciary department of the proposed government.

In unfolding the defects of the existing confederation, the utility and necessity of a federal judicature have been clearly pointed out. It is the less necessary to recapitulate the considerations there urged; as the propriety of the institution in the abstract is not disputed; the only questions which have been raised being relative to the manner of constituting it, and to its extent. To these points, therefore, our observations shall be confined.

The manner of constituting it seems to embrace these several objects: 1st. The mode of appointing the judges; 2nd. the tenure by which they are to hold their places; 3rd. The partition of the judiciary authority between different courts, and their relations to each other.

First. As to the mode of appointing the judges: This is the same with that of appointing the officers of the union in general, and has been so fully discussed . . . that nothing can be said here which would not be useless repetition.

Second. As to the tenure by which the judges are to hold their places: This chiefly concerns their duration in office; the provisions for their support; the precautions for their responsibility.

According to the plan of the convention, all the judges who may be appointed by the United States are to hold their offices *during good behavior;* which is conformable to the most approved of the state constitutions. . . . The standard of good behavior for the continuance in office of the judicial magistracy is certainly one of the most valuable of the modern improvements in the practice of government. In a monarchy, it is an excellent barrier to the despotism of the prince; in a republic, it is a no less excellent barrier to the encroachments and oppressions of the representative body. And it is the best expedient which can be devised in any government, to secure a steady, upright, and impartial administration of the laws.

Whoever attentively considers the different departments of power must perceive, that, in a government in which they are separated from each other, the judiciary, from the nature of its functions, will always be the least dangerous to the political rights of the constitution; because it will be least in a capacity to annoy or injure them. The executive not only dispenses the honors, but holds the sword of the community. The legislature not only commands the purse, but prescribes the rules by which the duties and rights of every citizen are to be regulated. The judiciary, on the contrary, has no influence over either the sword or the purse; no direction either of the strength or of the wealth of the society; and can take no active resolution whatever. It may truly be said to have neither FORCE NOR WILL, but merely judgment; and must ultimately depend upon the aid of the executive arm for the efficacious exercise even of this faculty.

This simple view of the matter suggests several important consequences: It proves incontestably, that the judiciary is beyond comparison, the weakest of the three departments of power, that it can never attack with success either of the other two; and that all possible care is requisite to enable it to defend itself against their attacks. It equally proves, that, though individual oppression may now and then proceed from the courts of justice, the general liberty of the people can never be endangered from that quarter; I mean so long as the judiciary remains truly distinct from both the legislature and executive. For I agree, that "there is no liberty, if the power of judging be not separated from the legislative and executive powers." It proves, in the last place, that as liberty can have nothing to fear from the judiciary alone, but would have everything to fear from its union with either of the other departments; that, as all the effects of such a union must ensue from a dependence of the former on the latter, notwithstanding a nominal and apparent separation; that as, from the natural feebleness of the judiciary, it is in continual jeopardy of being overpowered, awed or influenced by its coordinate branches; that, as nothing can contribute so much to its firmness and independence as PERMANENCY IN OFFICE, this quality may therefore be justly regarded as an indispensable ingredient in its constitution; and, in a great measure, as the CITADEL of the public justice and the public security.

The complete independence of the courts of justice is peculiarly essential in a limited constitution. By a limited constitution, I understand one which contains certain specified exceptions to the legislative no ex post facto laws, and the like. Limitations of this kind can be preserved in practice no other way than through the medium of the courts of justice, whose duty it must be to declare all acts contrary to the manifest tenor of the constitution void. Without this, all the reservations of particular rights or privileges would amount to nothing.

Some perplexity respecting the right of the courts to pronounce legislative acts void, because contrary to the constitution, has arisen from an imagination that the doctrine would imply a superiority of the judiciary to the legislative power. It is urged that the authority which can declare the acts of another void, must necessarily be superior to the one whose acts may be declared void. As this doctrine is of great importance in all the American constitutions, a brief discussion of the grounds on which it rests cannot be unacceptable.

There is no position which depends on clearer principles than that every act of a delegated authority, contrary to the tenor of the commission under which it is exercised, is void. No legislative act, therefore, contrary to the constitution, can be valid. To deny this would be to affirm, that the deputy is greater than his principal; that the servant is above his master; that the representatives of the people are superior to the people themselves; that men, acting by virtue of powers, may do not only what their powers do not authorize, but what they forbid.

If it be said that that legislative body are themselves the constitutional judges of their own powers, and that the construction they put upon them is conclusive upon the other departments, it may be answered, that this cannot be the natural presumption, where it is not to be collected from any particular provisions in the constitution. It is not otherwise to be supposed that the constitution could intend to enable the representatives of the people to substitute their *will* to that of their constituents. It is far more rational to suppose that the courts were designed to be an intermediate body between the people and the legislature, in order, among other things, to keep the latte. within the limits assigned to their authority. The interpretation of the laws is the proper and peculiar province of the courts. A constitution is, in fact, and must be, regarded by the judges as a fundamental law. It must therefore belong to them to ascertain its meaning, as well as the meaning of any particular act proceeding from the legislative body. If there should happen to be an irreconcilable variance between the two, that which has the superior obligation and validity ought, of course, to be preferred; in other words, the constitution ought to be preferred to the statute, the intention of the people to the intention of their agents.

Nor does his conclusion by any means suppose a superiority of the judicial to the legislative power. It only supposes that the power of the people is superior to both; and that where the will of the legislature declared in its statutes, stands in opposition to that of the people declared in the constitution, the judges ought to be governed by the latter, rather than the former. They ought to regulate their decisions by the fundamental laws, rather than by those which are not fundamental. . . .

It can be of no weight to say, that the courts, on the pretense of a repugnancy, may substitute their own pleasure to the constitutional intentions of the legislature. This might as well happen in the case of two contradictory statutes; or it might as well happen in every adjudication upon any single statute. The courts must declare the sense of the law; and if they should be disposed to exercise WILL instead of JUDGMENT, the consequence would equally be the substitution of their pleasure to that of the legislative body. The observation, if it proved anything, would prove that there ought to be no judges distinct from the body.

If then the courts of justice are to be considered as the bulwarks of a limited constitution, against legislative encroachments, this consideration will afford a strong argument for the permanent tenure of judicial officers, since nothing will contribute so much as this to that independent spirit in the judges, which must be essential to the faithful performance of so arduous a duty.

This independence of the judges is equally requisite to guard the constitution and the rights of individuals, from the effects of those ill-humors which the arts of designing men, or the influence of particular conjunctures, sometimes disseminate among the people themselves, and which, though they speedily give place to better information, and more deliberate reflection, have a tendency, in the meantime, to occasion dangerous innovations in the government, and serious oppressions of the minor party in the community. . . . Until the people have, by some solemn and authoritative act, annulled or changed the established form, it is binding upon themselves collectively, as well as individually; and no presumption, or even knowledge of their sentiments, can warrant their representatives in a departure from it, prior to such an act. But it is easy to see, that it would require an uncommon portion of fortitude in the judges to do their duty as faithful guardians of the constitution, where legislative invasions of it had been instigated by the major voice of the community.

But it is not with a view to infractions of the constitution only, that the independence of the judges may be an essential safeguard against the effects of occasional ill-humors in the society. These sometimes extend no farther than to the injury of the private rights of particular classes of citizens, by unjust and partial laws. Here also the firmness of the judicial magistracy is of vast importance in mitigating the severity, and confining the operation of such laws. It not only serves to moderate the immediate mischiefs of those which may have been passed, but it operates as a check upon the legislative body in passing them; who, perceiving that obstacles to the success of an iniquitous intention are to be expected from the scruples of the courts, are in a manner compelled by the very motives of the injustice they mediate, to qualify their attempts. . . .

That inflexible and uniform adherence to the rights of the constitution, and of individuals, which we perceive to be indispensable in the courts of justice, can certainly not be expected from judges who hold their offices by a temporary commission. Periodical appointments, however regulated, or by whomsoever made, would, in some way or other, be fatal to their necessary independence. If the power of making them was committed either to the executive or legislature, there would be danger of an improper compliance to the branch which possessed it; if to both, there would be an unwillingness to hazard the displeasure of either; if to the people, or to persons chosen by them for the special purpose, there would be too great a disposition to consult popularity to justify a reliance that nothing would be consulted but the constitution and the laws.

There is yet a further and a weighty reason for the permanency of judicial offices, which is deducible from the nature of the qualifications they require. It has been frequently remarked, with great propriety, that a voluminous code of laws is one of the inconveniences necessarily connected with the advantages of a free government. To avoid an arbitrary discretion in the courts, it is indispensable that they should be bound down by strict rules and precedents, which serve to define and point out their duty in every particular case that comes before them; and it will readily be conceived, from the variety of controversies which grow out of the folly and wickedness of mankind, that the records of those precedents must unavoidably swell to a very considerable bulk, and must demand long and laborious study to acquire a competent knowledge of them. Hence it is, that there can be but few men in the society, who will have sufficient skill in the laws to qualify them for the stations of judges. And making the proper deductions for the ordinary depravity of human nature, the number must be still smaller, of those who unite the requisite integrity with the requisite knowledge. . . .

From *Federalist 78* students can observe that the intent of the framers of the Constitution, at least as expressed and represented by Hamilton, was to give to the courts the power of judicial review over legislative acts. Students should note that this concept was not explicitly written into the Constitution. Although the cause of this omission is not known, it is reasonable to assume that the framers felt that judicial power implied judicial review. Further, it is possible that the framers did not expressly mention judicial review because they had to rely on the states for adoption of the Constitution; judicial power would extend to the states as well as to the coordinate departments of the national government.

The power of the Supreme Court to invalidate an act of Congress was stated by John Marshall in *Marbury* v. *Madison,* 1 Cranch 137 (1803). At issue was a provision in the Judiciary Act of 1789 which extended the *original jurisdiction* of the Supreme Court by authorizing it to issue writs of mandamus in cases involving public officers of the United States and private persons, a power not conferred upon the Court in the Constitution. Marbury had been appointed a justice of the peace by President John Adams under the Judiciary Act of 1801, passed by the Federalists after Jefferson and the Republican Party won the elections in the fall of 1800 so that President Adams could fill various newly created judicial posts with Federalists before he left office in March, 1801. Marbury was sched-

uled to receive one of these commissions, but when Jefferson took office
on March 4, with Madison as his Secretary of State, it had not been
delivered. Marbury filed a suit with the Supreme Court requesting it to exercise its original jurisdiction and issue a writ of mandamus (a writ to
compel an administrative officer to perform his duty) to force Madison to
deliver the commission, an act which both Jefferson and Madison were
opposed to doing. In his decision, Marshall, a prominent Federalist, stated
that although Marbury had a legal right to his commission, and although
mandamus was the proper remedy, the Supreme Court could not extend
its original jurisdiction beyond the limits specified in the Constitution;
therefore, that section of the Judiciary Act of 1789 permitting the court to
issue such writs to public officers was unconstitutional. Incidentally, the
Republicans were so outraged at the last-minute appointments of Adams
that there were threats that Marshall would be impeached if he issued a
writ of mandamus directing Madison to deliver the commission. This is
not to suggest that Marshall let such considerations influence him; however, politically his decision was thought to be a masterpiece of reconciling his position as a Federalist with the political tenor of the times.

58

MARBURY v. MADISON
1 Cranch 137 (1803)

Mr. Chief Justice Marshall delivered the opinion of the Court, saying in
part:
    . . . The authority, therefore, given to the Supreme Court, by the [Judi-
ciary Act of 1789] . . . establishing the judicial courts of the United States,
to issue writs of mandamus to public officers, appears not to be warranted
by the Constitution [because it adds to the original jurisdiction of the Court
delineated by the framers of the Constitution in Article III; had they wished
this power to be conferred upon the Court it would be so stated, in the
same manner that the other parts of the Court's original jurisdiction are
stated]; . . . it becomes necessary to inquire whether a jurisdiction so conferred can be exercised.
    The question whether an act repugnant to the Constitution can become
the law of the land, is a question deeply interesting to the United States; but,
happily, not of an intricacy proportioned to its interest. It seems only necessary to recognize certain principles supposed to have been long and well
established, to decide it.

That the people have an original right to establish, for their future government, such principles as, in their opinion, shall most conduce to their own happiness, is the basis on which the whole American fabric has been erected. The exercise of this original right is a very great exertion; nor can it nor ought it to be frequently repeated. The principles, therefore, so established, are deemed fundamental. And as the authority from which they proceed is supreme, and can seldom act, they are designed to be permanent.

This original and supreme will organizes the government, and assigns to different departments their respective powers. It may either stop here, or establish certain limits not to be transcended by those departments.

The government of the United States is of the latter description. The powers of the legislature are defined and limited; and that those limits may not be mistaken, or forgotten, the Constitution is written. To what purpose are powers limited, and to what purpose is that limitation committed to writing, if these limits may, at any time, be passed by those intended to be restrained? The distinction between a government with limited and un-limited powers is abolished, if those limits do not confine the persons on whom they are imposed, and if acts prohibited and acts allowed, are of equal obligation. It is a proposition too plain to be contested, that the Con-stitution controls any legislative act repugnant to it; or, that the legislature may alter the Constitution by an ordinary act.

Between these alternatives there is no middle ground. The Constitution is either a superior paramount law, unchangeable by ordinary means, or it is on a level with ordinary legislative acts, and, like other acts, is alterable when the legislature shall please to alter it.

If the former part of the alternative be true, then a legislative act con-trary to the Constitution, is not law; if the latter part be true, then written constitutions are absurd attempts, on the part of the people, to limit a power in its own nature illimitable.

Certainly all those who have framed written constitutions contemplate them as forming the fundamental and paramount law of the nation, and, consequently, the theory of every such government must be, that an act of the legislature, repugnant to the constitution, is void.

This theory is essentially attached to a written constitution, and is consequently to be considered, by this court, as one of the fundamental principles of our society. It is not, therefore, to be lost sight of in the further consideration of this subject.

If an act of the legislature, repugnant to the Constitution, is void, does it, notwithstanding its invalidity, bind the courts, and oblige them to give it effect? Or, in other words, though it be not law, does it constitute a rule as operative as if it was a law? This would be to overthrow in fact what was established in theory; and would seem, at first view, an absurdity too gross to be insisted on. It shall, however, receive a more attentive consideration.

It is emphatically the province and duty of the judicial department to say what the law is. Those who apply the rule to particular cases, must of necessity expound and interpret that rule. If two laws conflict with each other, the courts must decide on the operation of each.

So if the law be in opposition to the Constitution; if both the law and the Constitution apply to a particular case, so that the court must either decide that case conformably to the law, disregarding the Constitution, or conformably to the Constitution, disregarding the law, the court must determine which of these conflicting rules governs the case. This is of the very essence of judicial duty.

If, then, the courts are to regard the Constitution, and the Constitution is superior to any ordinary act of the legislature, the Constitution, and not such ordinary act, must govern the case to which they both apply.

Those, then, who controvert the principle that the Constitution is to be considered, in court, as a paramount law, are reduced to the necessity of maintaining that courts must close their eyes on the Constitution, and see only the law.

This doctrine would subvert the very foundation of all written constitutions. It would declare that an act which, according to the principles and theory of our government, is entirely void, is yet, in practice, completely obligatory. It would declare that if the legislature shall do what is expressly forbidden, such act, notwithstanding the express prohibition, is in reality effectual. It would be giving to the legislature a practical and real omnipotence, with the same breath which professes to restrict their powers within narrow limits. It is prescribing limits, and declaring that those limits may be passed at pleasure.

That it thus reduces to nothing what we have deemed the greatest improvement on political institutions, a written constitution, would of itself be sufficient, in America, where written constitutions have been viewed with so much reverence, for rejecting the construction. But the peculiar expressions of the Constitution of the United States furnish additional arguments in favor of its rejection.

The judicial power of the United States is extended to all cases arising under the Constitution.

Could it be the intention of those who gave this power, to say that in using it the Constitution should not be looked into? That a case arising under the Constitution should be decided without examining the instrument under which it arises?

This is too extravagant to be maintained.

In some cases, then, the Constitution must be looked into by the judges. And if they can open it at all, what part of it are they forbidden to read or to obey?

There are many other parts of the Constitution which serve to illustrate this subject.

It is declared that "no tax or duty shall be laid on articles exported from any State." Suppose a duty on the export of cotton, of tobacco, or of flour; and a suit instituted to recover it. Ought judgment to be rendered in such a case? Ought the judges to close their eyes on the Constitution, and only see the law?

The Constitution declares "that no bill of attainder or ex post facto law shall be passed."

If, however, such a bill should be passed, and a person should be prosecuted under it, must the court condemn to death those victims whom the Constitution endeavors to preserve?

"No person," says the Constitution, "shall be convicted of treason unless on the testimony of two witnesses to the same overt act, or on confession in open court."

Here the language of the Constitution is addressed especially to the courts. It prescribes, directly for them, a rule of evidence not to be departed from. If the legislature should change that rule, and declare one witness, or a confession out of court, sufficient for conviction, must the constitutional principle yield to the legislative act?

From these, and many other selections which might be made, it is apparent that the framers of the Constitution contemplated that instrument as a rule for the government of courts, as well as of the legislature.

Why otherwise does it direct the judges to take an oath to support it? This oath certainly applies in an especial manner to this conduct in their official character. How immoral to impose it on them, if they were to be used as the instruments, and the knowing instruments, for violating what they swear to support!

The oath of office, too, imposed by the legislature, is completely demonstrative of the legislative opinion on this subject. It is in these words: "I do solemnly swear that I will administer justice without respect to persons, and do equal right to the poor and to the rich; and that I will faithfully and impartially discharge all the duties incumbent on me as _____, according to the best of my abilities and understanding, agreeably to the Constitution and laws of the United States."

Why does a judge swear to discharge his duties agreeably to the Constitution of the United States, if that Constitution forms no rule for his government — if it is closed upon him, and cannot be inspected by him?

If such be the real state of things, this is worse than solemn mockery. To prescribe, or to take this oath, becomes equally a crime.

It is also not entirely unworthy of observation, that in declaring what shall be the supreme law of the land, the Constitution itself is first mentioned; and not the laws of the United States generally, but those only which shall be made in pursuance of the Constitution, have that rank.

Thus, the particular phraseology of the Constitution of the United States confirms and strengthens the principle, supposed to be essential to all written constitutions, that a law repugnant to the Constitution is void; and that courts, as well as other departments, are bound by that instrument.

The rule must be discharged.

Powers and Limitations
of the Supreme Court

Paul A. Freund, in his book *On Understanding the Supreme Court* (1949), notes that the Supreme Court has a definite political role. He asks:

"Is the law of the Supreme Court a reflection of the notions of 'policy' held by its members? The question recalls the controversy over whether judges 'make' or 'find' the law. A generation or two ago it was thought rather daring to insist that judges make law. Old Jeremiah Smith, who began the teaching of law at Harvard after a career on the New Hampshire Supreme Court, properly deflated the issue. 'Do judges make law?' he repeated. 'Course they do. Made some myself.' Of course Supreme Court Justices decide cases on the basis of their ideas of policy."

To emphasize this point today is to repeat the familiar. The Court makes policy. It would be difficult to conceive how a Court having the power to interpret the Constitution could fail to make policy, i.e., could fail to make rulings that have *general* impact upon the community as a whole. The essential distinction between policy-making and adjudication is that the former has a general effect while the latter touches only a specifically designated person or group.

If the Supreme Court has this power of constitutional interpretation, how is it controlled by the other governmental departments and the community? Is it, as some have claimed, completely arbitrary in rendering many of its decisions? Is it potentially a dictatorial body? The Supreme Court and lower courts are limited to the consideration of cases and controversies brought before them by outside parties. Courts cannot initiate law. Moreover, all courts, and the Supreme Court in particular, exercise judicial self-restraint in certain cases to avoid difficult and controversial issues and to avoid outside pressure to limit the powers of the judiciary. The discussion by John P. Roche deals with the background, the nature, and the implications of judicial doctrines of self-restraint.

59

John P. Roche

JUDICIAL SELF-RESTRAINT

Every society, sociological research suggests, has its set of myths which incorporate and symbolize its political, economic, and social aspirations. Thus, as medieval society had the Quest for the Holy Grail and the cult of numerology, we, in our enlightened epoch, have as significant manifestations of our collective hopes the dream of impartial decision-making and the cult of "behavioral science." While in my view these latter two are but different facets of the same fundamental drive, namely, the age-old effort to exercise human variables from human action, our concern here is with the first of them, the pervasive tendency in the American political and constitutional tradition directed toward taking the politics out of politics, and substituting some set of Platonic guardians for fallible politicians.

While this dream of objectivizing political Truth is in no sense a unique American phenomenon, it is surely true to say that in no other democratic nation has the effort been carried so far and with such persistence. Everywhere one turns in the United States, he finds institutionalized attempts to narrow the political sector and to substitute allegedly "independent" and "impartial" bodies for elected decision-makers. The so-called "independent regulatory commissions" are a classic example of this tendency in the area of administration, but unquestionably the greatest hopes for injecting pure Truth-serum into the body politic have been traditionally reserved for the federal judiciary, and particularly for the Supreme Court. The rationale for this viewpoint is simple: "The people must be protected from themselves, and no institution is better fitted for the role of chaperone than the federal judiciary, dedicated as it is to the supremacy of the rule of law."

Patently central to this function of social chaperonage is the right of the judiciary to review legislative and executive actions and nullify those measures which derogate from eternal principles of truth and justice as incarnated in the Constitution. Some authorities, enraged at what the Supreme Court has found the Constitution to mean, have essayed to demonstrate that the framers did not intend the Court to exercise this function, to have, as they put it, "the last word." I find no merit in this contention; indeed, it seems to me undeniable not only that the authors of the Constitution in-

From John P. Roche, "Judicial Self-Restraint," *The American Political Science Review*, 49 (September 1955). Reprinted by permission.

tended to create a federal government, but also that they assumed *sub silentio* that the Supreme Court would have the power to review both national and state legislation.

However, since the intention of the framers is essentially irrelevant except to antiquarians and polemicists, it is unnecessary to examine further the matter of origins. The fact is that the United States Supreme Court, and the inferior federal courts under the oversight of the high Court, have enormous policy-making functions. Unlike their British and French counterparts, federal judges are not merely technicians who live in the shadow of a supreme legislature, but are fully equipped to intervene in the process of political decision making. In theory, they are limited by the Constitution and the jurisdiction it confers, but, in practice, it would be a clumsy judge indeed who could not, by a little skillful exegesis, adapt the Constitution to a necessary end. This statement is in no sense intended as a condemnation; on the contrary, it has been this perpetual reinvigoration by reinterpretation, in which the legislature and the executive as well as the courts play a part, that has given the Constitution its survival power. Applying a Constitution which contains at key points inspired ambiguity, the courts have been able to pour the new wine in the old bottle. Note that the point at issue is not the legitimacy or wisdom of judicial legislation; it is simply the enormous scope that this prerogative gives to judges to substitute their views for those of past generations, or, more controversially, for those of a contemporary Congress and President.

Thus it is naive to assert that the Supreme Court is limited by the Constitution, and we must turn elsewhere for the sources of judicial restraint. The great power exercised by the Court has carried with it great risks, so it is not surprising that American political history has been sprinkled with demands that the judiciary be emasculated. The really startling thing is that, with the notable exception of the McCardle incident in 1869, the Supreme Court has emerged intact from each of these encounters. Despite the plenary power that Congress, under Article III of the Constitution, can exercise over the appellate jurisdiction of the high Court, the national legislature has never taken sustained and effective action against its House of Lords. It is beyond the purview of this analysis to examine the reasons for Congressional inaction; suffice it here to say that the most significant form of judicial limitation has remained self-limitation. This is not to suggest that such a development as statutory codification has not cut down the area of interpretive discretion, for it obviously has. It is rather to maintain that when the justices have held back from assaults on legislative or executive actions, they have done so on the basis of self-established rationalizations. . . .

The remainder of this paper is therefore concerned with two aspects of this auto-limitation: first, the techniques by which it is put into practice; and, second, the conditions under which it is exercised. . . .

TECHNIQUES OF JUDICIAL SELF-RESTRAINT

The major techniques of judicial self-restraint appear to fall under the two familiar rubrics: procedural and substantive. Under the former fall the various techniques by which the Court can avoid coming to grips with substantive issues, while under the latter would fall those methods by which the Court, in a substantive holding, finds that the matter at issue in the litigation is not properly one for judicial settlement. Let us examine these two categories in some detail.

Procedural Self-Restraint

Since the passage of the Judiciary Act of 1925, the Supreme Court has had almost complete control over its business. United States Supreme Court *Rule 38,* which governs the certiorari policy, states, (§ 5) that discretionary review will be granted only "where there are special and important reasons therefor." Professor Fowler Harper has suggested in a series of detailed and persuasive articles on the application of this discretion [*University of Pennsylvania Law Review,* vols. 99–101; 103] that the Court has used it in such a fashion as to duck certain significant but controversial problems. While one must be extremely careful about generalizing in this area, since the reasons for denying certiorari are many and complex, Harper's evidence does suggest that the Court in the period since 1949 has refused to review cases involving important civil liberties problems which on their merits appeared to warrant adjudication. As he states at one point: "It is disconcerting when the Court will review a controversy over a patent on a pin ball machine while one man is deprived of his citizenship and another of his liberty without Supreme Court review of a plausible challenge to the validity of government action." . . .

Furthermore, the Supreme Court can issue certiorari on its own terms. Thus in *Dennis* v. *United States,* appealing the Smith Act convictions of the American communist leadership, the Court accepted the evidential findings of the Second Circuit as final and limited its review to two narrow constitutional issues. This, in effect, burked the basic problem: whether the evidence was sufficient to demonstrate that the Communist Party, U.S.A., was *in fact* a clear and present danger to the security of the nation, or whether the communists were merely shouting "Fire!" in an empty theater.

Other related procedural techniques are applicable in some situations. Simple delay can be employed, perhaps in the spirit of the Croatian proverb that "delay is the handmaiden of justice." . . . However, the technique of procedural self-restraint is founded on the essentially simple gadget of refusing jurisdiction, or of procrastinating the acceptance of jurisdiction, and need not concern us further here.

Substantive Self-Restraint

Once a case has come before the Court on its merits, the justices are forced to give some explanation for whatever action they may take. Here self-restraint can take many forms, notably, the doctrine of political questions, the operation of judicial parsimony, and — particularly with respect to the actions of administrative officers of agencies — the theory of judicial inexpertise.

The doctrine of political questions is too familiar to require much elaboration here. Suffice it to say that if the Court feels that a question before it, e.g., the legitimacy of a state government, the validity of a legislative apportionment, or the correctness of executive action in the field of foreign relations, is one that is not properly amenable to judicial settlement, it will refer the plaintiff to the "political" organs of government for any possible relief. The extent to which this doctrine is applied seems to be a direct coefficient of judicial egotism, for the definition of a political question can be expanded or contracted in accordion-like fashion to meet the exigencies of the times. A juridical definition of the term is impossible, for at root the logic that supports it is circular: political questions are matters not soluble by the judicial process; matters not soluble by the judicial process are political questions. As an early dictionary explained, violins are small cellos, and cellos are large violins.

Nor do examples help much in definition. While it is certainly true that the Court cannot mandamus a legislature to apportion a state in equitable fashion, it seems equally true that the Court is without the authority to force state legislators to implement unsegregated public education. Yet in the former instance the Court genuflected to the "political" organs and took no action, while in the latter it struck down segregation as violative of the Constitution.

Judicial parsimony is another major technique of substantive self-restraint. In what is essentially a legal application of Occam's razor, the Court has held that it will not apply any more principles to the settlement of a case than are absolutely necessary, e.g., it will not discuss the constitutionality of a law·if it can settle the instant case by statutory construction. Furthermore, if an action is found to rest on erroneous statutory construction, the review terminates at that point: the Court will not go on to discuss whether the statute, properly construed, would be constitutional. A variant form of this doctrine, and a most important one, employs the "case or controversy" approach, to wit, the Court, admitting the importance of the issue, inquires as to whether the litigant actually has standing to bring the matter up. . . .

A classic use of parsimony to escape from a dangerous situation occurred in connection with the evacuation of the Nisei from the West Coast in 1942. Gordon Hirabayashi, in an attempt to test the validity of the regulations clamped on the American-Japanese by the military, violated the curfew and refused to report to an evacuation center. He was convicted on both counts by the district court and sentenced to three months for each offense, the sentences to run *concurrently.* When the case came before the Supreme Court, the justices sustained his conviction for violating the *curfew,* but refused to examine the validity of the evacuation order on the ground that it would not make any difference to Hirabayashi anyway; he was in for ninety days no matter what the Court did with evacuation.

A third method of utilizing substantive self-restraint is particularly useful in connection with the activities of executive departments or regulatory agencies, both state and federal. I have entitled it the doctrine of judicial *inexpertise,* for it is founded on the unwillingness of the Court to revise the findings of experts. The earmarks of this form of restraint are great deference to the holdings of the expert agency usually coupled with such a statement as "It is not for the federal courts to supplant the [Texas Railroad] Commission's judgment even in the face of convincing proof that a different result would have been better." In this tradition, the Court has refused to question *some* exercises of discretion by the National Labor Relations Board, the Federal Trade Commission, and other federal and state agencies. But the emphasis on *some* gives the point away; in other cases, apparently on all fours with those in which it pleads its technical *inexpertise,* the Court feels free to assess evidence de novo and reach independent judgment on the technical issues involved. . . .

In short, with respect to expert agencies, the Court is equipped with both offensive and defensive gambits. If it chooses to intervene, one set of precedents is brought out, while if it decides to hold back, another set of equal validity is invoked. Perhaps the best summary of this point was made by Justice Harlan in 1910, when he stated bluntly that "the Courts have rarely, if ever, felt themselves so restrained by technical rules that they could not find some remedy, consistent with the law, for acts . . . that violated natural justice or were hostile to the fundamental principles devised for the protection of the essential rights of property."

This does not pretend to be an exhaustive analysis of the techniques of judicial self-restraint; on the contrary, others will probably find many which are not given adequate discussion here. The remainder of this paper, however, is devoted to the second area of concern: the conditions under which the Court refrains from acting.

THE CONDITIONS OF JUDICIAL SELF-RESTRAINT

The conditions which lead the Supreme Court to exercise auto-limitation are many and varied. In the great bulk of cases, this restraint is an outgrowth of sound and quasi-automatic legal maxims which defy teleological interpretation. It would take a master of the conspiracy theory of history to assign meaning, for example, to the great majority of certiorari denials; the simple fact is that these cases do not merit review. However, in a small proportion of cases, purpose does appear to enter the picture, sometimes with a vengeance. It is perhaps unjust to the Court to center our attention on this small proportion, but it should be said in extenuation that these cases often involve extremely significant political and social issues. In the broad picture, the refusal to grant certiorari in 1943 to the Minneapolis Trotskyites convicted under the Smith Act is far more meaningful than the similar refusal to grant five hundred petitions to prison "lawyers" who have suddenly discovered the writ of habeas corpus. Likewise, the holding that the legality of Congressional apportionment is a "political question" vitally affects the operation of the whole democratic process.

What we must therefore seek are the conditions under which the Court holds back *in this designated category of cases.* Furthermore, it is important to realize that there are positive consequences of negative action; as Charles Warren has implied, the post-Civil War Court's emphasis on self-restraint was a judicial concomitant of the resurgence of states' rights. Thus self-restraint may, as in wartime, be an outgrowth of judicial caution, or it may be part of a purposeful pattern of abdicating national power to the states.

Ever since the first political scientist discovered Mr. Dooley, the changes have been rung on the aphorism that the Supreme Court "follows the election returns," and I see no particular point in ringing my variation on this theme through again. Therefore, referring those who would like a more detailed explanation to earlier analyses, the discussion here will be confined to the bare bones of my hypothesis.

The power of the Supreme Court to invade the decision-making arena, I submit, is a consequence of that fragmentation of political power which is normal in the United States. No cohesive majority, such as normally exists in Britain, would permit a politically irresponsible judiciary to usurp decision-making functions, but, for complex social and institutional reasons, there are few issues in the United States on which cohesive majorities exist. The guerrilla warfare which usually rages between Congress and the President, as well as the internal civil wars which are endemic in both the legislature and the administration, give the judiciary considerable room for maneuver. If, for example, the Court strikes down a controversial decision of the Federal Power Commission, it will be supported by a substantial bloc of congressmen; if it supports the FPC's decision, it will also receive considerable congressional support. But the important point is that *either* way it decides the case, there is no possibility that Congress will exact any vengeance on the Court for its action. A disciplined majority would be necessary to clip the judicial wings, and such a majority does not exist on this issue.

On the other hand, when monolithic majorities do exist on issues, the

Court is likely to resort to judicial self-restraint. A good case here is the current tidal wave of anti-communist legislation and administrative action, the latter particularly with regard to aliens, which the Court has treated most gingerly. About the only issues on which there can be found cohesive majorities are those relating to national defense, and the Court has, as Clinton Rossiter demonstrated in an incisive analysis [*The Supreme Court and the Commander-in-Chief,* Ithaca, 1951], traditionally avoided problems arising in this area irrespective of their constitutional merits. Like the slave who accompanied a Roman consul on his triumph whispering "You too are mortal," the shade of Thad Stevens haunts the Supreme Court chamber to remind the justices what an angry Congress can do.

To state the proposition in this brief compass is to oversimplify it considerably. I have, for instance, ignored the crucial question of how the Court knows when a majority *does* exist, and I recognize that certain aspects of judicial behavior cannot be jammed into my hypothesis without creating essentially spurious epicycles. However, I am not trying to establish a monistic theory of judicial action; group action, like that of individuals, is motivated by many factors, some often contradictory, and my objective is to elucidate what seems to be one tradition of judicial motivation. In short, judicial self-restraint and judicial power seem to be opposite sides of the same coin: it has been by judicious application of the former that the latter has been maintained. A tradition beginning with Marshall's *coup* in *Marbury* v. *Marshall* and running through *Mississippi* v. *Johnson* and *Ex Parte Vallandigham* to *Dennis* v. *United States* suggests that the Court's power has been maintained by a wise refusal to employ it in unequal combat.

What should be the proper role of the judiciary, and particularly the Supreme Court, in our system of government is a matter of much debate. The power of judicial review over national and state legislative and executive actions where federal questions are involved gives to the federal judiciary, and particularly to the ultimate spokesman of the judiciary — the Supreme Court — enormous potential power to shape public policies at all levels of government. The question is just how far the judiciary should be active in involving itself in matters of public policy that are normally within the jurisdiction of legislative bodies. Activist Supreme Courts have always brought down upon themselves the wrath of those who have opposing political philosophies, whether liberal or conservative. During the early New Deal, key legislation of President Franklin D. Roosevelt was declared unconstitutional by a conservative Supreme Court, which crippled the efforts of FDR to deal with the crisis of the depression. FDR responded by attempting to push through Congress a "court-packing" plan which would have given him the authority to appoint a new Supreme Court justice for each justice who was over seventy years of age. Since the majority of the Court at that time consisted of septuagenarian justices this bill would have given the President the authority to control the Court. This attack of FDR upon the Supreme Court was the most open effort in American history to undermine judicial independence and place the Supreme Court under presidential domination. The Roosevelt plan failed, due in large part to strong support from conservative elements of the community which were in turn reflected in Congress. In the early part of Roosevelt's second term the court majority switched in favor of the President which diminished the strong liberal attacks upon the Court.

After the Roosevelt era the Supreme Court exercised judicial self-restraint and did not become deeply involved in controversial political issues. It exercised judicial self-restraint on such important issues as the incorporation of the Bill of Rights under the Due Process Clause of the Fourteenth Amendment, carefully "nationalizing" only those parts of the Bill of Rights that it considered to be fundamental, historical, and essential to the maintenance of the democratic process. It also refused to involve itself in the question of equal apportionment of state and congressional legislative districts. However, an activist Supreme Court reasserted itself under the tutelage of Chief Justice Earl Warren, appointed by President Eisenhower in 1953. The Warren Court rendered the historic *Brown* v. *Board of Education* (1954) decision desegregating public education, nationalized most of the Bill of Rights, making its provisions applicable to the actions of state governments, established the one-man, one-vote rule in *Baker* v. *Carr* (1962), and strengthened the separation between church and state in *Engle* v. *Vitale* (1962). All of these decisions caused consternation and confusion within a broad cross-section of the community. Whereas liberals hailed the decisions of the Warren Court as necessary, justified, and long overdue, conservatives attacked the Court for undermining the Constitution and engaging in unauthorized "judicial legislation." The tables were turned from the New Deal. It was now the conservatives who were attacking the Court, and the liberals supporting it.

President Nixon in his election campaign of 1968 promised that if elected he would restore a conservative balance on the Supreme Court by appointing "strict constructionists." These presumably would be men who would adhere to the letter of the law and not engage in far-ranging judicial legislation. President Nixon did just that, and the Burger Court, although not directly overruling the decisions of the Warren Court, is returning to the doctrine of judicial self-restraint in many areas of constitutional law.

Judicial Decision Making

The preceding selections should dissuade students from accepting the commonly held assumption that judicial decision making is quasi-scientific, based upon legal principles and precedent, with the judges set apart from the political process. The interpretation of law, whether constitutional or statutory, involves a large amount of discretion. The majority of the Court can always read its opinion into law if it so chooses.

Justice William J. Brennan, Jr., a current member of the Supreme Court, discusses below the general role of the Court and the procedures it follows in decision making.

60
William J. Brennan, Jr.

HOW THE SUPREME COURT ARRIVES AT DECISIONS

Throughout its history the Supreme Court has been called upon to face many of the dominant social, political, economic and even philosophical issues that confront the nation. But Solicitor General Cox only recently reminded us that this does not mean that the Court is charged with making social, political, economic or philosophical decisions.

Quite the contrary, the Court is not a council of Platonic guardians for deciding our most difficult and emotional questions according to the Justices' own notions of what is just or wise or politic. To the extent that this is a government function at all, it is the function of the people's elected representatives.

The Justices are charged with deciding according to law. Because the issues arise in the framework of concrete litigation they must be decided on facts embalmed in a record made by some lower court or administrative agency. And while the Justices may and do consult history and the other disciplines as aids to constitutional decisions, the text of the Constitution and relevant precedents dealing with that text are their primary tools.

It is indeed true, as Judge Learned Hand once said, that the judge's authority

> depends upon the assumption that he speaks with the mouth of others: the momentum of his utterances must be greater than any which his personal reputation and character can command; if it is to do the work assigned to it — if it is to stand against the passionate resentments arising out of the

From William J. Brennan, Jr., "How the Supreme Court Arrives at Decisions," *The New York Times Magazine* (October 12, 1963). © 1963, by The New York Times Company. Reprinted by permission.

interests he must frustrate — he must preserve his authority by cloaking himself in the majesty of an over-shadowing past, but he must discover some composition with the dominant trends of his times.

ANSWERS UNCLEAR

However, we must keep in mind that, while the words of the Constitution are binding, their application to specific problems is not often easy. The Founding Fathers knew better than to pin down their descendants too closely.

Enduring principles rather than petty details were what they sought.

Thus the Constitution does not take the form of a litany of specifics. There are, therefore, very few cases where the constitutional answers are clear, all one way or all the other, and this is also true of the current cases raising conflicts between the individual and governmental power — an area increasingly requiring the Court's attention.

Ultimately, of course, the Court must resolve the conflicts of competing interests in these cases, but all Americans should keep in mind how intense and troubling these conflicts can be.

Where one man claims a right to speak and the other man claims the right to be protected from abusive or dangerously provocative remarks the conflict is inescapable.

Where the police have ample external evidence of a man's guilt, but to be sure of their case put into evidence a confession obtained through coercion, the conflict arises between his right to a fair prosecution and society's right to protection against his depravity.

Where the orthodox Jew wishes to open his shop and do business on the day which non-Jews have chosen, and the Legislature has sanctioned, as a day of rest, the Court cannot escape a difficult problem of reconciling opposed interests.

Finally, the claims of the Negro citizen, to borrow Solicitor General Cox's words, present a "conflict between the ideal of liberty and equality expressed in the Declaration of Independence, on the one hand, and, on the other hand, a way of life rooted in the customs of many of our people."

SOCIETY IS DISTURBED

If all segments of our society can be made to appreciate that there are such conflicts, and that cases which involve constitutional rights often require difficult choices, if this alone is accomplished, we will have immeasurably enriched our common understanding of the meaning and significance of our freedoms. And we will have a better appreciation of the Court's function and its difficulties.

How conflicts such as these ought to be resolved constantly troubles our whole society. There should be no surprise, then, that how properly to resolve them often produces sharp division within the Court itself. When problems are so fundamental, the claims of the competing interests are often nicely balanced, and close divisions are almost inevitable.

Supreme Court cases are usually one of three kinds: the "original" action brought directly in the Court by one state against another state or states, or between a state or states and the federal government. Only a handful of such cases arise each year, but they are an important handful.

A recent example was the contest between Arizona and California over the waters of the lower basin of the Colorado River. Another was the contest between the federal government and the newest state of Hawaii over the ownership of lands in Hawaii.

The second kind of case seeks review of the decisions of a federal Court of Appeals — there are eleven such courts — or of a decision of a federal District Court — there is a federal District Court in each of the fifty states.

The third kind of case comes from a state court — the Court may review a state court judgment by the highest court of any of the fifty states, if the judgment rests on the decision of a federal question.

When I came to the Court seven years ago the aggregate of the cases in the three classes was 1,600. In the term just completed there were 2,800, an increase of 75 percent in seven years. Obviously, the volume will have doubled before I complete ten years of service.

How is it possible to manage such a huge volume of cases? The answer is that we have the authority to screen them and select for argument and decision only those which, in our judgment, guided by pertinent criteria, raise the most important and far-reaching questions. By that device we select annually around 6 percent — between 150 and 170 cases — for decision.

PETITION AND RESPONSE

That screening process works like this: when nine Justices sit, it takes five to decide a case on the merits. But it takes only the votes of four of the nine to put a case on the argument calendar for argument and decision. Those four votes are hard to come by — only an exceptional case raising a significant federal question commands them.

Each application for review is usually in the form of a short petition, attached to which are any opinions of the lower courts in the case. The adversary may file a response — also, in practice usually short. Both the petition and response identify the federal questions allegedly involved, argue their substantiality, and whether they were properly raised in the lower courts.

Each Justice receives copies of the petition and response and such parts of the record as the parties may submit. Each Justice then, without any consultation at this stage with the others, reaches his own tentative conclusion whether the application should be granted or denied.

The first consultation about the case comes at the Court conference at which the case is listed on the agenda for discussion. We sit in conference almost every Friday during the term. Conferences begin at ten in the morning and often continue until six, except for a half-hour recess for lunch.

Only the Justices are present. There are no law clerks, no stenographers, no secretaries, no pages — just the nine of us. The junior Justice acts as guardian of the door, receiving and delivering any messages that come in or go from the conference.

ORDER OF SEATING

The conference room is a beautifully oak-paneled chamber with one side lined with books from floor to ceiling. Over the mantel of the exquisite marble fireplace at one end hangs the only adornment in the chamber — a portrait of Chief Justice John Marshall. In the middle of the room stands a rectangular table, not too large but large enough for the nine of us comfortably to gather around it.

The Chief Justice sits at the south end and Mr. Justice Black, the senior Associate Justice, at the north end. Along the side to the left of the Chief Justice sit Justices Stewart, Goldberg, White, and Harlan. On the right side sit Justice Clark, myself and Justice Douglas in that order.

We are summoned to conference by a buzzer which rings in our several chambers five minutes before the hour. Upon entering the conference room each of us shakes hands with his colleagues. The handshake tradition originated when Chief Justice Fuller presided many decades ago. It is a symbol that harmony of aims if not of views is the Court's guiding principle.

Each of us has his copy of the agenda of the day's cases before him. The agenda lists the cases applying for review. Each of us before coming to the conference has noted on his copy his tentative view whether or not review should be granted in each case.

The Chief Justice begins the discussion of each case. He then yields to the senior Associate Justice and discussion proceeds down the line in order of seniority until each Justice has spoken.

Voting goes the other way. The junior Justice votes first and voting then proceeds up the line to the Chief Justice, who votes last.

Each of us has a docket containing a sheet for each case with appropriate places for recording the votes. When any case receives four votes for review, that case is transferred to the oral argument list. Applications in which none of us sees merits may be passed over without discussion.

Now how do we process the decisions we agree to review?

There are rare occasions when the question is so clearly controlled by an earlier decision of the Court that a reversal of the lower court judgment is inevitable. In these rare instances we may summarily reverse without oral argument.

EACH SIDE GETS HOUR

The case must very clearly justify summary disposition, however, because our ordinary practice is not to reverse a decision without oral argument. Indeed, oral argument of cases taken for review, whether from the state or federal courts, is the usual practice. We rarely accept submissions of cases on briefs.

Oral argument ordinarily occurs about four months after the application for review is granted. Each party is usually allowed one hour, but in recent years we have limited oral argument to a half-hour in cases thought to involve issues not requiring longer arguments.

Counsel submit their briefs and record in sufficient time for the distribution of one set to each Justice two or three weeks before the oral argument. Most of the members of the present Court follow the practice of reading the briefs before the argument. Some of us often have a bench memorandum prepared before the argument. This memorandum digests the facts and the arguments of both sides, highlighting the matters about which we may want to question counsel at the argument.

Often I have independent research done in advance of argument and incorporate the results in the bench memorandum.

We follow a schedule of two weeks of argument from Monday through Thursday, followed by two weeks of recess for opinion writing and the study of petitions for review. The argued cases are listed on the conference agenda on the Friday following argument. Conference discussion follows the same procedure I have described for the discussions of certiorari petitions.

OPINION ASSIGNED

Of course, it is much more extended. Not infrequently discussion of particular cases may be spread over two or more conferences.

Not until the discussion is completed and a vote taken is the opinion assigned. The assignment is not made at the conference but formally in writing some few days after the conference.

The Chief Justice assigns the opinions in those cases in which he has voted with the majority. The senior Associate Justice voting with the majority assigns the opinions in the other cases. The dissenters agree among themselves who shall write the dissenting opinion. Of course, each Justice is free to write his own opinion, concurring or dissenting.

The writing of an opinion always takes weeks and sometimes months. The most painstaking research and care are involved.

Research, of course, concentrates on relevant legal materials — precedents particularly. But Supreme Court cases often require some familiarity with history, economics, the social and other sciences, and authorities in these areas, too, are consulted when necessary.

When the author of an opinion feels he has an unanswerable document he sends it to a print shop, which we maintain in our building. The printed draft may be revised several times before his proposed opinion is circulated among the other Justices. Copies are sent to each member of the Court, those in the dissent as well as those in the majority.

SOME CHANGE MINDS

Now the author often discovers that his work has only begun. He receives a return, ordinarily in writing, from each Justice who voted with him and sometimes also from the Justices who voted the other way. He learns who will write the dissent if one is to be written. But his particular concern is whether those who voted with him are still of his view and what they have to say about his proposed opinion.

Often some who voted with him at conference will advise that they reserve final judgment pending the circulation of the dissent. It is a common experience that dissents change votes, even enough votes to become the majority.

I have had to convert more than one of my proposed majority opinions into a dissent before the final decision was announced. I have also, however, had the more satisfying experience of rewriting a dissent as a majority opinion for the Court.

Before everyone has finally made up his mind a constant interchange by memoranda, by telephone, at the lunch table continues while we hammer out the final form of the opinion. I had one case during the past term in which I circulated ten printed drafts before one was approved as the Court opinion.

UNIFORM RULE

The point of this procedure is that each Justice, unless he disqualifies himself in a particular case, passes on every piece of business coming to the Court. The Court does not function by means of committees or panels. Each Justice passes on each petition, each time, no matter how drawn, in long hand, by typewriter, or on a press. Our Constitution vests the judicial power in only one Supreme Court. This does not permit Supreme Court action by committees, panels, or sections.

The method that the Justices use in meeting an enormous caseload varies. There is one uniform rule: Judging is not delegated. Each Justice studies each case in sufficient detail to resolve the question for himself. In a very real sense, each decision is an individual decision of every Justice.

The process can be a lonely, troubling experience for fallible human beings conscious that their best may not be adequate to the challenge.

"We are not unaware," the late Justice Jackson said, "that we are not final because we are infallible; we know that we are infallible only because we are final."

One does not forget how much may depend on his decision. He knows that usually more than the litigants may be affected, that the course of vital social, economic and political currents may be directed.

This then is the decisional process in the Supreme Court. It is not without its tensions, of course — indeed, quite agonizing tensions at times.

I would particularly emphasize that, unlike the case of a Congressional or White House decision, Americans demand of their Supreme Court judges that they produce a written opinion, the collective expression of the judges subscribing to it, setting forth the reason which led them to the decision.

These opinions are the exposition, not just to lawyers, legal scholars and other judges, but to our whole society, of the bases upon which a particular result rests — why a problem, looked at as disinterestedly and dispassionately as nine human beings trained in a tradition of the disinterested and dispassionate approach can look at it, is answered as it is.

It is inevitable, however, that Supreme Court decisions — and the Justices themselves — should be caught up in public debate and be the subjects of bitter controversy.

An editorial in *The Washington Post* did not miss the mark by much in saying that this was so because

> one of the primary functions of the Supreme Court is to keep the people of the country from doing what they would like to do — at times when what they would like to do runs counter to the Constitution. . . . The function of the Supreme Court is not to count constituents; it is to interpret a fundamental charter which imposes restraints on constituents. Independence and integrity, not popularity, must be its standards.

FREUND'S VIEW

Certainly controversy over its work has attended the Court throughout its history. As Professor Paul A. Freund of Harvard remarked, this has been true almost since the Court's first decision:

> When the Court held, in 1793, that the state of Georgia could be sued on a contract in the federal courts, the outraged Assembly of that state passed a bill declaring that any federal marshal who should try to collect the judgment would be guilty of a felony and would suffer death, without benefit of clergy, by being hanged. When the Court decided that state criminal convictions could be reviewed in the Supreme Court, Chief Justice Roane of Virginia exploded, calling it a "most monstrous and unexampled decision. It can only be accounted for by that love of power which history

informs us infects and corrupts all who possess it, and from which even the eminent and upright judges are not exempt."

But public understanding has not always been lacking in the past. Perhaps it exists today. But surely a more informed knowledge of the decisional process should aid a better understanding.

It is not agreement with the Court's decisions that I urge. Our law is the richer and the wiser because academic and informed lay criticism is part of the stream of development.

CONSENSUS NEEDED

It is only a greater awareness of the nature and limits of the Supreme Court's function that I seek.

The ultimate resolution of questions fundamental to the whole community must be based on a common consensus of understanding of the unique responsibility assigned to the Supreme Court in our society.

The lack of that understanding led Mr. Justice Holmes to say fifty years ago:

> We are very quiet there, but it is the quiet of a storm center, as we all know. Science has taught the world skepticism and has made it legitimate to put everything to the test of proof. Many beautiful and noble reverences are impaired, but in these days no one can complain if any institution, system, or belief is called on to justify its continuance in life. Of course we are not excepted and have not escaped.

PAINFUL ACCUSATION

> Doubts are expressed that go to our very being. Not only are we told that when Marshall pronounced an Act of Congress unconstitutional he usurped a power that the Constitution did not give, but we are told that we are the representatives of a class — a tool of the money power.
>
> I get letters, not always anonymous, intimating that we are corrupt. Well, gentlemen, I admit that it makes my heart ache. It is very painful, when one spends all the energies of one's soul in trying to do good work, with no thought but that of solving a problem according to the rules by which one is bound, to know that many see sinister motives and would be glad of evidence that one was consciously bad.
>
> But we must take such things philosophically and try to see what we can learn from hatred and distrust and whether behind them there may not be a germ of inarticulate truth.
>
> The attacks upon the Court are merely an expression of the unrest that seems to wonder vaguely whether law and order pay. When the ignorant are taught to doubt they do not know what they safely may believe. And it seems to me that at this time we need education in the obvious more than investigation of the obscure.

Justice William J. Brennan, Jr., in his discussion of how the Supreme Court arrives at decisions in the preceding selection, points out that inevitably Supreme Court decisions and the Justices are the subjects of public debate and often bitter controversy. It is not surprising that when Supreme Court Justices and lower court judges as well follow the early dictum of Chief Justice John Marshall, which he stated in *Marbury* v. *Madison* in 1803, that "It is emphatically the province and duty of the judicial department to say what the law is," they will become the center of political storms stirred up by those who feel the Court has overstepped its bounds.

The Supreme Court under Chief Justice Earl Warren was one of the most controversial in our history precisely because it, like the early Supreme Court under Chief Justice John Marshall, did not hesitate to say what the law is even in the face of stiff political opposition. The stage was set for heavy drama when Earl Warren was appointed Chief Justice by President Eisenhower in 1953. The school desegregation cases were already pending before the Court. The Vinson Court had noted probable jurisdiction of these cases in 1952, and in June of 1953 the cases were redocketed and scheduled for argument in the fall 1953 session of the Court. This meant that Chief Justice Warren, who was seated on October 4, 1953, was almost immediately confronted with one of the most momentous series of cases ever to confront the Supreme Court.

Although the final decision of Supreme Court in the *Brown* case as well as in the District of Columbia school desegregation case (*Bolling* v. *Sharpe,* 347 U.S. 497 [1954]) was unanimous in 1954, when the cases were initially brought up in 1952 the Court was far from a consensus to overrule the separate but equal doctrine of *Plessy* v. *Ferguson* (1896). From diaries kept by Associate Justice Harold Burton, who served on the Court from 1945 until 1958, it appears that in 1952 Justices Black, Douglas, Burton, and Minton were leaning toward reversal of the *Plessy* decision, while Chief Justice Vinson, and Justices Reed, Frankfurter, Jackson, and Clark were leaning toward affirmance or at least were doubtful as to the propriety of overruling *Plessy*.[1]

After Warren replaced Vinson as Chief Justice, skepticism still remained in the minds of many Justices about what course of action should be taken in the school desegregation cases. The first Supreme Court conference on the matter was held on December 12, 1953, after the first desegregation case was argued on December 7. At that conference Warren unequivocally stated that the Court should overrule de jure segregation in public schools, although he was careful to note that the problem was far from simple, and that the issue should be handled with as much delicacy as possible. At that conference only Justices Douglas and Minton fully agreed with the Chief Justice, although the tenor of the remarks of

---

[1] For a discussion of the background of the *Brown* decision, and the views of the justices as they were revealed in Burton's diaries, see S. Sidney Ulmer, "Earl Warren and the *Brown* decision," *Journal of Politics,* vol. 33 (1971): 689–702.

the other Justices suggested the possibility that they might be willing to go along with Warren. The final unanimity of the Court on the school desegregation cases was a credit to Warren's leadership skills as Chief Justice.

The following selection illustrates both the internal and the external politics of Supreme Court decision making. Dramatic oral argument took place before the Court. Just as the unanimity of the Court in the first *Brown* decision in 1954 was far from assured when the cases were first argued, the nature of the implementing decision in *Brown* II in 1955 was strongly debated before agreement was reached. External politics came into play not only in the acute awareness of the Court to southern resistance to an overturning of the *Plessy* decision, an awareness that apparently misgauged the extent of feelings in the South, but also in the attempt of President Eisenhower to influence Chief Justice Warren by making an ex parte representation to the Chief Justice after a White House dinner party where Warren was seated opposite the lawyer for the segregation states. President Eisenhower, who felt his appointment of Warren would bring a moderating influence to the Court, was apparently very disappointed with the *Brown* decision, and maintained coolly distant relations with the Chief Justice after the decision was announced.

61
Earl Warren

INSIDE THE SUPREME COURT

In a matter of hours after first coming to the Supreme Court, I learned more about the important cases that were lumped as the school desegregation cases.

There were five of them, from Kansas, Virginia, South Carolina, Delaware, and the District of Columbia. While the latter was in a somewhat different setting because it did not involve a state law, they all involved the "separate but equal" doctrine as established by the Supreme Court in the case of *Plessy* v. *Ferguson* (1896). That decision declined to prohibit separate railroad accommodations for blacks and whites. It sought to justify racial segregation for almost every movement or gathering so long as "separate but equal" facilities were provided, and it became known as the "Jim Crow" doctrine. The central issue in each of these school cases was,

> Does segregation of children in public schools solely on the basis of race, even though the physical facilities and other "tangible" factors may be equal, deprive the children of the minority group of equal educational opportunities?

The five cases had been argued during the 1952 term before I came to the Court but had not been decided and had been put over for re-argument, with a set of specific questions for discussion.

The United States government, through Assistant Attorney General J. Lee Rankin, supported by a brief signed also by Attorney General Herbert Brownell and other Justice Department attorneys, argued as a friend of the Court in favor of the positions maintained by the black students' lawyers. The first case was argued December 7, 1953, and it was easy to understand why the Court felt it necessary to have a full complement of Justices. Resubmission of the case for argument would normally indicate a difference of opinion within the Court. In these circumstances, particularly if any Justice is absent or disqualifies himself, the danger exists of an evenly divided, four-to-four Court, which means that the decision of the lower court is affirmed without opinion from the Supreme Court and without any precedential value.

Some of the cases under review had been decided against the black petitioners in the lower courts on the authority of the much eroded "separate but equal" doctrine of *Plessy* v. *Ferguson*.

To have affirmed these cases without decision and with the mere statement that it was being done by an equally divided Court, if such had been the case, would have aborted the judicial process and resulted in public frustration and disrespect for the Court. The Court was thoroughly conscious of the importance of the decision to be arrived at and of the impact it would have on the nation. With this went realization of the necessity for secrecy in our deliberations and for achieving unity, if possible.

We realized that once a person announces he has reached a conclusion, it is more difficult for him to change his thinking, so we decided that we would dispense with our usual custom of formally expressing our individual views at the first conference and would confine ourselves for a time to informal discussion of the briefs, the arguments made at the hearing, and our own independent research on each conference day, reserving our final opinions until the discussions were concluded.

We followed this plan until February, when we felt that we were ready to vote. On the first vote, we unanimously agreed that the "separate but equal" doctrine had no place in public education. The question then arose as to how this view should be written — as a *per curiam* (by the Court), or as a signed, individualized opinion. We decided that it would carry more force if done through a signed opinion, and some Justices thought it should bear the signature of the Chief Justice. I consented to this, and we discussed the importance of secrecy. We agreed that only my law clerks should be involved, and that any writing between my office and those of the other Justices would be delivered to the Justices personally. This practice was followed throughout and it was the only time it was required in my years on the Court. It was not done because of suspicion of anyone, but because of the sensitiveness of the school segregation matter and the prying for inside information that surrounded the cases. We thought we should confine our communications to the fewest possible people as a matter of security. Progress made in conference was discussed informally from time to time, and on occasion I would so inform Mr. Justice Jackson, who was confined to the hospital, recuperating from a heart attack which had incapacitated him for some time. Finally, at our conference on May 15, we agreed to announce our opinion the following Monday, subject to the approval of Mr. Justice Jackson. I went to the hospital early Monday morning, May 17, and showed the Justice a copy of the proposed opinion as it was to be released. He agreed to it, and to my alarm insisted on attending the Court that day in order to demonstrate our solidarity. I said that was unnecessary, but he insisted, and was there at the appointed time.

It was a momentous courtroom event and, unlike many other such events, it has not lost that character to this day.[1]

These five segregation cases all raised the same central issue and four of them are compendiously referred to as *Brown* v. *Board of Education of Topeka* (1954).

In the *Brown* decision, we decided only that the practice of segregating

---

[1] When Earl Warren took over as Chief Justice, the Court was quite divided. Justices Black and Douglas usually took a strongly liberal view in their opinions; Justices Jackson and Frankfurter were more conservative; the other Justices fluctuated in between. In addition, there were personality conflicts which provided a certain amount of bristling discord and admittedly had been beyond Chief Justice Vinson's powers to settle.

Some historians have given Warren credit for bringing greater amity and unity to the Court, at least for all-important racial decisions. Other observers, including the Chief Justice himself, have been more modest in their estimate of his harmonizing influence, holding that nothing could unify such differing spirits unless they individually *wanted* to be unified for a particular purpose. Memoranda in the Warren files for his Court years indicate that the Justices themselves gave Warren much credit for his leadership. A note to Warren from Mr. Justice Frankfurter on the day of the *Brown* decision says:

"Dear Chief: This is a day that will live in glory. It's also a great day in the history of the court, and not in the least for the course of deliberation which brought about the result. I congratulate you."

And from Mr. Justice Burton: "To you goes the credit for the character of the opinions which produced the all-important unanimity. Congratulations."

children in public schools solely because of their race was unconstitutional. This left other questions to be answered. For instance, could plaintiffs bring court actions as *class* actions for all who were similarly situated, or should persons actually joining in the action be entitled to relief only for themselves? What court should determine the decree in each case? For what reason could there or could there not be any delay in obeying the Court's mandate, and to what extent? All such questions we continued until the next term, inviting the United States and all states affected by our decision to file briefs and argue if they desired to do so.

These cases, postponed because of the death of Mr. Justice Jackson, which left an eight-man Court, came on for argument from April 11 to 14, 1955, with the newly appointed Mr. Justice Harlan in attendance. At the time of Mr. Justice Jackson's death in October 1954, John Harlan was a recent appointee to the Court of Appeals of the Second Federal Judicial Circuit. President Eisenhower nominated him to the Supreme Court on January 10, 1955, but those were the investigative days of Joe McCarthy, and Harlan was not approved by the Senate until March 17 because of the silly bulldozing he was given as a result of having been a Rhodes scholar, which some right-wingers vaguely associated with Red-tinged "internationalism."

Solicitor General Simon Sobeloff, in response to the Court's invitation, argued for the United States on behalf of the petitioners as a friend of the Court. The attorneys general or their assistants of the states involved in the litigation argued for their states, which included Arkansas, Florida, Maryland, North Carolina, Oklahoma, and Texas. All opposed school desegregation.

The principal arguments on this phase of the case, as well as in the original proceeding, were made by John W. Davis for the states and Thurgood Marshall, now an Associate Justice of the Supreme Court, for the plaintiffs' side. The arguments, for me at least, took a strange course. One might expect, as I did, that the lawyers representing black schoolchildren would appeal to the emotions of the Court based upon their many years of oppression, and that the states would hold to strictly legal matters. More nearly the opposite developed. Thurgood Marshall made no emotional appeal, and argued the legal issues in a rational manner as cold as steel. On the other hand, states' attorney Davis, a great advocate and orator, former Democratic candidate for the presidency of the United States, displayed a great deal of emotion, and on more than one occasion broke down and took a few moments to compose himself.

Again the Court was unanimous in its decision of May 31, 1955, reaffirming its opinion of May 17, 1954, by asserting the fundamental principle that any kind of racial discrimination in public education is unconstitutional, and that all provisions of federal, state, or local law requiring or permitting such discrimination must yield to this principle. Recognizing that because full application of these constitutional principles might require solution of a wide variety of local school desegregation problems, school authorities were given the primary responsibility for elucidating, assessing, and solving such problems. However, we stipulated that courts would ultimately have to consider whether the action of school authorities constituted implementation in good faith of the governing constitutional principles.

We discussed at great length in conference whether the Supreme Court should make the factual determinations in such cases or whether they should be left to the courts below. We decided finally to leave them to the latter, subject, of course, to our review, because they were getting closer to the problems involved, and were in a better position to engage in the fact-finding process. As guidelines for them, we directed that neither local law nor custom should be permitted to interfere with the establishment of an integrated school system, and that the process of achieving it should be carried out "with all deliberate speed" — a phrase which has been much discussed by those who are of the opinion that desegregation has not proceeded with as much celerity as might have been expected.

These people argued that the Supreme Court should merely have directed the school districts to admit Brown and the other plaintiffs to the schools to which they sought admission, in the belief that this would have quickly ended the litigation. This theory, however, overlooks the complexity of our federal system; the time it takes controversial litigation to proceed through the hierarchy of courts to the Supreme Court; the fact that the administration of the public school system is a state and local function so long as it does not contravene constitutional principles; that each state has its own system with different relationships between state and local government; and that the relationship can be changed at will by the state government if there should be a determination to bypass or defeat the decision of the Supreme Court. Evidence that such evasion would occur came immediately in some of the resolutions and laws initiated by certain states. In this, they were encouraged by the so-called Southern Manifesto, signed by over a hundred southern representatives and senators in the Congress of the United States. It urged all such states to defy the Supreme Court decision as being against their way of life and their "good" race relations, and to use "all lawful means" to make the decision ineffective. So reinforcing to southern defiance was this manifesto that the doctrine of "nullification" — first advanced by John C. Calhoun of South Carolina, discredited more than a century before and made forever inapplicable by the Civil War Amendments — was revived by southern governors, legislators, and candidates for public office. The doctrine, in simple terms, argued that states have the right to declare null and void and to set aside in practice any law of the federal government which violates their voluntary compact embodied in the United States Constitution. The doctrine, of course, did not prevail, but the delay and bitterness occasioned by it caused inestimable damage to the extension of equal rights to citizens of every race, color, or creed as mandated by the Fourteenth Amendment.

With courage drawn from this profession of faith in white supremacy by practically every southern member of Congress, together with oft-repeated congressional speeches and statements to the effect that no nine honest men could possibly have come to the conclusion reached by the Court in *Brown* v. *Board of Education,* excited and racist-minded public officials and candidates for office proposed and enacted every obstacle they could devise to thwart the Court's decision. This was aggravated by the fact that no word of support for the decision emanated from the White House. The most that came from high officials in the Administration was to the effect that they could not be blamed for anything done to enforce desegregation in education because it was the Supreme Court, not the Administration, that determined desegregation to be the law, and the executive branch of the government is required to enforce the law as interpreted by the Supreme Court. Bernard Shanley, the personal counsel of the President, in an effort to allay southern animosity against the Administration, was reported in the press to have said in a speech that the *Brown* case had set race relations in the South back by a quarter of a century. The aphorism (dear to the hearts of those who are insensitive to the rights of minority groups) that discrimination cannot be eliminated by laws, but only by the hearts of people, also emanated from the White House.[2]

A few years later, Governor George Wallace was emboldened to stand at the entrance to the University of Alabama and, in the face of the deputy attorney general of the United States, who had read to him the order of a United States district judge directing the university to admit Vivian Malone and James Hood, two black students, shout in defiance, "Segregation in the past, segregation today, segregation forever."

The Court expected some resistance from the South. But I doubt if any of us expected as much as we got. Nor did I believe that the Republican party, which freed the slaves through the Civil War and the Thirteenth Amendment and granted them all the attributes of citizenship through the Fourteenth and Fifteenth Amendments, would develop a southern strategy intended to restrict such rights in order to capture the electors of those states and achieve the presidency. I, for one, thought it would be wonderful if, by the time of the centennial of the Fourteenth Amendment (1968), the principle of desegregation in *Brown* v. *Board of Education* could be a reality throughout the land. And I still believe that much of our racial strife could have been avoided if President Eisenhower had at least observed that our country is dedicated to the principle that "We hold these Truths to be self-

---

[2] [The *Brown* decisions are discussed and presented, pp. 159–164.]

evident, that all Men are created equal, that they are endowed by their Creator with certain unalienable Rights, that among these are Life, Liberty and the Pursuit of Happiness . . ."

With his popularity, if Eisenhower had said that black children were still being discriminated against long after the adoption of the Thirteenth, Fourteenth, and Fifteenth Amendments, that the Supreme Court of the land had now declared it unconstitutional to continue such cruel practices, and that it should be the duty of every good citizen to help rectify more than eighty years of wrongdoing by honoring that decision — if he had said something to this effect, I think we would have been relieved of many of the racial problems which have continued to plague us. But he never stated that he thought the decision was right until after he had left the White House.

I have always believed that President Eisenhower resented our decision in *Brown* v. *Board of Education* and its progeny. Influencing this belief, among other things, is an incident that occurred shortly before the opinion was announced. The President had a program for discussing problems with groups of people at occasional White House dinners. When the *Brown* case was under submission, he invited me to one of them. I wondered why I should be invited, because the dinners were political in nature, and I could not participate in such discussions. But one does not often decline an invitation from the President to the White House, and I accepted. I was the ranking guest, and as such sat at the right of the President and within speaking distance of John W. Davis, the counsel for the segregation states. During the dinner, the President went to considerable lengths to tell me what a great man Mr. Davis was. At the conclusion of the meal, in accordance with custom, we filed out of the dining room to another room where coffee and an after-dinner drink were served. The President, of course, precedes, and on this occasion he took me by the arm, and, as we walked along, speaking of the southern states in the segregation cases, he said, "These are not bad people. All they are concerned about is to see that their sweet little girls are not required to sit in school alongside some big overgrown Negroes."

Fortunately, by that time, others had filed into the room, so I was not obliged to reply. Shortly thereafter, the *Brown* case was decided, and with it went our cordial relations. While Nina and I were occasionally invited to the White House after the decision for protocol reasons, when some foreign dignitary was being entertained, or were invited to some foreign embassy for a reciprocal honoring of the President, I can recall few conversations that went beyond a polite "Good evening, Mr. President" and "Good evening, Mr. Chief Justice."

Some southern states, and northern areas as well, have used every conceivable device to thwart the principle of the *Brown* case, and they have been successful in preventing full compliance or even that degree of compliance sufficient to create good will between the races. Because of these drawbacks, some people are of the belief that the Court's decree was a failure, but the fact is that real progress has been made. However, the tragedy of the situation is that because of die-hard segregationist resistance, advances have come about only after torrid litigation or after federal legislation which has emphasized the unfairness of the white supremacy theory to the point that deep bitterness against whites is felt by all minority groups — blacks, Chicanos, Puerto Ricans, Asians, and American Indians. That, too, can be remedied whenever we all realize the importance of the Thirteenth, Fourteenth, and Fifteenth Amendments to the Constitution in granting absolute equality of citizenship to "*Everyone* born or naturalized in the United States . . ."

Some more recent cases decided by the Supreme Court emphasize that these patterns die very hard. Despite the Court's condemnation of the principle of racial segregation and outlawing of it in public schools in 1954, not until 1962 was the separation of blacks and whites in state courtrooms likewise outlawed. Not until 1964 was a black witness given the right to be examined by counsel in the same spirit of deference accorded to white witnesses. Not until 1968, over one hundred years after the passage of the civil rights statute on which the Court belatedly relied, were blacks determined to have the same rights as whites to live where they choose. Despite an old holding by the Court that systematic exclusion of Negroes from juries is unconstitutional, that problem still persists. And as late as 1969, after I had retired from the Court, Mr. Justice Black was moved to say in the case of *Alexander* v. *Holmes County Board of Education* that ". . . there are many places still in this country where the schools are either 'white' or 'Negro' and not just schools for all children as the Constitution requires." In Justice Black's view, there was "no reason why such a wholesale deprivation of constitutional rights should be tolerated another minute."

An extremely touchy matter that has arisen out of the need to integrate schools is that of busing. Governor George Wallace of Alabama injected it into a presidential campaign, and others from Berkeley to Boston have brought the "busing issue" before the American public. Opponents hold it to be an undesirable principle whereby the courts are determined to wrench children from their neighborhoods and put them on buses for hours every day all over America in order to bring about a proportionate balance of black and white children in the schools. They have even argued that this must be prevented by depriving the courts of their constitutional jurisdiction.

This, however, is a complete distortion of the situation.

The Supreme Court has never held that there must be exact racial balance in the schools or that long-distance busing is desirable. Until recently, it has not recognized busing as a principle, only as a tool for the courts to use where the authorities have been reluctant to carry out the desegregation called for by *Brown* v. *Board of Education*. That decision was aimed at affording all children an equal opportunity for a good education, nothing more.

I believe that most parents would prefer having their children attend a school within walking distance of their home. They recognize, however, that it often becomes necessary or at least desirable to have pupils transported to a more distant school in order to educate them better. Busing is only one means to accomplish proper results when others have failed or been denied. There is much merit in a suggestion of Notre Dame's Father Hesburgh to the effect that busing can properly be used to transport underprivileged children to better schools but not the opposite; he would leave poorer schools to the bulldozer.

Harmony in race relations is not simply or easily achieved. No matter how comprehensive and clear the law is on this subject, there will always be bigots to promote tensions and patterns of resistance. But the vast majority of people must realize by now that racial equality under law is basic to our institutions and that we will not and cannot have peace in our nation until the race issue is properly settled. We have, we should be aware, 34 million members of minority groups whose civil rights have not been but must be fully respected. That calls for a combination of effective law and good will. In the absence of both or either of these elements, we can only expect chaos. If there is one lesson to be learned from our tragic experience in the Civil War and its wake, it is that the question of racial discrimination is never settled until it is settled right.

After the Supreme Court Decides

Although students may be familiar with a wide range of important Supreme Court decisions, they rarely have been given an opportunity to observe what happens to a case after the Supreme Court acts. In *Gideon* v. *Wainwright* (1963), the Court held that the right to counsel is fundamental to a fair trial and must be guaranteed by the states under the due process clause of the Fourteenth Amendment (see Chapter 3). Gideon, whose request for counsel had been turned down, had sought unsuccessfully to defend himself against a felony charge of breaking and entering a poolroom. Would it have made a difference to Gideon if the trial court had provided him with counsel as he requested? The following selection describes what happened to Gideon after the Supreme Court upheld his right to counsel.

62

Anthony Lewis

GIDEON'S TRUMPET: EPILOGUE

Resolution of the great constitutional question in *Gideon* v. *Wainwright* did not decide the fate of Clarence Earl Gideon. He was now entitled to a new trial, with a lawyer. Was he guilty of breaking into the Bay Harbor Poolroom? The verdict would not set any legal precedents, but there is significance in the human beings who make constitutional-law cases as well as in the law. And in this case there was the interesting question whether the legal assistance for which Gideon had fought so hard would make any difference to him.

Soon after the decision Abe Fortas wrote Gideon suggesting that in the future a local Florida lawyer should represent him. Fortas said he had written to a Florida Civil Liberties Union attorney about the case. This lawyer was Tobias Simon of Miami, who had signed the *amicus* brief presented to the Supreme Court by the American Civil Liberties Union. Gideon, who before the decision had expressed the hope that the A.C.L.U. would give him a lawyer, wrote Simon on April 9, 1963.

"I humbly am asking you for any help that you can give me in the present situation," Gideon said. "Because no one knows any better than me of what I am up against. I have no reason to believe now that I would receive a fair trial in the same court than I did before even with a court appointed attorney. I have my plea all ready to make but it probably will be denied me."

Simon replied on April 15th that someone from the Civil Liberties Union would represent him at his new trial. Gideon acknowledged that letter with thanks on April 29th, adding that he wondered how long the Supreme Court of Florida could take to act on his case now "without becoming contemptible of the United States Supreme Court."

A few days later Simon went to Raiford and interviewed Gideon for an hour and a half. He found Gideon to be "an irascible but spunky white male." Gideon spoke even more forcefully than in his letters. He was under the illusion that a new trial would constitute double jeopardy and that the Florida Supreme Court should already have released him outright. (A new trial won by a prisoner as a result of his own appeal is not double jeopardy under American law.) He said he could never get a fair trial in Panama City, and when Simon tried to reassure him Gideon "became exceedingly bitter and refused to discuss his case any further." But he "did agree that we would be able to represent him in the forthcoming new trial," Simon reported to the A.C.L.U.

The Florida Supreme Court had received the official notice of the United States Supreme Court decision — the mandate — in April; and on May 15th it issued an order entitling Gideon to a new trial. The circuit court of Bay County set July 5th as the trial date.

On July 4th Simon went to Panama City with Irwin J. Block, an experienced criminal lawyer, until recently the chief assistant prosecutor in Miami, who had agreed to help him. They interviewed some witnesses and former neighbors of Gideon who seemed to have "admiration for a man who fought so hard against odds so great." Then they went to see Gideon, who had been brought from Raiford to the local jail. Mr. Simon described the meeting.

"Gideon refused to be represented by either of us; he refused to be tried; he stated that the court had no power to try him, and that his trial in Panama City would only mean his return to the penitentiary. All efforts to calm him and to have him place some trust in us failed."

The next morning, the time set for trial, Simon and Block met with the prosecutors in the chambers of Robert L. McCrary, Jr., the judge who had presided over Gideon's first trial and was to handle the second. Gideon was also present. Judge McCrary began by noting that Simon had signed some papers and was appearing as defense counsel.

"I didn't authorize Mr. Simon to sign anything for me," Gideon said. "I'll do my own signing. I do not want him to represent me."

Judge McCrary asked warily, "Do you want another lawyer to represent you?"

"No," said Gideon. After a pause he added: "And I'm not ready for trial."

There must have been a touch of bewilderment in the judge's next question. "What do you want, then?"

"I want to file for an order to move my case from this court," Gideon replied. "I can't get a fair trial in this court; it's the same court, the same judge, everything, and everybody connected with the court is the same as it was before and I can't get a fair trial here. . . . You're not even going to let me plead my case."

At this point Simon explained his position in the case, reading to the judge, among other documents, Gideon's letter "humbly asking" for help. But Simon said that of course he and Block did not want to represent Gideon if he did not want them.

Gideon repeated his wish: "I want to plead my own case. I want to make my own plea. I do not want them to make any plea for me."

"You don't want Mr. Simon and Mr. Block to represent you?" Judge McCrary asked, making absolutely certain that all this was really happening.

"No," said Gideon, "I don't want them to represent me. I DO NOT WANT THEM." (The court reporter used capitals.)

The judge excused Simon and Block, but he also made clear that under no circumstances did he want Gideon to try his own case again. After ascertaining that Gideon had no money to hire a lawyer of his own choice, Judge McCrary asked whether there was a local lawyer whom Gideon would like to represent him. There was: W. Fred Turner.

"For the record," Judge McCrary said quickly, "I am going to appoint Mr. Fred Turner to represent this defendant, Clarence Earl Gideon."

A member of the prosecuting staff suggested that the public defender just appointed for that judicial circuit under the new Florida public-defender law assist Fred Turner.

"I don't want him in it," Gideon said, evidently preferring a private attorney with no touch of welfare.

The judge said, "We will just let Mr. Turner handle this case." Then he advised Gideon to get in touch with his new lawyer to file any motions he desired.

"I want to file my own motions," Gideon said. "If this is to be a matter of just sending me back to the penitentiary I want to do it my own way. It has been more than two years now since this crime is alleged to have been committed, and if I'm going back to the penitentiary for the same crime I want to do it my way. I want to file my own motions."

He pulled from his hip pocket two crumpled pages, typewritten single-spaced, that were the motions he had prepared. Judge McCrary asked Gideon to read them to the court reporter. The motions were full of legalistic language, and Gideon seemed to have some trouble reading them; finally the judge called a short recess to let Gideon look them over before reading them to the stenographer. These long documents made two main points: That a new trial was barred by the rule against double jeopardy and by Florida's two-year statute of limitations on his alleged crime. (The statute of limitations does not, in fact, apply when an appeal results in a new trial.)

Judge McCrary listened attentively during the reading of the motions and said he would rule on them later. Then he set a new trial date, August 5th, exactly one month later. The judge offered to free the prisoner on $1,000 bail, but Gideon could not raise it and was returned to the penitentiary.

Simon later wrote a report on the episode for the Florida Civil Liberties Union, which he subtitled, "How the Florida Civil Liberties Union Wasted $300, and How Two Attorneys Each Traveled over 1200 Miles and Killed an Otherwise Perfectly Enjoyable July Fourth Weekend." But by the end of the report his anger seems to have softened. He wrote:

"It has become almost axiomatic that the great rights which are secured for all of us by the Bill of Rights are constantly tested and retested in the courts by the people who live in the bottom of society's barrel. Thus, many of our freedom-of-religion cases developed out of efforts by members of small sects to force religious tracts upon people who did not want them; our freedom-of-speech cases have developed from the efforts of the police to jail persons who ranted and raved against others, including Catholics, Jews and Negroes. . . .

"In the future the name 'Gideon' will stand for the great principle that the poor are entitled to the same type of justice as are those who are able to afford counsel. It is probably a good thing that it is immaterial and unimportant that Gideon is something of a 'nut,' that his maniacal distrust and suspicion lead him to the very borders of insanity. Upon the shoulders of such persons are our great rights carried."

Gideon's new lawyer, Fred Turner, wrote to Judge McCrary on July 12th asking that the trial be postponed three weeks. He said there were "many, many legal problems" in this case — a case once considered so simple that the defendant could be required to try it himself on a few minutes' notice. Judge McCrary refused the postponement.

On August 1st the judge denied a series of motions including Gideon's own, presented by Turner, to dismiss the charges. Courtroom observers thought Gideon looked pleased at the denial and was looking forward to the new trial. Judge McCrary warned him not to interfere with Turner or try to take over his own defense.

The courthouse in Panama City is a large brick building, painted yellow, with peeling white columns. It stands on a rather seedy square set with palms. The courtroom is a simple, good-looking room with pale green walls and seats for about one hundred and fifty. It is air conditioned, a necessity in Panama City in August.

The trial began promptly at nine A.M. on August 5th. After the sheriff's traditional opening (". . . God save the United States of America, the State of Florida and this honorable court"), Judge McCrary read a prayer ending "and help us to do impartial justice, for Christ's sake. Amen." Forty-eight years old, with black hair, informal and gracious in his dealings with the lawyers but decisive when necessary, McCrary was not an awesome figure in his robes. To his left and below him was the court reporter, Mrs. Nelle P. Heath, a motherly figure with firmly upswept hair and pearl earrings. ("I reported this case originally, and I thought it was just another run-of-the-mill case. I never thought that Gideon was different from anyone else — that he would just keep on goin' and goin' and goin'.") The prosecution table was just in front of the bench. The original prosecutor, Assistant State Attorney William E. Harris, a tanned, bulky man, again sat there. But this time, indicating the importance the case had acquired, his boss was there, too — the state attorney for the circuit, J. Frank Adams, a foxy-looking figure in a bow tie — and also another assistant, J. Paul Griffith. The prosecutors seemed confident. Adams said, "If he'd had a lawyer in the first place, he'd have been advised to plead guilty."

Judge McCrary announced "the case of State of Florida versus Clarence Earl Gideon. Is the state ready for trial?" Harris said it was. Turner, who was sitting with Gideon at a table back near the rail that separated the spectators from the trial area, got up without waiting to be asked. "We're ready, your Honor," he said, enthusiastically rolling a pencil between his two flattened hands. Turner was thin and dapper, reminiscent of Fred Astaire, "forty-one summers" old, he said when asked.

Ordinarily a jury of six is used in Florida. There was a panel of twenty-eight white men in the courtroom. (Why no Negroes? "They just don't call any," a local newspaperman explained.) The first six men were called forward and questioned first by Harris for possible prejudice. Harris was satisfied with all of them. Then Turner questioned the same six; they said they had no prejudices in the case, and they agreed that they would give the defendant the benefit of any reasonable doubt. Without explanation, Turner excused two of the six. Later he said, privately, that he had gone over the whole jury list in advance — "you've got to know who they are, what they think" — and dropped the two men because he knew that one didn't like alcohol and that the other was "a convicter."

The jury was sworn just before ten A.M. Harris made a two-minute opening statement to the effect that the state expected to prove Gideon had broken into the Bay Harbor Poolroom through a rear window; a witness had seen him inside and in an alley after leaving. Turner waived his right to make an opening statement.

Henry Cook, the eyewitness, was the first to take the stand. He turned out to be a sallow-faced youth of twenty-two, with greasy black hair cut in a pompadour and long sideburns. Under Harris's questioning he told the same story he had at the first trial. He had come back to Bay Harbor from a dance in Apalachicola, sixty miles away, at five-thirty that morning and had spotted Gideon inside the poolroom; he had followed Gideon down the alley to a telephone booth, then back to the poolroom; Gideon's pockets bulged.

Turner began his cross-examination by asking who had driven Cook back from Apalachicola that night. When Cook had trouble remembering, Turner suggested some names. (Turner had driven to Apalachicola a few days earlier to try, without success, to find the other young men who had been in the car.) Cook said the car was "an old model Chevrolet."

"Why did they put you off two blocks from your home when they'd driven you sixty miles?" Turner asked.

Cook mumbled inaudibly, then said, "I was going to hang around there till the poolroom opened up — seven o'clock."

Turner began addressing the witness with irritating familiarity, "Well now, Henry . . . ," and took him back over the events of that night. Cook said he had had a beer or two, but then the stores had closed in Apalachicola at midnight. This brought Turner back to the question of why Cook and his friends had stopped outside the Bay Harbor Poolroom. Turner had a suggestion — an accusation.

"Mr. Cook," he said, "did you go into the Bay Harbor Poolroom?"

"No, sir."

"Did you all get a six-pack of beer out of there?"

"No, sir."

Turner led Cook over a detailed discussion of the geography of Bay Harbor and the poolroom, indicating an intimate acquaintance with it himself. (He had spent a day nosing around Bay Harbor and talking with people, to prepare for the trial.) Weren't there some advertising boards in the front window? How could Cook have seen past them and spotted Gideon, as he claimed? Weren't the windows on the alley too high to see through?

"You did not call the police then or later," Turner asked. It was as much a comment as a question.

"That's right."

After more questions, Turner asked, "Ever been convicted of a felony?"

"No, sir, not convicted. I stole a car and was put on probation."

That answer set off a long wrangle between the lawyers. At the first trial, when Gideon asked whether he had ever been convicted of a felony, Cook had answered: "No, sir, never have." Turner said that was a false answer that reflected on Cook's character and credibility as a witness. State Attorney Adams popped up and said it was not necessarily false because Cook had evidently pleaded guilty; that was not the same as being "convicted." Turner said it was the same. There was a suggestion that the plea might have been in a juvenile court, where there are no formal convictions. Finally the judge allowed this exchange, which closed the cross-examination:

Turner: "Have you ever denied being convicted of a felony?"

Cook: "Yes, sir."

Turner: "When and where did you deny your criminal record?"

Cook: "Right here — at his last trial."

On redirect examination Harris got Cook to say he had not understood the question about a felony at the first trial. Turner moved to strike this testimony, saying "I don't think this should go to the jury with any excuses or any embellishments. . . . I don't care if he's ignorant of the law or I am, that still doesn't change the spots on the leopard. He's a convicted felon." Judge McCrary let Cook's explanation stand, but Turner had made the score he wanted — impressing the jury with Cook's record.

The prosecution's second witness was the man who had operated the Bay Harbor Poolroom, Ira Strickland, Jr., twenty-nine years old, growing bald. He was no longer in the poolroom business; now he was a stock clerk. Questioning him, State Attorney Adams went into much greater detail about the poolroom and Gideon's relationship to it than at the first trial. Had Gideon worked for Strickland? "Never on the payroll," but he had helped out sometimes.

"Was he authorized to be in the poolroom on the morning of the third day of June, 1961?"

"No."

On cross-examination Turner asked whether others had not operated the poolroom for Strickland.

"Occasionally."

"Even this defendant, Gideon, operated it sometimes, didn't he?"

"Well, occasionally." There was no further explanation.

Turner pressed Strickland to say exactly what he missed from the poolroom when he arrived that morning, but Strickland said he could not be precise.

"Are you sure there was money in that cigarette machine [the night before]?"

"Yes."

"How can you be sure?"

"I bought a pack myself."

Shortly before noon Judge McCrary recessed the trial for lunch. Afterward the state called the detective who had arrested Gideon in 1961. Duell Pitts was a square-faced, handsome man, thirty-seven years old, wearing a sports jacket and salmon-colored tie. Like the other prosecution witnesses, he seemed to have no animus toward Gideon; indeed he spoke rather gently of him. On direct examination he testified that he had been called by the policeman who discovered the break-in, was given Gideon's name at the scene by Cook, and arrested Gideon in a downtown Panama City bar the same morning.

Under cross-examination Pitts produced his notes of what Strickland had told him was missing from the poolroom that morning: four fifths of wine, twelve bottles of Coca Cola, twelve cans of beer, about five dollars from the cigarette machine and sixty dollars from the juke box. Then Turner asked a question that boomeranged: "When you arrested Clarence

Pitts answered, "Twenty-five dollars and twenty-eight cents in quarters, nickels, dimes and a few pennies."

On redirect, that damning point was re-emphasized: "This twenty-five dollars and twenty-eight cents — he had no bills?"

"Not that I remember."

Preston Bray, the cab driver who was called by Gideon the morning of the crime and drove him downtown, testified that Gideon had paid him six quarters. He said that Gideon had told him: "If anyone asks you where you left me off, you don't know; you haven't seen me." But on cross-examination he said Gideon had told him the same thing on other occasions.

"Do you know why?"

"I understand it was his wife — he had trouble with his wife.' There were these further exchanges between Turner and Bray:

Q: "What was his condition as to sobriety?"

A: "What's that?"

Q: "Was he drunk or sober?"

A: "He was sober."

Q: "Did he have any wine on him?"

A: "No, sir."

Q: "Any beer?"

A: "No, sir."

Q: "Any Coca Cola?"

A: "No, sir."

Q: "Did his pockets bulge?"

A: "No, sir."

That was the prosecution's case. The jury was sent out; and then Turner moved for a directed verdict of acquittal, arguing that the evidence went only to show Gideon in the poolroom, not breaking into it. Judge McCrary listened politely and then said without hesitation: "The motion will be denied. Call the jury back."

Turner produced a surprise defense witness who had never appeared in the case before. He was J. D. Henderson, owner of the grocery in Bay Harbor. Between eight and nine on the morning of June 3, 1961, Henderson said, Henry Cook had come into his store and told the grocer that "the law had picked him up for questioning" about the break-in.

"Picked who up?" Turner asked with an air of mock disbelief.

"Henry Cook."

Henderson said Cook had told him about seeing someone in the poolroom but was "not sure who it was. He said, 'It looked like Mr. Gideon.' " If such a statement had been made by Cook, it was much less positive than his subsequent testimony.

On cross-examination Harris asked whether Henderson had ever had "any trouble with Henry Cook."

"No."

"Does he owe you any money?"

"He owes a grocery bill, forty-one dollars, for almost a year."

The second and last witness for the defense was Clarence Earl Gideon.

Q: "On the morning of June 3, 1961, did you break and enter the Bay Harbor Poolroom?"

A: "No, sir."

Q: "What was the purpose of your going into town?"

A: "To get me another drink."

Q: "Where'd you get the money?"

A: "I gambled."

Q: "What kind of games?"

A: "Mostly rummy."

Q: "Did you ever gamble with Henry Cook?"

A: "Sure, I gambled with all those boys."

Q: "Did you have any wine with you?"

A: "I don't drink wine."

Q: "Any beer? Any Coke?"

A: "No."

Q: "What did you purchase in town?"

A: "I didn't purchase nothin' except somethin' to drink."

Q: "That's what I mean. What did you purchase to drink?"

A: "Four or five beers, and I bought a half-pint of vodka."

Q: "What do you say to this charge that you broke and entered the pool hall?"

A: "I'm not guilty of it — I know nothing about it."

On cross-examination, Harris asked where Gideon was employed at the time. "I wasn't employed. I was gambling." There was a long exploration of when Gideon had last held a regular job. He had painted some rooms at the Bay Harbor Hotel and was given free rent (a $6-a-week room) in exchange. He had run poker games for Strickland in the poolroom. There followed some questions about gambling that Gideon answered with a puzzled air, as if bewildered at Harris's failure to understand.

Q: "Why did you have all that money in coins?"

A: "I've had as much as one hundred dollars in my pockets in coins."

Q: "Why?"

A: "Have you ever run a poker game?"

Q: "You would carry one hundred dollars in coins around for a couple of days at a time?"

A: "Yes sir, I sure wouldn't leave it in a room in the Bay Harbor Hotel."

Q: "Did you play rummy that night?"

A: "No — I was too busy drinking."

Q: "Have you ever been convicted or pled guilty to a felony?"

A: "Yes, five times, including this one."

At two-forty P.M. the testimony was all in. Judge McCrary recessed the trial and called the lawyers and Gideon into his chambers to discuss how he should charge the jury. The lawyers wrangled for half an hour, ending with a squabble over how much time they would have for closing arguments. Judge McCrary settled this by allowing each side forty-five minutes; as it turned out, neither used that much.

In his address to the jury Turner was the model of the practiced criminal lawyer — dramatic but not too dramatic. His whole argument focused on Henry Cook.

"This probationer," he said scornfully, "has been out at a dance drinking beer. . . . He does a peculiar thing [when he supposedly sees Gideon inside the poolroom]. He doesn't call the police, he doesn't notify the owner, he just walks to the corner and walks back [as Cook had testified]. . . . What happened to the beer and the wine and the Cokes? I'll tell you — it left there in that old model Chevrolet. The beer ran out at midnight in Apalachicola. . . . Why was Cook walking back and forth? I'll give you the explanation: He was the lookout."

Having accused Cook and his friends of actually committing the crime, Turner turned to the defendant.

"Gideon's a gambler," he said, "and he'd been drinking whiskey. I submit to you that he did just what he said that morning — he walked out of his hotel and went to that telephone booth [to call the cab]. . . . Cook saw him, and here was a perfect answer for Cook. He names Gideon."

For the state, Assistant Prosecutor Griffith had made a straightforward closing argument, summarizing the testimony without dramatics. Now, in rebuttal to Turner, Harris got a little more folksy.

"Twenty-five dollars' worth of change," he said, "that's a lot to carry in your pocket. But Mr. Gideon carried one hundred dollars' worth of change in his pocket." He paused and raised his eyebrows. "Do you believe ·that? . . . There's been no evidence here of any animosity by Cook toward Gideon. There's no evidence here that Cook and his friends took this beer and wine."

The jury went out at four-twenty P.M., after a colorless charge by the judge including the instruction — requested by Turner — that the jury must believe Gideon guilty "beyond a reasonable doubt" in order to convict him. When a half-hour had passed with no verdict, the prosecutors were less confident. At five twenty-five there was a knock on the door between the courtroom and the jury room. The jurors filed in, and the court clerk read their verdict, written on a form. It was *Not Guilty*.

"So say you all?" asked Judge McCrary, without a flicker of emotion. The jurors nodded.

Judge McCrary had written of Gideon's first trial: "In my opinion he did as well as most lawyers could have done in handling his case." But Gideon had not done as well as Fred Turner. He had none of Fred Turner's training, or his talent, or his knowledge of the community. Nor could he prepare the case as Turner had, because he had been in prison before his trial.

Turner had spent three full days before trial interviewing witnesses and exploring the case. He went out in the backyard and picked pears with Cook's mother to see what he could find out about the prosecution's star witness. Actually, Turner already knew a good deal about Cook because he had twice been Cook's lawyer — a coincidence that was not a great surprise in a small town like Panama City, where part of a lawyer's job is to know everyone. He had represented Cook in a divorce action and defended him successfully against a charge of leading a drunk out of the

Bay Harbor Poolroom, beating him up and robbing him of $1.98. Gideon's insistence on having a local lawyer — Fred Turner — may well have won the case for him. It is doubtful that the Civil Liberties Union lawyers from Miami could have been so effective with a Panama City jury.

After nearly two years in the state penitentiary Gideon was a free man. There were tears in his eyes, and he trembled even more than usual as he stood in a circle of well-wishers and discussed his plans. His half-brother, the Air Force sergeant, was coming home from Japan and would adopt Gideon's children. Gideon would see the children the next day, then go off to stay with a friend in Tallahassee. That night he would pay a last, triumphant visit to the Bay Harbor Poolroom. Could someone let him have a few dollars? Someone did.

"Do you feel like you accomplished something?" a newspaper reporter asked.

"Well I did."

The Constitution of the United States

We the People of the United States, in Order to form a more perfect Union, establish Justice, insure domestic Tranquility, provide for the common defence, promote the general Welfare, and secure the Blessings of Liberty to ourselves and our Posterity do ordain and establish this CONSTITUTION for the United States of America.

ARTICLE I

Section 1. All legislative Powers herein granted shall be vested in a Congress of the United States, which shall consist of a Senate and House of Representatives.

Section 2. [1] The House of Representatives shall be composed of members chosen every second Year by the People of the several States, and the Electors in each State shall have the Qualifications requisite for Electors of the most numerous Branch of the State Legislature.

[2] No Person shall be a Representative who shall not have attained to the Age of twenty-five Years, and been seven Years a Citizen of the United States, and who shall not, when elected, be an Inhabitant of that State in which he shall be chosen.

[3] [Representatives and direct Taxes[1] shall be apportioned among the several States which may be included within this Union, according to their respective Numbers, which shall be determined by adding to the whole Number of free Persons, including those bound to Service for a Term of Years, and excluding Indians not taxed, three fifths of all other Persons.] [2]

---

[1] The Sixteenth Amendment replaced this with respect to income taxes.
[2] Repealed by the Fourteenth Amendment.

The actual Enumeration shall be made within three Years after the first Meeting of the Congress of the United States, and within every subsequent Term of ten years, in such Manner as they shall by Law direct. The Number of Representatives shall not exceed one for every thirty Thousand, but each State shall have at Least one Representative; and until such enumeration shall be made, the State of New Hampshire shall be entitled to choose three, Massachusetts eight, Rhode-Island and Providence Plantations one, Connecticut five, New-York six, New Jersey four, Pennsylvania eight, Delaware one, Maryland six, Virginia ten, North Carolina five, South Carolina five, and Georgia three.

[4] When vacancies happen in the Representation from any State, the Executive Authority thereof shall issue Writs of Election to fill such Vacancies.

[5] The House of Representatives shall choose their Speaker and other Officers; and shall have the sole Power of Impeachment.

Section 3. [1] The Senate of the United States shall be composed of two Senators from each State, [chosen by the Legislature] [3] thereof, for six Years; and each Senator shall have one Vote.

[2] Immediately after they shall be assembled in Consequence of the first Election, they shall be divided as equally as may be into three Classes. The Seats of the Senators of the first Class shall be vacated at the Expiration of the second Year, of the second Class at the Expiration of the fourth Year, and of the third Class at the Expiration of the sixth Year, so that one-third may be chosen every second Year; [and if Vacancies happen by Resignation, or otherwise, during the Recess of the Legislature of any State, the Executive thereof may make temporary Appointments until the next Meeting of the Legislature, which shall then fill such Vacancies].[4]

[3] No person shall be a Senator who shall not have attained to the Age of thirty Years, and been nine Years a Citizen of the United States, and who shall not, when elected, be an Inhabitant of that State for which he shall be chosen.

[4] The Vice President of the United States shall be President of the Senate, but shall have no Vote, unless they be equally divided.

[5] The Senate shall choose their other Officers, and also a President pro tempore, in the absence of the Vice President, or when he shall exercise the Office of President of the United States.

---

[3] Repealed by the Seventeenth Amendment, Section 1.
[4] Changed by the Seventeenth Amendment.

[6] The Senate shall have the sole Power to try all Impeachments. When sitting for that Purpose, they shall be on Oath or Affirmation. When the President of the United States is tried, the Chief Justice shall preside: And no Person shall be convicted without the Concurrence of two thirds of the Members present.

[7] Judgment in Cases of Impeachment shall not extend further than to removal from Office, and disqualification to hold and enjoy any Office of honor, Trust or Profit under the United States: but the Party convicted shall nevertheless be liable and subject to Indictment, Trial, Judgment and Punishment according to Law.

Section 4. [1] The Times, Places and Manner of holding Elections for Senators and Representatives, shall be prescribed in each State by the Legislature thereof; but the Congress may at any time by Law make or alter such Regulations, except as to the Places of Choosing Senators.

[2] The Congress shall assemble at least once in every Year, and such Meeting shall [be on the first Monday in December,] [5] unless they shall by Law appoint a different Day.

Section 5. [1] Each House shall be the Judge of the Elections, Returns and Qualifications of its own Members, and a Majority of each shall constitute a Quorum to do Business; but a smaller number may adjourn from day to day, and may be authorized to compel the Attendance of absent Members, in such Manner, and under such Penalties as each House may provide.

[2] Each House may determine the Rules of its Proceedings, punish its Members for disorderly Behavior, and, with the Concurrence of two thirds, expel a Member.

[3] Each House shall keep a Journal of its Proceedings, and from time to time publish the same, excepting such Parts as may in their Judgment require Secrecy; and the Yeas and Nays of the Members of either House on any question shall, at the Desire of one fifth of those Present, be entered on the Journal.

[4] Neither House, during the Session of Congress, shall, without the Consent of the other, adjourn for more than three days, nor to any other Place than that in which the two Houses shall be sitting.

Section 6. [1] The Senators and Representatives shall receive a Compensation for their Services, to be ascertained by Law, and paid out of the Trea-

---

[5] Changed by the Twentieth Amendment, Section 2.

sury of the United States. They shall in all Cases, except Treason, Felony and Breach of the Peace, be privileged from Arrest during their Attendance at the Session of their respective Houses, and in going to and returning from the same; and for any Speech or Debate in either House, they shall not be questioned in any other Place.

[2] No Senator or Representative shall, during the Time for which he was elected, be appointed to any civil Office under the Authority of the United States, which shall have been created, or the Emoluments whereof have been increased during such time; and no Person holding any Office under the United States, shall be a Member of either House during his Continuance in Office.

Section 7. [1] All Bills for raising Revenue shall originate in the House of Representatives; but the Senate may propose or concur with Amendments as on other Bills.

[2] Every Bill which shall have passed the House of Representatives and the Senate, shall, before it become a Law, be presented to the President of the United States; If he approve he shall sign it, but if not he shall return it, with his Objections to that House in which it shall have originated, who shall enter the Objections at large on their Journal, and proceed to reconsider it. If after such Reconsideration two thirds of that House shall agree to pass the Bill, it shall be sent, together with the Objections, to the other House, by which it shall likewise be reconsidered, and if approved by two thirds of that House, it shall become a Law. But in all such Cases the Votes of both Houses shall be determined by Yeas and Nays, and the Names of the Persons voting for and against the Bill shall be entered on the Journal of each House respectively. If any Bill shall not be returned by the President within ten Days (Sundays excepted) after it shall have been presented to him, the Same shall be a Law, in like Manner as if he had signed it, unless the Congress by their Adjournment prevent its Return, in which Case it shall not be a Law.

[3] Every Order, Resolution, or Vote to which the Concurrence of the Senate and House of Representatives may be necessary (except on a question of Adjournment) shall be presented to the President of the United States; and before the Same shall take Effect, shall be approved by him, or being disapproved by him, shall be repassed by two thirds of the Senate and House of Representatives, according to the Rules and Limitations prescribed in the Case of a Bill.

Section 8. [1] The Congress shall have Power To lay and collect Taxes, Duties, Imposts and Excises, to pay the Debts and provide for the common Defense and general Welfare of the United States; but all Duties, Imposts and Excises shall be uniform throughout the United States;

[2] To borrow money on the credit of the United States;

[3] To regulate Commerce with foreign Nations, and among the several States, and with the Indian Tribes;

[4] To establish an uniform Rule of Naturalization, and uniform Laws on the subject of Bankruptcies throughout the United States;

[5] To coin Money, regulate the Value thereof, and of foreign Coin, and fix the Standard of Weights and Measures;

[6] To provide for the Punishment of counterfeiting the Securities and current Coin of the United States;

[7] To establish Post Offices and post Roads;

[8] To promote the Progress of Science and useful Arts, by securing for limited Times to Authors and Inventors the exclusive Right to their respective Writings and Discoveries;

[9] To constitute Tribunals inferior to the supreme Court;

[10] To define and punish Piracies and Felonies committed on the high Seas, and Offenses against the Law of Nations;

[11] To declare War, grant Letters of Marque and Reprisal, and make Rules concerning Captures on Land and Water;

[12] To raise and support Armies, but no Appropriation of Money to that Use shall be for a longer Term than two Years;

[13] To provide and maintain a Navy;

[14] To make Rules for the Government and Regulation of the land and naval Forces;

[15] To provide for calling forth the Militia to execute the Laws of the Union, suppress Insurrections and repel Invasions;

[16] To provide for organizing, arming, and disciplining the Militia, and for governing such Part of them as may be employed in the Service of the United States, reserving to the States respectively, the Appointment of the Officers, and the Authority of training the Militia according to the discipline prescribed by Congress;

[17] To exercise exclusive Legislation in all Cases whatsoever, over such District (not exceeding ten Miles square) as may, by Cession of particular States, and the acceptance of Congress, become the Seat of the Government of the United States, and to exercise like Authority over all Places purchased by the Consent of the Legislature of the State in which the Same shall be, for the Erection of Forts, Magazines, Arsenals, dock-Yards, and other needful Buildings; — And

[18] To make all Laws which shall be necessary and proper for carrying into Execution the foregoing Powers, and all other Powers vested by this Constitution in the Government of the United States, or in any Department or Officer thereof.

Section 9. [1] The Migration or Importation of such Persons as any of the States now existing shall think proper to admit, shall not be prohibited by the Congress prior to the Year one thousand eight hundred and eight, but a tax or duty may be imposed on such Importation, not exceeding ten dollars for each Person.

[2] The privilege of the Writ of Habeas Corpus shall not be suspended, unless when in Cases of Rebellion or Invasion the public Safety may require it.

[3] No Bill of Attainder or ex post facto Law shall be passed.

[4] No capitation, or other direct, Tax shall be laid, unless in Proportion to the Census or Enumeration herein before directed to be taken.[6]

[5] No Tax or Duty shall be laid on Articles exported from any State.

[6] No Preference shall be given by any Regulation of Commerce or Revenue to the Ports of one State over those of another: nor shall Vessels bound to, or from, one State, be obliged to enter, clear, or pay Duties in another.

[7] No Money shall be drawn from the Treasury, but in Consequence of Appropriations made by Law; and a regular Statement and Account of the Receipts and Expenditures of all public Money shall be published from time to time.

[8] No Title of Nobility shall be granted by the United States: And no Person holding any Office of Profit or Trust under them, shall, without the Consent of the Congress, accept of any present, Emolument, Office, or Title, of any kind whatever, from any King, Prince, or foreign State.

Section 10. [1] No State shall enter into any Treaty, Alliance, or Confederation; grant Letters of Marque and Reprisal; coin Money; emit Bills of Credit; make any Thing but gold and silver Coin a Tender in Payment of Debts; pass any Bill of Attainder, ex post facto Law, or Law impairing the Obligation of Contracts, or grant any Title of Nobility.

[2] No State shall, without the Consent of the Congress, lay any Imposts or Duties on Imports or Exports, except what may be absolutely necessary for executing its inspection Laws: and the net Produce of all Duties and Imposts, laid by any State on Imports or Exports, shall be for the Use of the Treasury of the United States; and all such Laws shall be subject to the Revision and Control of the Congress.

[3] No State shall, without the Consent of Congress, lay any duty of Tonnage, keep Troops, or Ships of War in time of Peace, enter into any Agreement or Compact with another State, or with a foreign Power, or engage in War, unless actually invaded, or in such imminent Danger as will not admit of delay.

---

[6] Changed by the Sixteenth Amendment.

ARTICLE II

Section 1. [1] The executive Power shall be vested in a President of the United States of America. He shall hold his Office during the Term of four Years, and, together with the Vice-President, chosen for the same Term, be elected, as follows

[2] Each State shall appoint, in such Manner as the Legislature thereof may direct, a Number of Electors, equal to the whole Number of Senators and Representatives to which the State may be entitled in the Congress; but no Senator or Representative, or Person holding an Office of Trust or Profit under the United States, shall be appointed an Elector.

[The Electors shall meet in their respective States, and vote by Ballot for two persons, of whom one at least shall not be an Inhabitant of the same State with themselves. And they shall make a List of all the Persons voted for, and of the Number of Votes for each; which List they shall sign and certify, and transmit sealed to the Seat of the Government of the United States, directed to the President of the Senate. The President of the Senate shall, in the Presence of the Senate and House of Representatives, open all the Certificates, and the Votes shall then be counted. The Person having the greatest Number of Votes shall be the President, if such Number be a Majority of the whole Number of Electors appointed; and if there be more than one who have such Majority, and have an equal Number of Votes, then the House of Representatives shall immediately choose by Ballot one of them for President; and if no Person have a Majority, then from the five highest on the List the said House shall in like Manner choose the President. But in choosing the President, the Votes shall be taken by States, the Representation from each State having one Vote; A quorum for this Purpose shall consist of a Member or Members from two-thirds of the States, and a Majority of all the States shall be necessary to a Choice. In every Case, after the Choice of the President, the Person having the greatest Number of Votes of the Electors shall be the Vice-President. But if there should remain two or more who have equal Votes, the Senate shall choose from them by Ballot the Vice-President.] [7]

[3] The Congress may determine the Time of choosing the Electors, and the Day on which they shall give their Votes; which Day shall be the same throughout the United States.

[4] No person except a natural born Citizen, or a Citizen of the United States, at the time of the Adoption of this Constitution, shall be eligible to the Office of President; neither shall any Person be eligible to that Office who shall not have attained to the Age of thirty-five Years, and been fourteen Years a Resident within the United States.

---

[7] This paragraph was superseded in 1804 by the Twelfth Amendment.

[5] In case of the Removal of the President from Office, or of his Death, Resignation, or Inability to discharge the Powers and Duties of the said Office, the same shall devolve on the Vice-President, and the Congress may by Law provide for the Case of Removal, Death, Resignation or Inability, both of the President and Vice-President, declaring what Officer shall then act as President, and such Officer shall act accordingly, until the Disability be removed, or a President shall be elected.[8]

[6] The President shall, at stated Times, receive for his Services, a Compensation, which shall neither be increased nor diminished during the Period for which he shall have been elected, and he shall not receive within that Period any other Emolument from the United States, or any of them.

[7] Before he enter on the Execution of his Office, he shall take the following Oath or Affirmation: — "I do solemnly swear (or affirm) that I will faithfully execute the Office of President of the United States, and will to the best of my Ability, preserve, protect and defend the Constitution of the United States."

Section 2. [1] The President shall be Commander in Chief of the Army and Navy of the United States, and of the Militia of the several States, when called into the actual Service of the United States; he may require the Opinion in writing, of the principal Officer in each of the executive Departments, upon any subject relating to the Duties of their respective Offices, and he shall have Power to Grant Reprieves and Pardons for Offenses against the United States, except in Cases of Impeachment.

[2] He shall have Power, by and with the Advice and Consent of the Senate, to make Treaties, provided two-thirds of the Senators present concur; and he shall nominate, and by and with the Advice and Consent of the Senate, shall appoint Ambassadors, other public Ministers and Consuls, Judges of the supreme Court, and all other Officers of the United States, whose Appointments are not herein otherwise provided for, and which shall be established by Law: but the Congress may by Law vest the Appointment of such inferior Officers, as they think proper, in the President alone, in the Court of Law, or in the Heads of Departments.

[3] The President shall have Power to fill up all Vacancies that may happen during the Recess of the Senate, by granting Commissions which shall expire at the End of their next Session.

Section 3. He shall from time to time give to the Congress Information of the State of the Union, and recommend to their Consideration such Measures as he shall judge necessary and expedient; he may, on extraordinary Occasions, convene both Houses, or either of them, and in Case of Dis-

---

[8] Changed by the Twenty-fifth Amendment.

agreement between them, with Respect to the Time of Adjournment, he may adjourn them to such Time as he shall think proper; he shall receive Ambassadors and other public Ministers; he shall take Care that the Laws be faithfully executed, and shall Commission all the Officers of the United States.

Section 4. The President, Vice President and all civil Officers of the United States, shall be removed from Office on Impeachment for, and Conviction of, Treason, Bribery, or other high Crimes and Misdemeanors.

ARTICLE III

Section 1. The judicial Power of the United States, shall be vested in one supreme Court, and in such inferior Courts as the Congress may from time to time ordain and establish. The Judges, both of the supreme and inferior Courts, shall hold their Offices during good Behavior, and shall, at stated Times, receive for their Services a Compensation which shall not be diminished during their Continuance in Office.

Section 2. [1] The judicial Power shall extend to all Cases, in Law and Equity, arising under this Constitution, the Laws of the United States, and Treaties made, or which shall be made, under their Authority; — to all Cases affecting Ambassadors, other public Ministers and Consuls; — to all Cases of admiralty and maritime Jurisdiction; — to Controversies to which the United States shall be a Party; — to Controversies between two or more States; — [between a State and Citizens of another State];[9] — between Citizens of different States; — between Citizens of the same State claiming Lands under Grants of different States, and [between a State, or the Citizens thereof, and foreign States, Citizens or Subjects].[10]

[2] In all Cases affecting Ambassadors, other public Ministers and Consuls, and those in which a State shall be Party, the supreme Court shall have original Jurisdiction. In all the other Cases before mentioned, the supreme Court shall have appellate Jurisdiction, both as to Law and Fact, with such Exceptions, and under such Regulations as the Congress shall make.

[3] The trial of all Crimes, except in Cases of Impeachment, shall be by Jury; and such Trial shall be held in the State where the said Crimes shall have been committed: but when not committed within any State, the Trial shall be at such Place or Places as the Congress may by Law have directed.

---

[9] Restricted by the Eleventh Amendment.
[10] Restricted by the Eleventh Amendment.

Section 3. [1] Treason against the United States, shall consist only in levying War against them, or in adhering to their Enemies, giving them Aid and Comfort. No Person shall be convicted of Treason unless on the Testimony of two Witnesses to the same overt Act, or on Confession in open Court.

[2] The Congress shall have power to declare the Punishment of Treason, but no Attainder of Treason shall work Corruption of Blood, or Forfeiture except during the Life of the Person attained.

ARTICLE IV

Section 1. Full Faith and Credit shall be given in each State to the public Acts, Records, and judicial Proceedings of every other State. And the Congress may by general Laws prescribe the Manner in which such Acts, Records and Proceedings shall be proved, and the Effect thereof.

Section 2. [1] The Citizens of each State shall be entitled to all Privileges and Immunities of Citizens in the several States.

[2] A Person charged in any State with Treason, Felony, or other Crime, who shall flee from Justice, and be found in another State, shall on demand of the executive Authority of the State from which he fled, be delivered up, to be removed to the State having Jurisdiction of the Crime.

[3] [No Person held to Service or Labor in one State, under the Laws thereof, escaping into another, shall, in Consequence of any Law or Regulation therein, be discharged from such Service or Labor, but shall be delivered up on Claim of the Party to whom such Service or Labor may be due.] [11]

Section 3. [1] New States may be admitted by the Congress into this Union; but no new State shall be formed or erected within the Jurisdiction of any other State; nor any State be formed by the Junction of two or more States, or parts of States, without the Consent of the Legislatures of the States concerned as well as of the Congress.

[2] The Congress shall have Power to dispose of and make all needful Rules and Regulations respecting the Territory or other Property belonging to the United States; and nothing in this Constitution shall be so construed as to Prejudice any Claims of the United States, or of any particular State.

Section 4. The United States shall guarantee to every State in this Union a Republican Form of Government, and shall protect each of them against Invasion; and on Application of the Legislature, or of the Executive (when the Legislature cannot be convened) against domestic Violence.

------

[11] This paragraph has been superseded by the Thirteenth Amendment.

ARTICLE V

The Congress, whenever two-thirds of both Houses shall deem it necessary, shall propose Amendments to this Constitution, or, on the Application of the Legislatures of two-thirds of the several States, shall call a Convention for proposing Amendments, which, in either Case, shall be valid to all Intents and Purposes, as part of this Constitution, when ratified by the Legislature of three-fourths of the several States, or by Conventions in three-fourths thereof, as the one or the other Mode of Ratification may be proposed by the Congress; Provided that no Amendment which may be made prior to the Year One thousand eight hundred and eight shall in any Manner affect the first and fourth Clauses in the Ninth Section of the first Article; and that no State, without its Consent, shall be deprived of its equal Suffrage in the Senate.

ARTICLE VI

[1] All Debts contracted and Engagements entered into, before the Adoption of this Constitution, shall be as valid against the United States under this Constitution, as under the Confederation.

[2] This Constitution, and the Laws of the United States which shall be made in Pursuance thereof; and all Treaties made, or which shall be made, under the Authority of the United States, shall be the supreme Law of the Land; and the Judges in every State shall be bound thereby, any Thing in the Constitution or Laws of any State to the Contrary notwithstanding.

[3] The Senators and Representatives before mentioned, and the Members of the several State Legislatures, and all executive and judicial Officers, both of the United States and of the several States, shall be bound by Oath or Affirmation, to support this Constitution; but no religious Test shall ever be required as a Qualification to any Office or public Trust under the United States.

ARTICLE VII

The Ratification of the Conventions of nine States, shall be sufficient for the Establishment of this Constitution between the States so ratifying the Same.

DONE in Convention by the Unanimous Consent of the States present the Seventeenth Day of September in the Year of our Lord one thousand seven hundred and Eighty seven and the Independence of the United States of America the Twelfth. In Witness whereof We have hereunto subscribed our Names.

Go WASHINGTON
President and deputy from Virginia

ARTICLES IN ADDITION TO, AND AMENDMENT OF, THE CONSTITU-
TION OF THE UNITED STATES OF AMERICA, PROPOSED BY CON-
GRESS, AND RATIFIED BY THE LEGISLATURES OF THE SEVERAL
STATES, PURSUANT TO THE FIFTH ARTICLE OF THE ORIGINAL
CONSTITUTION.

ARTICLE I [12]

Congress shall make no law respecting an establishment of religion, or prohibiting the free exercise thereof; or abridging the freedom of speech, or
of the press; or the right of the people peaceably to assemble, and to petition
the Government for a redress of grievances.

ARTICLE II

A well regulated Militia, being necessary to the security of a free State, the
right of the people to keep and bear Arms, shall not be infringed.

ARTICLE III

No Soldier shall, in time of peace be quartered in any house, without the
consent of the Owner, nor in time of war, but in a manner to be prescribed
by law.

ARTICLE IV

The right of the people to be secure in their persons, houses, papers, and
effects, against unreasonable searches and seizures, shall not be violated,
and no Warrants shall issue, but upon probable cause, supported by Oath
or affirmation, and particularly describing the place to be searched, and the
persons or things to be seized.

ARTICLE V

No person shall be held to answer for a capital, or otherwise infamous
crime, unless on a presentment or indictment of a Grand Jury, except in
cases arising in the land or naval forces, or in the Militia, when in actual
service in time of War or public danger; nor shall any person be subject
for the same offence to be twice put in jeopardy of life or limb; nor shall
be compelled in any criminal case to be witness against himself, nor be
deprived of life, liberty, or property, without due process of law; nor shall
private property be taken for public use, without just compensation.

---

[12] The first ten amendments were adopted in 1791.

ARTICLE VI

In all criminal prosecutions, the accused shall enjoy the right to a speedy and public trial, by an impartial jury of the State and district wherein the crime shall have been committed, which district shall have been previously ascertained by law, and to be informed of the nature and cause of the accusation; to be confronted with the witnesses against him; to have compulsory process for obtaining witnesses in his favor, and to have the Assistance of Counsel for his defence.

ARTICLE VII

In suits at common law, where the value in controversy shall exceed twenty dollars, the right of trial by jury shall be preserved, and no fact tried by a jury, shall be otherwise reexamined in any Court of the United States, than according to the rules of the common law.

ARTICLE VIII

Excessive bail shall not be required, nor excessive fines imposed, nor cruel and unusual punishments inflicted.

ARTICLE IX

The enumeration in the Constitution, of certain rights, shall not be construed to deny or disparage others retained by the people.

ARTICLE X

The powers not delegated to the United States by the Constitution, nor prohibited by it to the States, are reserved to the States respectively, or to the people.

ARTICLE XI [13]

The Judicial power of the United States shall not be construed to extend to any suit in law or equity, commenced or prosecuted against one of the United States by Citizens of another State, or by Citizens or Subjects of any Foreign State.

---

[13] Adopted in 1798.

ARTICLE XII [14]

The Electors shall meet in their respective states and vote by ballot for President and Vice-President, one of whom, at least, shall not be an inhabitant of the same state with themselves; they shall name in their ballots the person voted for as President, and in distinct ballots the person voted for as Vice-President, and they shall make distinct lists of all persons voted for as President, and of all persons voted for as Vice-President, and of the number of votes for each, which lists they shall sign and certify, and transmit sealed to the seat of the government of the United States, directed to the President of the Senate; — The President of the Senate shall, in presence of the Senate and House of Representatives, open all the certificates and the votes shall then be counted; — The person having the greatest number of votes for President, shall be the President, if such number be a majority of the whole number of Electors appointed; and if no person have such majority, then from the persons having the highest numbers not exceeding three on the list of those voted for as President, the House of Representatives shall choose immediately, by ballot, the President. But in choosing the President, the votes shall be taken by states, the representation from each state having one vote; a quorum for this purpose shall consist of a member or members from two-thirds of the states, and a majority of all the states shall be necessary to a choice. [And if the House of Representatives shall not choose a President whenever the right of choice shall devolve upon them, before the fourth day of March next following, then the Vice-President shall act as President, as in the case of the death or other constitutional disability of the President.] [15] — The person having the greatest number of votes as Vice-President, shall be the Vice-President, if such number be a majority of the whole number of Electors appointed, and if no person have a majority, then from the two highest numbers on the list, the Senate shall choose the Vice-President; a quorum for the purpose shall consist of two-thirds of the whole number of Senators, and a majority of the whole number shall be necessary to a choice. But no person constitutionally ineligible to the office of President shall be eligible to that of Vice-President of the United States.

ARTICLE XIII [16]

Section 1. Neither slavery nor involuntary servitude, except as a punishment for crime whereof the party shall have been duly convicted, shall exist within the United States, or any place subject to their jurisdiction.

---

[14] Adopted in 1804.
[15] Superseded by the Twentieth Amendment, Section 3.
[16] Adopted in 1865.

Section 2. Congress shall have power to enforce this article by appropriate legislation.

ARTICLE XIV [17]

Section 1. All persons born or naturalized in the United States, and subject to the jurisdiction thereof, are citizens of the United States and of the State wherein they reside. No state shall make or enforce any law which shall abridge the privileges or immunities of citizens of the United States; nor shall any State deprive any person of life, liberty, or property, without due process of law; nor deny to any person within its jurisdiction the equal protection of the laws.

Section 2. Representatives shall be apportioned among the several States according to their respective numbers, counting the whole number of persons in each State, excluding Indians not taxed. But when the right to vote at any election for the choice of electors for President and Vice-President of the United States, Representatives in Congress, the Executive and Judicial officers of a State, or the members of the Legislature thereof, is denied to any of the male inhabitants of such State, being twenty-one years of age, and citizens of the United States, or in any way abridged, except for participation in rebellion, or other crime, the basis of representation therein shall be reduced in the proportion which the number of such male citizens shall bear to the whole number of male citizens twenty-one years of age in such State.

Section 3. No person shall be a Senator or Representative in Congress, or elector of President and Vice-President, or hold any office, civil or military, under the United States, or under any State, who, having previously taken an oath, as a member of Congress, or as an officer of the United States, or as a member of any State legislature, or as an executive or judicial officer of any State, to support the Constitution of the United States, shall have engaged in insurrection or rebellion against the same, or given aid or comfort to the enemies thereof. But Congress may by a vote of two-thirds of each House, remove such disability.

Section 4. The validity of the public debt of the United States, authorized by law, including debts incurred for payment of pensions and bounties for services in suppressing insurrection or rebellion, shall not be questioned. But neither the United States nor any State shall assume or pay any debt

---

[17] Adopted in 1868.

or obligation incurred in aid of insurrection or rebellion against the United States, or any claim for the loss or emancipation of any slave; but all such debts, obligations and claims shall be held illegal and void.

Section 5. The Congress shall have power to enforce, by appropriate legislation, the provisions of this article.

ARTICLE XV [18]

Section 1. The right of citizens of the United States to vote shall not be denied or abridged by the United States or by any State on account of race, color, or previous condition of servitude —

Section 2. The Congress shall have power to enforce this article by appropriate legislation.

ARTICLE XVI [19]

The Congress shall have power to lay and collect taxes on incomes, from whatever source derived, without apportionment among the several States, and without regard to any census or enumeration.

ARTICLE XVII [20]

The Senate of the United States shall be composed of two Senators from each State, elected by the people thereof, for six years; and each Senator shall have one vote. The electors in each State shall have the qualifications requisite for electors of the most numerous branch of the State legislatures.

When vacancies happen in the representation of any State in the Senate, the executive authority of such State shall issue writs of election to fill such vacancies: *Provided,* That the legislature of any State may empower the executive thereof to make temporary appointments until the people fill the vacancies by election as the legislature may direct.

This amendment shall not be so construed as to affect the election or term of any Senator chosen before it becomes valid as part of the Constitution.

---

[18] Adopted in 1870.
[19] Adopted in 1913.
[20] Adopted in 1913.

ARTICLE XVIII [21]

Section 1. After one year from the ratification of this article the manufacture, sale, or transportation of intoxicating liquors within, the importation thereof into, or the exportation thereof from the United States and all territory subject to the jurisdiction thereof for beverage purposes is hereby prohibited.

Section 2. The Congress and the several States shall have concurrent power to enforce this article by appropriate legislation.

Section 3. This article shall be inoperative unless it shall have been ratified as an amendment to the Constitution by the legislatures of the several States, as provided in the Constitution, within seven years from the date of the submission hereof to the State by the Congress.

ARTICLE XIX [22]

The right of citizens of the United States to vote shall not be denied or abridged by the United States or by any State on account of sex.

Congress shall have power to enforce this article by appropriate legislation.

ARTICLE XX [23]

Section 1. The terms of the President and Vice-President shall end at noon on the 20th day of January, and the terms of Senators and Representatives at noon on the 3d day of January, of the years in which such terms would have ended if this article had not been ratified; and the terms of their successors shall then begin.

Section 2. The Congress shall assemble at least once in every year, and such meeting shall begin at noon on the 3d day of January, unless they shall by law appoint a different day.

Section 3. If, at the time fixed for the beginning of the term of the President, the president elect shall have died, the Vice-President elect shall become President. If a President shall not have been chosen before the time fixed for the beginning of his term, or if the President elect shall have

---

[21] Adopted in 1919. Repealed by Section 1 of the Twenty-first Amendment.
[22] Adopted in 1920.
[23] Adopted in 1933.

failed to qualify, then the Vice-President elect shall act as President until a President shall have qualified; and the Congress may by law provide for the case wherein neither a President elect nor a Vice-President elect shall have qualified, declaring who shall then act as President, or the manner in which one who is to act shall be selected, and such person shall act accordingly until a President or Vice-President shall have qualified.

Section 4. The Congress may by law provide for the case of the death of any of the persons from whom the House of Representatives may choose a President whenever the right of choice shall have devolved upon them, and for the case of the death of any of the persons from whom the Senate may choose a Vice-President whenever the right of choice shall have devolved upon them.

Section 5. Sections 1 and 2 shall take effect on the 15th day of October following the ratification of this article.

Section 6. This article shall be inoperative unless it shall have been ratified as an amendment to the Constitution by the legislatures of three-fourths of the several States within seven years from the date of its submission.

ARTICLE XXI [24]

Section 1. The eighteenth article of amendment to the Constitution of the United States is hereby repealed.

Section 2. The transportation or importation into any State, Territory, or possession of the United States for delivery or use therein of intoxicating liquors, in violation of the laws thereof, is hereby prohibited.

Section 3. This article shall be inoperative unless it shall have been ratified as an amendment to the Constitution by conventions in the several States, as provided in the Constitution, within seven years from the date of the submission hereof to the States by the Congress.

ARTICLE XXII [25]

Section 1. No person shall be elected to the office of the President more than twice, and no person who has held the office of President, or acted as President, for more than two years of a term to which some other person

---

[24] Adopted in 1933.
[25] Adopted in 1951.

was elected President shall be elected to the office of the President more than once. But this Article shall not apply to any person holding the office of President when this Article was proposed by the Congress, and shall not prevent any person who may be holding the office of President, or acting as President, during the term within which this Article becomes operative from holding the office of President or acting as President during the remainder of such term.

Section 2. This article shall be inoperative unless it shall have been ratified as an amendment to the Constitution by the legislatures of three-fourths of the several States within seven years from the date of its submission to the States by the Congress.

ARTICLE XXIII [26]

Section 1. The District constituting the seat of Government of the United States shall appoint in such manner as the Congress may direct:

A number of electors of President and Vice-President equal to the whole number of Senators and Representatives in Congress to which the District would be entitled if it were a State, but in no event more than the least populous State; they shall be in addition to those appointed by the States, but they shall be considered, for the purposes of the election of President and Vice-President, to be electors appointed by a State; and they shall meet in the District and perform such duties as provided by the twelfth article of amendment.

Section 2. The Congress shall have power to enforce this article by appropriate legislation.

ARTICLE XXIV [27]

Section 1. The right of citizens of the United States to vote in any primary or other election for President or Vice-President, for electors for President or Vice-President, or for Senator or Representative in Congress, shall not be denied or abridged by the United States or any state by reasons of failure to pay any poll tax or other tax.

Section 2. The Congress shall have power to enforce this article by appropriate legislation.

---

[26] Adopted in 1961.
[27] Adopted in 1964.

ARTICLE XXV [28]

Section 1. In case of the removal of the President from office or of his death or resignation, the Vice-President shall become President.

Section 2. Whenever there is a vacancy in the office of the Vice-President, the President shall nominate a Vice-President who shall take office upon confirmation by a majority vote of both Houses of Congress.

Section 3. Whenever the President transmits to the President pro tempore of the Senate and the Speaker of the House of Representatives has written declaration that he is unable to discharge the powers and duties of his office, and until he transmits to them a written declaration to the contrary, such powers and duties shall be discharged by the Vice-President as Acting President.

Section 4. Whenever the Vice-President and a majority of either the principal officers of the Executive departments or of such other body as Congress may by law provide transmit to the President pro tempore of the Senate and the Speaker of the House of Representatives their written declaration that the President is unable to discharge the powers and duties of his office, the Vice-President shall immediately assume the powers and duties of the office as Acting President.

Thereafter, when the President transmits to the President pro tempore of the Senate and the Speaker of the House of Representatives his written declaration that no inability exists, he shall resume the powers and duties of his office unless the Vice-President and a majority of either the principal officers of the Executive departments or of such other body as Congress may by law provide transmit within four days to the President pro tempore of the Senate and the Speaker of the House of Representatives their written declaration that the President is unable to discharge the powers and duties of his office. Thereupon Congress shall decide the issue, assembling within forty-eight hours for that purpose if not in session. If the Congress, within twenty-one days after receipt of the latter written declaration, or, if Congress is not in session, within twenty-one days after Congress is required to assemble, determines by two-thirds vote of both houses that the President is unable to discharge the powers and duties of his office, the Vice-President shall continue to discharge the same as Acting President; otherwise, the President shall resume the powers and duties of his office.

---

[28] Adopted in 1967.

ARTICLE XXVI [29]

Section 1. The right of citizens of the United States, who are 18 years of age or older, to vote shall not be denied or abridged by the United States or any state on account of age.

Section 2. The Congress shall have power to enforce this article by appropriate legislation.

ARTICLE XXVII [Proposed, not yet ratified] [30]

Section 1. Equality of rights under the law shall not be denied or abridged by the United States or by any State on account of sex.

Section 2. The Congress shall have the power to enforce, by appropriate legislation, the provisions of this article.

Section 3. This amendment shall take effect two years after the date of ratification.

---

[29] Adopted in 1971.

[30] Approved by Congress in 1972 and sent to the states for ratification. As of mid-1980, 35 states had ratified this "equal rights amendment," 3 short of the necessary 38 ratifications.